THE WORLD AROUND US

■ WORLD ■
REGIONS

No two places on earth are the same. This globe shows the rich variety of the landforms and bodies of water in part of our world. There are also exciting variations in the ways of life of the people of the earth. As you read, you will discover what makes each region of our world special.

JAMES A. BANKS   JEAN CRAVEN

BARRY K. BEYER   GLORIA LADSON-BILLINGS

GLORIA CONTRERAS   MARY A. McFARLAND

WALTER C. PARKER

MACMILLAN/McGRAW-HILL SCHOOL PUBLISHING COMPANY

NEW YORK   COLUMBUS

PROGRAM AUTHORS

Dr. James A. Banks
Professor of Education and Director of
 the Center for Multicultural Education
University of Washington
Seattle, Washington

Dr. Barry K. Beyer
Professor of Education and American Studies
George Mason University
Fairfax, Virginia

Dr. Gloria Contreras
Professor of Education and Director of
 the Office of Multicultural Affairs
University of North Texas
Denton, Texas

Jean Craven
District Coordinator of Curriculum
 Development
Albuquerque Public Schools
Albuquerque, New Mexico

Dr. Gloria Ladson-Billings
Assistant Professor of Education
University of Wisconsin
Madison, Wisconsin

Dr. Mary McFarland
Director of Staff Development and
 Instructional Coordinator of
 Social Studies, K-12
Parkway School District
Chesterfield, Missouri

Dr. Walter C. Parker
Associate Professor of Social
 Studies Education and Director
 of the Center for the Study of
 Civic Intelligence
University of Washington
Seattle, Washington

CONTENT CONSULTANTS

Virginia Arnold
Adjunct Professor of Reading, Language Arts,
 and Children's Literature
Virginia Commonwealth University
Richmond, Virginia

Yvonne Beamer
Resource Specialist
Native American Education Program
New York, New York

Joyce Buckner
Director of Elementary Education
Omaha Public Schools
Omaha, Nebraska

Sheila Clarke-Ekong
Director of Special Programming
James S. Coleman African Studies Center
University of California
Los Angeles, California

Walter Enloe
Director of Global Education
University of Minnesota
Minneapolis, Minnesota

Helen P. Gillotte
Associate Professor of English
San Francisco State University
San Francisco, California

Margaret Lippert
Literature Consultant
 and Story Teller
 North Bend, Washington

Narcita Medina
Reading Specialist
Middle School 135
New York, New York

Harlan Rimmerman
Director of Elementary Education
Kansas City Public Schools
Kansas City, Kansas

Joseph B. Rubin
Director of Reading and Language Arts
Fort Worth Independent School District
Fort Worth, Texas

Clifford E. Trafzer
Professor of Ethnic Studies and Director
 of Native American Studies
University of California
Riverside, California

Nancy Winter
Former Member of the Executive Board of the
 National Council for Geographic Education
Social Studies Consultant
Clark University
Worcester, Massachusetts

GRADE-LEVEL CONSULTANTS

John Allega
Seventh Grade Teacher
Whitin Intermediate School
Uxbridge, Massachusetts

Sister Judith Coreil
Former Assistant Director
National Catholic Education Association
Washington, D.C.

Nadine Kaufman
Principal and Seventh Grade Teacher
St. Francis Xavier School
Lake Station, Indiana

Linda Kuhlman
Seventh Grade Teacher
Trinity Lutheran School
Portland, Oregon

Mary Male
Seventh Grade Teacher
Sacred Heart School
Bethlehem, Pennsylvania

TRADITIONS WRITERS

Elza Dinwiddie Boyd
New York, New York

Blake Eskin
New York, New York

Carrie Evento
Waterford, Connecticut

Eric Kimmel
Portland, Oregon

Cheryl Haldane
Austin, Texas

Argentina Palacios
Fresh Meadows, New York

CONTRIBUTING WRITERS

Paula Franklin
New York, New York

Diana Reische
Pelham, New York

ACKNOWLEDGMENTS

The publisher gratefully acknowledges permission to reprint the following copyrighted material: Excerpt from "The Talking Cat" from THE TALKING CAT AND OTHER STORIES OF FRENCH CANADA by Natalie Savage Carlson. Illustrated by Roger Duvoisin. Copyright © 1952 by Natalie Savage Carlson. Reprinted by permission of Harper & Row, Publishers, Inc. Excerpt from A STORY—A STORY by Gail E. Haley. Copyright © 1970 by Gail E. Haley. Reprinted by permission of the Macmillan Publishing Company. Excerpt from ROOTS by Alex Haley. Copyright © 1976 by Alex Haley. Reprinted by permission of

Bantam Doubleday Dell Publishing Group, Inc. Excerpt from SUNDIATA: AN EPIC OF OLD MALI by D.T. Niane, translated by G.D. Pickett. Copyright © 1960 by Presence Africaine. Reprinted with permission. Simon & Schuster, Inc. for "The Role of the Griot" by D'jimo Kouyate. © 1989 by D'jimo Kouyate. Reprinted by permission of the publisher. Excerpt from "It's Time for Less Perilous Energy Sources" from *Los Angeles Times,* May 1, 1986. Reprinted by permission. Excerpt from "France Stands by Nuclear Power" from
continued on page 673

Macmillan/McGraw-Hill School Division
 10 Union Square East
New York, New York 10003

Printed in the United States of America
ISBN 0-02-146424-3
2 3 4 5 6 7 8 9 RRW 99 98 97 96 95

CONTENTS

UNIT 3 Western Europe 178

UNIT 4   Eastern Europe and Northern Asia 288

UNIT 7 Southern and Eastern Asia   486

REFERENCE SECTION

Building Citizenship

Traditions

Songs

Building Skills

THINKING/READING

GEOGRAPHY

STUDY/TIME

Charts, Graphs, and Diagrams

Maps

USING YOUR TEXTBOOK

TABLE OF CONTENTS
Lists all parts of
your book and tells
you where to find
them

Your textbook contains many
special features that will help
you read, understand, and
remember the people, geography,
and history of the world.

TRADITIONS
Lessons which give you a
deeper understanding of the
cultures of the regions you
are studying

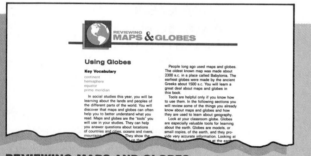

REVIEWING MAPS AND GLOBES
Reviews skills that will help you
use the maps in your book

LESSON OPENER

Logo identifies the focus for
each lesson

Important vocabulary, people, and
places introduced in the lesson

Lesson introduction

Asks you to think about what you
already know from previous lessons
or your own experience

Question you should keep in mind
as you read the lesson

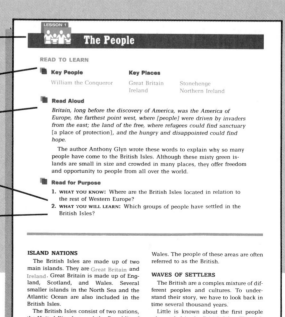

LESSON 1

The People

READ TO LEARN

Key People
William the Conqueror

Key Places
Great Britain   Stonehenge
Ireland   Northern Ireland

Read Aloud

*Britain, long before the discovery of America, was the America of
Europe, the farthest point west, where [people] were driven by invaders
from the east; the land of the free, where refugees could find sanctuary
[a place of protection], and the hungry and disappointed could find
hope.*

The author Anthony Glyn wrote these words to explain why so many
people have come to the British Isles. Although these misty green islands are small in size and crowded in many places, they offer freedom
and opportunity to people from all over the world.

Read for Purpose

1. **WHAT YOU KNOW:** Where are the British Isles located in relation to
the rest of Western Europe?
2. **WHAT YOU WILL LEARN:** Which groups of people have settled in the
British Isles?

ISLAND NATIONS

The British Isles are made up of two
main islands. They are Great Britain and
Ireland. Great Britain is made up of England, Scotland, and Wales. Several
smaller islands in the North Sea and the
Atlantic Ocean are also included in the
British Isles.

The British Isles consist of two nations,
the United Kingdom and the Republic of

Wales. The people of these areas are often
referred to as the British.

WAVES OF SETTLERS

The British are a complex mixture of different peoples and cultures. To understand their story, we have to look back in
time several thousand years.

Little is known about the first people
who settled in the British Isles. The first

2

REFERENCE SECTION

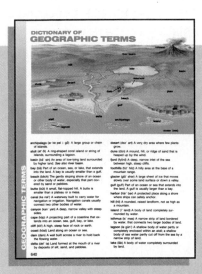

DICTIONARY OF GEOGRAPHIC TERMS

Definition and pronunciation of major geographic features

GAZETTEER

Location and pronunciation of major places discussed in your book and page where each is shown on a map

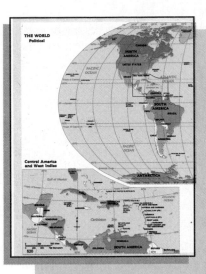

ATLAS

Maps of the eight culture regions of the world

GLOSSARY

Definition and pronunciation of all Key Vocabulary and page where each is introduced

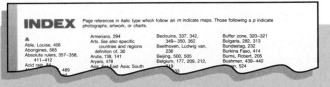

INDEX

Alphabetical list of important people, places, events, and subjects in your book and pages where information is found

Using Globes

Key Vocabulary

continent
hemisphere
equator
prime meridian

In social studies this year, you will be learning about the lands and peoples of the different parts of the world. You will discover that maps and globes can often help you to better understand what you read. Maps and globes are the "tools" you will use in your studies. They can help you answer questions about locations of countries and cities, oceans and rivers, mountains and deserts. They show the shapes and sizes of places on the earth. Maps and globes can also help you to make comparisons and determine distances and directions between places in the world.

People long ago used maps and globes. The oldest known map was made about 2300 B.C. in a place called Babylonia. The earliest globes were made by the ancient Greeks about 1500 B.C. You will learn a great deal about maps and globes in this book.

Tools are helpful only if you know how to use them. In the following sections you will review some of the things you already know about maps and globes and how they are used to learn about geography.

Look at your classroom globe. Globes are especially valuable tools for learning about the earth. Globes are models, or small copies, of the earth, and they provide very accurate information. Looking at a globe is a lot like looking at the earth from a point in outer space. On a globe shapes and relative sizes are shown correctly. Directions and relative distances are also shown correctly.

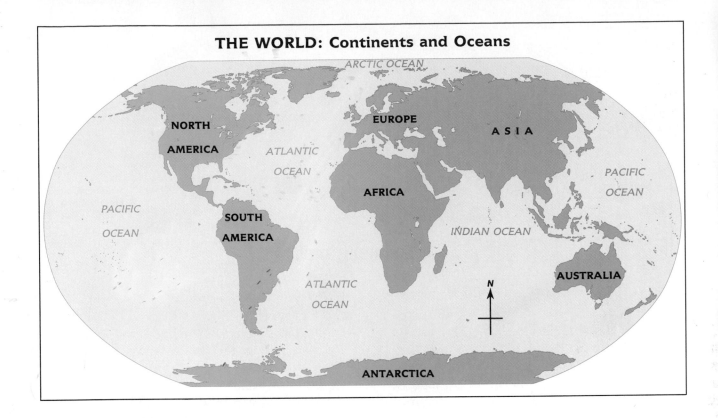

THE WORLD: Continents and Oceans

Maps are drawings on flat surfaces of all or part of the earth. Maps have some advantages that globes do not. Maps can be folded or rolled. They can be carried and stored easily. A map can show the world so that it can be seen all at once. On a globe only half the world can be seen at a time. You will be using maps as you read this book. Look at the many different maps in the book.

Continents and Oceans

The surface of the earth is made up of land and water. Globes show the parts of the earth's surface that are land and the parts that are water. Large bodies of land are called **continents**. You may know that there are seven continents on the earth: North America, South America, Europe, Asia, Africa, Australia, and Antarctica. Find these continents on the map of the world on this page.

As the map shows, most of the continents are separated, or nearly separated, from one another by water. If you look

carefully at a globe, you will see that most of the water on the earth's surface is part of a single, large connected body of water. This body of water, which covers more than half the earth, is divided into smaller parts, called oceans. You may know that the earth has four oceans: the Atlantic, the Pacific, the Indian, and the Arctic. Find these oceans on the map above.

Hemispheres

Do you know what a **hemisphere** is? If you break down the word into its parts, you can see what it means. A sphere is a round object, such as the earth. *Hemi* is a Greek word that means "half." Thus, the word *hemisphere* means "half a sphere." Geographers use the term *hemisphere* to refer to half of the earth.

By turning a globe or moving around it, you can see that the earth can be divided into an almost endless number of hemispheres. In order to simplify, geographers divide the earth in two ways.

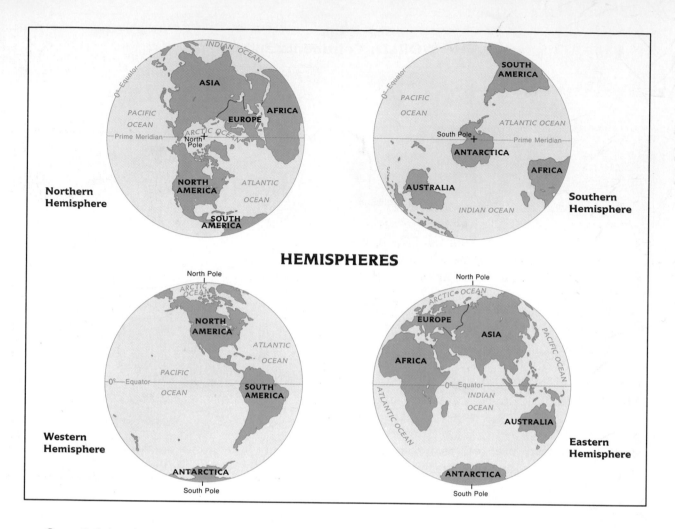

HEMISPHERES

One division is made along an imaginary line called the **equator**. The equator circles the earth halfway between the North Pole and the South Pole. As you can see from the maps above, it runs through South America and Africa. The equator divides the earth into the Northern Hemisphere and the Southern Hemisphere. The Northern Hemisphere is the part of the earth you would see if you were looking at the earth from a point in space directly above the North Pole. The Southern Hemisphere is the part of the earth you would see if you were looking at it from a point in space directly above the South Pole.

The earth can also be divided into the Eastern Hemisphere and the Western Hemisphere. These hemispheres are separated by another imaginary line around the earth. This line is known as the **prime meridian**. You will learn about the prime meridian on pages 50–51.

One way in which you can identify the hemispheres is by learning the names of the continents they contain. As you can see from the maps of the hemispheres on this page, most of the earth's landmasses are found in the Northern Hemisphere. Name the continents of the Eastern Hemisphere and the Western Hemisphere.

1. What is a continent?
2. What is a hemisphere?
3. Which imaginary line separates the Northern and Southern hemispheres?
4. Which imaginary line separates the Eastern and Western hemispheres?
5. How can using globes help you learn about the earth?

Using Maps

Key Vocabulary
cardinal directions
intermediate directions
scale
symbol
map key

While globes are the most accurate representations of the earth, maps are usually much more useful. Your book includes more than 100 maps. Some show the entire world, and others show only a part of the world.

In order to use maps effectively, you must know how to "read" them. Information on maps is presented in a special "language." The "language" of maps allows mapmakers to show a great deal of information in a small space. In this section you will learn to read the language of maps. When you understand this language, you will be able to read the maps in this book and the other maps you will find in books and magazines.

BRAZIL

⊛ National capital
• Other city

Directions

You already know that there are four cardinal directions—north, south, east, and west. North is the direction toward the North Pole. If you face north, south is directly behind you, east is to your right, and west is to your left. The letters *N*, *S*, *E*, and *W* are often used to stand for the cardinal directions.

There are also the four intermediate directions. *Intermediate* means "between." The intermediate directions are the directions halfway between the cardinal directions. Northeast (*NE*), for example, is the intermediate direction halfway between north and east. The other intermediate directions are northwest (*NW*), southeast (*SE*), and southwest (*SW*).

Most maps are drawn so that north is toward the top of the map. Many maps have a north pointer that shows which

way north is on the map. If you know where north is, you can easily find all the other directions. Look at the map of Brazil on this page. In what direction is Belém from Manaus? As you can see from the map, Belém lies east of Manaus.

Scale

All maps are smaller than the part of the earth they show. For this reason a short distance on a map stands for a much greater real distance on the earth.

The scale, or relative size, of a map will tell you how much smaller map distances are than real distances. The scale of a map can be shown in a few ways. On the maps in this book, scale is shown by lines, called line scales. Each map has two line scales, one for miles and the other for kilometers. Find the line scales on the map on this page.

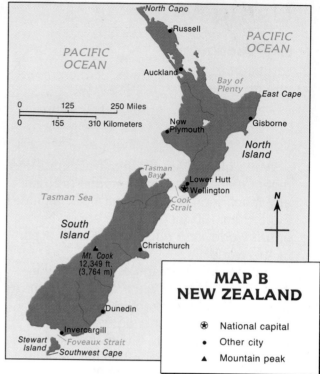

Now find the line scales on **Map A** of New Zealand on this page. The top line shows how many miles on the earth are represented by one inch on the map. The bottom line shows how many kilometers on the earth are represented by two centimeters on the map. How many miles on the earth does one inch on the map represent? How many kilometers do two centimeters represent? How many kilometers does one centimeter represent?

Suppose you want to know the distance between the cities of Auckland and Dunedin. Use a ruler to measure the map distance in inches between the two cities. Then multiply the number of inches by 350 to find the real distance in miles. To get the number of kilometers between Auckland and Dunedin, multiply the number of centimeters by 215 to find the real distance in kilometers. What is the approximate distance between the cities of Auckland and Dunedin in miles? What is the approximate distance between the cities in kilometers?

Now look at **Map B** on this page. It shows the same area shown on **Map A**. The shape of New Zealand is the same on both maps, but New Zealand appears larger on **Map B**. You know, of course, that New Zealand has not changed in size. What has changed is the scale of the map. One inch on **Map B** stands for a fewer number of miles than one inch stands for on **Map A**.

Use the line scale and a ruler to determine the distance between Auckland and Dunedin on **Map B** as you did on **Map A**. What is the distance in miles and in kilometers? If you measured and figured correctly, your answers will be the same as they were before, because the distance remains the same no matter which map you use.

The scale of **Map B** is larger than that of **Map A**. More details, that is, more information, can be shown on large-scale maps than on small-scale maps. Which things shown on **Map B** are *not* shown on **Map A**?

Symbols

Information on maps can be shown by **symbols**. A symbol is anything that stands for something else. Common map symbols are dots, squares, circles, triangles, lines, letters, and numbers. Color is a special symbol on maps. It is often used to show differences in height above sea level, rainfall, weather patterns, and plant life. Different colors are often used to distinguish one state or country from another. Blue is a commonly used symbol for water.

Some symbols look like the things they stand for. Others suggest the things they stand for. For example, a tiny drawing of an airplane may be a symbol for an airport. A small drawing of a tree may be a symbol for a forest or a small drawing of a fish may be a symbol for the fishing industry.

To find out what the symbols used on a map mean, you must look at the **map key**. The map key explains what each symbol stands for. It is important to check the map key on each map you use. A symbol that stands for one thing on one map may stand for a completely different thing on another map.

Look at the two maps on this page and check each map key. After studying the maps and their symbols, answer the following questions.

1. Where on maps is north usually shown?
2. In which direction would you travel going from Nairobi to Mount Kenya? From Nairobi to Mount Kilimanjaro?
3. Do both maps on this page have the same scale?
4. What does the color purple stand for on the map of Madagascar? What does the color orange stand for on the same map?
5. Which symbol is used to show cities?
6. Why do you think it is important to understand the different kinds of symbols that are used on maps?

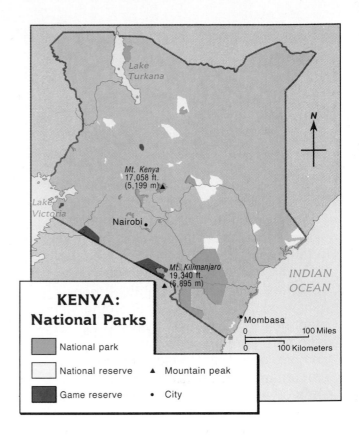

KENYA: National Parks

- National park
- National reserve
- Game reserve
- ▲ Mountain peak
- • City

0   100 Miles
0   100 Kilometers

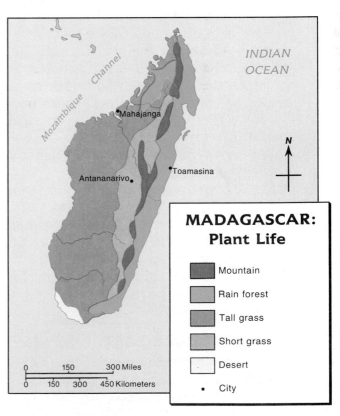

MADAGASCAR: Plant Life

- Mountain
- Rain forest
- Tall grass
- Short grass
- Desert
- • City

0   150   300 Miles
0 150 300 450 Kilometers

Different Kinds of Maps

Key Vocabulary

political map
physical map
landform map

grid map
distribution map

People study maps to understand the earth. The variety of information that can be shown on a map is endless. In order to keep things clear, most maps have a special purpose. Maps can be grouped according to the kind of information they provide. For example, **political maps** show countries, capitals, and other important political features. **Physical maps** show the natural features of the earth. For example, on physical maps you can find mountains, plains, lakes, rivers, deserts, and other kinds of land found on the earth.

Special-purpose maps provide information about particular subjects. The focus of a special-purpose map may be population, rainfall, language, or religion. No matter what you want to know about the world, there is sure to be a map for your purpose. As you read this book, think about the purpose of each of the maps that you come across.

Political Maps

This book has many different kinds of maps. In every unit you will find at least one political map. Political maps show political divisions such as countries and states. Political maps may also show national and state capitals and other important cities in countries.

The map on this page shows the countries of the Middle East. It is a political map. As you see, this map shows such political features as national boundaries,

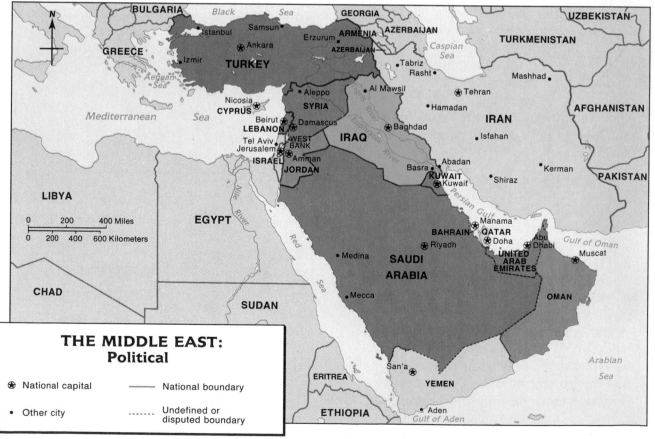

THE MIDDLE EAST:
Political

⊛ National capital

• Other city

——— National boundary

········ Undefined or disputed boundary

10

capitals, and other cities. Note that each country is shown in a special color. Also note that the land lying outside of the Middle East is shown in the same shade of gray. The map shows that some of the national boundaries are disputed, or uncertain. These boundaries appear as dotted lines on the map. Use the map to identify the capital of Turkey. Name the countries that border Syria.

Physical Maps

Physical maps emphasize the natural features of the earth. The earth's physical features include continents, oceans, islands, lakes, rivers, mountains, plains, and deserts. Some physical maps also show some political features, such as national boundaries and the names of cities and countries.

Landform maps are physical maps that show how the earth's surface varies from place to place. Landform maps use color to show the parts of the earth that are mountains, hills, plateaus, and plains. You may wish to use the Dictionary of Geographic Terms on pages 640–641 to help you picture some of these landforms. Some landform maps use shading to give a better idea of relief, or variation in height above sea level.

Look at the map of Scandinavia on this page. Check the key to see which colors are used to show mountains, hills, plateaus, and plains. Which country, Norway or Sweden, is more mountainous? Which part of Finland is mostly plains? Which country has plateaus? Find Denmark on the map. What kind of landform does Denmark have?

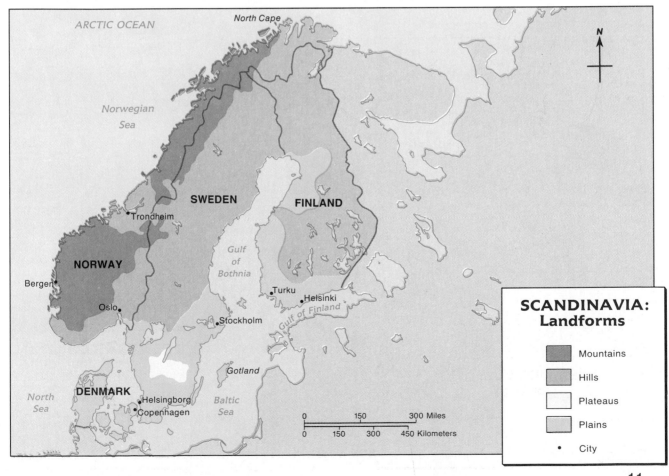

SCANDINAVIA:
Landforms

Mountains
Hills
Plateaus
Plains
• City

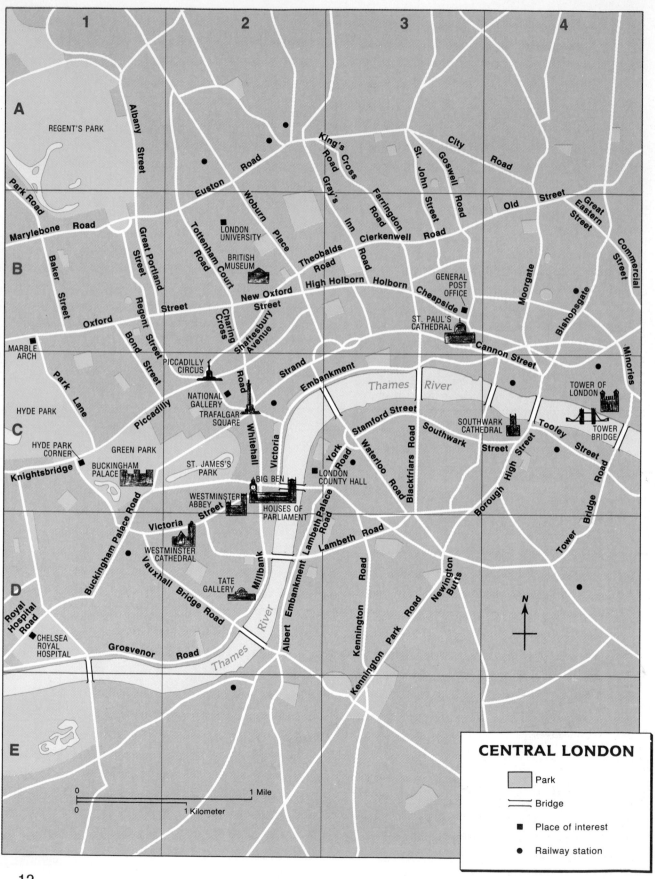

CENTRAL LONDON

- Park
- Bridge
- ■ Place of interest
- ● Railway station

12

Using a Grid Map

One kind of special-purpose map is a city map. Imagine that you are about to take a trip to London, the capital city of England. Imagine that you have only a few days to spend in this important city and that you do not know anything about its geography. How will you be able to find your way around London?

Those who have made the journey to London before suggest that you pick up a good city map. As the map on the opposite page shows, London's streets dart off in many directions. If you do not want to get lost, you will need to use this city map carefully.

City maps are special-purpose maps because they have a unique purpose: they help people find their way around a city. A good city map is also a grid map. For example, the map of London shows the central part of the city. This map has a number–letter grid that makes it easy to find places. Each square on the map can be identified by its letter and number. For example, St. Paul's Cathedral is found in square B–3. Find this place of interest on the map. Give the letter and number of the square in which Buckingham Palace is shown on the map.

Distribution Maps

Some maps show how such things as population, rainfall, language, and religion are distributed in different parts of the world. These kinds of maps are called distribution maps

The map on this page shows the distribution of population in India. Different colors are used to show the parts of India in which there are few people per square mile (or square kilometer) and in which there are many people per square mile (or square kilometer). Look at the map key. It shows different population categories. Which color shows areas where there are more than 500 people per square mile (200 people per square kilometer)?

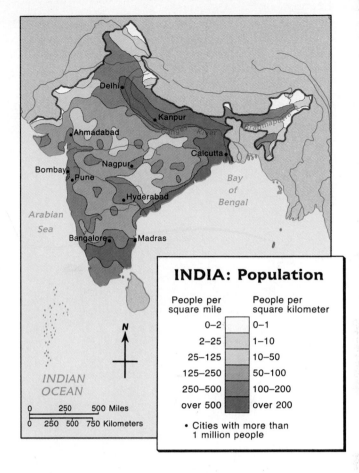

INDIA: Population

People per square mile	People per square kilometer
0–2	0–1
2–25	1–10
25–125	10–50
125–250	50–100
250–500	100–200
over 500	over 200

• Cities with more than 1 million people

Which parts of India have more than 500 people per square mile (200 people per square kilometer)? Where are there two or fewer people per square mile (one or fewer people per square kilometer)?

1. What are some of the things commonly shown on political maps?
2. What are some of the things commonly shown on physical maps?
3. What is a distribution map? Explain how distribution is shown on the map on this page.
4. What is a grid map?
5. In which grid on the map of Central London on page 12 are each of the following sites located? St. Paul's Cathedral; General Post Office; London University; St. James's Park; Parliament; Victoria Street.
6. How can a grid map help you find your way around a city?

THE IMPORTANCE OF GEOGRAPHY

They were searching for lands and straits they knew existed but which they had never seen. . . .

Author Barry Lopez wrote these words to describe how hundreds of years ago explorers searched for a passage through North America to Asia. These explorers reached lands, seas, and peoples previously unknown to them. You will carry on this spirit of exploration as you read this book and learn more about the land and people of our planet.

1 Geography's Five Fundamental Themes

Key Vocabulary

geography
physical geography
cultural geography
region

Read Aloud

What does the word *geography* mean to you? When you think of geography, perhaps you think of mountains, valleys, deserts, and other parts of the earth's land. Or maybe you think about people and how they live, from mountain villagers in thatched huts to big-city apartment dwellers. As you will read, all of these things are part of geography.

Read for Purpose

1. **WHAT YOU KNOW:** What are two things that you already know about geography?
2. **WHAT YOU WILL LEARN:** What are the Five Fundamental Themes of Geography?

STUDYING GEOGRAPHY

In the Read Aloud section you were asked to think about geography. Geography is the study of the earth and everything on it. Since this definition is very broad, let's look at how we study geography today.

Much of what we know about the earth is based on the findings of explorers. Some of the early explorers did not know much about geography, but they did have great courage. Supported by their courage, explorers traveled to all parts of the earth. These travels greatly increased our knowledge of geography.

Today the exploration of our world continues. We are no longer restricted to exploring our own planet. Astronauts have explored the moon, and satellites and probes have been sent to many other planets. As a result, we have learned not only about the remote areas of our planet, but about earth's place in the universe as well.

Look at the diagram on pages 16–17. It shows the solar system, or the group of planets that revolve around the sun. As you can see, the earth is but one part of a large system that includes a number of other planets. What are some of the other planets in our solar system?

PHYSICAL AND CULTURAL GEOGRAPHY

Clearly there is more to studying the universe than can be included in this book. So we will concentrate on our own planet, and try to learn as much as we can about its geography.

OUR SOLAR SYSTEM

NEPTUNE

PLUTO

MERCURY

SUN

EARTH

JUPITER

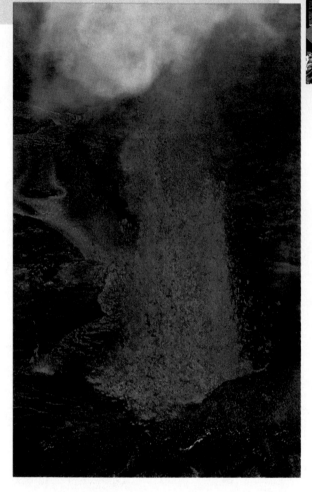

Physical geography is the study of the earth's surface, such as volcanoes.
Cultural geography deals with people, such as these people enjoying a shopping mall.

Since geography is such a broad subject, it is usually divided into parts. The two main parts of geography that you will study in this book are physical geography and cultural geography.

Physical geography is the study of the earth's surface—all of the different kinds of land that make up our planet. Physical geography also includes the study of weather over long periods of time, plant and animal life, and many other factors that affect the world in which we live. You will read more about physical geography in Part 2 of this introduction.

Cultural geography is the study of the earth's peoples—of the ways of life various peoples have developed as they have used and changed the earth. You will read more about cultural geography in Part 3.

FIVE THEMES

How do geographers study physical and cultural geography? There are many different ways, but in general the study of geography looks at five different themes. These themes are known as the Five Fundamental Themes of Geography. Let's look at each of them.

1. LOCATION

The first task of a geographer is to determine and describe the location of places on our planet. The geographer must identify the exact position of a place on the earth. This is called its absolute location.

To describe absolute location, geographers use maps and globes. You have already reviewed your knowledge of maps and globes. You have read how geographers divide the earth into hemispheres and use the cardinal directions of north, south, east, and west to show where places are located on the earth.

On pages 50–51, you will read about the lines of latitude and longitude that are shown on many maps and globes. These lines are the best way that geographers have to determine and describe the absolute location of places.

Relative location, or the relationship of one place to other places, is also very important to geographers. Think of how you would describe the relative location of your home. You might say that it was next to a park or ten blocks from a school. You would be relating your home to the location of something else in your community. Look at the map on this page. Describe the relative location of Chandler Park.

Knowing about relative location helps geographers understand why places develop the way they do. For example, the location of New Orleans, Louisiana, at the mouth of the Mississippi River helps to explain why it is a major port city.

2. PLACE

No two places on the earth are exactly alike. Geographers try to show how each place is unique. They also try to show the ways in which places are similar and the ways in which places are different. These are all part of the theme of place. As you read this book, remember that describing a place includes telling about both the aspects of its physical geography and the parts of its cultural geography.

Think about how you would describe the place where you live. You might talk about the types of buildings there are, whether you are near a body of water, what kinds of people live in your area, and what they do to earn a living. All of these are characteristics of a place that make it different from other places.

3. HUMAN–ENVIRONMENT INTERACTION

Geographers are interested in much more than simply knowing where places are and how they are described. They want to know in detail how people interact with the land on which they live. In other words, they want to know about human–environment interaction.

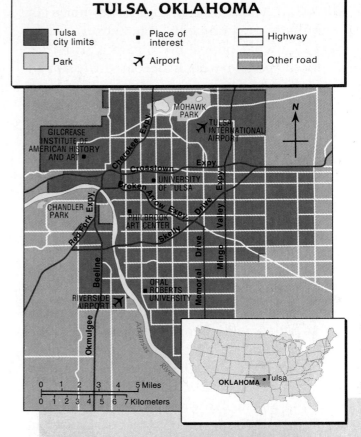

MAP SKILL: Maps are one way to determine absolute and relative location. This map shows the location of some important places in Tulsa, Oklahoma. How would you describe the location of Tulsa International Airport?

Think about your community. What happens there every day? How do people in the community get the food they eat every day? What is your area famous for? All of these things are part of the interaction of all the people of your community with their environment.

In daily life there are many examples of important interactions within places. In the United States it might be warm enough in November for people to relax on the beach in Palm Beach, Florida, or in southern California. On the other hand the people of International Falls, Minnesota, might be throwing snowballs after the first snowfall of the season.

Can you think of other examples of human–environment interaction? How about what people do to earn a living? A lot of people who live near the coast of Massachusetts fish for lobsters to earn their living. On the other hand, because Iowa has vast amounts of fertile farmland, many Iowans earn their living by farming.

All of these are human–environment interactions. Understanding them is an important part of geography.

4. MOVEMENT

The fourth theme in the study of geography is the movement of people, goods, and ideas around the world.

Have you ever moved to a new home, or do you know anyone who has? Why do people move? Of course there are many different reasons. One of the most common reasons is to start a new job. Geographers are interested in what causes certain jobs to be available in certain areas, and in studying the movement of people to be near these jobs.

Geographers are also interested in many other kinds of movement. Today a doctor in Sweden can contact a doctor in the United States and exchange important medical information by computer. Because of new equipment, ideas, information, and products can move very quickly around the world. Geographers study how these patterns of movement affect people and the way societies develop.

5. REGIONS

The last of the Five Fundamental Themes is one of the most important themes you will study about in this book. This is the theme of regions. A region is an area with common geographic or cultural features that set it apart from other areas.

Regions can vary greatly in size. They can range from a city and the areas around it to an entire hemisphere. Geographers divide the world into regions to study the different parts of the earth more closely.

Movement, such as this movement of cars through the city of Los Angeles, is one important theme of geography.

In this book the world is divided into eight large regions. In Part 3 of this introduction you will read about how and why the world is divided this way and about the different ways in which you will study the earth's major regions.

STUDYING OUR PLANET

Geography is the study of the earth and all the places and things on it. You have read that this study is divided into two kinds of geography, physical geography and cultural geography. You have also read about geography's five fundamental themes: location, place, human–environment interaction within places, movement, and regions. In the following sections you will read about how to apply these themes to your study of geography in this book.

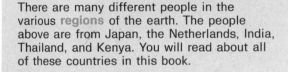

There are many different people in the various regions of the earth. The people above are from Japan, the Netherlands, India, Thailand, and Kenya. You will read about all of these countries in this book.

Check Your Reading

1. What is geography?
2. What is the difference between physical geography and cultural geography?
3. Describe the geography of the community where you live, using the Five Fundamental Themes of Geography.
4. **THINKING SKILL:** Look at the diagram on pages 16–17. Which planets in the solar system are closest to the earth?

2 Physical Geography

■ Key Vocabulary

environment	polar climate
landform	elevation
climate	natural resources
tropical climate	vegetation
temperate climate	fossil fuel

■ Read Aloud

Five, six, seven thousand feet and we turned eastward over the broad valley of the Juncal River and toward the mountains. We gained on them. At first they looked like colossal gobs of sponge cake sprinkled with a thin coating of powdered sugar. . . .The great gobs of sponge cake were not the Andes at all. They were only the foothills of the Andes. We hadn't started to climb.

This is how one writer described an airplane trip over the Andes mountains. Mountains are just one part of the amazingly different kinds of physical geography in the world.

■ Read for Purpose

1. **WHAT YOU KNOW:** What have people done over the years to change the land where you live?
2. **WHAT YOU WILL LEARN:** Why is it important to study physical geography?

STUDYING THE LAND

In this book you will study the regions of the earth. When you start to study each region, the first chapter you will read will be about the physical geography of that region. As you have read, physical geography is the study of the earth's surface. On the next few pages you will read in more detail about what is included in the study of physical geography.

ENVIRONMENTS

Every place on earth has its own special kind of physical geography. The earth has many different environments. An environment is made up of all of the surroundings of a place. It includes the land and the water, the weather patterns, and all the plants and animals that live in a place.

Physical geographers study the characteristics of all of the earth's environments. A physical geographer, for example, may study a mountain environment to determine how high the mountains are or how easy they are to travel through. Physical geographers also may study how such natural conditions affect things like rainfall and transportation.

LANDFORMS

Did you know that people can live on only a small part of the earth? More than 70 percent of our planet is covered with water. The 30 percent of the surface that is dry land is divided into different types of landforms, or physical features. Mountains, hills, plains, and plateaus are different kinds of landforms. Landforms vary greatly in size and shape.

If you look at pages 640–641 in the back of your book, you will find a Dictionary of Geographic Terms. This dictionary shows many of the earth's landforms and gives a definition of each. As you read this book, refer to this dictionary to read about each landform and to see what it looks like.

As you have read, geographers are very interested in studying landforms and how they affect the ways people live. Landforms are one of the most important parts of physical geography that you will study in this book.

CLIMATE

Climate is another important part of physical geography that you will study. Climate is the kind of weather a place has over a long period of time. Climate includes seasonal temperatures, the amount of precipitation (pri sip i tā′ shən), and wind patterns in a place. Precipitation is rain, snow, hail, sleet, and any other form of water that falls to the earth.

The climate where you live affects your everyday life. Think of your community and of places nearby. Do they almost always have cold winters? Are the summers long or short? Does it rain all year or only part of the year?

The answers to the above questions will help you to understand why climate is important to our lives. It affects how we live and work. It also affects the kinds of houses that we build and the types of

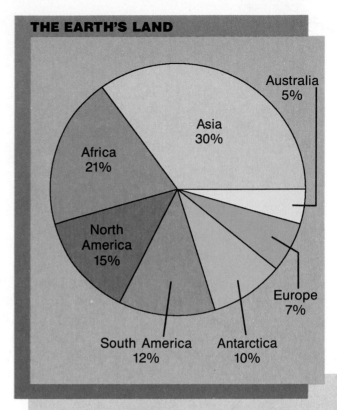

THE EARTH'S LAND

Australia 5%
Asia 30%
Africa 21%
North America 15%
Europe 7%
South America 12%
Antarctica 10%

GRAPH SKILL: The land surface of the earth is divided into seven continents. Which is the largest? Which is the smallest?

clothes that we wear. Finally, climate has a great effect on the kinds of crops, if any, that we grow in a region.

There are many different climates on the earth. Let's look at some of them.

THE EFFECT OF THE SUN

Do you know why some places on earth are warmer or colder than others? One important reason is the sun. Some places on the earth receive more of the sun's rays than other places receive. Because of the tilt of the earth as it revolves around the sun, places near the equator receive more direct rays of the sun than do places farther away from the equator. This helps to explain why places near the equator are warm most of the time, while the North and South poles tend to be very cold.

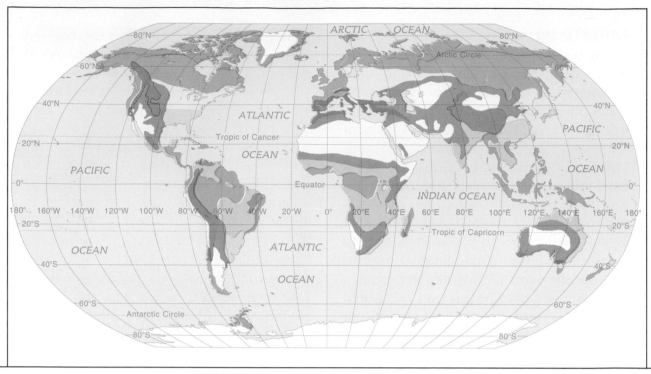

THE WORLD: Climate

☐ Ice cap	☐ Highlands, temperature and precipitation vary with elevation	☐ Mild winter, cool summer, wet
☐ Very cold winter, cold summer, dry	☐ Semi-dry, temperature varies with latitude	☐ Mild or warm winter, hot summer, wet
☐ Very cold winter, cool summer, wet	☐ Cold winter, hot or warm summer, wet	☐ Mild, wet winter; hot, dry summer

☐ Dry, temperature varies with latitude
☐ Warm all year, wet with one dry season
☐ Warm and wet all year

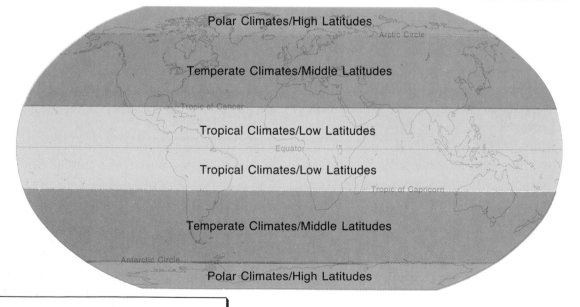

Polar Climates/High Latitudes

Temperate Climates/Middle Latitudes

Tropical Climates/Low Latitudes

Tropical Climates/Low Latitudes

Temperate Climates/Middle Latitudes

Polar Climates/High Latitudes

THE WORLD: Climate Zones

MAP SKILL: How many different types of **climate** are found in Africa? In which climate zone is most of Africa located?

CLIMATE ZONES

Look at the two maps on page 24. They show some of the different climate areas of the world.

Find the equator on the map at the bottom of the page. Now locate the area to the north and south of the equator—from the Tropic of Cancer to the Tropic of Capricorn. This area receives the most direct rays of the sun. Occasionally, temperatures here reach as high as 130°F. (54°C)! This is called the tropical climate zone. The word *tropical* comes from an ancient Greek word meaning "turning to the sun."

North and south of the tropics are the temperate climate zones. Places in the temperate climate zones have weather that changes considerably during four distinct seasons. Places located in these zones usually do not experience extremely high or low temperatures, or extremely large or small amounts of precipitation.

Some places on earth are always cold. The polar climate zones, which are located north and south of the temperate zones, receive only the most indirect rays of the sun. As a result, the polar zones are the coldest areas of the earth.

OTHER INFLUENCES ON CLIMATE

Look again at the map on the top of page 24. It shows that even though the world is divided into different climate zones, climates are not always the same within these zones. Why is this true?

In addition to heat from the sun's rays, other factors also affect climate. One of them is winds. Winds are currents, or masses, of air that blow around the earth. As the sun heats the earth, masses of air grow warmer and expand. When the warm air rises, it pushes out cold air. You may have seen a weather report on television that showed a cold front or a warm front coming to the area where you live. A front is air that is expanding or being pushed out of one area into another one.

Winds also carry moisture in the form of water vapor, which is tiny drops of water. The warm air that rises carries water vapor. The amount of moisture in the air determines the amount of precipitation that falls in a place.

Another factor that affects climate is elevation, or height above sea level. Areas with high elevations are cooler because temperatures become lower as the land grows higher. You will read more about how and why this happens in Unit 2.

Finally, distance from the ocean and the size and shape of landforms in a region also affect climate. You will read more about these factors throughout this book.

NATURAL RESOURCES

You have now looked at two of the important parts of physical geography, landforms and climate. The third important part is natural resources. Natural resources are the materials found in nature that people can use, such as water, air, soil, or animals.

In areas of high elevation, such as the Himalayas of Asia, many peaks are covered with snow all year.

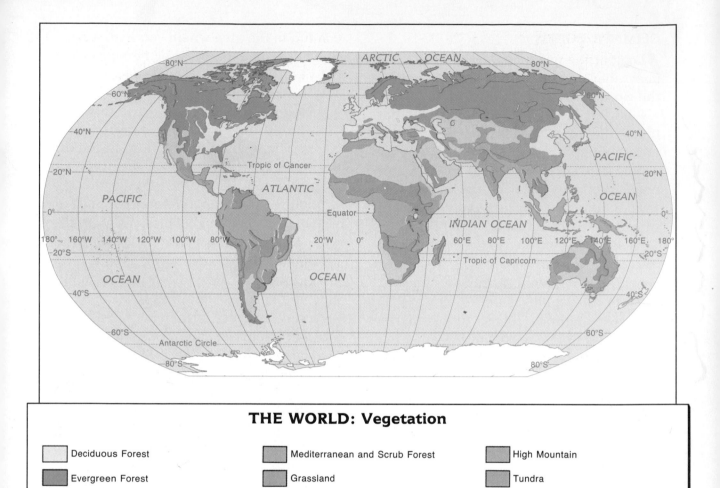

THE WORLD: Vegetation

- Deciduous Forest
- Evergreen Forest
- Tropical Rain Forest
- Mediterranean and Scrub Forest
- Grassland
- Desert
- High Mountain
- Tundra
- Little or no vegetation

MAP SKILL: In which part of the world is the vegetation mainly tundra? What kinds of vegetation are found on the continent of Antarctica at the South Pole?

Different parts of the world have natural resources in uneven amounts. What are some of the important natural resources of your area?

VEGETATION

Plants are one kind of natural resource. Trees, flowers, and grasses are all part of the vegetation, or plant life, that grows in an area. The main types of vegetation areas in the world are forest, grassland, desert, and tundra.

A forest is a place in which trees are the main type of vegetation. Forests require large amounts of water and are found in many climate zones.

Grasslands may be covered with many types of grasses. Grasses do not require as much water as trees and are found in most parts of the temperate zones.

Deserts are dry areas that have little plant life. Only plants that can live for long periods with little water can survive there.

A tundra is a type of plain found in polar zones. Although tundras have soil that is permanently frozen under the surface, the surface is warm enough to allow tiny plants and mosses to live.

The minerals shown here—azurite (*left*), copper (*center*), and placer gold (*right*)—have many uses, as does hematite (*below, left*). Malachite (*below, right*) is used in jewelry.

MINERALS AND FOSSIL FUELS

Other natural resources besides various kinds of vegetation are also found in the earth. Minerals are substances in nature that are not animals or plants. Some minerals are metals. Iron, copper, and gold are among the metals that people have used since very early times. Other minerals are nonmetals, such as table salt.

Coal, natural gas, and petroleum are fossil fuels, the remains of animals and plants that died thousands of years ago. Fossil fuels are important sources of energy used today for heating, lighting, and the running of machinery.

LANDFORMS, CLIMATE, NATURAL RESOURCES

In this section you have learned about the study of physical geography. You have read that there are three important parts of physical geography: landforms, climate, and natural resources. In this book there are chapters on the physical geography of each of the world's regions. As you read each chapter on physical geography, notice that it is divided into two lessons: one lesson on landforms and one lesson on climate and resources.

 Check Your Reading

1. Give some examples of the earth's landforms.
2. What is climate?
3. Why is it important to study the physical geography of the earth?
4. **THINKING SKILL:** List three questions you could ask to find out what kind of environment a place has.

3 Cultural Geography

■ Key Vocabulary

culture
ethnic group
custom

■ Read Aloud

The Chinese often talk about success in terms of food. "Having grains to chew" is an expression indicating a person has a job. If you "have an iron rice bowl" you have a very secure job. If you "have a porcelain rice bowl" you have an insecure job, while saying "the rice bowl is broken" means you are unemployed.

All of the peoples of the world find ways to express what is important to them and to their way of life. Studying these different ways through cultural geography will help you to understand what is special about people everywhere.

■ Read for Purpose

1. **WHAT YOU KNOW:** What are some of the groups you belong to besides your family?
2. **WHAT YOU WILL LEARN:** What are the main parts of culture?

CULTURE

As you can tell from its name, an important part of cultural geography is culture. Culture is the way of life of a group of people. Just as there are many environments, there are many cultures. Cultural geographers study how people use their environment to build their own special culture.

Cultural geography shows how people are alike and how they are different. All people, for example, have a way of greeting one another. However, people in different cultures greet one another in different ways. People in the United States shake hands when they meet, the Japanese bow, and the French kiss both cheeks.

WHAT MAKES UP CULTURE?

Culture includes all the ways in which people relate to one another. Social organizations, rules and governments, values, beliefs, languages, arts, and even sports and hobbies are all parts of culture.

In this book you will read about many cultures. In each unit, after you read a chapter about the physical geography of a region, you will read chapters about the cultural geography of each part of that region. These chapters will be divided into four lessons. Each lesson will cover one part of cultural geography. These parts are: people, economy, government, and arts and recreation. Let's look at them.

PEOPLE

One place to start studying a culture is to study the people in it and the groups they form. To understand a people, you need to know about their **ethnic groups**, languages, family structure, religions, and **customs**. An ethnic group is a group of people who share a language, history, and/or place of origin. Customs are the practices from the past that people continue to observe.

The family is the most important group in a culture. Geographers study families because they show how cultures provide for people's physical and emotional needs. Families provide food and shelter, raise children, teach values, and give love, affection, and a sense of purpose.

Studying language is another key to understanding culture. There are many different languages in the world. However, most languages belong to one of a few large language families. A language family is a group of languages that are similar to one another.

In addition to language, religion also helps to hold families and cultures together. For many people religion offers answers to important questions about how people should act in life and what will happen after they die. Thus religion strongly influences the way many people think and act. You will read more about many different religions as you study the cultural geography of the world.

ECONOMY

In Part 2 you read about the earth's environment. People all over the world have had to change their environments in order to earn a living. One way in which people have adapted their environments is by finding uses for their natural resources. For example, people may cut down trees to

Different **ethnic groups** have different **customs**. These Chinese Americans sometimes use chopsticks to eat their food.

sell. This wood is bought by different people to make a variety of products. All the ways in which people use their resources in order to earn a living are known as economic systems.

There are many kinds of economic systems because people respond to basic economic questions differently. Who or what determines what people will produce? How do goods get from one place to another? How should goods be shared?

Understanding the answers to these questions will help to explain differences in economic systems. In the United States, for example, individuals decide what and how much to produce. Most property is owned privately, by individuals or corporations, and goods are produced by privately owned businesses. By contrast, in China the government owns much of the property and most large factories.

In this book you will read about many of the economic systems in the world. As you read about them, think about how they answer the economic questions.

GOVERNMENT

In the different regions of the world people have found different ways to rule and

MAJOR FARM PRODUCTS OF THE WORLD-1992

Product	Major Producing Nations	Major Uses
Wheat	China, Russia, Ukraine, United States. India. France. Canada	Bread, breakfast foods, macaroni products, livestock feed
Rice	Vietnam, Thailand, Cambodia, Myanmar, Japan	Food
Corn	United States, China, Brazil, Mexico	Flour, starch, cooking oil, livestock feed
Potatoes	Russia, China, Poland, United States, India	Food
Soybeans	United States, Brazil, Argentina, China	Bean sprouts, tofu, soy sauce, livestock feed
Coffee	Brazil, Colombia, Indonesia, Côte d'Ivoire, Ethiopia	Beverage
Cacao	Côte d'Ivoire, Brazil, Ghana, Malaysia, Indonesia	Chocolate, cocoa butter, cocoa powder

CHART SKILL: What do wheat, corn, and soybeans have in common?

govern themselves. Long ago most governments developed from the need of a people to organize or defend themselves or to solve an environmental problem. Today almost all of the world's governments have many purposes.

When reading about one of the world's governments, ask yourself: How is the government and its leaders chosen? What responsibilities does it have? How does it share power? What rights do the people have? You will read in this book that, as with economic questions, different countries choose to answer these questions differently. In some governments people have a voice in running their country. Other governments are controlled by one person.

ARTS AND RECREATION

Studying the arts of a region also helps us to understand its culture. There are many different kinds of artists. For example, some paint beautiful pictures, some make sculptures, some write stories or poetry, and some compose and perform works of music and dance.

Leisure activities may also be special to a particular people. In Japan, for example, many people enjoy origami (ôr i gä′ mē), or the art of folding paper into the forms of animals, flowers, and other shapes.

CULTURE REGIONS

Geographers divide the world into culture regions. These are areas of the world in which people use their environment in similar ways and have developed a common culture.

Cultural geographers study culture regions to discover how cultures vary from place to place. First they study environments to determine what resources are available and how people have used them. Geographers look to see how people have changed the land. Have people built canals? What kinds of crops have farmers planted? Have people built many cities?

Cultural geographers also compare and contrast cultures of different regions. They identify the different kinds of ethnic groups, religions, economic and political

THE WORLD: Culture Regions

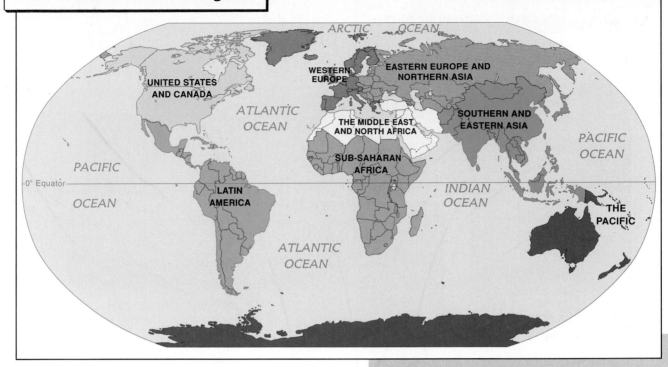

MAP SKILL: In this book you will study the world's eight culture regions. Which region contains South America? Which region contains countries in both Europe and Asia?

systems, and arts and types of recreation in the regions of the world. Such comparisons help geographers to identify what makes each culture region distinctive, or different from others.

EIGHT WORLD REGIONS

As a result of their studies, many geographers divide the world into eight major culture regions. In this book each of these regions will be studied as a separate unit. They are:

1. The United States and Canada
2. Latin America
3. Western Europe
4. Eastern Europe and Northern Asia
5. The Middle East and North Africa
6. Sub-Saharan Africa
7. Southern and Eastern Asia
8. The Pacific

In Part 2 you learned about physical geography. In each of the units listed above you will read a chapter about the physical geography of the region. Then you will read chapters about that region's cultural geography. As you read, compare each region to the others you have studied. How are they similar? How are they different? By the end of the book you will have found out what the world's cultures have in common, as well as the many ways in which they are different.

Check Your Reading

1. What is culture?
2. In which culture region do you live?
3. What are the four major parts of cultural geography?
4. **THINKING SKILL:** Look at the list of regions on this page. Classify the regions into two or more groups, and explain why you divided them the way you did.

THE IMPORTANCE OF GEOGRAPHY

 PART 1

- Geography is the study of the earth

- Two parts of geography: physical geography and cultural geography

- Five themes of geography: location, place, human-environment interaction, movement, regions

 PART 2

- Physical geography is the study of the earth's surface

- The environment includes: land, water, climates, plants, animals

- Climate is affected by: sun, winds, elevation, distance from the ocean, size and shape of the landform

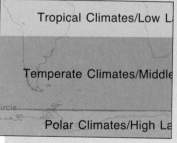

Tropical Climates/Low L

Temperate Climates/Middl

Polar Climates/High L

- Major climate zones: tropical, temperate, polar

 **PART 3**

- Culture is the way of life of a group of people

- Parts of cultural geography : people, economy, government, arts and recreation

- In a cultural region people use environments in similar ways and have a common culture

- This textbook discusses eight major culture regions of the world

IDEAS TO REMEMBER

- Geographers divide physical and cultural geography into five themes: location, place, human-environment interaction, movement, and regions.
- Physical geography is the study of the earth's environments.
- Many cultural geographers study the people, economies, governments, and arts and recreations of the world's eight culture regions.

REVIEWING VOCABULARY

vegetation	polar climate
environment	fossil fuel
cultural geography	region
custom	culture
physical geography	ethnic group

Number a sheet of paper from 1 to 10. Beside each number write the word or term from the list above that best matches the definition.

1. A large area with common features that set it apart from other areas
2. The weather pattern north and south of the temperate zones
3. Trees, flowers, and grasses
4. All the surroundings of a place
5. The energy source from the remains of plants and animals that died thousands of years ago
6. A practice from the past that people continue to observe
7. A group of people who share a language, history, or place of origin
8. The way of life of a group of people including their beliefs, customs, roles, and ways of relating to each other
9. The study of the earth's people and their ways of life
10. The study of all the different kinds of land that make up our planet

REVIEWING FACTS

1. List two ways in which exploration of our world continues today.
2. What is the difference between absolute location and relative location?
3. Why do geographers study the physical characteristics of places?
4. Explain why the existence of vast amounts of fertile farmland is an example of a relationship within a place.

5. Why do geographers divide the world into regions?
6. How does the sun affect climate?
7. List the major natural resources of the earth. Why are they important to the well-being of people?
8. What do cultural geographers study about ethnic groups to determine what makes them alike or different?
9. Which three questions could you ask to help find out what kind of an economic system a people have?
10. What are some of the ways in which governments may differ from one another?

WRITING ABOUT MAIN IDEAS

1. **Writing a List:** List four of the world's culture regions that are located nearest to the one in which you live.
2. **Writing a Paragraph:** Write a paragraph explaining why it is important to study the world's eight culture regions. Name the regions in your paragraph.
3. **Writing About Perspectives:** Imagine that you are visiting a place that has a very different climate from the place where you live. What place did you choose? Write a letter to someone back home. In it, describe the differences in temperatures, precipitation, and winds between the two places.

ASIA

+North Pole

ARCTIC
OCEAN

Bering Strait

Beaufort
Sea

75°N

Baffin
Bay

Arctic Circle

International Date Line

Bering
Sea

ALASKA

180

Gulf
of Alaska

Davis Strait

60°N

Labrador
Sea

165°W

45°N

Hudson
Bay

CANADA

150°W

PACIFIC

OCEAN

135°W

30°N

HAWAII

120°W

Gulf of
St.
Lawrence

Ottawa
✪

UNITED STATES

Washington, D.C.
✪

60°

Tropic of Cancer

75°W

15°N

Gulf of California

Gulf of Mexico

0°

Equator

Caribbean
Sea

CENTRAL
AMERICA

SOUTH
AMERICA

PACIFIC   OCEAN

105°W

90°W

15°S

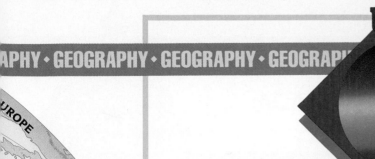

UNIT 1

THE UNITED STATES AND CANADA

WHERE WE ARE

You are about to begin an adventure that will take you all over the world around us. You will start your journey at home, in the region that consists of the United States and its neighbor to the north, Canada. As the map shows, these two countries cover a large part of the Western Hemisphere.

As you read about the landforms, climate, natural resources, people, economies, governments, and arts and recreation of the United States and Canada, think about how you would describe the region to a person from another land. Knowing what makes the part of the world in which you live special will help you to compare it with the other regions you will visit on your journey.

THE UNITED STATES AND CANADA

UNITED STATES

Capital ★
Washington, D.C.

Major language: English
Population: 250.4 million
Area: 3,623,420 sq mi; 9,384,658 sq km
Leading exports: machinery and
transportation equipment

CANADA

Capital ★
Ottawa

Major languages: English and French
Population: 26.8 million
Area: 3,851,798 sq mi; 9,976,140 sq km
Leading export: automotive products

CHAPTER 1

PHYSICAL GEOGRAPHY OF THE UNITED STATES AND CANADA

FOCUS

That dry aromatic odor . . . one could breathe that only on the bright edges of the world, on the great grass plains, or the sagebrush desert. . . .

Willa Cather, an American novelist, wrote these words in the 1920s. The grassy plains she wrote about stretch across much of the United States and Canada. But they are just one of many landforms in this region of variety and abundance.

Landforms

READ TO LEARN

Key Vocabulary

erosion
Continental Divide
population density
permafrost

Key Places

Appalachian Highlands
Interior Plains
Rocky Mountains
Pacific Mountains

Coastal Plains
Canadian Shield
Arctic Islands

Read Aloud

I think I shall never forget the scenery in the Santa Cruz Mountains. To me the most beautiful spot in our journey of thousands of miles was found among the stately pines on the mountaintop where a natural fountain poured its crystal waters into a granite basin . . .

These thoughts come from the diary of Susan Parrish, a young pioneer who traveled west across the United States with her family in 1850. Just as Willa Cather was struck by the beauty of the plains, Susan Parrish was excited by the mountains of the West.

Read for Purpose

1. **WHAT YOU KNOW:** What are the main geographic features of the area in which you live?
2. **WHAT YOU WILL LEARN:** What are the physical regions of the United States and Canada?

SEVEN GEOGRAPHIC REGIONS

People like Susan Parrish who travel through the United States and Canada come across many different landforms. Geographers group these landforms into seven physical regions. These regions are shown on the map of the United States and Canada on page 40.

The United States and Canada share four of these regions: the Appalachian Highlands, the Interior Plains, the Rocky Mountains, and the Pacific Mountains. One region, the Coastal Plains, is found only in the United States. The two remaining regions, the Canadian Shield and the Arctic Islands, are located almost entirely in Canada.

APPALACHIAN HIGHLANDS

Suppose you lived hundreds of years ago, before there were airplanes, trains, and cars. You are hiking across the land, starting in the East. Your first challenge is to cross the Appalachian Mountains. They are in the Appalachian Highlands region, which stretches from the southeastern part of the United States to Canada's Newfoundland Island.

Even though this region is called "highlands," the mountains here are not that

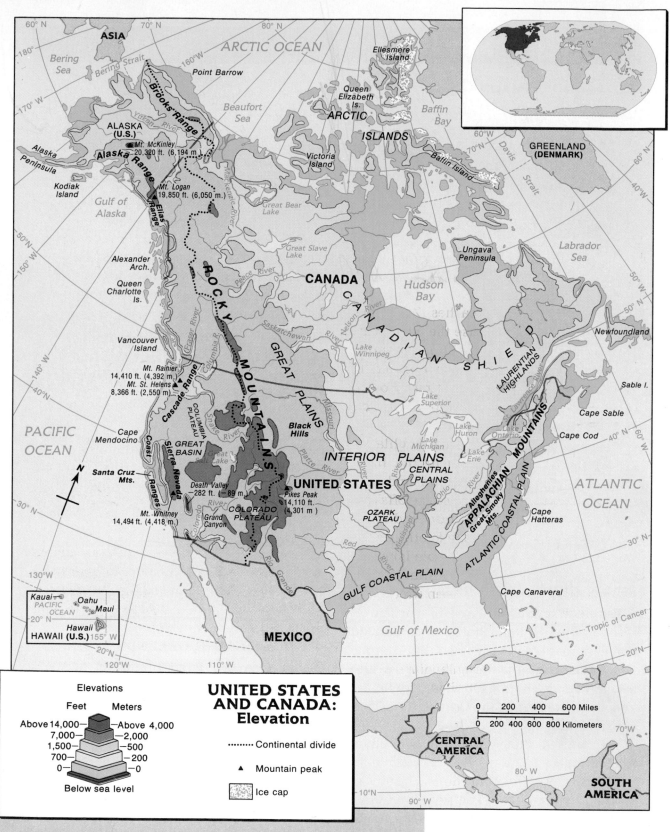

UNITED STATES AND CANADA: Elevation

Elevations

Feet	Meters
Above 14,000	Above 4,000
7,000	2,000
1,500	500
700	200
0	0

Below sea level

······· Continental divide

▲ Mountain peak

Ice cap

Scale:
0 200 400 600 Miles
0 200 400 600 800 Kilometers

MAP SKILL: The land of the United States and Canada varies greatly in elevation. What is the approximate elevation of the Black Hills?

The Appalachian Mountains (*above*) and the Great Plains (*below*) are examples of two major landforms found in the United States.

high. None of them reaches 7,000 feet (2,134 m). This is because the mountains are very old—about 500 million years old. As a result, they have been exposed to **erosion** over a long period of time. Erosion is the gradual wearing down of the earth's surface by water or wind.

In Canada the Appalachian Highlands end in Newfoundland. There the highlands meet the Atlantic Ocean and continue underwater. This makes the offshore waters dangerous in this area. Find Sable Island, off the coast of Nova Scotia, on the map on the opposite page. Sable Island is called the "graveyard of the Atlantic" because so many ships have been wrecked in its shallow waters.

INTERIOR PLAINS

After crossing the Appalachian Mountains, you enter a completely different region, called the **Interior Plains**. The Interior Plains extend through much of the central part of the United States and Canada.

Look at this region on the map on page 40. It is mostly flat land with rich soil. Most of the land is a prairie, an area of gently rolling grassland with few trees. As you travel west, the land gradually rises.

For centuries, people gathered plants and hunted animals on the Interior Plains. They also recognized that the Interior Plains offered good land for farming, and they planted crops there.

The western part of the Interior Plains, called the Great Plains, is drier than the rest of the region. The Great Plains are almost treeless, and you can see for miles in all directions.

ROCKY MOUNTAINS

From the flatlands of the Interior Plains, your westward journey would take you to the **Rocky Mountains**. These mountains stretch along most of the western part of North America.

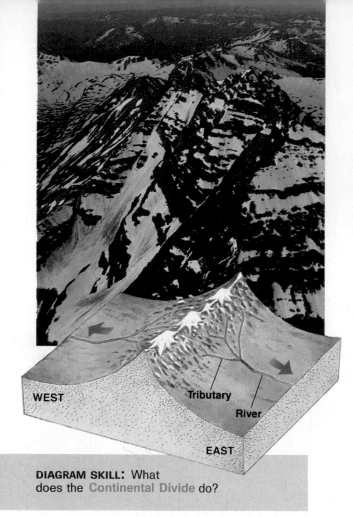

WEST

Tributary

River

EAST

DIAGRAM SKILL: What does the Continental Divide do?

canyons, and deserts. A plateau is an area of flat land that rises above the land around it. A canyon is just the opposite—a deep valley with steep sides.

The Grand Canyon in Arizona is one of the most famous canyons in the world. Over a period of about 6 million years, water from the Colorado River carved out the Grand Canyon. Today, from the floor of the canyon you can gaze at walls that rise upward for almost a mile (1.6 km). Brilliant colors glow on the canyon walls as the light changes.

PACIFIC MOUNTAINS

The Grand Canyon is beautiful, but you continue your journey into the Pacific Mountains region. Here, between the Rockies and the Pacific Ocean, you find both rich, rolling land and high mountains, such as the Cascade Range. Find this landform on the map on page 40.

Like the Appalachian Highlands, the Pacific Mountains extend into the ocean. Several peaks rise above the Pacific Ocean to form islands, such as Canada's Vancouver Island and Queen Charlotte Islands. The highest peak is Mount McKinley, which reaches 20,320 feet (6,194 m).

The Cascade Range has many active volcanoes, such as Mount St. Helens, which last erupted in 1980. Its ashes drifted across much of the United States.

COASTAL PLAINS

You have reached the West Coast of North America, and your journey has ended. Although you have visited many regions of the United States and Canada, you have missed some. For example, you have yet to visit the Coastal Plains, which are in the United States.

The Coastal Plains are divided into two parts. One part is the Atlantic Coastal

Look at the photograph above. Note that the Rockies are higher and more rugged than the Appalachians of the East. Many of the Rockies are over 10,000 feet (3,048 m) high. Unlike the Appalachians, the Rockies are young mountains — about 130 million years old. They have not been as worn down by erosion.

The summits, or peaks, of the Rockies form an imaginary line known as the Continental Divide. Sometimes called the "backbone of North America," the Continental Divide separates rivers flowing eastward and westward. Rivers west of the Continental Divide flow toward the Pacific Ocean. Those on the east flow toward the Atlantic Ocean or Gulf of Mexico.

As you descend west from the summits of the Rockies, you pass through plateaus,

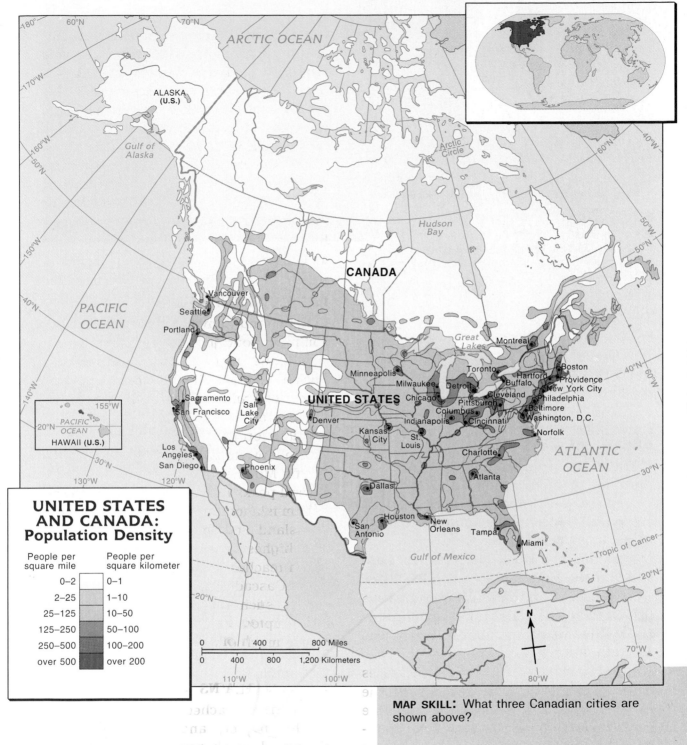

UNITED STATES AND CANADA: Population Density

People per square mile	People per square kilometer
0–2	0–1
2–25	1–10
25–125	10–50
125–250	50–100
250–500	100–200
over 500	over 200

MAP SKILL: What three Canadian cities are shown above?

Plain, which borders the Atlantic Ocean. The other part is the broad Gulf Coastal Plain, which borders the Gulf of Mexico.

Many people today live in the Coastal Plains. Look at the map above. It shows the **population density** of the United States and Canada. Population density is the number of people per square mile (or per square kilometer) in a given land area. As the map shows, the Coastal Plains include some of the most heavily populated areas of the United States today. This is

Because of the cold climate in parts of the Canadian Shield and Arctic Islands, only simple plant life such as that shown at left can live.

because some major port cities—such as New Orleans, New York City, and Boston—are here. Can you name some other major coastal cities?

CANADIAN SHIELD AND ARCTIC ISLANDS

There are two more regions to visit. In those far northern regions of Canada, the Canadian Shield and the Arctic Islands, you would expect to encounter a cold climate.

The Canadian Shield covers half of Canada. It has a landscape of low hills, lakes, and forests. Look again at the map on page 43. Why do you think a visitor to the Canadian Shield said that this region was "nothin' but miles and miles of miles and miles"?

North of the Canadian Shield are the Arctic Islands. Of the larger islands in this area, Victoria Island is very flat. Baffin Island and Ellesmere Island are marked by mountains and glaciers. A glacier is a large body of ice that moves slowly over the land.

The land of the Arctic Islands is tundra. This treeless plain has a thin layer of topsoil under which the soil is permanently

frozen. The frozen layer of soil is called permafrost. Only simple plant life, such as mosses and small woody plants, can survive in the permafrost of the tundra.

VARIED LANDS

During your travels across the United States and to the far northern reaches of Canada, you have visited all kinds of land, from wide plains to huge mountains. These two large countries offer a great variety of landforms. In the next lesson, you will learn how climate and resources also help to make this a region of great abundance.

Check Your Reading

1. What four physical regions are shared by the United States and Canada?
2. What two regions are located only in Canada?
3. Identify a major physical feature of each of the seven regions of Canada and the United States.
4. THINKING SKILL: The following words are taken from a traveler's journal: "We . . . stopped for the night, using water that . . . was the first water running west. . . . " What region do you think she was describing? Explain your answer.

Climate and Resources

Key Vocabulary

temperate	timberline
arable	hydroelectric power

Key Places

Great Lakes
St. Lawrence Seaway

Read Aloud

The Seneca Indians of eastern North America believe that once, long ago, Sky Woman, who lived high above the land, had a daughter who went to live on the earth. Years later, the daughter died. For many days afterward, Sky Woman's grandson, Good Mind, watered the earth above his mother's grave. Soon plants began to grow. From her body came corn and squash. From her hands came beans, looking like fingers. From her feet came potatoes, which look like large toes.

Today, most people in the United States and Canada have other explanations for the abundance of their land. But they still rely on the many resources it provides.

Read for Purpose

1. **WHAT YOU KNOW:** What are some of the natural resources of the area in which you live?
2. **WHAT YOU WILL LEARN:** What are the climate regions and the major natural resources of the United States and Canada?

A TEMPERATE CLIMATE

For humans, health depends greatly on body temperature. When a person's body temperature is too high or too low, he or she is likely to be sick. As with the human body, the health of the United States and Canada depends on temperatures that are neither too hot nor too cold. For instance, a sudden frost can destroy an orange crop in Florida. A long heat wave can destroy a corn crop in Iowa.

Too much or too little precipitation is also dangerous for many reasons. For example, if the Cascade Mountains do not receive enough rain, the forests there dry out. The chances of forest fires increase. What are some other examples of extreme weather that can cause damage?

Generally, the regions of the United States have a temperate climate. That means they are neither too hot nor too cold. Although temperate areas have few extremes in weather, their climates do change from place to place.

In general, as you go farther south in North America, the summers are longer and hotter and the winters are shorter and milder. As you go farther north, the summers are shorter and milder and the win-

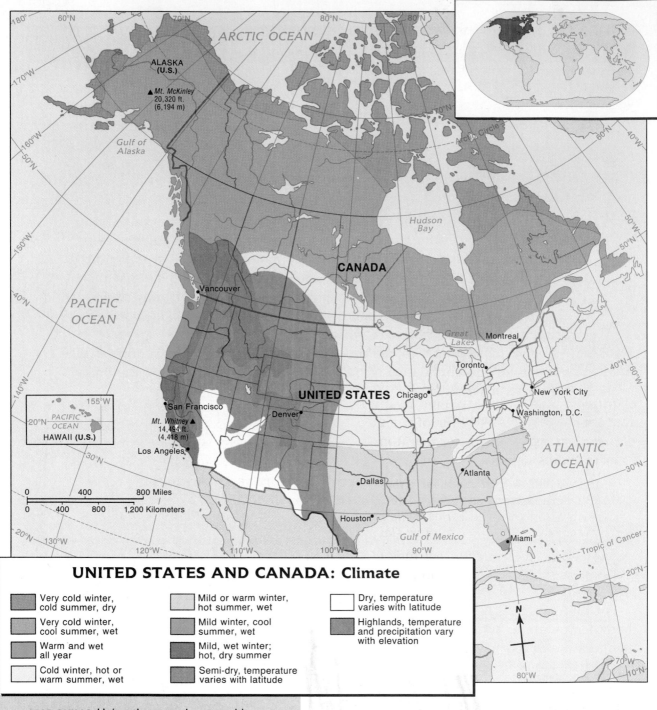

UNITED STATES AND CANADA: Climate

▢ Very cold winter, cold summer, dry	▢ Mild or warm winter, hot summer, wet	▢ Dry, temperature varies with latitude
▢ Very cold winter, cool summer, wet	▢ Mild winter, cool summer, wet	▢ Highlands, temperature and precipitation vary with elevation
▢ Warm and wet all year	▢ Mild, wet winter; hot, dry summer	
▢ Cold winter, hot or warm summer, wet	▢ Semi-dry, temperature varies with latitude	

MAP SKILL: Using the map, how would you describe the climate of the area around Washington, D.C.?

Climate also changes as the height of the land changes. The higher the land, the colder the temperature. In California's Pacific Mountain region, for instance, the peak of Mount Whitney is 14,494 feet (4,418 m) above sea level. It is so high that the peak is snow-capped all year. In contrast, the climate is much warmer in

ters are longer and colder. Look at the climate map of the United States and Canada above. What are some of the ways in which temperate climates differ?

46

California's sunny lowland valleys, where farming is a major industry.

Not all parts of the United States and Canada have temperate climates. Look again at the climate map. What other climates are found in these two nations?

SOIL AND CROPS

The United States grows more food than any other nation. This abundance is helped by the region's temperate climate, rich soil, and good water supply.

About half of the land in the United States is arable (ar' ə bəl), or good for farming. Major farming areas are found in the Interior Plains and the valleys of the Pacific Mountains and the Coastal Plains. Among the wide variety of crops grown in these areas are cotton, wheat, and corn.

Since much of Canada is cold and rocky, only about 5 percent of its land is arable. Yet Canadians make the most of what arable land they have. As one farmer from the Interior Plains says:

We farm as a family. On our farm three of our sons are farmers. . . . Wheat is our main crop, but we grow barley if the price is right, and the boys like to grow flax.

Many Canadian farmers feel they must grow those crops that they know will sell for high prices.

FORESTS

Forests cover about one third of the land in the United States and Canada. As a result, lumbering is an important economic activity in both countries.

In the Pacific Mountains region and the southern part of the Canadian Shield, broad forests are filled with evergreen trees such as pine and fir. Along the highways in these regions, you often see huge truckloads of lumber.

A long timberline divides the northern part of the Canadian Shield from the southern part. A timberline is the elevation above which, because of the cold climate at high elevations, trees cannot grow. Only small plants are able to live above the timberline.

WATERWAYS

Many important waterways are located in the United States and in Canada. Both countries share the Great Lakes, five of the largest freshwater lakes in the world. The Great Lakes are connected to the Atlantic Ocean by a system of rivers and canals

Forests are a major resource of the United States and Canada. Can you find the timberline in the photo at left?

47

called the St. Lawrence Seaway. Large ships are able to sail hundreds of miles inland on the seaway. Trace the routes that ships take on the map of the St. Lawrence Seaway on page 49.

Both the United States and Canada have many rivers that can be sailed far inland. The two nations share the Columbia River in the West. The Mississippi River in the United States, as well as the Mackenzie, Fraser, and other rivers in Canada, are all important transportation routes.

MAP SKILL: What is much of the land used for in the central part of the United States?

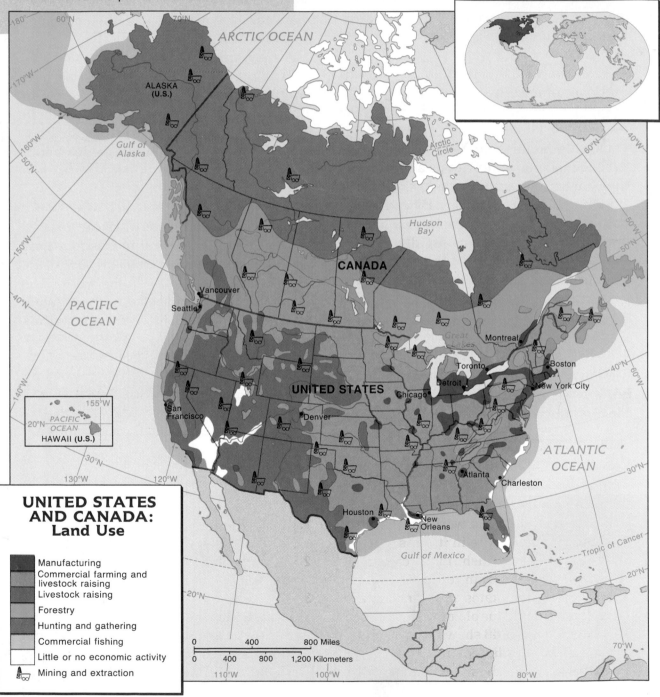

UNITED STATES AND CANADA: Land Use

- Manufacturing
- Commercial farming and livestock raising
- Livestock raising
- Forestry
- Hunting and gathering
- Commercial fishing
- Little or no economic activity
- Mining and extraction

0   400   800 Miles
0   400   800   1,200 Kilometers

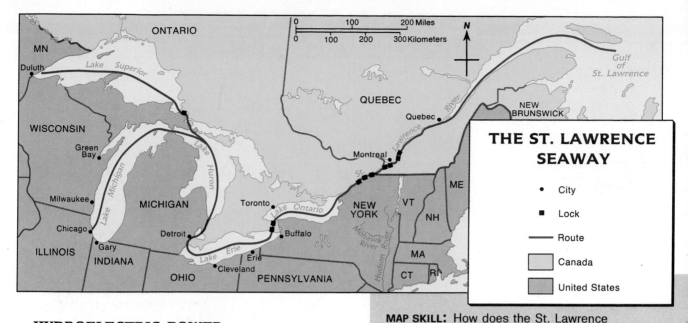

THE ST. LAWRENCE SEAWAY

- • City
- ■ Lock
- — Route
- ☐ Canada
- ▨ United States

MAP SKILL: How does the St. Lawrence Seaway help the United States and Canada?

HYDROELECTRIC POWER

People in the United States and Canada use many rivers to produce hydroelectric (hī drō i lek' trik) power. Hydroelectric power is electricity that is generated, or produced, by the force of rapidly moving water.

An advantage of hydroelectric power over other sources of energy is that it does not pollute the air. However, dams built for hydroelectric power block rivers, thus harming underwater life. For example, some fish need to migrate from place to place. Therefore, dams need to be planned and built carefully.

MINERALS AND MINING

A Canadian miner wrote that "rich nickel and copper deposits were actually found by accident" in his country about 100 years ago. Railroad workers who were blasting rock found ore in it. This started, he said, a "real land rush" in which miners "swarmed in and began to dig."

Both the United States and Canada have large reserves of valuable minerals. A look at the map on page 48 shows you the major mining areas of this region.

In recent times those coal and oil re-

serves that were easy to reach have nearly all been mined. However, new mining and drilling techniques are now making it possible to mine hard-to-reach reserves.

A LAND OF ABUNDANCE

The United States and Canada are very fortunate. As you have read, they form a region that has a temperate climate, abundant natural resources, and several rivers that can be sailed far inland. These factors allow the two nations to feed their people and to have many different kinds of industry.

 Check Your Reading

1. Why are temperate climates important to the United States and Canada?
2. Why is only 5 percent of Canada's land arable?
3. Describe the major resources of the United States and Canada.
4. **THINKING SKILL:** How are the climates of the United States similar to those of Canada? How are they different?

49

Understanding Latitude and Longitude

Key Vocabulary

latitude	prime meridian
longitude	meridian
parallel	global grid

As you have already seen, this book contains many maps. Have you noticed the system of lines drawn on many of them? The lines that extend east and west are called lines of latitude. The lines that extend north and south are called lines of longitude

Using Latitude

The equator is the starting line for measuring latitude. Latitude is distance, measured in degrees (°), north or south of the equator. The latitude of the equator is 0°. Lines of latitude north of the equator are labeled *N* for "north." Those south of the equator are labeled *S* for "south."

Look at the lines of latitude on the Lines of Latitude map on this page. These lines are also called parallels. Lines of latitude are always the same distance apart, or parallel. If you follow any two lines of latitude, you will see that they never meet.

Using Longitude

The prime meridian is the starting line for measuring longitude. All lines of longitude are called meridians. Longitude is distance, measured in degrees, east or west of the prime meridian. The longitude

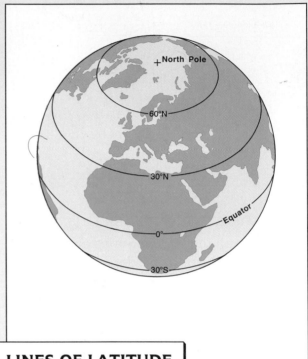

LINES OF LATITUDE

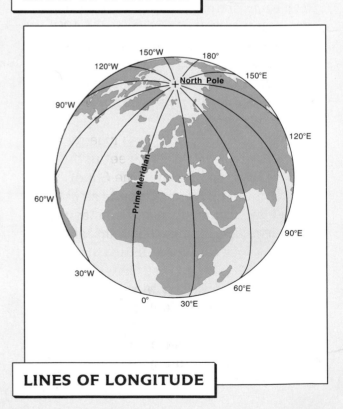

LINES OF LONGITUDE

GLOBAL GRID

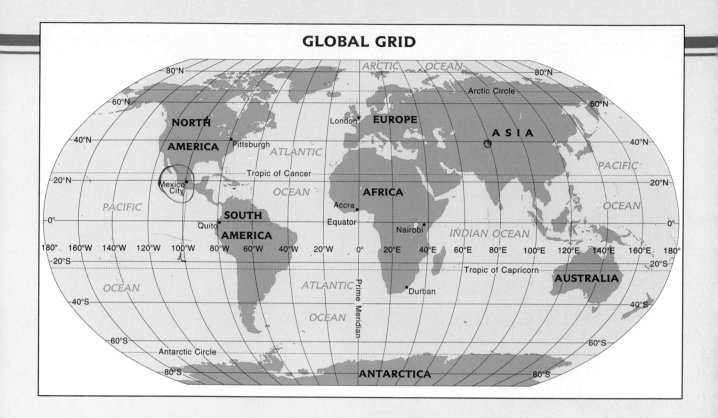

of the prime meridian is 0°. Meridians that lie east of the prime meridian are labeled *E.* Those west of the prime meridian are labeled *W.* If you traveled 180° eastward, you would be in the same place as you would be if you traveled westward 180°. Since 180°E and 180°W signify the same location, the line marking this longitude is not labeled *E* or *W.*

Look at the Lines of Longitude map. Notice how all meridians meet at the North Pole. They meet at the South Pole too. Distances between meridians increase as you move from the poles toward the equator. Meridians are farthest apart at the equator.

Finding Places on a Map

Together, lines of latitude and longitude make up the global grid. The global grid helps us to locate places on maps and globes. You can find any place on earth if you know its latitude and longitude. For

example, suppose you know that Pittsburgh, Pennsylvania, is located at approximately 40°N, 80°W. To find Pittsburgh on the map, first put your finger on the point where the equator and the prime meridian cross. Now move your finger north to the parallel labeled 40°N. Next move your finger west along this parallel to the point where it crosses the meridian, labeled 80°W. You have located Pittsburgh.

Reviewing the Skill

1. What are parallels and meridians? How do they help you to understand latitude and longitude?
2. Which city on the Global Grid map is located at approximately 20°N, 100°W?
3. Which South American city shown on the map is located very close to the equator?
4. At what longitude is Accra, Africa?
5. Why is it important to understand how to use latitude and longitude?

51

UNITED STATES AND CANADA: PHYSICAL GEOGRAPHY

LANDFORMS

- Mountains: Appalachian Highlands, Rocky Mountains, Pacific Mountains
- Plains: Interior Plains (includes Great Plains), Coastal Plains

- Northern Canada: Canadian Shield and Arctic Islands

CLIMATE

- Temperate climate: few extremes in weather

- Temperatures: Colder in mountains, warmer in lowlands

NATURAL RESOURCES

- Arable land: 50 percent of land in United States, only 5 percent in Canada

- United States grows more food than any other nation
- Forests cover one third of United States and Canada

- Waterways: Great Lakes, St. Lawrence Seaway, Mississippi River, Columbia River

IDEAS TO REMEMBER

- Mountains, plains, and other landforms divide the United States and Canada into seven physical regions.
- A temperate climate and abundant natural resources combine to provide this area with most of its needs.

REVIEWING VOCABULARY

arable   permafrost
Continental Divide   timberline
erosion

Number a sheet of paper from 1 to 5. Beside each number write the word or term from the list above that best matches each statement.

1. Harsh conditions resulting from a cold climate at high elevation keep trees from growing beyond this boundary.
2. This wearing-away process explains why the Appalachian Mountains are low and rounded compared with other mountain chains.
3. This term refers to land that is good for farming.
4. In North America this long line of mountain peaks divides rivers flowing eastward from those flowing westward.
5. In arctic regions this layer of permanently frozen soil allows only small plants and mosses to grow.

REVIEWING FACTS

1. Name the seven geographic regions of the United States and Canada. Which of the regions are found only in Canada? Which region is found only in the United States?
2. Why are the Rocky Mountains higher and more rugged than the Appalachian Mountains?
3. What is the difference between a *plateau* and a *canyon*? How was the Grand Canyon formed?
4. Name the two coastal plains in the United States. Why are these regions among the most heavily populated areas in the United States?
5. What is meant by the term *temperate climate*? In what ways does a temperate climate differ from an arctic or a tropical climate?

6. How does climate change as one moves north? As one moves south? How does altitude affect climate?
7. What are three reasons that the United States grows more food than any other country in the world?
8. How does the location of the Great Lakes and of the St. Lawrence Seaway encourage trade and transportation for both Canada and the United States?
9. Why is hydroelectric power cleaner than other forms of power generation?
10. Why do minerals, such as gold or oil, attract people to a place?

WRITING ABOUT MAIN IDEAS

1. **Writing an Outline:** Write an outline of the major physical regions of North America. Under each region list its important characteristics.
2. **Writing About Perspectives:** People in one country may view their country differently. Choose two cities of Canada and write descriptions of Canada as someone living in each city might see it.

BUILDING SKILLS: UNDERSTANDING LATITUDE AND LONGITUDE

1. What are lines of latitude and lines of longitude?
2. Which lines run north and south? Which lines run east and west?
3. Explain how the lines of latitude and lines of longitude are numbered.
4. What are the names of the lines at 0° latitude and 0° longitude?
5. How do lines of latitude and lines of longitude help you to read a map?

CHAPTER 2

THE UNITED STATES

FOCUS

I pledge allegiance to the flag of the United States of America and to the Republic for which it stands, one Nation under God, indivisible, with liberty and justice for all.

Millions of Americans know the Pledge of Allegiance of the United States by heart. In this chapter you will read why citizens of the United States are proud of their land, their freedom, and their way of life.

The People

Key Vocabulary

immigrant   discrimination
prejudice   megalopolis

Key Places

San Francisco

Read Aloud

It took us 12 days to cross the sea, and we thought we should die, but at last the voyage was over, and we came up and saw the beautiful bay and the big woman with the . . . lamp that is lighted at night in her hand.

These words were written in 1902 by Sadie Frowne, a garment worker in New York. Her joy at seeing the Statue of Liberty—of arriving in the United States—has been echoed in the words and thoughts of countless numbers of people coming to the United States to start a new life.

Read for Purpose

1. **WHAT YOU KNOW:** Do you know people who have come to the United States from other lands?
2. **WHAT YOU WILL LEARN:** Why have people from many different ethnic groups settled in the United States?

A FAMILY REUNION

It's the second Sunday in July, and in Dundee, Ohio, it's time for the annual Walter family reunion. More than 60 people, from 9 to 87 years old, have gathered at the schoolhouse. Many members of the Walter family live in Ohio. However, many others come all the way from Florida, California, and Massachusetts to be with the rest of the family.

Everyone sits down to a big dinner. First Glen Walter, who is the oldest, says a prayer. Then everyone starts to eat. The Walters have met in this way for 70 years.

Everyone at today's reunion is related to Remus and Abigail Walter, who ran a big farm near Dundee in the late 1800s. The Walter family traces its roots back to the Netherlands in Europe. In about 1780 a Dutch ancestor named Christian Walter sailed to the United States with his two brothers. They wanted a chance to better their lives, and they did so, buying land and turning it into successful farms.

PEOPLE FROM MANY LANDS

Like the Walters, people from all over the world have come to the United States. Many hoped to improve their lives.

They did not reach an empty land. For thousands of years, Indians had lived on this land and developed its resources. Many different Indian groups lived throughout North America and South America. They were the first people who lived in what is now the United States.

People like the Walters family, who arrived much later, are descendants of **immigrants**. An immigrant is a person who moves to a country other than the one where he or she was born. Most people now living in the United States are either immigrants or descendants of immigrants.

Not all of the people who reached the Western Hemisphere came voluntarily. Starting in the 1600s, millions of Africans were shipped to the Americas, where they were enslaved. Slavery in the United States ended after the Civil War. Those who had been enslaved were now free.

THE SEARCH FOR FREEDOM

Freedom attracted many immigrants to the United States. In the 1800s, great numbers of people immigrated to America from Europe. The main reason they came can be summed up in one word: *freedom*.

Many came for economic freedom—the opportunity to make a good living. Others came for religious freedom—the right to worship as they wished. Still others wanted political freedom—the right to have a say in the government of their country and be protected by its laws.

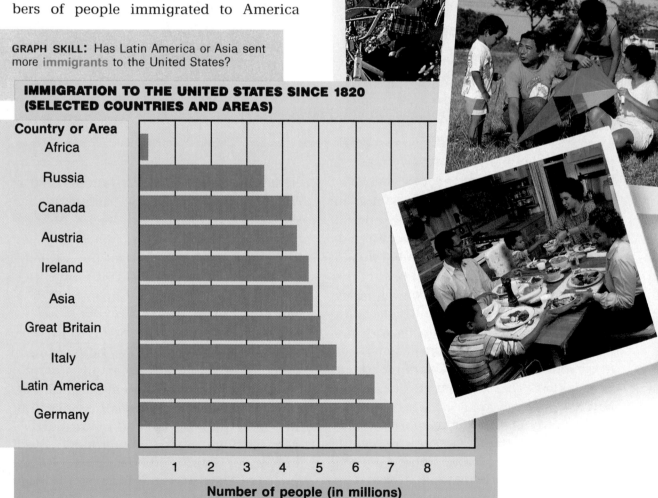

GRAPH SKILL: Has Latin America or Asia sent more **immigrants** to the United States?

IMMIGRATION TO THE UNITED STATES SINCE 1820 (SELECTED COUNTRIES AND AREAS)

Country or Area	Number of people (in millions)
Africa	
Russia	
Canada	
Austria	
Ireland	
Asia	
Great Britain	
Italy	
Latin America	
Germany	

Number of people (in millions)
1 2 3 4 5 6 7 8

Today immigrants continue to come to the United States for the same reasons. As one Cuban American explained:

When I came here from my country, I was living in New Jersey. . . . Very cold apartment, eight windows with no heat . . . It doesn't matter. . . . I was so happy to be here. The most important thing we were looking for was freedom. When you lose it once, you really know what freedom is.

ETHNIC GROUPS

During the early history of the United States most immigrants came to the country from Europe. Today, however, immigrants come from many parts of the world. Look at the graph on page 56. It shows where immigrants to the United States have come from. According to the graph, what areas have been the three largest sources of immigration to the United States since 1820?

Today the largest groups of immigrants come from Asia and Latin America—especially from Mexico. Spanish-speaking Americans from Latin America, called Hispanics, are the fastest-growing ethnic group in the United States today. An ethnic group is a group of people who share common roots, customs, and traditions.

The Spanish were the first Europeans to arrive in what is now the United States. Beginning in the 1500s, they began settlements in Florida and parts of the Southwest. Many Hispanics in the United States are descended from both Indians and Spanish people. They come from Latin America—from Mexico, Central America, South America, and from the Caribbean Islands.

Not all of America's ethnic groups came voluntarily. A few Africans immigrated to the United States in the 1600s, but soon after millions of Africans were forced to come to the Americas and were enslaved.

The influence of Chinese Americans can be clearly seen in the Chinatown neighborhood of San Francisco.

Slavery ended in 1865. However, African Americans have had to continue their struggle for certain rights, such as the freedom to vote and to live where they choose.

ETHNIC NEIGHBORHOODS

Many ethnic groups have left their marks on the American landscape and culture. Look at the photograph of Chinatown in San Francisco above. Note that many of the signs are in Chinese.

In addition to Chinatown, San Francisco has several other neighborhoods in which most of the residents are from a single ethnic group. The United States has many ethnic neighborhoods, but most American neighborhoods have people from many different ethnic groups living side by side.

Ethnic groups do not always live together peacefully. Prejudice (prej′ ə dis) and discrimination (di skrim ə nā′ shən) are problems that most ethnic groups have faced at some time in their history. Prejudice is one person or group's unfavorable opinion of another group that is formed unfairly, without knowing all the facts. Discrimination is the unfair treatment of a person or a group of people by another person or group. Today an ethnic group may still sometimes meet with prejudice and discrimination. However, laws have been passed to protect people in the United States against unfair treatment in jobs, housing, transportation, education, and other areas of life.

FROM FARMS TO CITIES

Most ethnic neighborhoods are in cities. When the Walter family you read about at

MAP SKILL: As you know, the United States is divided into 50 states. What state is in the northwest corner, south of Canada?

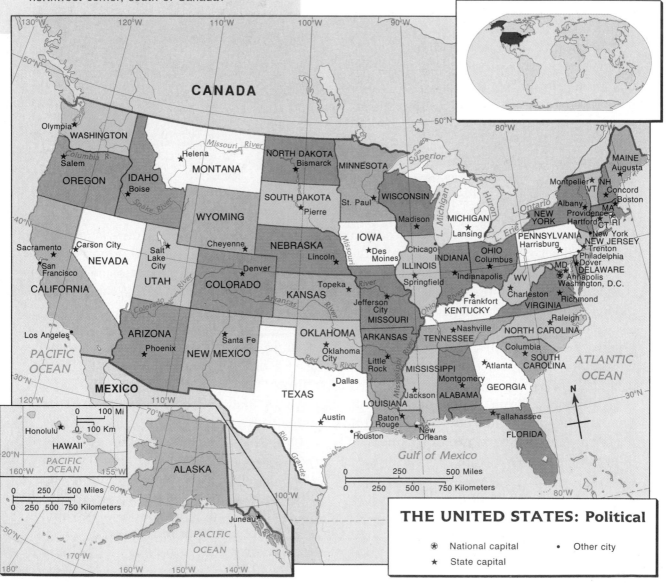

THE UNITED STATES: Political

⊛ National capital   • Other city
★ State capital

the beginning of the lesson came to the United States in the 1700s, most people in the United States lived on farms. Today less than one fourth of the people live in rural areas—that is, on farms or in towns with only a few thousand people. Each year, the number of farms gets smaller.

A LARGE POPULATION

Geographers can learn a lot about a country by studying its population. About 250 million people live in the United States. The country covers about 3.5 million square miles (9.1 million sq km), so it has an average of about 71 persons per square mile (27 per sq km). Each of these square miles could contain about 400 city blocks. That means that if people were spread out evenly across the nation, there would be one person every 5.6 blocks in the United States.

The United States has many areas where people live closely together. Often, people live in one city and work in another. At the beginning of the 1900s many people in the United States began moving to suburbs, the residential communities surrounding large cities. Today many suburbs have grown into towns and cities. Some places are so crowded that the entire area looks like one vast city. The name for such an area is a **megalopolis** (meg ə lop′ ə lis). The United States has megalopolises on the East and West coasts. Look at the map on page 58. Where are many cities close together?

ONE LAND, MANY PEOPLE

The people of the United States come from many different lands. Some lived here for centuries. Others immigrated to enjoy economic, religious, and political freedom. Still others were forced to come. Today, people of many backgrounds live throughout the land.

This photograph of Boston, Massachusetts, shows the city and the suburbs that have grown up around it.

Check Your Reading

1. What is an ethnic group?
2. Approximately what fraction of Americans lives in rural areas?
3. From what you have read in this lesson, how would you describe the origins of the people of the United States?
4. **THINKING SKILL:** List at least 10 freedoms Americans enjoy. Then group them by category: economic, political, and religious.

Decision Making

Every day you make many small decisions, like what to wear and what to eat. Some days you may also make big decisions that affect you and others around you. Decision making means selecting from a number of alternatives, or options, one option that will help you to achieve your goal. In this lesson you will learn one way to make good decisions.

Trying the Skill

In the last lesson you read about people who came from other countries to the United States. Here is a story about someone who is deciding whether or not to return to the country of his origin for his vacation.

Carlos Martinez is a 13-year-old boy who lives in New York City. Carlos and his family moved to New York from Honduras three years ago. The school year is nearly over, and Carlos has to decide how to spend his summer. His parents have told him he has two options. He can either stay at home and help in his father's grocery store or visit his grandparents in Honduras. Carlos enjoys helping in his father's store, but he would like to spend his summer outside the city, which gets very hot during the summer. He misses his grandparents in Honduras but does not want to be so far from his parents and friends.

Carlos's friend Eddy suggests another alternative. Eddy is spending the summer in the country with his family. He invites Carlos to spend one month with him on his family's farm in the country. Carlos thinks he would enjoy living on a farm. He wants to be away from the city but not too far from his family. He wonders, however, what it would be like living with Eddy's family.

1. What is Carlos's goal?
2. Which alternatives is he considering?
3. What do you think Carlos should do?

HELPING YOURSELF

The steps on the left can help you to make better decisions. The examples on the right apply these steps to Carlos's decision.

One Way to Make a Decision	Example
1. Identify and clearly define the goal(s) you wish to achieve.	Carlos's goal is to spend an enjoyable summer away from the city.
2. Identify all possible alternatives (options) by which you can achieve your goal(s).	Carlos can stay home, spend the summer with his grandparents, or visit Eddy on his family's farm in the country.
3. Predict the likely outcomes (consequences), both immediate and long range, of each alternative.	If Carlos stays home, he will spend the summer in the city. If he goes to Honduras, he might miss his family and friends. If Carlos visits Eddy, he will probably enjoy himself in the country.
4. Evaluate each outcome by determining whether it will benefit or harm you or others.	If Carlos does not enjoy the city during the summer, he will probably be unhappy if he stays home. If he goes to Honduras, he will probably miss his family and friends. If he goes to Eddy's farm, he will probably enjoy himself. However, he might miss his parents or have trouble adjusting to another family's way of life.
5. Choose the best alternative.	Which alternative did you choose?

Applying the Skill

Now apply what you have learned about the decision-making process. Read the following story.

Sam had always wanted to have a dog. One day he found a dog on the street. He called the animal shelter and looked in the newspaper for reports of lost dogs. When he could not find the dog's owner, he decided to keep the dog.

Then Sam saw a lost-dog sign with the dog's picture on it. Sam could call the phone number on the sign. But then he would miss his new pet. Or he could keep the dog and try to forget that he saw the sign. But then the owner of the dog would never get his pet back.

1. What was Sam's goal?
   a. to have a dog
   b. to return a lost dog
   c. to get a dog from an animal shelter
2. Which alternative did Sam probably not consider?
   a. returning the dog to its owner
   b. keeping the dog
   c. returning the dog and going to the animal shelter for a new dog
3. What do you think Sam should do? Explain your answer.

Reviewing the Skill

1. What does the term *decision making* mean?
2. What are some important steps to follow when you make a decision?
3. Why should you think of as many options as possible before making a choice?

The Economy

READ TO LEARN

Key Vocabulary

capitalism	import
free enterprise	developed economy
export	technology

Read Aloud

I took care of three cats for a few days. The cats' owners told other people. Now I've taken care of two dogs, five cats, a bird, and a gerbil. I earned $88. Doing a good job helps people notice you.

This account was written by a 12-year-old student from Gastonia, North Carolina. In this lesson you will learn why the student's pet-care business is a good example of how the economy of the United States works.

Read for Purpose

1. **WHAT YOU KNOW:** What are some jobs done by people in your community?
2. **WHAT YOU WILL LEARN:** Why is the economy of the United States known as a developed economy?

FREE ENTERPRISE

The United States has an economic system known as capitalism. In a capitalist system businesses are owned by individuals or groups of individuals rather than by the government. An important part of the capitalist system is free enterprise, the freedom to own property and run a business largely free of government control.

The pet-care business you read about in the Read Aloud is an example of the free enterprise system in practice. The student, like all Americans, is free to run a business with the goal of making a profit.

American businesspeople are also free to decide what to sell and what prices to charge. Consumers are free to buy whatever they can afford. However, in a free enterprise system, businesspeople must make sure there is a demand for things they want to sell and to price them carefully. If the price is too high, people will not get any business. If the price is too low, people cannot make a profit. By figuring out the right price, the student above can make more than $2,000 a year!

HOW AMERICANS EARN A LIVING

What kinds of jobs do people perform within a free enterprise system? Look at the graph on page 63. It shows the jobs in which most workers in the United States are employed.

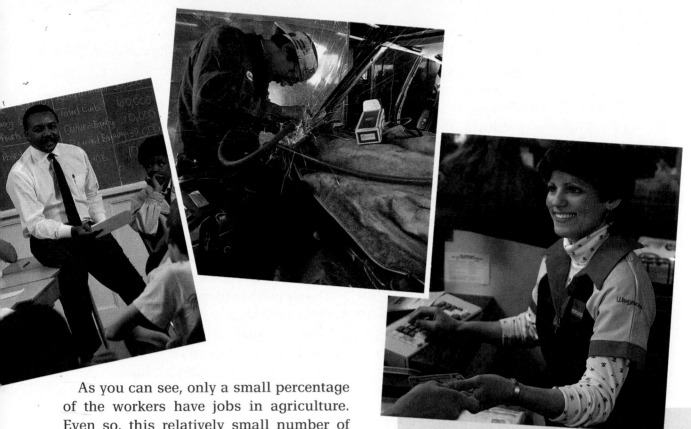

As you can see, only a small percentage of the workers have jobs in agriculture. Even so, this relatively small number of farm workers produces almost all the food the nation needs. Many United States farms are large, and farmers use huge machines to harvest their crops. These crops are sold all over the United States and the world.

The graph also shows that about 20 percent of the nation's workers have jobs in manufacturing and mining. Products that are manufactured include machinery, plastics, and chemicals.

How would you describe the pet-care business you read about on page 62? It is not farming, nor is it the manufacturing of a product. Neither is it trade, which is the business of buying and selling things. It is a type of economic activity called a service. That is, the worker helps people, or serves them, rather than makes or sells a product.

Service workers include government workers, secretaries, teachers, doctors, and lawyers. What other service jobs can you name?

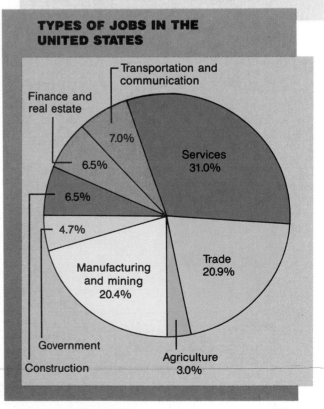

GRAPH SKILL: What are the three largest categories of jobs found in the United States? How are they shown above?

TYPES OF JOBS IN THE UNITED STATES

- Transportation and communication 7.0%
- Finance and real estate 6.5%
- Services 31.0%
- 6.5%
- 4.7%
- Manufacturing and mining 20.4%
- Trade 20.9%
- Government
- Construction
- Agriculture 3.0%

FOREIGN TRADE

Did you ever notice all the different places from around the world the products you buy come from? People in the United States buy and sell products from foreign nations as well as those from their own country.

The United States is one of the largest traders of goods in the world. People in the United States send many exports overseas. An export is any item sold to another nation. The leading exports are transportation equipment, machinery, chemicals, and different kinds of food.

The United States also receives imports such as petroleum, automobiles, clothing, food, and other goods. An import is an item bought from another nation.

Look at the chart below. What does it tell you about United States exports and imports since 1950?

A DEVELOPED ECONOMY

Many people in the United States have a comfortable way of life. The reason for this is that the United States has a developed economy. A developed economy is an economy that has many different economic activities, not just one or two. Most of the jobs in a developed economy are in the manufacturing and service industries rather than in agriculture.

Developed economies also make use of advanced technology. Technology is the methods, tools, and machinery that are used to meet human needs. Advanced technology, such as robots and computers, offers people new jobs. It also changes the way that many Americans do their work.

Today, for example, many factories are being automated. That means that machines controlled by other machines make

GRAPH SKILL: This chart shows United States imports and exports since 1950. Was the value of United States imports or exports greater in 1985?

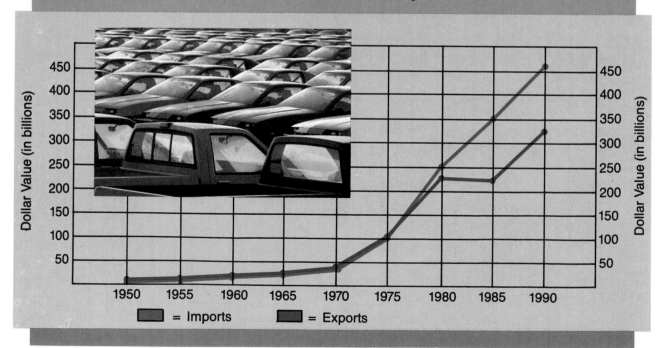

VALUE OF UNITED STATES EXPORTS AND IMPORTS, 1950-1990

Dollar Value (in billions): 50, 100, 150, 200, 250, 300, 350, 400, 450

Years: 1950, 1955, 1960, 1965, 1970, 1975, 1980, 1985, 1990

▬ = Imports   ▬ = Exports

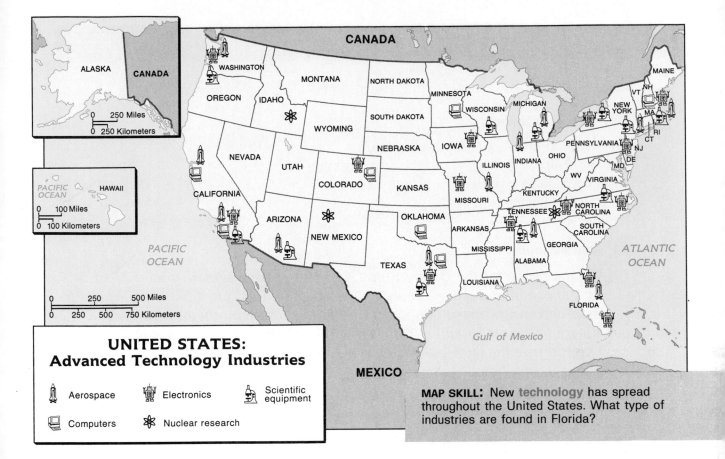

UNITED STATES: Advanced Technology Industries

- 🚀 Aerospace
- 🤖 Electronics
- 🔬 Scientific equipment
- 💻 Computers
- ⚛ Nuclear research

MAP SKILL: New technology has spread throughout the United States. What type of industries are found in Florida?

the products. In the past many automated machines were run from one large control room. Increasingly, though, workers are guiding the machines from computers at their desks. What do workers who must learn to use computers think of the change? According to one factory worker:

I used to be afraid I couldn't learn to use a computer. Now, I use one every day and I get more work out also. Our technology keeps changing and we have to change along with it.

Look at the map above. It shows some of the industries that make use of the latest technology. As the map shows, there are advanced technology industries throughout the United States.

ECONOMIC OPPORTUNITY

People in the United States seek economic opportunity under the system known as free enterprise, or capitalism. Today, as you have read, most workers in the United States are service workers, and fewer work in manufacturing and agriculture. The United States has a developed economy, which means that it involves many different economic activities and makes use of advanced technology.

 Check Your Reading

1. Define *technology*. How might you use technology during a normal day?
2. List the characteristics of a developed economy.
3. What are the three main areas of employment in the United States?
4. **THINKING SKILL:** Suppose you wanted to start your own small business. What three questions could you ask to learn how to go about it?

65

The Government

READ TO LEARN

Key Vocabulary

democracy   executive branch
republic   legislative branch
checks and balances   judicial branch
federal system

Read Aloud

We the people of the United States, in order to form a more perfect union, establish justice, insure domestic tranquility, provide for the common defense, promote the general welfare, and secure the blessings of liberty to ourselves and our posterity, do ordain and establish this Constitution for the United States of America.

These words form the Preamble, or introduction, to the Constitution of the United States. For more than 200 years the Constitution has served as the plan for the nation's government.

Read for Purpose

1. **WHAT YOU KNOW:** Which do you think is the most important of the ideas in the Preamble?
2. **WHAT YOU WILL LEARN:** How do the people of the United States govern themselves?

A REPUBLIC

The government of the United States is a form of democracy. A democracy is a government in which decisions are made by citizens. However, the United States has too many people to allow everyone to have a direct say in government. So the writers of the Constitution made the United States a representative democracy, or a republic. In a republic voters elect officials to represent them in government.

When the Constitution was being written in 1787, Americans did not know what kind of government they would have. Right after the Constitution was written, one of its writers, Benjamin Franklin, was asked, "What kind of government have you given us?" He answered, "A republic, madam, if you can keep it."

THE RESPONSIBILITIES OF CITIZENS

How have Americans kept their republic? One way has been through participation in government. It is the responsibility of every United States citizen 18 years and over to vote for their government representatives. You may be too young now to vote in elections for government leaders. But

66

Voting is one of the important responsibilities of American citizens. These people are registering to vote.

every time you vote for a class leader, you are practicing to become a responsible citizen.

Citizens of the United States have many other responsibilities, including obeying the laws and helping to solve problems in their own communities.

LIMITED POWER

The writers of the Constitution had lived under a powerful British king. Not surprisingly, after the United States gained its independence, its citizens wanted to make sure their new government did not become too powerful. One way to ensure this was to divide the powers of government.

A look at the organization of the United States government shows how this is done in our country. The national government is divided into three branches, or parts. The division of the government into three branches ensures that no one branch will hold too much power. The system by which each branch limits the power of the others is known as the system of checks and balances

Checks and balances are built into our system of government. Voters in the United States elect a President, a Vice President, and members of Congress. The President names judges to the Supreme Court but must gain congressional approval. Congress can propose that a bill become law. However, the President has the power to veto, or refuse to sign, the bill. If the President does not sign the bill, it usually does not become a law.

The Constitution also divides power between the national government and local governments. This division of power is called a federal system. The national government is sometimes called the federal government. It is responsible for tasks that concern the entire nation. Running the armed forces is one example. What are some other federal tasks?

THE THREE BRANCHES OF GOVERNMENT

EXECUTIVE BRANCH Carries out laws	LEGISLATIVE BRANCH Passes laws	JUDICIAL BRANCH Makes judgments about laws
President Vice President	Congress	Supreme Court
Cabinet — Independent Agencies	Senate ← → House of Representatives	Federal Courts

CHART SKILL: What are the three important parts of the executive branch?

THE NATIONAL GOVERNMENT

Look at the chart above. What are the names of the three branches of the national government? One branch is the executive branch, which is responsible for carrying out the laws of the United States. The President is head of the executive branch. Among the many duties of the President are creating programs to improve the welfare of the nation, heading the armed forces, and making treaties.

The executive branch includes the Cabinet, which consists of the heads of several federal departments to help the President. One Cabinet member heads the Department of the Treasury. It prints money, collects federal taxes, and pays federal bills.

The second branch of government, the legislative branch, is called Congress. Congress makes laws for the nation and decides how much money the government can spend. Congress is made up of two houses, the House of Representatives and the Senate. Each of the 50 states of the United States sends a number of representatives to the House, depending upon the size of the state's population. The Senate has 100 senators, 2 from each state.

The judicial branch is the third branch of government. The judicial branch interprets the nation's laws. That is, it makes sure that the laws are faithful to the law of the land as set down in the Constitution. This branch is headed by the Supreme Court, which has nine judges.

STATE AND LOCAL GOVERNMENTS

The national government does not make all the decisions in the United States. Some decisions, such as those concerning the enforcement of local laws, neighborhood schools, or garbage collection, are made by state and local governments.

The people of each of the 50 states elect their state governments. Each state has an executive branch (headed by a governor), a judicial branch, and a legislative branch. Among the many decisions made by state governments are how much money to spend on public education or what kind of mass transportation is needed.

Citizens of cities and towns elect a council of people to make local laws. Usually the citizens also elect or appoint a mayor or city manager to lead the city. This official chooses others to help govern the city.

State and local governments make many decisions every day. Who are some of your state and local representatives? What are some of the major issues that are important in your community?

A GOVERNMENT OF THE PEOPLE

The plan of government of the United States, called the Constitution, created a representative democracy. It also created a federal system in which power is divided between the national and local governments. In the national and state governments, power is divided among three branches of government. This division into the executive, legislative, and judicial branches is called the system of checks and balances. It ensures that no one branch becomes too powerful.

Check Your Reading

1. What is a republic?
2. Name the three branches of the United States federal government.
3. What are the three levels of government that operate in the United States?
4. **THINKING SKILL:** Look at the chart on page 68. What are two things it shows about the way the United States government is organized?

PHOTOGRAPHS of the HOMELESS

While Matthew Rothman was a college student in Providence, Rhode Island, he became interested in photography. Matthew started taking photographs of homeless people on the streets of Providence. Matthew soon met and became friendly with many of the people who lived on the streets. He photographed the shelters where homeless people slept and the soup kitchens where they ate.

Matthew wanted to help other people become aware of the problem of homelessness. One of his professors told him about a bill that had been proposed in the Rhode Island legislature. If the bill were to pass, the state government would provide $1 million for services to the homeless.

Next Matthew met with the sponsors of the bill. He arranged to exhibit his photographs in the Rhode Island Senate building, where the state senators would see them. The legislators remarked on the effect the photographs had on them.

With Matthew's help the bill was passed into law. Matthew had used his talents—his skill with a camera and his sense of caring—to make a difference in the lives of others.

Arts and Recreation

READ TO LEARN

 Key Vocabulary

freedom of expression

 Read Aloud

I was around 10 years old the first time I went skiing. . . . I pointed the skis straight down and somehow still had control. Snow flew everywhere. I loved the feeling of going so fast without being in some kind of vehicle.

These words were written by Shane Gregory, a young man who is training to be a professional dancer. Like other Americans Shane works hard. But he also enjoys relaxing in his spare time, and skiing is one of the things he does to relax. Through sports like skiing and other kinds of recreational activities, Americans make the most of their leisure time.

 Read for Purpose

1. **WHAT YOU KNOW:** What do you do to relax in your spare time?
2. **WHAT YOU WILL LEARN:** What are the major arts, leisure activities, and sports of the United States?

THE ARTS IN THE UNITED STATES

The United States is proud of its arts, which are known throughout the world. Dancers, painters, writers, musicians, and other artists from many nations come to the United States to study and work.

What makes the arts of the United States so well known? There are many reasons. But one of the most important reasons is that all artists in the United States have freedom of expression. As you have read, freedom is an important American value.

Freedom of expression means that artists in the United States are free to describe all aspects of American life. Given this freedom, American artists often use their art to help people to understand important facts about their nation. The

United States shows a willingness to look at its sorrows and problems as well as its successes and strengths. Knowing about their country's weaknesses can help the people of a nation to improve them.

Freedom of expression has been important to many different artists in the United States. Look at the song on the next page. What do you think its composer, Woody Guthrie, was trying to say about the United States?

Artists in other fields also use their freedom of expression to communicate their ideas. The Alvin Ailey American Dance Theater, for example, is known for works that often explore African American themes set to folk music or jazz. The company and its dancers are highly regarded

70

THIS LAND IS YOUR LAND

Words and music by Woody Guthrie

Refrain

This land is your land, This land is my land from Cal-i-for-nia to the New York is-land, From the red-wood for-est to the Gulf Stream wa-ters; This land was made for you and me. *Fine*

Verse

As I was walk-ing that rib-bon of high-way,
I've roamed and ram-bled and I fol-lowed my foot-steps
When the sun comes shin-ing and I was stroll-ing

I saw a-bove me that end-less sky-way.
to the spar-kling sands of her dia-mond des-erts,
and the wheat-fields wav-ing and the dust clouds rol-ling,

I saw be-low me that gold-en val-ley,
And all a-round me a voice was sound-ing,
As the fog was lift-ing a voice was chant-ing,

D.C. (Last time al Fine)

This land was made for you and me.
"This land was made for you and me."
"This land was made for you and me."

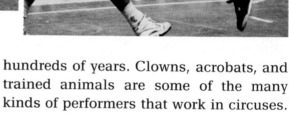

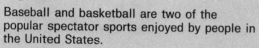

Baseball and basketball are two of the popular spectator sports enjoyed by people in the United States.

all over the world in the field of dance. Like so many other artists, they explore what it means to be an American.

WHAT PEOPLE DO FOR FUN

Many people in the United States have hours of free time after work or school every day. People use this time to enjoy many different hobbies and pastimes. The hobbies are as different as doll collecting, model building, quilting, stamp collecting, and photography.

In the United States, people are fond of reading, going to movies, and watching special events, such as rodeos and circuses. The skills seen in a rodeo include steer wrestling, lassoing, and horse taming. These were the same skills needed by the cowhands of the West during the 1800s. Circuses have been popular for

hundreds of years. Clowns, acrobats, and trained animals are some of the many kinds of performers that work in circuses.

SPORTS IN THE UNITED STATES

Do you have a favorite sport? Many of the sports popular in the United States were invented by North Americans. Baseball, football, and basketball are three examples. Baseball, often referred to as "the national pastime," is based on an earlier English game called rounders. Football also developed from an English sport, rugby. Basketball may have been invented by a Canadian living in Massachusetts.

People follow both professional and amateur sports, many of which they watch on television. Besides baseball, football, and basketball, professional sports include ice hockey, golf, bowling, and tennis. Do you play on any teams? Many schools and other organizations support amateur athletics.

People love to enjoy the outdoors in the national, state, and local parks of the United States.

Many of the best amateur athletes train hard for the Summer and Winter Olympics. The Olympics are held in a different country every four years. Athletes also take part in special contests, such as the Iditarod, which you will read about on pages 74–77.

Most people know that a good diet and exercise are important for a long and happy life. As a result, fitness sports such as weightlifting, bicycling, jogging, hiking, and swimming are very popular.

People in the United States also like to explore the outdoors. Throughout the country, large areas of land have been set aside as national, state, and local parks. Many families visit the nation's parks each summer to hike, picnic, camp, and enjoy the natural beauty of their country.

"THE PURSUIT OF HAPPINESS"

The Declaration of Independence says that one of the "unalienable rights" all citizens have is the right to the "pursuit of happiness." As you have read, the people of the United States pursue happiness in many different ways.

The arts are one important way. Freedom of expression guarantees that many different art forms flourish in the United States.

People in the United States also watch and participate in many different sports. Freedom of choice and expression makes for a rich and varied artistic and recreational life in the United States.

 Check Your Reading

1. Name three recreational activities enjoyed in the United States.
2. Name three different kinds of physical activities that Americans take part in.
3. Why is freedom of expression important to different artists in the United States?
4. THINKING SKILL: Sort the activities mentioned in this lesson into at least three groups.

IDITAROD

by Eric Kimmel

In the last lesson, you read about some of the most popular sports in the United States. These activities help people to have fun and stay in shape at the same time. Some sports also keep older customs alive. One such sporting event is the Iditarod (ī dit' ər äd), a race in Alaska that has become famous throughout the world. As you read, think about how an event like the Iditarod adapts and continues an Inuit tradition.

A JOURNEY THROUGH HISTORY

How would you travel in a land that lacked roads, bridges, or highways? Where the ground is covered with deep snow or thick ice for most of the year? The Inuit of Alaska long ago found a solution to this problem—the dogsled. They discovered that a team of 3 to 20 Alaskan huskies could haul a sled smoothly over the ice. The sled itself was made of light wood, with walrus-skin or ivory runners. Scientists have discovered traces of ivory sled runners dating back almost 2,000 years!

More recently, people have found other ways to travel during Alaska's winters, including planes and helicopters. Roads now connect most communities. Snowmobiles can go where cars can't. But meanwhile, the Iditarod Trail Sled Dog Race has become an Alaskan tradition.

The original Iditarod Trail was blazed by thousands of people during the early 1900s. Most of these people were searching for gold, which had been discovered in Alaska in the late 1800s. Many traveled to the gold rush town of Iditarod, which gave the trail its name.

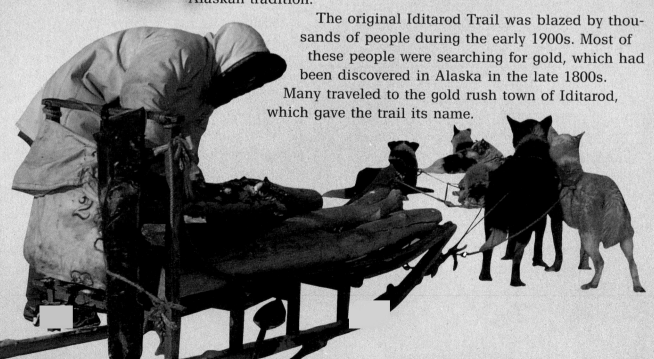

The trail became famous for another reason in 1925, when an illness called diphtheria (dif thîr′ ē ə) struck the town of Nome. A serum, or medicine, existed to fight this deadly illness. But how could the isolated community get the serum in time? A relay of dogsled teams rushed the precious medicine over hundreds of miles, saving many lives. In fact, several of the original "serum runners" were honored at Iditarod races during the 1970s.

In a sense, then, the Iditarod racers of today journey not only through Alaska's landscape, but through its history. "We travel through the country," says Jon Van Zyle, who has raced the Iditarod several times. "We're part of the past, and it's very much part of the race."

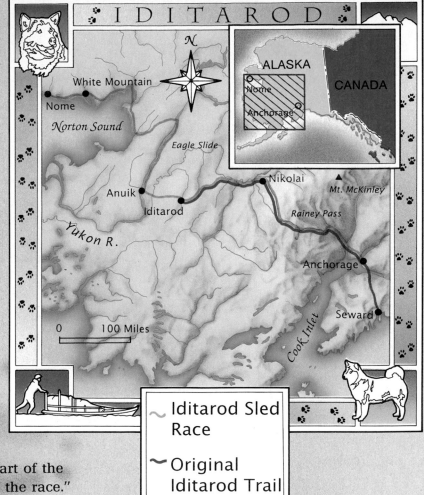

IDITAROD

Iditarod Sled Race

Original Iditarod Trail

A UNIQUE RACE

No other race of any kind matches the Iditarod as a test of skill and endurance. The race begins in Anchorage on the first weekend of every March. As you can see from the map on this page, the trail takes the racers over many different kinds of terrain. They cross icy tundra, frozen rivers, towering mountain ranges, dense forests, and a windswept seacoast. The dogsled teams fight their way through areas with names like Rainy Pass and Hell's Gate. After covering 1,049 miles (1,688 km), they finally reach Nome about 2 weeks later!

The man or woman driving the dog team is called a "musher"— a term that comes from *marcher* (mär shā′), a French word meaning "to march." In fact, the musher often cries out "Mush! Mush!" to urge the dogs on.

Each musher begins the race with between 7 and 20 huskies. The specific makeup of the team is important, since dogs cannot be added or switched once the race starts. If a dog weakens or becomes ill, however, it can be dropped off at checkpoints along the way.

A TEST OF ENDURANCE

Day in and day out, the mushers drive their teams over the snow and ice. Some of the time, the musher rides on the back of the sled runners. Often, though, he or she will jump off to help the dogs tug the sled over a rough patch of ground.

Some mushers stop each evening. Unpacking a portable stove, they build a fire, feed the dogs, and curl up in a cold-weather sleeping bag. Other mushers press on through the night. Sooner or later, however, every team must rest, and the rules specify at least one 24-hour stopover for each musher.

There's no such thing as an Iditarod "rain date"—the race continues no matter what the weather is like. This can make things very hard for the musher and the dog team. Take the case of Iditarod veteran Susan Butcher. During the 1982 race, a blizzard wiped out much of the trail, and Butcher's dogsled crashed into a tree. Then she was stranded for several days by a fierce storm, with winds blowing at 80 miles (129 km) per hour!

Butcher faced even worse problems during the 1985 Iditarod, when an enraged moose attacked her team. It killed 2 dogs and injured 13 others. Butcher tried to drive the moose away, but it might have killed her, too, if another musher hadn't come along and helped her.

A CHAMPION DOGSLEDDER

If anyone is capable of handling the problems you just read about, it's Susan Butcher. Winner of the 1986, 1987, 1988, and 1990 Iditarods, Butcher long held the Iditarod speed record: 11 days, 1 hour, 53 minutes, and 23 seconds. She also held records in several other dogsled races. How did this Massachusetts-born woman end up as one of the world's champion dogsledders?

Butcher moved to Fairbanks, Alaska, in 1975. Then she moved to rural Alaska to learn to be a musher. She took along three sled dogs, a sack of flour, two cats, a slab of bacon, and a jar of peanut butter! After a period of study and training, Butcher's dream came true in 1978 when she raced in the Iditarod for the first time.

"THE REAL CHAMPIONS"

Being a musher requires amazing skill and endurance. But according to Butcher, the dogs are the real champions. In fact, training and caring for the sled dogs is a tradition in itself. Butcher cares for her Alaskan huskies from the moment they are born. She talks to them, pets them, and plays with them. When the pups turn four-and-a-half months old, their training begins. Butcher teaches the unruly pups to work together. They pull a small sled at first and then move up to a larger one.

By the time they are ready for competition, the huskies pull as a team. Butcher never uses force to encourage them. Her dogs run because they love her, she says, and love what they are doing. As Susan Butcher knows, that combination is hard to beat.

The dogs also save lives. Butcher, her lead dog Tekla, and 14 other huskies were making a training run across a frozen river in 1977. Tekla kept trying to stray off the trail. Butcher couldn't understand why. Her lead husky had never disobeyed her before. Soon she decided to let Tekla go where she wanted. Moments after the team pulled aside, the trail collapsed into the river. "That day I learned that the wilderness is their domain," Butcher later said. "The dogs know more about it than I do, and I'm better off trusting their instincts."

 How does the Iditarod race of Alaska keep an Inuit tradition alive?

THE UNITED STATES: CULTURAL GEOGRAPHY

 **PEOPLE**

- Many different ethnic groups in the United States today

- People from many lands came to the United States searching for freedom and opportunity

- Hispanics: fastest growing ethnic group

ECONOMY

- Capitalist system: freedom and economic opportunity

- Free enterprise: freedom to own property and run a business

- Large foreign trade: exports and imports
- Developed economy: many different economic activities, advanced technology

GOVERNMENT

- Representative democracy

- Three branches: executive, legislative, and judicial
- Federal republic: divides power between national and local governments

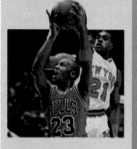 **ARTS AND RECREATION**

- Freedom of expression provides opportunities for artists

- Americans enjoy hobbies: reading, movies, sports

- Exploring the outdoors: Americans enjoy national, state, and local parks

IDEAS TO REMEMBER

- The population of the United States is made up of a mixture of many different ethnic groups.
- The developed economy of the United States, with its advanced technology, employs many workers in services, manufacturing, trade, and other fields.
- The United States is a federal republic with elected representatives and with power divided between national and state governments.
- Freedom of expression provides artists in the United States with opportunities to express themselves in many different ways.

REVIEWING VOCABULARY

capitalism ✓   federal system ✓
checks and balances ✓ immigrant ✓
democracy ✓   megalopolis ✓
developed economy ✓   republic ✓
discrimination ✓   technology ✓

Number a sheet of paper from 1 to 10. Beside each number write the word or term from the list above that best completes each sentence.

1. _____ is an economic system in which businesses and factories are owned by individuals or private groups.
2. In a _____ governmental power is divided between the national government and state and local governments.
3. _____ is the unfair treatment of a person or a group of people because of race, class, ethnic origin, or other factors.
4. A country that employs many people in a variety of manufacturing and service jobs is said to have a _____.
5. A large area of interconnected cities, suburbs, and towns is called a _____.
6. A _____ is a type of democracy in which citizens elect people to represent them in government.
7. An _____ is a person who moves to a country other than the country in which he or she was born.
8. _____ refers to any method, machine, or tool that is used to meet human needs.
9. By dividing power among three branches of government, the framers of the Constitution established a system of _____ to limit governmental power.
10. A _____ is a form of government in which decisions are made by citizens.

REVIEWING FACTS

1. Why is the United States a land of many people? From where are the largest numbers of immigrants to the United States coming today?
2. How have the living patterns of Americans changed since the 1700s?
3. List three economic freedoms that Americans enjoy under the free enterprise system of the United States.
4. Name the two houses of Congress. What is the function of each house?
5. What is meant by the phrase "freedom of expression"? List three ways this freedom is practiced in the United States.

◀◀ WRITING ABOUT MAIN IDEAS

1. **Writing a Pamphlet:** Write a pamphlet for foreign visitors entitled "Democracy in Action: How the United States Government Works."
2. **Writing an Essay:** Write a short essay explaining the meaning of the phrase "the pursuit of happiness." How do you exercise this right in your own life?
3. **Writing About Perspectives:** Citizens in the United States have the right to vote, a right many other people in the world do not have. Yet many citizens do not vote. Write a paragraph giving your point of view about why people do or do not vote.

BUILDING SKILLS: DECISION MAKING

1. What is another word or phrase that means *decision making*?
2. Write a set of instructions for a student who is not familiar with the steps to making a decision.
3. Why is it important to consider many alternatives when making a decision?

CHAPTER 3

CANADA

FOCUS

The Mounties—the Royal Canadian Mounted Police—have become, like the beaver and the maple leaf, a symbol of Canada.

These words were written by Jennifer Malcolm, a teacher and a writer. As you read this chapter, you will learn what lies behind the symbols of Canada. You will learn about Canada's people and cultures.

As a minority, French Canadians have fought to keep their French way of life—French language, Roman Catholicism and French customs. Roman Catholicism is the branch of Christianity that is headed by the pope in Rome.

In the 1960s some French Canadians believed their way of life was in danger. They felt they had to break away from Canada in order to preserve their culture. This kind of movement is called separatism. In 1980 the people of Quebec voted on whether or not to remain part of Canada. After a heated debate Quebec elected to stay a Canadian province. You will read more about this issue on pages 84–85.

CANADA AND THE UNITED STATES

Some Canadians also worry about what they see as a different threat to their way of life. This threat comes from across the border—from the United States. According to one Canadian:

We are already inundated with American magazines and televison shows that don't reflect Canadian opinions and values. We have much in common with Americans but not enough to justify merging our thinking.

One reason for the great influence of the United States is that most Canadians live close to the United States–Canadian border. Although Canada is the world's second-largest nation in area, much of it is made up of land that is difficult to live on. Almost three fourths of all Canadians live in a narrow belt below the Canadian Shield. All of this belt is within 100 miles (160 km) of the United States border. It has Canada's most fertile land and its warmest climates. According to the Canadian writer Pierre Berton:

The Shield and the wilderness bear down upon us, a crushing weight, squeezing us like toothpaste along the border.

Traditional parades like this one in Quebec City show the influence of British culture in Canada.

THE CULTURES OF CANADA

Canada, as you have read, is a mosaic of different groups that live together in this vast country. The earliest, and now the smallest, of these groups are the Indians and the Inuit. The British Canadians and the French Canadians are the two largest groups of people in the country today. Most of them live in a narrow belt of land bordering the United States.

 Check Your Reading

1. What two languages are commonly spoken in Canada?
2. Why do the Inuit not want to be called "Eskimos"?
3. What are some of the important groups in the "mosaic" of Canada?
4. **THINKING SKILL:** What causes nearly three fourths of all Canadians to live close to the United States border? Give at least two causes.

Bilingualism in Canada

As you have read, Canada has two official languages, French and English. If you were to visit Canada, you would notice that road signs appear in both languages. Canadian postage stamps and money are also printed in both English and French.

Forty years ago English was the only official language of Canada. French was not seen on signs in public places and was rarely heard outside Quebec or New Brunswick, where most of the French-speaking Canadians live. During the 1960s many French-speaking Canadians felt that their way of life was being threatened because they were the minority in Canada. As you have read, in an attempt to preserve Quebec's French culture and language, a movement developed in that province to make it independent.

In response to the unrest of the French-speaking population, a program of bilingualism was established in 1969. People who worked for the government were required to speak both English and French. Universities began offering classes in both languages. Canada became a bilingual nation.

Today many English-speaking Canadians are unhappy with the bilingual policy of the government. Some of them object to being required to speak French. Others think that the government spends too much money on French-language programs.

POINT ☆\☞

Canada Should Continue to Be a Bilingual Nation

In 1988 the Official Languages Act became law in Canada. Under this law government offices must make sure that people who work for the government are able to speak both English and French.

Graham Fraser, a member of Parliament, commented on the Official Languages Act in a Canadian newspaper.

I think Canadians are far more open now to accepting the fact that we are a bilingual nation. Canadians who happen to speak French should be entitled to the same basic level of services, wherever they may be in the country. . . . It's a very small price to pay for national unity.

Fraser thinks that Canadians have become more comfortable with bilingualism during the past ten years.

I remember the uproar about a French-language television station in my community, and the criticism I got for supporting it. That wouldn't have happened today. It's taken for granted.

● Why does Graham Fraser believe that Canada should continue to be a bilingual nation?

COUNTERPOINT ☜\☆

Canada Should Not Continue to Be a Bilingual Nation

Isaac Bar-Lewaw, a Canadian professor of linguistics, had the following to say about the effects of Canada's official language policy.

Unfortunately, it [bilingualism] is an illusion—and a costly one. The reality is different from the dreams. . . . Canada was and still is bilingual on paper only. . . . One has to admit that Canada, with the exception of Quebec, and to a certain degree New Brunswick, has never been, is not, and will never be *truly* bilingual.

Many English-speaking Canadians think the bilingual policy results in unfair treatment of certain employees. Author Peter Brimelow, who writes about Canada, said:

It [the government] has been able to require bilingualism of shop assistants in the airports of English-speaking cities and of post office employees in remote English-speaking villages. In some instances this has meant firing locals and importing [people] from Quebec.

● According to Peter Brimelow, in what way is the policy of bilingualism unfair to some Canadians?

UNDERSTANDING THE POINT/COUNTERPOINT

1. Who do you think presents a better argument about whether Canada should be a bilingual nation?
2. Canada has immigrants from many other countries. What might some of these people think about the issue of bilingualism?
3. Can you suggest a compromise that might be acceptable to both those who support bilingualism and those who do not?

LESSON 2

The Economy

READ TO LEARN

Key Vocabulary

fossil fuel   acid rain   tariff

Read Aloud

Today mining is big business in Canada. There are more than 300 operating mines across the country and the various companies that own them employ 7 percent of all working Canadians. From these mines about 60 different commodities are [taken out], including nickel, copper, gold, silver, platinum, coal, and iron.

These words were written by Robin Rose, a driller in a mine in Sudbury, in southeastern Ontario. They help to explain why mining is so important to the economy of Canada. Many of the nation's industries are based on obtaining raw materials or using them to make goods.

Read for Purpose

1. **WHAT YOU KNOW:** What is a free enterprise economy?
2. **WHAT YOU WILL LEARN:** In what ways does the Canadian economy depend on the country's natural resources?

MINING

Canada, like the United States, has a developed economy. More than in many other countries with developed economies, Canada's wealth comes from its natural resources.

The most profitable industry in Canada is mining. The nation's abundant mineral resources make it one of the world's largest producers of minerals. In 1990 it was the third-largest exporter of minerals after the United States and the Soviet Union.

Canada has the world's largest nickel mine, near Sudbury, Ontario. The Sullivan Mine, in Kimberley, British Columbia, is the world's largest source of lead, zinc, and silver. Canada is also a leading producer of fossil fuels—coal, petroleum, and natural gas.

THE POLARIS MINE

Many of Canada's most valuable resources are located in areas where the climate is extremely cold. How do people live and work there?

In one mine, far beneath the Arctic ice and snow, electric lights burn 24 hours a day. Heavy machinery drills through the permafrost and scoops out tons of ore that contain lead and zinc. This is the Polaris Mine, located on desolate Cornwallis Island, in far northern Canada.

Here, north of the Arctic Circle, more than 200 men and women work to mine lead and zinc. Because of ice on the Arctic Ocean, the sea route to the Polaris Mine is open fewer than 50 days a year. During this time, a year's worth of ore from the mine is shipped out.

86

The Polaris Mine is located in one of Canada's most remote regions. But it produces shiploads of lead and zinc every year.

The workers have learned to live with this schedule and with many other features of life in the frozen north. In the winter it is dark 24 hours a day. It is so cold that door handles break off in people's hands. Motors must be left running from October to May so that they do not freeze.

The Polaris Mine is expensive to run. However, the ore is of high quality—much richer than ores mined farther south. Therefore, the mine can make a big profit. The maps on page 88 show where some of Canada's minerals are located.

FARMING

Canadians also make use of resources other than minerals. Farmland is one of these resources. As you read in Chapter 1, only about 5 percent of Canada's land is arable.

In some areas, such as Quebec, small plots of land are farmed using traditional methods of agriculture. However, most of the nation's farmers depend on modern technology to run large farms. They use giant machines to plant and harvest their crops.

Large-scale farming is carried out mainly on the flat expanses of the Interior Plains. So much wheat is grown there that Canada is one of the world's leading wheat exporters. Canada also produces corn, oats, barley, and dairy products.

MANUFACTURING

Canada is one of the world's leading manufacturing nations. Canadian industries use the products from its mines, forests, and farms to produce many different goods. With its huge forests, Canada is the world's leading producer of newsprint, the inexpensive paper on which newspapers are printed.

The center of Canadian manufacturing is called the "Golden Horseshoe." This is the urban area along Lake Ontario that has the city of Toronto near its center. Many cars and metal products are made here.

FOREIGN TRADE

Canada exports more natural resources than most nations. About 25 percent of Canada's total exports consist of natural resources. In comparison, natural resources make up only about 10 percent of United States exports. Canada's leading exports are minerals such as zinc, petroleum, natural gas, and steel. Canada is also the world's leading exporter of fish and forest products.

Because Canada produces many more goods than it can use, it depends upon other nations to buy them. This can cause problems. For example, the United States

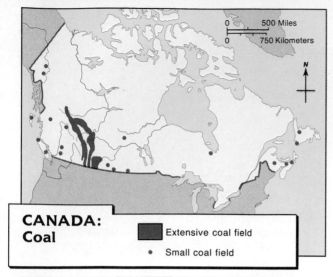

CANADA: Coal

⬛ Extensive coal field
• Small coal field

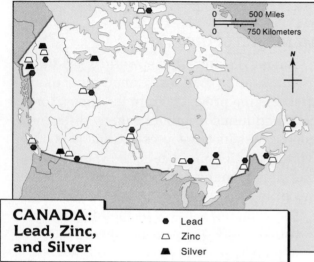

CANADA: Lead, Zinc, and Silver

● Lead
△ Zinc
▲ Silver

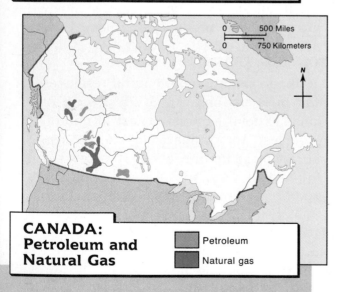

CANADA: Petroleum and Natural Gas

⬜ Petroleum
⬛ Natural gas

MAP SKILL: Canada is rich in minerals. Where are most of its natural gas reserves located?

is Canada's major trading partner. But this partnership is not balanced. About 20 percent of American exports go to Canada, while about 75 percent of Canada's exports are sold to the United States.

In 1989, the United States and Canada began a free-trade agreement. Under that agreement, most goods traded between the countries will not be subject to a tariff. A tariff is a tax on goods. A free-trade agreement between Canada, the United States, and Mexico was signed in 1993.

ACID RAIN

Factories in both the United States and Canada cause pollution. But a great deal of the acid rain in Canada comes from the United States. Acid rain is rain mixed with chemicals from the burning of coal and other fuels. Acid rain pollutes lakes and other waterways, killing fish and other water life. It also damages trees and buildings. For this reason both countries have cooperated to control acid rain.

A WORLD ECONOMIC LEADER

Canada has one of the world's leading economies. You have read that much of the nation's wealth comes from its abundant natural resources. Mining is the most important industry in Canada. Agriculture, forestry, fishing, and manufacturing also are important to the Canadian economy.

 Check Your Reading

1. What is unusual about the Polaris Mine?
2. To which nation do most of Canada's exports go?
3. Explain why natural resources are so important to Canada's economy.
4. **THINKING SKILL:** Suppose a Canadian firm wants to develop a mine in far northern Canada. What are some of the difficulties it must consider?

Using the Library

Key Vocabulary

reference   almanac
dictionary   atlas
encyclopedia

As you read about the regions of the world, you may want to learn more about certain subjects. For example, you may want answers to such questions as: How do the Inuit live today? What is it like to live near the Arctic Circle?

Reference Books

You can find information about many subjects in a library. The reference section is a good place to begin looking. Here you will find reference books, or books that are sources of information. Dictionaries, encyclopedias, almanacs, and atlases are reference books that are useful for research.

A dictionary provides the meanings of words and indicates their pronunciation. An encyclopedia has information about many subjects written in the form of articles. An almanac is published every year and contains up-to-date facts on many subjects. When you want to locate a certain place on a map, use an atlas.

Finding Books

You may also want to find informational books that are not in the reference section. As you may know, a card catalog or a computer is used to tell you where these books are located. Each book is listed three different ways—by author, by title, and by subject. The card in the catalog or entry in the computer lists the author's last name, followed by the first name. Each card or entry has a call number to help you to find the book you are looking for.

Reviewing the Skill

1. Name four kinds of reference books.
2. Which reference book would you use to find out how to pronounce *mosaic*?
3. How would you go about finding a book on the Arctic Circle?
4. Why is it important to know how to use the library?

The Government

READ TO LEARN

■ Key Vocabulary

parliamentary democracy
prime minister
cabinet
Commonwealth of Nations
monarchy

■ Read Aloud

A Member of Parliament's function is to represent his political party and [the people who elect him] at the federal level, to gain for them whatever aid and support he can.

This is how John Crosbie, a member of the Canadian Parliament, explained how the people who serve in Canada's national legislature view their roles. They believe that it is their duty to aid and support the people who voted them into office. In Canada, as in the United States, this belief is the foundation of representative government.

■ Read for Purpose

1. **WHAT YOU KNOW:** What is a representative democracy?
2. **WHAT YOU WILL LEARN:** How is Canada's parliamentary democracy organized, and how does it fit within the Commonwealth of Nations?

CANADA'S GOVERNMENT

In 1988, after they were criticized for "betraying the people," important members of the Canadian government suddenly resigned. Why did this happen? The Canadian government was trying to win approval of a trade treaty with the United States. There were bitter debates between Canada's political parties. These debates were televised both in French and in English. Opponents of the treaty kept criticizing it, and it appeared that people were losing confidence in the government. When that happens in Canada, the government leaders resign. New elections are then held.

Like the United States, Canada has a representative government in which the voters elect the people they wish to represent them at both the national and local levels. However, the Canadian government has kept more of its British heritage than has the United States.

Great Britain governed Canada as a colony for about a century. Canada won the right to govern itself in 1867, but it did not win full independence from British rule until 1982. Canada's government is still much like Great Britain's. You will read more about the government of Great Britain in Chapter 9.

PARLIAMENTARY DEMOCRACY

Canada is a **parliamentary democracy**. The country has a national legislature called Parliament, which meets in Ottawa, the national capital. The Canadian Parliament is made up of the House of Commons and the Senate. Representatives of the lower house, the House of Commons, are elected. Members of the upper house, the Senate, are appointed by the governor general, whom you will read about later in this lesson.

The leader of Canada's national government is the **prime minister**. A prime minister is the leader of the political party that has a majority of members in the House of Commons. A majority is more than half the total number.

You have read that in the United States the President heads the executive branch of government. In Canada the prime minister heads both the executive and the legislative branches of government. The two branches are not separate in Canada as they are in the United States. The prime minister governs with the help of the **cabinet**. The cabinet is made up of the prime minister and about 30 members of the House of Commons. The cabinet members advise the prime minister and help him or her carry out the law.

The prime minister depends on the support of Parliament to stay in office. Without support from Parliament, the prime minister must resign, as Canada's prime minister did after the events you read about at the beginning of this lesson. In any parliamentary democracy, the prime minister and Parliament must work together to govern the country.

The representatives to the Canadian Parliament meet in Ottawa, the capital of Canada.

The members of the British royal family are still treated with great respect in Canada.

Canada is one of the members of the **Commonwealth of Nations.** This is a group of independent nations once ruled by Great Britain. Commonwealth nations think of the British monarch—the king or queen—as the head of their governments. A **monarchy** is any government headed by a hereditary ruler, such as a king or queen. However, in Canada the British monarch is leader in name only.

In Canada the British monarch is represented by an official called the governor general. The governor general has little power. For the most part, this official approves decisions made by Parliament and the prime minister. For example, the prime minister recommends people to serve in the Senate, and the governor general officially appoints them.

CANADA'S PARLIAMENTARY DEMOCRACY

You have read that Canada's government is a democracy in which people choose their representatives. They elect the members of the House of Commons, the lower house of Parliament. The members of the upper house, the Senate, are appointed.

Canada inherited a parliamentary democracy from Great Britain. In a parliamentary democracy the legislative and executive functions are not separate, as they are in the United States. The prime minister leads both the executive and legislative branches.

Check Your Reading

1. How does Canada have elements of a monarchy in its government?
2. Why is the prime minister and his or her government sometimes forced to resign in Canada?
3. What is a parliamentary democracy?
4. **THINKING SKILL:** What three questions could you ask to learn how Canada won its independence from Great Britain?

Arts and Recreation

READE TO LEARN

■ Key Places

Edmonton, Alberta

■ Read Aloud

Once in another time, my friends, a great change came into Tante Odette's life although she was already an old woman . . . It all happened because of a change that came over [her cat] Chouchou . . . As Tante Odette worked at her loom every evening, Chouchou would lie on the little rug by the stove and stare at her with his big green eyes. "If only you could talk, what company you would be for me." Suddenly . . . a thump, thump . . . came from the door. . . .

In this French Canadian folktale, called "The Tale of the Talking Cat," the knock at the door was a woodsman named Pierre Leblanc. Tante Odette refused him entry. Suddenly her cat miraculously began to speak and told her to let him in. How could this be? Leblanc had used ventriloquism, the ability to throw his voice, to get his way. The story warned, "If you must follow the advice of a talking cat, be sure you know who is doing the talking for him." Folktales are just one part of Canada's cultural heritage.

■ Read for Purpose

1. **WHAT YOU KNOW:** What is distinctive about the arts of the United States?
2. **WHAT YOU WILL LEARN:** What do the arts and recreation of Canada tell you about Canada and its people?

LOVE OF THE OUTDOORS

Canada has many traditional arts. The Inuit, American Indians, French Canadians, and British Canadians are just a few of the groups whose artistic traditions go back hundreds of years in Canada. Inuit sculpture in soapstone, a soft soapy-feeling stone, American Indian masks and poems, and folktales such as "The Tale of the Talking Cat" are well known throughout the world.

Even though the arts of different groups may differ, many of them deal with the same topics. One such topic is nature and the beauty of the Canadian land. Canada, as you know, is a land of beautiful mountains, forests, and rivers. Canadian writings, paintings, and songs often describe the country's landscape. From Canada's artists we know Canadians have a great love of the outdoors.

93

ETHNIC IDENTITY

Another topic that interests Canadians is ethnic identity. Because Canada is a mosaic of cultures, groups often are concerned with keeping their cultures alive or learning to live with other ethnic groups. A Canadian television program or a modern dance, for example, may show what it is like to be a French Canadian in British Canada. Programs may also show what it is like to be an Inuit or Indian in Canada or to be a Canadian in a culture that is dominated by the United States.

SPORTS AND OTHER AMUSEMENTS

The Canadian interest in nature is expressed not only in the arts but also in sports and other amusements. Canadians excel in many sports.

According to one story, on Christmas Day in 1855 soldiers at Kingston, Ontario, were bored. So they tied blades to their boots and took to the ice with field hockey sticks and an old lacrosse ball. This was the beginning of Canada's national sport, ice hockey. Today ice hockey is played all over the world. Canadian players are included on many of the world's professional hockey teams.

Canadian sports fans like baseball and basketball, too. It was probably a Canadian living in Massachusetts—James Naismith—who invented the game of basketball, using a soccer ball and two peach baskets that he nailed to a wall in a gym.

Ice hockey is sometimes called the national sport of Canada. Rodeo and skiing are also popular sports in Canada.

94

Water sports and other amusements, in addition to stores and restaurants, are found at the West Edmonton Mall.

A Canadian sports event that draws thousands of spectators to Alberta every year is the Calgary Stampede. This ten-day spectacle is a combination agricultural fair and rodeo, with Indian displays and stage shows.

Because of Canada's cold climate, many recreational activities in the country take place indoors. Even in warmer areas of Canada, cities are built with the cold winter in mind. Canada has the world's largest indoor shopping mall, the West Edmonton Mall in Edmonton, Alberta. Edmonton is the northernmost of Canada's major cities. The West Edmonton Mall is the size of 108 football fields. It boasts 800 stores, an indoor lake, and the world's largest parking lot. Farther south, Montreal has a huge underground shopping mall. It includes restaurants and many different kinds of stores. Advanced technology and vast energy resources make it possible for such malls to remain lighted and warm, even in the coldest weather.

CULTURAL TRADITIONS

Canada has a variety of cultural traditions. Within these traditions, Canada's artists often express their concern for the environment, for ethnic identity, and with what it means to be a Canadian today.

For recreation, many Canadians love being outdoors. Canadian athletes excel in many different sports and are supported by avid fans.

 Check Your Reading

1. What are some of the traditional arts of Canada?
2. What is Canada's national sport?
3. How do the arts in Canada reflect the people's love for the outdoors?
4. THINKING SKILL: What do you think the activities shown in the photographs on page 94 say about the arts and recreation of Canada?

95

CANADA: CULTURAL GEOGRAPHY

PEOPLE

- First people: Indians
- French and British colonized Canada
- Today: people of British and French descent dominate population
- United States influence is strong

ECONOMY

- Developed economy: mining, farming, fishing, manufacturing
- Vast natural resources: make up about 25 percent of exports
- Acid rain: threatens Canada's environment

GOVERNMENT

- Parliamentary democracy
- House of Commons elected; Senate appointed
- Prime minister leads government
- Member of Commonwealth of Nations

ARTS AND RECREATION

- Artists and writers: reflect a love of the outdoors
- Popular sports: ice hockey, skiing, basketball, baseball

IDEAS TO REMEMBER

- Canada is a "mosaic" of different ethnic groups living together.
- Canada's natural wealth has made it a leading world economic power.
- Canada's system of government is a parliamentary democracy, with an elected parliament and a prime minister.
- Many of the arts and popular recreational activities of Canada reflect a love of the outdoors.

REVIEWING VOCABULARY

Each of the following statements contains an underlined vocabulary word or term. Number a sheet of paper from 1 to 10. Beside each number write whether each of the following statements is true or false. If the statement is true, write "true." If it is false, rewrite the sentence using the vocabulary word or term correctly.

1. Acid rain, or rain mixed with certain forms of air pollution, has caused great damage to Canada's lakes and rivers.
2. A monarchy is a government that is headed by a king or queen, or by another hereditary ruler.
3. Canadians describe their country as a mosaic because of the many different groups of people living there.
4. Like the United States President, the Canadian prime minister heads only the executive branch of government.
5. Canada is one of many countries that belongs to the Commonwealth of Nations.
6. A province is an area that is ruled by a monarch.
7. Canada is a parliamentary democracy in which the Prime Minister and the Parliament work closely together.
8. Separatism, or the desire to break away from a larger country, has been a powerful political force in Quebec.
9. Canada is a leading producer of fossil fuels such as lead, zinc, and silver.
10. The Canadian cabinet is a group of business and labor leaders who recommend legislation in the Parliament.

REVIEWING FACTS

1. Name two things that many Canadians feel are threats to their country.
2. In which part of Canada do most Canadians live? Why?
3. Only a small percentage of Canada's land is good for farming, yet agriculture is one of Canada's most important industries. Explain why.
4. Name two ways in which the governments of Canada and the United States are similar. In what two ways are they different?
5. What is one way in which people in Canadian cities adapt to harsh northern winters? How do Canada's vast natural resources help its people to do this?

WRITING ABOUT MAIN IDEAS

1. **Writing a Help Wanted Ad:** Imagine that you are the director of the Polaris Mine in extreme northern Canada. How would you interest people in coming to the Arctic to work? Write a help wanted ad for mining jobs in your company.
2. **Writing a Paragraph:** Write a paragraph describing how the present form of Canadian government reflects the country's British heritage.
3. **Writing About Perspectives:** Imagine that you are an Indian who must learn French and English as well as your own language. Write a letter to a friend telling how you feel about having to speak three languages.

BUILDING SKILLS: USING THE LIBRARY

1. Name four kinds of reference books.
2. Which reference book would you use to find out how to pronounce monarchy?
3. What kind of information is found in an atlas?
4. Why is it important to know how to use the library?

UNITED STATES AND CANADA: PHYSICAL GEOGRAPHY

 LANDFORMS

- Mountains (Appalachian Highlands, Rocky Mountains, Pacific Mountains) and Plains (Interior Plains, Coastal Plains)

- Northern Canada: Canadian Shield and Arctic Islands

 CLIMATE

- Temperate climate: few extremes in weather
- Temperatures: colder in mountains and north, warmer in lowlands and south

NATURAL RESOURCES

- Arable land: 50 percent of land in Unites States, only 5 percent in Canada
- United States grows more food than any other nation
- Forests cover one third of United States and Canada
- Waterways: Great Lakes, St. Lawrence Seaway, Mississippi River, Columbia River

UNITED STATES AND CANADA: CULTURAL GEOGRAPHY

 PEOPLE

- Indians came to the region more than 40,000 years ago
- Inuit came to Canada about 6,000 years ago, still alive in the north today
- In the United States, many different ethnic groups; in Canada, most people are of British or French descent
- Hispanics are fastest-growing ethnic group in the United States today
- Immigrants came from many lands searching for opportunity

 **ECONOMY**

- Developed economies: many different economic activities, advanced technology
- Capitalist system: freedom and economic opportunity
- Free enterprise: freedom to own property and run a business
- Foreign trade: extensive in both countries, especially with each other
- Acid rain: threatens the environment of Canada and the United States

 GOVERNMENT

- Democratic government: representative democracy in the United States, parliamentary democracy in Canada
- United States: power divided between national and local governments, federal government divided into three branches (executive, legislative, judicial)
- Canada: House of Commons elected, Senate appointed; prime minister leads government

ARTS AND RECREATION

- Freedom of expression provides opportunities for artists

- Popular sports: baseball, football, basketball, ice hockey, skiing, and many others
- People use leisure time for hobbies: reading, movies, sports

REVIEWING VOCABULARY

cabinet   republic

capitalism   timberline

prime minister

Number a sheet of paper from 1 to 5. Beside each number write the word or term from the list above that best matches each statement.

1. Trees cannot grow above this line because of high elevation or cold climate.
2. This head of state depends on the support of Parliament to remain in office.
3. Canada's prime minister governs with the help of this group of advisers.
4. In this type of economic system, an individual may establish his or her own business largely free of government control.
5. The United States is an example of this form of democracy in which citizens elect people to represent them in government.

WRITING ABOUT THE UNIT

1. **Writing a Myth:** The Seneca used the myth of Sky Woman to explain how the land became fruitful. Write a myth of your own explaining a natural event you have read about, such as the eruption of Mount St. Helens or the creation of the Rocky Mountains.

2. **Writing an Essay:** Many people throughout the world have marveled at the strength of democracy in the United States. Write an essay entitled "Why Democracy Works in the United States."

3. **Writing About Perspectives:** Write a "letter to the editor" expressing your opinion for or against Quebec's independence.

ACTIVITIES

1. **Constructing a Chart:** Use almanacs, encyclopedias, and atlases to find the following geographical data about both Canada and the United States: capital, area (in square miles and kilometers), population, and gross national product. Then make a chart comparing the data.

2. **Making a List:** Make a list of states that border on a province, territory, or body of water in Canada. Next to each state on the list, write the province, territory, or body of water on which it borders.

3. **Working Together to Research Canadian-American Issues:** Work in groups to find information on the current issues affecting both the United States and Canada. Use newspapers and magazines to find articles about acid rain, trade policies, or United States influence on Canada. Then present summaries of the issues to the class.

LINKING PAST, PRESENT, AND FUTURE

During the past, large segments of our nation's population have been employed in farming and in manufacturing. Today increasing numbers of people are employed in services. In which of these industries do you think you will be employed in the future? Is your prediction related to the results reflected by today's trends in industry and employment?

NORTH AMERICA

30°N   Gulf of Mexico   Tropic of Cancer

MEXICO

CENTRAL AMERICA
AND THE CARIBBEAN

15°N   ATLANTIC

                                                                        OCEAN

0°   Equator

                                        SOUTH AMERICA

PACIFIC   OCEAN

15°S

Tropic of Capricorn

105°W   90°W   75°W   45°W   30°W

135°W   120°W
        30°S

45°S

60°S

100   South Pole
                                              +

AFRICA

15°W   0°

UNIT 2

LATIN AMERICA

WHERE WE ARE

In Unit 2 your journey through the world around us continues, south of the United States, to the part of the world known as Latin America. This region includes not only the entire continent of South America, but also Mexico and the countries of Central America and the Caribbean Sea.

On your journey through Latin America you will visit a land of high mountain peaks and vast river valleys. You will meet people like Alfredo Rios Perez, who lives and works in Mexico City. As you read about Latin America, think about how it compares to the region in which you live. What makes Latin America unique?

LATIN AMERICA

BARBADOS

Capital ★
Bridgetown

Major language: English
Population: 0.3 million
Area: 166 sq mi; 430 sq km
Leading export: sugar

ANTIGUA AND BARBUDA
Capital ★
St. Johns

Major language: English
Population: 0.1 million
Area: 170 sq mi; 440 sq km
Leading export: clothing

BELIZE

Capital ★
Belmopan

Major languages: English and Spanish
Population: 0.2 million
Area: 8,865 sq mi; 22,960 sq km
Leading export: sugar

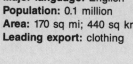

ARGENTINA

Capital ★
Buenos Aires

Major language: Spanish
Population: 32.7 million
Area: 1,068,299 sq mi; 2,766,890 sq km
Leading exports: meats and corn

BOLIVIA
Capital ★
Sucre (judicial)
and La Paz
(administrative)

Major languages: Spanish, Quechua, and Aymará
Population: 7.5 million
Area: 424,163 sq mi; 1,098,580 sq km
Leading exports: tin and copper

BAHAMAS

Capital ★
Nassau

Major language: English
Population: 0.3 million
Area: 5,382 sq mi; 13,940 sq km
Leading export: lobster

BRAZIL

Capital ★
Brasília

Major language: Portuguese
Population: 153.3 million
Area: 3,286,480 sq mi; 8,511,970 sq km
Leading exports: iron ore and coffee

CHILE

Capital ★
Santiago

Major language: Spanish
Population: 13.4 million
Area: 292,259 sq mi; 756,950 sq km
Leading export: copper

DOMINICA

Capital ★
Roseau

Major language: English
Population: 0.1 million
Area: 290 sq mi; 750 sq km
Leading export: bananas

COLOMBIA

Capital ★
Bogotá

Major language: Spanish
Population: 33.6 million
Area: 439,734 sq mi; 1,138,910 sq km
Leading export: coffee

DOMINICAN REPUBLIC

Capital ★
Santo Domingo

Major language: Spanish
Population: 7.3 million
Area: 18,816 sq mi; 48,730 sq km
Leading export: sugar

COSTA RICA

Capital ★
San Jośe

Major language: Spanish
Population: 3.1 million
Area: 19,652 sq mi; 50,900 sq km
Leading export: coffee

ECUADOR

Capital ★
Quito

Major languages: Spanish and Quechua
Population: 10.8 million
Area: 109,483 sq mi; 283,560 sq km
Leading export: oil

CUBA

Capital ★
Havana

Major language: Spanish
Population: 10.7 million
Area: 42,803 sq mi; 110,860 sq km
Leading export: sugar

EL SALVADOR

Capital ★
San Salvador

Major language: Spanish
Population: 5.4 million
Area: 8,124 sq mi; 21,040 sq km
Leading export: coffee

103

FRENCH GUIANA

Capital ★
Cayenne

Major languages: French and Creole
Population: 0.1 million
Area: 35,135 sq mi; 91,000 sq km
Leading export: shrimp

HONDURAS

Capital ★
Tegucigalpa

Major language: Spanish
Population: 5.3 million
Area: 43,277 sq mi; 112,090 sq km
Leading export: coffee

GRENADA

Capital ★
St. George's

Major language: English
Population: 0.1 million
Area: 131 sq mi; 340 sq km
Leading export: nutmeg

JAMAICA

Capital ★
Kingston

Major language: English
Population: 2.5 million
Area: 4,243 sq mi; 10,990 sq km
Leading export: aluminum

GUATEMALA

Capital ★
Guatemala City

Major language: Spanish
Population: 9.5 million
Area: 42,042 sq mi; 108,890 sq km
Leading export: coffee

MEXICO

Capital ★
Mexico City

Major languages: Spanish
Population: 85.7 million
Area: 761,604 sq mi; 1,972,550 sq km
Leading exports: oil and cotton

GUYANA

Capital ★
Georgetown

Major languages: English, Hindi, and Urdu
Population: 0.8 million
Area: 83,000 sq mi; 214,970 sq km
Leading exports: sugar and bauxite

NICARAGUA

Capital ★
Managua

Major language: Spanish
Population: 3.9 million
Area: 49,998 sq mi; 129,494 sq km
Leading export: coffee

HAITI

Capital ★
Port-au-Prince

Major languages: French and French Creole
Population: 6.3 million
Area: 10,714 sq mi; 27,750 sq km
Leading export: coffee

PANAMA

Capital ★
Panama City

Major language: Spanish
Population: 2.5 million
Area: 30,193 sq mi; 78,200 sq km
Leading export: bananas

PARAGUAY

Capital ★
Asunción

Major languages: Spanish and Guaraní
Population: 4.4 million
Area: 157,047 sq mi; 406,750 sq km
Leading export: copper

ST. VINCENT AND THE GRENADINES

Capital ★
Kingstown

Major language: English
Population: 0.1 million
Area: 131 sq mi; 340 sq km
Leading export: bananas

PERU

Capital ★
Lima

Major languages: Spanish, Quechua, and Aymará
Population: 22.0 million
Area: 496,225 sq mi; 1,285,220 sq km
Leading export: copper

SURINAME

Capital ★
Paramaribo

Major languages: Dutch, English, and Hindi
Population: 0.4 million
Area: 63,039 sq mi; 163,270 sq km
Leading exports: bauxite and aluminum

PUERTO RICO

Capital ★
San Juan

Major languages: Spanish and English
Population: 3.5 million
Area: 3,515 sq mi; 9,104 sq km
Leading exports: chemicals

TRINIDAD AND TOBAGO

Capital ★
Port-of-Spain

Major language: English
Population: 1.3 million
Area: 1,980 sq mi; 5,130 sq km
Leading export: oil

ST. KITTS AND NEVIS

Capital ★
Basseterre

Major language: English
Population: 40,000
Area: 139 sq mi; 360 sq km
Leading export: sugar

URUGUAY

Capital ★
Montevideo

Major language: Spanish
Population: 3.1 million
Area: 68,039 sq mi; 175,220 sq km
Leading export: meat

ST. LUCIA

Capital ★
Castries

Major language: English
Population: 0.2 million
Area: 239 sq mi; 620 sq km
Leading export: bananas

VENEZUELA

Capital ★
Caracas

Major language: Spanish
Population: 20.1 million
Area: 352,143 sq mi; 912,050 sq km
Leading export: oil

CHAPTER 4

PHYSICAL GEOGRAPHY OF LATIN AMERICA

▼ FOCUS

I've never seen anything to compare with the richness and beauty of the land over which we've been flying. The patterning of fields covering all but the steepest slopes with those emerald pile carpets is fantastic.

Selden Rodman, the author of many books about Latin America, used these words to describe the view he had from his plane as he flew over the mountain valleys of South America. The "richness and beauty of the land" is just one of the qualities of this region.

Landforms

READ TO LEARN

Key Vocabulary

archipelago
altiplano
river system

Key Places

Central America
Caribbean Islands
Mexico
South America

Andes Mountains
Amazon River
Río de la Plata
Orinoco River

Read Aloud

In 1911 Hiram Bingham, an American explorer, discovered Machu Picchu (mäch′ ü pēk′ chü)—the "Lost City" of the ancient Inca Indians—deep in the Andes Mountains of Peru. The city Hiram Bingham saw consisted of several massive stone buildings on a lonely strip surrounded by steep cliffs. Today people visit Machu Picchu by train. They continue to be amazed at finding massive stone buildings in such an isolated area. But even today, many Latin Americans live in isolation, separated from each other by major landforms.

Read for Purpose

1. WHAT YOU KNOW: Where is Latin America located?
2. WHAT YOU WILL LEARN: What are the major landforms of Latin America, and how do they separate people?

LATIN AMERICA

The region of Latin America is vast in size and includes land on two continents. Central America, the Caribbean Islands, and Mexico—all of which are located in North America—are part of the region. All of the countries located on the continent of South America are also part of the region of Latin America.

Latin America gets its name from Latin, the language of ancient Rome. Languages that developed from Latin are spoken by many people today. These "Latin languages" include Spanish and Portuguese. When Spain and Portugal conquered large parts of the Western Hemisphere in the 1500s, they started colonies there. The colonies formed a large region where either Spanish or Portuguese became the official language. This region came to be called Latin America.

HIGH MOUNTAINS AND LONG RIVERS

After the Spanish conqueror Hernando Cortés captured Mexico from the Aztecs in the 1500s, he was asked to describe its landscape. Cortés took a piece of paper, crumpled it up, and tossed it onto a table, saying, "This is a map of Mexico." This dramatic description applies to most parts of the region of Latin America.

Look at the map on page 108. It shows that two contrasting physical features

107

dominate the Latin American landscape. They are high, rugged mountains and vast river valleys. These two features wind their way through most of Latin America.

The **Andes Mountains** of South America are more than 4,000 miles (6,437 km) long. They are the longest mountain chain in the world.

The mountains contain many volcanoes. When they erupt, the volcanoes can cause great damage. Yet people still live close to them because the ash from the eruptions makes the soil fertile.

One of the most famous Latin American volcanoes, Popocatépetl (pō pō kä tā′ pə təl),

is in southern Mexico. According to an Indian legend, Popocatépetl, "Smoking Mountain," and the nearby volcano Ixtaccihuatl (ēs tä sē′ wät əl), "Sleeping Woman," were once a prince and princess. After the two were forbidden to marry, the princess died of a broken heart. Now when Smoking Mountain rumbles, the Indians say the prince mourns his sweetheart.

The **Amazon River** in South America is 3,900 miles (6,275 km) long. It is the world's second longest river, after the Nile River in Africa. The Amazon flows eastward across almost all of the northern part of South America.

The Andes Mountains and the Amazon River Valley have a great influence on the South American continent. They affect the climate and limit the land that can be

MAP SKILL: High, rugged mountains run along the western coasts of Mexico, Central America, and South America. In which nations are the highest elevations located?

LATIN AMERICA: Elevation

farmed. They also separate people and form barriers to trade and transportation.

ISLANDS OF THE CARIBBEAN

Most of the islands of the Caribbean Sea are also part of Latin America's mountain system. They are contained in a large circle of mountains under the sea whose peaks rise above the water. The mountain tops form the archipelago (är kə pel' i gō), or island group, known as the Caribbean Islands or West Indies. They are divided into smaller archipelagos called the Greater Antilles (an til' ēz), Lesser Antilles, and Netherlands Antilles. Find these island groups on the map on page 108.

The Bahamas are among the few islands in the area that are not mountain peaks. The Bahamas are coral islands. They were formed by layers of tiny sea animals.

THE ANDES

The Andes Mountains stretch along most of western South America. They are higher and more rugged than the mountains of Mexico and Central America. The highest peaks of the Andes are on the border between Argentina and Chile. There, peaks reach over 20,000 feet (6,000 m) above sea level.

Maria Yupanqui (ū pän' kē) of Argentina lives in the Andes. She explains that because the mountains are so high, there "is less oxygen up here than at sea level." The weather is hot during the day, but the elevation makes it "very cold at night."

Look at the population density map on page 110. It shows that many people live in the Andes today. This area is more crowded than the lowlands in the middle of the continent. One crowded Andean area is the altiplano (äl ti plän' ō). The altiplano is a high, cold, flat area between two mountain ranges in Bolivia and Peru. Lake Titicaca, the highest navigable lake in the world, is on the altiplano.

Popocatépetl, a volcano in Mexico, is North America's fifth-highest peak. It gives off smoke but has had no major eruption since 1702.

GREAT RIVER SYSTEMS

South America's continental divide is on the west coast, in the Andes Mountains. From the eastern peaks of the Andes, many rivers flow thousands of miles east to the ocean. No other continent has so many long rivers flowing in one direction.

In other parts of Latin America, though, rivers are short, with many waterfalls and rocks. As a result, ships cannot travel along them for long distances. South America is the only part of Latin America that has long, navigable rivers.

South America has three large river systems: the Amazon, the Río de la Plata and the Orinoco River. A river system, or river basin, is the land drained by a river and its tributaries. This land is often shaped like a bowl. One of the world's greatest river systems, the Amazon flows through an area about three fourths the size of the United States.

Latin America's second-largest river system is the Río de la Plata. Made up mainly of the Paraná and Uruguay rivers,

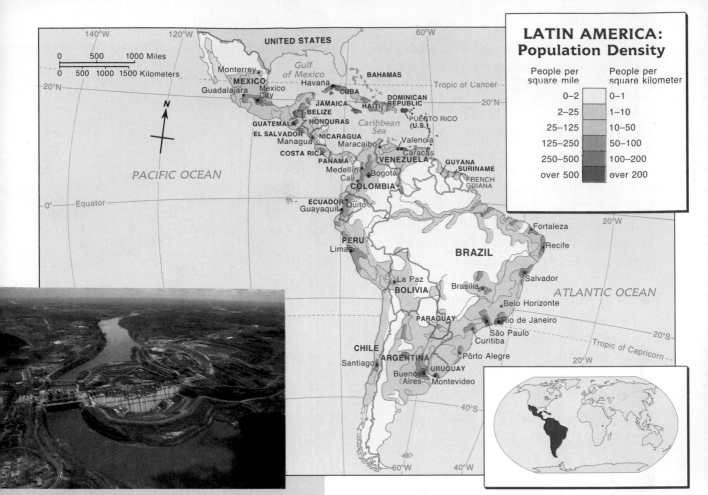

LATIN AMERICA: Population Density

People per square mile	People per square kilometer
0–2	0–1
2–25	1–10
25–125	10–50
125–250	50–100
250–500	100–200
over 500	over 200

MAP SKILL: The Itaipu Dam provides energy for southern Brazil's most crowded areas. Name two cities that are located in these crowded areas.

it flows through east-central South America. The Río de la Plata system is a major transportation route for southeastern South America. The Itaipu (ē tī′ pü) Dam, the world's largest hydroelectric project, is on a tributary of the Río de la Plata.

The third large river system in Latin America is the Orinoco. In the north, the Orinoco's tributaries flow mainly across Venezuela and eastern Colombia.

MOUNTAINS AND TROPICAL LOWLANDS

Latin America is made up of Mexico, Central America, the Caribbean Islands, and South America. This region is dominated by its high mountains and the Amazon River Valley. Latin America has three great river systems—the Amazon, the Río de la Plata, and the Orinoco. High mountains and tropical forests make farming difficult and form barriers to travel.

 Check Your Reading

1. What are the main parts of the Latin American region?
2. Name the three major river systems of Latin America.
3. What are the two main features of the physical geography of Latin America?
4. **THINKING SKILL:** Look at the map on page 108. Why do you think Brazil has so many rivers that flow into the Amazon River? Explain.

Climate and Resources

READ TO LEARN

■ Key Vocabulary

rain forest

■ Read Aloud

The land animals here have all fled or died. . . . We are looking for tree animals like . . . anteaters and felines.

These words were spoken by a member of an animal rescue mission in Brazil. Every day this mission sends boats into a part of the Amazon River Valley that is being flooded by water to form a reservoir. Some scientists question whether it was wise to begin developing this area because of its poor soil and difficult climate.

■ Read for Purpose

1. **WHAT YOU KNOW:** What are Latin America's most important landforms?
2. **WHAT YOU WILL LEARN:** What are the major climates and resources of Latin America?

EL DORADO

Latin America is rich in natural resources. Before the Europeans arrived, Indians created beautiful objects of gold and jewels.

Stories of precious metals and jewels drew many Europeans seeking to become rich from American treasure. They heard tales about a land where gold was lying around for anyone to pick up. This legendary kingdom was called *El Dorado*, the Spanish words for "the golden one."

No treasure hunter ever found the legendary El Dorado. However, conquerors found and took gold, silver, tin, emeralds, and other resources. Today new resources are being discovered. Mexico and Venezuela have huge petroleum reserves. Mexico also has considerable reserves of natural gas. However, mineral resources are often not easy to find. As one author has written:

Although nature has blessed the region in great abundance . . . it has jealously hidden the keys to this treasure house. Much of this wealth [cannot be reached] because of the barriers of jungles, mountains, and rivers.

UNEVEN DISTRIBUTION OF RESOURCES

Latin America's natural resources are unevenly spread around. A number of countries, especially in Central America and the Caribbean Islands, have few minerals, or none at all.

Some Latin American nations have large ore deposits but lack other resources needed to use them for industry. Brazil, for example, has iron ore but no coal to turn

111

the iron into steel. So Brazil must import coal in order to make steel.

AGRICULTURE

As the map on this page shows, very little land in Latin America is good for farming. In South America only about 5 percent of the land can be farmed. That's an area slightly smaller than the nation of Bolivia. The main reasons for the lack of arable land are the mountains and the fact that there is too much or too little rain in many areas. The daily rain in the rain forests, for example, washes away the nutrients in the soil.

Some of the best farmland in Latin America is found in the islands of the Caribbean. Other good farmland is in mountain valleys and in some lowlands.

GRASSLANDS

From Buenos Aires, Argentina, south almost to Patagonia are miles and miles of flat grasslands. They are Latin America's largest plains. In the north the plain is called the Chaco and is about 200,000 square miles (518,000 sq km) in area. In the south the plain is called the Pampas and is almost 300,000 square miles (777,000 sq km) in area.

The Chaco is a harsh land covered with thorn bushes, but the Pampas is green and gentle. In the Pampas the summers are long, the winters are mild, and the soil is fertile. It is both a cattle range and one of the world's great producers of grain.

MAP SKILL: Only the largest manufacturing centers are shown on the map. Which countries have manufacturing centers inland?

LATIN AMERICA: Land Use

- Manufacturing
- Commercial farming and livestock raising
- Livestock raising
- Subsistence farming
- Forestry with farming, hunting, and gathering
- Commercial fishing
- Little or no economic activity
- Mining and extraction
- Tourism

112

FORESTS

Trees are one of Latin America's most valuable resources. About two fifths of Latin America is covered with trees. Most of these trees are in the rain forest of the Amazon River Valley. One writer has written that there "even the trees war with each other for a place in the soil and the sun . . . ." Among the many kinds of trees in the tropical rain forest are hardwood trees, such as rosewood and mahogany.

Now much of the Amazon forest is being cleared for dams, roads, farms, and factories. Some people, however, say that too much is being cleared. You can read about this issue on pages 168–169.

THREE CLIMATE ZONES

Most of Latin America is in the tropics. So you might expect the region to have a warm climate. Yet, as you can see from the map on page 114, the region has several different climates. Latin America is mountainous. The high elevation in the mountains causes them to be cooler than you might think.

Latin America has three different climate zones in the mountains. The diagram on this page shows you these zones and the crops that grow in each one. Look at the diagram and find the *tierra caliente* (tē âr′ ə käl ē en′ tä), meaning "hot land." This lowland tropic zone is hot all year.

The second climate zone is the higher *tierra templada* (tē âr′ ə tem plä′ də), or "temperate land." The Central Plateau of Mexico and many of Latin America's highland plateaus and valleys are in this mild climate zone. As you might expect, the tierra templada is the most heavily populated part of Latin America.

The *tierra fría* (tē âr′ ə frē′ ə), Latin America's "cold land," is the highest climate zone. It is made up of land above 6,000 feet (1,800 m). Even in the tropics,

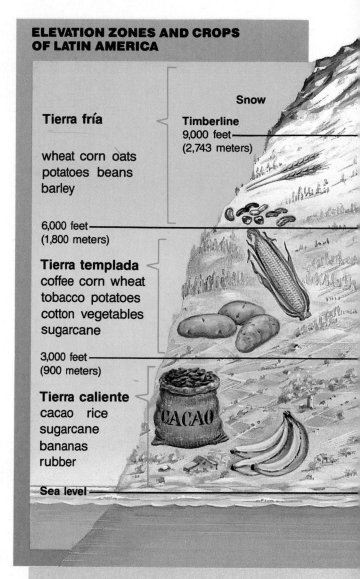

ELEVATION ZONES AND CROPS OF LATIN AMERICA

Tierra fría

wheat corn oats potatoes beans barley

Snow

Timberline 9,000 feet (2,743 meters)

6,000 feet (1,800 meters)

Tierra templada
coffee corn wheat tobacco potatoes cotton vegetables sugarcane

3,000 feet (900 meters)

Tierra caliente
cacao rice sugarcane bananas rubber

CACAO

Sea level

DIAGRAM SKILL: Which climate zone has mild temperatures, average rainfall, and crops that do not need much heat and moisture?

high peaks such as Mount Aconcagua (ak ən kä′ gwə) in Argentina are snow-capped all year. Mount Aconcagua is 22,831 feet (6,959 m) above sea level.

RAINFALL

Latin America has the largest rainy area in the world—the Amazon River Valley. It rains almost every day here. You can see this wet area on the map on page 114.

Throughout Latin America the amount of rainfall varies, depending on whether

113

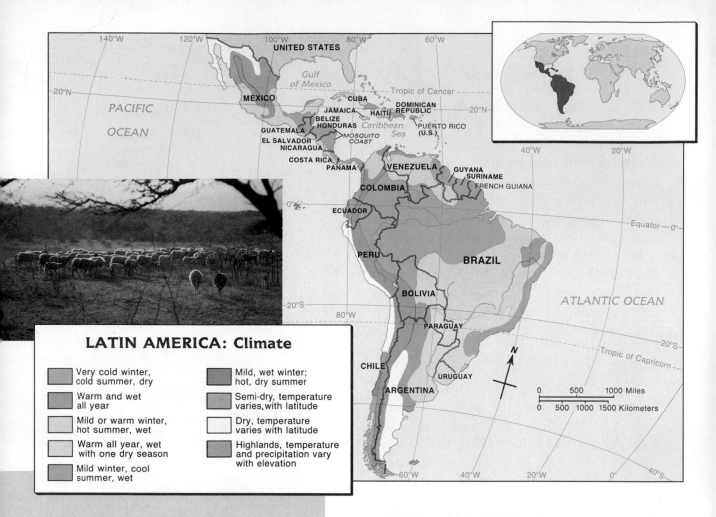

LATIN AMERICA: Climate

- Very cold winter, cold summer, dry
- Warm and wet all year
- Mild or warm winter, hot summer, wet
- Warm all year, wet with one dry season
- Mild winter, cool summer, wet
- Mild, wet winter; hot, dry summer
- Semi-dry, temperature varies with latitude
- Dry, temperature varies with latitude
- Highlands, temperature and precipitation vary with elevation

MAP SKILL: Name a part of Latin America in which a semidry climate is found.

rain-bearing winds blow onshore and where they hit the mountains. The heaviest rains fall along the eastern part of the region. Some places have too much rain. Along the Mosquito Coast of Nicaragua and Honduras, more than 200 inches (500 cm) of rain can fall in a year.

Latin America also has the driest place in the world, the Atacama Desert of Chile. Imagine having to "travel overland by mule and afoot across . . . burning flats where it hasn't rained for a thousand years." This is what miners traveling here in the 1800s experienced. They said that nothing grew or moved there.

DIFFERENT CLIMATES AND RESOURCES

Although most of Latin America is in the tropics, the high elevation of its mountains form hot, temperate, and cold climate zones. Latin America also has areas of high rainfall and of low rainfall. The region is rich in natural resources. However, many resources are difficult to reach or are unevenly distributed.

Check Your Reading

1. What are the Chaco and the Pampas?
2. What are some important natural resources found in Latin America?
3. Name Latin America's climate zones.
4. **THINKING SKILL:** What effect do Latin America's mountains have on the climate of the region?

Relating Latitude, Elevation, and Climate

Key Vocabulary
low latitudes
middle latitudes
high latitudes

In the last lesson you read about Latin America's climate. You learned that although most of Latin America lies in a tropical zone, the region has a wide variety of different climates. In fact, there are three different climate zones in Latin America. In order to understand the reasons for this fact, it is important to know how latitude, elevation, and climate are related to each other.

How Latitude Affects Climate
You may recall that the amount of heat received by any location on earth depends on its latitude. Regions near the equator generally have the hottest temperatures because they receive more of the sun's rays all year long. These areas are said to be located in the low latitudes. Regions farther from the equator have generally cooler temperatures and experience changing seasons throughout the year. These milder areas are said to be in the middle latitudes. The lands around the North and South poles are the coldest places on earth because they receive less direct sunlight. These areas, which are covered by snow and ice, are in the high latitudes. In general, the latitude of an area tells us a great deal about the temperatures found there.

How Elevation Affects Climate
Imagine you are in Ecuador, which is located on the equator in South America. In the lowlands of Ecuador temperatures are very warm. In the mountains, however, temperatures are much colder. Higher elevation means lower temperatures. In fact, for each 1,000-foot (300-m) increase in elevation, the temperature drops about 3.6°F. (2°C).

You have read that the higher elevations in Latin America are called the *tierra friá*, or "cold land." Only a few crops grow in the higher elevations of the *tierra friá*, where temperatures are very cold. In fact, if you were to climb to the top of one of Ecuador's higher mountains, you would most likely find snow, ice, and freezing temperatures.

Latitude and Elevation
Climate is affected by many factors: Latitude and elevation are two of the most important. Much of Latin America lies in the low and middle latitudes and therefore has a warm climate. But because of variations in elevation, some mountainous regions in Latin America are very cold.

Reviewing the Skill
1. How does latitude affect climate?
2. In which latitudes are temperatures coldest? In which are they hottest?
3. How does elevation affect climate?
4. Why are some regions of Latin America very cold?
5. Why is it important to understand the relationships among latitude, elevation, and climate?

LATIN AMERICA: PHYSICAL GEOGRAPHY

 LANDFORMS

 CLIMATE

NATURAL RESOURCES

- High mountains: Andes

- Vast river systems: Amazon, Río de la Plata, Orinoco

- Three climate zones:
  a) Tierra caliente ("hot land")
  b) Tierra templada ("temperate land")
  c) Tierra fría ("cold land")

- Gold, silver, tin, and other minerals

- Volcanoes: Popocatépetl
- Caribbean Islands: formed into archipelagos

- Rainiest place in the world: Amazon River Valley
- Driest place in the world: Atacama Desert

- Mexico and Venezuela: huge petroleum reserves
- Uneven distribution: some countries have many resources, some have few

IDEAS TO REMEMBER

- High mountains and vast rivers dominate the Latin American continent.
- Latin America has a variety of natural resources and, because of its mountains, three different climate zones.

REVIEWING VOCABULARY

Each of the following statements contains an underlined vocabulary word or term. Number a sheet of paper from 1 to 5. Beside each number write whether each of the following statements is true or false. If the statement is true, write "true." If it is false, rewrite the sentence using the vocabulary word or term correctly.

1. The islands of the West Indies are an example of an <u>archipelago.</u>
2. The land drained by a major river and its tributaries is called a <u>rain forest.</u>
3. A <u>river system</u> is a tropical area of dense trees where rain falls almost every day.
4. The <u>altiplano</u> is a high, flat region that has a cold climate and the world's highest navigable lake.
5. The Andes Mountains are an example of an <u>archipelago.</u>

REVIEWING FACTS

1. Which of the four main areas of Latin America are part of North America?
2. Why is this region called Latin America? What are the two main European languages spoken by people in Latin America today?
3. Which mountain system is the largest in Latin America?
4. Name three effects that the Andes Mountains have on the continent of South America.
5. What is the name of the second longest river in the world?
6. In which part of South America are the Andes Mountains located? Between which two countries are the chain's highest peaks found?
7. Why are temperatures very low in some Andean regions even though these mountains are located in the tropics?
8. Which region in South America is among the wettest in the world? Which region is among the driest in the world?
9. What does *El Dorado* mean? How did El Dorado affect the European exploration and settlement of Latin America?
10. Name two reasons that only a small percentage of land in Latin America is suitable for farming.

WRITING ABOUT MAIN IDEAS

1. **Writing a Paragraph:** Look again at the diagram of mountain climates on page 113. Write a paragraph describing the changes in climate from the lowlands to the mountains.
2. **Writing a Travel Brochure:** Imagine that you will be leading a tour of the Amazon rain forest. Describe in several paragraphs the sights and sounds the tourists will see.
3. **Writing About Perspectives:** Imagine that you are moving from the *tierra caliente* to the *tierra fría*. Write a letter to a friend describing some of the changes you have to make in the way you live.

BUILDING SKILLS: RELATING LATITUDE, ELEVATION, AND CLIMATE

1. How do latitude and elevation affect climate?
2. What are the three climate zones of Latin America?
3. Why does Latin America have more than one climate zone?
4. Why is it important to understand how latitude and elevation affect climate?

CHAPTER 5

MEXICO

FOCUS

Mexicans have an incredible attachment to their country.

These words by the writers Lynn and Lawrence Foster describe how many Mexicans feel about their country. In the following chapter you will read about Mexico and the ways of life that are special to its people.

The People

READ TO LEARN

Key Vocabulary

civilization
mestizo
extended family

Key People

Hernando Cortés

Key Places

Tenochtitlán
Mexico City

Read Aloud

Have you ever eaten a taco? The outside is a corn-flour pancake called a tortilla (tôr tē′ yə). The tortilla is fried and folded around a filling that often includes pieces of beef or chicken. The tortilla pancake is Indian, a product of thousands of years of growing corn. The filling for the taco comes from animals like cattle and chickens. These animals were brought to Mexico by the Spanish. The tasty food that results is neither Spanish nor Indian. It is Mexican.

Read for Purpose

1. WHAT YOU KNOW: Who were the first people known to have lived in North America?
2. WHAT YOU WILL LEARN: In what ways is Mexico a blend of cultures?

EARLY INDIAN CIVILIZATIONS

As you may remember from Chapter 2, the first peoples in North America were Indians. The first peoples in Latin America were also Indians. Thousands of years ago Indian groups in Mexico created civilizations (siv ə li zā′ shənz). A civilization is a culture that has developed systems of government, religion, and learning.

Among the earliest Indian civilizations was that of the Mayas (mä′ yəz). About 1,500 years ago these skilled farmers and mathematicians built stone temples and palaces in the rain forests of the Yucatán Peninsula. The Mayas were also splendid craftworkers, decorating their buildings with both fine paintings and sculptures.

During the 1200s the Mexica, whom the Spanish called the Aztecs, settled in Mexico's high Central Plateau. Their capital city was called Tenochtitlán (te nôch tē tlän′). It stood where Mexico City, the capital of Mexico, stands today.

THE ARRIVAL OF THE SPANISH

The Spanish military leader Hernando Cortés reached Mexico in 1519. He was amazed at the wealth and beauty of Tenochtitlán, which he called "the most beautiful city in the world." Yet Cortés and his followers destroyed the city in order to defeat the Aztecs. Although the Aztecs fought bravely, their weapons were no match for Spanish horses and guns and the help of the Aztecs' enemies who aided the Spanish.

119

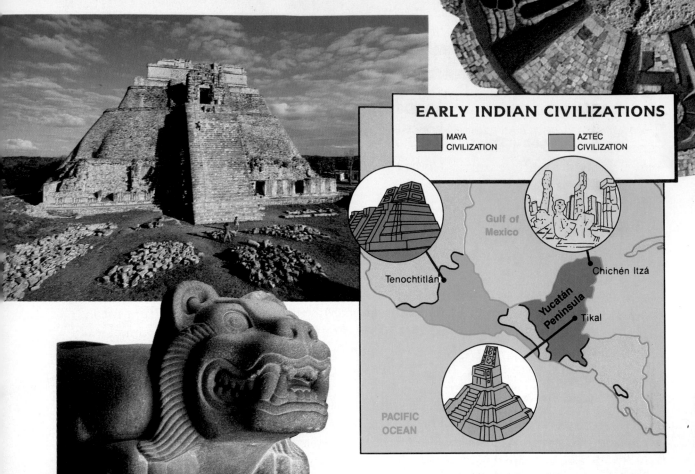

EARLY INDIAN CIVILIZATIONS

MAYA CIVILIZATION

AZTEC CIVILIZATION

Gulf of Mexico

Tenochtitlán

Chichén Itzá

Yucatán Peninsula

Tikal

PACIFIC OCEAN

MAP SKILL: Which of the two civilizations shown on the map extended onto the Yucatán Peninsula? Near which bodies of water were the Mayas located?

The Spanish conquest of Mexico in 1521 changed the history and culture of the country. The Indians lost control of their land and their lives. They were forced to work on Spanish farms and ranches and in mines. Thousands of Indians died from diseases brought by Europeans. Many Indians also had to convert, or change their religion, to Christianity. As a result, the way of life of Mexico's people became a mixture of the Spanish and Indian cultures.

MEXICANS TODAY

Today most of the people of Mexico are a blend of Indian and Spanish. About 55 percent of Mexico's 86 million people are considered to be mestizos (mes tē′ zōz). That is, they are of mixed Indian and Spanish ancestry. Another 29 percent are Indian. Most of the rest are of Spanish ancestry. Some of Mexico's people have come from other European countries as well as from Africa, Asia, and North and South America.

Spanish is the official language of Mexico. However, some Mexicans speak one of about 50 Indian languages, including the Aztec and Mayan languages. And like American English, Mexican Spanish has adopted some words from different Indian languages.

RELIGION

The Spanish who conquered Mexico were Roman Catholics and wanted to convert the Indians to Christianity. The Indians had followed traditional religions, which included worship of nature gods such as the gods of rain, thunder, and agriculture. The Spanish destroyed the temples to these gods.

Today more than 90 percent of all Mexicans are Roman Catholic, and most villages have a Catholic Church. In Mexico there are also many shrines, or holy places named for a special religious figure.

Mexico has a patron saint, the Virgin of Guadalupe (gwäd ä lü' pā), for the entire country. The shrine of the Virgin of Guadalupe is located near Mexico City. The shrine of Guadalupe is devoted to Mary, the mother of Jesus.

Leobardo Lopez, a photographer at the shrine, tells the story of its origin.

> In 1531, it is said that the Virgin [Mary] appeared to a young Indian boy named Juan Diego, and asked him to build a church in her memory. . . . To convince the priests of her wishes, Juan was to go to the hills of "El Tepayac" and pick all the roses he could find there. . . . When he returned to the town [and took] the flowers from his shirt, . . . the image of the Virgin [was] printed on Juan's shirt.

The shrine was built where Juan Diego said Mary appeared to him. About 6 million people visit the shrine every year.

HOLIDAYS

Many Mexican cities and towns celebrate religious holidays with a *fiesta,* or festival. Fiestas often involve costumes and traditions kept alive from the time of the Aztecs.

Mexico also celebrates holidays that mark important days in its history. September 16 is Mexico's Independence Day. It marks the beginning of a struggle against Spanish rule. Cinco de Mayo, May 5, celebrates an important battle in 1862 when a Mexican army defended the city of Puebla from French invaders.

Fiestas may be celebrated with traditional music and dance (*above*). Revolution Day in Mexico is often marked with a modern parade (*below*).

121

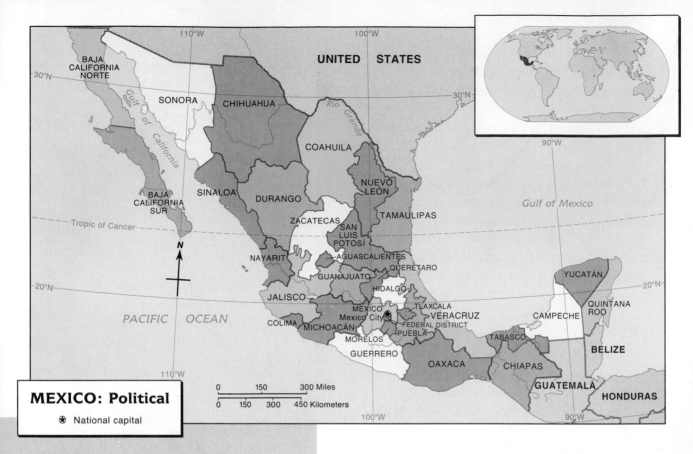

MEXICO: Political

⊛ National capital

MAP SKILL: Find the national capital of Mexico. At about what latitude and longitude is the capital located?

FAMILIES

Family life is important to most Mexicans. Often people live with or near their **extended families.** An extended family includes parents, children, and other family members, such as aunts, uncles, grandparents, and cousins. When family members leave a rural area to find work elsewhere, they often go to stay with their extended families.

Godparents are an important part of a Mexican family. As in many countries, a godparent is an adult sponsor who promises to oversee a child's religious upbringing. In Mexico, godparents are like a second set of parents to whom children may turn for help.

A BLEND OF INDIAN AND SPANISH

You have read that Indians were the first settlers of Mexico and that Indian groups such as the Mayas and Aztecs developed civilizations. Mexico's culture changed after the Spanish conquered Mexico in the 1500s and introduced Spanish ways of life. Today most Mexicans are Catholics and mestizos.

Check Your Reading

1. Who are the mestizos?
2. Why are most present-day Mexicans Roman Catholics?
3. What are some important holidays people in Mexico celebrate?
4. **THINKING SKILL:** List some ways in which families in the United States are different from families in Mexico. How are they similar?

122

The Economy

READ TO LEARN

◼ Key Vocabulary

metropolitan area	commercial farming
campesino	developing economy
subsistence farming	petrochemical

◼ Read Aloud

I left home maybe six months ago. Why? To better myself!

As Alfredo Rios Perez speaks these words, he proudly straightens his mud-spattered hard hat. He works on a construction project in Mexico City. But he was born in a village to the north. When he worked on a farm, he earned about six dollars a week. Now he makes six times as much—enough to bring his wife and three children to the capital.

◼ Read for Purpose

1. **WHAT YOU KNOW:** Why do workers sometimes move to different places to work?
2. **WHAT YOU WILL LEARN:** What are the major features of Mexico's developing economy?

MEXICO CITY—A SPRAWLING GIANT

Alfredo Rios Perez is only one of about 1,000 Mexicans who move to Mexico City every day. Besides being the nation's capital, Mexico City is also the economic and cultural center of the nation.

Mexico City is a bustling, modern city. Among its high buildings is the 44-story Latin America Tower—the tallest skyscraper in Latin America. Mexico City's subway riders travel for the world's cheapest fare. A ride costs one peso, which is less than one United States cent. City leaders encourage people to take the subway because more than 2 million automobiles are used in the city daily.

No other city in Mexico offers more opportunities than Mexico City does. As a result, the constant movement of people to the city caused its population to reach 18 million by the late 1980s. The table on page 124 shows that Mexico City is one of the largest metropolitan areas in the world. A metropolitan area includes a large city and all of its surrounding suburbs and towns.

AGRICULTURE

Outside the large cities most Mexicans farm for a living. Their lives are similar to those described by Rosa Valdepeñas, a teacher in Tlaxcala, east of Mexico City:

Most of my pupils' parents are farmers with small plots of land and very low incomes. After school, many of my pupils spend the afternoon helping their parents farm the land.

WORLD'S LARGEST URBAN AREAS	
Urban Area	**Population**
Tokyo-Yokohama, Japan	27.2 million
Mexico City, Mexico	20.8 million
São Paulo, Brazil	18.7 million
Seoul, South Korea	16.7 million
New York City, U.S.A.	14.6 million
Osaka-Kobe-Kyoto, Japan	13.8 million
Bombay, India	12.1 million
Calcutta, India	11.8 million
Rio de Janeiro, Brazil	11.6 million
Buenos Aires, Argentina	11.6 million

CHART SKILL: How many of the large urban areas listed in the chart are located in Latin America? Name them.

These village farmers, or **campesinos** (käm pə sē' nōz), grow just enough corn, beans, and squash for their families. Farming of this type is called **subsistence farming**. Without surplus, or extra, food, subsistence farmers have little to trade at markets. Moreover, the little money they earn is often just enough to buy other kinds of food. As a result, large trade centers have not developed in Mexico's poor farming areas.

Only 11 percent of Mexico's land can be farmed. Besides the campesinos, the other people who own this land cultivate mainly sugarcane, cotton, and tropical fruits on large farms. This type of farming in which all the crops are grown for sale is called **commercial farming**. Many commercial crops are exported to other nations.

INDUSTRIALIZATION

Mexico is working to increase its mineral manufacturing industries. Mexico has great amounts of silver and gold—the treasure that may have been behind the legend of El Dorado that you read about earlier. For centuries about one third of the world's silver came from Mexico's mines. This ore was not used in Mexico to develop the nation's businesses and factories but went instead to other countries. Partly for this reason, Mexico today has a **developing economy**. A developing economy is one that is only partly industrialized.

Mexico also has other minerals—coal, iron, zinc, and petroleum. Large deposits of petroleum, discovered in the 1970s, helped Mexico's economy. The discovery of oil has created new industries, like the **petrochemical** industry. Petrochemicals are chemicals, like ammonia and benzene, that are made from petroleum. Mexico has the largest petrochemical industry in Latin America.

124

Petroleum is one of Mexico's major natural resources. All oil reserves, inland and offshore, are developed by PEMEX, the state-owned oil company of Mexico.

THE GROWING POPULATION

Despite its new industries, Mexico's economic growth slowed in the 1980s. The main reason for this was that as Mexico became industrialized, the nation's living conditions and the health of its population improved. People began to live longer and have larger families. As a result, the population doubled between 1972 and 1982. Today Mexico's population is growing twice as rapidly as that of the United States and faster than the nation's ability to provide jobs for everyone. In the late 1980s about one third of Mexico's 86 million people could not find jobs.

CHALLENGES FOR THE FUTURE

Mexico, as you have read, has a developing economy that is partially industrialized. Most of its industry is concentrated in Mexico City and a few other cities. Because it has poor farmland and a rapidly growing population, Mexico finds it difficult to provide jobs, goods, and services for all of its people.

Check Your Reading

1. Why is Mexico's economy called a developing economy?
2. Why is Mexico City important?
3. What is the difference between subsistence farming and commercial farming?
4. **THINKING SKILL:** What factors might you consider if you were trying to decide whether or not to move to a large city in Mexico?

Determining the Accuracy of Information

Suppose a friend shows you a baseball card and tells you that it is worth $6.35. The card is one of your favorites. Your friend offers to sell it to you, telling you it will increase in value each year. Before you buy the card, wouldn't you want to know if your friend is giving you accurate information? You need accurate information to make good decisions. Information that is accurate is free of errors. Therefore, when you check information for errors, you are determining the accuracy of that information.

Trying the Skill

Suppose you were to read the following in a magazine article about Mexico dated January 1990.

According to Mexico's Minister of Public Education, there has been a dramatic increase in public school enrollment since the 1950s. Enrollment in secondary schools today is five times higher than it was in 1955. About 86 percent of children ages 6–14 are now attending primary schools. A major effort is being made to promote education in rural areas.

1. Do you think the above information is accurate? Why?
2. What could you do to determine the accuracy of the information given?

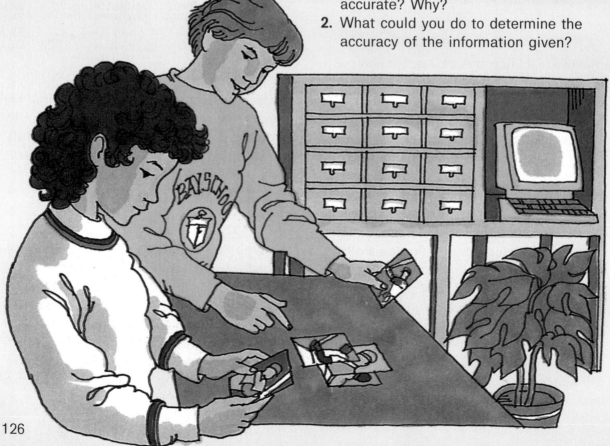

HELPING YOURSELF

The steps on the left can help you to determine the accuracy of information. The examples on the right show how these steps can be used to evaluate the information about education in Mexico.

One Way to Determine the Accuracy of Information	Example
1. Identify the source of the information.	The source is Mexico's Minister of Public Education.
2. Determine the credibility, or believability, of the source by asking the following questions. • Is the author or speaker an expert or well informed about the topic? • Does the author or speaker have anything to gain by giving inaccurate information?	The speaker is the Minister of Public Education and is therefore likely to be well informed about the topic. The speaker appears to have nothing to gain by giving inaccurate information.
3. Determine if the information is current.	The article was written in 1990, so the education figures provided for "today" are current.
4. Compare the information with similar information in other sources.	Checking the same information in other sources helps you to determine its accuracy. In this case, you might look for information in current world almanacs and encyclopedias. If all the sources agree, the information is probably accurate.

Applying the Skill

Now apply what you have learned. Determine the accuracy of the following information from a book about Mexico written in 1979. The author of the book is a geography professor who has taught at a university in Mexico City for 20 years.

Since 1950 economic growth has been steady in Mexico. Oil and gas reserves were discovered in 1975, making Mexico self-sufficient in petroleum. Tourism is at a record high. The Mexican stock market is on an upswing.

1. Is the information presented accurate? How can you tell?

2. Is the source of the information a credible source? How do you know that the source is credible?
3. What are two sources you might check to determine the accuracy of the information above?

Reviewing the Skill

1. What does the word *accuracy* mean?
2. What are three things you can do to determine the accuracy of information?
3. Why is it important to determine whether or not information is accurate?

The Government

Key People

Carlos Salinas de Gortari

Read Aloud

I take office at a complicated moment, between . . . the necessity to build for the future and the urgency of immediate achievements. . . . I am determined to move ahead with a democratic reform, and I have invited political parties to join me. . . .

Carlos Salinas de Gortari spoke these words when he was sworn in as president of Mexico in 1988, after the most troubled election in modern Mexican history. Like many other Mexican leaders before him, he faced the prospect of turmoil in the country he was to lead.

Read for Purpose

1. **WHAT YOU KNOW:** What is a federal republic?
2. **WHAT YOU WILL LEARN:** How is Mexico's representative democracy different from that of the United States?

A STRONG PRESIDENT

Mexico gained its independence from Spain in 1821. However, independence did not bring stability to the country. Instead a series of strong leaders, usually from the military, ruled Mexico. Finally in 1910, a popular revolution swept across Mexico. When it was over, Mexicans wrote a constitution that guaranteed basic rights for all of its citizens. Today Mexicans are proud of what they accomplished in their popular revolution.

Mexico's constitution made the country a representative democracy. However, its government is a little different from the governments of the United States and Canada in that it provides for strong leadership by one person.

The Mexican constitution gives its president more power than the Constitution of the United States gives to the President of the United States. The president of Mexico can remove local officials from office and change laws with the approval of the Senate. However, the Mexican president can be elected for only one six-year term.

The Mexican constitution also established a legislature of two houses. One house, the Chamber of Deputies, passes laws and is responsible for elections. The second house, the Senate, approves or disapproves treaties and presidential appointments. Mexico also has a federal system of government. This means that its 31 states control many local affairs. A Supreme Court interprets laws.

LEADERSHIP BY ONE PARTY

Unlike the United States, Mexico has only one strong political party, the Party of Institutional Revolution (PRI). It was formed in 1929 to include many interests—labor, agriculture, professional people, and the military. The reason for this union was to prevent different groups from clashing and causing unrest.

For about 60 years the PRI won elections easily. In the 1988 election, however, the PRI was losing until the last minute. After it was declared the winner by less than 1 percent, Carlos Salinas de Gortari became president. But some people believed that the party had really lost the election. Critics said the PRI had "fixed" the returns to make the party win.

Critics of the PRI today say it is time to make the government more directly responsible to the people and to allow parties to air their differences in public. They say that Mexico "needs [several] political parties . . . to express those divisions—of class, of racial background, of politics."

INTERNATIONAL COOPERATION

Despite its party troubles, Mexico has one of the most stable governments in Latin America. This fact enables Mexico to be very active in international affairs.

Many Mexicans took part in the 1988 presidential election. Carlos Salinas de Gortari (*below*), who won, was the candidate of the PRI. The party's emblem is shown above.

129

The Organization of American States Building and its emblem are in Washington, D.C.

OVER 70 YEARS OF DEMOCRACY

Mexico's government combines strong presidential leadership with democracy. Until 1988 one party, the PRI, easily won elections in Mexico. After the PRI almost lost the 1988 election, critics of the government said that it was time for a multiparty system to be formed in Mexico.

One of the Latin American organizations in which Mexico is very active is the Organization of American States (OAS). The main goals of the OAS are to improve the lives of Latin American people and to keep peace in the Western Hemisphere. Mexico has also been a strong supporter of the United Nations (UN), the world's largest international organization. The UN was formed in 1945 to keep peace among nations and to help poor people.

 Check Your Reading

1. List two ways in which the presidency of Mexico is different from the presidency of the United States.
2. Describe Mexico's legislature.
3. Briefly describe the political party system of Mexico.
4. **THINKING SKILL:** Classify the powers of the Mexican government into its executive and legislative branches.

Arts and Recreation

READ TO LEARN

Key Vocabulary

mural

Key People

Diego Rivera

José Orozco

Read Aloud

La Cucaracha, La Cucaracha,
Just the same as you and I,
He got the jitters, the sweets, and bitters,
Lived and loved and said "Goodbye."

This is the last chorus from "La Cucaracha," or "The Mexican Cockroach Song." It was a favorite marching song of the Mexican revolutionaries in 1910. Today it is still one of the most popular Mexican songs.

Read for Purpose

1. **WHAT YOU KNOW:** What songs express the way people in the United States feel about their country?
2. **WHAT YOU WILL LEARN:** How are Mexico's arts and amusements the products of different cultures?

1910 AND THE ARTS

You read in Lesson 3 that the Mexican Revolution, which changed the country into a republic, began in 1910. After the revolution, Mexicans started to think of themselves as one people. Indians, mestizos, and Mexicans of Spanish ancestry had fought together. They had succeeded in creating a government that guarantees people's rights. One writer explains:

The 1910 Revolution was the revolution of the campesinos. Before this time they were a forgotten people. But the campesinos gave their hearts and their lives to create a new Mexico. Now let their voices be heard!

The people's pride in their achievement inspired Mexico's artists. They began to explore what it meant to be Mexican.

INDIAN AND MESTIZO CULTURES

A number of artists explored their Indian heritage. Well-known composers, such as Carlos Chávez, began to use Indian melodies in their music.

The mestizo heritage was also explored. Two Mexican painters are identified with the mestizo art of their country. They are Diego Rivera (dyā′ gō ri ver′ ə) and José Orozco (hō sā′ ō rô′ skō). Both artists painted large murals, or works of art on building walls.

With simple lines and bold colors Rivera and Orozco captured the spirit of Mexico—both the past sufferings and the hopes for the future. Their murals are among the first and best works of modern Mexican art. Every year thousands of people visit Mexico City, Guadalajara, and

131

Among Mexico's famous art works is the **mural** *Mexico Through the Centuries* by Diego Rivera. It highlights Mexico's fight for land and freedom. Craftworkers like the weaver below also create works of art.

Cuernavaca (kwâr nə väk′ ə) to see the beautiful murals painted by these artists.

CRAFTS

After the Mexican Revolution the Mexican government began to support traditional Mexican crafts. It gave craftworkers awards and helped them export their best works. In so doing, Mexico hoped to maintain its traditions, give people income, and produce goods for export.

Today craftworkers produce a wide variety of colorful and well-made products, including pottery, woven goods, jewelry, and objects made of wood, reeds, bark, and cactus. Usually each town specializes in a particular craft, such as silvermaking or goldmaking. Craft skills are handed down from one generation to the next.

Celestino Bautista, who lives in the state of Oaxaca (wä häk′ ə) learned to weave when he was young. He says, "My father taught me to weave when I was 11, and now my youngest son, José, is that age, and I am teaching him the same skills."

SPORTS

Among the favorite sports in Mexico are baseball, soccer, and jai alai (hī' lī), which is a form of handball. Mexicans have long played handball. Paintings more than 1,000 years old show that Indians of that time played a game like handball. The game was part of a religious ceremony. Losers of the game sometimes lost their freedom and wealth, and even their lives.

Many Mexicans are skilled horseback riders. The Spanish brought horses to the Americas in the 1500s. But the riding skills used in Mexico today are both Spanish and Indian. Luis Bernal, a welder, describes a Mexican rodeo.

Horsemen wearing richly embroidered costumes, topped by massive sombreros with specially shaped brims, perform spectacular feats of riding as they lasso young bulls and wild horses.

BLENDING THE TRADITIONAL AND THE MODERN

Almost everything in Mexico—from the people themselves to the arts and amusements they enjoy—reflects a blend of different cultures. Writers, painters, and craftworkers have combined Indian and Spanish traditions to create a distinctive Mexican style.

Check Your Reading

1. What are two popular sports in Mexico?
2. What is a mural? How are Mexico's cultures combined in its murals?
3. How did the 1910 Revolution affect the arts in Mexico?
4. **THINKING SKILL:** Look at the mural *Mexico Through the Centuries* by Diego Rivera on page 132. What does this mural tell you about the people of Mexico and the blend of cultures in the country?

PRESERVING
FOLK ART

Maria Teresa Pomar was born soon after the Mexican Revolution. At that time artists and composers were creating new ways to work, and traditional craftsworkers were being encouraged by the government to develop their skills.

Maria, whose father was a famous musician, learned at a young age to appreciate the work of artists. In time she became especially interested in the traditional crafts of Mexico.

Later Maria visited Mexican craftsworkers all over the country. After years of travel and study she became an expert on Mexico's traditional crafts. By examining a piece of art, Maria could identify the person who had made it.

In 1976 Maria was asked to manage the National Museum of Folk Arts in Mexico City. Later she opened museums throughout Mexico to further spread the traditions of Mexican crafts.

In 1985 the president of Mexico awarded Maria the Gamio Prize, one of Mexico's highest honors. On behalf of all Mexicans he honored her hard work to preserve the history and protect the future of traditional Mexican art.

by Argentina Palacios

Long ago the great ancient civilizations of Mexico created spectacular buildings and beautiful works of art. Among the most impressive artwork they left behind were beautiful murals painted on the walls of stone buildings. You can still see these beautiful ancient murals in Mexico today.

As you read in Lesson 4, modern Mexican artists are still painting murals such as this one by Diego Rivera. Mural painting is a Mexican tradition that is centuries old. The artists of modern Mexico paint murals that combine the artistic traditions of their Indian and European ancestors. As you read this lesson, think about how the tradition of mural painting connects past, present, and future generations in Mexico.

AN ARTIST AND TEACHER

It was the early 1900s, and Dr. Atl (ot′ əl) had just come home from a trip through Europe and Eastern Asia. He was returning to his position as a teacher at San Carlos Academy, a school of fine arts in Mexico City. Dr. Atl was an expert on art, architecture, and volcanoes, as well as a fine painter of portraits and landscape scenes. When he was born, he had been given the name Gerardo Murillo (mü rē′ yō). He had changed his name to Dr. Atl in honor of the Aztecs—his Indian ancestors who had created one of Mexico's great civilizations. *Atl* means "water" in the Aztec language.

During his travels through Europe, Dr. Atl had been particularly impressed by the murals of a great Italian artist, Michelangelo. He described these murals in detail to his students. Dr. Atl believed that painting murals could provide a perfect way to honor the artistic traditions of the Indian and European ancestors of modern Mexicans. Some of his students were to become the finest muralists in Mexico.

MEXICO'S ANCIENT MURALS

Dr. Atl was drawn to murals because he knew that mural painting has a long history. Beautiful murals had been painted by the artists of the Aztecs, the Mayas, and Mexico's other Indian civilizations. Perhaps the most beautiful ancient murals in Mexico are found in the Mayan city of Bonampak (bō näm päk'), located in the present-day Mexican state of Chiapas. In fact, the name *Bonampak* means "painted wall" in the Mayan language.

The Bonampak murals were painted in about A.D. 700 but their existence was unknown in modern times until 1946. The largest of them is divided into three parts, each showing a different stage of warfare. One part shows a battle scene in which soldiers dressed in scary headdresses attack their enemies with knives and long spears.

PUBLIC ART

Dr. Atl and many of his students believed that murals painted in public places are a powerful way of communicating ideas to the Mexican people. They wanted to produce art that would be enjoyed in public by all Mexicans, not just by collectors in their own homes. Many of the muralists also hoped to teach Mexicans about their history. In many of their murals and other paintings,

they used symbols and images that were directly drawn from the murals of the Aztecs, the Mayas, and other Mexican civilizations.

Dr. Atl and his followers were aided by supporters in the Mexican government who made it possible for the artists to paint on walls in public places. Sometimes, as in this photograph, the artists covered the walls of buildings with mosaic (mō zā′ ik) murals. A mosaic is a picture or design made by fitting together colored pieces of stone, glass, or other hard materials.

DIEGO RIVERA

One of Mexico's greatest muralists and most famous artists was Diego Rivera. From an early age, Rivera displayed great artistic ability. He started taking art classes when he was 10 years old and at age 16 became a student of Dr. Atl. Rivera was fascinated by Mexico's ancient Indian civilizations. He saw his mural paintings as "visual books" that could teach people Mexican history. He also hoped that his murals would make people care more about the welfare of Mexico's surviving Indians.

Rivera put together a large collection of ancient Indian art objects. More than once he made himself nearly penniless after purchasing a prized and expensive piece of art. Toward the end of his life, Rivera built a large house that displayed designs based on Aztec and Mayan architecture. He called the house *Anahuacalli* (än ä hwä kä′ yē), which is a combination of two Aztec words. *Anahuac* is the Aztec name for the valley where Mexico City is located, and *calli* is the Aztec word for "house." Rivera combined traditional and modern styles in this house, just as he did in his mural paintings.

One of Rivera's most famous murals shows over 1,000 years of Mexican history. The huge mural, called "The History of Mexico," covers more than 1,900 square feet (176 sq m). It is located on a wall above a large staircase in the Palacio Nacional, a

government building in Mexico City. Rivera worked on the mural for 22 years, from 1929 to 1951. The mural shows Mexico's great Indian civilizations, their conquest by the Spanish, and the history of modern Mexico. Some experts consider Rivera's mural one of the most dramatic historical paintings in the world.

In the center of Rivera's huge mural is a large golden eagle. The image of the eagle is based on an Aztec sculpture and is a symbol of modern Mexico. Another large part of the mural shows Aztec rulers, gods, and ways of life. Underneath the golden eagle, Rivera painted Aztecs fighting Spanish invaders. He was reminding Mexicans that the time of the Aztec Empire was an important part of their history.

A TRADITION FOR THE PEOPLE

You may know that many artists in the United States have also painted murals in public places. Art in public places becomes a part of people's lives. People see mural art on their way to work and school and at other times during the day.

Mural painting is a tradition in Mexico that goes back centuries to the time of the great Mayan and Aztec civilizations. Like the artists of Mexico's great Indian civilizations, Mexico's modern mural painters have created large works of art that can be seen by everyone. The tradition of mural painting teaches Mexicans of today about their past. It also adds to their enjoyment of the world in which they live.

How does the tradition of mural painting connect past, present, and future generations in Mexico?

MEXICO: CULTURAL GEOGRAPHY

PEOPLE

- First people: Indians (Mayan civilization, Aztec civilization)
- Spanish conquerors came in 1500s: Hernando Cortés
- Today: blend of Indian and Spanish cultures

- Religion: mostly Roman Catholic
- Extended families

ECONOMY

- Mexico City: world's largest metropolitan area

- Outside cities: campesinos (village farmers) live by subsistence farming
- Developing economy
- Rapidly growing population

GOVERNMENT

- Representative democracy, with strong leadership by president

- Until recently, only one strong political party: PRI

ARTS AND RECREATION

- Important painters: Diego Rivera, José Orozco

- Crafts: traditional, handed down from generation to generation
- Sports: baseball, soccer, jai alai, horseback riding

IDEAS TO REMEMBER

- The culture of Mexico is a blend of the Spanish and the Indian.
- Mexico, one of the fastest-growing countries in the world, has a developing economy that is only partly industrialized.
- The Mexican constitution provides for a representative democracy, but with strong leadership by the president.
- The Spanish and Indian cultures are both reflected in the arts, crafts, and sports of Mexico.

REVIEWING VOCABULARY

subsistence farming extended family
campesino mestizo
civilization metropolitan area
commercial farming petrochemical
developing economy mural

Number a sheet of paper from 1 to 10. Beside each number write the word or term from the list above that best matches the definition.

1. A product developed from petroleum
2. Large work of art painted on building walls
3. A family that includes aunts, uncles, cousins, and grandparents
4. A culture that has developed systems of government, religion, and learning
5. A form of agriculture that produces only enough food for a family's immediate needs
6. A person of mixed Spanish and Indian ancestry
7. A large city and the smaller towns surrounding it
8. An economy that is still in the process of becoming industrialized
9. A farmer in a Mexican village
10. A form of agriculture in which crops are raised for profit and sometimes for export

REVIEWING FACTS

1. List three ways in which the Spanish conquest changed the people and the culture of Mexico.
2. What is the relationship between rural poverty and the tremendous growth of Mexico City?
3. How did improvements in health and living conditions affect Mexico's population growth?

4. How did the 1988 election reflect a change in public attitude toward the PRI?
5. How has the Mexican government contributed to the arts in Mexico?

WRITING ABOUT MAIN IDEAS

1. **Writing a Time Line:** Write a time line showing important events in the history of Mexico from the Mayan civilization to the national elections in 1988.
2. **Writing a Brief Biography:** Diego Rivera and José Orozco painted murals that expressed the Mexican culture. Choose one of the artists and write a brief biography that also explains how his art reflected the Mexican experience.
3. **Writing About Perspectives:** Imagine that you are a Mexican campesino deciding whether to move to a city or remain on the farm. Make your decision. Then write a letter to a friend explaining the reasons for your choice. In your letter, tell both the advantages and the drawbacks of your decision.

BUILDING SKILLS: DETERMINING THE ACCURACY OF INFORMATION

1. What does the word *accuracy* mean?
2. Name three steps you can take to determine the accuracy of information.
3. What questions can you ask to determine the credibility of a source?
4. When would it be helpful to know how to determine the accuracy of information?

CHAPTER 6

CENTRAL AMERICA AND THE CARIBBEAN

▼ FOCUS ▼

This world isn't all white! This world isn't black neither! This world isn't blue, and it isn't pink and it isn't yellow. It's all colors. And it's beautiful 'cause it's all colors. We're one family.

This is how a Jamaican artist described the many different people who live in Central America and the Caribbean.

The People

READ TO LEARN

Key Vocabulary

Maroon
sect

Key Places

Guatemala
Belize

Costa Rica
Montego Bay

Read Aloud

Looking at Central America and the Caribbean is like looking through a kaleidoscope. Every time you glance into the tube you see a different pattern of people.

A kaleidoscope is a tube in which a new colored design forms whenever the tube is turned. As the journalist who wrote the observation above says, the people of Central America and the Caribbean form an ever-changing kaleidoscope.

Read for Purpose

1. **WHAT YOU KNOW:** Who are the mestizo people?
2. **WHAT YOU WILL LEARN:** How are the people of Central America and the Caribbean like a kaleidoscope?

LATIN AMERICA'S KALEIDOSCOPE

Central America and the Caribbean form the southernmost part of North America. Central America is a thin ribbon of land that connects Mexico to the continent of South America. The Caribbean Islands are scattered throughout the Caribbean Sea between North America and South America. The entire area is made up mainly of mountains and volcanoes.

This area is one of the most ethnically diverse in the world. According to one writer, "Three streams of people flowed from the Eastern Hemisphere to create one of the most amazing blending of peoples that history has ever seen." These streams of people were the Indians, the Europeans, and the Africans.

THE FIRST STREAM OF PEOPLE

Indians were the first peoples to live in Central America and the Caribbean. In addition to several small groups of Indians who lived in the Caribbean, the Mayan civilization extended beyond Mexico to what is now **Guatemala, Belize** (be lēz'), and western Honduras. Find these places on the map on page 142.

Today many of the people living in these areas, especially in Guatemala, are descendants of the Mayas. In fact, Guatemala is the only nation in Central America where most of the people are Indian.

As in Mexico, the Indians of Guatemala often live in small mountain villages. Many Indians prefer to live with their own people, speak their own language, and

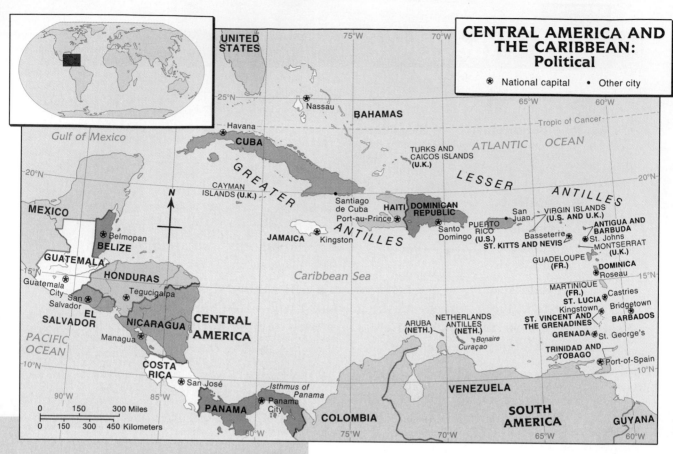

CENTRAL AMERICA AND THE CARIBBEAN: Political

⊛ National capital   • Other city

MAP SKILL: Which three countries are on the two largest Caribbean Islands?

follow the customs of their group. They often observe both their traditional religion and Roman Catholicism, which was brought by Europeans. For example, some Mayas continue to worship *mams*, spirits who live in the "wind, the rain, the lakes, the rivers, and the mountains. . . . "

THE SECOND STREAM

Led by the Spanish, the Europeans were the second stream of people to settle Central America and the Caribbean. The Spanish claimed vast areas of the Americas after Christopher Columbus arrived in 1492. However, they settled only in areas rich in natural resources. If an area was mountainous and poor, few Spanish people stayed there.

However, in Costa Rica, with its mild climate and few Indians, many Spanish people came to live and divided the land among themselves. As a result, Costa Rica's present population is mainly of Spanish ancestry. In other parts of Central America, most people are of mixed Spanish and Indian origin.

The Spanish were the dominant force in Central America and the Caribbean, but sometimes they lost control of their holdings. In the 1600s the British, French, and Dutch gained control of some Caribbean Islands. These islands were mainly in the Lesser Antilles and the Netherlands Antilles. Find these islands on the map above.

THE THIRD STREAM

After the Europeans arrived, thousands of Indians were killed. This lack of people was a problem for the British and French, who wanted to start sugarcane, tobacco, and other plantations there. They solved this problem by bringing captured Africans to the plantations to work as slaves. These Africans were the third stream of people to come to Latin America.

South of Montego Bay in northwestern Jamaica is a dry, rugged, hilly land called "Cockpit Country," or "Look Behind Country." Find Jamaica on the map on page 142.

Cockpit Country is the home of the descendants of the Maroons. "Maroon" comes from the Spanish *cimarrones* (sē mä rō' nes), which means "peak dwellers." The Maroons were enslaved Africans who escaped from the Spanish, set up their own communities, and later fought the British, who tried to conquer them, for more than 100 years.

East Indians, people whose ancestors came from India, Pakistan, and other countries of southern Asia, also live in the Caribbean region. Forty percent of the population of Trinidad and Tobago is of East Indian descent.

Smaller numbers of people came from other Asian countries. It is not unusual to find people who are part Asian and part African or European.

ONE CARIBBEAN PEOPLE

The combination of historical events, customs, and different ethnic groups makes the individual Caribbean Islands unique. Jamaica has many British customs because it was long a colony of Great Britain. Its population, however, includes many different ethnic groups. In addition to people of African ancestry, Jamaica is made up of people of British, Chinese, and East Indian origin. This mixture of peoples that developed over hundreds of years is the reason that Jamaica took as its motto, "Out of many, one people."

Like children in the United States, children of all the different ethnic groups of Central America and the Caribbean attend school to learn the skills they need.

LANGUAGE

If you traveled through Central America and the Caribbean, what differences would you expect to find? As you might expect, you would hear French spoken if you visited the French Caribbean island of Martinique (mär ti nēk'). People in the areas long held by Spain—Cuba, the Dominican Republic, and Puerto Rico—speak Spanish.

In general, the people of Central America and the Caribbean speak the languages of the Europeans who colonized their countries. An exception is Haiti, where many people speak Creole, a mixture of French and African languages. In the Netherlands Antilles, Papiamento, a language that combines Dutch, English, and Spanish, is used.

Haiti has been independent of France since 1804. Yet many signs of French culture remain. In Port-au-Prince, the capital, French bread is sold in the market at the harbor.

RELIGION

The major religions of Central America and the Caribbean were also determined by the colonists who settled there. Most of the colonists were Roman Catholics and Protestants. The Caribbean Islands also have several religious sects. A sect is a religious group that is outside the mainstream of large, organized religions. Rastafari, one of the newest sects, is the fastest-growing one in Jamaica. Rastafarians honor the last emperor of Ethiopia, Haile Selassie (hī′ lē sə·las′ ē), whom they call Ras Tafari, as a god.

A BLENDING OF PEOPLE AND TRADITIONS

The area that is made up of Central America and the Caribbean is one of the most ethnically diverse in the world. Indians were its first settlers. Then came the Spanish, followed by the British, French, and Dutch. These colonists brought enslaved Africans to the area. In Central America and the Caribbean, the African, the European, and the Indian cultures blended to form new cultures.

Check Your Reading

1. Where did most of the languages and religions in Central America and the Caribbean come from?
2. Why are there many people of African ancestry in the Caribbean Islands?
3. How are the people and culture of Central America and the Caribbean like a kaleidoscope?
4. THINKING SKILL: Do you think the following statement is correct?: "Colonialism changed the historical path of Central America and the Caribbean Islands." Give evidence to support your answer.

The Economy

READ TO LEARN

Key Vocabulary

plantation   dictator
one-crop economy   communism

Key People

Fidel Castro

Key Places

Barbados
Cuba

Read Aloud

If God wills and my wife's health improves, we'll soon move to our new house.

Andres Ramirez expresses the hope of many people in Central America and the Caribbean—the hope of raising their standard of living. Ramirez raises corn and beans on his farm in southern Honduras. He also works on a nearby sugarcane plantation to earn extra money. Ramirez lived with his in-laws for years before he could save enough money to buy material to build his home.

Read for Purpose

1. **WHAT YOU KNOW:** What is commercial farming?
2. **WHAT YOU WILL LEARN:** Why are most Central American and Caribbean economies limited in what they can produce?

PLANTATION AGRICULTURE

The story of Andres Ramirez is typical of thousands of families in Central America and the Caribbean. Most of the countries in this area do not have developed economies. More than half the people farm small plots of land that do not produce much food because of the poor quality of the soil.

As in the rest of Latin America, the best land in the area is used for plantations. These are large farms that grow crops for sale. Central America and the Caribbean have more plantations than do most areas of the world. About 15 percent of the world's coffee is grown in this area, as is about 10 percent of the world's bananas. Other fruits, sugarcane, cacao, and spices are also grown in abundance on plantations in the area.

Most economies of Central America and the Caribbean are one-crop economies. That is, countries often depend on a single crop for income. Over half of Panama's exports are bananas, for example, and sugar makes up over 75 percent of the exports of the Caribbean Island country of St. Kitts and Nevis.

Depending heavily on one crop is risky for a nation. If world prices for that crop fall, or a natural disaster strikes, nations may lose money or the main cash crop they export. In addition, many businesses could close and thousands of people could lose their jobs.

MANUFACTURING

One reason that the economies of Central America and the Caribbean depend on agriculture is that they are poor in minerals. Many of the nations in this part of the world do not have coal or other minerals needed for manufacturing. Moreover, most manufacturing jobs are related to agriculture. Costa Rica, Guatemala, and Puerto Rico, for example, are the most industrialized areas of Central America. Yet most of their factories process food and beverages.

Jamaica is one of the few Caribbean nations that has a large mining industry. Bauxite, a mineral used in making aluminum, is mined in Jamaica. Other places with valuable resources and industries are Trinidad, which has oil, and the islands of Curaçao (kyùr′ ə sō) and Aruba, which refine petroleum imported from Venezuela.

TOURISM

Tourism is the major industry of the Caribbean Islands. According to a resident of Barbados, one of the most beautiful of the area's islands: "God made the world. Then He said, 'I must have somewhere for Myself—a place to rest.' So He made Barbados."

Barbados has few natural resources. However, it has one of the strongest economies in the Caribbean. Most people there work in tourism and earn more money than people in other parts of the Caribbean. Barbados is very small, only 21 miles (33 km) long and 14 miles (22.4 km) wide. Yet the island is dotted with almost 140 tourist hotels and many golf courses.

MAP SKILL: What products do Cuba and the Dominican Republic both produce? Where is nutmeg grown?

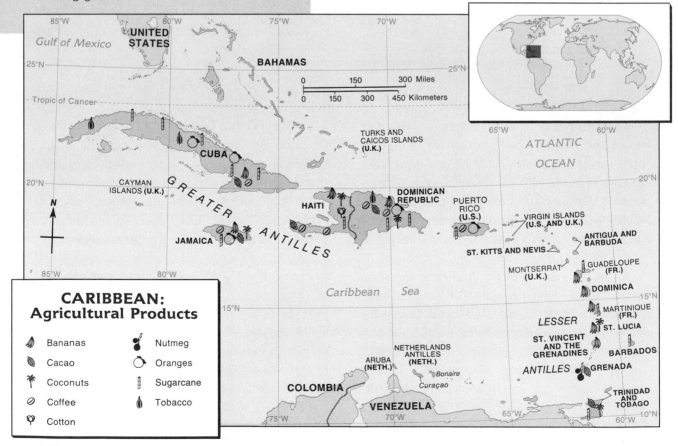

CARIBBEAN: Agricultural Products

- 🍌 Bananas
- 🍫 Cacao
- 🌴 Coconuts
- Ø Coffee
- 🌿 Cotton
- Nutmeg
- 🍊 Oranges
- Sugarcane
- Tobacco

Although the nations of the area welcome tourism, they seek new industries. Tourism helps economies by giving jobs mainly to unskilled workers. A healthy nation also needs jobs for skilled workers.

A REVOLUTION IN CUBA

The region's leaders have made many attempts to solve economic problems in Central America and the Caribbean. In Cuba, for example, a revolution brought in a completely new kind of government.

In 1959 Fidel Castro led a revolution in Cuba and overthrew the Cuban dictator. A dictator is a ruler who has total control over a country.

Castro said he wanted all Cubans to have an equal share in their country. So he set up a system called communism. You will read more about communism in Chapter 15.

Under communism, the government controls the economy and way of life. Castro's government seized private property from most foreigners and wealthy citizens and redistributed it.

Did the Cuban revolution solve the nation's problems? Some people think of Castro as another dictator. But Elena Santos, a Cuban, said, "In the past, many black and mestizo Cubans didn't have a chance to hold good jobs, but life has improved." Health care, schooling, and many services are free.

Yet the Cuban economy remains weak. The map on the opposite page shows that Cuba grows several crops, but sugar makes up 75 percent of Cuba's exports.

For many years, the Soviet Union helped support Cuba. But changes in the Soviet Union, which began in the late 1980s, lessened Soviet support of Cuba. The island nation is now on its own more than ever before.

Beautiful beaches, such as this one on the Caribbean Island of Barbados, attract tourists who like to sail, swim, and relax in the sun.

LIMITED CHOICES

Central America and the Caribbean Islands have limited natural resources. So the people make use of the resources they have. Usually, this means good farmland, as well as warm weather and sandy beaches that draw tourists. Jamaica has bauxite and Trinidad has some petroleum. Still, the economies of most countries are developing ones.

 Check Your Reading

1. Why is it risky to have a one-crop economy?
2. Why do so many Caribbean islands depend upon tourism?
3. What is a dictator?
4. THINKING SKILL: List some of the questions you would ask if you were planning to start a business in a Central American or Caribbean nation.

Understanding Transportation Routes

Today the nations of the world are connected by transportation routes that make trade and travel direct and convenient. Air and water routes, railroads, and highways crisscross the earth, bringing countries closer together than ever before.

Countries in Central America and the Caribbean depend heavily on trade with other countries in Latin America. For people in these countries, it is very important that goods move quickly from one country to another. The Pan-American Highway is one transportation route that has been developed to meet the needs of people in Latin America.

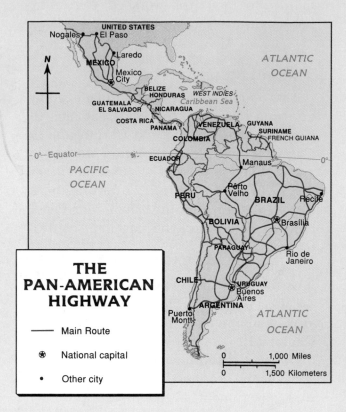

THE
PAN-AMERICAN
HIGHWAY

—— Main Route

✪ National capital

• Other city

The Pan-American Highway

The Pan-American Highway extends from the United States-Mexico border in the north to the southern tip of Chile in the south. It also connects the east and west coasts of South America, linking many major cities. The entire highway system with its interconnecting routes is about 45,000 miles (72,000 km) long.

The Pan-American Highway is of great importance to the Latin American economy because it provides routes for the transportation of raw materials, agricultural products, and other goods. The highway cuts through dense jungles, passes through scorching deserts, and crosses some of the highest mountains in the world—areas that are otherwise difficult to reach.

The map on this page shows the main routes of the Pan-American Highway. Find

Rio de Janeiro, located on the east coast of Brazil. Imagine how important the highway is to people in this city. Without it they would have to depend on air or water transportation for many goods and products. Which other major cities are connected by this highway?

Reviewing the Skill

1. What is the southernmost city on the Pan-American Highway?
2. What is the approximate distance along the Pan-American Highway between Laredo, Texas, and Puerto Montt, Chile?
3. Name five countries the Pan-American Highway passes through.
4. Why is the Pan-American Highway an important transportation route?

The Government

READ TO LEARN

Key Vocabulary

commonwealth

Key People

François Duvalier

Key Places

Haiti
Puerto Rico
Panama Canal

Read Aloud

Who would not give his life for the land in which he was born?

The man who wrote these words, José Martí (hō sā′ mär tē′), did just that. A Cuban patriot and poet, Martí died in 1895 fighting to free Cuba from Spain. Other Cubans carried on the struggle, and they won their freedom a few years later. Then another struggle began—to keep the freedom they had won.

Read for Purpose

1. **WHAT YOU KNOW:** How would you describe the people of Central America and the Caribbean?
2. **WHAT YOU WILL LEARN:** What types of government do the nations of Central America and the Caribbean have?

COLONIES AND OVERSEAS AREAS

As you read in Lesson 1, all of Central America and the Caribbean was once divided into European colonies. Today only a few colonies are left. Great Britain has five colonies—more than any other nation. They are Montserrat, the British Virgin Islands, the Turks and Caicos (kā′ kəs) Islands, the Cayman Islands, and Bermuda. The people who live in the colonies are citizens of Great Britain and have a voice in their own government.

Some parts of the Caribbean are also "overseas areas" of European countries. An overseas area is a place that is part of a nation far away across the ocean. The island of Martinique, for example, is an overseas area of France. Aruba is part of the Netherlands.

REPUBLICS AND DICTATORSHIPS

Almost all of the 21 nations of Central America and the Caribbean have constitutions that give them representative governments. Some of these governments are true republics. However, unrest and economic problems have made it difficult for others to govern themselves as republics. In some nations, dictators have taken advantage of political divisions to seize power. Some dictators rule for 20 or 30 years. Long-term rule by one leader is common in many countries of the region.

THE LEADERS AND THE PEOPLE

Dictators often take power when there is a wide gap between the ordinary people and their leaders. In Haiti, for example, most of the people were, and are, descen-

149

Haiti's **dictator** François Duvalier (*above*) ruled from 1957 until his death in 1971. Unlike Duvalier, who was elected, Fidel Castro of Cuba (*below*) took power through revolution.

dants of enslaved Africans. The rulers, however, were French or people of mixed blood. Most Haitians spoke Creole, while the rulers spoke French.

In an election in 1957, Francois Duvalier (fran swä′ dü val yā′), called "Papa Doc," was elected president of Haiti. The people hoped he would lead a democratic government. But Duvalier was not only another dictator, he stripped the people of much of their remaining wealth. When Haitians forced the Duvalier family to flee the country in 1986, Haiti was one of the poorest nations in the world. Its people earned an average of $300 a year.

What do Haitians think about the future? According to one leader:

Haiti needs peace and good leadership. Everyone wants democracy, but after so many dictators, Haiti has to go slowly to find the right way.

Since 1986, Haiti has had several changes of government. In late 1990, Jean-Bertrand Aristide was elected president in the first free elections ever held in Haiti. He was forced out in a coup a year later.

UNITED STATES INTERESTS

The United States watches events in the Caribbean closely because the area is very near to its borders. At various times in the past, the United States has sent troops or advisers to most of the Central American nations, as well as to Cuba, Haiti, the Dominican Republic, and Grenada.

The United States also has possessions in the Caribbean. One of the most important is Puerto Rico. This is how one Puerto Rican describes his life:

I have two names. When I am in Puerto Rico my name is Federico, and I speak Spanish. When I am in New York my name is Freddy, and I speak English. My last name is Ramirez in both places.

Many Puerto Ricans live like Ramirez. They move back and forth between their island home and the United States. Puerto Rico is part of the United States. However, it is not a state, but a self-governing territory known as a commonwealth.

Puerto Ricans choose their own governor and legislators. They also elect a nonvoting representative to the United States Congress. Many Puerto Ricans like living

in a commonwealth. Others want the island to become a state of the United States or else to have it become completely independent. You can read two opinions about this topic in the Point/Counterpoint feature on pages 152–153. In an election on this issue in 1993, Puerto Ricans voted to remain a commonwealth.

PANAMA CANAL

Another reason the United States is interested in Central America and the Caribbean is the Panama Canal. Find the canal on the map on this page. The United States built the canal from 1903 to 1914 to provide a direct water route between the Pacific and Atlantic oceans.

The United States controlled the canal for a long time. In 1978, the United States and Panama signed a treaty that turned the ownership of the Panama Canal Zone over to Panama. Panama will have complete control of the canal by the year 2000.

VARIETIES OF GOVERNMENT

The countries of Central America and the Caribbean have many types of government. These include republics, dictatorships, colonies, overseas areas, and commonwealths. Many nations in the region suffer from economic and social unrest.

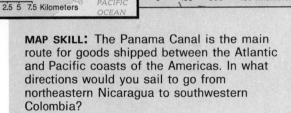

MAP SKILL: The Panama Canal is the main route for goods shipped between the Atlantic and Pacific coasts of the Americas. In what directions would you sail to go from northeastern Nicaragua to southwestern Colombia?

Check Your Reading

1. Describe the kind of leader that François Duvalier was.
2. Why has the United States been so active in Central America and the Caribbean?
3. What bodies of water does the Panama Canal connect?
4. **THINKING SKILL:** Classify the following countries into three or more categories, based on their governments: Bermuda, Martinique, Cuba, Puerto Rico.

Should Puerto Rico Become a State?

As you have read, in 1993 Puerto Ricans voted for Puerto Rico to remain a commonwealth. Why do you think the island should remain a commonwealth? Why did others disagree?

Puerto Rico has been a self-governing commonwealth since 1952. As a commonwealth Puerto Rico is a possession of the United States, but it is governed by its own constitution. Citizens of Puerto Rico have many of the rights and responsibilities of United States citizens. But Puerto Ricans do not have the right to vote in national elections, and they are not required to pay federal taxes.

But some people in Puerto Rico wanted Puerto Rico to become a state of the United States. These citizens believe that statehood would help Puerto Rico economically. With statehood Puerto Rico would be directly represented in the United States Senate and the House of Representatives. Federal funds would become available to provide housing and jobs for people who are unemployed.

POINT

Puerto Rico Should Become a State

The movement to make Puerto Rico a state has gained wide support during recent years. Supporters believe that political, social, and economic conditions in Puerto Rico would improve if statehood were acquired.

Baltasar Corrada del Río, the former mayor of San Juan, explains his view.

Statehood provides local self-government as well as more political participation in Washington. As a state, Puerto Rico would continue to elect its own governor, as well as senators and representatives to its legislature. In addition, Puerto Ricans would be . . . afforded equal participation in the U.S. Senate and proportionate [fair] representation in the House of Representatives.

We will share in the responsibility to pay federal taxes. . . . By giving, we will provide more dignity to our receiving.

The island will continue to have its two flags and its two anthems—a national flag and anthem and a state flag and anthem. We can be good Puerto Ricans and good Americans at the same time.

● What does Baltasar Corrada del Río believe Puerto Rico would gain from statehood?

COUNTERPOINT

Puerto Rico Should Remain a Commonwealth

Many Puerto Rican citizens prefer that the island remain a commonwealth. They believe that commonwealth status lets them keep and protect their Hispanic culture. They fear that if Puerto Rico becomes a state, Congress might impose English as the official language, an action which would lead to a lessening of the island's Hispanic culture. Miguel A. Hernández Agosto, president of the Puerto Rican Senate, explains his view.

We are historically a Spanish-speaking people who cherish our Hispanic culture and would not exchange it for any material benefits. We are also proud of our linkage with the United States. . . . But we are not willing to relinquish [give up] Spanish as our first language nor to change our Hispanic culture for the "American way of life."

No one would gain culturally from changing the status quo [the way things currently are]—neither the people of Puerto Rico nor the people of the United States, who would be losing a valuable cultural link with the other half of America.

● What are the disadvantages that Miguel A. Hernández Agosto believes would result from Puerto Rican statehood?

UNDERSTANDING THE POINT/COUNTERPOINT

1. Explain which side you think presents the stronger argument.
2. What are some other groups of people who might have an opinion on whether Puerto Rico should become a state? What might they say?
3. Can you think of a way in which the two sides could reach a compromise? Explain your answer.

Arts and Recreation

READ TO LEARN

Key Vocabulary
calypso
reggae

Key Places
Dominican Republic   San Pedro de Macorís

Read Aloud

A favorite Haitian folktale says that many of the island's pigeons were flying to New York. A turtle wanted to go, too, but he had no wings. Feeling sorry for the turtle, a pigeon said "Turtle, I'll take you with me. I'll hold one end of a piece of wood in my mouth and you hold on to the other end. But do not let go, or you'll fall into the water." As they flew over the shore, the turtle saw a group of animals waving good-bye. He was so pleased, he called out the one English word he knew, "Bye-bye!" He fell into the sea. For that reason, according to the tale, there are many pigeons in New York, but turtles are still in Haiti.

Read for Purpose

1. **WHAT YOU KNOW:** What group of people first lived in Central America and the Caribbean?
2. **WHAT YOU WILL LEARN:** What are the artistic achievements and main entertainments of Central America and the Caribbean?

MUSIC

Have you ever heard a steel drum? This musical instrument was developed in Trinidad in the 1930s. An inventor—nobody knows who—took an oil drum, sliced off the end, and hammered the other end into sections that produced different tones. Melodies are played by hitting these sections of the drum with mallets, or wooden hammers. With drums of different sizes, steel bands can play any form of music.

One style of music associated with steel bands is calypso. Calypso developed from music that enslaved Africans sang while they worked.

Another form of music that developed in the Caribbean is reggae (reg' ā). Reggae mixes American pop music and calypso rhythms. Reggae music is popular in many parts of the world.

SPORTS

Sports are popular in the area, and soccer is one of the favorites. So, too, is baseball. The nations in which baseball is played most frequently are Nicaragua, Cuba, and especially the Dominican Republic. Over 200 Dominicans also play on major and minor league teams in the United States. Remarkably, half of this number come from just one town, San Pedro de Macorís (mä kô rēs'), which is in the southeastern part of the nation. This

Calypso music is often played by steel drum bands (*above left*). Bob Marley was the most popular reggae musician of his time (*above right*). Baseball is a popular sport in the Caribbean (*below*).

city of about 110,000 people has about 200 teams. According to one of the townspeople, "Baseball is in the blood here."

Many of the people in San Pedro de Macorís have few possessions. Nevertheless, the baseball-crazy youngsters of this area often make bats out of palm leaves and balls out of wadded socks.

CREATIVITY AND TRADITION

Indian, Spanish, African, and other ethnic traditions have blended in Central America and the Caribbean to create unique forms of art. Steel-drum bands, calypso and reggae singers, and many other artists perform music. Sports like soccer and baseball are very popular.

 Check Your Reading

1. What are calypso and reggae?
2. What is the town of San Pedro de Macorís famous for?
3. What are three popular pastimes in Central America and the Caribbean?
4. **THINKING SKILL:** What are three questions you could ask to learn more about the arts and entertainment in Central America and the Caribbean?

155

CENTRAL AMERICA AND THE CARIBBEAN: CULTURAL GEOGRAPHY

PEOPLE

- First stream of peoples: Indians

- Second stream: Europeans (Spanish, British, French, and Dutch)

- Third and fourth streams: Africans and Asians

- Today: blend of Indian, European, African, and Asian people

- Religion: Roman Catholic and Protestant

ECONOMY

- Plantations: coffee, bananas, sugarcane, spices

- Most countries have one-crop economies

- Caribbean's major industry: tourism

- Cuba: communist system led by Fidel Castro

GOVERNMENT

- Dictatorships: Cuba and Haiti

- Only a few European colonies left

- United States interests: Puerto Rico and the Panama Canal

ARTS AND RECREATION

- Popular forms of music: calypso, reggae, and steel drum bands

- Sports: baseball and soccer very popular

IDEAS TO REMEMBER

- The population of the Caribbean and Central America is ethnically diverse.
- The region, which has limited economic resources, depends largely on agriculture and tourism.
- Many types of government are found in the region, including republics, colonies, dictatorships, and commonwealths.
- Unique forms of music and art have evolved from the mixed cultural traditions of Central America and the Caribbean.

REVIEWING VOCABULARY

Each of the following statements contains an underlined vocabulary word. Number a sheet of paper from 1 to 5. Beside each number write whether each of the following statements is true or false. If the statement is true, write "true." If it is false, rewrite the sentence using the vocabulary word correctly.

1. <u>Plantations</u> are large farms on which crops are grown for sale.
2. <u>Calypso</u> is a type of fruit that is grown for export in Central America and the Caribbean Islands.
3. Puerto Rico is a self-governing territory known as a <u>commonwealth</u>.
4. Although a <u>dictator</u> has many powers, he or she must act within the limits of a constitution and a legislature.
5. A <u>sect</u> is a religious group whose beliefs and practices are outside those of mainstream religions.

REVIEWING FACTS

1. Why is it important for countries to develop more than one industry?
2. Why is the United States watchful of developments in the Caribbean Islands?
3. What conditions have enabled dictators to take control of several countries in Central America and the Caribbean?
4. Which island is the United States' most important possession in the Caribbean Islands?
5. Which Central American country has given the world an unusually large number of baseball players?

WRITING ABOUT MAIN IDEAS

1. **Writing a Paragraph:** Write an opening paragraph for a travel article about the Caribbean Islands. Tell why the Caribbean is a particularly attractive area for tourists to visit.
2. **Writing a Summary:** Think about the three groups of people who settled the Caribbean Islands and Central America. Choose one of these groups and write a summary about them. Describe the group's development from their arrival in the area through the present.
3. **Writing About Perspectives:** Imagine that you live in more than one place like Federico (Freddy) Ramirez, who is mentioned on page 150. One place you live is your town in the United States. The other place is a country you choose in the Caribbean or Central America. Name the country. Then write one paragraph describing your life in each place. In a final paragraph, write about the differences between each place.

BUILDING SKILLS: UNDERSTANDING TRANSPORTATION ROUTES

1. Name three different kinds of transportation routes.
2. What geographical feature makes land transportation difficult in the countries of Central America?
3. Which continents does the Pan-American Highway connect?
4. Why is it helpful to understand transportation routes?

SOUTH AMERICA

FOCUS

South America is a continent of contrasts and surprises. Much of its land is empty, yet its population is growing faster than that of Asia. . . . Its two main languages, Portuguese and Spanish, are European, and yet its people have come from every corner of the world.

The writer William E. Carter mentions just a few of the contrasts that exist in South America. In this chapter you will learn how the Spanish and Portuguese settlers joined American Indians, Africans, and many others to form unique South American cultures.

The People

READ TO LEARN

Key Vocabulary

gaucho

Key Places

Argentina
Uruguay
Pampas

Read Aloud

October 12 is an important day for us [South Americans]. *North Americans call this holiday Columbus Day, but we call it* El Día de la Raza, *the "Day of the Race." It was the beginning of Latin America.*

In South America, October 12 is set aside to celebrate the birth of the new "race" of mestizos that formed after the coming of the Europeans. South Americans are proud of the many people and traditions that have blended to make their culture unique.

Read for Purpose

1. **WHAT YOU KNOW:** What is the meaning of the term *Latin America*?
2. **WHAT YOU WILL LEARN:** How have the ethnic groups of South America shaped life on the continent?

INDIAN HERITAGE

The continent of South America is the largest part of Latin America. South America is a little smaller in size than the United States and Canada together.

The population of South America consists of people of many different ethnic groups. As in other parts of Latin America, Indians were the first people in South America. By the 1300s, an Indian people called the Incas had created a great civilization in the Andes Mountains. Some stone buildings the Incas built long ago are still standing.

Today many Indians live in the Andean nations of Peru, Bolivia, and Ecuador. About half of the people who live in Bolivia and Peru and about a quarter of the people in Ecuador are Indians.

EUROPEANS

South America also has many European immigrants—more than the rest of Latin America. In fact, almost all of the people of Argentina and Uruguay are European or of European ancestry. Juan Roberts of Patagonia, in Argentina, is Welsh. His story is similar to that of many Europeans whose ancestors left their homelands to seek a better life.

I'm a direct descendant of one of the 153 Welsh people who landed . . . in 1865. They were poor people who were escaping from the crowded mining valleys. . . .

Between 1857 and 1930 more than 6 million immigrants entered Argentina alone. Today both Argentina and Uruguay have many Italian, Spanish, French, English, and German people.

CENTRAL
AMERICA
NICARAGUA

COSTA
RICA
PANAMA

Caribbean Sea

Baranquilla
Cartagena
Maracaibo
*Lake
Maracaibo*
Caracas
VENEZUELA
Orinoco River

Georgetown
GUYANA
Paramaribo
SURINAME
Cayenne
FRENCH
GUIANA (FR.)

Medellín
Bogotá
Cali
COLOMBIA

Negro River

Amazon River
Belém

ECUADOR
Quito
Equator
Guayaquil
Iquitos

Ucayali River
PERU

Manaus

Madeira River

Fortaleza

Recife

BRAZIL

São Francisco River

Lima
Cuzco
*Lake
Titicaca*

BOLIVIA
La Paz
Sucre

Paraguay River

Brasília

Salvador

Belo
Horizonte

Antofagasta
Tropic of Capricorn

PACIFIC
OCEAN

PARAGUAY

Asunción

Paraná River
Uruguay River

São Paulo
Río de Janeiro

ATLANTIC
OCEAN

Pôrto Alegre

Valparaíso
Santiago

Córdoba
Rosario

URUGUAY

CHILE

Buenos
Aires
ARGENTINA

Montevideo
Río de la Plata

N

Strait of
Magellan
Tierra
del
Fuego
Cape Horn

Falkland
Islands
(U.K.)

South
Georgia
(U.K.)

| 0 | 300 | 600 Miles |

| 0 | 300 | 600 | 900 Kilometers |

SOUTH AMERICA:
Political

⊛ National capital   • Other city

MAP SKILL: South America has only two countries that do not have coast lines.
What are these two countries? What are their capital cities? Which countries do
not share a border with Brazil?

South America has many different peoples and ways of life. Buenos Aires, Argentina (*left*), for example, has many European-style cafés. In Peru (*right*), Indians follow traditional ways.

GAUCHOS

The population of Paraguay, Venezuela, Chile, and Ecuador consists mainly of mestizos. Perhaps the best known of South America's mestizo groups are the gauchos of the Pampas. The Pampas is Argentina's vast inland plain. The gauchos are cowhands who roam the Pampas herding cattle. Life changed for the gauchos after the Pampas was fenced in. Nevertheless, the gaucho spirit remains alive today.

> *To be a gaucho is to belong to a big fraternity where there is a code of honor and friendship. After a hard day's work, gauchos still meet around an open fire . . . and express our feelings through music and song.*

RELIGION

As you might expect from a continent that was ruled by Spain and Portugal, many South Americans are Roman Catholics. Guyana, a British colony until 1966, has many Protestants. So does Suriname, which was a Dutch colony until 1975. Yet about half the people in Suriname are East Indian. Many of them are Hindus. The Hindu religion is discussed in Chapter 25.

South America also has different religious sects. Some sects, such as candomblé (kan dōm blä'), follow African beliefs and practices. One spiritual leader explains that believers "call on the gods and spirits of Africa." During ceremonies, she says, they "beat drums, chant, dance, and meditate as our ancestors did."

PEOPLE FROM ALL OVER THE WORLD

South America is made up of many different ethnic groups. Indians, Europeans, and Africans are the largest of these groups. Their different ways of life form the cultures of present-day South America.

 Check Your Reading

1. Name two countries in South America made up largely of Europeans and their descendants.
2. Where did the Incas build their civilization?
3. Name three ethnic groups found in South America today.
4. **THINKING SKILL:** How are South America's people similar to people in the rest of Latin America? How do they differ?

161

Distinguishing Facts from Opinions

Key Vocabulary
value judgment
reasoned opinion

Have you ever read a story in which a detective solved a mystery by gathering the facts? If so, you know that a fact is information that can be proved to be true.

Statements of opinion, however, cannot be proved true. An opinion is a personal view or belief. There are two types of opinions. One type of a personal opinion is a **value judgment**. A value judgment tells how someone feels about something, such as "this is the best cookie I ever ate."

Sometimes an opinion is supported by evidence or reasons. "This is the best novel I have read because it has an exciting plot and interesting characters" is a **reasoned opinion**. The speaker or writer tells you the reasons on which the opinion is based.

It is important to distinguish among facts, value judgments, and reasoned opinions.

Trying the Skill
As you read this description of life in the Amazon Basin in Brazil, decide whether each sentence states a fact or an opinion.

Life for the people living in the Amazon Basin is harsh and lonely. They find it difficult to grow food and to make a living from the forest. Their only contact with the outside world is with traders who stop at settlements along the rivers. More than 60 percent of these people, most of whom are part-Indian and part-Portuguese, cannot read. Their rate of infant mortality is high. I would rather live in a modern city than in the villages of the Amazon Basin.

1. What facts did you find?
2. What opinions did you find?
3. Which opinion was supported by reasons?

HELPING YOURSELF

The steps on the left show one way to distinguish between facts and opinions. The examples on the right show how these steps can be used to identify facts and opinions in the paragraph on the Amazon Basin.

One Way to Distinguish Between Facts and Opinions	Example
1. Recall the definitions of a fact, a reasoned opinion, and a value judgment.	A fact is something that can be checked and proved true. A reasoned opinion is a personal view or belief supported by evidence. A value judgment is a personal opinion about a subject.
2. Look for clues to statements of fact. Look for statements that can be proved to be true.	The percentage of a population that is literate and infant mortality rates are facts that can be checked.
3. Look for clues to value judgments. Clues such as "I think" and adjectives such as "best" signal statements of opinion.	"Harsh and lonely" and "I would rather live" are clues to the writer's opinion.
4. Look for clues to reasoned opinions. Look for words such as "because" and judgments supported by evidence.	Sentences 2 and 3 give evidence to support the opinion that life is "harsh and lonely."
5. Read each statement carefully to find clues to facts, value judgments, and reasoned opinions.	The first sentence is an opinion, supported by the next sentences, which are facts. The last sentence states a value judgment.

Applying the Skill

Read the following description of another South American country.

Bolivia is the most "Indian" of the countries in the Andes Mountains. Three fourths of the population are of almost pure Indian heritage. I saw Indian sheepherders on the high, remote plains. They were wrapped in dark ponchos. They stood guard over their flocks of sheep on cold, windy days. I believe their way of life is very difficult.

1. Which sentence states a fact?
   a. I saw Indian sheepherders on the high, remote plains.
   b. Bolivia is the most "Indian" of the countries in the Andes mountains.
   c. I believe their way of life is very difficult.

2. What value judgments can you find in the passage?
   a. They were wrapped in dark ponchos.
   b. Three fourths of the population are of almost pure Indian heritage.
   c. I believe their way of life is very difficult.

3. Which of the opinions in the passage are supported by reasons or evidence?

Reviewing the Skill

1. What is the difference between a fact and a value judgment?
2. What clue words can help you to distinguish facts from opinions?
3. Why is it important to be able to distinguish a fact from an opinion?

LESSON 2

The Economy

READ TO LEARN

Key Vocabulary

per capita income

Key Places

Venezuela
Brasília

Read Aloud

With its simple wooden houses and horses tied to hitching posts, [this town] looks a lot like towns in the western United States 100 years ago. And well it might, for it is located on Brazil's frontier, the western Amazon Basin.

The government of Brazil is trying to get more people to move to the cleared land of the rain forest in the Amazon River Valley. The nation's leaders describe this area as "a land without people for a people without land." However, Indian groups already live in this land.

Read for Purpose

1. **WHAT YOU KNOW:** What are some of Latin America's natural resources?
2. **WHAT YOU WILL LEARN:** How are the nations of South America trying to develop their economies?

THE SEARCH FOR OPPORTUNITY

Like people all over Latin America, many South Americans are searching for better jobs and better opportunities. The desire for a better life has led thousands of people to the Amazon rain forest. Some of them want to "get rich quick." Others just want to have enough land to feed their families and improve their lives. Think of what you know about United States history. Why were these immigrants willing to leave their homes?

One Brazilian, Raimundo Pinho, has spent five years clearing 125 acres (50 ha) in the rain forest. He thinks his hard work will pay off. "Take my word for it," he says. "In five more years there will be a bus stop in front of my house. . . ."

Many people do not agree with Pinho. They say that the soil of the rain forest is poor and cannot be used for long. Others believe that cutting down the rain forest harms the world's environment by destroying plants and animals. You can read about this issue on pages 168–169.

COMMERCIAL AGRICULTURE AND RANCHING

The economy of South America is largely based on agriculture. Profits in agriculture come from cash crops that plantation owners sell to other countries. Ecuador, for example, sells more bananas than any other nation. Colombia and Brazil grow some of the world's finest coffee.

164

Many South Americans work in logging camps in the rain forests (*left*), in copper mines (*above*), and on cattle ranches (*below*).

South America is also a major producer of meat and wool. The Pampas and other plains areas are good for raising cattle, sheep, and other grazing animals. Wheat and cotton are also grown in these areas.

MINING AND MANUFACTURING

South America wants to develop more kinds of manufacturing businesses. Most of South America's manufacturers process, or treat, agricultural resources. For example, some businesses squeeze fruit for juice, while others make cheese. Colombia and Ecuador are leading food-processing nations. Argentina is a leader in meat packing and leather production.

South Americans want to use more of their own minerals to make products. This will give people jobs. Only about 20 percent of the workers in South America are in manufacturing and mining jobs.

Several South American countries have large mineral and fuel deposits. However, most of what is mined is sold to other countries. In Bolivia, for example, 90 percent of the money made by exports comes

from tin. About 80 percent of Suriname's export income comes from bauxite. Copper brings in almost half of Chile's income. This situation is risky, as you will read.

VENEZUELA

Look at the map showing Venezuela on page 166. Venezuela is a nation that has used a major resource, petroleum, to help its economic development.

Venezuela was a leader in forming the Organization of Petroleum Exporting Countries (OPEC) in 1960. OPEC wanted to control the price and amount of petroleum produced around the world. After OPEC raised the price of oil, Venezuela became one of the richest nations in South America. Its yearly per capita income, or average income for each person, rose to about $3,000. This was one of the highest per capita incomes in Latin America.

During the 1980s, world oil prices fell and hurt Venezuela's economy. But by the 1990s, Venezuela once again had the fastest-growing economy in South America, followed by Chile.

Oil still makes up the greatest part of Venezuela's trade, but the country is also developing its natural gas, coal, steel, and aluminum resources.

Like other Latin American countries, Venezuela has debts it owes to other countries. Venezuelans hope that they can find the right mix of industries to keep the country's economy strong.

TRANSPORTATION

Because much of South America is rugged, dry, or thickly forested, most people live along the coasts. The continent's big cities are found here. These cities are joined by modern systems of travel and communication.

Efforts have been made to develop the interior. In 1960 Brazil built a new capital city, Brasília, inland. This city was to be the first step toward settling the central part of Brazil. Today more than a million

MAP SKILL: Venezuelan oil wells produce about 2 million barrels of oil a day. Several oil pipelines help to transport this oil to refineries or ports. Name two bodies of water within Venezuela that have pipelines near them.

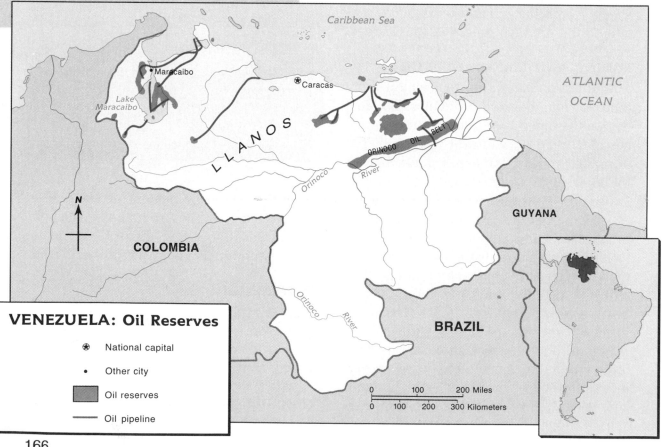

VENEZUELA: Oil Reserves

⊛ National capital
• Other city
▨ Oil reserves
— Oil pipeline

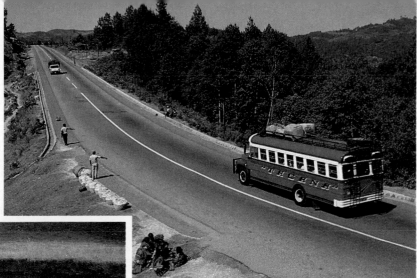

people live in Brasília. But few people have moved to the very dry area around the city. Hundreds of thousands of people living in the center of South America have never seen a railroad, ridden in a car, or used a telephone.

Airplanes and railroads are South America's major means of transportation. More and more, though, the Pan American Highway is making it easier for South Americans to reach more places by automobile. This highway begins in Mexico and continues south through much of Chile. As you read earlier, it also connects the east and west coasts of South America.

DEVELOPING ECONOMIES

South America has very little good farmland, but most people still farm small plots of land for a living. Throughout the continent new solutions are being tried to develop modern, strong economies.

South Americans depend upon many types of transportation. People use buses (*above*) and horses and carts (*left*) daily. Trains (*right*) connect most parts, even the most mountainous and densely forested areas, of the continent.

 Check Your Reading

1. What is *per capita income*?
2. Why are people settling in the Amazon rain forest?
3. How did Venezuela achieve one of the highest per capita incomes in South America?
4. **THINKING SKILL:** List three questions that you could ask to find out about the economy of a typical South American country.

Preserve or Develop the Amazon Rain Forest?

During the past 15 years huge areas of land in the Amazon forest have been destroyed. Thousands of acres of trees in the forest have been cut down and burned to clear the land for settlers in the rain forest. As you read in the last lesson, people in Brazil are moving to the Amazon region in search of a better life. Just as the United States government supported people settling the West, Brazilian leaders have encouraged their country's citizens to develop the Amazon region.

Some people in Brazil and around the world object to the Brazilian government's effort to develop the Amazon region. They think the Amazon region should be protected and preserved. They fear that development, particularly in agriculture and the lumber industry, will destroy the soil and the forest.

POINT ☆▷

The Amazon Should Be Preserved

Paulo Neto, a Brazilian, explains why he thinks the Amazon rain forest should be protected.

> [W]e are destroying the rain forests. Fire has no place at all in the ecology of the rain forests. We are in real danger if this trend of destroying most of Amazonia continues.
>
> Around half of the land of Amazonia should never be used for any kind of agriculture or cattle ranching simply because the soils there are extremely fragile.
>
> We still have time to protect large parts of Amazonia. We are beginning to run out of time. If we do not act now, then it might be too late.

Many people in Brazil agree with Paulo Neto's view of the rain forests. In fact, people all over the world support the protection of this region. Since the Amazon rain forest supplies one fifth of the earth's oxygen, Brazil's choices affect the rest of the world. Environmentalists from many other countries have asked the Brazilian government to limit destruction of the rain forest.

● Why does Paulo Neto want the Amazon rain forest to be preserved?

COUNTERPOINT ▷☆

The Amazon Should Be Developed

Marcilio Marques Moreira, who was Brazil's ambassador to the United States, made the following comments about the development of Brazil.

> Brazil has an enormous potential to be developed. We Brazilians hope to make our development [hopes agreeable] with preservation of our natural heritage.

José Sarney, the former president of Brazil, hoped to develop the natural resources of the Amazon region without interference from the rest of the world. In April 1989 President Sarney announced a program to divide the rain forest into zones for agriculture, mining, and conservation. President Sarney made his position clear when he said, "The Amazon is ours."

Fernando César Mesquita, the head of a new environmental agency, agreed with President Sarney about the interference of other countries.

> We are seeing a[n] . . . international effort to hold back development in Brazil.

● Why does President José Sarney want to develop the Amazon region?

UNDERSTANDING THE POINT/COUNTERPOINT

1. Which point of view do you think represents the stronger position? Why do you believe it is the stronger position?
2. What point of view might other Brazilians have about the rain forests? What might people in other countries believe?
3. What compromise do you think the two sides might reach?

169

The Government

READ TO LEARN

Key Vocabulary
caudillo
junta
coup

Key People
Juan Perón

Key Places
Argentina

Read Aloud

Yaya is someone who knows a lot. He is the oldest. He knows how to talk. Children learn from him. . . .

The villagers of Hualcan in the Peruvian Andes respect their *yaya*—their "father of fathers." Yayas are older people who once served in the village government. Many South American communities that depend upon the advice of such leaders are far from other communities, in the mountains or rain forests.

Read for Purpose

1. **WHAT YOU KNOW:** What is a dictator?
2. **WHAT YOU WILL LEARN:** Why has South America been troubled by frequent political change and social unrest?

CAUDILLOS

Most Latin American colonies gained their independence in the 1800s. However, few people in the new governments had experience governing large areas. This sometimes made it possible for local military leaders called caudillos (kou dē′ yōz) to gain great power. Some caudillos became so powerful that they were able to form their own armies. One such caudillo was the Argentine gaucho Juan Quiroga (kē rō′ gä), who was called *El Tigre*, meaning "the Tiger." Quiroga used fear and cruelty to control people.

RULE BY DICTATORSHIP

Today all the countries of South America except French Guiana have constitutions that require them to have democratic governments. French Guiana is an overseas area of France.

But in many countries, democracy exists only on paper. Instead, presidents rule as dictators. Sometimes these presidents stop government leaders from meeting. Sometimes, to prevent laws from being carried out, they declare national emergencies. In a state of emergency, the president rules with complete power.

In some countries the army and not the president plays the most important role. This situation occurs when the army is the only group in the nation that is well organized and has the power to bring about change. When an army assumes control, military leaders may choose to rule through a group of officers called a junta (hùn′ tə).

Other times, military leaders do not rule directly, but through the president whom they control. Without orderly systems for changing governments, changes occur often. These changes may be violent.

A STRUGGLE FOR DEMOCRACY

For many years Argentina was ruled by a president who became a dictator. Juan Perón (pə rōn') became the president of Argentina in 1946. He maintained power by creating labor unions, schools, and new industries to help Argentina's "shirtless ones." His wife, Eva Perón, helped him by encouraging workers to support the government's programs. Meanwhile, however, Perón became a dictator. He took control of the press, businesses, labor unions, and the army.

Juan Perón's enemies overthrew him in a coup (kü) in 1955. A coup is the sudden overthrow of a government. But after years of unrest, Perón was elected again in 1973. He died in 1974. For several years afterward, Argentina was ruled by dictators. They arrested and killed people without cause, and many people "disappeared."

Though many problems remain, Argentina, its neighbor Chile, and several other Latin American countries have recently made progress towards improving their economies and becoming more democratic. Other countries are still ruled by military dictators.

STRONG LEADERS, WEAK GOVERNMENTS

Almost all the countries of South America have constitutions that guarantee representative government. But for hundreds of years, these same countries have been plagued by dictatorships and military governments. This has caused unrest and lack of stability throughout the continent.

Argentina's President Juan Perón and Eva Perón rode through Buenos Aires in 1952 after he took the oath of office for a new presidential term.

Check Your Reading

1. What is the difference between a caudillo and a junta?
2. Why have many military leaders been able to gain control of national governments in South America?
3. What are some methods dictators use to stay in power in South America?
4. **THINKING SKILL:** From what you read about Juan Perón and his rule, what conclusions can you draw about the political life of Argentina?

Arts and Recreation

READ TO LEARN

Key People

Pablo Neruda
Gabriel García Márquez

Key Places

Rio de Janeiro

Read Aloud

It's a great language . . . we inherited from the [Spanish] conquerors. They carried everything off, [yet still] left us everything. They left us the words.

The above words were written by a Chilean poet. He tells of the pride that many South Americans have in their Spanish heritage, especially in their language.

Read for Purpose

1. **WHAT YOU KNOW:** What are some of the major ethnic groups of South America?
2. **WHAT YOU WILL LEARN:** How have South American arts been shaped by the continent's many ethnic groups?

LITERATURE

South America has many famous poets and novelists. They have told the stories of the continent's Indians, gauchos, and other peoples. Among the topics most often described are the problems of ethnic identity and poverty.

South America's writers also help people to understand what it is like to live in a tropical environment. The Chilean poet Pablo Neruda, for instance, describes the rain that often fell on the tin roof over his room as "the piano of my childhood." He also wrote about the rain forests.

South American authors are noted for their imaginative writing. Because they live in a land where many people believe in myths, South American writers feel comfortable writing about things that are out of the ordinary.

One South American novel that uses this style is *One Hundred Years of Solitude* by Gabriel García Márquez of Colombia. Many of his readers think that through the imaginary town of Macondo, the author tells the whole history of South America. In the novel, he mixes real life with events that are out of the ordinary. No one in Macondo finds it strange that it rains flowers one day or that for a time all the villagers lose their memories.

MUSIC AND CELEBRATIONS

South America's artistic tradition also includes music, dancing, and many different kinds of celebrations.

One of the best known examples of South American dance is the tango, the national dance of Argentina. A dramatic dance based on Spanish dances, the tango

Many South Americans join Rio de Janeiro's Carnaval (*above*) and play or watch soccer. Argentina's soccer team (*left*), in blue and white, plays Trinidad's soccer team, in red uniforms.

is recognized internationally as a serious art form.

Another national dance, the samba of Brazil, has African roots. Every year in **Rio de Janeiro**, during a huge celebration known as Carnaval, different samba bands plan the parades. Band members decorate their own floats and gather dancers. The good times of Carnaval bring happiness to even the poorest people of Brazil and of many other South American countries. It is summed up in a recent Carnaval song: "You must find in imagination what you lack in your wallet."

SOCCER

South Americans are fans of many sports. Among the most popular sports are baseball, tennis, jai alai, and polo. Above all, though, South Americans love the game of soccer.

Soccer player João Nuñes de Oliveira (zhwou nün′ yāz dā ol ə vâr′ ə), known

also as "Nuñes," says that Brazilian soccer is special.

When a Brazilian player gets hold of the ball, he does some wonderfully artistic and skillful things with it. He creates a special relationship between the man and the ball.

ARTS AND SPORTS

Through literature, the arts, sports, and many other traditions, South Americans celebrate their heritage and share their culture with the world.

✔ **Check Your Reading**

1. What is Carnaval?
2. Who is Gabriel García Márquez? What does he do?
3. Describe two South American dance forms.
4. **THINKING SKILL:** What do the photographs above tell you about the arts and recreation in South America?

173

CHAPTER 7 ▪ SUMMARY

SOUTH AMERICA: CULTURAL GEOGRAPHY

PEOPLE

- Incas: ancient civilization in Andes Mountains
- European immigrants: came in great numbers in 1800s and 1900s
- Gauchos: mestizo group on the Pampas
- Religion: mostly Roman Catholic

ECONOMY

- Rain forest: much of it has been cleared in recent years
- Agriculture: coffee, wheat, cotton, bananas, and other products
- Venezuela: developed petroleum resources
- Transportation: new systems needed to develop interior

GOVERNMENT

- Argentina, Chile dictatorships yielding to democracies
- Caudillos: powerful local military leaders
- Rule by junta: military dictatorship

ARTS AND RECREATION

- Literature: Pablo Neruda and Gabriel García Márquez
- Popular dances: tango, samba
- Carnaval: huge annual celebration in Rio de Janeiro
- Sports: soccer, baseball, tennis, jai alai, polo

IDEAS TO REMEMBER

- Most of the people of South America are a blend of Indian, Spanish, Portuguese, and African ethnic groups.
- The nations of South America are trying to develop their economies by creating modern mining, manufacturing, and transportation systems.
- South American governments are marked by unrest.
- South American arts and recreational activities include literature, dances, Carnaval, and popular sports such as soccer.

REVIEWING VOCABULARY

caudillo   junta
coup   per capita income
gaucho

Number a sheet of paper from 1 to 5. Beside each number write the word or term from the list above that best completes each sentence.

1. Control of the government by a _____, or small group of military officers, has been common in South America.
2. Similar to a cowboy of the American West, a _____ herds cattle on Argentina's Pampas.
3. The average yearly earnings per person, or _____, is generally low in the countries of South America.
4. In many countries of South America, inexperience in self-government led to harsh rule by a _____, a powerful local military leader.
5. Political instability in Latin America has often resulted in a _____, or sudden overthrow of a government.

REVIEWING FACTS

1. Which area of Brazil is being cleared for thousands of settlers who are looking for a better life?
2. Why did Venezuela's economy suffer during the 1980s?
3. Which South American leader became a dictator after becoming president of Argentina?
4. Why is it important for South American nations to develop orderly systems by which to change political leadership?
5. Which Argentine dance has become popular worldwide?
6. Why did Brazil build its new capital in the country's interior?
7. What is the dominant religion in South America?
8. What is the primary economic activity in South America?
9. Name five European countries that have contributed large numbers of immigrants to Argentina and Uruguay.
10. What are some topics often described by South American writers?

WRITING ABOUT MAIN IDEAS

1. **Writing a Summary:** Reread the description on page 171 of Juan Perón's rise to power in Argentina. Then write a summary of the events in Perón's political career.
2. **Writing About Perspectives:** If you were an Argentinian worker, why might you prefer to live under an elected leader instead of army rule? Write a letter in which you explain your position to a friend.

BUILDING SKILLS: DISTINGUISHING FACT FROM OPINION

1. Explain how a fact is different from an opinion. Write an example of each.
2. List some key words that indicate that an opinion is being expressed.
3. What are some steps you could take to distinguish a fact from an opinion?
4. When would it be helpful to be able to distinguish a fact from an opinion?

UNIT 2 · SUMMARY

LATIN AMERICA: PHYSICAL GEOGRAPHY

 LANDFORMS

- High mountains (Andes) and vast river systems: Amazon, Río de la Plata, Orinoco

- Volcanoes: Popocatépetl
- Caribbean Islands: formed into archipelagos

 CLIMATE

- Three climate zones:
  a) Tierra caliente ("hot land")
  b) Tierra templada ("temperate land")
  c) Tierra fría ("cold land")
- Rainiest place in the world: Amazon River Valley
- Driest place in the world: Atacama Desert

NATURAL RESOURCES

- Gold, silver, tin, and other minerals
- Mexico and Venezuela: huge petroleum reserves
- Uneven distribution: some countries have many resources, some have few

LATIN AMERICA: CULTURAL GEOGRAPHY

 PEOPLE

- First inhabitants were Indians: Mayas, Aztecs, and Incas had prominent ancient civilizations
- Europeans came, starting in the 1500s: Spanish, British, French, and Dutch
- Third and fourth streams of settlers: enslaved Africans and Asians
- Today: blend of Indian, European, and African people
- Religion: most people are Roman Catholics

 ECONOMY

- Many countries have one-crop economies
- Mexico has rapidly growing population: Mexico City is world's largest metropolitan area
- South America: new transportation systems needed to develop the interior
- Crops: coffee, bananas, sugarcane, wheat, cotton, spices
- Brazilian rain forest: much of it has been cleared
- Venezuela: has developed petroleum resources

 **GOVERNMENT**

- Return to democracy in Argentina
- Mexico: representative democracy, with strong rule by the president
- Cuba: communist dictatorship led by Fidel Castro
- Only a few European colonies left

ARTS AND RECREATION

- Many important painters, such as Diego Rivera and José Orozco
- Literature: famous writers such as Pablo Neruda and Gabriel Garcia Márquez
- Sports: soccer, baseball, jai alai, tennis, horseback riding
- Traditional crafts handed down from generation to generation

176

REVIEWING VOCABULARY

archipelago	mestizo
coup	metropolitan area
developing economy	mural
dictator	per capita income
junta	sect

Number a sheet of paper from 1 to 10. Beside each number write the word or term from the list above that matches the definition.

1. The average yearly income per person in a given country
2. A leader who assumes total control of a country, often by force
3. A large city with its surrounding towns and suburbs
4. Large work of art painted on building walls
5. The sudden overthrow of a government, often by army officers
6. A person of mixed Spanish and Indian ancestry
7. An island system such as the Caribbean Islands
8. Religious group other than mainstream religions
9. A country with very little industry and a strong dependence on agriculture
10. A type of military government that is often set up after a government is overthrown

WRITING ABOUT THE UNIT

1. **Writing an Explanation:** Look at the places in Latin America listed below. Which of them probably has the coldest climate? Explain why.
   a. a village in the Andes
   b. Brasília, the capital of Brazil
   c. San Juan, Puerto Rico
2. **Writing About Perspectives:** Write a dialogue between a Brazilian of African descent and one of Indian descent. Have them discuss whether the arrival of Europeans in the Americas was good or bad, in the long run.

ACTIVITIES

1. **Constructing a Bar Graph:** Make a bar graph to show the per capita income of five Latin American countries. After you have chosen five countries, look in encyclopedias or almanacs for the information you need to make the bar graph.
2. **Working Together to Research Volcanoes:** As a class, find out more information about the volcanoes of Latin America. Some members of the class may use the library to learn how volcanoes are formed, how and why they erupt, and how they become inactive. Other students may draw diagrams of the various volcanoes to illustrate the information.

LINKING PAST, PRESENT, AND FUTURE

For centuries the United States has focused its attention on the countries of Europe. Today many people believe that Latin America will soon replace Europe and Japan as the United States' main interest. What do you think of that opinion? Tell why you agree or disagree with it.

NORTH AMERICA

North Pole

ARCTIC
OCEAN

Arctic Circle

Barents
Sea

60°N

SCANDINAVIA

ATLANTIC

North

THE
BRITISH
ISLES

45°N

Baltic Sea

FRANCE AND
THE LOW
COUNTRIES

CENTRAL
EUROPE

ASIA

OCEAN

30°N

Tropic of Cancer

SOUTHERN

EUROPE

Caspian Sea

Black Sea

Mediterranean Sea

30°W

15°W

15°N

INDIAN

0°

AFRICA

OCEAN

15°N

45°E

60°E 0°

Equator

15°S

Tropic of Capricorn

UNIT 3

WESTERN EUROPE

WHERE WE ARE

You have read about the regions of the Western Hemisphere. It is now time to journey to the Eastern Hemisphere, on the other side of the globe. You will start with Western Europe, a region that is small in size but, as you will read in the following chapters, of great importance.

As the map shows, Western Europe is divided into five areas—the British Isles, France and the Low Countries, Central Europe, Southern Europe, and Scandinavia. Let's look at the physical geography of this compact region and at the way of life of the people who live there today.

WESTERN EUROPE

ANDORRA
Capital ★
Andorra la Vella

Major languages: Catalan, French, and Spanish
Population: 53,000
Area: 174 sq mi; 450 sq km
Leading export: stamps

GERMANY
Capital ★
Berlin

Major language: German
Population: 79.5 million
Area: 137,803 sq mi; 356,910 sq km
Leading exports: machinery and manufactured goods

AUSTRIA
Capital ★
Vienna

Major language: German
Population: 7.7 million
Area: 32,375 sq mi; 83,850 sq km
Leading exports: iron and steel products, and machinery

GREECE
Capital ★
Athens

Major language: Greek
Population: 10.1 million
Area: 50,942 sq mi; 131,940 sq km
Leading exports: fruits and vegetables, and textiles

BELGIUM
Capital ★
Brussels

Major languages: Dutch and French
Population: 9.9 million
Area: 11,779 sq mi; 30,510 sq km
Leading exports: machinery, and iron and steel products

ICELAND
Capital ★
Reykjavik

Major language: Icelandic
Population: 0.3 million
Area: 39,768 sq mi; 103,000 sq km
Leading export: fish

DENMARK
Capital ★
Copenhagen

Major language: Danish
Population: 5.1 million
Area: 16,629 sq mi; 43,070 sq km
Leading exports: food and machinery

IRELAND
Capital ★
Dublin

Major languages: English and Irish
Population: 3.5 million
Area: 27,135 sq mi; 70,820 sq km
Leading exports: machinery and food

FINLAND
Capital ★
Helsinki

Major languages: Finnish and Swedish
Population: 5.0 million
Area: 130,128 sq mi; 337,030 sq km
Leading exports: paper and machinery

ITALY
Capital ★
Rome

Major language: Italian
Population: 57.7 million
Area: 116,305 sq mi; 301,230 sq km
Leading exports: machinery and manufactured goods

FRANCE
Capital ★
Paris

Major language: French
Population: 56.7 million
Area: 211,209 sq mi; 547,030 sq km
Leading exports: machinery and manufactured goods

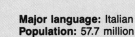

LIECHTENSTEIN
Capital ★
Vaduz

Major language: German
Population: 30,000
Area: 62 sq mi; 160 sq km
Leading export: stamps

LUXEMBOURG

Capital ★
Luxembourg

Major languages: Letzeburgesch, German, and French
Population: 0.4 million
Area: 998 sq mi; 2,586 sq km
Leading exports: iron and steel products

SAN MARINO

Capital ★
San Marino

Major language: Italian
Population: 23,000
Area: 23 sq mi; 60 sq km
Leading export: stamps

MALTA

Capital ★
Valletta

Major languages: Maltese and English
Population: 0.4 million
Area: 123 sq mi; 320 sq km
Leading exports: machinery and clothing

SPAIN

Capital ★
Madrid

Major languages: Spanish and Catalan
Population: 39.0 million
Area: 194,884 sq mi; 504,750 sq km
Leading exports: iron and steel products, and manufactured goods

MONACO

Capital ★
Monaco

Major languages: French and Monégasque
Population: 30,000
Area: 0.7 sq mi; 1.9 sq km
Leading export: stamps

SWEDEN

Capital ★
Stockholm

Major language: Swedish
Population: 8.6 million
Area: 173,730 sq mi; 449,960 sq km
Leading export: machinery

NETHERLANDS

Capital ★
Amsterdam

Major language: Dutch
Population: 15.0 million
Area: 14,405 sq mi; 37,310 sq km
Leading exports: machinery, chemicals, and manufactured goods

SWITZERLAND

Capital ★
Bern

Major languages: German, French, Italian, and Romansh
Population: 6.8 million
Area: 15,942 sq mi; 41,290 sq km
Leading exports: machinery and chemicals

NORWAY

Capital ★
Oslo

Major language: Norwegian
Population: 4.3 million
Area: 125,182 sq mi; 324,220 sq km
Leading exports: oil and natural gas

UNITED KINGDOM

Capital ★
London

Major language: English
Population: 57.5 million
Area: 94,525 sq mi; 244,820 sq km
Leading exports: machinery and manufactured goods

PORTUGAL

Capital ★
Lisbon

Major language: Portuguese
Population: 10.4 million
Area: 35,552 sq mi; 92,080 sq km
Leading exports: machinery, manufactured goods, and timber

VATICAN CITY

Capital ★
Vatican City

Major languages: Italian and Latin
Population: 750
Area: 0.17 sq mi; 0.44 sq km

CHAPTER 8

PHYSICAL GEOGRAPHY OF WESTERN EUROPE

FOCUS

Europe is a mystery and a challenge, a puzzling mixture and a problem, a temptation and a delight, even to the European.

These words were written by an American writer named Lewis Mumford. He, like many others, was interested in the "puzzling mixture" of lands, climates, and societies that makes up Western Europe. Let's find out about the different parts of this mixture.

Landforms

Key Vocabulary

fjord

Key Places

Scandinavian Peninsula	Balkan Peninsula
Jutland Peninsula	British Isles
Iberian Peninsula	Low Countries
Italian Peninsula	

Read Aloud

On the opposite side of the ship, so near that a [person] could swim it, was Europe! I had no idea whether it was France, Belgium, England, Italy, or perhaps even one of the Scandinavian coasts, but it glistened in the dawn, and seemed so clean and peaceful. This was Europe and I, a child from a prairie state, was looking at it with my own eyes!

These words were written by a young American sailor as he first gazed at the continent of Europe. In this lesson you will learn that Europe is a land of great geographical variety, from tall mountains to flat farmlands, from sparkling blue lakes to rushing mountain streams. As you read on, try to imagine that you are seeing Europe for the first time "with your own eyes."

Read for Purpose

1. **WHAT YOU KNOW:** What are some of the major landforms of the earth?
2. **WHAT YOU WILL LEARN:** What are the main geographic features of Western Europe?

A SMALL REGION

Look at the map of Western Europe on page 628 of your Atlas. You can see that it is a small region. In fact, it is the smallest region that you will study in this book. It covers slightly more than 1,431,826 square miles (3,708,430 sq km). That means that it is less than half the size of the United States. But unlike the United States, Western Europe is divided into many different countries. As you read this lesson, think about how the geography of Western Europe might have contributed to the creation of so many nations.

THE SHAPE OF THE LAND

Many thousands of years ago, glaciers covered all of northwestern Europe. These thick sheets of ice inched slowly forward, crushing the land under their enormous weight. As the ice moved, it smoothed hills and mountains, polished rocks, and deepened valleys.

About 10,000 years ago the ice began to melt. As sunshine warmed the land, trees and grass grew and covered huge areas. Birds, animals, and fish moved into this new wilderness. So did people. As they settled every part of the continent, they

WESTERN EUROPE: Elevation

Elevations

Feet		Meters
Above 14,000		Above 4,000
7,000		2,000
1,500		500
700		200
0		0

Below sea level

▲ Mountain peak

MAP SKILL: Which is at a generally higher elevation, the United Kingdom or Spain?

learned how to use the resources of this large and lovely land.

The shape of the land of Western Europe can be divided into two main landforms: peninsulas and islands. Let's find out about each of them.

A PENINSULA OF PENINSULAS

If you look at the map above, you will see that most of Western Europe is a giant peninsula jutting out from a huge land area. Geographers call this large area Eurasia (ū rā′ zhə). As you might have guessed, the name *Eurasia* comes from combining the words *Europe* and *Asia*.

184

To the west of Western Europe lies the Atlantic Ocean. Among the other large bodies of water that surround the continent are the Arctic Ocean, the North Sea, the Baltic Sea, and the Mediterranean Sea. Over the years Europeans have used these waterways as transportation routes to the rest of the world.

Not only is Western Europe itself a large peninsula, but it also contains many smaller peninsulas. Several long pieces of land jut out from the northern and southern sides of the continent. To the north the Scandinavian Peninsula is made up of Norway and Sweden. To the south is the much smaller Jutland Peninsula, which includes Denmark. Together, these two peninsulas are known as Scandinavia. Extending southward into the Mediterranean Sea are three other peninsulas. One of these, the Iberian Peninsula, contains the countries of Spain and Portugal.

Can you find the two other peninsulas on the map? First find the piece of land that is shaped like a long boot. This is called the Italian Peninsula because it contains the country of Italy.

Finally, east of Italy lies the Balkan Peninsula, on which lies the country of Greece. Some people think that Greece is shaped like a large hand. The pieces of land that extend from the mainland remind them of long fingers.

THE ISLANDS OF WESTERN EUROPE

Western Europe also includes many islands. Rising out of the Atlantic Ocean in the north is Iceland. To the south, and closer to the mainland, lie the British Isles. The English Channel cuts the British Isles off from the rest of Europe.

The Mediterranean Sea also contains several large islands. The three largest are Corsica, Sicily, and Sardinia.

A LONG COASTLINE

Because of its many peninsulas and islands, Western Europe has thousands of miles of coastline. Look at the map on the opposite page. Find France and the Low Countries—Belgium, the Netherlands, and Luxembourg. The coastline of three of these countries—France, Belgium, and the Netherlands—stretches for more than 600 miles (965 km).

In some parts of Europe, the coastline is rugged. For example, the western coast of

Many of the islands of Western Europe are located in the Mediterranean Sea. This one, Mykonos Island, is in Greece.

Norway is cut by great bays and long **fjords** (fyôrdz). A fjord is a deep, narrow inlet of the sea between high cliffs.

Because of Western Europe's long coastline, most people do not live far from the sea. In fact, there is no spot within this entire region that is more than 300 miles (480 km) from a seacoast.

Many port cities have developed along the bays on Europe's coastline. These bays form naturally protected harbors where people can load and unload goods from ships easily.

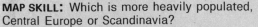

MAP SKILL: Which is more heavily populated, Central Europe or Scandinavia?

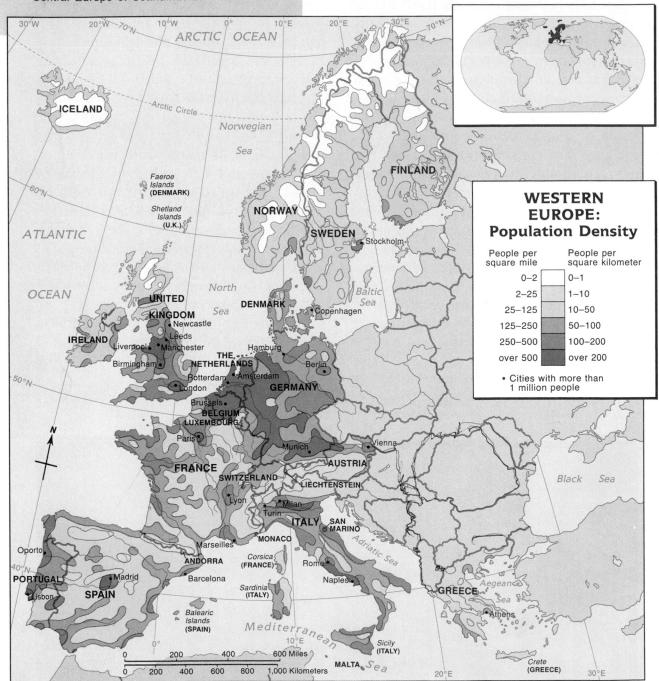

WESTERN EUROPE: Population Density

People per square mile	People per square kilometer
0–2	0–1
2–25	1–10
25–125	10–50
125–250	50–100
250–500	100–200
over 500	over 200

• Cities with more than 1 million people

Because Western Europe has many good bays and harbors, and because it is so close to the sea, the region has become a world crossroads. Throughout their history, Western European people have used the sea to transport their products and their ideas all over the globe. At the same time, Western Europe has absorbed other products and ideas from many of the world's other cultures.

POPULATION

Although Western Europe is small in size, it has many people. Over 370 million people live in this compact region.

Look at the map on the opposite page. This map shows you where people live in Western Europe. The population density of this region is about 265 people per square mile (102 people per sq km). You read in Chapter 2 that the United States has a population density of about 71 persons per square mile (27 people per sq km). These figures should tell you that little land in Western Europe is uninhabited.

As you may have guessed, most of Western Europe's people live in urban areas. Almost three fourths of all Western Europeans live in or near cities.

Look again at the population density map. It shows the cities of Western Europe that have more than 1 million people living in them.

A LAND OF MANY WONDERS

You have read that Western Europe is a land of peninsulas and islands. Although it is a small region, it is divided into many countries by its mountains, rivers, and seas. Yet these same mountains, rivers, and seas have not created barriers between the different parts of the land. Over the years Western Europe has developed into a region where people can move, trade, and share ideas with ease.

London is one of the most densely populated cities in Western Europe.

 Check Your Reading

1. Name three peninsulas found in Western Europe.
2. What has the long coastline of Western Europe meant to the region throughout its history?
3. How would you describe the shape of the land that makes up the countries of Western Europe?
4. **THINKING SKILL:** Look at the map on page 184. Compare and contrast the elevations of France and Norway.

Understanding Map Projections

Key Vocabulary

distortion
projection

cylindrical projection
equal-area projection

You can learn about the geographic features of Western Europe by looking at a globe. Because a globe is a sphere like the earth, it can show the earth accurately. All the countries that appear on the globe are in correct proportion to one another.

Distortion and Projection

Maps are less accurate representations of the earth than globes. Imagine trying to flatten a globe. You would have to cut or stretch some parts of the earth, causing distortions, or errors in size, shape, distance, and or direction.

Mapmakers solve the problem of distortion by using projections. A projection is a way of showing locations on the earth on a flat map. The people who make maps have developed many different kinds of projections.

Cylindrical Projection

One common type of map projection is called a cylindrical projection. On a cylindrical projection distances measured along the equator are correct because there is little distortion in the areas near the equator. Distortion increases as you move toward the poles.

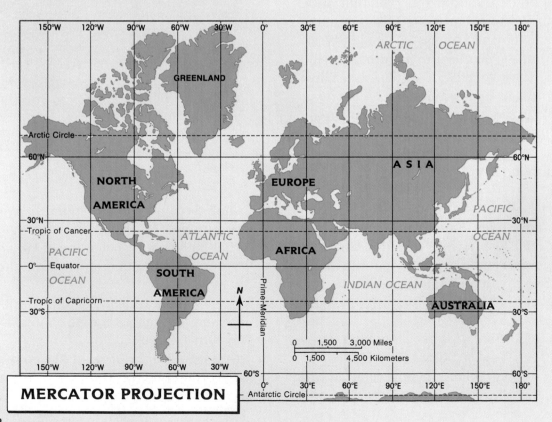

MERCATOR PROJECTION

ROBINSON PROJECTION

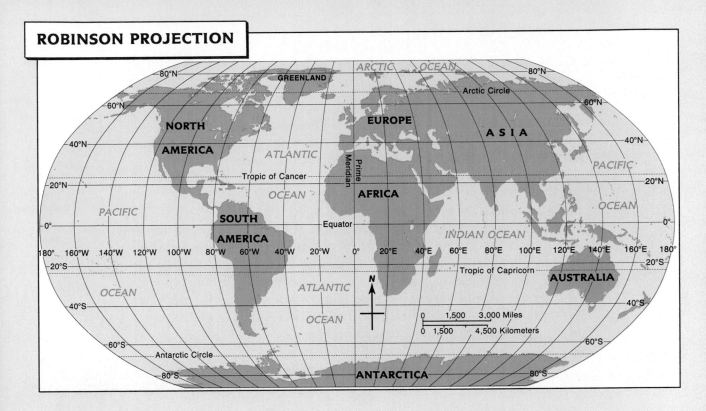

The Mercator projection on page 188 is an example of a cylindrical projection. Notice that the island of Greenland, which is actually much smaller than the continent of Africa, appears almost as large as Africa on the map. Remember that Greenland appears distorted in size because it is located near to the North Pole.

On cylindrical maps north is always directly toward the top of the map, east is to the right, west is to the left, and south is toward the bottom. Cylindrical projection is useful to navigators of ships, who use it to draw their ships' courses in straight lines.

Equal-area Projection

Another type of projection is called an **equal-area projection**. On equal-area maps sizes and shapes are shown fairly accurately, and distances are nearly correct. For these reasons, equal-area projec-

tions are useful when different places on the earth are compared.

The Robinson projection on this page is an example of an equal-area map. Find Greenland on this map and compare it to Africa. Notice that Greenland is shown as smaller than Africa.

On this Robinson projection only the lines of latitude are always drawn as straight lines. Other than the prime meridian, all the lines of longitude are curved. As a result, north is not always in a straight line to the top of the map.

Reviewing the Skill

1. What is a map projection? What is distortion?
2. Which kind of map would be most useful to someone who wants to compare the size of two continents?
3. Why is it useful to understand different kinds of map projections?

The Use of Nuclear Energy

You have read that Western Europe supports a large population even though the region covers a small geographical area. In recent years the growth of industry in Western Europe has made enormous demands on the energy sources of the region. Leaders in government and industry have had to look for new ways to meet the increasing demands for energy.

One of the alternative methods they have found is the use of nuclear power to produce electricity. The French government, in particular, with the strong support of its people, has started a vast program to produce nuclear energy. Recently, however, people in France and throughout the world have expressed their concerns about France's and other countries' dependence on nuclear energy. Some environmental groups think that the dangers to health and safety will make the production of nuclear power too risky.

POINT ☆✍

Nuclear Plants Should Continue To Be Built

In France a government group called *Electricité de France* (EDF) is responsible for the design, construction, and operation of nuclear plants. During a visit to the United States in April 1989, Remy Carle, the assistant director general of EDF, explained his country's policy.

Japan has a nuclear program, probably for the same reason we do, because they have no domestic resources in the ground. Some countries have abundant coal or hydropower. We have some, and we want to use a mix of these different sources. . . .

We export about 10 percent of our electricity to neighboring countries. Those people recognize by this fact that our electricity is cheaper than the electricity they can produce by their own means. . . . We think that the safety of present nuclear plants is good and sufficient. We don't think it's possible to have what you call a . . . safe reactor, a reactor that cannot fail in any situation.

But safety can, of course, be improved . . . We have a lot of experience now. We have time. We prepare the next generation for a decision after the end of the century.

- According to Remy Carle, why should France continue to build nuclear plants?

COUNTERPOINT ✍☆

Nuclear Plants Should Not Be Built

Many environmentalists throughout the world fear that nuclear plants are dangerous to life everywhere. They say that if the radioactive waste produced by nuclear plants comes in contact with living things, it can cause serious health problems and even death. Environmental groups also fear that radioactive waste cannot be disposed of safely.

One environmentalist who opposes the continued development of nuclear plants expressed the following opinion.

Nuclear energy is super-dangerous, and we must face up to the fact. . . . Nuclear plants . . . do have accidents.

Forty years into the nuclear era, the world still doesn't have the means to dispose of the highly radioactive waste accumulating at nuclear plants. Each year about one third of the used fuel loaded with highly dangerous . . . products is placed in pools of water . . . waiting for a decision on what to do with it—or for some accident . . . to spread it around the countryside.

It appears essential, then, to provide humanity with alternate choices of energy supply.

- Why do some environmentalists think that nuclear plants are dangerous and should no longer be built?

UNDERSTANDING THE POINT/COUNTERPOINT

1. Which side do you think makes the stronger argument? Why?
2. What other groups might have an opinion on this issue? What do you think members of those groups might say?
3. Do you think that the two sides could reach a compromise on this issue? Explain.

Climate and Resources

AN OCEANIC CLIMATE

If you actually visited Great Britain and Ireland, you would find that the climate there is much warmer than Canada's. In January, London is about as warm as Washington, D.C., which is almost 900 miles (1,450 km) south of Canada's Hudson Bay.

The main reason for this difference in climate is a special "river" that flows in the Atlantic Ocean. It is called the Gulf Stream. The Gulf Stream brings warm water from the Gulf of Mexico to the Atlantic coast of Europe. The photograph on page 193 shows what the Gulf Stream looks like from miles above the earth.

Western Europe's climate is mild also because the ocean waters off its Atlantic coast heat up in summer and cool off in winter more slowly than the land does. In winter, winds blowing off the Atlantic Ocean warm coastal areas. In summer ocean breezes keep places near the coast cooler than the inland areas. Look at the climate map on page 194. In which areas do you think the climate is affected by ocean breezes?

Ocean winds also bring plenty of rain to the coastal areas of Western Europe. Every year these areas get more than 20 inches (50 cm) of precipitation.

In the northern part of Western Europe, the moderating effect of the Gulf Stream and the Atlantic Ocean is not nearly as strong. As a result, the winters are long, cold, and snowy. In northern Sweden and most of Finland, the ground is covered with snow, and temperatures are very cold for several months of the year.

A completely different type of climate is found in the southern part of Western Europe. You can see from the climate map that Portugal, Spain, Greece, and Italy have mostly hot summers and mild winters. Two mountain ranges, the Alps and the Pyrenees, prevent Atlantic breezes from reaching this area. This explains why summers are mostly sunny and dry and winters are usually mild or even warm in Southern Europe. Every winter tourists from the rainy or snowy countries of northern Europe flock to Spain and Italy to enjoy the blue seas and warm, sandy beaches of these countries.

Although Western Europe has different climate regions, the weather in the region is generally temperate. Only in the farthest northern lands of Scandinavia is the winter bitterly cold.

Most of Western Europe also gets plenty of rainfall. The area around the Mediterranean Sea is one of the few areas of the region in which there is little rainfall during part of the year.

GRAPH SKILL: The path of the **Gulf Stream** is shown in the satellite photo above. Is London or Stockholm more strongly affected by the Gulf Stream?

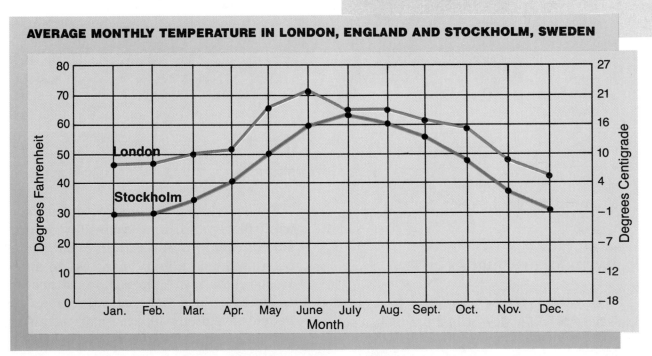

193

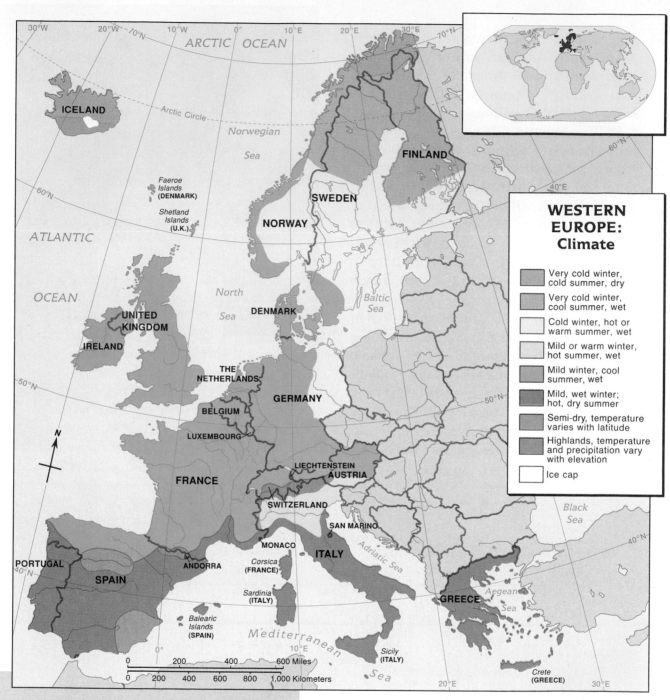

	WESTERN EUROPE: Climate

Very cold winter, cold summer, dry

Very cold winter, cool summer, wet

Cold winter, hot or warm summer, wet

Mild or warm winter, hot summer, wet

Mild winter, cool summer, wet

Mild, wet winter; hot, dry summer

Semi-dry, temperature varies with latitude

Highlands, temperature and precipitation vary with elevation

Ice cap

MAP SKILL: What type of climate covers most of the central part of Western Europe?

NATURAL RESOURCES

Under an ash-colored sky, the fields have been combed and rolled till they appear to have been finished with a pencil instead of a plough.

The American poet Ralph Waldo Emerson wrote these words to describe the countryside of Great Britain. But they could have been written about many places in Western Europe. This region is rich in farmland and other natural resources. People have been using these resources for so many years that the landscape has a cared-for look that contrasts sharply with the areas of wilderness often found in other parts of the world.

FORESTS AND SOIL

Look around you. How many things do you see that are made of wood or paper? All these products come from an important natural resource—forests.

In the past, much of Western Europe was covered with dense forests. But over the years most of the trees were cut down to make room for farms. The wood was burned as fuel and used for buildings and furniture.

Today there are few large forests left in Western Europe. And the forests that remain are threatened not only by logging, but also by acid rain. As you may remember from Chapter 3, acid rain is rain mixed with chemicals from the burning of coal and other fuels. Much of the Black Forest, which was once a huge forest in West Germany, has been destroyed by acid rain.

As the map on page 196 shows, Western Europe has ample rich soil for farming. About 25 percent of the soil is arable. In some countries, like the Netherlands, more than half the land can be farmed. Raising livestock is also an important economic activity throughout the region.

RIVERS AND OTHER WATERWAYS

You read in Lesson 1 that most countries in Western Europe have access to oceans and seas. The region is also fortunate in having several important inland rivers. Because of Western Europe's temperate climate, most rivers are open all year long. Ships can navigate in ice-free waters around most European ports.

Many of Western Europe's major cities, like London, Paris, and Rome, developed along the banks of rivers. Having good inland waterways has also meant that even the landlocked countries of Western Europe—Luxembourg, Switzerland, Austria, Andorra, and Liechtenstein—have ade-

Herding reindeer in Lapland in northern Scandinavia is one of many activities that occurs in Europe.

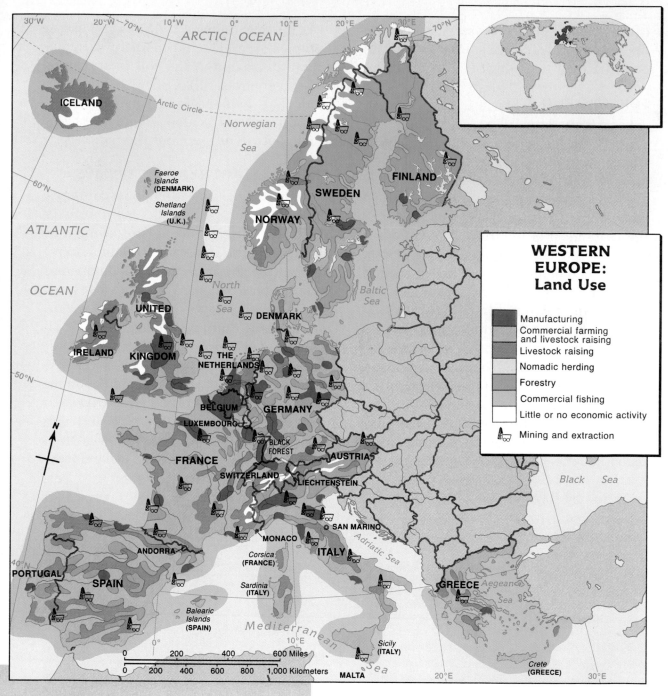

WESTERN EUROPE: Land Use

- Manufacturing
- Commercial farming and livestock raising
- Livestock raising
- Nomadic herding
- Forestry
- Commercial fishing
- Little or no economic activity
- Mining and extraction

MAP SKILL: What is the major economic activity of Scandinavia?

quate transportation. A landlocked country is one that is entirely surrounded by land.

The longest river in Western Europe is the Danube (dan′ ūb) River. It flows for nearly 1,800 miles (2,900 km). That makes it slightly longer than the Rio Grande in the United States. The Danube flows from the Black Forest in Germany to the Black Sea in Romania. On its way it passes through seven countries in Western and Eastern Europe.

The Rhine (rīn) River is another important river in Western Europe. The Rhine is

The Rhine River is a major transportation route and runs through some of the best farmland in Western Europe.

a large navigable river. That means it is wide and deep enough for ocean-going ships to use. More ships travel on the Rhine every year than on any other waterway in the world.

The Rhine begins in Switzerland, where it is fed by streams rushing down the slopes of the Alps. The Rhine then flows through the center of Western Europe and empties into the North Sea on the north coast of the Netherlands. The Rhine and its tributaries form a water highway that stretches from the heart of Western Europe to the North Sea.

The American poet Henry Wadsworth Longfellow described the Rhine this way:

O, the pride of the German heart is this noble river! And right it is; for of all the rivers of this beautiful earth there is none so beautiful as this.

In the Scandinavian countries, the rivers are shorter and narrower than those in other parts of Western Europe. But Scandinavians have found ways to put these waterways to work. In the north, swift rivers have been dammed where they emerge from the mountains in order to make hydroelectricity. In Finland factories producing paper and pulp have been built near sources of hydroelectric power.

MILD CLIMATE, RICH SOIL

Western Europe is a land with many advantages. It has rich soil and a mild climate for growing crops. It has navigable rivers that are free from ice during the winter. And it has a central location that makes it accessible to all of the world.

In this chapter you learned that the countries of Western Europe mostly share these advantages. In the next five chapters you will learn what makes each country different. No traveler today would mistake London for Athens or confuse the Swiss countryside with that of Spain. The special character of the individual countries of Western Europe is one of the things that makes this region so interesting.

 Check Your Reading

1. What problems threaten the forests of Western Europe today?
2. How does the Gulf Stream affect Western Europe's climate?
3. Why are rivers important to Western Europeans?
4. **THINKING SKILL:** What are three questions you could ask to find out about the climate of Scandinavia?

197

WESTERN EUROPE: PHYSICAL GEOGRAPHY

 LANDFORMS

 CLIMATE

NATURAL RESOURCES

- Peninsulas: Scandinavian, Jutland, Italian, Balkan, Iberian

- Islands: British Isles, Greece, Corsica, Sardinia, Sicily
- Thousands of miles of coastline

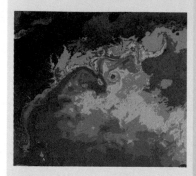

- Gulf Stream: brings warm waters that help create mild climate in coastal areas
- Ocean winds bring plenty of rainfall to most areas

- Northern part of the region: winters are long and cold
- Southern part: summers are sunny and dry, winters short and mild

- Forests: important resource, but few large ones are left

- Many long inland rivers and waterways, such as Danube and Rhine rivers

- Rich soil: used for farming and raising livestock

IDEAS TO REMEMBER

- Western Europe is made up of two main landforms: islands and peninsulas.
- Western Europe's climate is generally temperate, and its major resources include rich soil and long waterways.

REVIEWING VOCABULARY

Number a sheet of paper from 1 to 5. Read the definition of each underlined word. Beside each number write **T** if the definition is true and **F** if it is false.

1. The dense forests of Finland are called <u>fjords</u>.
2. Countries that are entirely surrounded by water are <u>landlocked</u>.
3. A <u>fjord</u> is a deep, narrow inlet of seawater between high cliffs.
4. <u>Landlocked</u> countries are entirely surrounded by land.
5. The <u>fjords</u> bring warm water from the Gulf of Mexico to Europe.

REVIEWING FACTS

1. What are the two main geographic features of Western Europe?
2. What does the term *Eurasia* mean?
3. Name the five major peninsulas of Western Europe.
4. Name three European islands in the Mediterranean Sea.
5. What is a fjord? In which country are most fjords found?
6. What two factors are responsible for the mild climate of Western Europe?
7. How do the Alps and the Pyrenees affect the climate in the southern part of Western Europe?
8. Why are there few large forests in Europe today?
9. What is a landlocked country? Name three countries in Western Europe that are landlocked.
10. Name the two largest rivers in Western Europe. How have rivers been used to help Europe's landlocked countries?

WRITING ABOUT MAIN IDEAS

1. **Writing a List:** Bodies of water are important resources in Western Europe. List the ways in which countries of Western Europe are affected by the Atlantic Ocean, the Danube River, and the Rhine River.
2. **Writing a Magazine Article:** Imagine that the Gulf Stream has suddenly shifted its course away from Western Europe. What do you think would happen to the people of the region? Write a magazine article describing the change and the efforts of Western Europeans to cope with it.
3. **Writing a Travel Log:** You have read that Europe is divided into many different countries. Imagine that you are taking a trip from Sweden to Greece. Name the countries and the bodies of water you would pass through or over on your trip.
4. **Writing About Perspectives:** Choose the country in Western Europe that you would most like to visit. Then write a letter to a pen pal in that country, asking questions about what life there is like.

BUILDING SKILLS: UNDERSTANDING MAP PROJECTIONS

1. What is meant by the term *distortion* as it relates to mapmaking?
2. What is a map projection?
3. How is a grid system useful in determining a map's distortion?
4. Why is it important to understand map projection and distortion?

CHAPTER 9

THE BRITISH ISLES

FOCUS

Heavy Fog Over Channel, Continent Isolated.

This headline from an English newspaper tells something important about life in Great Britain and Ireland. The British Isles are separated from the European continent by the English Channel. Today you can travel between Britain and the European mainland in about half an hour. But in the days before modern transportation, the waters of the English Channel set the British Isles apart from the rest of Europe.

The People

READ TO LEARN

Key People

William the Conqueror

Key Places

Great Britain   Stonehenge
Ireland   Northern Ireland

Read Aloud

Britain, long before the discovery of America, was the America of Europe, the farthest point west, where [people] were driven by invaders from the east; the land of the free, where refugees could find sanctuary [a place of protection], and the hungry and disappointed could find hope.

The author Anthony Glyn wrote these words to explain why so many people have come to the British Isles. Although these misty green islands are small in size and crowded in many places, they offer freedom and opportunity to people from all over the world.

Read for Purpose

1. **WHAT YOU KNOW:** Where are the British Isles located in relation to the rest of Western Europe?
2. **WHAT YOU WILL LEARN:** Which groups of people have settled in the British Isles?

ISLAND NATIONS

The British Isles are made up of two main islands. They are Great Britain and Ireland. Great Britain is made up of England, Scotland, and Wales. Several smaller islands in the North Sea and the Atlantic Ocean are also included in the British Isles.

The British Isles consist of two nations, the United Kingdom and the Republic of Ireland. The United Kingdom is made up of Great Britain and the northern part of Ireland. The people of the United Kingdom live mainly on the island of Great Britain, which includes England, Scotland, and Wales. The people of these areas are often referred to as the British.

WAVES OF SETTLERS

The British are a complex mixture of different peoples and cultures. To understand their story, we have to look back in time several thousand years.

Little is known about the first people who settled in the British Isles. They left no written records. Like the first Americans, they did not have a system of writing. The chief remains of their existence are a group of enormous gray stones called Stonehenge The purpose of this huge

THE BRITISH ISLES: Political

⊛ National capital   • Other city   ▪ Point of interest

MAP SKILL: The United Kingdom and the Republic of Ireland make up the British Isles. What is the capital of the Republic of Ireland?

In about A.D. 43 the Romans invaded the British Isles. By this time the Celts had spread throughout the islands. Within the next four years, the Romans gained control of most of Britain. They ruled this area for more than 400 years. Today the remains of a wall that the Romans built all the way across the northern part of England still exist.

When the Romans left Britain in around A.D. 450, the area was invaded by several groups of warriors from northern Europe. Together these people were known as Anglo-Saxons. They called the land they settled *Angleland*, or England. Over the years the Anglo-Saxons pushed the Celts north and west into Wales, Scotland, and Ireland. Find these on the map.

In 1066 the world of the Anglo-Saxons changed forever. A group of invaders led by William the Conqueror took over England. This group was called the Normans, because they came from the western part of France known as Normandy. They brought with them their own culture and their own language, French. Several centuries would pass before the Anglo-Saxon and French languages would blend together to form the English language that is spoken today.

MODERN NEWCOMERS

After 1066 no other group or nation invaded the British Isles. Since that time, however, millions of people have crossed the waters of the English Channel and settled in the British Isles. During the 1900s immigrants from outside Europe flooded into Great Britain. To these people, the British Isles represented opportunity. Here they could find land, work, and freedom.

Today more than 60 million people live in the British Isles. Great Britain is the fourth most crowded nation in the world. The largest groups of newcomers come

stone structure, which was built in southern England about 4,000 years ago, is still a mystery. Some historians think Stonehenge was built as a means to study the stars and the planets. Others think that it was for religious celebrations.

In the early history of the British Isles, the islands were invaded several times. After the builders of Stonehenge, the oldest known inhabitants of the British Isles were the Celts. They came from the mainland of Europe in about 800 B.C. Most Celts were either farmers or metalworkers.

202

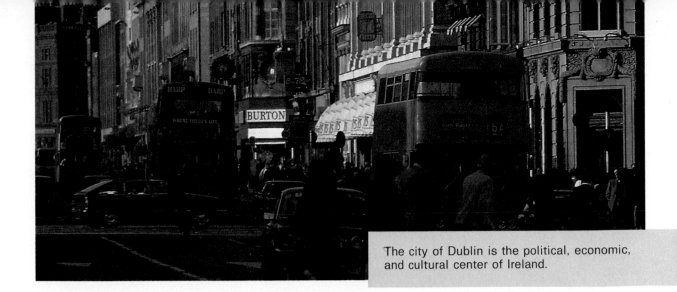

The city of Dublin is the political, economic, and cultural center of Ireland.

from countries once ruled by Britain—India, Pakistan, and other parts of Asia, the West Indies and parts of Africa. Like earlier immigrants they come seeking freedom and opportunities for a better life.

TROUBLES IN NORTHERN IRELAND

The United Kingdom began as the small nation of England. As it grew more powerful, it took over Wales, Scotland, and Ireland. Today the people in each of these areas are proud of their separate customs. But different traditions have sometimes led to bloody conflicts.

For example, religious differences in Northern Ireland have torn that area apart. About 60 percent of the people living in Northern Ireland are Protestants. The rest are Roman Catholics.

After Britain gave southern Ireland its independence in 1921, Catholics in Northern Ireland hoped to join their southern neighbors in forming an Irish Republic. But their dream was never realized. Angry Protestants in Northern Ireland feared that such a union would leave them outnumbered by Catholics.

Since the 1960s British soldiers have been stationed in Northern Ireland. Violence has broken out repeatedly in the area. Thousands of people have been killed. Hope for peace came in 1993. The British announced that Northern Ireland would be free to choose whether or not to stay in the United Kingdom. But first the Irish Republican Army, the group committing much of the violence in Northern Ireland, had to abandon their violence.

TWO NATIONS, MANY PEOPLES

The British Isles consist of two countries with many groups of people. You have read how the Celts were the first people to come to the British Isles. They were followed by several other groups of invaders. Later, immigrants from other countries came to work in these island nations. Like newcomers before them, they saw the British Isles as a land of opportunity.

 Check Your Reading

1. Which two main islands make up the British Isles?
2. What happened to the Celts who lived in the British Isles thousands of years in the past?
3. Why has Northern Ireland been a land of conflict?
4. THINKING SKILL: Beginning with the Celts, list in order the groups of people that have invaded the British Isles.

Reading Time Zone Maps

Key Vocabulary

time zone
International Date Line

When it is noon in London, England, it is 7:00 A.M. in Washington, D.C., and it is 2:00 P.M. in Cairo, Egypt. As you can see from the map below, the world is divided into 24 **time zones**, one for every 15° of longitude on a map or globe.

Time and Space

Why does time differ from place to place? As you know, the earth completes one rotation on its axis every 24 hours. Because the earth rotates 360° each day, it follows that in one hour it rotates 15°. This is the reason that each of the world's time zones is about 15° of longitude wide.

The time on which all time zones are based is located on the prime meridian in Greenwich, England. Find the prime meridian on the map. The times given at the top of the map show how the time changes as a person moves away from the prime meridian.

Because the earth rotates from west to east, the time in any zone east of you is always later than it is in your zone. As you move east, you add one hour for each time zone that you cross. The time in any zone west of you is always earlier than it is in your zone. As you move to the west, you subtract an hour for each time zone crossed.

For example, suppose it is 10:00 A.M. in Washington, D.C. To find the time in Houston, which is one time zone west of Washington, D.C., you subtract one hour.

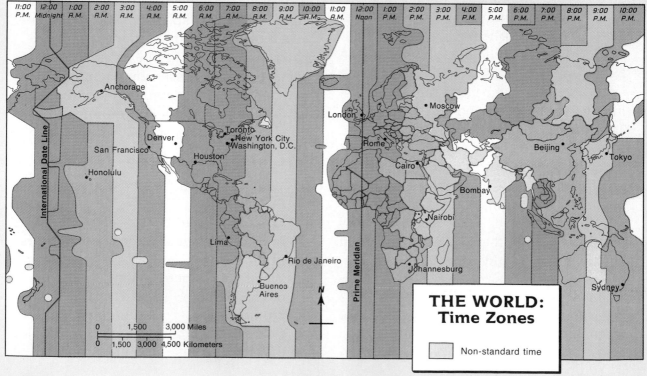

THE WORLD:
Time Zones

Non-standard time

Now find Lima on the map. When it is 7:00 P.M. in Lima, what time is it in Rio de Janeiro? Since Rio de Janeiro is two time zones east of Lima, you must add two hours to the time in Lima.

The International Date Line

Halfway around the world from the prime meridian is the International Date Line, located on the 180° meridian of longitude. The International Date Line is an imaginary line that marks the boundary between one day and the next. Because of the International Date Line, two different days always exist at the same time throughout the world.

At the International Date Line you gain or lose a day, depending on the direction in which you are traveling. For example, suppose you are on a ship which sails west across the International Date Line on Tuesday at 3:00 P.M. Your time would change one full day to Wednesday at 3:00 P.M. What do you think would happen if you crossed the International Date Line traveling east on Friday at 5:00 P.M.? You would go back one full day to Thursday at 5:00 P.M.

Look at the time zone map. You will see that the red line marking the International Date Line is not a straight line. It zigzags so that eastern Siberia and Russia are on the same side of the International Date Line. The line has also been redrawn so that it does not cross land areas. Similarly, time zones around the world zigzag to follow national boundaries or to prevent one city from having two different time zones.

Using the Time Zone Map

To understand how to use a time zone map, look at the map on page 204 and read the following examples.

A. When it is 7:00 A.M. Monday in Toronto, it is 3:00 A.M. Monday in Anchorage. (As the map shows, Anchorage is four time zones west of Toronto.)

B. When it is 9:00 P.M. Friday in Tokyo, it is 2:00 A.M. Thursday in Honolulu. (As the map shows, Honolulu is five time zones east of Tokyo, and the International Date Line was passed.)

C. When it is 10:00 P.M. Thursday in Sydney, it is 5:00 A.M. Wednesday in Denver. (As the map shows, Sydney is seven time zones west of Denver, and the International Date Line was passed.)

D. When it is 6:00 A.M. Tuesday in San Francisco, it is 12:00 P.M. Tuesday in Sydney. (Sydney is six time zones west of San Francisco, and both the midnight time zone and the International Date Line were passed.)

Reviewing the Skill

1. What is a time zone?
2. What is the prime meridian?
3. What is the International Date Line?
4. Why are the world's time zones about 15° of longitude wide?
5. If you were traveling through time zones from west to east, would you turn your clock ahead or back?
6. If it is noon in London, what time is it in Beijing? In Sydney? In Houston?
7. If it is 6:00 A.M. Monday in Moscow, what day and time is it in Lima?
8. If it is 5:00 P.M. Friday in San Francisco, what day and time is it in Nairobi? In Tokyo?
9. What day and time will it be when you arrive in Denver, if your three-hour flight left New York on Wednesday at 4:00 P.M.?
10. Why is it important to know how to use a time zone map?

The Economy

READ TO LEARN

 Key Vocabulary

Industrial Revolution
nationalize
mixed economy

Read Aloud

It was a town of machinery and tall chimneys, out of which interminable [endless] *serpents of smoke trailed themselves for ever and ever. It had a . . . river that ran purple with ill-smelling dyes and vast piles of buildings . . . where the piston of the steam engine worked monotonously up and down like the head of an elephant in a state of melancholy madness.*

These words by the writer Charles Dickens describe the factory towns of England during the 1800s. In this lesson you will read how the British economy has changed since the days when English factories first filled the air with dark clouds of smoke.

Read for Purpose

1. **WHAT YOU KNOW:** Why have millions of immigrants moved to the British Isles?
2. **WHAT YOU WILL LEARN:** What economic challenges do the British face today?

THE INDUSTRIAL REVOLUTION

At the time when Charles Dickens was writing about factory towns in England, the country was in the middle of the Industrial Revolution of the 1800s. Jobs that were once done by hand were being done by machine. Products that once were made at home or in small workshops were being produced in factories. Machines helped factory workers to produce goods faster than ever before. In 1865 a shoe factory could turn out 300 pairs of machine-made shoes in a day. This was as many as a cobbler making shoes by hand could produce in an entire year.

The Industrial Revolution made Great Britain the economic leader of the world. Meanwhile, the Republic of Ireland was developing at a much slower pace. Ireland, which was a colony of Great Britain for hundreds of years, has few natural resources. Today the average income of the Irish is about half that of the British.

A MIXED ECONOMY

In the 1940s the British government took over large sections of industry. The government nationalized several businesses, including coal mines, gas and electric utilities, and railroads. To nationalize an industry means to place it under the control or ownership of the government.

In recent years, however, many nationalized industries have been made private again. This means that today the United Kingdom has a **mixed economy**. A mixed economy is an economy consisting of a mixture of both private enterprises and government-run businesses.

The Republic of Ireland also has a mixed economy. The Irish government owns and operates the railroad and airline industries, and television and radio stations. Most other industries are controlled by private companies.

NEW RESOURCES

Things have changed in Great Britain since the days of the Industrial Revolution. The United Kingdom is no longer the world's leading industrial nation as it was in the 1800s. Today people in other countries are building new factories and setting up new businesses. They can produce goods more cheaply than the British because many British factories are outdated. But the British have recently discovered some valuable new resources.

During the 1960s huge oil and natural gas fields were found beneath the waters of the North Sea. When the price of oil increased dramatically in the 1970s, North Sea oil became very valuable. This pumped money into the British economy, which helped offset the loss of income from manufacturing industries.

FARMING

Every day John O'Leary tends the cows and sheep on his 22-acre (9-ha) farm in western Ireland. He adds to his income by cutting turf, or peat—the half-formed coal that the Irish dig out of the ground to burn as fuel. O'Leary is known as a *crofter*—a person who owns or rents a small farm.

Large platforms have been set up in the North Sea to get at valuable oil reserves far below the sea waters.

The countryside of Ireland is dotted with small farms. At right, a man and a girl load turf they have cut for fuel onto a donkey.

The O'Leary family members are among those Irish workers who farm for a living. Like other crofters they grow potatoes and oats in addition to raising livestock. Today most Irish farms are smaller than 30 acres (12 ha). But they provide enough food to feed most of the people living in Ireland.

In Great Britain farming is different. Only about 2 percent of the people there are farmers. But most farms are large, modern, and efficient. Despite these farms' productivity, however, there is simply not enough farmland to feed Britain's large population. Every year the British import tons of food from countries around the world.

A WORLD LEADER

The Industrial Revolution made Great Britain a wealthy and powerful nation. Today Britain faces new economic prob-

lems. Because of its small size, its natural resources are limited. In addition, British factories now find it hard to compete against more modern factories in other countries. So the British now produce and sell fewer goods than in the past. The key to Britain's economic future may lie in resources buried under the North Sea.

Check Your Reading

1. What was the Industrial Revolution?
2. What does it mean to say that Great Britain has a mixed economy?
3. How is farming in Ireland different from farming in Great Britain?
4. **THINKING SKILL:** What is the correct order of the major events discussed in this lesson?

The Government

READ TO LEARN

Key Vocabulary

Magna Carta
constitutional monarchy
welfare state

Key People

Margaret Thatcher

Read Aloud

Imagine that you are visiting London. It is autumn, and the leaves are turning bright shades of red and orange. Suddenly you see a stately procession winding through the streets. Soldiers in glittering uniforms escort a gilded horse-drawn coach. Why all the fuss? Because in that coach rides the queen of England.

Read for Purpose

1. **WHAT YOU KNOW:** What countries make up the British Isles?
2. **WHAT YOU WILL LEARN:** What are the important features of the governments of the British Isles?

TRADITIONS OF RULE

You read in Chapter 3 that Canada has a form of government called a parliamentary democracy. This kind of government is headed by a prime minister who rules through a national legislature. The system of parliamentary democracy began to be adopted by Canadians from the British during the 1700s.

The roots of British government go back hundreds of years. Early kings, such as William the Conqueror, whom you read about in Lesson 1, had great power. They could make laws, choose officials, and declare war or peace. Over the centuries, however, English thinking changed. Some people began to argue that all individual citizens had certain rights that ought to be protected.

Over time the British Parliament limited the power of the king and assumed more power. The rights and freedoms of each individual, argued Parliament leaders, were just as important as the powers of the king. In 1215 King John of Great Britain was forced to sign the Magna Carta, a document that limited the powers of the monarch. The Magna Carta is one of the most important documents in the history of the world.

Great Britain became the world's first constitutional monarchy. It is a monarchy because it is headed by a king or queen. It is constitutional because the monarch's powers are limited by a constitution that guarantees the rights of the people, especially the right to elect representatives to make laws.

Unlike the United States Constitution and most of the world's constitutions, the British constitution is not a single written document. Instead, it is made up of

Great Britain's royal family includes Queen Elizabeth (*left*), and Prince Charles and his son Prince William (*right*).

important laws and charters adopted over many centuries. A charter is a formal written document, like the Magna Carta, issued by a government.

PARLIAMENT AND THE MONARCHY TODAY

The British Parliament consists of two parts called "houses." The upper house, known as the House of Lords, has more than 1,000 members. The House of Lords is made up largely of aristocrats who hold titles granted to them by English monarchs. The Duke of Kent, for example, is a member of the House of Lords. Some judges and leaders of the Church of England also belong to the House of Lords.

The lower house of Parliament is called the House of Commons. Its 650 members are elected by the British people. In the twentieth century the House of Commons has become more and more powerful. It now has the right to pass any measure into law. Now, unlike in the past, the House of Lords cannot interfere with any bills dealing with finances. Today few of its members play an active role in government.

The leader of the political party with the most seats in Parliament is the prime minister. The prime minister meets regularly with the cabinet, all of whom must be members of Parliament. Britain's legislative and executive branches of government are not separated.

In 1979 Margaret Thatcher became Britain's first woman prime minister. She was the first prime minister in more than 150 years who was elected for three consecutive terms. She resigned in 1990.

Under the British system of government, the monarch does not play a direct role in making policy. But the king or queen carries out many public functions. The monarch opens and closes Parliament, visits hospitals and factories, and represents Great Britain in foreign countries. The monarch also heads the Commonwealth of Nations. As you may remember from Chapter 3, the Commonwealth of Nations includes Great Britain and more than 40 other countries that were once ruled by the British.

Above all, the monarch inspires the loyalty of the British people. Today it costs the British over $40 million a year to maintain the "royals"—Queen Elizabeth and her family. But most British people believe that it is a good investment. "In laying out millions on the monarchy," explained one British woman, "the public is paying partly for a unique product—magic." An inhabitant of London put it more simply: "There's no one like her [the queen], that's all. We'd be lost without her."

The Republic of Ireland, like Great Britain has a parliament with two houses. But unlike Great Britain, Ireland does not have a monarch.

THE BRITISH INFLUENCE

As you have already read, democracies around the world have different forms of government. The United States, for example, is not headed by a hereditary ruler. Yet the world's democracies all have one thing in common: they are all modeled on the British system of government. The people who wrote the Declaration of Independence and the Constitution were familiar with British theories of government and documents like the Magna Carta. They were influenced by the long British tradition of respect for the individual rights and liberties of citizens.

NEW APPROACHES

During the 1940s the United Kingdom became a welfare state. Under this system, the government of the country took responsibility for the well-being of all its citizens. New programs aimed at protecting people "from the cradle to the grave" were established. The most far-reaching program was the National Health Service. The government provides free medical care to all British citizens.

Today some people say the health service is becoming too expensive. Others say that health care is worth the cost.

Margaret Thatcher became the first woman prime minister of Great Britain in 1979 and remained prime minister until 1990.

A LONG TRADITION

As you have seen, government in the British Isles is a complex system that tries to balance ancient traditions with modern concerns for the individual. The British are very proud of their government. One observer has noted:

The typical Englishman believes that his government is incomparably the best in the world. . . . He does not, of course, always agree with the course of policy pursued . . . but he is certain that the general form of government is well-nigh perfect.

 Check Your Reading

1. How has the role of the British monarch changed over the years?
2. Why is the House of Commons more powerful than the House of Lords?
3. Why is the British government called a constitutional monarchy?
4. **THINKING SKILL:** Compare and contrast the governments of Great Britain and the United States.

Arts and Recreation

READ TO LEARN

 Key People

William Shakespeare

 Read Aloud

It is late afternoon on a hot summer's day. On the village green in the center of town several people dressed in white pants and shirts are playing a game called cricket. Now and then spectators applaud or call out, "well played!" Soon it will be time for a tea break. After tea the two teams will return to the field and finish the game.

You have read that the British came up with many new ideas about government. But did you also know that they have had a great effect on the games played and the books read around the world?

 Read for Purpose

1. **WHAT YOU KNOW:** What sports are popular in the United States?
2. **WHAT YOU WILL LEARN:** What are the literary and sporting traditions of the British Isles?

SPORTS

Cricket is just one of many sports enjoyed in the British Isles. The British people believe that good sportsmanship is important in all sports. A famous poem expresses this attitude:

For when the one Great Scorer comes
To write against your name.
He marks not that you won or lost,
But how you played the game.

Soccer, which is called "football" in the British Isles, is the most popular British spectator sport. It was invented in England and is enjoyed today in countries from Europe to South America.

Different sports are popular in different parts of the British Isles. In Scotland, for example, many people love to play golf. The game was invented there, and players all over the world follow the rules estab-lished by the Royal and Ancient Golf Club of St. Andrews in Scotland.

LITERARY TRADITIONS

Assassination, countless, gloomy, and *laughable*—do you know what these words have in common? All of them, and many more, were invented by the great English playwright **William Shakespeare** Whether or not you have yet read any of Shakespeare's plays, you are probably familiar with several characters in his plays. Do you know the sad stories of Romeo and Juliet, Hamlet, King Lear, and Macbeth?

English writers created many of the world's first novels. The fame of novelists and poets like Charlotte Brontë, Elizabeth Barrett Browning, Charles Dickens, and Thomas Hardy has spread around the

212

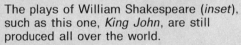
The plays of William Shakespeare (*inset*), such as this one, *King John*, are still produced all over the world.

world. Ireland has produced such giants as the poet William Butler Yeats and the novelist James Joyce. The best-known Welsh poet of recent times is Dylan Thomas. And Scots like to memorize and recite the poems of the writer, Robert Burns.

THE INFLUENCE OF THE BRITISH

Although Great Britain and Ireland are small in size, the people living there have had a huge impact on the rest of the world. In addition to soccer and cricket, Britain has given the world many great works of literature. Britain also gave the world the English language. English is the main language of about 400 million people all over the world, and a second language for 600 million more. As you read the rest of this book, remember that it is written in English because of the wide influence of the people of the British Isles.

 Check Your Reading

1. Name some of the major writers who came from the British Isles.
2. Name three sports that are enjoyed by people in Great Britain and Ireland.
3. List two examples of the influence British literature and sports have had on the rest of the world.
4. **THINKING SKILL:** Is the following statement a fact or an opinion? Explain your answer. "The British [are] sport-mad. Whatever else may be going on in the world . . . [they] will prefer both to talk and to think about sport."

THE BRITISH ISLES: CULTURAL GEOGRAPHY

 **PEOPLE**

- First People: Celts

- Anglo-Saxons invaded from northern Europe
- 1066: Norman invasion: William the Conqueror
- Today: many immigrants from Asia, West Indies, and Africa

Ireland
NORTHERN IRELAND
REPUBLIC
⊛ Dublin
OF IRELAND
Shannon
Channel

- Northern Ireland: constant conflict during modern period

ECONOMY

- Industrial Revolution: made Britain world economic leader
- Mixed economy: private enterprise and government-run businesses

- 1960s: oil and natural gas discovered in North Sea

- Farming: small farms in Ireland, large farms in England

GOVERNMENT

- Parliamentary democracy and constitutional monarchy
- Parliament: House of Lords and House of Commons

- British influence: their form of democracy has spread all over the world
- Welfare state: government takes great responsibility for well-being of citizens

ARTS AND RECREATION

- Sports: cricket, rugby, and soccer

- Great literary tradition: William Shakespeare, Charlotte Brontë, Elizabeth Barrett Browning, Charles Dickens, and many more

IDEAS TO REMEMBER

- The people of the British Isles are a complex mixture of peoples and cultures.
- Though Great Britain was once an industrial leader, today the country faces economic problems.
- The government of Great Britain provides for both a parliamentary democracy and a constitutional monarchy; the Republic of Ireland has a parliamentary democracy.
- Arts and sports that originated in Great Britain are popular the world over.

REVIEWING VOCABULARY

Industrial Revolution   nationalize
Magna Carta   welfare state
mixed economy

Number a sheet of paper from 1 to 5. Beside each number write the word or term from the list above that best completes each sentence.

1. Because it set limits on royal power, the ____ became one of the greatest political documents of all time.
2. A ____ has both government-owned and privately owned businesses.
3. In a ____ the government takes responsibility for the well-being of its citizens by providing free health care and other services.
4. During the ____ machines began to be used to do many jobs that had once been done by hand.
5. To take government control of a business is to ____ it.

REVIEWING FACTS

1. Which two nations make up the British Isles?
2. Which body of water separates the British Isles from the European mainland?
3. Which powerful group conquered England in A.D. 1066? Who was its leader?
4. Which two religious groups are involved in the conflict in Northern Ireland?
5. What is a mixed economy? How has Great Britain changed its economy in recent years?
6. Why must Britain import thousands of tons of food each year?
7. How does a constitutional monarchy limit the power of a king or queen?
8. What are the main functions of the monarch in present-day Great Britain?
9. Describe the two houses of the British Parliament.
10. Which two sports now popular worldwide began in Great Britain?

WRITING ABOUT MAIN IDEAS

1. **Writing an Essay:** The quotation by a British writer at the beginning of the chapter suggests that Great Britain was "the America of Europe." Write an essay expressing agreement or disagreement with the writer's suggestion.
2. **Writing a Poem:** Write a poem about some aspect of England that you have read about or seen in an illustration.
3. **Writing About Perspectives:** Imagine that you live in Great Britain. Write a paragraph telling five things that make your country a place in which you are glad to live.

BUILDING SKILLS: READING A WORLD TIME ZONE MAP

1. If you are traveling, by how many hours should you adjust your watch for each time zone you cross?
2. What happens when you cross the International Date Line?
3. If you cross the International Date Line from east to west on a Sunday, what day does it become?
4. Why is it helpful to understand world time zones?

CHAPTER 10

FRANCE AND THE LOW COUNTRIES

FOCUS

Both as individuals and as a nation the French like to be the best and first in everything.

These words from a book about France sum up how the French take pride in themselves and in their approach to life. This pride is typical among many of the residents of France and the Low Countries.

The People

READ TO LEARN

Key Vocabulary

guest worker

Key Places

Belgium
the Netherlands
Luxembourg

Read Aloud

Every yard of Europe has, at one time or another, belonged to some other nation, race, or clan; every foot has been fought for, given, or stolen.

The words above are especially true of France and the Low Countries. For thousands of years, other Europeans have envied these lands along the Atlantic Coast. In this lesson you will read how different groups of people have lived and worked in France and the Low Countries.

Read for Purpose

1. **WHAT YOU KNOW:** What are the Low Countries?
2. **WHAT YOU WILL LEARN:** Which groups of people have settled in France and the Low Countries?

AN ATTRACTIVE LAND

Can you guess the reason Belgium, the Netherlands, and Luxembourg are called the Low Countries? Their land is among the lowest-lying in all of Europe. For thousands of years, invading armies were attracted to these fertile lowlands. They were also attracted to the wide, navigable rivers and to the long flat coastlines that provided natural ports for trade. For these reasons, France and the Low Countries have been a crossroads of people for many centuries.

CELTS, FRANKS, AND OTHERS

On the walls of a cave at Lascaux, France, wonderful pictures show prehis-toric animals. Stone Age hunters painted them about 20,000 years ago. Thousands of years later, new groups moved in from the north and south. Among them were the Celts, whom you read about in Chapter 9. In France one group of Celts were known as the Gauls. They called the land that they settled Gaul.

The Romans also took an interest in France, just as they did in Great Britain. In 58 B.C. Julius Caesar led a powerful Roman army into Gaul. After seven years of fighting, his soldiers conquered part of what is now France and the Low Countries.

Roman colonists spread their language— Latin — throughout much of southern

FRANCE AND THE LOW COUNTRIES: Political

⚝ National capital   • Other city   ■ Point of interest

MAP SKILL: What body of water is located off the coast of Belgium and The Netherlands?

like Notre Dame in Paris were built by hand, stone by stone.

Although the Franks ruled France for more than 400 years, they constantly had to fight off invaders from all sides. In the A.D. 800s, for example, ships from Scandinavia filled with warriors called the Vikings attacked settlements on the North Atlantic coast. Fortresses had to be built all over France to keep out invaders like the Vikings.

The Vikings were not the last people to invade France and the Low Countries. But until the 1900s no other group settled there in very large numbers. From the ninth century until the middle of the twentieth, the people of France and the Low Countries developed their own cultures.

FRANCE: A NATION OF INDIVIDUALISTS

Today each part of France has its own individual groups. In Bordeaux (bôr dō′), for example, some family names sound English. This is due to the fact that for 300 years Bordeaux was ruled by the English. Find the Bordeaux region on the map on this page.

People living in the rugged slopes of the Pyrenees Mountains speak Basque, a language unrelated to any other tongue. And the Bretons of Brittany came to France from across the English Channel. Many still speak an ancient Celtic language similar to languages in Wales and Ireland.

In recent years immigrants from many lands have added to France's diversity. Some newcomers, called **guest workers**, have moved to France in search of work. They come mostly from Southern Europe. Usually they cannot become citizens.

Another group of immigrants left Algeria and Morocco to live in France. These North African lands had been under French control for many years. After

Europe. But people in Gaul had trouble pronouncing the Latin words correctly. They added new terms and phrases to the language until they created a brand new one, which became known as French.

As the power of the Romans weakened, warlike groups swept across many parts of Europe. One group, called the Frisians, conquered the Celts of the Netherlands. Another group called the Franks took control of what is today Belgium.

Soon, the kingdom of the Franks spread southward from Belgium. This kingdom became known as France. Under the powerful ruler Charlemagne, France became a Roman Catholic country. Great cathedrals

The Eiffel Tower (*right*) is one of the popular landmarks of Paris, France. People in Paris enjoy gathering at sidewalk cafés (*left*).

Morocco became independent in 1956 and Algeria won its independence in 1962, thousands of French colonists from these countries poured into France. Like almost everyone else in the country, these newcomers knew how to speak French. And in France, that is essential.

THE FRENCH LANGUAGE

The French consider their language to be a national treasure. In 1635 King Louis XIII of France founded the French Academy to write a dictionary of *bon usage* (good and proper use). To this day the Academy is still busy revising definitions and deciding on the correct use of the French language. Every three months the Academy publishes a list of new errors that creep into common use.

Today the French government tries to preserve the purity of the French language by preventing American phrases from being used. Road signs, menus, and other printed materials are constantly examined to root out French words that have been taken over from American phrases. Businesses can be fined for using terms like *le jogging* or *le compact disc.*

Today at least 122 million people speak French. It is one of the official languages of Belgium, Luxembourg, Switzerland, Canada, and 20 other countries. It is one of the six official languages of the United Nations.

THE LOWLANDERS

If language is the connecting thread in French life, it is the dividing wedge in nearby Belgium. Unlike Canada, which is a bilingual nation, Belgium is divided into language areas. In the southern part of Belgium are the Walloons. They speak French, and French is the official language of their area, called Wallonia. In the

219

Visiting a traditional cheese market, such as this one in the Netherlands, is just one popular activity in the Low Countries.

north are the Flemings, who speak a form of Dutch known as Flemish. Dutch is the official language of this area, but many Flemings are bilingual. A small group of Belgians near the southeastern border speak German. The capital city of Belgium, Brussels, is bilingual.

Family ties are strong among the people of Belgium. Many Belgians rarely travel far from home. They prefer to spend time with their families than to travel overseas or to other European countries.

The people of the Netherlands do not have the language divisions that the Belgians do. But the Dutch have other problems. They live in a very crowded country. With more than 900 people per square mile (347.5 people per sq km), the Netherlands is one of the most densely populated countries in Western Europe.

A RICH LAND

The people who settled in France and the Low Countries found a rich land. As you have read, there was fertile soil on the coastal plain. The climate was mild most of the year. And navigable rivers made the area easy to reach.

For thousands of years, migrating groups of people and attacking armies crisscrossed France and the Low Countries. Over the years the Celts, Gauls, Romans, and Vikings who lived here formed the different people of this region. Today immigrants from southern Europe and North Africa come to live and work in this prosperous part of the world.

 Check Your Reading

1. Which groups of people have invaded France and the Low Countries in the past?
2. How was the French language created? How does it unite the people of France?
3. Which languages are commonly spoken in Belgium?
4. **THINKING SKILL:** How are the people of Belgium and France similar? How are they different?

The Economy

READ TO LEARN

Key Vocabulary

vineyard   polder
canal   European Community
dike

Read Aloud

France and the Low Countries have highly developed economies. They produce everything from tulips to supersonic jets. In this lesson you will read how these countries, individually and in cooperation with the rest of Western Europe, work to keep their economies strong.

Read for Purpose

1. **WHAT YOU KNOW:** What is a mixed economy?
2. **WHAT YOU WILL LEARN:** What makes the economies of France and the Low Countries strong?

FOOD AND FARMING PATTERNS

Although today less than 8 percent of the working people in France and the Low Countries are farmers, the countrysides are dotted with well-tended and highly productive farms. Most are small, family-owned businesses.

You might not think of flowers as a farm product, but the Dutch do. Dutch flowers and bulbs are exported all over the world. One of the world's largest flower markets is held at Aalsmeer, near Amsterdam. Aided by computers, farmers sell more than 12 million flowers and 1 million houseplants every day.

In France family farms often specialize in just one product. A small farm might grow only tiny green beans picked while they are young and tender. Or it might raise chickens for only the most demanding French chefs. In Normandy farmers are famous for their apples and pork. And in Bordeaux, hundreds of **vineyards** (vin' yərdz) produce grapes for some of the finest wines in the world. A vineyard is an area used for growing grapes.

INDUSTRIAL POWER

Farming is only one small part of the economies of France and the Low Countries. These countries also have advanced technological industries.

Many French industries specialize in finely crafted goods, while others produce complicated electronic equipment. Several factories in southern France produce satellites, missiles, and sophisticated weapons. The Concorde jet is assembled in the French city of Toulouse.

The Netherlands has few mineral resources. So the Dutch have to import many resources, such as iron ore, from other countries. Later, skilled Dutch workers turn these resources into everything from ships, airplanes and trucks, to toys.

THE NETHERLANDS: Reclaimed Land

- Land reclaimed from the sea
- Land being reclaimed from the sea
- Canal
- ⊛ National capital
- • Other city
- ∕ Dam

SERVICES

Imagine for a moment that you are lucky enough to be on vacation in France. One day you might visit the Riviera and enjoy its warm, sandy beaches. Or you might decide to go to Paris and wander through its ancient cathedrals and magnificent art museums. Or perhaps you'll spend an afternoon just relaxing in an outdoor café. France, as its citizens are proud to tell you, is a country "with everything."

Service industries, such as tourism, banking, and shipping, also play an important part in the economies of the Low Countries. For example, the city of Rotterdam, in the Netherlands, is the world's busiest port. Another Dutch city, Amsterdam, is an international banking center.

TRADE AND TRANSPORTATION

France and the Low Countries are fortunate in having excellent transportation networks. There are many roads, railroads, and airports. In addition, wide, navigable rivers flow from the heart of Western Europe, through the Low Countries, into the North Sea. For hundreds of years, these rivers have provided the region with great trade and transportation advantages.

The Dutch landscape is covered by a network of waterways. Where rivers did not connect people to each other, people built **canals**. A canal is a waterway that has been dug for boat travel. Unlike rivers, canals can be built to flow wherever people want them to.

But if water has been a friend to the Netherlands, it has also been a foe. For a thousand years the Dutch have had to invent ways to protect their land from the sea. First they built huge walls called **dikes** to keep the water back. Then they pumped out the sea water from inside the dikes, and used canals to drain the water from the low ground back into the North Sea. Look at the map above. It shows the lowland areas that have been reclaimed from the sea. They are called **polders**. "God created the earth," goes an old saying, "but the Dutch created Holland."

THE COMMON MARKET

Western Europe, including France and the Low Countries, has been a center of world trade for hundreds of years. However, in the past the nations of this region often set up trade barriers against each other. They passed tariffs, or taxes on imports, to protect their own industries. Tariffs raise the price of imported goods, so people will buy fewer of them.

After World War II, some countries of Western Europe formed the European Economic Community to promote free trade and link transportation routes among themselves. That organization later became part of the European Community, or EC. The members of the EC, also called the Common Market, are listed on the chart on this page.

The Common Market changed the way France, the Low Countries, and the rest of Western Europe did business. It ended most trade barriers so that people and goods could move freely among its nations.

In the coming years the Common Market will change even more. Member countries want to join together economically, so they work together much as the 50 states of the United States now do. Eventually, plans are to have one kind of currency (money) for all member countries and one European banking system, perhaps by the year 2000. Western Europeans hope that working together will make their region a world economic power in the years to come.

STRONG ECONOMIES

France and the Low Countries have developed economies that produce a wide variety of farm products and manufactured goods. Services play an important economic role in these countries.

The creation of the Common Market has ended most trade barriers among the 12 members of the European Community. This

THE EUROPEAN COMMUNITY (COMMON MARKET)

Country	Currency	Year Joined
Belgium	Franc	1958
Denmark	Krone	1973
France	Franc	1958
Great Britain	Pound	1973
Greece	Drachma	1981
Ireland	Pound	1973
Italy	Lira	1958
Luxembourg	Franc	1958
The Netherlands	Guilder	1958
Portugal	Escudo	1986
Spain	Peseta	1986
Germany	Mark	1958

CHART SKILL: Someday the countries of the European Community may all use the same currency. Who are the two newest members of the Common Market?

links France and the Low Countries more closely with the rest of Western Europe.

Check Your Reading

1. How would you describe farming in France?
2. What have the Dutch done to reclaim their land from the sea?
3. Why was the Common Market created?
4. **THINKING SKILL:** How has the geography of France and the Low Countries influenced the economies of the countries of this area?

223

Using Maps at Different Scales

Key Vocabulary

small-scale map
large-scale map

As you know, maps can be used to show the world in many different ways. They can be used to show areas as large as the whole world or areas as small as a city block.

One important way in which maps differ is in scale. As you have seen, most of the maps in this book have a scale of miles and kilometers. The scale for a particular map tells how distance shown on that map translates into actual distance on the earth.

Maps can be drawn to many different scales. When mapmakers want to show a large area in a small space, they draw a **small-scale map**. For example, suppose you wanted to know how far Marseilles is from Paris. You would look on a small-scale map, such as **Map A**, that shows many of the important cities in France.

Small-scale Maps

Map A will help you understand what the term *small-scale map* means. On small-scale maps a very small unit of

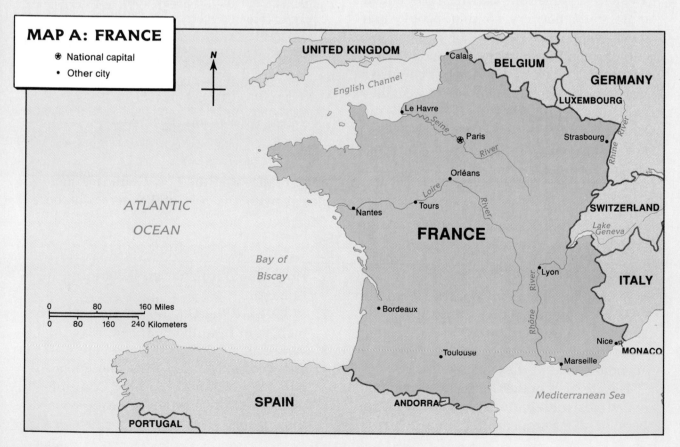

MAP A: FRANCE

⊛ National capital
• Other city

UNITED KINGDOM
Calais
BELGIUM
GERMANY
LUXEMBOURG
English Channel
Le Havre
Seine
Paris
Strasbourg
Rhine River
River
Orléans
Loire
SWITZERLAND
Nantes
Tours
River
Lake Geneva
ATLANTIC
OCEAN
FRANCE
Bay of
Biscay
Rhône River
Lyon
ITALY
Bordeaux
0   80   160 Miles
0   80   160   240 Kilometers
Toulouse
Nice
MONACO
Marseille
SPAIN
ANDORRA
Mediterranean Sea
PORTUGAL

N

measure, such as 1 inch (2.54 cm), stands for a large distance, such as 500 miles (805 km). Small-scale maps usually show large areas in a fairly small space.

Looking at a small-scale map can be very helpful when you are studying about all the countries of Western Europe. **Map A** shows you the size and location of France in relation to the countries it borders. France is larger than any of the countries it borders. The map shows the location of major rivers and important cities in France.

Large-scale Maps

Suppose that you wanted more detailed information about a city, such as Paris, in France. This type of information can be shown on a large-scale map, such as **Map B** on this page. Compare the information shown on **Map A** with that shown on **Map B**. Notice the details about Paris that are found on **Map B**. For example, the map shows the names and locations of many streets in Paris. It also shows the location of some important points of interest, such as Notre Dame, the Louvre, and the Eiffel Tower.

Paris appears larger on **Map B** than it does on **Map A** because on a large-scale map, a unit of measure stands for a smaller distance than it does on a small-scale map. For example, on **Map B**, 1 inch (2.54 km) stands for 1.25 miles (2 km). Notice that the map of Paris is only about 3.75 miles (6 km) across, while the map of France is about 560 miles (900 km) across. Remember that even though maps are often drawn to different scales, real distances do not change.

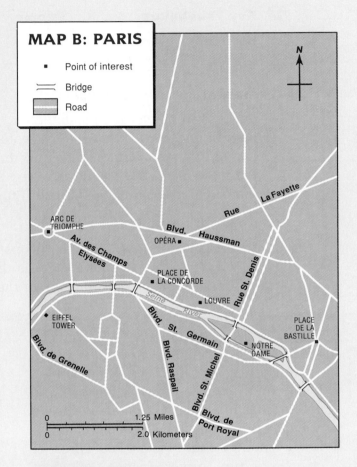

Reviewing the Skill

1. Which map, **Map A** or **Map B**, shows more details about Paris?
2. Which map, **Map A** or **Map B**, covers a larger area?
3. Which map, **Map A** or **Map B**, is drawn to a larger scale?
4. Look at the map on page 224. What river flows northwest into Le Havre? Now look at the map on this page. What river flows through the center of Paris?
5. How can using maps drawn to different scales be useful?

The Government

READ TO LEARN

Key Vocabulary

premier

Key People

Charles de Gaulle

Read Aloud

Liberté! Égalité! Fraternité!

These three words, translated as "Liberty! Equality! Fraternity!" were the rallying cry of the French Revolution in 1789. That revolution marked the end of monarchy and the start of republican government in France. Since 1789 the ideas of the French Revolution have spread to almost every country in Western Europe.

Read for Purpose

1. **WHAT YOU KNOW:** What is a constitutional monarchy?
2. **WHAT YOU WILL LEARN:** What is the structure of the government of France? Of the governments of the Low Countries?

GOVERNING FRANCE

France has long had the reputation of being a difficult nation to govern. The country has many individual areas that do not always act together. "How can you govern a country that makes 265 kinds of cheeses?" the former French President Charles de Gaulle once joked.

The government of France has changed many times since the French Revolution. The country has been governed by kings, emperors, presidents, and elected national assemblies.

Unlike the United States, France has had several constitutions. "How can you live with the same old constitution for two centuries?" one French politician asked an American. "Don't you think it's good to freshen up now and then?"

The current French constitution, which was adopted in 1958, calls for a government named the Fifth Republic. The Fifth Republic has a strong president who is elected by the people for a seven-year term. The president makes the important decisions on matters of defense and foreign affairs. He or she has the authority to dismiss the elected National Assembly, thus bringing about new elections. The president also names the prime minister, who heads the day-to-day activities of the government. In France the prime minister is called the premier.

Why does the Fifth Republic give the president so much power? In the first four republics, the National Assembly argued so much that little was accomplished. Now the French support the idea of a strong national leader.

THREE MONARCHIES

Like Great Britain, the Netherlands, Belgium, and Luxembourg are constitutional monarchies. The head of state inherits his or her throne. King Baudouin of Belgium, Grand Duke Jean of Luxembourg, and Queen Beatrix of the Netherlands are mostly ceremonial rulers. Like Queen Elizabeth of Britain, they are symbols of their nations as a whole.

The people of the Low Countries treat their monarchs more casually than the British do. Dutch monarchs, for example, are not crowned. To the Dutch, crowns symbolize too much power. Members of the Dutch royal family live much like other people. They ride around town on bicycles just as everybody else does.

In each of the Low Countries, a two-house legislature not only passes laws but also makes most of the important decisions. In Belgium, for example, the king can appoint officials, declare war, and make treaties. But all of these actions must be approved by the Parliament.

REPRESENTATIVE GOVERNMENTS

France and the Low Countries all have representative governments. But, as you have read, there are some important differences in these governments. France's Fifth Republic gives wide powers to the president. The three Low Countries are all constitutional monarchies, and they have elected legislatures.

Check Your Reading

1. What do the governments of the Low Countries have in common?
2. How many republics has France had since the French Revolution?
3. How are the governments of France and the Low Countries similar?
4. **THINKING SKILL:** What alternatives did the people of France have to consider in deciding how much power to give their president?

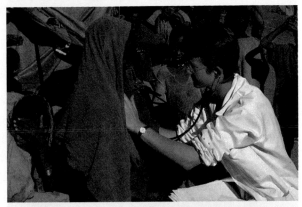

DOCTORS WITHOUT BORDERS

Every year disasters, such as earthquakes, hurricanes, and floods, strike all over the world. At such times huge numbers of people require immediate medical care. In 1971 five French medical doctors decided to form an organization to respond to emergencies throughout the world. Today when disasters strike, the group they formed, *Médecins Sans Frontières* (MSF), responds. *Médecins Sans Frontières* means "Doctors Without Borders."

When natural disasters like floods and volcanoes occur, the volunteers of MSF must be ready at a moment's notice. Their mission is to get to disaster scenes fast in order to save lives. They set up clinics, distribute medicines, and provide clean drinking water. The volunteers of MSF have brought their medical skills to people in more than 80 countries.

Depending upon the particular situation, MSF teams may live in an area for a few days, for several months, or for years at a time. Some of the teams build hospitals, some train doctors, and some work at controlling the spread of a disease.

The volunteers of MSF treat all people regardless of race, religion, or politics, and they do so free of charge. Their sole commitment is to save lives.

Arts and Recreation

READ TO LEARN

Key Vocabulary

Impressionism
Tour de France

Key People

Jan van Eyck
Pieter Brueghel
Vincent van Gogh
Claude Monet
Edgar Degas

Read Aloud

Other cities are cities. Paris is a world.

This is what Emperor Charles V of France said about his country's capital city. In Paris and throughout France and the Low Countries, there is much to see and do. For thousands of years, the people of France and the Low Countries have had the time and wealth to create and support great works of art.

Read for Purpose

1. **WHAT YOU KNOW:** What kinds of sports are popular in the British Isles?
2. **WHAT YOU WILL LEARN:** Which arts and sports have developed in France and the Low Countries?

A RICH HERITAGE OF THE ARTS

As Great Britain is famous for its writers and playwrights, so France and the Low Countries are well known for their many fine painters.

From the 1300s to the 1600s, Europe produced many great painters known as the Old Masters. Several of these came from Flanders, an area in western Belgium. Jan van Eyck (yän' van īk') helped invent new ways to show light in paintings. Today Belgians looking at the paintings of Pieter Brueghel (pē' tər broi' gəl) can see how their ancestors lived 400 years in the past.

A famous Dutch painter, Vincent van Gogh (van gō), worked during the late 1800s. Van Gogh sold only one painting in his lifetime. But artistic tastes change. In 1988 a painting of sunflowers by Van Gogh sold for almost $40 million.

Van Gogh worked for a while in Paris, the center of the art world during the late nineteenth century. In this period, a style of painting known as Impressionism was developed by French artists like Claude Monet (mō nā') and Edgar Degas (dā gä'). Impressionists did not paint scenes exactly as they appeared. They tried to capture the feeling of a place in a moment of time. The light-filled paintings of the Impressionists are among the world's most popular works of art.

Horse races and the sporting life of Western Europe were popular subjects with Impressionist painter Edgar Degas.

BICYCLING AND OTHER SPORTS

The people of France and the Low Countries share a passion for bicycling. For three weeks every summer they are glued to their television sets to watch the famous Tour de France, a 2,500-mile (4,023-km) bicycle race that winds around the perimeter of France.

The colored jerseys of racers on the Tour de France help enthusiastic fans identify them. For example, the first-place cyclist on each day wears a yellow jersey. The rider who goes fastest on sprints up mountains gets to wear a polka-dotted shirt.

Eddy Merckx of Belgium has won the Tour de France five times. He says cycling is part of the Belgian way of life. "It would be very difficult to find a town or village here that doesn't have a bike race."

In France and the Low Countries, soccer is also a favorite sport—unless it happens to be ski season. Then people head for the Alps. Some ski runs in the Alps are so long that skiers need to ride up the mountain only once or twice a day.

ARTS AND SPORTS

France and the Low Countries have rich cultural traditions. As you have read, these countries have produced many great painters. Sports are also very popular. "I'm passionate about various kinds of sports," said one French citizen. "To keep fit, yes, but also because I enjoy the competition. That's the French way."

 Check Your Reading

1. What is Impressionism? How would you describe this style of painting?
2. What is the Tour de France?
3. Which sports are popular in France and the Low Countries?
4. THINKING SKILL: Classify the painters mentioned in this lesson into these two groups: The Old Masters and The Impressionists.

229

FRANCE AND THE LOW COUNTRIES: CULTURAL GEOGRAPHY

PEOPLE

- Early settlers and conquerors: Celts, Gauls, Romans, Franks
- Guest workers: have come to France and Low Countries to work

- Language: ties French people together
- Belgium: divided into Walloons and Flemings

ECONOMY

- Highly developed economies

- Farming: small-scale, but highly productive

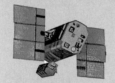

- Industry: highly developed, advanced technology
- Services: tourism, banking and shipping important in Low Countries
- European Community: helps link France and Low Countries with rest of Western Europe

GOVERNMENT

- Fifth Republic: provides for a strong president to govern France
- Low Countries: three constitutional monarchies

ARTS AND RECREATION

Painters:
a) Belgian: Jan van Eyck, Pieter Brueghel
b) Dutch: Vincent van Gogh
c) French Impressionism: Edgar Degas, Claude Monet

- Tour de France: popular bike race in France

IDEAS TO REMEMBER

- The people of France and the Low Countries are a mixture of Celts, Gauls, Romans, Franks, and other groups who settled in the area.
- France and the Low Countries have industrial economies and are linked to the rest of Western Europe by the European Community.
- France and the Low Countries all have representative governments, but France is a republic and the Low Countries are constitutional monarchies.
- The area is characterized by a rich artistic heritage (particularly painting) and a great interest in competitive sports such as bicycle racing.

REVIEWING VOCABULARY

Each of the following statements contains an underlined vocabulary word or term. Number a sheet of paper from 1 to 10. Beside each number write whether each of the following statements is true or false. If the statement is true, write "true." If it is false, rewrite the sentence using the vocabulary word or term correctly.

1. A polder is an area reclaimed from the sea so that it can be used as land for farming.
2. A vineyard is a farm where flowers grow on vines.
3. The Dutch have built and maintained dikes for hundreds of years in order to protect their land from the sea.
4. Like the powers of the British monarch, the powers of the French premier are limited to ceremonial and symbolic functions.
5. A vineyard is a place for growing grapes.
6. Canals, or waterways, are used to transport goods and people.
7. Guest workers are servants, maids, and cooks employed only by wealthy families in France.
8. The European Community was established to promote free trade and to link transportation routes among its member countries.
9. The Tour de France is a large-scale tourist group for visitors to France from many countries.
10. Impressionism is a style of painting in which objects are painted realistically, to look exactly as they do in real life.

REVIEWING FACTS

1. What are the names of the three Low Countries?
2. Why have the Low Countries and France attracted invaders throughout their history?
3. Why does the French constitution allow for a strong president with broad powers?
4. Who were the Old Masters?
5. Which city was the center of the art world in the late nineteenth century?

WRITING ABOUT MAIN IDEAS

1. **Writing an Explanation:** The Netherlands—a tiny, densely populated country with few natural resources—has one of the world's highest standards of living. Write a paragraph explaining why.
2. **Writing About Perspectives:** Imagine that you live in one of the Low Countries. Write a letter to the editor of your local newspaper expressing your opinion on whether Europe should be unified. Give reasons for your opinion.

BUILDING SKILLS: USING MAPS OF DIFFERENT SCALES

1. What are the differences between large-scale maps and small-scale maps?
2. Look at the map on page 225. How many miles does 1 inch represent on the map?
3. Which map on pages 224–225 shows a larger area—Map A or Map B?
4. Which map, A or B, uses a larger scale?
5. How can using maps of different scales be helpful?

231

CENTRAL EUROPE

FOCUS

*This feat of Tell, the archer, will be told
While yonder mountains stand upon their base.*

That was how the German poet Johann Friedrich von Schiller described the skill and courage of the legendary Swiss patriot William Tell. Throughout their history the Swiss, Germans, and Austrians have used their skill and courage to develop their countries. In this chapter you will read about these people and their countries that make up Central Europe.

The People

READ TO LEARN

Key Vocabulary

reunification
dialect
Holocaust

Key People

Martin Luther

Key Places

Germany   Alps
Switzerland   Berlin
Austria   Vienna

Read Aloud

It is a very positive thing. . . . It overcomes a division that never represented the will of the people.

These words were spoken in 1990 by Peter Perbandt, a German businessperson who had fled from East Berlin four years before. He was talking about the end of a division that for 45 years had split Germany into two countries. In this lesson you will read about the people of Germany. You will learn how their country was split up and then brought together again. You will also read about the people of the two other countries—Austria and Switzerland—that together with Germany make up Central Europe.

Read for Purpose

1. **WHAT YOU KNOW:** How does language unify the people of France?
2. **WHAT YOU WILL LEARN:** What roles do language and religion play in unifying the people of Central Europe?

IN THE CENTER OF EUROPE

Central Europe is made up of Germany, Switzerland, Austria, and Liechtenstein. Germany is the largest country in Central Europe. It stretches from the shores of the North Sea south to the snow-covered Bavarian Alps. Many major rivers flow through Central Europe, but Germany is the only country with a coastline.

DIVIDED GERMANY

People have lived in present-day Germany for at least 50,000 years. Around 500 B.C. groups of Celtic people settled in Germany's forests and plains. About 500 years later, the Romans arrived. They built roads and fortresses and introduced their system of law. Hundreds of years after that the Huns, groups of warriors on horses, made their way from Asia into Germany.

Germany had more than 1,800 separate kingdoms whose people shared one language. In 1871 it finally became one nation.

Then, in 1945, after its defeat in World War II, Germany was divided again. The western part was controlled by Great Britain, France, and the United States. In 1949 it became the Federal Republic of Germany, known as West Germany. The same year, the eastern part, controlled by the

233

CENTRAL EUROPE: Political

⊛ National capital   • Other city

MAP SKILL: Central Europe includes Germany, Austria, Liechtenstein, and Switzerland. On which river is the capital of Austria located?

man government built a huge wall to separate East and West Berlin. Many Germans longed for the Berlin Wall to topple and the barriers to come down so they would once again live in one country. Many people in East Germany tried to flee to West Germany by getting past the Berlin Wall and other barriers.

A REUNITED COUNTRY

By 1989 many people began to find new ways to get out of communist countries including East Germany. As a new spirit of freedom and democracy spread across Europe, the Soviet Union could no longer control East Germany. East Germans overthrew the Soviet-controlled government. Then, with the help of West Germans, they began to tear down the Berlin Wall. Germany was united again.

On October 3, 1990, 1 million people poured into Alexanderplatz, the main square of East Berlin. They came to celebrate **reunification** [rē ū nə fi kā′ shən], being united again. Look at the map on this page to see the present borders of Germany along with its Central European neighbors, Austria and Switzerland.

Reunification was a time for family reunions. Here is an account of one such reunion.

Over a 12-year period, three Grabowski children, a son and two daughters, had fled to the West. Their daughters, they explained, had risked arrest and prison by hiding illegally in the trunks of automobiles that carried them across the armed checkpoints that vanished with the Berlin Wall.

"Now they can visit us freely, we can visit them," Mr. Grabowski said.

LANGUAGE AND DIALECTS

People in Germany share the German language. So do most people in Switzerland and Austria. Yet not everyone who

Soviet Union, became the German Democratic Republic, or East Germany. Barriers were built between the two areas.

The city of **Berlin**, the traditional capital of Germany, was also divided. West Berlin became part of West Germany, and East Berlin became part of East Germany.

West Germany was encouraged to become a democracy. East Germany and other countries of Eastern Europe became communist countries under the control of the Soviet Union. About 3 million people emigrated from East Germany to West Germany through Berlin.

In 1961, to keep people from moving to the west, the Soviet-controlled East Ger-

speaks German sounds the same. The official language of Germany is called High German, and all German schoolchildren learn to read and write High German. But there are many dialects, or local variations, of the language.

"Up here we have our own dialect, which we often use when we're with friends or members of the family," explains Hanna Bumann, a German who lives near the Baltic Sea. "It's almost totally different from standard [High] German."

German is also Austria's official language. But Switzerland has four national languages. About 70 percent of Swiss citizens speak German. Another 20 percent speak French. The language of the Swiss city Ticino (ti chē' nō), near Lake Lugano, is Italian. Some Swiss speak Romansh (rō mänsh'). This language comes from Latin. Despite differences in their languages, the Swiss people remain united.

RELIGION

Most Central Europeans practice some branch of Christianity. In Austria, 85 percent of the people are Roman Catholics. In Germany and Switzerland about half are Roman Catholics, and the other half Protestants.

Protestantism began in Germany in the 1500s after a young priest named Martin Luther "protested" against some actions taken by the Catholic Church. Luther and his followers broke away from the Roman Catholic Church and formed a new branch of Christianity called Protestantism.

Until World War II, many Jews lived in Germany and other countries of Central and Eastern Europe. But Adolf Hitler, the dictator of Germany, had more than 6 million Jewish men, women, and children in these countries put to death. This destruction of nearly half the world's Jewish population is called the Holocaust.

Martin Luther founded the Protestant movement in Germany in the 1500s. Today many people in Germany and throughout Central Europe are Protestants.

CITIES AND OPEN SPACES

Since the end of World War II, most Central Europeans have lived in cities and large towns. Yet huge areas are set aside for parks, farms, and forests. Berlin, the largest city in Central Europe, has over 50 square miles (130 sq km) of parks, forests, and lakes. There are even farms within the city limits.

Most German and Austrian cities were badly damaged in World War II, but many have been rebuilt. The mayor of Lübeck, a German city on the Baltic Sea, is proud that so many historic buildings have survived. "Only as a last resort," he said, "do we knock down a building. Preservation of our rich heritage is always uppermost in our minds."

Vienna's people believe no other city in the world can match this Austrian city for style and elegance. Vienna is the capital and cultural center of Austria. Splendid palaces dating back many hundreds of years are found throughout the city.

FOUR COUNTRIES

Central Europe is made up of Switzerland, Austria, Liechtenstein, and the newly reunited Germany. The German language and the Christian religion unite many people of this area. There are many large forests and farms in Central Europe, but most people live in large cities.

Check Your Reading

1. Which four countries make up Central Europe?
2. How do language and religion help to unite the people of Central Europe?
3. What does reunification mean for the people of Germany?
4. **THINKING SKILL:** What effect might the Alps have had in keeping Switzerland and Austria separate countries?

THE RIGHT LIVELIHOOD AWARD

A NEW Award

Jakob von Uexkull (yä′ küp fôn uk′ skəl) grew up in Hamburg, Germany, but his mother came from Sweden. Each year he and his mother listened to the announcement of the Nobel prizes from Sweden. These prizes honor writers, scientists, and humanitarians from all over the world.

Jakob knew that the Nobel prizes were very important, but he had another idea. He thought that people who try to solve world problems, such as pollution and poverty, should also be honored for their important work.

When he grew up, Jakob sold the stamp collection he had started when he was nine years old. With the money he received he decided to establish The Right Livelihood Awards. Jakob traveled all over the world looking for people who were trying to solve problems, such as cleaning up the environment and educating children.

Now the Right Livelihood Awards are announced in Sweden the day before the Nobel prize ceremonies. Since 1980 Jakob has awarded prizes to people from over 25 countries. The idea he had as a boy is today a reality.

The Economy

READ TO LEARN

Key Vocabulary

standard of living
pollution

Key Places

Ruhr Valley
Basel

Read Aloud

It's very good, very hopeful. . . . Maybe things won't be rosy at first, but the future will be better.

These words were spoken by Doris Bruch (brükh), who lives in a town near Berlin, as she and her family celebrated the reunification of Germany. Although problems lie ahead for Doris and other former East Germans, she is optimistic about the future for her newly united country. Her confidence is common to the people of Central Europe.

Read for Purpose

1. **WHAT YOU KNOW:** What are the four countries of Central Europe?
2. **WHAT YOU WILL LEARN:** How have the countries of Central Europe developed strong economies?

COMMUNISM IN EAST GERMANY

After World War II East Germany built its economy under the system of communism. As you read in Chapter 6, under communism the government controls the entire economy.

Doris Bruch, whose words you just read, lives in Bernau (bûr′ nō). East Germans like Doris worked hard and enjoyed the most advanced economy of communist Eastern Europe. Wages were low, yet Doris could afford many basic goods because the government kept prices low. The East German government also guaranteed everyone a job.

Most East Germans worked in mining, agriculture, and industry. The goods that they made were often of poor quality because many factories in East Germany were old and inefficient.

If Doris had owned a television set, she might have received programs from nearby West Berlin. She would have seen that West Germany's economy had become much more successful than the economy of East Germany.

Few people could have predicted West Germany's growth after World War II. Most factories had been destroyed. Bridges, canals, and roads lay in ruins. Yet, under the economic system of capitalism and with hard work, planning, and efficiency, West Germany was transformed into a prosperous nation within 20 years.

West German factories make a wide variety of products, from cars and computers to chemicals and steel. The farms of West Germany are efficient, often using advanced technology.

237

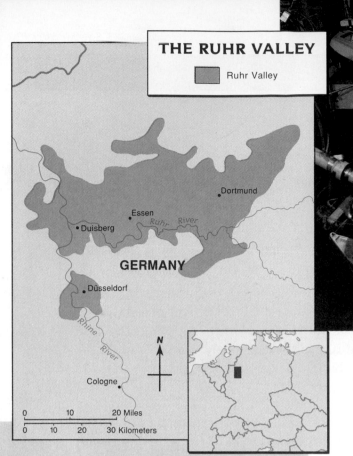

THE RUHR VALLEY

◼ Ruhr Valley

Dortmund

Essen

Ruhr River

• Duisberg

GERMANY

• Düsseldorf

Rhine River

Cologne

N

0   10   20 Miles

0   10   20   30 Kilometers

MAP SKILL: Auto-making is just one of the important industries of the Ruhr Valley. What are some important cities in this area?

The map on this page shows you the main cities along the Ruhr Valley, Europe's biggest industrial center. The Ruhr Valley is crowded with coal and iron mines, oil refineries, chemical plants, and heavy industries.

COMBINING TWO ECONOMIES

Through reunification, East Germany exchanged communism for capitalism. Now the people of what was once East Germany want to improve their lives, but conditions may get worse first.

Economic reunification is expensive for both western and eastern Germany. It will eventually cost Germany billions of dollars to help build the economy in the east. But it has already cost the former East Germany nearly half its jobs. Inefficient fac-

tories have been forced to close. Their goods cannot compete with goods from Western Europe.

SWITZERLAND AND AUSTRIA

Unlike Germany, Switzerland has few natural resources and little arable land. But the Swiss people have the highest standard of living in Europe. A country's standard of living is measured by the goods and services that its people have. A high standard of living offers people good medical care, decent housing, and the chance for an education and a good job.

The Swiss have worked hard for their prosperity. They pride themselves on making high-quality goods that include machinery, tools, and watches.

Tourists arrive to enjoy the majestic scenery or to ski down the snow-covered Swiss Alps. Since tourists are vital to the Swiss economy, the Swiss try hard to make them feel welcome.

Switzerland is a safe place to keep money. People all over the world keep their money in Swiss banks. Banking is an important part of the Swiss economy.

Today many people want to live and work in this prosperous, productive na-

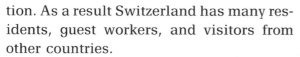
Pollution has caused many problems in Central Europe, from killing fish to damaging outdoor statues.

tion. As a result Switzerland has many residents, guest workers, and visitors from other countries.

Like Switzerland, Austria has little arable land and few natural resources. Austria's massive snow-covered peaks, shimmering blue lakes, and thick green forests also attract many visitors. The income from tourism, along with industries such as steel and machinery, play a key part in Austria's economy.

PROBLEMS AND PROSPECTS

In 1986 a fire in a factory in Basel, Switzerland, sent clouds of foul-smelling smoke over the city. Deadly chemicals poured into the Rhine River. Many fish died. The chemical spill caused problems in areas far beyond Switzerland.

Pollution, or dirty and dangerous elements in the environment, is a serious problem in Central Europe. It is one price the area has paid for its factories. No country in Central Europe remains unaffected by its neighbors' problems. The air and rivers cross national borders. That means that countries need to cooperate to solve pollution problems.

A PROSPEROUS REGION

Central Europe is an industrial region with a high standard of living based on manufacturing, advanced technology, and service industries. While Switzerland and Austria have strong economies, reunited Germany faces economic challenges. Together, these countries must fight common problems such as air and water pollution.

 Check Your Reading

1. How have the countries of Central Europe developed strong economies?
2. What impact did German reunification have on the country's economy?
3. Name three businesses that are important to Switzerland's economy.
4. THINKING SKILL: Before reunification, how was life in East Germany and West Germany similar? How was it different?

The Government

READ TO LEARN

Key Vocabulary

chancellor   neutral

canton

Key Places

Bonn

Geneva

Read Aloud

At the beginning of World War I in 1914, Austria was the center of a huge empire called Austria-Hungary. Germany was a unified nation that stretched from the Low Countries to Russia.

The face of Central Europe has changed greatly since World War I. Today, Austria is a small republic. Germany has recently become a re-united country after having been divided into two countries. As you read this lesson, you will learn how some of these changes came about.

Read for Purpose

1. **WHAT YOU KNOW:** What is a federal system of government?
2. **WHAT YOU WILL LEARN:** What are the structures of the governments of Germany, Austria, and Switzerland?

ONE GERMAN GOVERNMENT

On July 1, 1990, East and West Germany united their economies. Three months later, they also united their governments. They dissolved East Germany's government and kept West Germany's form of government.

Now East Germans will have to relearn how to make choices in electing their leaders. Under communism, they did not have choices when they voted.

The united government of Germany has a two-house national legislature. It is called the Bundestag [bùn′ dəs täk]. German citizens elect representatives to the Bundestag but do not directly elect the heads of the government. Instead the two houses of the Bundestag elect a president as the country's head of state. The president performs ceremonial duties and, with the approval of the Bundestag, appoints a prime minister, called a chancellor. The chancellor is head of government.

Like many other democracies, Germany has a federal system of government. Political power is divided between a central government and 16 states—called *Lander*. The *Lander* have more power than states in the United States.

Before reunification, the Bundestag met in the city of Bonn. After reunification, Germans agreed to move their government to Berlin, which had been Germany's capital until the end of World War II. That means thousands of people and all their office files had to be moved. The move is expected to take at least ten years!

TWO OTHER DEMOCRACIES

Austria's government is similar to Germany's. A chancellor leads the government, while a president heads the nation.

Less than a year after East and West Germans celebrated the destruction of the Berlin Wall in 1989, they celebrated the reunification of their country.

Switzerland is made up of 26 cantons. A canton is a small political unit, like a state or province. A Swiss canton is one of the few places in the world where direct democracy is at work. Its citizens hold regular meetings to decide all local issues.

Switzerland has been a self-governing democracy since the 1500s—longer than any other nation in Europe. Yet Swiss women could not vote on a national level until 1971. Even then several cantons refused to allow women full political rights at the local level. It was not until 1991 that the last canton recognized the full political rights of women.

Switzerland has remained at peace for hundreds of years. Since 1815 the country has been officially neutral. This means that Switzerland refuses to take sides in wars or disputes. It was neutral in World Wars I and II.

Because of Switzerland's neutrality, the city of Geneva is the headquarters of about 200 world organizations. Among them is the International Red Cross.

MAINTAINING DEMOCRACIES

Austria, Switzerland, and the newly reunited Germany all have democratic governments. As you have read, each country has a legislature with elected representatives.

Check Your Reading

1. What became of the government of East Germany after reunification?
2. How are the governments of Germany, Austria, and Switzerland organized?
3. What are cantons? Describe how they are governed.
4. **THINKING SKILL:** How could you determine the accuracy of this statement: "Switzerland has been a self-governing democracy since the 1500s"?

Recognizing Bias

Key Vocabulary
bias

Imagine that you went to a rock concert that you really enjoyed. The next day you read a newspaper review. The reviewer wrote that he thought all rock musicians were amateurs and that all rock music was boring. He could not understand why the audience was so excited about the music.

The reviewer had decided in advance that he did not like any rock music. This kind of one-sided view is known as bias. A person can be biased for or against something. Recognizing bias will help you to determine the accuracy of information you hear or read.

Trying the Skill

Read the following comments made by a German farmer. He lives on land in northern Bavaria that has been farmed by his family for generations.

Farming used to be a pleasant way of life around here, but now it's terrible. The price we get for our milk is outrageously low. The soil is thin and rocky. Our three sons have factory jobs. They never wanted to farm. We'd like to sell, but only a crazy person would buy this farm. Nobody wants to be a farmer. Soon there will be no farms left.

1. Does this account show any bias?
2. What did you do to determine if this account was biased?
3. Did you find any clues to bias in the account? What clues did you find?

HELPING YOURSELF

The steps on the left will help you to recognize bias. The examples on the right show one way to apply these steps to the farmer's comments.

One Way to Recognize Bias	Example
1. Recall the definition of *bias*.	*Bias* is a one-sided or slanted presentation of information.
2. Recall clues to bias.	Clues to bias include: • loaded or emotionally charged words such as *massacre* or *fantastic*, • exaggerations, especially *always* or *never*, • presentation of only one side of an issue.
3. Examine the information presented, sentence by sentence, looking for clues.	*Outrageously low* and *crazy* are words loaded with emotional impact. "Soon there will be no farms left" is an exaggeration.
4. Ask yourself: Do the clues I find give a one-sided view or impression for or against something?	Only the negative side of farming is given. The farmer does not talk about the positive aspects of farming or the possibility of improvement in the future.
5. State the bias, if any.	The farmer shows a bias against farming in his area of Germany.

Applying the Skill

Read the two passages below. Each discusses the Black Forest in Germany. Which passage shows bias?

Passage A

The Black Forest has long been a favorite place for hikers in the summer and skiers in the winter. Now, however, the forest is showing the effects of air pollution. Acid rain has caused many trees to become diseased, and some have died. Steps are being taken to curb pollution, but these are costly steps, both in money and in jobs, since industry causes much of the pollution.

Passage B

I looked at the trees of the forest. Some were already dead. Others were dying, their needles yellow, their branches drooping wearily, their trunks stained. It was the saddest sight I have ever seen. Our highest priority must be to save this beautiful forest, no matter what it costs.

1. Which passage shows bias?
2. What are some clues that helped you to recognize the bias?
3. Describe the bias in your own words.

Reviewing the Skill

1. What does the word *bias* mean?
2. What are some steps you can follow to recognize bias?
3. Name two clues that will help you to identify bias.
4. Give some examples of when you should be alert to bias.

Arts and Recreation

READ TO LEARN

Key People

Johann Sebastian Bach
Ludwig van Beethoven
Johannes Brahms
Wolfgang Amadeus Mozart

Key Places

Munich

Read Aloud

On Christmas Eve in 1818, mice chewed through a church organ in an Austrian town. The organ would have provided the music for church services, and the villagers were upset. So the schoolmaster wrote music that could be played on a guitar. The priest wrote words to accompany the music. The song they composed, "Silent Night," became one of the most popular Christmas songs of all time. "Silent Night" is just one of many contributions that Central Europeans have made to the world of music.

Read for Purpose

1. **WHAT YOU KNOW:** What kinds of recreational activities are popular in France and the Low Countries?
2. **WHAT YOU WILL LEARN:** How is music an important part of the artistic heritage of Central Europe?

MUSIC YESTERDAY AND TODAY

Any list of great composers includes a large number of Germans and Austrians. You can start with the famous "3 Bs" of German music—Johann Sebastian Bach (bäk), Ludwig van Beethoven (bā′ tō vən), and Johannes Brahms (brämz). Then add still another name, Wolfgang Amadeus Mozart (mō′ tsärt), an Austrian.

Beethoven was born in 1770 in Germany. He moved to Vienna, Austria, in 1792 to study music. For hundreds of years, Vienna has been a center of opera and music. Mozart also worked in Vienna.

Today Central Europe celebrates its musical heritage through yearly music festivals. One of the biggest festivals is held every year at Mozart's birthplace, Salzburg, Austria. The city of Bonn, Germany, stages a Beethoven festival. And Bayreuth (bī roit′), Germany, hosts a third major music festival presenting operas by composer Richard Wagner.

Almost every major city in Central Europe has an opera house or a concert hall. But the people of Central Europe also enjoy their traditional songs and brass bands.

FESTIVALS AND CELEBRATIONS

Festivals of all kinds provide welcome breaks from work in Central Europe. Peo-

244

Marching bands are just one part of the entertainment at festivals in Germany and the other countries of Central Europe.

ple listen to brass bands, dress in colorful costumes, and eat many kinds of delicious foods.

Every year about 6 million people attend a festival in **Munich** (mū′ nik), Germany, known as *Oktoberfest*. This city-wide celebration marks the end of the growing season. Munich's many breweries—places where beer and ale are made—put up huge tents at the fair grounds. Some of the tents hold up to 7,000 people!

SPORTS AND LEISURE

Central Europeans love to participate in outdoor recreation. Hiking, rock climbing, skiing, ice skating, track, and bicycling are all very popular activities.

Switzerland's snow-capped Alps attract skiers from around the world. Many come to train for international competitions. The Swiss themselves—with their natural "home-field advantage"—are often winners in these events.

Before reunification, both East and West Germany were extremely successful in many international sports competitions. East Germany spent a great deal of effort developing outstanding athletes. For example, Katarina Witt won Olympic gold medals for figure skating in 1984 and 1988. Both East and West Germans won gold medals for team sports. From now on, German athletes will be representing one country at the Olympics.

OLD TRADITIONS

Central Europe has produced many great musicians. Central Europeans have always strongly supported their musical, ballet, and theater groups. They also enjoy festivals, sports, and outdoor recreation.

Check Your Reading

1. Name four great German and Austrian composers who are part of the heritage of Central Europe.
2. What is *Oktoberfest*?
3. What are some activities that Central Europeans do in their spare time?
4. **THINKING SKILL:** Explain why the following statement is biased: "To people like me, who live in Vienna, there never was a musician as great as Mozart."

245

CHAPTER 11 - SUMMARY

CENTRAL EUROPE: CULTURAL GEOGRAPHY

PEOPLE

- Early peoples: Celts and Romans
- Today: People of a divided Germany have been reunited

- Language: German, with many local dialects

- Religion: Christianity, about evenly divided between Catholics and Protestants

ECONOMY

- Germany is a prosperous nation, but must rebuild former East Germany
- Standard of living is high throughout area

- Pollution: serious environmental problems
- Tourism: very important economic activity

GOVERNMENT

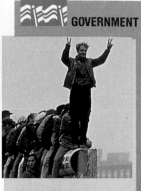

- Germany: parliamentary democracy, headed by a chancellor

- Federal system in Germany: power divided between national and local governments
- Switzerland: oldest working democratic government in Europe

ARTS AND RECREATION

- Many famous composers: Mozart, Bach, Brahms, Beethoven

- Popular outdoor sports: hiking, rock climbing, skiing, bicycling

- Festivals: Oktoberfest

IDEAS TO REMEMBER

- Most of the people of Central Europe are united by language and by the Christian religion.
- Central Europe is a highly industrialized and prosperous region.
- The countries of Central Europe have democratic governments with elected representatives and power divided between central and local governments.
- Central Europe has produced many great composers and musicians.

REVIEWING VOCABULARY

canton   pollution
dialect   reunification
neutral

Number a sheet of paper from 1 to 5. Beside each number write the word from the list above that best matches the definition.

1. A local variation of speech, such as that found in the German regions of Central Europe
2. The bringing together of parts that had been separated
3. One of the areas, resembling a state or province, into which the country of Switzerland is divided
4. Not taking sides in a war or dispute
5. The act of making something dirty or dangerous, as with harmful wastes or chemicals

REVIEWING FACTS

1. Name the three largest countries of Central Europe. What is the main language of these countries?
2. Why do Germans sometimes have difficulty understanding each other even though they speak the same language?
3. What are the four national languages of Switzerland?
4. Why was Germany divided into two parts?
5. What is the name of Western Europe's greatest industrial region?
6. Which nation has Western Europe's highest standard of living?
7. Why is pollution a serious problem in Central Europe? Why can no one country solve the pollution problem by itself?
8. In Austria and Germany, what is the title of the person who runs the government?
9. Why has the city of Geneva, Switzerland, become the headquarters for many international organizations?
10. Which city has an annual festival in honor of the composer Wolfgang Amadeus Mozart? Of the composer Ludwig van Beethoven?

WRITING ABOUT MAIN IDEAS

1. **Writing an Essay:** Write an essay comparing the democracy of the United States with the "pure" democracy of the Swiss canton.
2. **Writing a Letter:** Imagine that you are visiting a town or city in Germany, Switzerland, or Austria. Write a letter to a friend at home describing the city or town— its people, environment, culture, and economy.
3. **Writing About Perspectives:** Imagine that you live in a Central European country and are concerned about pollution. Write a plan telling five things people could do to help curb pollution in your country.

BUILDING SKILLS: RECOGNIZING BIAS

1. What is the meaning of *bias*?
2. What are some of the clues that will help you to recognize bias?
3. Write a statement that expresses strong bias about a topic that interests you.
4. Why is it important to recognize an author's use of bias?

COUNTRIES OF SOUTHERN EUROPE

FOCUS

Every bird likes its own nest.

This Italian expression is another way of saying, "There's no place like home." In this chapter you will find out what home is like for the Italians and their neighbors in Southern Europe.

The People

READ TO LEARN

Key Vocabulary

siesta

Key Places

Spain   Greece
Portugal   Vatican City
Italy   Athens

Read Aloud

Have you ever read about the ancient Greeks and the spread of their advanced civilization? Have you read about the Spanish and Portuguese who built large empires in the Amercias hundreds of years ago? Do you know what these people had in common? They all came from Southern Europe.

Read for Purpose

1. **WHAT YOU KNOW:** What peninsula contains the countries of Spain and Portugal?
2. **WHAT YOU WILL LEARN:** What do the people of Southern Europe have in common?

SETTLERS AND EXPLORERS

In the region we call Southern Europe are four large countries: **Spain**, **Portugal**, **Italy**, and **Greece**. Thousands of years ago, the people of this area began leaving their homes to explore faraway lands. Because much of this area is too rocky and steep for farming, many of its more adventurous sailors set sail in search of new lands to settle. The people of ancient Greece and Rome played an especially important role in the development of all of the region of Western Europe.

The ancient Greeks, for example, were among the first people to use shipping to import and export food. Early in Greek history the Greeks traveled to the plains north of the Black Sea and returned with wheat and animal hides. In return the Greeks exported wine to these areas.

Over the years the Greeks established trading posts around the Black Sea, along the shores of western Asia and northern Africa, and in far-off France. They also settled on the hundreds of islands that surround mainland Greece.

Like the Greeks, the Romans also spread their civilization throughout Europe. From their capital in Italy, the Romans ruled lands that stretched from North Africa to England and from Spain to Syria. The Mediterranean Sea became the center of a vast Roman Empire. In fact, during the Roman Empire the Romans called the Mediterranean Sea *Mare Nostrum*—the Latin words for "our sea."

Portugal and Spain were two of the great exploring nations of later times. In the 1400s and the 1500s, Spanish and Portuguese explorers discovered new trade routes and explored the Americas. In Latin America they found huge amounts of gold and silver. Eventually Spain and Portugal controlled empires that reached from Latin America all the way to Asia.

Recently, people from Southern Europe have flocked to areas farther north in search of work. Today guest workers from Spain and Portugal hold a variety of jobs in other European countries. They send much of the money they earn back home to support their families.

LANGUAGE AND RELIGION

Each of the four Southern European countries has a different language. But if you were to listen to people speaking Portuguese, Spanish, and Italian, you would notice many similarities among these languages. The reason is that they all come from Latin, the language of the Roman Empire. Let's take the word *milk* as an example. It is *leite* in Portuguese, *leche* in Spanish, and *latte* in Italian.

In Greece the people speak a language that can be traced back thousands of years. Greek is written in a different alphabet from that of the other languages you have read about so far. Although many of the letters of the Greek alphabet sound similar to the letters of our Roman alphabet, they sometimes look very different. The letter *mu*, for example, begins with an "*m*" sound, but it looks like this: μ.

Two groups of people living in Spain speak languages all their own. The Catalans, who live in and around the city of Barcelona, speak a language that is a cross between Spanish and French. The Basques, who live in the Pyrenees mountains of northern Spain and southern France, have a language unlike any other in the world. Some people think that the Basque language is the oldest in Europe.

In religion as well as in language, Portugal, Spain, and Italy are similar. Most people in these three countries belong to the Roman Catholic Church. In Greece nearly

MAP SKILL: Many different countries border on the Mediterranean Sea. Which large Southern European country is not on the Mediterranean?

SOUTHERN EUROPE: Political

⊛ National capital   • Other city

MAP SKILL: St. Peter's Square in Vatican City is thronged with spectators on special occasions. Where is St. Peter's Square in the map at left?

all the people belong to the Greek Orthodox Church.

Although the Roman Catholic and Greek Orthodox religions have much in common, there are several differences. For example, the leader of the Roman Catholic Church is the pope. The pope lives in Vatican City, shown on the map, a tiny independent state located within the city of Rome. Vatican City is the world headquarters of the Roman Catholic Church. The archbishop of Athens, not the pope, is the head of the Greek Orthodox Church. In addition, Greek Orthodox priests, unlike Roman Catholic priests, are permitted to marry.

PATTERNS OF LIVING

Imagine for a moment that you could spend a day living in Southern Europe. What do you think a typical day would be like? You might be surprised at some of the differences between the average day of a person living in Southern Europe and a typical day in your life.

Most working people in Southern Europe leave their jobs at 1:00 or 2:00 P.M. and return home for a large meal. A typical meal might consist of baked fish, stewed chicken, fruit, black coffee, and wine. The whole family spends a few hours together, enjoying their delicious meal.

In the middle of the afternoon, most people take a long nap, which is called a siesta in Spanish. People rest at this time

Like children in the United States, children in Southern Europe use their free time for hobbies such as playing guitar.

because it is usually the hottest part of the day. After the siesta people return to work for several more hours.

Most children come home from school around 5:30 or 6:00 P.M. After a filling snack of cakes, pastries, and tea, they either do their homework or go out to play with friends. Several hours later, at around 10:00 or 11:00 P.M., it's time for supper. The family does not go to bed until after midnight.

TRAFFIC AND SMOG

Since most people in Southern Europe come home for lunch, they have to travel back and forth to work twice each day. "The only trouble with our two days in one," explains a Greek businessman, "is four rush hours instead of two." All this commuting creates a special problem in **Athens**, the Greek capital. Athens is home to half the country's 10 million people. Every day car exhaust fills the air. As a result, Athens is the most polluted city in Western Europe. Heavy smog not only endangers people's health, but it also damages the priceless buildings of ancient Athens, many of which still stand.

SHARED TRADITIONS

The people of Southern Europe have much in common. As you have read, they are alike in many ways. The sea has played an important role in each of their countries. The Latin-based languages that developed in Portugal, Spain, and Italy are very similar. Except for the Greeks, most people in the area are Roman Catholics. Finally, the people of Southern Europe lead similar daily lives.

 Check Your Reading

1. Name the four major countries that are part of Southern Europe.
2. Describe an average day in Southern Europe.
3. Why does Athens have an air pollution problem?
4. **THINKING SKILL:** How does the lifestyle of people in Southern Europe help contribute to pollution problems in the area?

252

Reading Graphs and Charts

Key Vocabulary
graph
chart

Throughout this book you will often see graphs and charts as you study the people and places around the world. Graphs show numbers in picture form. Charts are used to organize more detailed information in a form that you can read easily.

Reading a Bar Graph
A bar graph is used to compare different amounts. Bar graphs have a horizontal axis that runs along the bottom of the graph and a vertical axis that runs up the side of the graph. The bar graph on this page uses bars to represent the populations of two cities in Mediterranean Europe. Which city had the smaller population in 1970?

Reading a Chart
Charts are often used to show numbers and other, more detailed kinds of information. To read a chart, first look at the title, and then read the labels at the top of each column and along each row. The chart on this page shows the capital cities, the populations, and the people per square mile for two countries in Southern Europe.

Using Graphs and Charts
Notice that the graph and the chart on this page each presents information in a different way. For example, the graph shows at a glance which city had the larger population in 1960. The chart

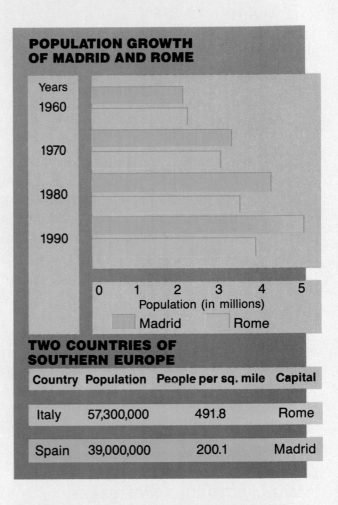

POPULATION GROWTH OF MADRID AND ROME

Population (in millions) — Madrid / Rome

TWO COUNTRIES OF SOUTHERN EUROPE

Country	Population	People per sq. mile	Capital
Italy	57,300,000	491.8	Rome
Spain	39,000,000	200.1	Madrid

presents actual population figures more accurately than does the graph.

Would you use the chart or the graph to find out which city had the larger population in 1980? Which would you use to find the population of Italy, the graph or the chart?

Reviewing the Skill
1. What is the population of Italy?
2. Which city had the larger population in 1980?
3. Which city's population is growing faster, Madrid or Rome?
4. Why is it useful to be able to use both graphs and charts?

253

The Economy

READ TO LEARN

Key Places

Turin   Rome
Madrid   Oinoussai
Marbella

Read Aloud

The two Basile brothers, Gianni and Salvatore, own and manage a handbag factory in the Italian city of Naples. Housed in a small building, the factory has just ten employees—all of them relatives. The Basile's factory produces about 50 handbags a day and provides a good living for everyone who works there.

Many companies in Southern Europe are small family operations like that of the Basiles. In this lesson you will read about how the economies of the Southern European countries are different from those in other parts of Europe.

Read for Purpose

1. **WHAT YOU KNOW:** Why does Germany have such a strong economy?
2. **WHAT YOU WILL LEARN:** What economic challenges does Southern Europe face today?

MANUFACTURING AND TRADE

Today about 40 percent of the workers in Southern Europe have jobs in manufacturing. Important industries include food and beverage processing, textiles, and chemicals. Factories in Italy, Portugal, and Spain make handbags, shoes, and other small leather goods.

Not all the factories in Southern Europe are as small as the one owned by the Basile brothers. Fiat, the largest privately owned company in Italy, employs almost 60,000 workers. Every year more than 1 million cars roll off Fiat's assembly lines in Turin. Automobiles and trucks are also manufactured in factories in the Spanish city of Madrid. Workers there produce Ford and General Motors cars for sale throughout Europe.

All four of these countries are members of the European Community. Every year they buy products from and sell goods to other European countries, such as Germany, France, and the United Kingdom. Italy and Spain also trade extensively with the United States.

FARMING

In many parts of Southern Europe, the land is not good for growing crops. The soil is poor, and the rainfall is scanty. Yet today more than 22 percent of the working

Picking olives (*left*) and gathering hay (*right*) are only two of the important farm activities of Southern Europe.

people of this region are farmers. Many of them are too poor to buy machinery, fertilizers, and the types of seeds that would make their land as productive as possible.

Although all four of these countries ship oil and wine around the world, the main crops of the region are cereal grains, such as wheat and barley. Farmers also grow olives, citrus fruits, nuts, tobacco, and cotton. "Our oranges and tangerines are sweeter than those from other countries," explains one Portuguese farmer. "The high temperatures . . . allow the fruit to ripen earlier and at the same time develop a higher concentration of sugar."

TOURISM

In the 1940s the Spanish coastal town of Marbella was a small fishing village that had only a few paths down to the beach and about 10,000 inhabitants. Today it is a very different place. Huge hotels and apartment buildings line its busy streets. Boutiques sell everything from designer sunglasses to gleaming yachts. The popu-

lation has grown and now includes 170,000 visitors. Every spring and summer, they come to enjoy the ocean beaches in this once quiet town.

Tourism has come to Marbella. The money spent by visitors at local hotels, restaurants, and stores has brought prosperity to many people in the area. Yet economic success has come at a high price: today Marbella is often crowded, noisy, and polluted.

Hundreds of towns like Marbella dot the Mediterranean shore. But, as any travel agent will tell you, the sea and the sand are not the only attractions of this area. In Greece and Italy visitors wander through such ancient remains as the Parthenon in Athens and the Forum in Rome. "Everywhere you go in Italy," noted one American tourist, "you look up in wonderment at the unequaled architecture of churches, cathedrals, palaces, and towers."

In Greece and the other countries of Southern Europe, fishing is still an important economic activity.

SHIPPING

Near the eastern end of the Mediterranean Sea lies a tiny Greek island called Oinoussai (ē nü′ sā). Less than 12 miles square (31 sq km), the island has a population of only about 400.

What makes Oinoussai special is that it is the home of 30 millionaire shipping families. Together, Greek shipowners control the largest merchant fleet in the world, a third of whose vessels come from this small island. One of the owners from Oinoussai is the richest shipper of all, Constantine Lemos, who is said to make 1 million dollars a day.

The sea is important to the economies of all the Southern European countries. Both Italy and Portugal have large merchant fleets. Fishing is a major industry throughout the area.

DEVELOPING ECONOMIES

Economically, the countries of Southern Europe have trouble keeping up with the rest of the European Community. Three of the four countries—Greece, Portugal, and Spain—are among Western Europe's poorest nations. They hope that closer ties with the European Community will bring greater investment and improving economies.

In recent years, much of the income in these nations has come from tourism. Another source of income has been money that Southern European guest workers have made in other countries and sent back to their own countries.

AN ECONOMIC STRUGGLE

As you have read, the people of Southern Europe are trying to develop the economic strengths of their region. Shipping and tourism are two of Southern Europe's successful industries. In addition, many of its people have manufacturing jobs, often in small family-owned businesses. And many other people work hard to get the most from this area's limited farmland.

Check Your Reading

1. What are some of the problems that farmers in Southern Europe face today?
2. Why do tourists choose to visit southern Europe?
3. How do the economies of the Southern European countries compare with those of countries in other parts of Western Europe?
4. **THINKING SKILL:** What kinds of jobs could you choose from if you lived in Southern Europe? Which job would you choose? Why?

The Government

Key Vocabulary
coalition
autonomy
terrorism

Key People
Juan Carlos

Key Places
Sicily
Gibraltar

Read Aloud

On a bright spring morning in 1974, thousands of Portuguese soldiers and sailors overthrew their country's dictator. But instead of using bullets and bombs, they stuffed red carnations into the barrels of their guns. The troops paraded down the streets in triumph. Only a few shots were fired. Freedom had arrived in Portugal.

Although Portugal's "carnation revolution" was unusual, its earlier control by a dictator was not. At one time or another, all the countries of Southern Europe have been dictatorships. In addition, all of these countries have also once been controlled by monarchs. Yet today, as you will read, each country of Southern Europe has a democratic form of government that is responsible to the people it governs.

Read for Purpose

1. **WHAT YOU KNOW:** What do all of the governments of Western Europe that you have studied so far have in common?
2. **WHAT YOU WILL LEARN:** How are the governments of Southern Europe similar?

GREECE

As you may already know, the Greeks were the first people in the history of the world to develop a democratic system of government. In the days of ancient Greece, each Greek city ruled itself. Today there is one national government for the country.

Greece has a parliamentary democracy. Unlike legislatures in most other democracies, the Greek parliament has just one house, consisting of more than 200 members. The government is headed by a prime minister, who is usually the leader of the political party that has the most members in the parliament.

Greece also has a president, who is elected by the parliament. The president leads the armed forces and has the power to declare war and make treaties with other nations.

The central government of Greece oversees each of the country's local governments. There is one exception to this rule, however. That is the community of Mount Athos, which is completely self-governing. Mount Athos is a small peninsula jutting out from the Greek mainland, on which 1,400 monks live in 20 monasteries. Women cannot set foot on Mount Athos.

ITALY

Like Greece, Italy is a parliamentary democracy. The parliament is made up of two houses—the Chamber of Deputies and the Senate. As in many other republics, a president serves as the head of state but has little political power. The real power is in the hands of the prime minister, who runs the country from day to day.

The government of Italy has been unstable for many years. Since World War II, Italy has had more than 40 different governments. No single political party has ever been strong enough to gain control. As a result, Italy has been ruled by a series of coalition governments. A coalition is a temporary union between different political parties that agree to work together for a common purpose.

One of the greatest difficulties faced by Italy's coalition governments has been a lack of national unity. Although the country has been united for more than 100 years, there are still huge differences between the north and the south. Most indus-try in Italy is located in the fertile north, around the cities of Milan and Turin. People there have a high standard of living.

In southern Italy and on the island of Sicily, however, the land is poor, as are many of the people. In the past, workers from the south have moved north in search of jobs. But they have often been unwelcome. Recently the Italian government has tried to improve the southern economy by bringing new industries there. As American journalist Flora Lewis explains, "Italians say the north produces the wealth and Rome spends it, mainly on the south."

PORTUGAL

As you have read at the beginning of this lesson, Portugal today is a democracy. But the Portuguese, like the Italians, have found political stability hard to achieve. Since the revolution in 1974, more than 15 national governments have come and gone in Portugal.

Under Portugal's current plan of government, executive power is shared by a president and a prime minister. The legislative branch of the government, like that of Greece, has only one house.

These posters are used to promote three of many different political parties in Italy.

The Portuguese people are proud of their country's democratic government. One member of parliament says: "Our parliamentary democracy must be defended. We can't go back to the years of darkness under a dictatorship again."

SPAIN

Like Portugal, Spain emerged from a long dictatorship to become a peaceful, democratic country. But Spain's government is somewhat different from the governments of the other Southern European countries. Spain is governed by an elected parliament, but it also has a monarch. In this respect Spain's government is like that of Great Britain.

In 1975 Prince Juan Carlos became King of Spain. He took over after the death of Francisco Franco, who had ruled the country as a dictator.

Under Franco's rule free elections and political parties had not been allowed in the country. When Juan Carlos came to power, the government of Spain was completely changed. First the Spanish people elected a new parliament. Then a new constitution was both written and approved in 1978. It established a parliamentary democracy with King Juan Carlos as head of the government.

Under the new constitution the legislative branch, called the Cortes, is divided into two houses. Most of the power is in the lower house, called the Congress of Deputies, which is made up of 350 members elected by the people. The upper house is called the Senate.

A NATION OF SEPARATE GROUPS

Spain, like Italy, has long been troubled by differences among areas. After Juan Carlos became king, one of his first acts was to lift a ban on traditional local languages and flags in Spain. Yet some

King Juan Carlos rules Spain under its new constitution written in 1978.

groups of people, like the Catalans and the Basques, were still not satisfied. They wanted much more.

The Catalans live in an area called Catalonia in northeastern Spain that is cut off by mountains from the rest of the country. Catalonia has always been more closely tied to France than to Spain. Although the Catalans do not want complete independence, they do want full autonomy. Autonomy is the right to self-government. Today Catalonia has an elected regional assembly. In addition, all direction signs and advertising billboards in the area are in both Spanish and Catalan.

For thousands of years, the Basques have wanted to preserve their independence. You may remember from Lesson 1 that the Basques live in the rugged Pyrenees on the border between northern Spain and France. When democracy came to Spain, the Basques were granted autonomy. But despite the changes, many Basques are still separatists. They want to split their area off from both Spain and France and set up their own country.

259

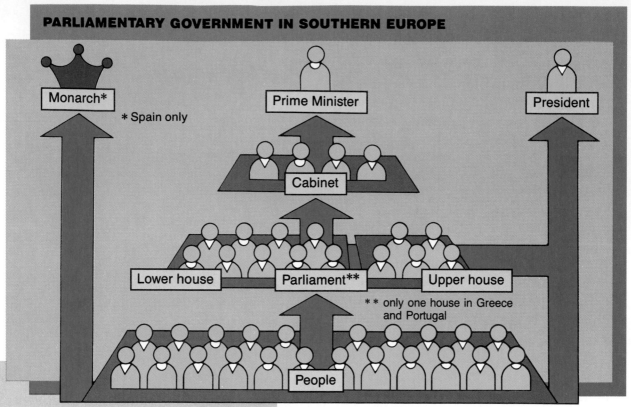

PARLIAMENTARY GOVERNMENT IN SOUTHERN EUROPE

Monarch*

* Spain only

Prime Minister

President

Cabinet

Lower house

Parliament**

Upper house

** only one house in Greece and Portugal

People

DIAGRAM SKILL: Which Southern European countries have a parliament with only one house?

In order to draw attention to their cause, some Basques have resorted to terrorism. Terrorism is the use of violence and the threat of violence, usually to gain political ends. Today the bombings and murders in the Basque areas still go on.

Another problem area for the Spanish government is Gibraltar. This rocky point at the southernmost tip of Spain has belonged to the British since the early 1700s. Now Spain wants the territory back. But the people of Gibraltar have voted to remain under British control.

FOUR DEMOCRACIES

As you have read, the governments of the four major countries of Southern Europe are all democratic. The diagram above shows a typical government. Spain and Portugal are the youngest democracies in Southern Europe.

Many parts of the area have been torn apart by conflicts. In Italy differences between the north and the south remain strong. In Spain, the Catalans and Basques have long fought the country's national government. If these countries are to grow and prosper, they need to solve the internal conflicts they have with different groups of people.

Check Your Reading

1. In what ways did the government of Spain change in 1975?
2. What problems does Italy's government face today?
3. What do the governments of Southern European countries have in common?
4. **THINKING SKILL:** Find three statements of fact in the section of this lesson titled "Spain." How could you prove these statements are true?

Arts and Recreation

READ TO LEARN

Key Vocabulary

Renaissance
pilgrimage

Key Places

Florence
Santiago de Compostela

Fátima

Read Aloud

Southern Europe has a rich artistic history that dates from the ancient Greek writers to the Italian painters of the Renaissance to the writers and painters of the present time. In this lesson you will read about this artistic heritage and about the festivals and celebrations that are so important to the people of Southern Europe today.

Read for Purpose

1. **WHAT YOU KNOW:** What are some things that the people of Southern Europe have in common?
2. **WHAT YOU WILL LEARN:** What are the popular arts and recreational activities of Southern Europe?

ARTISTIC ACHIEVEMENTS

The artistic heritage of Southern Europe stretches back thousands of years. The world's oldest dramas were written by the Greek poets Aeschylus (es′ kə ləs), Sophocles (sof′ ə klēz), and Euripides (ū rip′ ə dēz) in the 400s B.C. But these plays are still staged today in Greece and all over the world.

Few countries can match Italy's impressive achievements in the arts. During the 1300s and 1400s, a period of great activity in the arts began in the city of Florence. This was the Renaissance (ren′ ə säns), which means "rebirth." Artists of the Renaissance wanted to imitate nature and even improve on it. Their goal was to create an image of the ideal human being.

Today museums all over the world display works by such Italian painters of the Renaissance as Leonardo da Vinci and Raphael. Another great artist of the period was Michelangelo, whose works include both heroic statues and paintings. His paintings done on the ceiling of the Sistine Chapel in Vatican City are among his best-known works.

Other Renaissance painters include the Spaniard Diego Velázquez and El Greco, who was born in Crete but spent much of his life in Spain. In more recent times, Spain has produced such master artists as Pablo Picasso.

Some outstanding music has also been produced in Southern Europe. For example, opera was invented in Florence in about 1600, when several musician-poets began experimenting with dramas set to music. Later operas, such as those of Giuseppe Verdi and Giacomo Puccini thrill audiences around the world.

261

OH, CATERINA!

Italian Folk Song

Ci va al monte, ci va al mon-te a far la le - gna:
Oh, _____ where has gone our mer - ry Ca - te - ri - na?

ma dir - le qua ve - gna, ma dir - le que ve - gna.
Has an - y - one seen her? Has an - y - one seen her?

Ci va al mon - te, ci va al mon-te a far la le - gna;
Oh, _____ where has gone our mer - ry Ca - te - ri - na?

ma dir - le que ve - gna, a fa - re l'a - mor. _____
Go tell her we need her, We want _ to dance. _____

Oh, Ca - te - ri - na! Oh, Ca - te - ri - na! Col - pia - mo le man,
We're clap - ping our hands,

1. Col - pia - mo i pie'.
We're rea - dy to dance!

2. Col - pia - mo i pie'. _____
We're rea - dy to dance! _____

Trans. by Mary S. de Saettone. Eng. by ADZ. © 1962 CRS, Inc. Songs to Keep

FESTIVE TIMES

People in all the Southern European countries observe major Christian holidays, such as Christmas and Easter. Traditional costumes are often worn during festivals and celebrations on these and other holidays. In Spain, for example, girls and women may wear lace headdresses that are called *mantillas*.

Among the special events that take place are **pilgrimages**, or journeys that people make to sacred places. In Spain, pilgrims have been going to **Santiago de Compostela**, in the northwest, for nearly a thousand years. Huge crowds of people gather on July 25, the feast day of Santiago (St. James). Santiago is the patron saint of Spain. A saint is a person who is honored after his or her death by Christians, for being a holy person worthy of deep love and respect.

In **Fátima**, a small town north of Lisbon, Portugal, a major site is the shrine of Our Lady of Fátima. On May 13, 1917, three children reported having a vision of Mary, the mother of Jesus, at Fátima. According to the children the vision reappeared on the thirteenth of each month until October. Today people come from all over the world to be in Fátima between May and October.

The most important holiday in Greece is Easter. It is usually celebrated a week or two later than in other Western European countries because the Greek Orthodox calendar is different.

On the night before Easter Sunday, people gather at their local church, carrying candles. At midnight the priest appears, dressed in scarlet and gold, and announces "Christ is risen!" Everyone in the crowd shouts back, "He is risen indeed." At this cry all eyes turn toward the sky, where fireworks explode overhead. On Easter day Greek Orthodox families gather to eat a large feast of roasted lamb.

EVERYDAY AMUSEMENTS

After a day's work, many people in Southern European countries enjoy relaxing at outdoor restaurants and cafés. In Greece only the men gather at the cafés, where they drink small cups of strong coffee and play a board game called backgammon. The women often meet at the local church.

Because Southern Europe has a mild, sunny climate, it is not surprising that its people tend to spend much of their leisure time outdoors. Many enjoy golf, cycling, and tennis. During the winter months crowds of people gather on the ski slopes of the Alps and the Pyrenees to ski. And traditions like the Palio races, which you will read about on pages 264–267, remain strong.

As in many other parts of the world, folk songs are an important part of the culture of Southern Europe. One of the most popular folk songs of Italy appears on page 262.

DISTINCTIVE TRADITIONS

The nations of Southern Europe have cultural traditions that go back hundreds of years. In this lesson you read that Greek poets wrote the world's first dramas and that Italy led the Western world in painting, sculpture and opera. You also read how people in these countries celebrate religious holidays that are centuries old.

Check Your Reading

1. What was the Renaissance?
2. Why is the town of Fátima important to many people?
3. What do people in Greece do to celebrate Easter?
4. **THINKING SKILL:** What three questions could you ask to learn more about the Renaissance?

The Palio

by Eric Kimmel

In the last lesson, you read about the festivals and celebrations that play an important role in the culture of Mediterranean Europe. One of these celebrations, called the Palio (pä' lē ō), takes place twice every summer in the Italian city of Siena (sē en' ə). As you read, think about what makes this tradition special, and how it keeps Siena's history alive.

A CITY OF NEIGHBORHOODS

Siena is located in a hilly area of central Italy. This ancient city dates back to Roman times, when it was the site of a fortress. During the early years of the Renaissance, it became a center for the arts. Michelangelo, whom you read about in the last lesson, carved decorations for the city's Duomo (dwō' mō), or cathedral. Other painters and sculptors helped to make Siena one of Italy's most beautiful cities.

Along with its beauty, Siena is also famous for its *contrade* (kon trä' dā), or neighborhoods. The 17 contrade are very important. Each one has a name such as Shell, Tower, Forest, Eagle, or Goose. When two Sienese meet, they never fail to mention the names of their respective contrade. Why? The people in each neighborhood feel a tightly knit sense of community, as though they were members of a single family. They live together and work together. They may even go on vacations together!

The Sienese are proud of their contrade. Often this pride encourages a friendly rivalry between the various neighborhoods. The Sienese long ago discovered an exciting way for these rivals to compete. This is the Palio.

THE PALIO

The Palio is a horse race held in the main square of the city. It was first run in July 1656 to celebrate a Christian religious holiday, the Feast of the Madonna of Provenzano. Over the years it also became a celebration of Siena's past and its rival contrade.

The rules have remained the same for more than three centuries. Each neighborhood is represented by a horse and jockey—a person who races horses as a profession. But this "battle of the neighborhoods" is no ordinary horse race. For one thing, the jockeys ride bareback, without a saddle. For another, the jockeys are allowed to strike out at each other with whips as they fight for position. And a horse can win the race even if its jockey falls off!

In this race, even the prize is unusual. The winner receives no money, no crown, no silver trophy. Instead he is presented with a special silk flag, painted with religious symbols. This flag has been the traditional prize since the 1600s. The winner usually hangs it in his neighborhood's church.

In fact, the Palio gets its name from this prize. The original meaning of the Italian word *palio* was "flag." For centuries the word has also been used to refer to the race itself.

PREPARATIONS

The people of the neighborhoods start planning early for the Palio. Each contrada hires a jockey. Often rival neighborhoods try to persuade talented jockeys to switch sides. Horses, on the other hand, are chosen by lottery, and matching the horse and jockey can be a tricky process. If a neighborhood draws a horse with a good chance of winning, it may fire its jockey and hire a better one. If a neighborhood draws a poor horse but has already hired a good jockey, it may allow the jockey to ride for a different, friendly neighborhood.

Several events take place before the actual race. First the Palio opens with an elaborate parade. Representatives of each neighborhood dress in the Renaissance costumes of Siena's "golden age." Marching through the streets, carrying their neighborhood banners, they are followed by excited crowds of children and adults.

Next there are several days of trial races. These trials allow the horses and jockeys to get used to the narrow, curving course around the main square. After the last trial, all the horses are led into the neighborhood churches to be blessed for the race.

THE RACE BEGINS

Palio Day—the day of the race—begins with another parade. Some people march on foot. Others ride on horseback, dressed in armor and Renaissance clothing. An ox-drawn chariot follows, carrying the flag that the winner will receive.

Now it is time for the jockeys to mount their horses. Each jockey splashes water on his pants to make it easier to grip the horse's back. Then police search them thoroughly. Why? Jockeys are not allowed to carry anything but the official whip.

Mounted, the jockeys raise their whips in salute, and the judges assign them starting positions. The horses line up. The signal is given. They're off!

The crowd lets out a mighty roar. Each jockey immediately begins fighting for a good position. At the same time, he tries to block his rivals.

The crowd cheers wildly as the horses enter the third and final lap. As the front-runners near the dangerous San Martino curve, the horse from the Forest neighborhood stumbles. It knocks into the Shell horse, and the Eagle horse plows into both. Three horses are down!

The others surge ahead. Tower and Goose are in the lead. The jockeys lash at each other with whips as they round the Casato corner. Suddenly the jockey on Goose loses his balance and falls to the ground. But his riderless horse pulls ahead and thunders across the finish line. Goose has won!

A TRADITION CONTINUES

That night there is feasting in the Goose neighborhood and its "allies" among the other contrade. The Tower neighborhood is quiet. But the losers can't feel too bad—after all, the Palio will be run next summer! In only months the crowds will gather again for this traditional celebration of Siena's past and present.

How does the tradition of the Palio keep Siena's history alive?

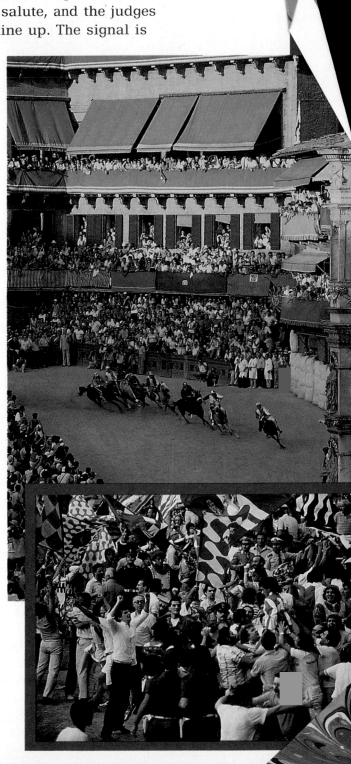

CHAPTER 12 SUMMARY

SOUTHERN EUROPE: CULTURAL GEOGRAPHY

PEOPLE

- Greeks: used shipping to import and export food
- Romans: spread their civilization throughout Europe
- Spanish and Portuguese: discovered new trade routes
- Languages: different but based on Latin in three countries
- Religions: Roman Catholic and Greek Orthodox

ECONOMY

- Industries: shipping, manufacturing, tourism
- Farming: cereal grains, olive oil, wine
- Standard of living: improving, but not as strong as other areas of Western Europe

GOVERNMENT

- Greece, Italy, and Portugal: parliamentary democracies

- Spain: constitutional monarchy
- Italy and Spain: plagued by regional conflicts

ARTS AND RECREATION

- Rich cultural heritage that stretches back thousands of years
- Renaissance: Italy: Leonardo da Vinci, Michelangelo

- Festivals: used to celebrate religious and other holidays
- Outdoor activities: golf, cycling, tennis, skiing, Palio races

IDEAS TO REMEMBER

- Most of the people of Southern Europe share a way of life that includes the Christian religion and three languages that are based on Latin.
- Industries such as shipping and tourism are helping to develop the economies of Southern Europe.
- Greece, Italy, and Portugal are governed by parliamentary democracies, while Spain is led by a constitutional monarchy.
- The region has a long cultural heritage and has produced many of the world's greatest writers, artists, and musicians.

REVIEWING VOCABULARY

autonomy   siesta
coalition   terrorism
Renaissance

Number a sheet of paper from 1 to 5. Beside each number write the word from the list above that best completes each sentence.

1. Since World War II, Italy has been run by a series of unstable _____ governments.
2. The _____ was a period of artistic flowering that began in Italy in the 1300s and 1400s and spread throughout Europe.
3. It is customary in Southern Europe to take a _____, or long nap, during the hottest part of the day.
4. Some separatist groups have tried to achieve independence through _____, a method of frightening people with the threat of violence.
5. Although they do not want to separate completely from Spain, the Catalans seek _____, or the right to govern themselves.

REVIEWING FACTS

1. Name the four major countries of Southern Europe. What body of water is important to three countries in this region?
2. Which two great ancient civilizations emerged from Southern Europe?
3. Why did the ancient Romans call the Mediterranean Sea *Mare Nostrum*, or "our sea"?
4. What is the name of the tiny state in Rome that is the home of the leader of the Roman Catholic Church?
5. Which region of Europe, northern or southern, has a greater percentage of people who are farmers?
6. Why is tourism a mixed blessing for towns like Marbella, Spain?
7. Name two factors that have heavily influenced Italian politics since World War II.
8. In which region are most Italian industries located?
9. How do the goals of the Catalans and the Basques differ?
10. What is a pilgrimage? Why are pilgrimages common in Southern European countries?

WRITING ABOUT MAIN IDEAS

1. **Writing a Paragraph:** Write a paragraph that discusses why the economies of Spain, Portugal, and Greece are sometimes called "developing economies."
2. **Writing a List:** List five sights in Southern Europe that you would like to see on a vacation to the region.
3. **Writing About Perspectives:** Imagine that you live in one of the countries of Southern Europe. Which country did you choose? Write a letter to a friend in the United States describing the different pace of life, the culture, and the physical environment of the country in which you live.

BUILDING SKILLS: READING GRAPHS AND CHARTS

1. What is the difference between a graph and a chart?
2. What do the labels on each axis tell you about the graph?
3. What kind of information does a chart give you?
4. When might it be useful to understand the difference between a graph and a chart?

CHAPTER 13

SCANDINAVIA

FOCUS

Throughout Scandinavia at this time of year, the effect of the long daily periods of sunlight on people's behavior, temperament, and work habits is strikingly different. People, it seems, are like plants: they blossom in the sunlight.

You probably have felt the uplifting effects of spring yourself. The newspaper article from which these sentences come tells us that Scandinavians "think bright" under the spring sunlight. In this chapter you will learn about the ways of life that have developed in the north.

The People

READ TO LEARN

Key Places

Norway	Denmark	Faeroe Islands
Sweden	Finland	Stockholm
Iceland	Greenland	Copenhagen

Read Aloud

Imagine what it would be like to stand outside in the middle of the night with the sky still light. Every year, because of the angle of the earth as it circles the sun, the night sky is light in parts of Scandinavia. Every June this event is celebrated during a holiday called Midsummer Eve. In Helsinki, the capital of Finland, the sun is still shining brightly at 11:00 P.M. About two hours later dawn begins. At midnight the sky is still bright.

During winter the opposite happens. Some days the sun barely rises. To help keep their homes cheerful during the dark winter, Scandinavians decorate them with brilliant colors. This is just one of the many ways in which they make the most of what they have. In this lesson you will read how the Scandinavians, a proud, self-reliant people, live in their home in the far north.

Read for Purpose

1. **WHAT YOU KNOW:** Where is the Scandinavian Peninsula located?
2. **WHAT YOU WILL LEARN:** What ways of life do the people of Scandinavia share today?

LANDS OF THE NORTH

Before you read about how Scandinavians live, it is important to know where they live. As you may remember from Chapter 8, the Scandinavian Peninsula is one of the many peninsulas in Western Europe. It includes the countries of Norway and Sweden. The term *Scandinavia* is also used for a larger area. It includes Iceland, Denmark, and Finland. The Danish island of Greenland, which is the world's largest island, and the Faeroe (fār′ ō) Islands are also part of Scandinavia.

THE EARLY SCANDINAVIANS

Scandinavia is a rugged land, much of it mountainous or snow-covered. It has produced some of the most hardy, rugged, and self-reliant people in the world.

Hundreds of years ago the Scandinavians were a warlike people. In Chapter 10 you read about daring Scandinavian seafarers called Vikings who raided many European communities. But the Vikings were also skilled shipbuilders and traders. Sturdy Viking ships traveled as far away as North America.

271

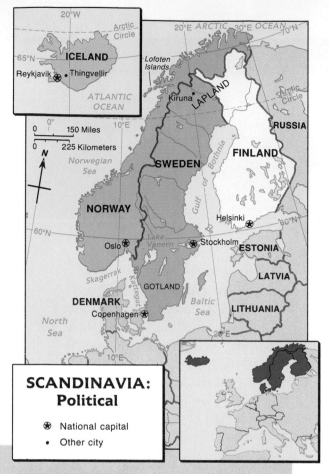

SCANDINAVIA: Political

⊛ National capital

• Other city

MAP SKILL: Copenhagen is one of the most important cities in Scandinavia. Where is Copenhagen located?

After the Viking period ended, Scandinavians turned their energies toward developing their own land. Today they work hard to make the most out of what their land has to offer.

SIMILARITIES OF LANGUAGE

What ties the Scandinavian people together? Their language does, for one thing. Most of the early settlers of Scandinavia spoke the same language. Over thousands of years, this one language has developed into different Scandinavian languages. But even today Danes, Swedes, and Norwegians can understand each other. Look at the table on the opposite page. It shows the similarity of the Scandinavian languages.

The languages of Finland are exceptions to this language similarity. One group of people in Finland, the Finns, are descended from people who probably came from Asia. They also speak an entirely different language. Look at the chart again to see the differences between the Finnish language and the other languages.

Another group of people in Finland—the Lapps—also speak their own language. The Lapps live in Lapland. As the map on this page shows, Lapland includes parts of northern Finland, Norway, and Sweden. The Lapp language is similar to Finnish.

A SMALL POPULATION

The Scandinavians are a people who have taken on many challenges, such as cold climate and scarce resources. Scandinavians have won a reputation as a people who get things done. Today their towns, governments, and businesses are known for the efficiency with which they are run. In the next two lessons you will read about the governments and economies of the Scandinavian countries.

The size of the population helps Scandinavians get things done. The area has few people—its 23 million residents represent only about 6 percent of the total population of Western Europe. Most of the people live in or near cities. However, Scandinavian cities are both small and uncrowded. Stockholm, the capital of Sweden and the largest city in Scandinavia, has about 1.5 million people. By contrast, the cities of Paris, Vienna, and Rome each have more than 2 million people. London has more than 6 million residents.

CLOSE-KNIT FAMILIES

How do the Scandinavian people live? Let's look at one Scandinavian family.

Leise Abrahamson lives in a small city near Copenhagen, the capital of Denmark. She and her brother Neel often bicycle with their mother to do the food shopping. Their mother is a weaver. In the evening their father, an architect, sometimes reads to the family.

Leise's parents, like many others throughout Scandinavia, spend much of their spare time with their children. Family occasions are especially important. Relatives travel miles to attend graduations, weddings, or other family events. On birthdays—especially on the milestone birthdays that fall every 10 years—relatives and friends stop by. Such celebrations can be tiring, as visits may start as early as 7:30 in the morning!

LIVING IN THE NORTH

Scandinavians, as you have read, share a common heritage of efficiency and hard work. They are a peaceful people who make the most of their rugged land. Because they are few in number, Scandinavians make up a small percentage of the population of Western Europe. They are united by a common language and close-

COMPARING WORDS IN SCANDINAVIAN LANGUAGES

	day	house	man
Danish	dag	hus	mand
Finnish	päivä	talo	mies
Icelandic	dagur	hús	mandur
Norwegian	dag	hus	mann
Swedish	dag	hus	man

CHART SKILL: The people of Scandinavia speak very similar languages. Which three languages use the same word for *day*?

knit families. In the following lessons you will read about the economic, political, and social lives of these people of the North.

Check Your Reading

1. Which countries and areas make up Scandinavia?
2. Where is Lapland located, and what group of people lives there?
3. What do the Scandinavian people have in common?
4. **THINKING SKILL:** In what ways are Scandinavians like people in other parts of Western Europe? In what ways are they different?

LESSON 2

The Economy

READ TO LEARN

Key Vocabulary

diversified economy
cooperative

Key Places

Lofoten Islands

Read Aloud

The trouble is, we don't have any means of making the trees grow faster or persuading the herring to come back.

The Norwegian economist who spoke these words describes a problem that Scandinavians have had for many years—dependence on a few natural resources. In the past, Scandinavians relied on a few resources to earn a living. Today, however, things have changed.

Read for Purpose

1. **WHAT YOU KNOW:** What are natural resources?
2. **WHAT YOU WILL LEARN:** How have the Scandinavian countries developed diversified economies?

HAULING IN THE LINES

It's 2:30 A.M., and Edmund, Ole, and the rest of their Norwegian fishing crew are already out of bed. After breakfast they board their boat and chug out to the sea around the Lofoten (lō′ fōt ən) Islands. These islands are located in some of the richest fishing waters in the world.

When they reach the fishing grounds, the members of the crew haul in the three long lines they had dropped overboard a day or two earlier.

Each of the these lines is 2 miles (3.2 km) long and baited with hundreds of mackerel. Now the three lines each have hundreds of cod caught on them.

Most crews like Edmund and Ole's come to the Lofotens for three months, beginning in February. This is a lonely stretch of time for the crews because they come

without their families. Many crew members live in a large dormitory called a *fiskerheimen*, which means "home for fishers." The work is hard—16-hour days are common. But the large catches make the hard work worthwhile.

DEVELOPING NEW RESOURCES

Edmund and Ole play an important part in Norway's oldest and most important industry—fishing. The economies of Norway and Iceland have long been dependent on the sea. But lately these and other Scandinavian countries have found new resources to develop. In Iceland, for example, sheep have become a major resource.

Oil is another example of a new resource that has come to play a major role in the economies of the Scandinavian countries. Norway has Western Europe's largest

274

fields of offshore petroleum and natural gas. That country now plays an important part in the world oil market.

The economies of Finland and Sweden have been based on their huge forests for hundreds of years. These countries are two of the most heavily forested nations in Europe. About 70 percent of Finland is covered with forests.

Lumbering still plays a key role in the economies of Finland and Sweden. But today these countries also have highly developed manufacturing industries. Sweden, now the most industrialized country in Scandinavia, produces steel, automobiles, furniture, and other products. Finland produces clothing and chemicals.

Denmark, too, has made great strides. As one Dane says, "Denmark is a little country. We have no wood, no metals, nothing in the ground." But, he added, "We have fantastically good craftsmen." Today Denmark is renowned for its furniture, glassware, and toys.

Scandinavian factories are among the most efficient in the world. These factories were among the first to use robots. Many lumber camps and farms in the area are automated as well.

Because of their hard work in developing new resources, most Scandinavian countries have **diversified economies**. This means that they produce a wide range of goods. From automobiles and airplanes to processed wood and fish, Scandinavia's economies produce a wide range of products for world markets.

In the past most Scandinavians earned their living either by fishing, farming, or lumbering. This is no longer true. Today less than 8 percent of workers earn their living by farming, fishing, or lumbering. Instead, because of diversified economies, most workers have jobs in service industries, mining, or manufacturing.

Fishing is now just one part of the **diversified economies** of Scandinavian countries.

PLANNING AND SHARING

How has Scandinavia developed such successful diversified economies? Government has played a large role. All five Scandinavian countries have mixed economies. As you read in Chapter 9, in a mixed economy the government owns some businesses while private companies own others. In most of Scandinavia, the telephone and electric power companies are owned and operated by the government. Governments control other large industries, such as the oil industry.

Scandinavians also work together in another way. Scandinavia is known for its many **cooperatives**. A cooperative is a business organization owned by its members. Denmark was a pioneer in the development of the agricultural cooperative,

Many people in Scandinavia buy consumer goods at retail **cooperatives** such as this one in Stockholm, Sweden.

which helps farmers buy supplies and market their products.

Retail cooperatives are also common in Scandinavia. Many food and department stores are owned by consumers. The consumers save money because items in the stores are sold at the same price that the store paid to purchase them.

Finally, Scandinavian nations cooperate with one other. Trade flows freely among the five countries, and it is easy for people to move from one country to another to find work. Scandinavians also share television programs as well as a commercial airline.

Cooperation and planning have enabled Scandinavia to have one of the highest standards of living in Western Europe. The area has virtually no city slums and few poor people. In Norway, the wealthiest country in Scandinavia, the average yearly family income is over $15,000, one of the highest incomes in the world.

SHARING THE GOOD LIFE

The countries of Scandinavia have developed diversified economies, and their people enjoy a high standard of living. As you have read, traditional industries such as fishing, farming, and lumbering are still important. However, fewer people today work in these areas than did people in the past. Scandinavia has prospered through government planning, cooperation, and the production of quality goods.

 Check Your Reading

1. What are the main natural resources of Scandinavia?
2. What is a cooperative? How do cooperatives help their members?
3. What is the meaning of the following statement: "Scandinavia has diversified economies"?
4. **THINKING SKILL:** List three questions you could ask to find out whether or not the following statement is true: "Scandinavians make the most of what they have to work with."

276

The Government

READ TO LEARN

Key Vocabulary   **Key Places**

ombudsman   Thingvellir

Read Aloud

I would rather have a welfare state where people are not fully satisfied than the old world where people had no choice but to suffer.

This is how the Finnish author Vaino Linna explained why many Scandinavians want to keep the types of governments they have. In this lesson you will read about the welfare states of Scandinavia.

Read for Purpose

1. **WHAT YOU KNOW:** What is a welfare state?
2. **WHAT YOU WILL LEARN:** What beliefs about government are shared by the countries of Scandinavia?

DRIVERS CHANGE TO THE RIGHT

September 3, 1967, was a special day in Sweden. On that day all drivers switched from driving on the left-hand side of the road to driving on the right-hand side of the road. Swedes called it H-Day, from *hoger*, the Swedish word for "right."

Sweden made this change so that driving would be the same there as it is in most other Western European countries. Experts believed—rightly, as it turned out—that the number of accidents in Scandinavian countries would decrease if drivers did not have to change from one system of driving to another.

H-Day took four years of planning. It was very costly. Road signs and traffic lights had to be changed—almost 350,000 lights were changed in Stockholm alone. Buses had to be changed so that passengers could board from the right side instead of from the left side.

In spite of all these changes, H-Day went smoothly. This fact says a lot about how government works in Sweden and all of Scandinavia. The governments of Scandinavia are known for their efficiency. In all of the Scandinavian countries, people have put great trust in their governments. Citizens work hard to make government work well for them and to provide them with the services they need.

Although the governments of Scandinavia share a reputation for efficiency, they are not all the same. Let's look at the different kinds of government found in the countries of Scandinavia—three monarchies and two republics.

THREE MONARCHIES

Denmark, Norway, and Sweden, like many countries of Western Europe, are constitutional monarchies. As you may remember, this means they have both elected representative governments and royal families.

Unlike Queen Elizabeth and the "royals" of the United Kingdom, Scandinavia's ruling families live simply and with little special treatment. They are treated just the same as other citizens of their countries.

Denmark, Norway, and Sweden all have one-house legislatures. In each country a prime minister is chosen from the parliament to head the executive branch of government. The prime minister, not the monarch, is the true head of the government.

TWO REPUBLICS

Many visitors to Iceland travel to a tiny southwestern settlement of Thingvellir (thēng' vet lēr). There, overlooking a deep gorge, is the "law rock"—the place where Iceland's parliament used to meet. The Icelandic legislature, formed in the year 930, is the oldest working lawmaking body in the world. For this reason this legislature is sometimes called "the grandmother of parliaments."

Both Iceland and Finland are republics. They have both a prime minister and a

The welfare states of Scandinavia have many social programs for their people. In most countries medical care is free.

president. Unlike Norway, Sweden, and Denmark, they do not have monarchs.

Finland is also different in another way. Unlike other countries in Scandinavia and the rest of Western Europe, Finland had close ties to the former Soviet Union. You will read more about the former Soviet Union in Unit 4. In the 1940s, after World War II, Finland and the Soviet Union signed a friendship treaty. Finland keeps up close relations with countries, like Russia, that were part of the Soviet Union.

THE OMBUDSMAN

Whatever form their governments take, Scandinavians demand that they perform well and respond to the needs of the people. Let's look at how one country—Sweden—has responded to this demand.

Almost 200 years ago Sweden created a special officer called the ombudsman (om' budz mən). The ombudsman receives complaints from citizens who are not satisfied with a government service or action. Complaints may be about such things as the courts, the environment, or taxes.

The ombudsman cannot take legal action. But he or she informs government representatives about the problems and tries to persuade them to make changes. This, the Swedes say, gives people a close link to their elected representatives.

WELFARE STATES

At the beginning of this lesson, you read a quote about the Finnish welfare state. As you may remember from Chapter 9, a welfare state is one that ensures the well-being of its citizens through a variety of government programs. These include health care, unemployment insurance, child care, pensions, and various housing programs.

The countries of Scandinavia are some of the best-known welfare states in the world. In Denmark, for instance, workers who are sick or out of a job receive about 90 percent of what they would normally earn. In Sweden parents can take up to 60 days off each year for every child under 12 who is ill. A new mother in Sweden can automatically take a year off at 90 percent of her salary. Most medical care is free or low-cost.

Of course, all of these social programs do not come without a price. Taxes in Scandinavia are very high. In Sweden, which has the highest taxes in the world, some people have to pay more than 75 percent of their earnings to the government.

But most people in Scandinavia would not have it any other way. They ask their governments to do a lot and to do it well. As one young Finnish worker says, "Being born in this country is like winning the lottery of life."

EFFICIENT GOVERNMENTS

Three of the Scandinavian governments are constitutional monarchies and two are republics. Also, as you have read, all five nations have efficient governments that provide necessary services for their citizens through far-reaching welfare programs. Such programs are costly and cause taxes to be high. But to the people of Scandinavia, the investment in their governments is worth the cost.

Check Your Reading

1. Why was H-Day important to the people of Sweden?
2. What is an ombudsman?
3. Why are the nations of Scandinavia called welfare states?
4. **THINKING SKILL:** Reread the Read Aloud passage on page 277. What is the author's bias about welfare states and countries that have them?

Ecological Development

For generations the people of the rural villages of Suomussalmi, Finland, had supported themselves by fishing, farming, and logging. However, as these industries modernized, fewer workers were needed and people began moving to the cities.

The people wanted to improve their economy, but they did not want to endanger their peaceful way of life. Kauko Heikurainen (kou′ kō hā kə rān′ ən) believed the economy could be developed without destroying the beauty of the villages. His idea was to apply new methods to traditional ways of using the land.

Under Kauko's leadership, the villagers started an experiment called "ecological development." Farmers learned how to grow crops without using harmful chemicals. Other villagers learned new methods of fishing and forestry.

The "ecovillages" experiment was a success. Today the farmers can barely meet the demand for their products. The many visitors who come to Suomussalmi to study the "ecovillages" have created a tourist industry. "When we started," Kauko remembers, "we were afraid these villages would die. Now we see they are healthy and thriving. We are eagerly planning for the future with great hope."

Determining Point of View

Key Vocabulary

point of view

Last winter Karen thought rabbits were adorable, furry little animals. This summer Karen thinks rabbits are nasty, greedy pests. Karen changed her thinking because rabbits have eaten most of the vegetables she planted in her garden. She now has a different **point of view**. Point of view is the way a person looks at or feels about something.

It is important to determine people's point of view when they are speaking or writing. How a person feels about a subject often affects the accuracy of what he or she says. Someone who had an unhappy time at camp, for example, might tell you that going to camp is boring. You might really enjoy camp, but if you believe this camper's stories you might never go.

Trying the Skill

Read the following passage about education in one of the Scandinavian countries. As you read, think about how the writer feels about the subject.

The most striking feature of Finnish education is the emphasis on learning foreign languages. In Finland all students must learn two foreign languages. Third-graders begin to study English, Russian, German, or French. Students begin to study a second foreign language in seventh grade.

I believe the study of languages is just as important as the study of science or math. The world is growing smaller because of improved transportation and communication techniques. American schools should require all students to learn two foreign languages.

1. What is the writer's point of view about the study of foreign languages?
2. How did you determine the writer's point of view?

HELPING YOURSELF

The steps on the left will help you to determine a writer's or speaker's point of view. The example on the right shows one way to apply these steps to the passage on Finnish education.

One Way to Determine Point of View	Example
1. Identify the subject or topic.	Foreign language study in Finland.
2. Identify statements of fact.	Students study English, Russian, German, or French in third grade and a second foreign language in seventh grade.
3. Identify value judgments and reasoned opinions.	Look for clues to how the writer feels or what the writer believes. For example, *I believe*, *just as important*, and *should* in the second paragraph.
4. Look for any biases the writer or speaker has. Identify information that was left out but could have been included, loaded words, and exaggerations.	Finns need to learn other languages because Finnish is not spoken in other countries. English, however, is spoken in many different countries. The writer states only one view about learning languages.
5. Describe the point of view from which the author writes. What is the writer for or against?	The author's point of view is that studying foreign languages is as important for Americans as it is for Finns.

Applying the Skill

Read the following passage describing one person's view of sports. Look for clues that will help you to determine the writer's point of view.

In the United States there are many professional sports teams. People go to football or baseball games or watch them on TV. In Norway we don't have any professional teams. We love sports of all kinds, but we like to "do it ourselves." We prefer to exercise and to have a good time playing sports rather than to watch others play. Winning is not the important thing. It's having a healthy body and enjoying some exercise.

1. Which is a statement of fact?
   a. In Norway we don't have any professional teams.
   b. Winning is not the important thing.
   c. We prefer to exercise and have a good time playing sports rather than to watch others play.
2. What information is left out?
   a. Americans enjoy playing sports.
   b. There are professional teams in America.
   c. Sports are very popular in Norway.
3. Which of the following do you think the writer would most enjoy: attending a soccer game or going skiing?

Reviewing the Skill

1. What does *point of view* mean?
2. Which five steps can you follow to recognize a person's point of view?
3. Where, outside of school, would it be useful to try to determine the point of view of a writer or a speaker?

Arts and Recreation

READ TO LEARN

Key Vocabulary

Edda
saga

Key People

Hans Christian Andersen
Selma Lagerlöf

Henrik Ibsen
Sigrid Undset

Read Aloud

The sea was all green to look at, and round there floated large icebergs. . . . She had seated herself on one of the largest, and all the ships made a wide circle in fear, away from the place where she was sitting and letting the wind set her long hair flying.

This was how the heroine of the story "The Little Mermaid" first saw the world above the ocean floor where she lived. In this tale by Hans Christian Andersen, the mermaid gave up her fish's tail and then her life to gain the love of a human prince. Today a bronze statue of the Little Mermaid sits on a rock in the harbor of Copenhagen, Denmark. Andersen's story, like so many other Scandinavian tales, celebrates the heroes and heroines of Scandinavia and the rugged land in which they live.

Read for Purpose

1. **WHAT YOU KNOW:** Which winter sports are popular in the United States?
2. **WHAT YOU WILL LEARN:** How do the arts and recreational activities of Scandinavia show the Scandinavians' love of their land and its people?

SCANDINAVIAN LITERATURE

Hans Christian Andersen is only one of many writers honored in Scandinavia. Scandinavian stories and poems date back hundreds of years. They describe many kinds of heroes—some larger than life, and some ordinary people.

The Vikings were among the earliest Scandinavian storytellers. They created long poems called Eddas. The Eddas tell stories about early Scandinavian gods, such as Woden, the chief god, and Thor, the god of thunder.

In Iceland a group of lengthy stories called sagas tell the history of that country. Most of the sagas tell about the deeds of kings and heroes. One saga tells how the explorer Leif Ericson reached North America in about the year 1000.

In the modern era Scandinavians have continued the storytelling tradition. Selma Lagerlöf (sel' mä läg' ər löv) of Sweden updated the folktales she heard as a child. Other modern Scandinavian writers highlighted the daily lives of ordinary people. Henrik Ibsen of Norway wrote many plays

Cross-country skiing is just one of the many popular outdoor sports of Scandinavia.

about the problems of contemporary people. Sigrid Undset (sig′ rē ůn′ set) of Norway wrote books that explored the history of her country as well as books that examined present-day life.

ENJOYING THE OUTDOORS

Scandinavians do not just write and tell stories about their land. They also explore the land themselves.

Many Scandinavians like being outdoors. Even the coldest of winters do not keep them inside. Many Scandinavians love to fish, sail, and hike. Even in the winter they fish through ice and swim outdoors in heated pools.

The favorite—and perhaps the oldest—winter sport in Scandinavia is skiing. Wooden skis about 6,000 years old have been found in Sweden and Finland.

Every year crowds of Scandinavians take to the ski slopes and fields just for fun. The largest cross-country ski meet in the world is held yearly in Dalarna, Sweden. There is even a ski meet in July at a glacier in western Norway.

People all over the world who exercise are grateful for a Finnish invention, the sauna (sô′ nə). A sauna is a kind of steam bath taken in a special wooden room. The steam cleans people's skin and relaxes their muscles.

A LOVE FOR THE LAND

Through their arts and recreational activities, Scandinavians celebrate their land and its people. Ancient works, such as the Eddas and sagas, and modern writings tell about the heroes, heroines, and ordinary people of these northern lands. When Scandinavians aren't reading about their countries, they are exploring them by skiing, sailing, swimming, hiking, and in many other ways.

Check Your Reading

1. What is the difference between an Edda and a saga?
2. What is the favorite winter sport in Scandinavia?
3. How do literature and the recreational activities of Scandinavia reflect a love for the land?
4. **THINKING SKILL:** Classify the people mentioned in this lesson into two or more groups. What do your groupings tell you about Scandinavians?

SCANDINAVIAN COUNTRIES: CULTURAL GEOGRAPHY

 **PEOPLE**

- Peaceful, hard-working people live in or near small cities

- Challenges: cold climate and scarce resources

- Languages are very similar except in Finland

- Close-knit families typical in the area

ECONOMY

- Diversified economies produce a wide range of goods—autos, airplanes, furniture

- Cooperatives: workers organize together to produce and sell goods

- New resources being developed: petroleum, natural gas

GOVERNMENT

- Constitutional monarchies: Denmark, Sweden, Norway

- Republics: Iceland, Finland

- Welfare states: many welfare programs, high taxes

 **ARTS AND RECREATION**

- Rich storytelling tradition, from Viking poems, modern stories, and plays

- Popular outdoor activities: fishing, sailing, hiking, skiing

IDEAS TO REMEMBER

■ The peaceful, hard-working Scandinavians are linked together by similar languages and close-knit family traditions.

■ Cooperation and planning have been combined to make Scandinavia a region with a very high standard of living.

■ The Scandinavian nations are run by efficient governments with far-reaching welfare programs.

■ Scandinavians express their love for their land through their enjoyment of the outdoors.

REVIEWING VOCABULARY

cooperative   ombudsman
diversified economy   saga
Edda

Number a sheet of paper from 1 to 5. Beside each number write the word or term from the list above that best matches each definition.

1. A Swedish official who helps citizens to resolve problems involving governmental policies and actions
2. A type of economy that produces many different kinds of goods and services
3. A long poem that describes the deeds of Scandinavian gods and goddesses
4. A business organization owned and operated by its members
5. One of the group of long stories that tell the history of Iceland

REVIEWING FACTS

Number a sheet of paper from 1 to 10. Determine whether each statement is true or false. If the statement is true, write "true" next to the appropriate number. If the statement is false, rewrite it to make it true.

1. Scandinavian people live in a rugged land that has a cold climate.
2. People in Sweden and Finland speak the same language.
3. Stockholm, a typical Scandinavian capital, is overpopulated.
4. Family events and activities are especially important to Scandinavians.
5. Norway's most important industry is fishing.
6. Most Scandinavian countries have recently developed diversified economies.
7. The countries of Scandinavia cooperate and trade freely with one another.
8. The standard of living in Scandinavia is one of the lowest in the world.
9. The governments of Denmark, Norway, and Sweden are constitutional monarchies with royal families as well as elected representatives.
10. Taxes in Sweden are lower than in any other country.

WRITING ABOUT MAIN IDEAS

1. **Writing a List:** List five things you have read about Scandinavia that show that cooperation is an important principle among its people.
2. **Writing a Summary:** Reread the section in this chapter about H-Day in Sweden. Then write a summary of what happened on H-Day and why.
3. **Writing a Report:** Write a report about some aspect of Scandinavia. Topics might include a particular town, a group such as the people of Lapland, or a way of life such as that of the people who fish the waters near the Lofoten Islands.
4. **Writing About Perspectives:** Imagine that you lived in a Scandinavian country. Write a paragraph describing a day in the middle of winter, how you feel about having little sunlight, and what you do to deal with it.

BUILDING SKILLS: DETERMINING POINT OF VIEW

1. What is meant by the term *point of view*?
2. Name some steps you could take to determine an author's point of view.
3. Write a statement that expresses your point of view on a topic that interests you.
4. When would it be helpful to know how to identify an author's point of view?

UNIT 3 · SUMMARY

WESTERN EUROPE: PHYSICAL GEOGRAPHY

 LANDFORMS

- Peninsulas: Scandinavian, Jutland, Italian, Balkan

- Islands: British Isles, Greece, Corsica, Sardinia, Sicily
- Thousands of miles of coastline

 CLIMATE

- Gulf Stream: brings warm waters that help create mild climate in coastal areas
- Northern part of the region: winters are long and cold
- Southern part: summers are sunny and dry, winters short and mild
- Ocean winds bring plenty of rainfall to most areas

NATURAL RESOURCES

- Forests: important resource, but few large ones are left
- Rich soil: about 25 percent of land is arable
- Many long inland rivers and waterways, such as Danube and Rhine

WESTERN EUROPE: CULTURAL GEOGRAPHY

 PEOPLE

- Early peoples: Celts, Gauls, Franks, Vikings, ancient Greeks and Romans
- Language: ties some people together (such as French) and separates others (such as Flemings and Walloons in Belgium)
- Guest workers: come from Southern Europe to France, the Low Countries, and Central Europe
- Religion: mostly Christians (Roman Catholic, Protestant, Greek Orthodox)

 ECONOMY

- Mixed economies common: private enterprise and government-run businesses
- European Community: links many countries of the region together
- Highly developed economies with advanced technology industries in many parts of the region
- Services: tourism, banking and shipping are all important
- Pollution: has caused serious environmental problems

 **GOVERNMENT**

- Each country in the region has some form of democracy
- Great Britain has a constitutional monarchy with parliamentary democracy; British form of democracy is widespread
- Other constitutional monarchies: Low Countries, Spain, Denmark, Sweden, Norway
- Welfare states: government takes great responsibility for well-being of citizens; common in Scandinavia

 ARTS AND RECREATION

- Great Britain: great literary tradition

- France and the Low Countries: many famous painters
- Central Europe: many famous composers
- Southern Europe: rich cultural heritage
- Scandinavia: rich storytelling tradition

REVIEWING VOCABULARY

Each of the following statements contains an underlined vocabulary word or term. Number a sheet of paper from 1 to 10. Beside each number write whether the statement is true or false. If it is false, rewrite it to make it true.

1. A <u>neutral</u> country is one that refuses to take sides in international disputes.
2. <u>Fjords</u> are long, narrow inlets of the sea, bordered by steep cliffs.
3. A <u>constitutional monarchy</u> is a form of government in which a monarch is given absolute power by a constitution.
4. Groups striving for <u>autonomy</u> seek stronger political ties with the national governments of their countries.
5. The Swiss <u>canton</u> is one of the most democratic political units in the world.
6. A <u>diversified economy</u> depends on only one or two industries to provide jobs and consumer goods.
7. <u>Terrorism</u> is the use or threat of violence to frighten people.
8. People who live in a <u>welfare state</u> receive little assistance from the government while they are sick or unemployed.
9. The <u>coalition</u> governments of Italy have generally tended to be unstable.
10. The French <u>premier</u>, elected by the people, makes defense and foreign affairs decisions.

WRITING ABOUT THE UNIT

1. **Writing an Essay:** The following events or movements that took place in Europe had enormous impact on the world: the Renaissance, the Industrial Revolution, communism, World War I, and World War II. Choose one of these events or movements and write an essay describing how it affected world history.
2. **Writing About Perspectives:** You have read about the diverse regions of Western Europe. Yet there is also much that unites the regions of Western Europe. Imagine that you are a citizen of Iceland. Write a paragraph describing ideas and attitudes that would link you to other Europeans.

ACTIVITIES

1. **Writing a Report:** Use magazines and newspapers to find an article that interests you about a country in Western Europe. Summarize the article in an oral report to the rest of the class.
2. **Working Together to Make a Bar Graph:** Use an almanac to find the population densities (average number of persons per square mile or square kilometer) for ten countries of Western Europe. Then make a bar graph to show the relative population densities of the countries.

LINKING PAST, PRESENT, AND FUTURE

For centuries the countries of Europe have shared common interests. Today some Europeans believe that these shared interests will be unified under a political group—the United States of Europe. Do you agree with this prediction? Do you believe such a union would have positive or negative consequences? Explain your answer.

NORTH AMERICA

North Pole

ARCTIC OCEAN

Arctic Circle

60°N

Barents Sea

NORTHERN ASIA

ATLANTIC OCEAN

45°N

North Sea

Baltic Sea

EASTERN EUROPE

30°N

Caspian Sea

Tropic of Cancer

Black Sea

Mediterranean Sea

30°W

15°W

15°N

INDIAN OCEAN

0°

AFRICA

15°E

Equator

60°E 0°

45°E

15°S

Tropic of Capricorn

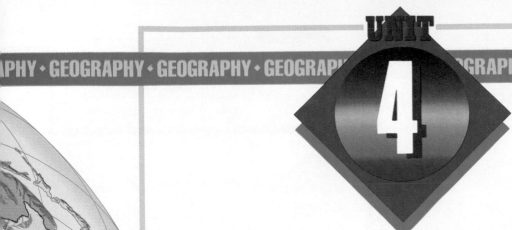

UNIT

4

EASTERN EUROPE AND NORTHERN ASIA

WHERE WE ARE

In Unit 3 you read about tremendous changes that have taken place in Germany. The same forces that brought about the reunification of Germany have brought even greater changes to the region we call Eastern Europe and Northern Asia. The huge country known as the Soviet Union ceased to exist at the end of 1991. In its place there are now 15 independent countries. Seven other countries in this region were not part of the Soviet Union but were strongly influenced by Soviet policies.

The first chapter of this unit describes the region's physical geography. Chapter 15 discusses the countries that were once part of the Soviet Union. The map on these pages shows that area in light purple. The following chapter refers to the countries of Eastern Europe that were not part of the Soviet Union. The map shows that area in darker purple. You are about to read about a region of the world that is changing rapidly.

EASTERN EUROPE AND NORTHERN ASIA

CROATIA
Capital ★
Zagreb

Major language: Croatian
Population: 4.8 million
Area: 21,829 sq mi; 56,538 sq km

ALBANIA
Capital ★
Tiranë

Major language: Albanian
Population: 3.3 million
Area: 11,100 sq mi; 28,750 sq km
Leading export: minerals

CZECH REPUBLIC
Capital ★
Prague

Major languages: Czech and Slovak
Population: 10.4 million
Area: 30,450 sq mi; 78,864 sq km
Leading exports: glassware, textiles, and machinery

ARMENIA
Capital ★
Yerevan

Major language: Armenian
Population: 3.3 million
Area: 11,490 sq mi; 29,800 sq km
Leading exports: rubber and electronic parts

ESTONIA
Capital ★
Tallinn

Major languages: Estonian and Russian
Population: 1.6 million
Area: 17,413 sq mi; 45,100 sq km
Leading exports: agricultural and wood products and textiles

AZERBAIJAN
Capital ★
Baku

Major languages: Azerbaijani, Russian, and Armenian
Population: 7.1 million
Area: 33,430 sq mi; 86,600 sq km
Leading exports: oil and textiles

GEORGIA
Capital ★
Tbilisi

Major languages: Georgian and Russian
Population: 5.5 million
Area: 26,900 sq mi; 69,700 sq km
Leading exports: agricultural products and machinery

BELARUS
Capital ★
Minsk

Major languages: Belarusian and Russian
Population: 10.3 million
Area: 80,134 sq mi; 207,800 sq km
Leading export: tractors

HUNGARY
Capital ★
Budapest

Major language: Hungarian
Population: 10.4 million
Area: 35,919 sq mi; 93,030 sq km
Leading export: machinery

BOSNIA AND HERZEGOVINA
Capital ★
Sarajevo

Major language: Serbo-Croatian
Population: 4.5 million
Area: 19,741 sq mi; 51,129 sq km

KAZAKHSTAN
Capital ★
Alma-Ata

Major languages: Kazakh and Russian
Population: 16.7 million
Area: 1,049,155 sq mi; 2,717,300 sq km
Leading exports: oil, gas, and machinery

BULGARIA
Capital ★
Sofia

Major languages: Bulgarian and Turkish
Population: 9.0 million
Area: 42,822 sq mi; 110,910 sq km
Leading export: machinery

KYRGYZSTAN
Capital ★
Bishkek

Major languages: Kyrgyz, Russian, and Uzbek
Population: 4.4 million
Area: 76,640 sq mi; 198,500 sq km
Leading exports: metals and agricultural products

LATVIA
Capital ★
Riga

Major languages: Latvian and Russian
Population: 2.7 million
Area: 24,595 sq mi; 63,700 sq km
Leading exports: metals and agricultural products

SLOVAKIA
Capital ★
Bratislava

Major languages: Slovak, Czech, and Hungarian
Population: 5.3 million
Area: 18,932 sq mi; 49,035 sq km
Leading exports: consumer goods, industrial products, and chemicals

LITHUANIA
Capital ★
Vilnius

Major languages: Lithuanian and Russian
Population: 3.7 million
Area: 25,170 sq mi; 65,200 sq km
Leading exports: machinery, food, and chemicals

SLOVENIA
Capital ★
Ljubljana

Major language: Slovenian
Population: 2.0 million
Area: 7,819 sq mi; 20,251 sq km
Leading exports: manufactured goods and aluminum

MACEDONIA
Capital ★
Skopje

Major language: Macedonian
Population: 2.1 million
Area: 9,928 sq mi; 25,713 sq km
Leading exports: agricultural and mining products

TAJIKISTAN
Capital ★
Dushanbe

Major languages: Tajik and Russian
Population: 5.3 million
Area: 55,240 sq mi; 143,100 sq km
Leading exports: aluminum and textiles

MOLDOVA
Capital ★
Kishinev

Major languages: Moldovan, Ukrainian, and Russian
Population: 4.4 million
Area: 13,000 sq mi; 33,700 sq km
Leading exports: wine, fur, and clothing

TURKMENISTAN
Capital ★
Ashkhabad

Major languages: Turkmen and Russian
Population: 3.6 million
Area: 186,400 sq mi; 488,100 sq km
Leading exports: gas, oil, and cotton

POLAND
Capital ★
Warsaw

Major language: Polish
Population: 38.2 million
Area: 120,726 sq mi; 312,680 sq km
Leading export: machinery

UKRAINE
Capital ★
Kiev

Major languages: Ukrainian and Russian
Population: 51.8 million
Area: 231,990 sq mi; 445,000 sq km
Leading exports: wheat, beets, and coal

ROMANIA
Capital ★
Bucharest

Major language: Romanian
Population: 23.4 million
Area: 91,699 sq mi; 237,500 sq km
Leading export: machinery

UZBEKISTAN
Capital ★
Tashkent

Major languages: Uzbek and Russian
Population: 20.3 million
Area: 172,741 sq mi; 447,400 sq km
Leading export: cotton

RUSSIA
Capital ★
Moscow

Major language: Russian
Population: 148.0 million
Area: 6,592,813 sq mi; 17,075,000 sq km
Leading exports: consumer goods, industrial equipment, and foods

YUGOSLAVIA
Capital ★
Belgrade

Major languages: Serbo-Croatian, Slovene, and Macedonian
Population: 10.6 million
Area: 39,448 sq mi; 102,173 sq km
Leading export: machinery, food products, and textiles

CHAPTER 14

PHYSICAL GEOGRAPHY OF EASTERN EUROPE AND NORTHERN ASIA

FOCUS

I love my country, but that love is odd:
My reason has no part in it at all! . . .
Ask me not why I love, but love I must her fields' cold silences,
Her somber forests swaying in a gust,
Her rivers at the floodlike seas.

These lines are from the poem "My Country" by Mikhail Lermontov (myik ə ēl′ ler′ mən tôf), a Russian poet of the early 1800s. His words express the feelings of many Russians—and of other people in the region as well—toward their homeland.

Landforms

READ TO LEARN

Key Places

Eastern Europe	Soviet Union	Central Asia
Northern Asia	Caucasus Mountains	Volga River
Ural Mountains	Siberia	Danube River
Russia	Caspian Sea	

Read Aloud

There is something solemn about crossing the [boundary] line the first time. Thousands of kilometers lie behind you. Ahead thousands of kilometers . . . stretch . . . endlessly before you. At a moment like this you have a physical sensation of your country's vastness.

This is how one journalist described the experience of crossing the Ural Mountains, which form the boundary line between the European and Asian parts of the region. The region is so vast that it spans two continents.

Read for Purpose

1. **WHAT YOU KNOW:** What is Eurasia?
2. **WHAT YOU WILL LEARN:** What are the main physical features of Eastern Europe and Northern Asia?

SPANNING TWO CONTINENTS

If you were to travel from east to west across the vast expanse that makes up the region of **Eastern Europe** and **Northern Asia**, you would cross more than half the world's time zones. When people in the eastern part of Northern Asia are waking up in the morning, people in the western part of Eastern Europe are eating their dinner or getting ready to go to sleep for the night.

As you read above, the **Ural Mountains** form the boundary between Europe and Asia. The Urals are not very high mountains. They rarely rise above 3,000 feet (900 m). Because they are so low, they never became a barrier for travelers.

MANY LANDFORMS AND CLIMATES

Cold, icy, forested—these words are often used to describe the land of Eastern Europe and Northern Asia. They are good descriptions because much of this region spans the northern part of the Eastern Hemisphere. A long northern coastline borders the frigid Arctic Ocean.

Dry and *dusty*—these words are also accurate descriptions because parts of the region reach as far south as 35°N latitude, which is the same latitude as northern Africa. In fact, almost any words you could think of to describe landforms and climates would fit some part of the region.

Russia, the largest country in the world, is spread over more than half the region.

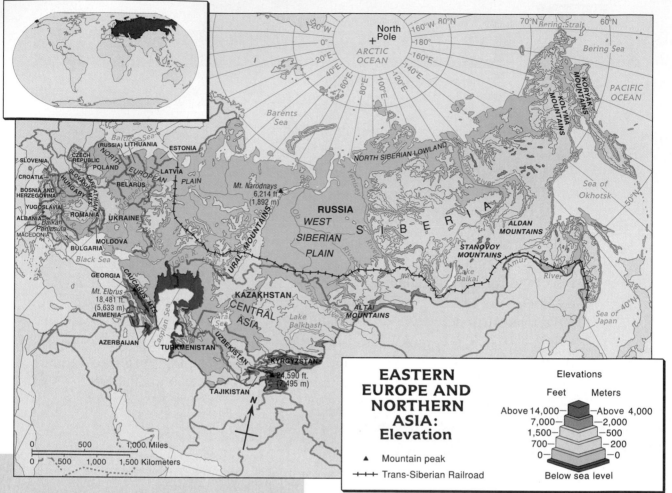

Map labels (clockwise / as shown):

North Pole
ARCTIC OCEAN
Barents Sea
Bering Strait
Bering Sea
PACIFIC OCEAN
KORYAK MOUNTAINS
KOLYMA MOUNTAINS
Sea of Okhotsk
NORTH SIBERIAN LOWLAND
RUSSIA
WEST SIBERIAN PLAIN
SIBERIA
Mt. Narodnaya 6,214 ft. (1,892 m)
ALDAN MOUNTAINS
STANOVOY MOUNTAINS
Lake Baikal
Amur River
Sea of Japan
URAL MOUNTAINS
NORTH EUROPEAN PLAIN
(RUSSIA) LITHUANIA
ESTONIA
LATVIA
SLOVENIA
CZECH REPUBLIC
POLAND
CROATIA
HUNGARY
SLOVAKIA
BELARUS
BOSNIA AND HERZEGOVINA
YUGOSLAVIA
ALBANIA
Balkan Peninsula
MACEDONIA
ROMANIA
UKRAINE
BULGARIA
MOLDOVA
Black Sea
GEORGIA
CAUCASUS MTS.
Mt. Elbrus 18,481 ft. (5,633 m)
ARMENIA
AZERBAIJAN
Caspian Sea
Volga River
Aral Sea
KAZAKHSTAN
CENTRAL ASIA
Lake Balkhash
ALTAI MOUNTAINS
TURKMENISTAN
UZBEKISTAN
KYRGYZSTAN
24,590 ft. (7,495 m)
TAJIKISTAN
N

0   500   1,000 Miles
0   500   1,000   1,500 Kilometers

EASTERN EUROPE AND NORTHERN ASIA: Elevation

Elevations

Feet   Meters
Above 14,000—   Above 4,000
7,000—   2,000
1,500—   500
700—   200
0—   0
Below sea level

▲ Mountain peak
+++ Trans-Siberian Railroad

MAP SKILL: What is the area of lowest elevation in Eastern Europe and Northern Asia?

PLAINS AND MOUNTAINS

Imagine an area of vast plains surrounded by mountains. Much of the land of Eastern Europe and Northern Asia is very flat. Find some of the plains and mountains on the map above.

Use the map above to locate the Caucasus (kô′ kə səs) Mountains in the southwestern part of the region. These mountains separate Europe from southwestern Asia. This area has had many severe earthquakes.

To the east of the Caucasus Mountains lie a series of other mountain ranges, which you can find on the map. These mountain ranges stretch eastward for thousands of miles, all the way to the shores of the Pacific Ocean.

Until late 1991 Russia was part of an even larger country, the Soviet Union. But in 1991 the republics that made up the Soviet Union separated into 15 independent countries. You will read more about the former Soviet Union in Chapter 15.

To the west of the former Soviet Union are the countries that you will study in Chapter 16. These countries were dominated by the Soviet Union in the years following World War II. East Germany was also one of these countries, but as you read in Chapter 11, East Germany is now part of a united Germany. The Eastern European countries have also become fully independent.

Farther west in Eastern Europe you will also find many mountain ranges. As you can see on the map on page 294, the Balkan Peninsula contains several mountain ranges. In fact, the name *Balkan* comes from the Turkish word meaning "mountain." Throughout history, the Balkan Peninsula has served as a crossroads for Europe, Asia, and Africa.

All of these mountain ranges form a great circle around a land of wide plains with few geographical barriers. In the past conquering armies often swept back and forth across these plains. Now people cross these plains to find jobs and homes.

The population of the region is mainly concentrated in the warmer western plains and plateaus. As the map on page 296 shows, Moscow, St. Petersburg (formerly called Leningrad), Budapest, Prague, Warsaw, and many other cities each have more than 1 million people. The region's major industrial centers and its most important rivers are also found mainly in the European part of the area.

SIBERIA

At the beginning of this lesson, you read a description by a journalist who made his way across the Ural Mountains. The Urals are an important dividing line between Europe and Siberia (sī bêr' ē ə). Siberia is the name for a former political region made up of the entire Asian portion of Russia and a small part of land that now belongs to Kazakhstan (kä zäk stan'). Siberia extends across roughly three fourths of the entire region of Eastern Europe and Northern Asia. Siberia alone is larger than the entire United States.

The vast West Siberian Plain is the largest single area of level land on the surface of the earth. It has many marshes, or wetlands, that are frozen for up to eight months a year.

Climbing steep hills is an everyday activity in this Caucasus Mountain town.

For a long time Siberia was a very remote region. As one writer noted, Siberia was "a land of exiles, religious refugees, . . . and fugitive rebels." An exile is a person who is sent either out of the country or to a remote area because the government of that country thinks he or she is dangerous. The father of Nina Kosterina, a young student, was exiled to a camp in Siberia in 1937. Nina wrote in her diary that her father described the camp as being in a beautiful area, near a "wild canyon, [and] a cold . . . , rapid forest stream."

Nina Kosterina's diary, though, also helps to explain why few people escaped from Siberia. She wrote that one November her father's camp "was moved in a frost of −50°C (−58°F.) to another river that is not even on the map. Before pitching their tents, the exiles had to dig through a 1-meter-thick (3.2-ft) layer of snow."

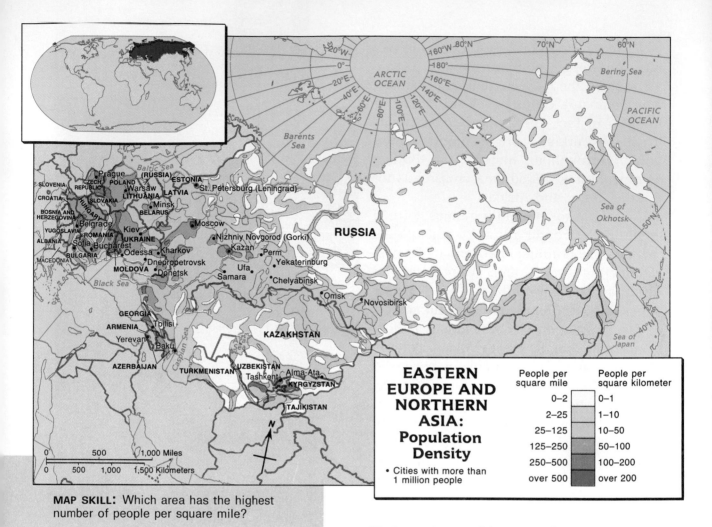

Barents Sea, Baltic Sea, Black Sea labels, ARCTIC OCEAN, PACIFIC OCEAN, Bering Sea, Sea of Okhotsk, Sea of Japan, Caspian Sea

RUSSIA

SLOVENIA, CZECH REPUBLIC, POLAND, ESTONIA, CROATIA, SLOVAKIA, LATVIA, LITHUANIA, HUNGARY, BELARUS, BOSNIA AND HERZEGOVINA, YUGOSLAVIA, ROMANIA, UKRAINE, ALBANIA, BULGARIA, MOLDOVA, MACEDONIA, GEORGIA, ARMENIA, AZERBAIJAN, KAZAKHSTAN, TURKMENISTAN, UZBEKISTAN, KYRGYZSTAN, TAJIKISTAN

Prague, (RUSSIA), Warsaw, St. Petersburg (Leningrad), Minsk, Moscow, Belgrade, Kiev, Nizhniy Novgorod (Gorki), Sofia, Bucharest, Kazan, Perm, Odessa, Kharkov, Yekaterinburg, Dnepropetrovsk, Ufa, Donetsk, Samara, Chelyabinsk, Omsk, Novosibirsk, Tbilisi, Yerevan, Baku, Tashkent, Alma-Ata

0 500 1,000 Miles
0 500 1,000 1,500 Kilometers

N

EASTERN EUROPE AND NORTHERN ASIA: Population Density

• Cities with more than 1 million people

People per square mile	People per square kilometer
0–2	0–1
2–25	1–10
25–125	10–50
125–250	50–100
250–500	100–200
over 500	over 200

MAP SKILL: Which area has the highest number of people per square mile?

To live in Siberia today requires the use of special technology. In many places houses have to be built in such a way that they don't melt the permafrost under them. If the ice melts, the houses begin to sink.

Although there are many settlements in Siberia, only a small number of people live there. Look at the population density map above. It shows where most of the people in the region live.

CENTRAL ASIA

Find the Caspian Sea on the map above. To its east is a large, dry lowland that is part of Central Asia. Central Asia includes the countries of Kazakhstan, Uzbekistan (ùz bek′ i stän), Tajikistan (tä jik′ i stän), Turkmenistan (tûrk men′ i stän) and Kyrgyzstan (kîr giz′ stän). It continues into China and Mongolia.

High mountains form the southern border of Central Asia. Because these mountains block rain-bearing clouds that blow from the south, the climate of Central Asia is very dry. Hundreds of years ago, the "Silk Route," an important trade route between China and southwestern Asia, ran through this area. This route was also used by invaders from the east and the west.

LONG RIVERS

Travel between the widely separated areas of Eastern Europe and Northern Asia has always been difficult. Only after the Trans-Siberian Railroad was built in 1916

296

were the eastern and western parts of the region linked. Because severe cold breaks up the surfaces of roads, even today no major highway connects the east with the west.

In the past rivers were the most important transportation routes. Russia has some of the world's longest rivers, as you can see from the table on this page. Yet most of Russia's rivers do not provide good transportation routes. The reason for this is that no major rivers flow from east to west. Almost all Russia's rivers flow from south to north. Because these rivers are so far north, almost all of them are frozen solid for at least four months of each year. During the winter the sight of large sleds, snowmobiles, and even trucks traveling across the frozen rivers is common.

One of Russia's most important rivers is the **Volga River**, the longest river in Europe. The Volga, which is sometimes called the "Main Street" of Russia, flows 2,194 miles (3,531 km) through Russia before emptying into the Caspian Sea. The Volga is linked by canals to the Baltic Sea, the Don River, and the Black Sea.

The most heavily traveled river in Eastern Europe is the **Danube River**. It links many countries in Eastern Europe and Western Europe as well as the cities of Vienna, Budapest, and Belgrade.

AN IMMENSE REGION

The region of Eastern Europe and Northern Asia spans a large portion of two continents. Most of the population is concentrated in the European part of the region. The Asian part has two distinct areas—Siberia and Central Asia.

It is a region of vast plains with few geographic barriers, except in the south. Yet the great distances that stretch across these plains have traditionally made travel throughout the region difficult.

LONGEST RIVERS OF THE WORLD

River	Country	Length in Miles (Kilometers)
Nile	Egypt	4,100 (6,560)
Amazon	Brazil	4,000 (6,400)
Chang (Yangtze R.)	China	3,964 (6,342)
Mississippi-Missouri	United States	3,710 (5,936)
Ob	Russia	3,362 (5,379)
Huang (Yellow R.)	China	2,903 (4,644)
Congo	Zaire	2,900 (4,640)
Amur	Russia	2,744 (4,390)
Lena	Russia	2,734 (4,374)
Mackenzie	Canada	2,635 (4,216)
Mekong	China	2,600 (4,160)
Yenisey	Russia	2,543 (4,068)
Paraná	Brazil	2,485 (3,976)
Murray Darling	Australia	2,310 (3,718)
Volga	Russia	2,194 (3,531)

CHART SKILL: Which is Russia's third-longest river?

Check Your Reading

1. Which is the largest country in Eastern Europe and Northern Asia?
2. Why is Siberia's population density lower than other parts of the region?
3. Describe the region's major landforms.
4. **THINKING SKILL:** How are the geographic features of Siberia and Central Asia alike? How are they different?

Climate and Resources

■ Key Vocabulary

taiga   steppes

■ Read Aloud

In one Eastern European folk tale a girl named Marushka is forced by her stepmother to search for violets, then for strawberries, and finally for apples in the dead of winter. Marushka is able to find all of these through the kindness of Great January, King of the Months. This powerful ruler then punishes Marushka's stepmother by sending her a blizzard.

The story of Marushka is a reminder that winter in many parts of Eastern Europe and Northern Asia is a serious matter. Snow, ice, and freezing temperatures are a reality for at least half the year.

■ Read for Purpose

1. **WHAT YOU KNOW:** How long does winter last where you live? How cold does it get during winter?
2. **WHAT YOU WILL LEARN:** What are the major climates and natural resources of Eastern Europe and Northern Asia?

CLIMATE

Many stories describe the climate of Siberia—its blizzards and freezing temperatures. Because of these stories, some people think all of Eastern Europe and Northern Asia has a harsh climate.

In fact, the region has several climates. However, as the climate map on page 299 shows, most of the region falls within two large climate zones. The first zone includes the western part of Northern Asia and all of Eastern Europe. This zone has different kinds of temperate climates, ranging from warm to hot summers and from mild to cold, snowy winters.

The second large climate zone is in Siberia and the northern part of Eastern Europe. It has short, cool summers and long, cold winters. Most of this zone is inland, far from large bodies of water that help make temperatures milder. The northern part of Russia is tundra and has an Arctic climate.

SOIL AND VEGETATION

In countries that have large plains—such as Poland and Hungary—people can farm more than 50 percent of the land. Even in more mountainous countries of Eastern Europe, such as Slovakia, the Czech Republic, and Romania, at least one third of the land can be cultivated.

Less than 20 percent of Russia's land is arable, mainly because of the cold climate of much of the country. Hardly anything can grow in the bleak northern tundra, where permafrost lies just below the earth's surface. Even south of the tundra,

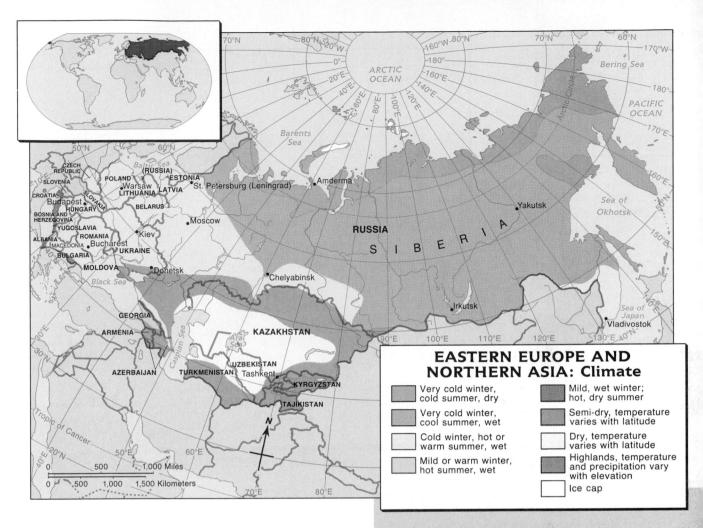

EASTERN EUROPE AND NORTHERN ASIA: Climate

- Very cold winter, cold summer, dry
- Very cold winter, cool summer, wet
- Cold winter, hot or warm summer, wet
- Mild or warm winter, hot summer, wet
- Mild, wet winter; hot, dry summer
- Semi-dry, temperature varies with latitude
- Dry, temperature varies with latitude
- Highlands, temperature and precipitation vary with elevation
- Ice cap

MAP SKILL: What kind of climate does Moscow have? How does Moscow's climate compare with the climates of the major cities in Eastern Europe?

summers are too short for the growing of many crops.

FORESTS AND GRASSLANDS

In addition to its farmland, Eastern Europe is heavily forested, with trees covering about one third of the land. Russia has a vast region of evergreen forests south of the tundra. It is called the taiga (tī′ gə), and it stretches all the way from Finland to the Pacific Ocean.

South of the taiga are the steppes (steps). Steppes are dry, grassy plains. These grasslands cover much of Russia, Ukraine, parts of Eastern Europe, as well as western Siberia. The steppes of Europe contain some of the world's richest soil.

In the 1950s the government of what was then the Soviet Union sent people to

Northern Asia to cultivate the steppes. When the first settlers arrived, they found that cultivating the land was backbreaking work. One settler wrote:

Slowly, first one then another plow dug into the black soil, which cracked like a torn [canvas] all interlaced with strong roots. . . .

But the pioneers refused to give up. As a result, the steppes of Northern Asia are a major grain-growing area today.

MINERALS

Russia is richer in minerals than all of its neighbors in Eastern Europe combined.

299

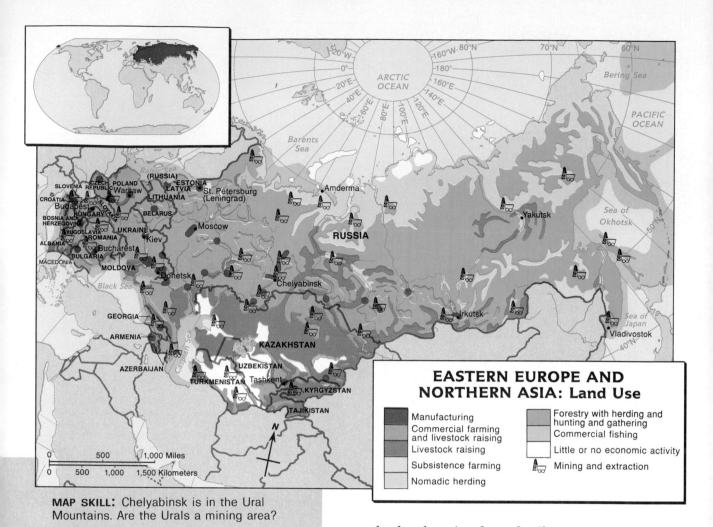

EASTERN EUROPE AND
NORTHERN ASIA: Land Use

Manufacturing
Commercial farming
and livestock raising
Livestock raising
Subsistence farming
Nomadic herding

Forestry with herding and
hunting and gathering
Commercial fishing
Little or no economic activity
 Mining and extraction

MAP SKILL: Chelyabinsk is in the Ural Mountains. Are the Urals a mining area?

Russia has about one third of all the coal in the world. It also has huge oil reserves in Siberia. The countries in the Caucasus Mountains and Central Asia also possess productive oil fields.

In general, the countries of Eastern Europe are not rich in minerals. There are some exceptions. Poland has large deposits of coal, while Romania is one of Eastern Europe's few oil-producing nations.

DIFFERENT CLIMATES AND RESOURCES

You have read that most of Eastern Europe and Northern Asia is located within two climate zones. You have also read that the land varies from fertile steppes to dry land. Russia has coal and oil reserves. Oil is also found in the Caucasus Mountains, Central Asia, and Romania. Poland has large deposits of coal.

Check Your Reading

1. List two major climate zones of Eastern Europe and Northern Asia.
2. What is the difference between the taiga and the steppes?
3. Why was it difficult to begin to cultivate the steppes of Northern Asia?
4. **THINKING SKILL:** Imagine that you plan to visit Moscow and then the Caspian Sea in March. Use the climate map on page 299 to decide what kind of clothing you might pack for your trip.

Reading Climographs

Key Vocabulary
climograph

In this chapter, as well as throughout this book, you have seen climate maps of the world's regions. These maps tell a lot about the climate of a place. Another way to learn about the climate of a place is to look at a climograph. A climograph is a graph that shows information about the temperature and precipitation of a particular location over a period of time.

Parts of a Climograph
Climographs are useful because they give a picture of the weather in a particular place for each month of the year.

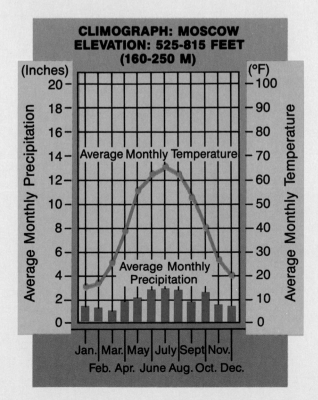

CLIMOGRAPH: MOSCOW
ELEVATION: 525-815 FEET
(160-250 M)

Notice that the climograph on this page includes two graphs—a bar graph and a line graph. The bar graph shows the average monthly precipitation in Moscow. The line graph shows the average monthly temperature in Moscow.

To read the climograph, first look at the title. The title tells you the location of the place whose climate is being described. What else does it tell you? Then read the labels on the sides and along the bottom of the graph. What do these labels tell you about the graph?

Next look at the vertical bars along the bottom of the bar graph. The bars tell you the average precipitation during each month. Now look at the line on the line graph that shows the average temperature for each month. What is the average temperature in Moscow during May? Which is the driest month on average in the city?

Reviewing the Skill
1. What does a climograph show?
2. Which is the coldest month of the year in Moscow?
3. During which months of the year is there more than 2 inches (5 cm) of rain in Moscow?
4. In which month of the year does the most rain fall in Moscow?
5. According to the climograph, would the precipitation in February be in the form of rain or snow?
6. In which month do you think it would be best to visit Moscow if you like mild, dry weather?
7. When might you find climographs especially helpful for understanding climate?

EASTERN EUROPE AND NORTHERN ASIA: PHYSICAL GEOGRAPHY

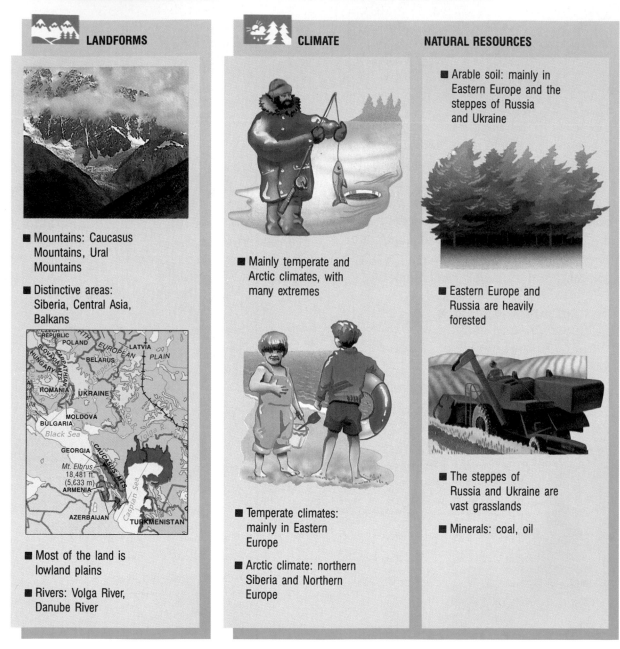

LANDFORMS

- Mountains: Caucasus Mountains, Ural Mountains
- Distinctive areas: Siberia, Central Asia, Balkans
- Most of the land is lowland plains
- Rivers: Volga River, Danube River

CLIMATE

- Mainly temperate and Arctic climates, with many extremes
- Temperate climates: mainly in Eastern Europe
- Arctic climate: northern Siberia and Northern Europe

NATURAL RESOURCES

- Arable soil: mainly in Eastern Europe and the steppes of Russia and Ukraine
- Eastern Europe and Russia are heavily forested
- The steppes of Russia and Ukraine are vast grasslands
- Minerals: coal, oil

IDEAS TO REMEMBER

- The region of Eastern Europe and Northern Asia spans two continents and is made up mainly of lowland plains.
- Russia has several climate zones and is richer in minerals than all of the Eastern European countries combined.

REVIEWING VOCABULARY

Each of the following statements contains an underlined vocabulary word. Number a sheet of paper from 1 to 5. Beside each number, write whether the following statements are true or false. If a statement is true, write true. If a statement is false, rewrite the sentence using the vocabulary word correctly.

1. The <u>steppes</u> are regions of high mountains and heavily wooded foothills.
2. The <u>taiga</u> is a vast arctic plain where almost nothing grows and where a layer of permafrost lies just below the surface.
3. Russia is heavily forested by a vast region of evergreen forests called the <u>taiga</u>.
4. The <u>steppes</u> are dry, grassy plains covering vast areas of Russia, Ukraine, and parts of Eastern Europe.
5. The European part of the <u>steppes</u> contains some of the world's most fertile soil.

REVIEWING FACTS

1. Which mountain range divides Eastern Europe from Northern Asia? Which mountain range divides Eastern Europe from southwestern Asia?
2. In the region of Eastern Europe and Northern Asia, where is most of the population concentrated?
3. Why does only a small percentage of the region's population live in Siberia?
4. About what fraction of Eastern Europe and Northern Asia does Siberia cover?
5. Why do no major highways in this region link the east and west? How are the eastern and western parts linked?
6. What drawbacks make river transportation very difficult in Russia?
7. Why is Central Asia, the lowland south of Siberia, a dry area?
8. What is the main reason that while roughly 50 percent of Hungary's land is arable, only 20 percent of Russia's land can be farmed?

9. Which area of Northern Asia has been turned into a major grain-growing area in the past few decades?
10. Which two minerals are found in large quantities in Russia?

WRITING ABOUT MAIN IDEAS

1. **Writing an Explanation:** Look at the places listed below. Which of the choices in each pair probably has a colder climate? Explain why.
   a. a village in Siberia; the city of Moscow
   b. the city of St. Petersburg; a village in the Ural Mountains
2. **Writing a Paragraph:** Look at the climate map on page 299. What kind of climate would you be living in if you lived in St. Petersburg? Write a paragraph comparing the climate where you live with the climate in St. Petersburg.
3. **Writing About Perspectives:** Imagine that you are a member of a family that is riding the Trans-Siberian Railroad across Russia from Moscow to your new home in eastern Siberia. Write a letter to a friend describing the vastness of Russia's land, its diverse geography, and its climate.

BUILDING SKILLS: READING CLIMOGRAPHS

Look at the climograph on page 301 to answer the following questions.
1. What does a climograph show?
2. Which month of the year is the warmest in Moscow?
3. When might you find climographs especially helpful for your own use?

CHAPTER 15

RUSSIA AND ITS NEIGHBORS

FOCUS

Our leaders have often praised the people as the country's greatest resource.

Dmitry Kotler, a Russian student, is proud of the achievements of the people of his country. This chapter describes some of these achievements, as well as the enormous changes that are taking place in Russia as well as the 14 other countries that used to make up the Soviet Union.

LESSON 1

The People

READ TO LEARN

Key Vocabulary
Soviet

Key Places
Latvia
Lithuania
Estonia
Georgia

Armenia
Uzbekistan
Moscow
Azerbaijan

Read Aloud

The unity of the multinational Soviet people is as solid as a diamond.

History has proved Leonid Brezhnev, leader of the Soviet Union from 1964 to 1982, to be wrong in describing his country as solidly unified. In this lesson you will read about the different groups of people that live in Russia and the other 14 countries that until 1991 made up the Soviet Union. You will also learn about the enormous changes that have caused the unity among the countries, once "solid as a diamond," to crumble.

Read for Purpose

1. **WHAT YOU KNOW:** In which parts of Russia do most of its people live?
2. **WHAT YOU WILL LEARN:** What changes have been taking place in Russia and the other 14 countries that were once part of the Soviet Union?

A TIME OF CHANGE

In 1991 **Latvia**, **Lithuania**, and **Estonia** gained their independence from the Soviet Union. These three countries along the eastern shore of the Baltic Sea had been the last to become part of the Soviet Union. In 1991 they were the first to break away. Within a few months, the enormous country known as the Soviet Union ceased to exist. In its place were 15 separate, independent countries.

By far the largest of these countries is Russia. Even before the birth of the Soviet Union in 1917, Russia had dominated its neighbors and had conquered many of them throughout the centuries.

MANY ETHNIC GROUPS

The word **Soviet** describes people who lived in the former Soviet Union and their government. It does not describe an ethnic group. As you know, an ethnic group is made up of people who share a common language, history, and customs. More than 150 different ethnic groups lived in the Soviet Union. Some of these groups are huge. The Russians, with about 145 million people, are the largest. The smallest group has only about 500 people.

While the Soviet Union existed, some people in other countries mistakenly called all Soviet people *Russians*. That practice annoyed many non-Russians.

Russians are part of a larger group of people called *Slavs*. Two other ethnic groups, the Ukrainians and Belarusians (bel ə rüs′ ənz), are also Slavs. Together these three Slavic groups make up nearly 75 percent of the population of present-day Russia and its neighboring countries. Even though they are all Slavs, Russians, Ukrainians, and Belarusians consider themselves to be very different from one another.

In addition to the Slavic groups, many other ethnic groups live in the region. Georgians and Armenians, for example, live in the Caucasus Mountain region. Each of these groups has its own distinctive language and culture. Find **Georgia** and **Armenia** on the map on this page.

The Uzbeks make up the third largest ethnic group after the Russians and Ukrainians. Uzbeks, Kazakhs (kä zäks′), and Tajiks (tä jiks′) are a few of the ethnic groups of Central Asia. Use the map below to locate the five countries of Central Asia—**Uzbekistan**, Tajikistan, Kazakhstan, Turkmenistan, and Kyrgyzstan.

MAP SKILL: In 1991 the people of Estonia celebrated their independence from the Soviet Union. On which body of water is Estonia located?

RUSSIA AND ITS NEIGHBORS: Political

⊛ National capital　　• Other city

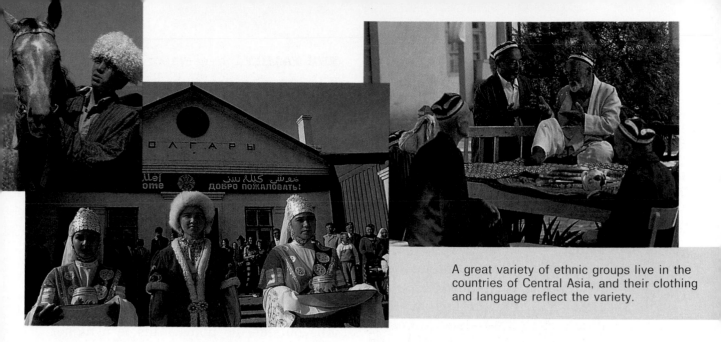

A great variety of ethnic groups live in the countries of Central Asia, and their clothing and language reflect the variety.

Farther east in northeastern Siberia live the Chukchi (chuk′ chē). This ethnic group is related to the Inuit, or Eskimos, of North America.

INDEPENDENT COUNTRIES

As you know, Russia is the largest country of this region. Russia's capital city, Moscow, was also the capital of the Soviet Union. You have read that Russia dominated many of its neighbors. Today people are wondering whether Russia will continue to dominate its neighbors.

Many Russians also live in the countries that were once part of the Soviet Union. In the past the rulers of Russia and the Soviet government sent Russians to fill jobs throughout the region. Often Russians had the best jobs, and other people objected.

While the Soviet Union existed, it was divided into 15 republics. Today each of those republics is a separate country. Each country is known by the name of its major ethnic group. However, within each country there are many people who do not belong to the main ethnic group. Many groups live side by side peacefully, but others have long histories as enemies.

One such rivalry exists between Armenians and Azerbaijanis. Many Armenians live in Azerbaijan (äz ər bī jän′), and some Azerbaijanis live in Armenia. Find these countries on the map on page 306. Armenians and Azerbaijanis speak different languages and practice different religions. Armed fights have often occurred between the two groups. While they were part of the Soviet Union, the Soviet government sent troops to the area to keep the peace.

RELIGION

During the more than 70-year period that the Soviet Union existed, its Communist government made it very difficult for people to practice their religion. Soviet leaders feared that any form of religion could endanger the communist government because some religious leaders had been powerful under previous governments. Soviet leaders wanted people to be loyal only to the government, not to their religious groups.

Houses of worship were closed. Some were kept as museums or public buildings. Others were allowed to fall apart.

In spite of years of discouraging religion, the Soviet leaders never destroyed it.

You will read more about the survival of religious traditions on pages 310-313.

Many Russians belong to the Russian Orthodox Church. Ukraine and Georgia each has its own Orthodox church. Like the Greek Orthodox Church, which you read about in Chapter 12, these Orthodox churches are Christian churches that are not headed by the Roman Catholic pope in Rome. Each of the Orthodox churches has its own leader.

Most Estonians and Latvians are Protestant. The majority of Lithuanians are Roman Catholic. Armenia has its own Christian church that separated from the Roman Catholic Church and the Orthodox churches hundreds of years ago.

Followers of Islam form the largest non-Christian religious group in the region. You will read more about this religion in Chapter 18.

Jews have lived throughout the region for centuries. Even before the Soviet Union was created Jews were often treated harshly. Some Jews emigrated to Israel and the United States. Today Jews, like other religious groups, are free to worship as they choose.

Most women hold full-time jobs. Many work in factories such as this textile factory in Tajikistan employing 10,000 workers.

THE FAMILY

When the whole family is together, the soul is in place.

These are the words of an old Russian proverb, or saying. In the major cities, where apartments are tiny and hard to find, families tend to be small and close-knit. In Siberia and Central Asia, where more space is available, families are also close, but they tend to be somewhat larger than in the cities.

Whether families are large or small, both men and women usually work. About 85 percent of all women of working age have jobs outside the home. This is a higher percentage than in any other industrialized region. Women hold many different kinds of jobs, from street cleaner to construction worker to judge. Almost 75 percent of all the region's doctors are women. There are more female engineers in the countries of this region than in any other region of the world.

Some families have a live-in *babushka*, or grandmother, to look after the children while the parents work. But most children of preschool age are cared for in day-care centers run by the government.

Life is hard for working mothers in the region, as it is everywhere. After a full day at their jobs, women do most of the shopping and housekeeping. There are few supermarkets. Shopping often means waiting for hours in long lines to buy food and other goods. When shoppers reach the front of the line, they often find that there is very little left to buy.

EDUCATION

"Give me a generation to train the children," wrote one Soviet leader, "and the seed I sow [plant] will never be uprooted." Soviet leaders saw education as a way to teach children about communism as well as to train them for jobs and professions.

This farm family in Georgia shares a traditional breakfast of meat, cucumbers, scallions, and bread.

Before the Soviet Union was formed, only a small percentage of children in the region attended school. The creation of the Soviet Union changed that. Schooling became free and available to everyone in the country. All children went to school until they were at least 15 years old.

In the Soviet Union children of all ethnic groups studied Russian. Many studied their own languages as well. Students throughout the country learned the same subjects. Their textbooks were produced by the Soviet government. Until the late 1980s, Soviet textbooks did not mention events in the country's history that might reflect badly on its communist leaders.

Now that there is no Soviet Union, the schools remain. But the system of education has changed because it no longer trains students in communism. Education in the region may vary from country to country because each of the 15 countries must design and operate its own school system.

A REGION OF MANY PEOPLE

Russia is a huge land with many different ethnic groups. Its neighboring countries also have a great variety of ethnic groups. Russians outnumber all the other ethnic groups in the region. As you have read, each group in the 15 countries follows its own customs and traditions.

For years the Soviet government kept a tight control over its people, but changes began to take place. In 1991, the Soviet republics became independent countries. In the next two lessons, you will read more about how these countries have been changing.

Check Your Reading

1. How many countries are in the region?
2. Which ethnic group is the largest in the region?
3. How did the Soviet government change the availability of education?
4. **THINKING SKILL:** What was the Soviet government's point of view regarding religion?

SURVIVAL of RELIGION

by Blake Eskin

In the last lesson you read that the Soviet Union broke up into 15 independent countries in 1991. Until then many ethnic groups were ruled by the Soviet government. Each of these groups has its own distinctive customs. In many cases, these groups also have religious traditions that are centuries old. However, until recently, the communist government of the Soviet Union opposed all religious practices. In this lesson you will read about how these traditions survived despite the government's opposition. As you read, think about how religion and its survival can be important to a culture.

A WAR ON RELIGION

As you know, the communist leaders of the 1917 revolution tried to abolish religion in their country. They insisted that the existence of many different religious groups would divide the Soviet Union. Using this argument, the government closed most houses of worship. The few that remained open were converted to museums. The government also tried to replace traditional religious holidays with newly invented holidays such as the Anniversary of the Revolution.

The Soviet government also refused to allow people to write or read books about religion. In response, people began printing such books in secret. This custom was called *samizdat* (säm' ēz dät), which means "self-publishing." In many cases, people were sent to prison or were executed for possessing samizdat literature or illegal printing presses. Still, these homemade books continued to circulate among friends and relatives. Samizdat was a method of struggle shared by many faiths. But just as each religious group in the Soviet Union had its own history, each group also had its own way of keeping religious traditions alive.

THE SURVIVAL OF CHRISTIANITY

The people of what was once the Soviet Union practice many different kinds of Christianity, including Roman Catholicism and Protestantism. However, the oldest and largest Christian church in the region is the Russian Orthodox Church.

The Orthodox Church originally developed in Byzantium (bə zant′ ē əm)—the ancient name for the modern-day city of Istanbul. According to tradition, a Russian noble named Prince Vladimir of Kiev decided to convert to Orthodox Christianity in A.D. 988. His conversion had a major impact on his country's history. Many Russians—including Russia's rulers—became Orthodox Christians. Churches in the Byzantine style, with high ceilings and onion-shaped domes, began appearing throughout Russia. Inside, worshipers prayed in front of icons. An icon is a painting of a saint or religious leader. Many Russians also hung icons on the walls of their houses and worshiped at home.

Russian Orthodoxy enjoyed the support of Russian governments for hundreds of years. After 1917, however, Orthodox Christians were subject to the same oppression as other groups in the Soviet Union. Most churches were boarded up. Others were converted to museums, warehouses, and even factories. The government asked people to stop praying and to remove icons from their houses.

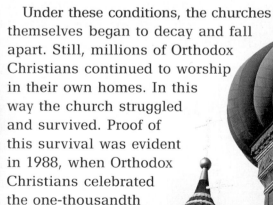

Under these conditions, the churches themselves began to decay and fall apart. Still, millions of Orthodox Christians continued to worship in their own homes. In this way the church struggled and survived. Proof of this survival was evident in 1988, when Orthodox Christians celebrated the one-thousandth anniversary of Prince Vladimir's conversion. In many parts of the country, churches and religious schools were restored and reopened. The icons that many people had been hiding in their homes were now openly and proudly displayed on their walls.

THE SURVIVAL OF ISLAM

Followers of Islam, who are called Muslims, have lived in the Caucasus and Central Asian areas of what was the Soviet Union for over 1,200 years. They have succeeded in preserving their traditions through centuries of foreign rule. When the Soviet government tried to restrict their customs, they found ways to adapt them to the new political situation.

For example, Muslims are commanded to make a pilgrimage to their holy city of Mecca in Saudi Arabia. But for many years, the Soviet government allowed no more than 20 Soviet Muslims to make this pilgrimage each year. Khadzhi Adil Zeinalov (käd′ zhē ä dēl′ zā′ nə lov), the head of a mosque in Baku, Azerbaijan, summed up the problem this way:

> *You know, to a Muslim, there are ten sacred things one must do, and among them [is] . . . going to Mecca, if health and finances permit. Here we have always had to add "and if the Government allows."*

How could Soviet Muslims make this required pilgrimage? For many years, their solution was to visit other places called *mazars*, which means "holy tombs." One such mazar is the Shah-i-zind tomb in the city of Samarkand, in Uzbekistan. This tomb is the burial site of Kusam-bin-Abbas, who brought Islam to Uzbekistan centuries ago. Thousands of Soviet Muslims made pilgrimages to Shah-i-zind every year.

More recently, the persistence of this tradition was officially acknowledged by the government. In April 1990 Soviet officials announced that special airline flights to Mecca would be arranged for Soviet Muslims. Zeinalov was elated by this good news. "For us, this announcement is a gift," he said. "It is like we are celebrating a holiday."

THE SURVIVAL OF JUDAISM

As you read in Lesson 1, Jewish people living in the Soviet Union have been treated harshly for many years. But like the Christians and Muslims, the Jews have fought to preserve their religious traditions. One such tradition is the study of the Torah and other Jewish holy books written in Hebrew. After 1917 the Soviet government refused to allow Jews to study Hebrew books. It also made sure that the Hebrew language was not taught in any state-run schools.

Many people broke these rules. For example, a Soviet Jew named Josif Begun (bā′ gün) secretly taught himself Hebrew and decided that he wanted to study the Torah. Since it was a crime to undertake such study in the Soviet Union, Begun asked permission to emigrate. Government officials refused his request. They also punished Begun by making sure he lost his job.

However, Begun refused to give up. To support himself and to help keep Jewish traditions alive, he began teaching Hebrew. On several occasions he was arrested, and spent a total of eight years in prison. He was finally allowed to immigrate to Israel in 1988, where he now pursues the Jewish tradition of study.

Although the Soviet Union has ceased to exist, many Jews fear continued persecution. Thousands have recently immigrated to Israel, the United States, and other countries. But many remain, looking for signs of hope. One such sign came in 1990, when a visiting American rabbi named Arthur Schneier led a Jewish prayer service in the Kremlin, the headquarters of the Soviet government! "It was very, very moving, the fact that we were obviously chanting and singing Hebrew prayers," said Schneier. "And they echoed throughout the Kremlin."

A PROMISING FUTURE

The independent governments of Russia and its neighbors now permit the practice of religion. Millions of young people have begun reclaiming ancient customs. By attending religious schools or quizzing their grandparents about religious practice, they are demonstrating how these traditions have survived, changed, and once again flourished.

Why did people struggle to keep their religious traditions alive in spite of government oppression?

313

The Economy

Key Vocabulary

command economy
capital goods
consumer goods
reform
perestroika
Commonwealth of Independent States

Key People

Mikhail Gorbachev
Boris Yeltsin

Read Aloud

This country produces 24 percent of all the world's milk and now we produce machines that can package all that milk efficiently and safely. But still, there's no milk in the stores.

These words were spoken by Alexander Panchenko, a manager of a factory that manufactured milk cartons. Shortages of basic goods such as milk were common in the Soviet Union. When Russia and its neighbors became independent, these shortages continued. But now these countries are free to work out new ways of organizing their economies.

Read for Purpose

1. **WHAT YOU KNOW:** How does a free-enterprise economic system work?
2. **WHAT YOU WILL LEARN:** How are the countries of the region trying to change their economies?

AN ECONOMIC SYSTEM ENDS

Imagine this. You live in a family in which the head of the family makes all the economic decisions. These include which businesses to begin, who will do which jobs, what products the business will produce, and how much each person will be paid. You as an individual cannot go into business for yourself and set your own prices. Suddenly the head of the family disappears. Family members now must make all the decisions that the head of the family once made. But family members have no experience in making decisions.

The situation described above is similar to what happened when the communist government of the Soviet Union ceased to exist and 15 separate countries had to work out their own economies. Until 1991 Soviet government officials in Moscow had made the decisions about where to build factories, what and how much to produce, how much to charge for products, and how much to pay workers.

Now these countries have to build new economies using what they can from the old Soviet Union. They must decide how much to cooperate with each other and with other countries. To understand the changes that must be made, you must first understand the old system.

314

A COMMAND ECONOMY

The Soviet economy was not working. Although it provided jobs for Soviet citizens, the economy did not produce enough of the goods and services that the people needed and wanted.

From 1917 until the late 1980s, Soviet citizens lived under the communist system of a command economy. In a command economy, the government makes most of the economic decisions. The government owns and operates land, factories, banks, and businesses. Everything from coal mines to taxicabs is owned and operated by the government.

Planners who worked for the Soviet government decided how many businesses needed to be established. They decided what goods would be manufactured, and they set all prices and wages. Often only one factory in the entire Soviet Union made a particular product.

For many years Soviet planners concentrated on producing capital goods. These are products that are used by industries to make other products. Soviet factories turned out huge quantities of capital goods, such as heavy machinery, tractors, trucks, and chemicals. But they failed to produce enough consumer goods, such as stoves, refrigerators, clothing, and furniture. Consumer goods satisfy people's needs and wants. Often the Soviet people simply did without them.

Workers did not have to worry about losing their jobs. In fact, the Soviet government guaranteed everybody a job. Keeping a job and getting paid had nothing to do with how good a job a worker did, so workers were not motivated to work hard. Most consumer goods were very scarce. Goods were bought and workers were paid even if the quality of the goods they produced was poor. As a result, the Soviet economy suffered.

This truck factory on the Kama River, west of the Ural Mountains, has been a major supplier of tractors for the region.

CHANGING THE ECONOMY

In 1985, Mikhail Gorbachev (mik ə ēl′ gôr′ bə chôf) became the head of the Soviet Union. Gorbachev wanted to reform the entire economy. To *reform* means "to make a change for the better."

Gorbachev called his plan of reforms perestroika (per ə stroi′ kə), or "restructuring." He hoped to reform the Soviet Union's economy by taking decision making out of the hands of the government officials. He wanted to give greater control to managers of factories and businesses. Workers who produced more would earn more.

Perestroika did not take place quickly enough for most Soviet citizens. Consumer

315

goods were still hard to find, and their quality was still poor.

MANY PROBLEMS TO SOLVE

In June 1991 a historic election took place in the Soviet Union. Boris Yeltsin was elected as the president of the Russian republic. Yeltsin was chosen from five candidates in the first free presidential election in Russia's history. Yeltsin wanted to abandon the communist command economy in favor of a capitalist free-enterprise system. He wanted to proceed at a much faster pace than that set by Gorbachev.

Yeltsin wanted to plunge the Russian republic into a kind of "shock therapy." The plan he supported was to lift all controls on prices for most foods and other goods. For years the government had set prices for meat, cooking oil, gasoline, and hundreds of other items. Yeltsin wanted prices to be determined by what buyers were willing to pay and what sellers were willing to be paid.

Although there have been frequent shortages of food in government stores in Moscow, food is often available in private outdoor markets.

Yeltsin put his "shock therapy" plan into effect in Russia at the end of 1991. Prices shot up overnight. Some foods cost three or four times what they cost the day before. Meat was often ten times more expensive. Many people became angry because their salaries had not been raised, and they could not afford to buy necessary foods.

Once Russia removed price controls, other countries in the region also raised prices. Otherwise people from Russia would have crossed national borders to buy goods at lower prices. That would have created shortages outside of Russia.

CREATING SEPARATE ECONOMIES

When Russia and its neighbors became independent countries, they realized that they were all connected by a single economic system. Many problems had to be solved and many questions had to be answered.

All 15 republics had used the ruble as their money. The independent countries had to decide whether to continue using rubles or to create their own currency. The Soviet Union had owned all the factories. The countries had to decide how to divide

Farmers in Ukraine grow a great deal of wheat. In Georgia, sheep-raising is an important economic activity.

the factories among themselves. Each country also had to decide who would now own the factories—the governments of the countries or private companies. They had to decide how the countries that had no plants for generating electric power could get a fair share of electricity. The countries also had to work out how to guarantee people the pensions and other benefits they had earned as citizens of the Soviet Union.

These were only a few of the economic problems that 15 countries had to solve. They needed a way to work together to solve them.

A NEW FORM OF UNION

Most of the countries realized that they could not solve their problems without cooperating. Some leaders suggested that they begin a new form of cooperation. They called the new organization they began in 1991 the Commonwealth of Independent States, or C.I.S.

Like the European Community, or E.C., which you read about in Chapter 10, the Commonwealth of Independent States offered a way to join the economies of a group of countries. The countries would remain independent, but they could link their economies.

The task of the C.I.S. was different from that of the E.C. The E.C. began with economies that were not strongly connected and worked to connect them. The C.I.S. began with a single economic system and tried to find ways to separate it while keeping some of the links.

LOOKING TO THE FUTURE

The economic system that existed in the Soviet Union underwent great changes even before the country ceased to exist. What had been a command economy is gradually changing to a mixed economy or a free-enterprise system. Each country must choose its own way.

Check Your Reading

1. What is a command economy?
2. What are capital goods and consumer goods?
3. Describe some economic problems that the newly independent countries had to solve.
4. **THINKING SKILL:** How could you check the accuracy of this statement, "This country produces 24 percent of all the world's milk."

317

1991: Should Economic Change Be Fast or Slow?

In this chapter you have read that before it fell the Soviet Union had a command economy. In a command economy the government owns and operates all the businesses. You have also read that one of the problems with the Soviet command economy was that consumer goods were in short supply. Shortages of clothing, televisions, cars, and shoes were common. Even food products were not easily found in stores. People often stood in long lines for many hours waiting to buy a loaf of bread. These difficult conditions have changed very little.

When Russia and its neighboring countries became independent, most leaders agreed that the command economy should be replaced by a capitalist economic system. In this system many businesses would be privately owned. However, people disagree about how that change should take place. Some people say that only quick and complete privatization—the selling of state-run businesses to private owners—could encourage economic growth. Others say that although privatization is a future goal, it is impossible to achieve in a short time. Meanwhile, the people of the countries that used to be part of the Soviet Union have continued to suffer shortages of food and other goods, and the leaders are still deciding what to do.

POINT ☆◁☞

The Change to Private Enterprise Should Be Fast

Grigory Yavlinsky, a Soviet economist, believes that the change to capitalism should happen quickly. He and Graham Allison, an American economist, wrote the following just before the fall of the Soviet Union.

> The goal of the program of economic transformation [*change*] is to create a *normal market economy* in the Soviet Union in the shortest possible time. Experience in other countries...dictate[s] that the reforms must be rapid...to have a chance of success. The reforms must also...aim to create an economy whose fundamental features will resemble those of the advanced industrial economies. . . .
>
> These steps will begin to narrow the growing gap between the living standards of Soviet citizens and the living standards of the advanced industrial economies.

- Why does Grigory Yavlinsky think economic change should be fast?

COUNTERPOINT ☜▷☆

The Change to Private Enterprise Should Be Slow

Roy A. Medvedev is a well-known Russian historian. Medvedev believes that a rapid change in the economy is a very difficult task which cannot be accomplished in a short time.

> It is impossible to carry out a really comprehensive [complete] privatization of our economy. You can't privatize the railway system, for example, or the telephone system. . . . KAMAZ [a huge vehicle manufacturer] will continue to exist and to operate as a large state enterprise, because it is connected by thousands of links to enterprises throughout the entire territory of the country. . . .
> So I think this argument between the privatizers and the supporters of the large state enterprises will end in a compromise, because both forms of enterprise are needed. It is necessary to develop a system of small private enterprise, and where large-scale production exists it is necessary to retain it.

- Why does Roy A. Medvedev think economic change should be slow?

UNDERSTANDING THE POINT/COUNTERPOINT

1. Who do you think has the stronger argument—Yavlinsky or Medvedev?
2. What other opinions might the people in the region have about economic change?
3. Is there a way that both sides in this discussion might reach a compromise? Explain your ideas.

LESSON 3

The Government

READ TO LEARN

Key Places

Kremlin	Minsk
Ukraine	Kazakhstan
Belarus	

Key People

Karl Marx
Lenin

Read Aloud

People have a free soul now. It's a hard time but nevertheless a happy time. The free spirit compensates [makes up] for the deficiencies [shortages] in food, and so forth. The process of democracy is a living organism. It has just been born. It has to grow.

These words capture the optimism of Vladimir Tikhonov. He was a Soviet citizen who was excited by the changes that had begun to take place in the Soviet Union even before the 15 countries became independent. Now even greater changes are taking place.

Read for Purpose

1. **WHAT YOU KNOW:** How have the economic systems of Russia and its neighbors been changing?
2. **WHAT YOU WILL LEARN:** What changes took place in the governments of Russia and its neighboring countries after the Soviet Union collapsed?

CHANGING GOVERNMENTS

During 1991, change was taking place so rapidly in the Soviet Union that map makers and textbook writers had difficulty keeping up. At the beginning of the year there was a country called the Soviet Union. It was made up of 15 republics that were all part of one nation. By the end of the year there was no country called the Soviet Union. One after another, each of the 15 republics had declared that it was independent. Maps had to be redrawn and textbooks had to be rewritten.

In this lesson you will learn about how those countries and their people began adapting to the change. You will learn more about the Commonwealth of Independent States. Above all you will learn that the breakup of the Soviet Union was only the start of many changes.

ABANDONING THE SOVIET SYSTEM

Even before the end of the Soviet Union many leaders had decided to try to introduce democracy. The communist system of the Soviet Union had been based on ideas of government described by a German thinker and writer named Karl Marx.

In the 1800s Marx described an idea of social organization in which all property is owned in common. He called this system communism. In a communist nation,

320

the government also runs the nation's economy. Marx believed that, eventually, there would be no need for government because everyone's needs would be met. Then true communism would be established and everyone would be treated equally. The Soviet Union was the first country to apply some of Marx's ideas.

As you know, the United States and many other countries have a free-enterprise system, one in which individuals, called capitalists, own property and make economic decisions. Marx believed that capitalists kept workers poor in order to maintain their own power. Sooner or later, he said, the workers would revolt against the rich. Then people would be equal, and property would be commonly owned.

In the early 1900s Vladimir Ilyich Ulyanov, better known as Lenin, came to believe that Marx's ideas could be used in Russia. Lenin believed that the revolution against the wealthy should be led by a few strong leaders. In 1917 Lenin selected a group of people to help him guide the Russian Revolution. This group later became the core of the Communist party.

In 1917, the old Russian government fell apart as a result of the Russian Revolution. Lenin and the Communist party came to power. Lenin argued that the Communists should seize all private property and control it for the benefit of the people. The Communists controlled the government, and the government took full control of the nation's economy.

COMMUNISM IN THE SOVIET UNION

Communism in the Soviet Union did put an end to most private property. The government seized the ownership of most farms and factories. Almost all workers worked for the government.

Yet all workers were not equal. Government officials received better apartments

Pictures of Lenin, the founder of the Soviet Union, were displayed throughout the country.

and more money and benefits than ordinary workers. Athletes, ballet dancers, and a few other people also had better standards of living than ordinary workers.

The Soviet Union's constitution stated that all citizens had the right to a job, vacation, and free education, as well as to freedom of speech, press, assembly, and religion. But the Soviet government failed to guarantee these freedoms for individuals. Thus, many people, especially writers and scientists, found their freedoms denied. Many people who disagreed with the government were forced to live in Siberia or were sent to jail.

In 1989 the Soviet constitution was amended to provide greater protection for the freedom of individuals. However, many people were still unhappy because the constitution still did not provide adequate protection for certain freedoms.

THE COMMUNIST PARTY

Between 1917 and 1990 the Communist party was the "leading and guiding force of Soviet society." By law, it was the only political party allowed. For many years all

Boris Yeltsin, president of Russia, stood on a tank to defy a communist group that tried to stop the move to democracy.

the real power for ruling the Soviet Union was in the hands of the Communist Party. The party controlled the government and the economy.

A HISTORIC ELECTION

In March 1989, for the first time since the Communists came to power in 1917, the people of the Soviet Union were given a choice of candidates in a national election. Previously, only approved Communist party candidates had been on the ballot.

Throughout the country members of the Communist party were voted out of office. Even party leaders who ran unopposed lost because they failed to win 50 percent of the vote. Voters had simply crossed their names off the ballots.

By the end of 1991 the Communist party had lost all its power. Many Communists had lost elections. Other former Communists had declared that they no longer belonged to the party.

In August 1991 some government officials who were unhappy about the Communist party's loss of power tried to stage a coup, a sudden seizing of the government. Russian President Boris Yeltsin de-

fied the coup leaders, and the coup failed. Mikhail Gorbachev rapidly lost power.

STRUGGLES FOR POWER

After all the republics had become independent countries, Gorbachev found that he was head of a country that did not exist. His job had disappeared.

The 15 new countries faced problems of government similar to those they faced with the economy. For example, they had to decide which country would be in charge of the army and navy. Several countries said that the portion of the army or navy stationed in their country belonged to them. But soldiers and sailors wanted to serve in their own country's forces. The Soviet Union had many nuclear weapons. Which country would keep them? Or should they all be destroyed?

Moscow, the capital of Russia, had also been the capital of the Soviet Union. After independence, Russia claimed all buildings in the Kremlin, the Soviet government offices. On December 25, 1991, the Russian flag was raised over the Kremlin.

CONTINUED UNREST

The three Slavic countries of Russia, Ukraine, and Belarus began the Commonwealth of Independent States (C.I.S.). They chose Minsk, the capital of Belarus, to be the headquarters of the C.I.S.

COMMONWEALTH OF INDEPENDENT STATES: Political

⊛ National capital   • Other city

▢ Members of the Commonwealth   ▢ Former Soviet Republics not part of the Commonwealth

MAP SKILL: The Commonwealth of Independent States was established in 1991 at a meeting in Alma-Ata. In which country is Alma-Ata located?

Kazakhstan was the first non-Slavic nation to join.

The C.I.S. is a plan of economic and governmental relations. However, the C.I.S. has not been able to prevent Armenia, Azerbaijan, and other members from fighting over ethnic and other differences.

Russia, too, has had its problems. Immediately after being elected president in 1991, Yeltsin faced many economic and political challenges. Among them were rapidly rising prices. This caused some parliamentary leaders who had been communists to try and stop Russia's move to democracy. They staged a coup in 1993 that President Yeltsin quickly put down.

THEN AND NOW

The Soviet Union has ceased to exist, and 15 independent countries have taken its place. The Communist party, which ruled the Soviet Union for about 70 years, has lost its power. Economic, political, and ethnic unrest have troubled Russia and its neighbors in the early 1990s.

Check Your Reading

1. Describe the theory of communism.
2. Who was Lenin?
3. What changes have taken place in Russia and its neighboring countries?
4. **THINKING SKILL:** What questions could you ask to find out what changes are still taking place in this region?

Drawing Conclusions

When you draw a conclusion, you put facts together so that they mean something to you. Suppose you walk into your backyard just in time to see a raccoon disappearing into the bushes. The garbage pail is overturned, with its lid removed and garbage spread out on the lawn. You would probably conclude that the raccoon had knocked over the pail, opened the lid, and started to eat some garbage. You could tell what had happened even though you had not seen it happen.

Trying the Skill

Read the facts listed below. Think about what the facts mean. State a conclusion based on the facts.

- The average shopper in Russia spends 14 hours a week standing in shopping lines.
- Because most consumer goods, even ordinary ones like toothpaste, are often unavailable, shoppers rush to join a line even when they don't know what is for sale.
- In most Russian stores making a purchase requires waiting in three lines: one line to select the item, a second line to pay for it, and a third line to pick up the item purchased.

1. What conclusion did you draw?
2. What did you do to draw your conclusion?

HELPING YOURSELF

The steps on the left will help you to draw conclusions. The example on the right shows one way to apply these steps to the facts about Russian shoppers.

One Way to Draw Conclusions	Example
1. Identify the topic or subject.	The subject is consumer shopping in Russia.
2. Read the information given.	In this step you quickly read the information to get a general sense of the facts.
3. Look for ideas that are common to all the pieces of information.	Each piece of information is about Russian shoppers waiting in line.
4. Write a sentence stating how the subjects or ideas common to all the pieces of information relate to one another. This is your conclusion.	One conclusion that you might draw is that shopping in Russia is difficult and time-consuming.

Applying the Skill

Now apply what you have learned by drawing a conclusion from the following pieces of information.

- In Kazakhstan, the Kazakhs make up only 36 percent of the population. Russians and Ukrainians together make up the largest ethnic groups there, with about 50 percent of the population.
- Most Kazakh familes have five or six children. The Russian and Ukrainian families usually have two or three.
- The Kazakh population is likely to increase at two or three times the rate of the Russian and Ukrainian populations for the foreseeable future.

1. What is the topic of the information given above?
   a. Infant deaths among the people of Kazakhstan
   b. Population figures for some groups in Kazakhstan
   c. Ethnic groups in Kazakhstan

2. What patterns do you see in this information?
   a. Birthrates are the same for both the Kazakhs and the Russians and Ukrainians in Kazakhstan.
   b. Birthrates are increasing faster for Kazakhs than for Russians and Ukrainians.
   c. Birthrates are declining among Kazakhs, Russians, and Ukrainians.

3. Write a sentence that states a conclusion you can draw from the information given above.

Reviewing the Skill

1. Tell in your own words what it means to draw a conclusion.
2. List some steps you can follow to help you to draw conclusions.
3. Name some occasions when you find it necessary or useful to draw conclusions in school.

Arts and Recreation

READ TO LEARN

Key Vocabulary

censor
glasnost

Key People

Alexander Pushkin
Feodor Dostoyevsky
Leo Tolstoy

Peter Ilyich Tchaikovsky
Boris Pasternak
Alexander Solzhenitsyn

Read Aloud

For many years the Soviet government strictly controlled the right to print newspapers and to produce art such as poetry. Today the glorious tradition of arts, long held captive by the government of the Soviet Union, is being returned to the people of Russia and its neighbors.

Read for Purpose

1. **WHAT YOU KNOW:** What had been the Soviet government's attitude toward the rights of its citizens?
2. **WHAT YOU WILL LEARN:** What changes are taking place for the region's artists and athletes?

LITERATURE, PAST AND PRESENT

For many years Russian literature astounded the world with the richness of its prose and poetry. The poet and story writer Alexander Pushkin, who wrote in the 1800s, is called the father of Russian literature. He was followed by great novelists, such as Feodor Dostoyevsky (fyō dôr dos tə yef′ skē) and Leo Tolstoy.

Russian writers have written about everything from the beauty of the Russian countryside to the tragedy of unhappy love. During the time of the Soviet Union some writers' works opposed the government. They were not allowed to publish in the Soviet Union, but some writings were passed around secretly.

Not all of the great literature of the region has been produced by Russians. Many other ethnic groups have their own literature. For example, Georgia has a long history of beautiful poetry and songs. Unfortunately, few people outside of Georgia can read the Georgian language and little has been translated.

MUSIC

Among the many famous Russian composers, several wrote music especially for the ballet. One of the best known of these composers is Peter Ilyich Tchaikovsky (il′ yich chī kof′ skē). About 100 years ago he wrote the music for the famous ballet *The Nutcracker*. Adults and children around the world have delighted in the tale of a magical nutcracker that comes alive.

GOVERNMENT AND THE ARTS

Writers and other artists were supported and controlled by the Soviet government. Government-approved artists often received training and jobs that allowed them to concentrate on their work. But works of art that criticized the government or its leaders were censored. To censor is to prevent something from being made public.

Until the 1980s control of what was written and published in the Soviet Union was strict. But well-known Soviet writers were able to publish censored works in other countries. When writer Boris Pasternak was awarded the Nobel Prize for literature in 1958, the Soviet government forced him to turn it down. Alexander Solzhenitsyn (sol zhə nēt′ sən), who wrote about life in Soviet labor camps, lost his citizenship and was sent into exile.

In the 1980s Mikhail Gorbachev introduced a new policy known as glasnost, or "openness." For the first time since the Russian Revolution, state controls over the press were outlawed. As a result, there was an explosion of free speech. Soviet citizens gained the freedom to see plays and read literature that had been banned for more than 60 years. As one writer said:

Even if [glasnost] were to end today, what has already been accomplished in the past three years will go down in the history of Russian literature.

Glasnost had an effect on music as well. Until 1986 all rock music had been carefully controlled by a government agency. Today anyone can listen to their favorite rock groups.

SPORTS AND LEISURE

Television shows and movies are also very popular in Russia and its neighbors. Another favorite pastime is the game of chess. Chess players from Russia and its neighboring countries have won many international chess competitions.

Even when the weather is cold, people like to be outdoors. On even the coldest days both children and adults enjoy skating, skiing, hiking, and sledding.

Russia's Kirov Ballet is world famous for the skill and grace of its dancers.

For many years talented young Soviet athletes received special training in sports academies. The academies prepared these athletes for international events such as the Olympics. As a result, Soviet athletes won many Olympic medals.

NEW FREEDOMS

As you have read, the people of this region have made many contributions to literature and music. Government control of the arts has ended, and artists now enjoy a greater variety of free expression.

Check Your Reading

1. Name three major Russian writers.
2. What effect did glasnost have on the arts?
3. What do people in the region do to relax?
4. **THINKING SKILL:** What were the effects of the Soviet Union's decision to censor many of its artists?

327

RUSSIA AND ITS NEIGHBORS: CULTURAL GEOGRAPHY

 PEOPLE

- The Slavs are the largest of the more than 150 ethnic groups in the region
- The Soviet Union was officially atheistic

- Religions: Eastern Orthodox, Islam, Roman Catholicism, Judaism

- Soviet families are close-knit
- Education is highly valued

ECONOMY

- The Soviet government owned most land, most factories, and most banks
- Perestroika, or economic restructuring began to introduce capitalism
- Each newly independent country has its own economic system

- A change to a free-enterprise system has caused hardships

GOVERNMENT

- Soviet system: communism developed by Karl Marx and shaped by Lenin, the founder of the Soviet state
- The real power in the Soviet Union was the Communist party

- 15 former republics are now independent countries
- Some newly independent countries formed the Commonwealth of Independent States to cooperate on mutual interests

 ARTS AND RECREATION

- Famous writers: Tolstoy, Dostoyevsky, Pushkin, Pasternak, Solzhenitsyn

- The Russian ballet is world famous
- Tchaikovsky wrote the music for The Nutcracker ballet
- Many ethnic groups have their own traditions of arts

- Many people enjoy television, movies, skating, skiing, hiking, and sledding

IDEAS TO REMEMBER

- The Slavs belong to the largest of more than 150 ethnic groups in Russia and its neighboring countries.
- The Soviet Union had a planned economy, but most newly independent countries in the region have encouraged free enterprise.
- The 15 independent countries have established new governments and are also trying to cooperate with one another.
- The region has produced many famous writers and composers, and its people enjoy a variety of sports.

REVIEWING VOCABULARY

capital goods consumer goods
censor reform
command economy

Number a sheet of paper from 1 to 5. Beside each number write the word or term from the above list that best completes the sentence.

1. To prevent works of art it disliked from being made public, the Soviet government acted to ＿＿ them.
2. In a ＿＿, the government makes most economic decisions for a country.
3. Products, like heavy machinery, tractors, and trucks, that industries make for use by other industries are called ＿＿.
4. To make a change for the better in something is to ＿＿ it.
5. Products like stoves, refrigerators, clothing, and furniture that satisfy people's needs and wants, are called ＿＿.

REVIEWING FACTS

1. Which three countries were the first to gain independence from the Soviet Union in 1991?
2. To which larger ethnic group do Russians, Ukrainians, and Belarusians all belong?
3. What are the five countries of Central Asia?
4. Name three major religions practiced by the people of Russia and neighboring countries.
5. Toward what kind of economic system have Russia and its neighbors been trying to move?
6. What does *perestroika* mean? Which leader of the Soviet Union introduced it?
7. How did Boris Yeltsin's "shock therapy" affect prices in Russia and neighboring countries?

8. Who was the leader who helped to bring the Communist Party to power and establish the Soviet Union in 1917?
9. Why was the Commonwealth of Independent States established? What were some its first economic goals and challenges?
10. What was glasnost and what effect did it have on the arts in the former Soviet Union?

WRITING ABOUT MAIN IDEAS

1. **Writing a List:** Write a list of statements about the many ethnic groups that live in Russia and its neighboring countries.
2. **Writing a Paragraph:** "Gorbachev opened a volcano, and I don't think he realized the lava was so deep," stated a candidate in the 1989 Soviet elections. What do you think the writer meant? Write a paragraph giving facts that support the quotation.
3. **Writing About Perspectives:** Imagine that you and your family are Russians who are undergoing the challenge of living with a new economic system in your country. Write a letter to a pen pal in the United States explaining what changes you are going through and what you hope for in the future.

BUILDING SKILLS: DRAWING CONCLUSIONS

1. What does it mean to draw a conclusion?
2. List some of the steps you could follow to draw conclusions.
3. Why is it important that you be able to draw conclusions?

CHAPTER 16

EASTERN EUROPE
FOCUS

For us, there is no Eastern Europe. It is a collection of countries. . . . You should not see us as a single entity.

This statement by the Czech Nobel Prize-winning poet Jaroslav Seifert expresses the opinion of many Eastern Europeans. In this chapter you will read that each nation in Eastern Europe has its own distinct history and its own customs. You will also read about the many recent changes that most of the countries of Eastern Europe have been experiencing.

The People

READ TO LEARN

Key Vocabulary

satellite
nationalism
Cyrillic

Key Places

Poland
Czechoslovakia
Hungary
Bulgaria

Romania
Albania
Yugoslavia

Read Aloud

For the first time in my life, I feel proud singing the national anthem.

These are the words of Andrea Ernyeiova, a 16-year-old student from the Czech Republic. Across much of Eastern Europe, people are rediscovering their national pride after years of domination by the Soviet Union.

Read for Purpose

1. **WHAT YOU KNOW:** How do the ethnic groups of Russia and its neighbors contribute to the cultures of their countries?
2. **WHAT YOU WILL LEARN:** How do the ethnic groups of Eastern Europe contribute to the cultures of their countries?

SATELLITES NO MORE

Great changes took place in Eastern Europe in 1989. Beginning with Poland, five countries freed themselves from Communist rule and became independent of the Soviet Union.

Until 1989 Poland, the former country of Czechoslovakia, Hungary, Bulgaria, and Romania were called satellites of the Soviet Union. Like planets, they all "revolved" around the same "sun"—the Soviet Union. After World War II the Soviet Union kept tight control of these countries. The former country of East Germany was also a satellite nation.

The Soviet Union placed severe limits on people's freedom in the satellite countries. In Hungary in 1956, and in Czechoslovakia in 1968, the people rose up against their Soviet-controlled governments to demand more freedom. Both times the Soviet army moved in to crush the uprisings.

In the late 1980s the Soviet Union could no longer control the demand for freedom that the people of the satellite countries expressed. By 1989 all the satellite countries had broken free.

Two other Eastern European countries had not been Soviet satellites. Albania and the former country of Yugoslavia had cut their ties with the Soviet Union many decades ago. Although both were communist nations, they were very different from each other. Albania had strict rules about what its people could do, where they could go, and even what they could wear. In Yugoslavia people often enjoyed greater freedom than people in the Soviet Union.

EASTERN EUROPE:
Political

✸ National
   capital

• Other
   city

MAP SKILL: Eastern Europe is made up of twelve countries, the poorest of which is Albania. Which three seas border this region?

MANY ETHNIC GROUPS

Eastern Europeans are known for their nationalism, or a strong love of one's country. In fact, Eastern Europe consists of many ethnic groups, each one proud of its heritage. The map on this page shows you the countries in which they live.

Many ethnic groups in Eastern Europe are descended from Slavs who migrated into the area about 1,500 years ago from lands to the east of the area where they now live. Large Slavic groups live in many countries of Eastern Europe.

Poland, Hungary, and Albania each have a majority population of one ethnic group and small minorities of other groups. The Hungarians are not Slavs. They descended from people called *Magyars* who came from the east 1,000 years ago.

Other Eastern European countries are home to more than one large ethnic group. The former Czechoslovakia, for instance, had roughly 10 million Czechs and nearly 4 million Slovaks. Both the Czechs and the Slovaks cling to their own identities. That was one reason why Czechoslovakia was split into two nations—Slovakia and the Czech Republic—at the beginning of 1993.

Several major ethnic groups lived in former Yugoslavia. Many of these people lived in their own republic in Yugoslavia and spoke their own language. After the Soviet Union ended in 1991, the republics began to declare their independence. By 1992 Yugoslavia had split into five countries: Slovenia, Croatia, Bosnia and Herzegovina, Yugoslavia, and Macedonia.

That same year, a bitter civil war broke out among the Serbs, Croats, and Muslims in Bosnia and Herzegovina. World leaders tried to end the war, but it was fueled by strong feelings of nationalism. Despite common Slavic roots, the Serbs and the Croats maintain a fierce rivalry. There are also rivalries between Slavic and non-

Slavic groups, such as the Christian Serbs and the Muslim Bosnians.

The Gypsies are another non-Slavic ethnic group in Eastern Europe. These wandering people once earned a living mainly by mending pots and pans, telling fortunes, and trading horses. Believing that these people originated in Egypt, Europeans called them Gypsies. However, the Gypsies probably came to Europe from India. Gypsies call themselves the *Rom* and their language, *Romany.*

LANGUAGES

According to an often quoted Czech proverb, "As long as the language lives, the nation is not dead." Each Eastern European ethnic group takes pride in its language, knowing that language helps to preserve people's ethnic identity.

Most Eastern European languages are Slavic in origin. These related languages contain many similar words. For example, the word *please* is *prosím* (pro' sēm) in Czech and *prosze* (pro' shē) in Polish.

As the chart on this page shows, Eastern European languages are written in several different alphabets. Usually the alphabet is Roman, which is used in English, or Cyrillic (sə ril' ik), which is used in Russian. Some languages were once written in the Greek and Arabic alphabets. The alphabet for a language may contribute to feelings of belonging to a group. For example, Serbians and Croatians speak the same language, called Serbo-Croatian, but Croatians use the Roman alphabet, and Serbians use Cyrillic.

RELIGION

Christians have lived in Eastern Europe for over 1,000 years. The Eastern Orthodox Church and the Roman Catholic Church are the two largest religious groups in the region. Muslims have lived in Eastern Eu-

LANGUAGES OF EASTERN EUROPE

Language	Language Family	Alphabet
Albanian	separate branch of Indo-European	Roman
Bulgarian	Slavic	Cyrillic
Croatian	Slavic	Roman
Czech	Slavic	Roman
Hungarian (Magyar)	Finno-Ugric	Roman
Macedonian	Slavic	Cyrillic
Montenegrin	Slavic (Serbian)	Cyrillic
Polish	Slavic	Roman
Romanian	Romance	Roman
Serbian	Slavic	Cyrillic
Slovak	Slavic	Roman
Slovene	Slavic	Roman

CHART SKILL: The chart shows many of the languages spoken in Eastern Europe. Which of these languages are not Slavic?

rope for over 500 years. Until the end of World War I, many Eastern European countries were ruled by the Muslims of the Ottoman Empire.

While under the influence of the Soviet Union, most Eastern European governments tried to discourage the practice of religion. Yet religious feelings ran so high in Eastern Europe that the governments often had no choice but to allow the people to follow their faith. As Eastern Europe broke away from the Soviet Union, people gained more religious freedom.

In parts of Eastern Europe, religion is a very strong force that binds people together. Nearly all Poles are Roman Catholics. The importance of the Roman Catho-

Prague, the capital of the Czech Republic, is considered by many to be one of the most beautiful cities in Eastern Europe.

lic Church was made clear in 1978 when one of its leaders, Karol Wojtyla (voi ti′ wə) became Pope John Paul II. The Roman Catholic Church in Poland also helped to lead the country to independence from the Soviet Union.

Eastern Europe once had a large Jewish population. During World War II, 3 million Jews in Poland alone died in concentration camps. As a result of the Holocaust, few Jews live in Eastern Europe today.

WAYS OF LIFE

Many Eastern European families are small. Most families have just one or two children. Both men and women typically work outside the home.

About half of all Eastern Europeans live in or near cities. Many Eastern European cities have preserved many of their traditional buildings. In Prague, the capital of the Czech Republic, ancient churches with gold-topped spires stand side by side with lovingly restored buildings from before the turn of the century. Most cities contain both traditional and modern buildings.

Housing shortages are common. People often crowd together in small apartments. The three members of the Novak family of Hungary, for example, live in two city rooms. According to Peter Novak:

Even in a family as close and loving as ours, everyone has to be very patient so that we can live together in such a small, crowded place.

Modern ways of life have reached rural areas. Yet traditional ways of life are also preserved. In rural areas, families tend to be larger, and farming is a way of life.

ETHNIC HERITAGE

As you have read, the different ethnic groups of Eastern Europe are proud of their heritage. Despite decades of Soviet control, the various ethnic and religious groups maintained their identity. Today a spirit of nationalism is sweeping through the region. This spirit has served to unite certain countries and to tear others apart.

 Check Your Reading

1. Why were some countries called "satellites" of the Soviet Union?
2. Why is nationalism important to the people of Eastern Europe?
3. How does language affect people's sense of belonging in Eastern Europe?
4. **THINKING SKILL:** What are two questions you might ask to learn more about why nationalism is so strong in Eastern Europe?

The Economy

Key Vocabulary

quota

Read Aloud

I have courage. Every day is exciting.

These are the words of Malgorzata Zuch, who runs a small business in Poland. Malgorzata is one of many people who are bringing new energy to Poland's economy. After Soviet control ended, the economic condition of many Eastern European countries changed almost overnight. As a result, new laws and attitudes are developing as people adjust to changing business needs. Some Eastern European economies are changing at a dizzying pace, while economic change in other countries is slower.

Read for Purpose

1. **WHAT YOU KNOW:** What changes are taking place in the economies of Russia and its neighbors?
2. **WHAT YOU WILL LEARN:** What changes are taking place in the economies of the countries of Eastern Europe?

CHANGING THE SYSTEM

Until the late 1980s the Soviet Union controlled nearly all economic matters in the satellite countries. The Soviet Union maintained communist systems in these countries. A Soviet-controlled trade group set quotas, or fixed amounts, for the types of goods that each Eastern European country could produce and sell. There were also quotas that required each country to buy a certain amount of goods. Hungary, for example, may have had to buy a set amount of steel from the Soviet Union and sell a set number of buses to the Soviet Union.

Today the former satellite countries are pursuing independent economic paths. Some countries, such as Poland, have taken great strides by making a complete change to a free-market system. Other countries are experimenting with a mixed economy.

ALBANIA AND YUGOSLAVIA

As you read in Lesson 1, both Yugoslavia and Albania broke their ties with the Soviet Union several decades ago. Yugoslavia followed an economic path that was much freer than that of the Soviet Union and the satellite countries. Trade with the West was encouraged. Workers had the power to own and manage their industries. A Croatian leader noted, "Here workers feel they participate, that the decisions are in their own hands."

In Albania the government has had almost total control over the nation's economy. Albania's government hoped that in

Among Eastern Europe's many large factories are this textile factory in Hungary (*above*) and this aircraft factory in Yugoslavia (*below*).

this way Albania would become entirely self-sufficient. However, as Albanian industry and agriculture suffered, the country slowly began to trade with other countries. It remains to be seen whether Albania will expand its trade or whether it will emphasize production from within.

INDUSTRY AND RESOURCES

About one third of the workers in Eastern Europe have jobs in mining and manufacturing. High-quality coal is mined in Poland, and various other mineral resources are mined in Yugoslavia. Look at the map on page 337 to see the areas where mining and manufacturing take place in Eastern Europe.

Given the satellite countries' former ties to the Soviet Union, it is not surprising that Eastern Europe, as did the Soviet Union, has several factories that are huge. It is also not surprising that for many years these countries produced more capital goods than consumer goods.

Many state-run enterprises are being transformed from state ownership to private ownership. In the process, factories are being modernized in order to produce goods that will be competitive with goods produced in other countries.

The transition from a controlled economy to a free-market economy has been difficult. Tough decisions determine how much of a product to manufacture and where the products should be sold. The larger the enterprise, the harder it is to make these decisions. For the time being, small businesses will probably lead the transition to a free-enterprise system.

AGRICULTURE

Until the 1950s Eastern Europe was mainly an agricultural area. The top map on page 337 shows that much of Eastern Europe contains major farming areas. Today many of the workers in Eastern Europe still have jobs in agriculture. Eastern European agricultural products include grain, potatoes, sugar beets, and livestock. Regional specialties abound, one of which is paprika, a type of red pepper that Hungarians use to spice many dishes.

In the late spring a valley in the Balkan Mountains of Bulgaria blossoms with millions of roses. The roses are grown for one purpose—to make perfume. The perfume is produced from rose oil. Rose oil is expensive to make because 3 tons (2.7 metric t) of rose petals produce only about 1 quart (0.95 l) of oil. Hundreds of workers are needed to pick the roses by hand. They start work at 4:00 A.M. and quit at sunrise because the sunlight causes the rose oil to evaporate. Bulgaria is the world's leading producer of rose oil. Much of the oil is exported to other nations.

Under the influence of the Soviet Union, most farmers in Eastern Europe were encouraged to work on collectives or state farms. On collectives, land is owned by a group of farmers who work together and share the earnings. State farms are owned and operated by the government.

Private ownership of small farms is now common. Even under Soviet control, many farmers were allowed to own their own small plots of land. For the time being, many agricultural products are produced by large farms that are run by the government. As with factories, the people of Eastern Europe are slowly working to transfer the ownership of certain agricultural enterprises to private hands.

PRIVATE ENTERPRISE

While under Soviet control, limited private ownership was allowed in Hungary and Poland. After gaining control of their economies, these countries had a head start in leading other Eastern European nations toward private ownership and a free-market system. In Bulgaria and Romania, the move toward private ownership has been slower.

You had read in Lesson 1 that Czechoslovakia split into two countries because of ethnic differences. It also separated because western Czechoslovakia, now the Czech Republic, wanted to tie itself closer to Western Europe. Eastern Czechoslovakia, now Slovakia, wanted to make economic changes more slowly. To prevent unrest, Czechoslovakia's leaders decided to divide the nation into two countries.

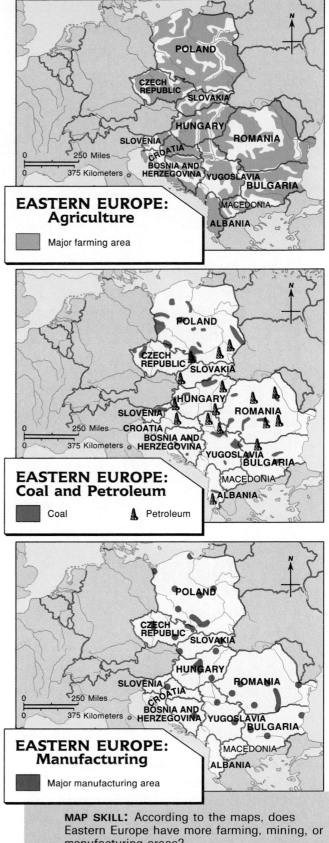

EASTERN EUROPE: Agriculture

☐ Major farming area

EASTERN EUROPE: Coal and Petroleum

■ Coal   ⚲ Petroleum

EASTERN EUROPE: Manufacturing

■ Major manufacturing area

MAP SKILL: According to the maps, does Eastern Europe have more farming, mining, or manufacturing areas?

Many privately owned businesses have developed in Eastern European countries since the communist government was overthrown.

One Hungarian factory worker, Gyula Balogh, has embraced free enterprise by selling herbal teas. With a growing business, he is succeeding in a way that had been impossible. "Ten or 20 years ago," he says, "I never could have done all this."

LIVING WITH ECONOMIC CHANGE

You have read that in the past the Soviet Union controlled the economies of most of Eastern Europe. These economies were based on central planning and featured collective farms and industries that produced capital goods.

Today many of the countries of Eastern Europe are making the transition from a command to a free-market economy. Some countries have made more progress than others. Given the difficulty of the transition, much work remains to be done.

 Check Your Reading

1. List the agricultural products that are produced in Eastern Europe.
2. What is a quota?
3. How have the economies of the former satellite countries of Eastern Europe changed in recent times?
4. **THINKING SKILL:** Compare and contrast a controlled economy and a free-enterprise economy. List at least two ways in which they are different.

338

The Government

READ TO LEARN

Key Vocabulary
buffer zone
Warsaw Pact

Key People
Vaclav Havel
Lech Walesa

Read Aloud

*From a democracy to a dictatorship, sometimes you need a day,
. . . from a dictatorship to a democracy, the way is very
much longer.*

These are the words of Romania's prime minister, Petre Roman. In the following lesson you will read that many of the countries of Eastern Europe suddenly broke away from the influence of the government of the Soviet Union. You will also read about the steps that these countries are taking as they learn to govern themselves.

Read for Purpose

1. **WHAT YOU KNOW:** How are Eastern European countries changing their economies?
2. **WHAT YOU WILL LEARN:** How have Eastern European countries been changing their governments since 1989?

A NEW FREEDOM

I learned in prison that everything is possible, so perhaps I should not be amazed. But I am.

These were the words of Vaclav Havel (väk′ lav häv′ el) as he reflected on the sudden changes that took place in Eastern Europe in 1989. Havel is a playwright who helped lead the opposition to Soviet control over the government of Czechoslovakia. Havel has been a firm believer in freedom for his people. His outspoken views on freedom led him to be jailed several times by the communist government. Yet Havel's spirit remained unbroken.

In 1989 the people of Czechoslovakia rallied around Havel in demanding freedom from Soviet control. Similar demands were made by the people of Hungary, Bulgaria, Poland, and Romania. One by one the Soviet-backed governments in each country fell. These revolutions were accomplished with little violence, except for Romania where several hundred people died and the former communist leader was quickly executed. In Czechoslovakia Vaclav Havel was elected as the country's president. He became the president of the Czech Republic in 1993.

With the removal of the communist governments in the former satellite countries, many Eastern Europeans enjoyed a fresh breath of freedom. Soon, however, it became clear that the new freedom had brought with it a new set of responsibilities.

Decisions had to be made as to what kind of government to establish. New constitutions and new laws had to be written. New leaders had to be chosen, and people had to decide what to do with their former leaders. After years of living under the influence of the Soviet Union, people had to learn how to live in a democracy in which they could rule themselves.

AN END TO THE WARSAW PACT

At the end of World War II, the Soviet Union extended its sphere of influence to include Eastern Europe, partly to protect itself. Because the land of the Soviet Union and Germany had fought two major wars within 30 years, the Soviets decided to make Eastern Europe a buffer zone, or a region between hostile powers. However, unlike many buffer zones, Eastern Europe was not expected to remain neutral, but to be friendly to the Soviet Union.

The buffer-zone countries of Eastern Europe were joined to the Soviet Union by a military alliance called the Warsaw Pact. The Warsaw Pact included East Germany and all of the other countries of Eastern Europe except Yugoslavia and Albania. As part of the pact, the Soviet Union was allowed to station troops in Eastern Europe. The Warsaw Pact formally came to an end on July 1, 1991. Troops from the Soviet Union began to leave Eastern Europe.

After Hungary overthrew its communist leaders, voters chose a new government in a democratic election.

Lech Walesa (*left*), a former leader of Poland's Solidarity union, and Vaclav Havel (*right*), a Czech playwright, each became president of his country.

NEW POLITICAL PARTIES

In working to throw off the influence of the Soviet Union, the countries of Eastern Europe began to form new political parties. One of the earliest "new" parties in Eastern Europe developed in Poland. Under the leadership of Lech Walesa (lek vä len′ sə), an independent workers' union called Solidarity was organized in 1980. In the beginning, the union was broken up by the government, but after years of struggle Solidarity won the right to form a political party in 1989. During the elections that followed, the party won. A Solidarity candidate explained:

In 1981 they first legalized us, then crushed us. . . . We fear that the same thing can happen again. So we are creating democratic institutions to make it less likely.

In 1990 Lech Walesa was elected as Poland's president. Upon his election, Walesa declared, "since we defeated the system without one gunshot or one drop of blood, we can dare to build a new system."

The Czech Republic and Hungary are also daring to build new systems. These countries have avidly embraced the right to form new political parties and to hold elections for government leaders.

CHANGING ATTITUDES

Eastern European attitudes about the limits on their freedom have changed greatly over the last few years. Until recently many people might have agreed with this quotation from a factory worker.

Why waste time worrying about how to change something that cannot be changed? . . . We prefer to keep quiet and have a reasonably comfortable life.

Today the Czech Republic, Poland, and Hungary are well on their way to abolish-

341

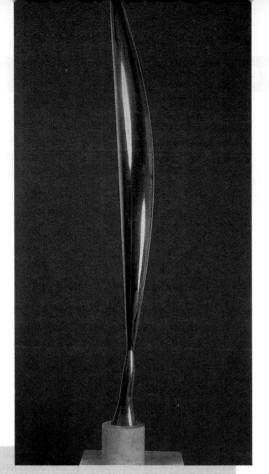

The work of Constantin Brancusi, a Romanian sculptor, has influenced many artists around the world. This sculpture, called Bird in Space, is one of his most famous works.

works were written in defiance of the communist government of Czechoslovakia. As a result, he was imprisoned several times and his plays were banned. Today, Havel's plays are freely performed and, as you have read, he became the president of Czechoslovakia. When that country split in 1993, Havel became the president of the Czech Republic.

Several Eastern European writers have described what can happen to people who find themselves in frightening circumstances. The Czech Karel Capek (kä rel chä pek), for example, introduced the word *robot* in his play *R.U.R.*, which is about what happens when technology gets out of control.

Another Czech, Franz Kafka, wrote about people who find themselves in circumstances that they do not understand. His short stories and novels were often about the difficulties that people face in a world that does not seem to make sense.

EXCELLENCE IN SPORTS

If you had watched the Olympics on television in the past, you may well have seen Romanian gymnasts, Czechoslovakian hockey players, and the Yugoslavian soccer team. Over the years the Olympic teams fielded by the countries of Eastern Europe have enjoyed remarkable success.

While under Soviet control, the Eastern European countries placed a great deal of emphasis on sports. Within the schools, sports training was given a high priority. As in the Soviet Union, talented athletes were recognized early in their lives and given special training. Athletes from Eastern Europe will no doubt continue to excel.

PRIDE IN ONE'S COUNTRY

As you have read, nationalism is a strong creative force among Eastern Europe's musicians, writers, and other artists. Many of them have taken themes from their homelands and integrated them into their work. Nationalism has also been evident in the region's competitive sports.

 Check Your Reading

1. What is the origin of the word *robot*?
2. How have Eastern European composers shown their love of their homelands in their music?
3. Why have Eastern European athletes excelled in sports?
4. THINKING SKILL: The countries of Eastern Europe are no longer satellites of the Soviet Union. What effect do you think this fact will have on the Eastern Europeans' pursuit of sports?

Reading a Newspaper

Key Vocabulary

news article   editor
feature article   headline
editorial   dateline

You have read about Eastern Europe in this chapter. But new events are taking place there every day. You can learn more about them by reading a newspaper.

The Parts of a Newspaper

All newspapers contain several different forms of information. They usually begin with news articles. A news article is a story about an important event that has just taken place. News articles can be about important local, national, or international events.

Inside the newspaper you will usually find feature articles and editorials. A feature article is a detailed report on a person, an issue, or an event. An editorial is an article in which the editors, or the people who run the newspaper, give their opinion on an important issue.

Parts of a News Article

News articles are an important source of information. Look at the news article on this page. Can you find the headline? It is printed in large type across the top of the story to catch your attention.

Each news article usually also has a dateline. The dateline tells when and where the story was written. Find the dateline in the story on this page.

In the first paragraph of a news article, the reporter tries to get the reader interested in the story. The reporter also answers some important questions: *Who*

Walesa Asked to Lead New Government

WARSAW, August 17—Solidarity leader Lech Walesa was asked today to form a cabinet and to lead a new government in Poland.

Legislators from Solidarity and two smaller political parties met and agreed to propose that General Wojciech Jaruzelski (voi′ chek yär ü zel′ skē), Poland's Communist president, allow Walesa to form a cabinet and govern the country as its premier. The legislators said that Walesa "is capable of forming a government of national responsibility in which there can be represented all the political forces of our country that have decided to act for political and economic reforms."

Walesa said he had not made a final decision on whether or not he would accept the proposal.

was involved in the story? *What* happened? *When* did the event take place? *Where* did it occur? These points are called the *Who, What, When,* and *Where* of the story.

Reviewing the Skill

1. What three types of articles can be found in a newspaper?
2. What is the difference between a news article and an editorial?
3. What are the *Who, What, When,* and *Where* of the story on this page?
4. Why is it important to understand how to read newspapers?

EASTERN EUROPE: CULTURAL GEOGRAPHY

PEOPLE

- Ethnic groups: many Slavic groups, Gypsies

- Religions: Christianity, Roman Catholicism (and Eastern Orthodox) Islam

- Families tend to be small

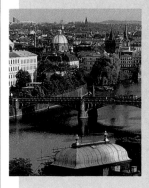

- 55% of people live near cities

ECONOMY

- Most Eastern Europe countries are now encouraging free enterprise

- Agriculture: collective farms and state farms are gradually being replaced with private farms

- Workers: 1/4 are in agriculture; 1/3 are in mining and manufacturing

- Products: coal, petroleum, perfume made from roses

GOVERNMENT

- Had been a buffer zone between Western Europe and the Soviet Union

- All but Albania and former Yugoslavia were tied to Soviet Union by Warsaw Pact, which ended in 1991

- The Communist party was the major party until the late 1980s

- Poland's Solidarity Union won a majority in 1989 elections

- Many countries are encouraging democracy

ARTS AND RECREATION

- Major characteristic: nationalistic themes

- Famous composers: Frédéric Chopin, Anton Dvorák

- Well known writers: Czeslaw Milosz, Vaclav Havel

- Famous sculptor: Constantin Brancusi

- Popular sports: tennis, track, gymnastics, ice skating

IDEAS TO REMEMBER

- Eastern Europe has many ethnic groups, most of whom are Slavic in origin.
- The area's planned economies are being replaced by free-enterprise systems.
- The area was long a buffer zone in which most nations were tied to the Soviet Union but many of these countries have recently held free elections.
- Nationalism is important in the arts and in the sports of Eastern Europe.

REVIEWING VOCABULARY

buffer zone   satellite
Cyrillic   Warsaw Pact
quota

Number a sheet of paper from 1 to 5. Beside each number write the word or term from the above list that best matches the definition.

1. A military alliance that joined most countries of Eastern Europe with the former Soviet Union until 1991
2. A country that is controlled or dominated by another, more powerful country
3. A fixed amount allotted to or expected from a country, state, or person
4. An area that lies between two hostile powers
5. The alphabet that is used by some Eastern European languages, like Russian and Serbian

REVIEWING FACTS

1. Which five Eastern European countries were long-time satellites of the Soviet Union? Which two Eastern European countries were not controlled by the Soviets?
2. What is the main language family of countries in Eastern Europe?
3. What is nationalism? What are some of its effects in Eastern Europe?
4. How did the Holocaust affect the size of the Jewish population in Eastern Europe?
5. What kinds of farm ownership can be found in Eastern Europe?
6. What gave Poland and Hungary a head start in developing free market systems? Which two Eastern European countries are finding it more difficult to begin free market systems?
7. Why did the Soviet Union want to create a buffer zone in Eastern Europe?

8. How did Lech Walesa help to establish one of Eastern Europe's earliest "new" political parties in Poland?
9. Who is Vaclav Havel and how has he helped his country on the road to democracy?
10. What Romanian sculptor influenced the work of many modern artists?

WRITING ABOUT MAIN IDEAS

1. **Writing an Explanation:** Read the Read Aloud quote on page 339 concerning democracy and dictatorship. Write an explanation of why you think it takes longer to go from dictatorship to democracy than the other way around.
2. **Writing a Paragraph:** The people of Eastern Europe are learning that their new freedom brings with it a new set of responsibilities. Write a paragraph in which you explain why this is so.
3. **Writing About Perspectives:** Imagine that you are a farmer working on a large government-run farm and that you are given the opportunity to begin your own small agricultural enterprise. Write a journal entry in which you debate whether or not to make this change.

BUILDING SKILLS: READING A NEWSPAPER

1. What types of articles can be found in a newspaper?
2. What kind of information would you find in a news article?
3. What kind of information would you find in an editorial?
4. Why is it important to read newspapers?

347

EASTERN EUROPE AND NORTHERN ASIA: PHYSICAL GEOGRAPHY

- Mountains: Caucasus Mountains, Ural Mountains
- Distinctive areas: Siberia, Central Asia, Balkans
- Most of the land is lowland plains
- Rivers: Volga River, Danube River

- Temperate climates: mainly in Eastern Europe and the western part of Northern Asia
- Arctic climate: Siberia

- Arable soil: mainly in Eastern Europe and the steppes of Russia and Ukraine
- Eastern Europe and Russia are heavily forested
- The steppes of Russia and Ukraine are vast grasslands
- Minerals: coal, oil

EASTERN EUROPE AND NORTHERN ASIA: CULTURAL GEOGRAPHY

- The region has more than 150 ethnic groups; Slavs are the largest
- Religions: Eastern Orthodox, Islam, Roman Catholicism

- Under the communist system, the government owned most land, banks, and factories
- The command economies are trying to change to free-enterprise economies
- Each country is now free to establish its own economic system
- Each country must determine how to convert huge government-run farms to private farms
- The change from command economies has caused hardship

- The country that was the Soviet Union is now broken up into 15 independent countries
- The Communist party has lost its power to control the governments of these countries
- The Warsaw Pact, which tied Eastern Europe to the Soviet Union, ended in 1991
- Many countries held their first democratic elections between 1989 and 1991

- Famous writers: Tolstoy, Dostoyevsky, Pushkin, Pasternak, Solzhenitsyn, Milosz
- Famous composers: Tchaikovsky, Chopin, Dvorák

- The region has some of the best-trained and most successful athletes in the world

REVIEWING VOCABULARY

Each of the following statements contains an underlined vocabulary word or term. Number a sheet of paper from 1 to 10. Beside each number write whether the statement is true or false. If a statement is true, write true. If it is false, rewrite the sentence using the vocabulary word correctly.

1. In a <u>command economy</u>, the government makes most economic decisions.
2. To <u>censor</u> is to prevent something from being made public.
3. <u>Capital goods</u> are products that are used to produce other products.
4. A <u>buffer zone</u> is an area that lies between two hostile powers.
5. The word <u>Soviet</u> has the same meaning as "Russian."
6. The <u>Warsaw Pact</u> was a way to join the economies of several Eastern European countries to the economy of the Soviet Union.
7. <u>Perestroika</u> refers to attempts at economic reforms in the Soviet Union.
8. <u>Glasnost</u> describes the attempts made to limit freedom in the Soviet Union.
9. <u>Nationalism</u> is a purely political movement found only in Eastern Europe.
10. The <u>steppes</u> are dry, treeless, grassy plains that cover much of Russia, Ukraine, and parts of Eastern Europe.

WRITING ABOUT THE UNIT

1. **Writing a Tall Tale:** You have read about the cold and harsh climate of Siberia. Write a tall tale telling how Siberia's environment and climate were formed.
2. **Writing About Perspectives:** Write a dialogue between an elderly Russian who accepted and lived under communism all his life and a young Russian who supports a change to democratic rule. Have each discuss which is better for Russia.

ACTIVITIES

1. **Constructing a Bar Graph:** Construct a bar graph showing the populations of the following countries: Albania, Bulgaria, Slovakia, Hungary, Kazakhstan, Poland, Romania, Russia, Ukraine, and Uzbekistan. Use Unit 4 opening pages 290–291 to find the information you need.
2. **Producing Progress Reports:** You have read about ways that both the Eastern European countries and the countries that once made up the Soviet Union have been trying to strengthen their individual political and economic systems. Work together in groups, each dealing with a different country, to produce progress reports on each. Look in newspapers and magazines to find the information you need.

LINKING PAST, PRESENT, AND FUTURE

Imagine it is the year 2017—the one-hundredth anniversary of the Bolshevik Revolution that transformed Russia into the world's first communist state. Describe what has happened to communism in Russia since it was first established in 1917.

+North Pole

Arctic Circle

60°N

45°N

EUROPE

30°N

Black Sea

Caspian Sea

Tropic of Cancer

Mediterranean Sea

NORTH AFRICA

THE
MIDDLE
EAST

Persian
Gulf

15°N

Red Sea

Arabian Sea

Gulf of Aden

AFRICA

ATLANTIC
OCEAN

Equator   0°

INDIAN

30°W

15°S

Tropic of Capricorn

30°S

15°W

0°

15°E

30°E

45°E

60°E   45°S

75°E

UNIT

5

THE MIDDLE EAST AND NORTH AFRICA

WHERE WE ARE

Now and throughout the past, three great continents—Asia, Africa, and Europe—have been linked by the region described in this unit. Many different groups of people have lived in and traveled through this region, making it a crossroads of peoples and cultures. Three of the world's great religions arose here and spread to other parts of the world. This region is known as the Middle East and North Africa.

As the map shows, the Middle East and North Africa covers the southwestern part of Asia and the northern part of Africa. Some of the world's earliest known civilizations developed in this region. Now you will read about the people who make this region their home today. Turn the page to continue your journey through the world around us.

THE MIDDLE EAST
AND
NORTH AFRICA

IRAQ

Capital ★
Baghdad

Major languages: Arabic and Kurdish
Population: 17.1 million
Area: 167,923 sq mi; 434,920 sq km
Leading export: oil

ALGERIA

Capital ★
Algiers

Major languages: Arabic, Berber,
and French
Population: 26.0 million
Area: 919,592 sq mi; 2,381,740 sq km
Leading exports: oil and natural gas

ISRAEL

Capital ★
Jerusalem

Major languages: Hebrew and Arabic
Population: 4.9 million
Area: 8,091 sq mi; 20,770 sq km
Leading exports: diamonds and
machinery

BAHRAIN

Capital ★
Manama

Major language: Arabic
Population: 0.5 million
Area: 239 sq mi; 620 sq km
Leading export: oil

JORDAN

Capital ★
Amman

Major language: Arabic
Population: 3.4 million
Area: 35,475 sq mi; 91,880 sq km
Leading exports: phosphates and
chemicals

CYPRUS

Capital ★
Nicosia

Major languages: Greek and Turkish
Population: 0.7 million
Area: 3,571 sq mi; 9,250 sq km
Leading exports: clothing, fruit and
potatoes

KUWAIT

Capital ★
Kuwait

Major language: Arabic
Population: 1.4 million
Area: 6,880 sq mi; 17,820 sq km
Leading export: oil

EGYPT

Capital ★
Cairo

Major language: Arabic
Population: 54.8 million
Area: 386,661 sq mi; 1,001,450 sq km
Leading export: oil

LEBANON

Capital ★
Beirut

Major languages: Arabic and French
Population: 3.4 million
Area: 4,015 sq mi; 10,400 sq km
Leading exports: jewelry, clothing,
and metal products

IRAN

Capital ★
Tehran

Major languages: Farsi, Azerbaijani,
and Kurdish
Population: 58.6 million
Area: 636,294 sq mi; 1,648,000 sq km
Leading export: oil

LIBYA

Capital ★
Tripoli

Major language: Arabic
Population: 4.4 million
Area: 679,360 sq mi; 1,759,540 sq km
Leading export: oil

MOROCCO

Capital ★
Rabat

Major languages: Arabic, Berber, and French
Population: 26.6 million
Area: 172,413 sq mi; 446,550 sq km
Leading exports: food and phosphates

TUNISIA

Capital ★
Tunis

Major languages: Arabic and French
Population: 8.4 million
Area: 63,170 sq mi; 163,610 sq km
Leading export: oil

OMAN

Capital ★
Muscat

Major language: Arabic
Population: 1.6 million
Area: 82,013 sq mi; 212,460 sq km
Leading export: oil

TURKEY

Capital ★
Ankara

Major languages: Turkish and Kurdish
Population: 58.5 million
Area: 301,383 sq mi; 780,580 sq km
Leading exports: textiles and food

QATAR

Capital ★
Doha

Major languages: Arabic and English
Population: 0.5 million
Area: 4,247 sq mi; 11,000 sq km
Leading export: oil

UNITED ARAB EMIRATES

Capital ★
Abu Dhabi

Major language: Arabic
Population: 2.4 million
Area: 32,278 sq mi; 83,600 sq km
Leading export: oil

SAUDI ARABIA

Capital ★
Riyadh

Major language: Arabic
Population: 15.5 million
Area: 829,997 sq mi; 2,149,690 sq km
Leading export: oil

YEMEN

Capital ★
San'a

Major language: Arabic
Population: 10.1 million
Area: 203,850 sq mi; 527,970 sq km
Leading exports: oil and coffee

SYRIA

Capital ★
Damascus

Major languages: Arabic and Kurdish
Population: 12.8 million
Area: 71,498 sq mi; 185,180 sq km
Leading exports: oil and textiles

PHYSICAL GEOGRAPHY OF THE MIDDLE EAST AND NORTH AFRICA

FOCUS

I never knew what desert was till I came here; it is a very wonderful thing to see; out of nothing, out of a little water, springs up a garden.

When people such as this English writer first travel through the Middle East, they are struck by how much of the land is desert. But most of the people in this region live in cities and towns. The people of the Middle East have met the challenge of their environment by making imaginative use of water—a precious resource that is often in short supply.

Landforms

READ TO LEARN

Key Vocabulary
desert
oasis
irrigation

Key Places
Sinai Peninsula
Arabian Peninsula
Anatolia
Sahara

Nile River
Tigris River
Euphrates River

Read Aloud

Two of the world's earliest civilizations—ancient Egypt and ancient Sumer—began in North Africa and the Middle East. The people of these ancient societies invented farming, the wheel, and writing. They invented many new forms of technology, and they traveled and traded throughout the Middle East and North Africa. Later, people in the Middle East and North Africa founded three of the world's great religions—Judaism, Christianity, and Islam. In order to understand the people of this historic region better, it is important to begin by learning about the land.

Read for Purpose

1. **WHAT YOU KNOW:** What is a crossroads?
2. **WHAT YOU WILL LEARN:** What are the main physical features of the Middle East and North Africa?

A CROSSROADS

The region of the Middle East and North Africa is considered to be one of the world's most important crossroads. The main reason for this is that the region spans two continents, Asia and Africa. These two continents are connected by a land bridge called the Sinai Peninsula. They also share with Europe a coastline along the Mediterranean Sea. Find the Sinai Peninsula and the Mediterranean Sea on the map on page 356. In what ways do you think the Sinai Peninsula and the Mediterranean Sea may have helped to make this region a major crossroads?

Even in ancient times traders and explorers used the currents of the Mediterranean Sea to carry them from shore to shore in the Middle East and North Africa. For example, more than 3,500 years ago North African traders from Egypt sailed along Asia's Mediterranean coast.

Similarly, many different groups from Asia migrated into North Africa across the Sinai Peninsula. For example, the ancient Hebrews made the journey after a drought destroyed their crops. You have read in previous chapters that when different cultures meet, ideas are often exchanged. Because this is what has happened in the Middle East and North Africa, many geographers consider this region to be an important crossroads.

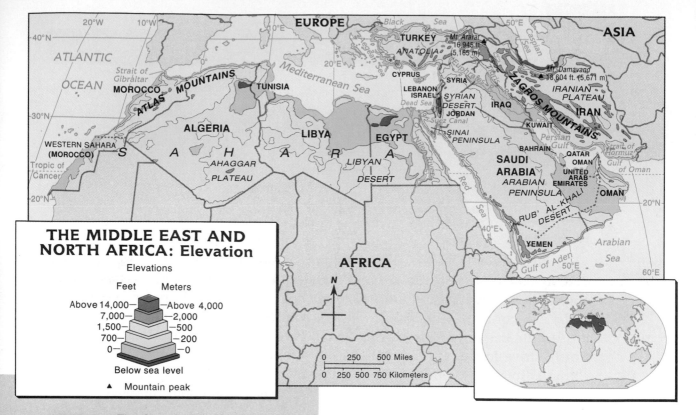

THE MIDDLE EAST AND NORTH AFRICA: Elevation

Elevations

Feet	Meters
Above 14,000	Above 4,000
7,000	2,000
1,500	500
700	200
0	0

Below sea level

▲ Mountain peak

MAP SKILL: The Suez Canal (*below*) is between the Red and Mediterranean seas. In which country is the Suez Canal located?

IMPORTANT PENINSULAS

In addition to the Sinai Peninsula, the region of the Middle East and North Africa also has two larger peninsulas. Find the Arabian Peninsula on the map above. As you can see, it is separated from Africa by the Red Sea and from the rest of Asia by the Persian Gulf.

In the northern part of the Middle East, you will find a peninsula called Anatolia. Geographers often call this peninsula Asia Minor. Anatolia has a special place in history. According to archaeologists, many of the world's first villages were built on this peninsula.

A REGION OF CONTRASTS

This region has some of the driest land on earth. But it also has some of the most fertile farming valleys. Rich farmlands are even found close to deserts. A desert is a dry, sandy, or rocky region that receives very little rainfall. Very few people live in deserts.

The deserts of the Middle East and North Africa exist because a vast area of the region receives little rainfall. Many parts of this region receive an average of less than 10 inches (25.4 cm) of annual rainfall.

The world's largest desert, the Sahara, is located in North Africa. You can find the Sahara on the Atlas map on page 633. The word *Sahara* comes from the Arabic word for "wilderness."

You might think that the landscape of a desert is all the same. But desert landscapes vary from place to place. Some parts of the Sahara look like great oceans of sand dunes. Dunes, as you may know, are mounds or ridges of sand formed by wind. Other parts of the Sahara have a gray, rocky surface. Little vegetation grows in any part of the desert, except after a rare rainstorm, when even flowers have been known to bloom suddenly. Use the diagram below to compare some of the different kinds of desert landscapes.

Most of the region's area is covered by desert, but the desert is not where most of

the people live. Most people live along the narrow river valleys or on the seacoasts. Others live in the highlands or mountains, especially in Turkey, Syria, Iraq, and Iran.

DESERT DWELLERS

Only a small percentage of the region's people live in the deserts. Those who do need special skills to live there. The Bedouins (bed′ ü inz) are one group that has developed the skills to survive in the desert. *Bedouin* is an Arabic word meaning "desert dweller." Many Bedouins tend herds of sheep and goats. However, the camel is their most important animal.

Camels are well suited to desert life. They can walk for many days without drinking, carry heavy loads, and exist on

DIAGRAM SKILL: The desert contains many different types of landforms. Which form has an oasis nearby? Which form was created by the flow of old rivers?

DESERT SURFACES OF THE SAHARA

Erg: Vast stretches of shifting sand dunes

Hammada: Worn-down rock platforms surrounding oasis

Wadi: Dry river valleys with flat bottoms

Reg: Plains covered with deposits of sand and gravel

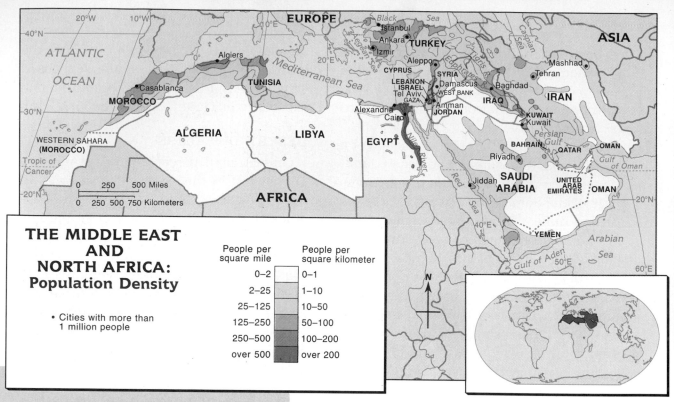

THE MIDDLE EAST AND NORTH AFRICA: Population Density

People per square mile	People per square kilometer
0–2	0–1
2–25	1–10
25–125	10–50
125–250	50–100
250–500	100–200
over 500	over 200

• Cities with more than 1 million people

MAP SKILL: Which areas have the greatest population? Are most of them near water?

sparse vegetation. The Bedouins depend on their camels. They drink the camels' milk and they make tents out of camel skins. They also use camel hair and skin to make many useful products.

These animals can survive without food and water for many days because the humps on their backs store fat, which the camels burn for energy when they must go without food. The kind of camel found in the Middle East and North Africa is a single-humped beast, called a dromedary. Another variety of camel is the Bactrian camel, which has two humps. It is found in Central Asia.

Desert dwellers carry their food with them as they travel across the desert. When they need new supplies, they stop at an **oasis** to find food and water. An oasis is a green, fertile spot in the desert that has a water supply. Many oases have de-veloped into large towns or cities. For example, Riyadh (rē yäd′), the capital of Saudi Arabia, began as an oasis.

FERTILE FARMLANDS

More than 200 million people live in the Middle East and North Africa. As you can see from the map above, most of the region's people live along its narrow river valleys or on its seacoasts. For example, more than 95 percent of Egypt's 55 million people live along the banks of the **Nile River**, the world's longest river. From an airplane the Nile River Valley looks like a long, thin green ribbon on a vast brown blanket. The Nile River Valley is one of the earth's most densely populated areas.

Along the river valleys of the Middle East and North Africa, **irrigation** helps to make farming possible. Irrigation is the watering of dry land by means of streams, canals, or pipes. Irrigation was invented by this region's first farmers more than 8,000 years ago. Today farmers still use irrigation to provide the water to grow their crops. You will read more about irrigation in the Middle East and North Africa in the following chapters of this unit.

As the map on page 358 shows, important centers of population have also formed around other rivers in this region. In the Middle East, the **Tigris River** and the **Euphrates** (ū frā′ tēz) **River** flow through a rich river-valley region that some geographers call the Fertile Crescent because of its crescentlike shape.

Parts of the Fertile Crescent are watered by irrigation. Other areas rely upon a string of oases. These oases are sustained by the Tigris, the Euphrates, and the other rivers that flow through this area. Sumer, one of the world's earliest civilizations, developed in the Fertile Crescent.

OTHER FARMLANDS

Not all parts of the Middle East and North Africa depend on irrigation for farming. Along the coast of North Africa, some areas get enough rainfall for farms. In fact, for part of its history, the coastal farming areas of North Africa provided southern Europe with much of its wheat and other farm products.

Some areas depend on a combination of rainfall and irrigation to supply enough water for farming. The highlands of Turkey, Syria, and Iran often get enough rain for crops, but additional irrigation can guarantee a supply of water.

VARIED ENVIRONMENTS

In this lesson you have been introduced to the physical geography of the Middle East and North Africa. You have learned that large parts of the region are covered by deserts. However, most of the region's people live in areas in which rivers provide one of the region's most important resources—water.

Irrigation has helped create fertile farmland in Jordan. Along the Nile River, the desert is next to fertile fields (*above*), and people live on the desert to save farmland.

Check Your Reading

1. What land bridge connects the Middle East and North Africa?
2. Name the world's largest desert and describe a desert environment.
3. Use the map on page 358 to identify three very densely populated parts of the Middle East and North Africa.
4. **THINKING SKILL:** Based on your reading of the section "Fertile Farmlands" in this lesson, what conclusions can you draw about the Nile River Valley?

Reading Contour Maps

Key Vocabulary

contour map   relief
contour line   contour interval

The geography of the Middle East and North Africa is varied, ranging from the extremes of vast, flat deserts to rugged mountain peaks. Today we can refer to maps to find the exact locations of these landforms. But imagine the difficulties before accurate maps were available.

Long ago people did not know the extent of a desert's vastness or the height of a mountain. As you know, cartographers, or the people who make maps, now can represent actual distances and elevations on the maps they draw.

In this book you have seen a number of elevation maps that use different colors to represent the height of land above sea level. In this lesson you will find out about another way cartographers show elevation on a map.

Contour Maps

The elevation and features of a place can be shown on a **contour map**. *Contour* means "shape." Contour maps help us to picture the shape of the earth's surface. These kinds of maps represent the actual elevation of an area.

Contour maps show landforms and use lines or colors to show different elevations. A **contour line** on a map connects areas that have the same elevation. As you know from reading the maps in this book, elevation is given in either feet or

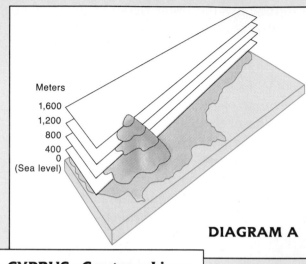

DIAGRAM A

CYPRUS: Contour Lines

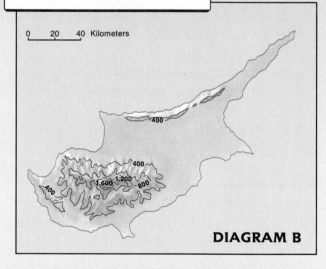

0   20   40 Kilometers

DIAGRAM B

meters. If you were to walk along an area represented by a contour line, you would not go up or down. You would remain at the same elevation.

Using the Diagrams

Diagram A on this page will help you to understand contour lines. It shows a model of Cyprus, an island in the Mediterranean Sea. This diagram illustrates how

360

CONTOUR MAP OF LEBANON

- • City or town
- ▲ Mountain peak
- —— International boundary

Contour interval is 500 meters

Map labels: Mediterranean Sea, Tripoli, Qurnat al-Sawda 3083 m, Halimah 2464 m, LEBANON MOUNTAINS, Jubayl, Baalbek, Tal 'at Musa 2629 m, ANTI-LEBANON MTS., Harfel Mreffi 2628 m, Beirut, Zahlé, SYRIA, Sidon, Mount Hermon 2814 m, Tyre, ISRAEL

Scale: 0 10 20 Miles / 0 10 20 30 Kilometers

closed, somewhat circular lines of **Diagram B** show the varied elevations of Cyprus.

Contour Maps Show Relief

When you look at a contour map, you see the relief of an area. Relief is variation in elevation. Rugged mountains with great variation in elevation have high relief. But flat plains with little variation in elevation have low relief.

Cartographers show relief on a map by the spacing of contour lines. For example, widely spaced contour lines mean that the land is flat or gently sloping. A steep slope, or mountainside, is shown by lines that are drawn close together. The contour map of Lebanon on this page shows low relief in the coastal areas and high relief in the mountains.

When reading contour maps, it is important to check first the contour interval of the map. This is the difference in elevation between any two contour lines. The contour interval, which may vary from map to map, is usually shown in the legend. Look at the map of Lebanon. You can see that the contour interval is 500 meters.

the island can be cut into layers by using horizontal sheets that intersect the land. Note the elevation of each sheet. Imagine that you can push the sheets completely through the model, line them up directly above one another, and trace the outline of each "cut" on the sheet below it. If you took each outline in turn and positioned it correctly over a piece of paper, you would have a simple contour map of Cyprus as shown in **Diagram B**.

If you now compare **Diagram A** with **Diagram B**, you will see that the contour lines reflect the shape of the land. The

Reviewing the Skill

1. What is a contour line? A contour interval?
2. What is the contour interval on the map of Lebanon on this page?
3. According to the map of Lebanon, Tripoli is located how many meters below the highest peak in the Lebanon Mountains?
4. How do contour maps help you to picture the elevation of the land?

Climate and Resources

READ TO LEARN

Key Vocabulary
arid
aquifer
qanat
petroleum

Key Places
Plateau of Iran
Zagros Mountains
Atlas Mountains
Persian Gulf

Read Aloud

In the 1930s an American oil company asked King Ibn Saud of Saudi Arabia for permission to drill wells to test for oil in his desert kingdom. When the company struck oil, the king is said to have been disappointed. He had hoped the drillers would find water.

Oil has brought great wealth to Saudi Arabia and much of the Middle East. Yet the need for fresh water in these dry lands is more urgent today than ever. Populations are growing fast, creating a greater demand for water.

Read for Purpose

1. **WHAT YOU KNOW:** Has your community ever had to conserve water? What did people do to use less water?
2. **WHAT YOU WILL LEARN:** Why are water and oil key resources in the Middle East and North Africa?

SHARP CONTRASTS IN CLIMATE

You read in Lesson 1 that the region of the Middle East and North Africa has vast deserts and fertile farmland. Some of this region's deserts are the most arid, or dry, places in the world. They also are among the hottest places in the world. The world's record for high temperature is 136°F. (58°C), and it was recorded at Al-'Aziziyah (al az ē zē′ yä), in the Libyan Desert. Due to the high temperature in this region, any rain that falls evaporates quickly.

"Between 11:00 A.M. and 3:30 P.M. even the camels lie down," wrote Wayne Eastep, a writer who lived in Saudi Arabia one summer. "The desert baked. We seemed immersed in a [glowing] furnace." He also noted that his thermometer burst one day when the temperature reached 125°F. (52°C).

Yet other parts of the region are mild and wet, or even cold and snowy. As the map on page 363 shows, people who live along the Mediterranean coast from Morocco to Turkey enjoy a climate that is hot and dry in summer and mild and wet in winter, with 30 inches (75 cm) or more of rainfall a year.

As you move inland from the coast, the climates are more arid. In the higher ele-

362

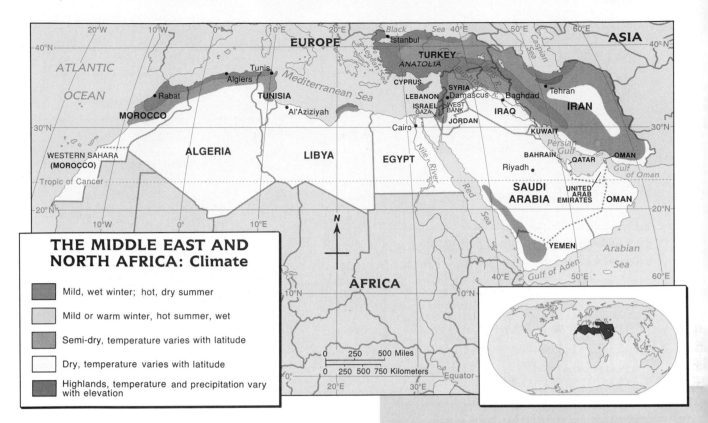

THE MIDDLE EAST AND NORTH AFRICA: Climate

- Mild, wet winter; hot, dry summer
- Mild or warm winter, hot summer, wet
- Semi-dry, temperature varies with latitude
- Dry, temperature varies with latitude
- Highlands, temperature and precipitation vary with elevation

MAP SKILL: In which type of climate do you think farming would be most difficult in North Africa and the Middle East?

vations of Anatolia and the **Plateau of Iran**, the weather is like that of Wyoming or Colorado. Summers are hot, while winters are long and cold. You can find the Plateau of Iran on the Atlas map on page 633. Enough snow covers the mountains north of Tehran, Iran, in winter to create good conditions for skiing.

WATER—A PRECIOUS RESOURCE

According to an ancient legend, a prince once lived in an African kingdom near Lake Victoria. Enemies threatened his life and forced him to flee. The prince ran northward. As he fled from his enemies, his sword trailed behind him. Wherever it touched the ground, the earth opened and poured forth water to protect him. When he reached the Mediterranean Sea, the prince disappeared. But the river that sprang up behind him remained. It is called the Nile.

The Nile River has been so vital that the people of Egypt call their country the "gift of the Nile." The river provides Egyptians with 85 percent of the water they use.

As you read in Lesson 1, irrigation from rivers such as the Nile, the Tigris, and the Euphrates helps make farming possible throughout the region. According to one Egyptian farmer, irrigation "helps the farmer harness the water to his advantage."

Not all water for irrigation comes from rivers. For example, **aquifers** are important sources of water in some areas. An aquifer is an underground layer of rock that holds water or carries water to springs or wells.

In Iran, for example, people have built underground tunnels called **qanats** (kä′nats). The water that runs through the qanats comes from the **Zagros Mountains** in southwestern Iran. Some qanats are 40 miles (64 km) long, and a few extend as far as 300 feet (91 m) underground.

363

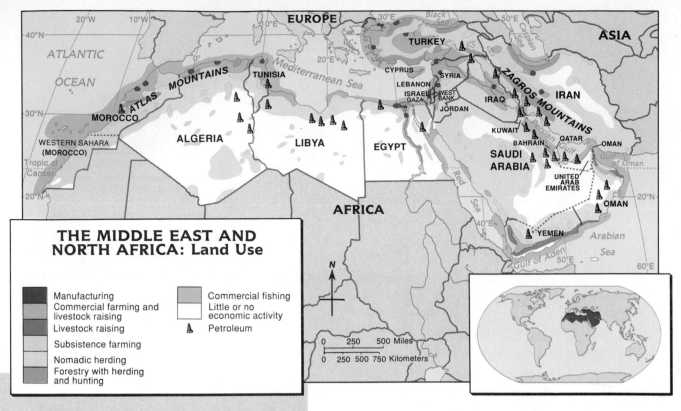

THE MIDDLE EAST AND NORTH AFRICA: Land Use

Manufacturing
Commercial farming and livestock raising
Livestock raising
Subsistence farming
Nomadic herding
Forestry with herding and hunting
Commercial fishing
Little or no economic activity
Petroleum

0   250   500 Miles
0 250 500 750 Kilometers

MAP SKILL: Why do you think many parts of this region have little or no economic activity?

The first qanats were dug more than 2,000 years ago in Persia (the old name for Iran). About 50,000 qanats still provide water to 75 percent of Iran's farms. Since qanats are underground, the water cannot evaporate, as it can from an open canal.

USING THE LAND

Fertile, well-watered land is scarce in the region of the Middle East and North Africa. About 10 percent of the land is farmed today. The distribution of the arable farmland that does exist is very uneven. For example, Turkey and Iran have large areas of fertile land, while in Saudi Arabia only 1 percent of the land can be farmed. Less than 4 percent of Egypt's land is used for farming. Yet Egyptian farmers along the Nile River can grow two or more crops on the same field each

year. Scientists have tried to increase the cultivatable land in Egypt with irrigation, but the desert soil is too salty for farming.

Fertile land with enough natural moisture to grow crops is found only in a few other areas. They include Lebanon, the Nile Delta, and Yemen, which gets abundant yearly rains from the Indian Ocean.

On the slopes of the Atlas Mountains of North Africa, enough rain falls to support forests of cork, oak, and evergreen trees. Northern Iran also has major forests along the Caspian Sea. Look at the map above to find other forested areas.

A WEALTH OF OIL

The discovery of petroleum, or oil, in the 1930s has greatly affected the Middle East and North Africa. The rulers of the oil kingdoms in this region are among the world's richest people. These rulers use some of the oil wealth to build schools, roads, and hospitals to improve the lives of their countries' citizens.

The Middle East produces nearly one third of the petroleum in the world today. An even larger share—two thirds—of the earth's known oil reserves is found in the Middle East. Reserves are supplies of a resource that are available for future use.

Most of the Middle East's oil is located beneath the lands bordering the **Persian Gulf**. Saudi Arabia alone has about one fourth of the world's known oil reserves. Tiny Kuwait had another 15 to 20 percent, but Iraq set Kuwait's oil fields on fire in a war in 1990, and Kuwait lost huge amounts of petroleum. Iraq and Iran are also oil giants.

Libya is the largest oil-producing country in North Africa. This makes Libya the richest nation in North Africa.

Many countries have invested in the oil-rich Middle East and North Africa. Japan gets nearly all of its oil supply from the region.

USING PETROLEUM

A Saudi Arabian leader once said that petroleum was too valuable to burn. But today, petroleum's greatest value is as a fuel. The Saudis and Kuwaitis are trying to find more ways to use their greatest resource. Petroleum is already used to make plastics and fertilizer. It is also used in other, more surprising ways.

For example, in its fight to prevent the sand dunes of the Sahara from covering valuable farmland, Libya planted 400 million trees. Each tree was first sprayed with oil. The sticky oil held the shifting sands against the trees, stopping the dunes from moving over farmland.

So much oil lies beneath Saudi Arabia and Kuwait that these countries rarely bother to save the natural gas that is often discovered with petroleum. By contrast, Iran, which has the world's second-largest supply of natural gas, has built pipelines that send this resource to markets in neighboring countries. Other than oil and natural gas, the Middle East and North Africa have few natural resources.

WATER AND OIL

As you have read, the Middle East and North Africa is a hot, dry region. Because water is scarce, the rivers and aquifers provide water for irrigation. Most farmers in the region depend heavily on irrigation. If more water were available for irrigation, more than the 10 percent of the land now being farmed could be used for crops.

The discovery of oil in the 1930s has transformed the region and brought great wealth to some of its countries. The nations bordering the Persian Gulf have two thirds of the world's known oil reserves.

 Check Your Reading

1. What is an oil reserve?
2. What are qanats?
3. Are water and oil key resources in this region for the same reason? Explain your answer.
4. **THINKING SKILL:** In what ways do you think the countries of the Middle East would be affected if large new oil reserves were found in North America?

MIDDLE EAST AND NORTH AFRICA: PHYSICAL GEOGRAPHY

 LANDFORMS

 CLIMATE

NATURAL RESOURCES

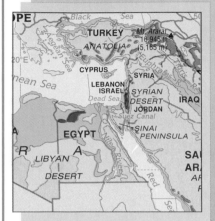

- Peninsulas: Sinai Peninsula, Arabian Peninsula, Anatolian Peninsula

- Arid climate: hot and dry in deserts

- Mild climate: warm and wet along Mediterranean coast

- Cold climate: long, cold winters in Anatolia and Plateau of Iran

- Fertile land in Lebanon; the Nile Delta; and parts of Yemen, North Africa, Iran, and Turkey

- Forests in Atlas Mountains, northern Iran, and Turkey

- Abundant resources: oil, natural gas, phosphates

- Deserts: Sahara, Syrian, Rub-al-Khali

- Fertile river valleys: Nile River Valley, Tigris River Valley, Euphrates River Valley

- Mountains: Zagros Mountains, Atlas Mountains, Lebanon Mountains

- The Middle East produces one third of the world's supply of oil

IDEAS TO REMEMBER

- The region has vast deserts and also fertile, irrigated farmland.
- Although the region has some of the hottest and driest places in the world, it also has warm, wet sections and some areas with cold winters.
- Oil and natural gas, which are abundant in the region, have brought great wealth to the countries that have them.

CHAPTER 17 • REVIEW

REVIEWING VOCABULARY

aquifer   oasis
arid   petroleum
irrigation

Number a sheet of paper from 1 to 5. Beside each number write the word or term that best completes the sentence.

1. An _____ is a layer of rock that holds large amounts of underground water.
2. _____, another word for oil, has brought great wealth to several nations in the Middle East and North Africa.
3. Some cities grew up around an _____, or a fertile and well-watered spot in the desert.
4. Because they are so dry, deserts are often called _____ regions.
5. _____, or bringing water to dry land, has made farming possible in many desert regions.

REVIEWING FACTS

1. Why is the Middle East and North Africa often called a crossroads?
2. Name three major peninsulas in the Middle East and North Africa. Which peninsula is also called Asia Minor?
3. Describe ways in which people have used the camel to help them survive in the desert.
4. Where do most people live in the Middle East and North Africa? What percentage of Egypt's population lives along the Nile River?
5. What is the Fertile Crescent? What was the earliest civilization to develop in this region?
6. Which climate in the Middle East and North Africa is the mildest? What are the characteristics of this climate?
7. Name two regions in the Middle East in which the climate is similar to that of the American West.
8. Why have the people of Iran built huge qanats underground?
9. What fraction of the world's oil production comes from the Middle East?
10. Which country in North Africa has the largest oil supply?

WRITING ABOUT MAIN IDEAS

1. **Writing a Paragraph:** Even though Kuwait and Saudi Arabia are desert countries with almost no farmland, they are among the world's wealthiest nations. Write a paragraph explaining why.
2. **Writing a Myth:** You read about an ancient African myth describing the origin of the Nile River. Write your own myth describing the origin of the great deserts of the Middle East and North Africa.
3. **Writing About Perspectives:** Imagine that you live in a country that is rich in petroleum. First, decide whether you are a ruler or an ordinary citizen. Then write a paragraph that explains your plan for using the money made from selling oil to benefit the people of your country and perhaps other people in the world.

BUILDING SKILLS: READING CONTOUR MAPS

1. What is the purpose of a contour map?
2. Which type of landform would be shown by lines drawn very close together? Very far apart?
3. When do you think you might find contour maps useful?

CHAPTER 18

THE MIDDLE EAST

FOCUS

Allah Akbar! Allah Akbar!

For millions of people in the Middle East, the day begins with the above prayer, which is translated, "God Is Great! God Is Great!" Later in the day people in Middle Eastern offices, oil fields, and farms will stop working and will pray again. Religion is deeply important to most people in the Middle East.

The People

READ TO LEARN

Key Vocabulary   **Key People**   **Key Places**

Islam   Muhammad   Israel
hajj

Read Aloud

Prince Sultan Salman al-Saud is a grandson of the founder of Saudi Arabia. He is also the first Middle Eastern astronaut. On his space flight aboard the United States space shuttle *Discovery* in 1985, the prince launched a communications satellite owned by Middle Eastern countries. His life aboard the shuttle was busy. But, he said, "I still had time to read the Koran [the holy book of the Muslims] in space from beginning to end. I am more proud of that than all my other achievements."

Read for Purpose

1. **WHAT YOU KNOW:** Where do most people of the Middle East live?
2. **WHAT YOU WILL LEARN:** What role does religion play in the lives of the people of the Middle East?

THE MIDDLE EASTERN CROSSROADS

What is the Middle East? It is the southwestern part of the continent of Asia. It begins in the northwest with Turkey and continues south and east to the Arabian Peninsula and Iran. Europeans called it the "Middle East" because the region is located in the "middle" of the land area between Europe and the area Europeans call the "Far East," which means China and its neighbors.

As you read in Chapter 17, the Middle East is one of the world's great crossroads. People and ideas from Asia, Africa, and Europe have long mingled in the Middle East. The alphabet that is used in the West, as well as the Western way of writ-ing numbers, began here. The Middle East is also the birthplace of three of the world's great religions—Judaism, Christianity, and Islam. You will read about Islam in this chapter.

ARABS, THE MAIN CULTURE GROUP

Although the Middle East has hundreds of ethnic groups, the Arabs are the largest group. The Arab culture and language are important in many countries of the Middle East. Two large non-Arab groups who live in the region are the Persians and the Turks.

The first Arabs lived in the Arabian Peninsula. The language they spoke was called Arabic. Today the term Arab also includes most people who speak Arabic and share a common culture. They live throughout the Middle East and North Africa and in many other parts of the world.

Most Arabs live in cities and towns. Some, such as the Bedouins, live in deserts, but even many former nomads have moved to settled communities.

Arabs are united by their language and by many customs. Even more important, most Arabs are united by their religion.

THE BEGINNINGS OF ISLAM

Until the sixth century, the small group of Arab people worshiped many different gods. Then an Arab merchant named Muhammad (mù ham′ əd) began to teach that there was only one *Allah*, the Arabic word for "God." Muhammad said that he was God's messenger. Muhammad's teachings about Allah were the foundation of the religion of Islam. The word *Islam* means "submission, or surrender, to the will of God." People who follow Islam are called Muslims (muz′ limz).

Muhammad died in A.D. 632. After that, people who had been inspired by his preaching left their homeland on the Arabian Peninsula. Their goal, they explained, was to spread the religion of Islam "in the name of Allah." They spread their religion throughout the Middle East and North Africa. Within 100 years after Muhammad's death, Islam had spread westward to Spain and other parts of southern Europe and as far east as India and southern Asia. Islam also spread southward into other parts of Africa.

Today Islam is the second largest religion in the world. There are now more than 800 million Muslims in the world.

MAP SKILL: All Muslims turn to Mecca to pray five times a day. In which country is Mecca located?

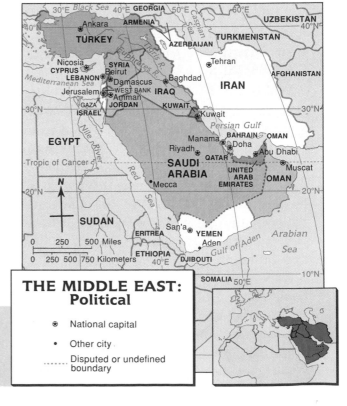

THE MIDDLE EAST: Political

⊛ National capital

• Other city

...... Disputed or undefined boundary

370

ISLAMIC BELIEFS

No matter where they live, all Muslims hold certain beliefs. "I suppose the high spot of my life was performing the **hajj** in the company of my son," says one Saudi Arabian. The *hajj* is the name Muslims give to the pilgrimage they make to the city of Mecca, the birthplace of Muhammad. A pilgrimage, as you may remember, is a trip to a religious shrine or holy place. As one Muslim says:

> *This pilgrimage is one of the "five pillars of Islam," the other four being the belief in one God; prayer five times a day; the giving of alms [charity]; and fasting during the holy month of Ramadan.*

NON-ARAB MUSLIM PEOPLE

Some Muslim people in the Middle East are not Arabs. Find Turkey on the map on this page. Turkey is a Muslim nation, but most of its people are not Arab.

The Turks probably originated in Central Asia and moved westward. Most of them converted to Islam some time after the Arabs became Muslims. In the past, great Turkish empires have ruled large parts of Europe, the Middle East, and North Africa. Although most Turks share the Muslim religion, their customs and languages are different from Arab customs and language.

The Persian people are not Arabs either. Most people in Iran descend from the people of ancient Persia. They speak a language called *Farsi*, or Persian. Like the Turks, the Persians are Muslims but have their own language and customs.

Another Muslim group, the Kurds, live mostly in the mountainous areas of Turkey, Iran, Iraq, Syria, and Armenia. Their language is related to Persian, but their customs are different from those of most Persians. For a long time, Kurds have wanted their own country, but the coun-

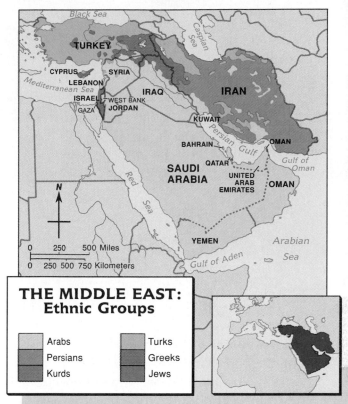

THE MIDDLE EAST: Ethnic Groups

Arabs
Persians
Kurds
Turks
Greeks
Jews

MAP SKILL: Arabs live in most of the countries in the Middle East. In which countries of the Middle East do most non-Arab groups live?

tries in which they live oppose Kurdish independence.

NON-MUSLIM PEOPLES

Some people in the Middle East are neither Muslims nor Arabs. Many of the people in Cyprus and Lebanon are Christians. Some are Christian Arabs. The majority of the people in **Israel** are Jews.

Israel was founded in 1948 as a homeland for Jewish people from all over the world. Jews had lived in Israel, which was part of a region called Palestine, and in other parts of the Middle East since ancient times. But until after World War II, they did not have their own country.

During the 1930s and 1940s, many Jews fled persecution in Europe and made their way to Palestine. They fled because of the

While many women in the Middle East wear veils, the types of veils range from a full cover of face and body to a head scarf.

Holocaust in Germany and other countries of Europe. The Jews in Palestine joined small groups of other Jews who had left Europe earlier to live in what they believed to be their historic homeland. Since Israel became a country, Jews from many continents have left their countries to live in Israel. In the following lessons you will read more about Israel and its relations with Arab countries.

WOMEN IN THE MIDDLE EAST

In many countries of the Middle East, men and women are expected to live apart more than they do in the United States or Western Europe. However, the idea of separate lives varies from country to country and even in regions of a country.

Some countries, such as Saudi Arabia, have very strict rules about what women may or may not do. For example, women are not allowed to drive automobiles, and they are not allowed to shop in some stores. Other countries, like Turkey, make few rules to limit what women may or may not do.

Women in all countries of the Middle East may work at jobs outside their homes.

Some women are doctors, lawyers, teachers, bankers, or nurses. In some Middle Eastern countries they may work with both women and men. In other countries, women may work only with other women.

Women in some Muslim countries are expected to veil their faces when they leave their homes. But while women in Iran have had to wear full coverings since 1979, women in many other Muslim countries wear smaller veils or even head scarves and sunglasses.

ARAB AND NON-ARAB COUNTRIES

As you have read, religion is very important throughout the Middle East. Most of the nations of this area have largely Arab populations. In these lands and in Iran and Turkey, people organize their lives around the Islamic religion. In Israel, the majority of the people practice the Jewish religion.

 Check Your Reading

1. How did the Middle East get its name?
2. What are the "five pillars of Islam"?
3. In what ways does religion affect the daily lives of the Islamic people of the Middle East?
4. THINKING SKILL: List three questions you could ask to find out more about how the country of Israel developed.

The Economy

READ TO LEARN

Key Vocabulary

bazaar   moshav

labor-intensive kibbutz

Key Places

Bahrain

Read Aloud

For months in 1932, a small group of workers had been drilling through rock and pockets of tar on the sandy island of Bahrain in the Persian Gulf. Finally, on a June day, their drills struck oil. With a mighty rumble, a black torrent of oil burst upward before raining down on the jubilant crew. Bahrain—a small island of pearl divers and traders—soon became one of the world's richest countries.

Read for Purpose

1. **WHAT YOU KNOW:** Name three countries in the Middle East.
2. **WHAT YOU WILL LEARN:** How has the discovery of oil changed the economies of many of the countries in the Middle East?

MONEY MADE FROM OIL

"Bahrain lies in just the right time zone for international trading," says Bachir Barbir, a banker in the island country. He buys and sells stocks on the stock exchanges of the world. Barbir explains:

That is why we work 12 hours a day, from 8 A.M. until 8 P.M., Bahrain time. Our day begins before the Tokyo and Singapore [stock] markets close, and we keep going . . . until after New York opens.

Mr. Barbir works for one of the more than 170 banks in Bahrain. You might wonder how such a small country has come to be a world banking center. The answer, as you read above, is oil money. Bahrain is the financial center of the countries around the Persian Gulf.

The contrast between Bahrain now and Bahrain 60 years ago is dramatic. The Bahrain oil discovery you read about above was not the first oil struck in the Middle East. Petroleum had already been found in Iran earlier in the 1900s. But the discovery in Bahrain began the era of large-scale development.

This development increased rapidly after the founding of the Organization of Petroleum Exporting Countries, or OPEC, in 1960. The Middle Eastern countries that helped to found OPEC agreed to work together to sell their oil. By doing so, they were able to raise the price of oil.

The richest oil-producing countries of the Middle East are located on the Arabian Peninsula. Kuwait, Qatar, and the United Arab Emirates have the world's highest per capita incomes. In Qatar, for example, the average yearly income per person is $27,000. This is almost twice the $14,500 average yearly income per person in the

WORLD OIL PRODUCTION-1992

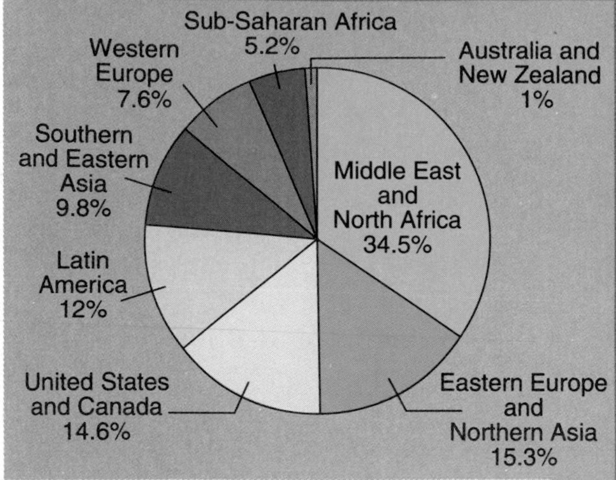

Pie chart labels:
- Sub-Saharan Africa 5.2%
- Western Europe 7.6%
- Southern and Eastern Asia 9.8%
- Latin America 12%
- United States and Canada 14.6%
- Australia and New Zealand 1%
- Middle East and North Africa 34.5%
- Eastern Europe and Northern Asia 15.3%

OPEC OIL PRODUCTION

Country	Barrels of oil annually
Saudia Arabia	2,970,005,000
Iran	1,261,075,000
Venezuela	846,070,000
United Arab Emirates	834,025,000
Nigeria	694,230,000
Libya	544,945,000
Indonesia	490,925,000
Kuwait	321,200,000
Algeria	281,780,000
Iraq	155,125,000
Qatar	155,125,000
Ecuador	117,165,000
Gabon	109,500,000

GRAPH/CHART SKILL: How does the Middle East and North Africa's oil production compare with that of other regions? Which country produces the most oil?

United States. Look at the chart and graph above. They show that the oil-rich countries of the Middle East produce a large part of the world's oil.

Other than oil, however, the Middle East has few natural resources. Therefore, nations in this area that are without oil are usually poor. For example, Yemen, Lebanon, and Jordan have little oil. They are among those countries with the world's lowest per-capita incomes. Turkey also has little oil. While its per-capita income is not as low as those of Yemen, Lebanon, and Jordan, it is lower than those of its oil-rich neighbors. Nearly 2 million Turkish citizens have left their homeland to find work in Europe, the Middle East, and North Africa.

WORKERS FROM MANY COUNTRIES

The wealthy countries of the Middle East have used some of their money to build modern schools, airports, highways, ports, hospitals, and factories. These nations often need to hire guest workers from other countries. Some guest workers come from other countries in the Middle East. Others come from Asia and Africa.

These guest workers are welcome to come and work, but they may not be allowed to become citizens. As one Jordanian who lived in Kuwait explained:

> My son was born here but will never be a citizen. An uncle worked a lifetime in Kuwait. When he retired, they gave him a week to leave the country.

Guest workers usually send money home to their own countries. Often this money makes it possible for their families to survive.

THE EFFECTS OF A WAR

In August 1990 Iraq invaded Kuwait. After asking Iraq to withdraw, the United States and other countries sent troops to the Persian Gulf area to drive the Iraqis out of Kuwait. War broke out in January 1991. In less than two months Iraq was defeated. During the war Iraq blew up hundreds of Kuwait's oil fields causing long-lasting fires that polluted the air and

The fruit of the date palm tree is a favorite food in the Middle East. The trees also provide sugar, oil, and fiber for weaving.

stopped much of Kuwait's oil production. Then fighting broke out in Iraq between the Kurds and the Iraqi government.

As a result of the war, nearly 5 million people were forced to leave the Middle Eastern countries where they lived and worked. Many departing guest workers lost both the money and their savings.

COMMERCE

Despite the changes brought about by oil, most of the people in the Middle East earn their livings in traditional ways—mainly by commerce, or trade, and farming the land.

Hundreds of years ago caravans traveled long distances to large trading centers such as Baghdad in Iraq, Damascus in Syria, and Istanbul in Turkey. Today trucks and railroads have replaced most of the caravans in the Middle East. But at city bazaars, or outdoor markets, some of the same products that were traded long ago are still traded today. Textiles and fine carpets made in Iran and Turkey are exchanged for farm products. Farm products

are in high demand because, as you read in the last chapter, much of the soil in the Middle East is not good for farming.

FARMING METHODS

In those parts of the Middle East where the land can be farmed, many farms continue to employ labor-intensive methods. That is, they use people rather than machinery to do the work. On labor-intensive farms whole families work in the fields.

Some farmers, however, make use of the latest technology. For example, some farmers on the Arabian Peninsula now get water from huge plants that turn salt water from the sea into fresh water.

One Saudi Arabian farmer tells how his family created a farm in the desert near the city of Riyadh. They used both traditional and modern methods to make the farm a success. First they planted rows of fast-growing tamarisk trees to act as wind-breaks. Next the family planted date palms. Date palms grow well in the dry climate and are sources of fruit, sugar, oil, and fiber. After drilling deep water wells, the family also was able to grow alfalfa and vegetables. Funds to drill the deep water wells were provided by the Saudi Arabian government from its petroleum profits.

People on each Israeli kibbutz own and work the land in common. Children on a kibbutz share the work of taking care of animals.

AGRICULTURE IN ISRAEL

In one Middle Eastern country, Israel, modern methods of farming are extensively used. When Israel was created in 1948, it lacked raw materials, energy resources, and industries. Jewish immigrants from Europe and other parts of the world worked hard to make their new country a success. They also received economic aid from the United States and Europe. Today Israel has a highly developed economy.

To farm their harsh land, the early settlers of Israel developed two special kinds of farms. One is the moshav (mō shäv'), a cooperative farm. Under the moshav system, each farm family owns its own land but sells its produce through the moshav.

The other kind of Israeli farm community is the kibbutz (ki bùts'), or collective farm. Members of a kibbutz own and work the land in common. They eat together in communal dining halls. About one third of Israel's farmers cooperate in their work either on a moshav or a kibbutz.

Sometimes a kibbutz also produces manufactured goods. One kibbutz, for instance, makes drip irrigation systems. In these systems water is trickled to the roots of plants. That way no water is wasted by evaporation in the dry air.

THE TRADITIONAL AND THE MODERN

Most of the people of the Middle East earn their living in traditional ways, like farming and commerce. Yet, as you read in this lesson, money from oil has changed the economies of some of the countries of this area. In these countries money from oil is used to build schools, highways, factories, and power plants. As a result very modern ways of life exist along with very traditional ones.

Check Your Reading

1. Why is oil so important to some nations in the Middle East?
2. How did the war in the Persian Gulf affect the people of the Middle East?
3. How are the economies of the Middle East a mix of the traditional and the modern?
4. THINKING SKILL: If you were deciding whether or not to start a farm in the Middle East, what important facts would you need to know to help you make your decision?

The Government

Key Vocabulary

absolute ruler
sharia
Islamic Republic

Key People

Qaboos bin Saud
Golda Meir

Read Aloud

This behavior is against the will of Allah.

This statement was made in 1991 by Sheik Ibn Baz, a Saudi Arabian religious leader. He was criticizing some other Islamic leaders for opposing Saudi Arabia's education system, especially the education of women.

Like other countries in the Middle East, Saudi Arabia has many people who want their country's laws to be based on a strict interpretation of the Koran. Other people in these countries also want laws to follow the Koran but are concerned that some religious leaders interpret the Koran too strictly and keep their countries from being part of the modern world.

Read for Purpose

1. **WHAT YOU KNOW:** Who makes the laws in your community?
2. **WHAT YOU WILL LEARN:** What kinds of government are most common in the Middle East?

ABSOLUTE RULE

During the 1950s the nation of Oman was led by a ruler called Sultan Said. The sultan was determined to keep the nation as it had been for hundreds of years. He succeeded in keeping most Western influences out of Oman. He banned Western medicine and education and refused to allow people to wear Western clothes, ride bicycles, and even to wear eyeglasses.

However, the Sultan did send his son, Qaboos bin Saud, to England to be educated. By the time Qaboos returned to Oman, oil had been discovered there. When Sultan Said refused to use the country's new wealth to modernize it, his son led a peaceful revolt against his father and became sultan.

Less than 20 years later, Oman has almost 500 schools and many hospitals. The changes in the country came about because one person wanted them. Oman has no constitution and no elections. Sultan Qaboos is an absolute ruler, one with complete power whose authority cannot be challenged.

Most of the Middle East's rulers with traditional titles, such as *sultan* or *emir*, have been absolute rulers. In some of these countries, attempts are being made to make the rule less absolute. Jordan's king, who is officially a constitutional monarch, is no longer exercising absolute authority. Since the war in the Persian Gulf ended, Kuwait has been pressured to allow more democracy. Yet Kuwait, Bahrain, Qatar, Saudi Arabia, and the United Arab Emirates still have absolute rulers.

GOVERNMENT AND RELIGION

Most governments in the Middle East rely on Islamic law, or sharia, to govern them fully or partially. Some governments in the Middle East have constitutions that combine sharia and western law. Others rely entirely on sharia.

In 1979 the people of Iran overthrew the Shah, their ruler, and then declared Iran to be an Islamic republic, a nation ruled by sharia. In Iran there is not a sharp difference between religious laws and state laws. Religious leaders make up a majority of Iran's parliament and play an important role in its government.

Saudi Arabia, which is ruled by a king, is also heavily influenced by Islamic religious leaders. In addition to regular police, Saudi Arabia has a religious police force. They patrol to see that religious laws are enforced. These include laws that forbid alcohol and drugs as well as laws that do not permit women to drive.

In Israel Judaism plays a special role. Israel has no official constitution, and the government is influenced by Jewish law. Every Jew in the world has the legal right to enter Israel and become a citizen. Israel is also a democracy.

DEMOCRACY IN THE MIDDLE EAST

Israel has a parliamentary system of government. It is one of the few countries in the Middle East that have elected a female head of state in modern times. Golda Meir, an emigrant from the United States, worked to help create Israel in 1948. She became its premier in 1969.

The Jewish, Christian, and Muslim citizens of Israel all enjoy the right to vote and to practice their religions. However, many Palestinian Arabs living in areas that Israel had occupied after wars have not had the same rights as Israeli citizens. One such area is the West Bank. Find the West Bank on the map on this page. It is the home of a large number of Palestinians.

Turkey, a Muslim country, has had a democratic form of government since it became a republic in 1923. Tansu Ciller became its first female prime minister in 1993.

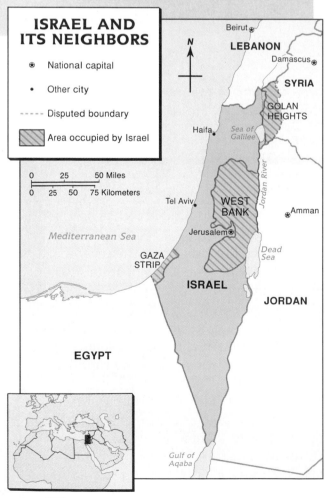

MAP SKILL: Besides the West Bank, what other areas have been occupied by Israel?

ISRAEL AND ITS NEIGHBORS

⊛ National capital

• Other city

- - - - Disputed boundary

▨ Area occupied by Israel

0   25   50 Miles
0 25 50 75 Kilometers

Beirut⊛
LEBANON
Damascus⊛
SYRIA
GOLAN HEIGHTS
Haifa
Sea of Galilee
Jordan River
Tel Aviv
WEST BANK
Amman⊛
Jerusalem⊛
Mediterranean Sea
Dead Sea
GAZA STRIP
ISRAEL
JORDAN
EGYPT
Gulf of Aqaba

HISTORY OF CONFLICT

Often different groups in the Middle East claim the same homeland. One serious conflict involves Israel and the Palestinians. As you have read, Israel was formerly part of a region called Palestine. The Palestinians are Arabs who have traditionally lived in this region. The Palestinians along with the Muslim countries of the region opposed the creation of Israel in 1948. They thought that Palestine should be an Arab homeland. As a result, Israel's neighbors attacked Israel several times. In 1967 Israel gained control of the West Bank, Golan Heights, and some other areas. Palestinians and Arab countries demanded that these lands be returned.

A large step toward peace was taken in 1993. Yitzhak Rabin, the prime minister of Israel, and Yasir Arafat, the Palestinian leader, shook hands after a peace agreement was signed in Washington, D.C. They also agreed to a timetable for self-rule in the West Bank and Gaza Strip. Jordan also met with Israel.

BENEFITS OF COOPERATION

Cooperation often exists among many of the Muslim countries of the Middle East. Many are members of OPEC, whose goal is to establish and agree on oil-production policy. Several of these countries joined with the United States and other nations to force Iraq to end its occupation of Kuwait.

Check Your Reading

1. What is an absolute ruler?
2. What role does *sharia* play in some Middle Eastern nations?
3. What kinds of government are most common in the Middle East?
4. **THINKING SKILL:** Compare and contrast absolute rule with democratic rule.

LIFELINE
For The Old

Myriam Mendilow, who lives in Jerusalem, noticed that more and more elderly people were wandering the streets and that some of them were asking passersby for money. Myriam discovered that many of these lonely people felt that they had outlived their usefulness.

Myriam decided to help these people to find meaningful work. She founded a workshop, called Lifeline for the Old, to train the elderly to bind books. Myriam convinced elderly people that joining the workshop would help to restore their self-respect. They learned that saying no to Myriam was not easy. When they protested she told them, "If a person has just one finger, I'll put that finger to work."

Today Lifeline for the Old is an active center for young people with disabilities as well as the elderly. Together they have found dignity in a shared activity.

Myriam is a fine example of the Lifeline for the Old motto: "Give me work while I live and life while I work." Even though she was nearly 80 years old, Myriam used her energy and enthusiasm to help make life worthwhile for many elderly poor people in Jerusalem. As one of the workers at the center said, "As I keep working here, I get younger and younger."

BUILDING SKILLS

GEOGRAPHY SKILLS

Comparing Maps

While reading about the Middle East, you were often referred to maps for specific information. For example, a political map provides a general picture of an area, showing the locations of countries and their capitals. A population-density map shows the distribution of people within a given area.

Sometimes information is best described by showing two or more different maps of the same area. Then these maps can be compared and conclusions can be drawn from the comparison. When you compare maps, you can acquire information that either map alone might not provide. In this lesson you can compare similar maps to find new information and draw conclusions.

Comparing Temperature Maps

Look at the two maps of Egypt on this page. On both maps the average temperature in Egypt is shown. Notice that **Map A** shows temperatures in January while **Map B** shows temperatures in July. **Map A** shows how the average January temperature varies in Egypt. **Map B** shows the variation in average July temperature.

By comparing **Map A** with **Map B**, you see that it is hotter in Egypt in July than it is in January. You can also see that in general there is a greater difference between January and July temperatures in southern Egypt than in northern Egypt. What is the average January temperature in Cairo? What is the average July temperature in the city?

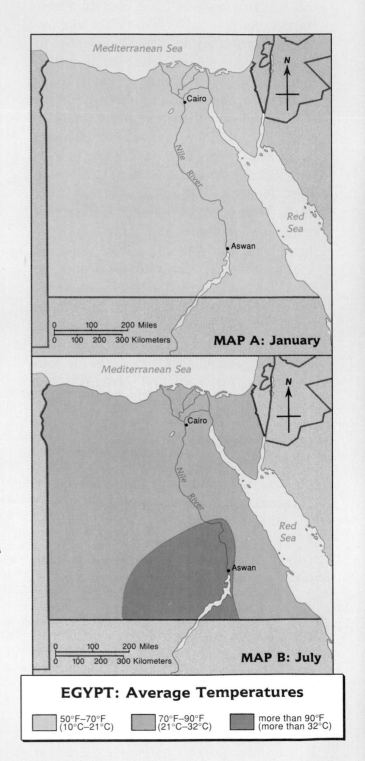

MAP A: January

MAP B: July

EGYPT: Average Temperatures

50°F–70°F (10°C–21°C)

70°F–90°F (21°C–32°C)

more than 90°F (more than 32°C)

380

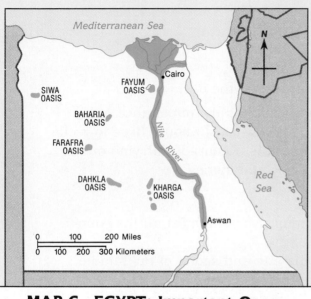

MAP C EGYPT: Important Oases

Oasis   Color shows extent of irrigated land.

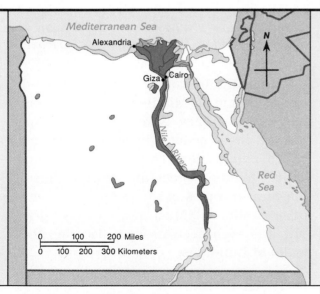

MAP D EGYPT: Population Density

People per square mile 0 2 25 125 250 500

People per square kilometer 0 1 10 50 100 200

• Cities with more than 1 million people

Comparing Other Maps

Comparing maps can help you to understand relationships or to draw conclusions. Look at **Map C** and **Map D** on this page. The titles of these maps tell you that the maps have different subjects. **Map C** shows the location of oases in Egypt. You can see that the color green represents the location of oases on the map.

Map D shows the population density of Egypt. Look at the legend to see which color represents each population category. Which color represents the greatest number of people per square mile? Which color represents the lowest number of people per square mile? In which areas of Egypt is the population density greatest?

Now compare **Map C** with **Map D**. Are the most densely populated areas near oases? Which areas of Egypt are the least densely populated? Are these areas located near oases? By using the maps, what conclusions can you draw about the relationship between population density and the location of oases in Egypt?

Reviewing the Skill

1. What is the purpose of comparing maps?
2. During which month are temperatures lower in Cairo than in Aswan?
3. Which city is cooler in July, Cairo or Aswan?
4. Which area in Egypt is the most densely populated?
5. What is the relationship between oases and population in Egypt?
6. Why is it helpful to understand how to compare maps?

Arts and Recreation

READ TO LEARN

Key Vocabulary

calligraphy

Read Aloud

Baghdad is, for me, a city full of the spirits of the past.

This is how Iraqi poet Khalil Khoury explains the importance of his home city to his work. As he works on new poems, Khoury likes to recite them aloud to his family. When he does this, Khoury is carrying on the Middle Eastern tradition of spoken poetry and stories.

Read for Purpose

1. **WHAT YOU KNOW:** Which ethnic group lives in almost all the countries of the Middle East?
2. **WHAT YOU WILL LEARN:** How are the arts and sports of the Middle East a blend of the traditional and the modern?

THE WRITTEN AND SPOKEN WORD

People like Khalil Khoury have been sharing their poems and stories for centuries in the Middle East. The importance of the skill of storytelling is highlighted in the Middle East's most famous collection of tales, the *Arabian Nights*. In these tales a ruler tells his new wife, Scheherazade (shə här ə zäd′), that she will be put to death if she fails to amuse him. So each night, to save her life, she tells a story. Her stories are so interesting that each day the ruler puts off giving the death order.

Hundreds of years ago few people could read. So storytellers memorized poetry and stories. Early tales from the Middle East were passed on by word of mouth. Poems about heroes and famous events became favorites. As one writer explained:

The Arabian poet was regarded as one gifted with knowledge beyond ordinary humans, and . . . began to assume many roles, including that of leader, . . . teacher, and priest.

Eventually, of course, the poems and stories told in the Middle East were written down. When they were, they often appeared in a beautiful form of writing called **calligraphy**. This type of writing, which features graceful, flowing lines, appears in copies of the Koran and many other Arabic and Muslim works. Calligraphy has even been used to decorate the walls of buildings.

DETAILS IN DESIGN

The Islamic religion has had and continues to have a great effect on the arts of the Middle East. Islam discourages the painting of pictures of humans and animals in public buildings such as mosques in order to keep people from praying to idols. To avoid portraying images of living beings, many Muslim artists turned to and perfected the art of design. The finest, most elaborate designs decorate mosques.

Yet there is also a rich history of Muslim artists portraying people and animals in their famous miniature paintings.

Designs like those on mosques also appear on carpets. The carpets of the Middle East are both works of beauty and useful objects.

OLD AND NEW ENTERTAINMENTS

In the Middle East, as in other parts of the world, popular pastimes keep old traditions alive. Today training and racing camels has become a sport. Most of the riders are boys ten years old or younger.

"The races keep alive one of our most important traditions," says Sheik Abdul Aziz of Sharjah, a small Middle Eastern kingdom. In Sharjah, camel races take place every other Friday in winter.

Many sports and pastimes are thousands of years old. Men in the Middle East have competed in wrestling since their ancestors learned it from the Greeks thousands of years ago.

Falconry is also popular among men of the Middle East. Falconry is the practice of raising and training hawk-like birds called falcons. Men use these birds for hunting.

Sports from other parts of the world are also popular, especially soccer. Women have their own sports clubs at which they enjoy swimming, tennis, volleyball, and other athletics.

ARTS AND LEISURE

The spoken and written word are considered forms of art in the Middle East. As you have read, poetry and storytelling are especially popular. Because Islam discourages showing the human figure and

Middle Eastern art often includes examples of **calligraphy**, a beautiful form of writing.

animals, most artists paint beautiful designs based on flowers or trees or geometric shapes. Camel races and soccer are two of the many leisure activities popular in the Middle East. Sports and recreational activities in the area combine old and new pastimes.

 Check Your Reading

1. Why were storytellers held in such high regard by the ancient Arabs?
2. What is calligraphy?
3. Name two traditional Middle Eastern pastimes.
4. **THINKING SKILL:** Is the following statement from this lesson a fact or an opinion: "The Islamic religion has had and continues to have a great effect on the arts of the Middle East."? Why?

MIDDLE EAST: CULTURAL GEOGRAPHY

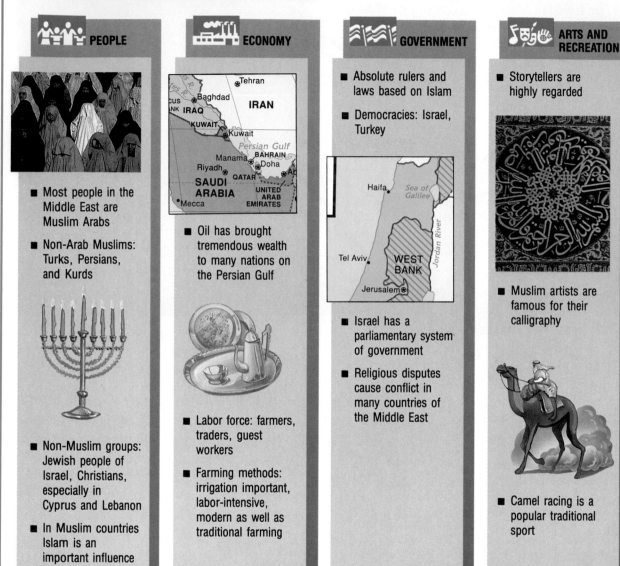

PEOPLE

- Most people in the Middle East are Muslim Arabs
- Non-Arab Muslims: Turks, Persians, and Kurds
- Non-Muslim groups: Jewish people of Israel, Christians, especially in Cyprus and Lebanon
- In Muslim countries Islam is an important influence

ECONOMY

- Oil has brought tremendous wealth to many nations on the Persian Gulf
- Labor force: farmers, traders, guest workers
- Farming methods: irrigation important, labor-intensive, modern as well as traditional farming

GOVERNMENT

- Absolute rulers and laws based on Islam
- Democracies: Israel, Turkey
- Israel has a parliamentary system of government
- Religious disputes cause conflict in many countries of the Middle East

ARTS AND RECREATION

- Storytellers are highly regarded
- Muslim artists are famous for their calligraphy
- Camel racing is a popular traditional sport

IDEAS TO REMEMBER

- Most people in the Middle East are Muslim Arabs.
- Commerce and farming are the main ways of earning a living, although oil has brought wealth to some countries.
- Some governments of the area have absolute rulers as well as laws that are based on Islam; some governments are democratic.
- Storytelling, calligraphy, carpet making, camel racing, and falconry have long been popular in the Middle East.

REVIEWING VOCABULARY

absolute ruler	Islamic Republic
bazaar	kibbutz
calligraphy	labor-intensive
hajj	moshav
Islam	sharia

Number a sheet of paper from 1 to 10. Beside each number write the word or term from the above list that best matches the definition.

1. An outdoor market that has been the center of Middle Eastern economic life for hundreds of years
2. The pilgrimage Muslims make to the city of Mecca
3. A kind of collective farm in Israel on which people share the work
4. A leader who has complete authority over his subjects
5. A world religion based on the teachings of Muhammad
6. A writing style that features beautiful, graceful lines
7. A nation ruled by sharia
8. A type of production that is based on human strength instead of machinery
9. A set of Islamic rules based on the Koran
10. A cooperative Israeli farm system under which each family owns its own land

REVIEWING FACTS

1. Name two non-Arab Muslim nations in the Middle East. In which Middle Eastern country is Judaism the main religion?
2. Why did many Jews leave Europe and move to Palestine in the 1930s and 1940s?
3. Why are Middle Eastern nations that do not have oil generally poor?
4. How did the war in the Persian Gulf affect guest workers in the Middle East?
5. Why are many works of art in Muslim countries more likely to portray designs rather than people or animals?

WRITING ABOUT MAIN IDEAS

1. **Writing a Paragraph:** "In the Middle East the family performs many services that must be performed by institutions in the United States." Do you agree or disagree with this statement? Write a paragraph explaining why.
2. **Preparing an Interview:** Imagine that you are planning to interview someone in the Middle East. Whom would you interview? Make a list of five questions that you would ask.
3. **Writing About Perspectives:** Imagine that you are the son or daughter of guest workers and you were born in the Middle Eastern country in which your parents work. Write a diary entry about your feelings when it is time to leave the country in which you have lived all your life and return to a country you do not know.

BUILDING SKILLS: COMPARING MAPS

1. What is the purpose of comparing maps?
2. Look at the maps on pages 380 and 381. Which city is warmer in July, Cairo or Aswan?
3. Why is it useful to understand how to compare maps?

CHAPTER 19

NORTH AFRICA

FOCUS

North Africa has always been at the crossroads of civilizations, absorbing influences from everywhere but never quite losing its own essence.

As this writer notes, North Africa's location near Europe, Asia, and Sub-Saharan Africa has made this region a unique blend of peoples and civilizations.

The People

READ TO LEARN

Key Vocabulary

muezzin

Key Places

Marrakesh
Cairo

Read Aloud

To outsiders the name of Egypt's capital is Cairo. But Egyptians often call the city *Misr* (mis′ rə), which means "big city" or "home." When Egyptians say, "I am going to Misr," they are heading for Cairo, whether it is their home or not. Today about 10 million people live in this sprawling city, and its population is growing by almost 1,000 people a day. Cairo is just one place in North Africa in which the population is growing quickly. In this lesson you will read how the countries of North Africa have tried to deal with their rapidly increasing populations.

Read for Purpose

1. **WHAT YOU KNOW:** Which type of landscape covers much of North Africa?
2. **WHAT YOU WILL LEARN:** What challenges do the people of North Africa face today?

PEOPLE AND LANGUAGES

When an American writer walked through Marrakesh (mar ə kesh′), Morocco, he was amazed at what he saw.

Never have I seen so much diversity in one place, like a great party with a thousand guests. Many men wore djellabas, ankle-length robes of brown, white, or gray, with turbans or crocheted skull-caps. . . . Women in flowing caftans, often sheltered by their special form of invisibility, the veil, moved with graceful dignity among them.

Some of the people shopping in the market at Marrakesh were Berbers, descendants of the first known group of people to live in North Africa. Today the Berbers, a tall, light-skinned people, live mostly in the mountains of southern Morocco and Algeria. One group of Berbers are Tuareg (twä′ reg) nomads who live in the desert. They stand out in a crowd of North Africans because the Tuareg men, not the women, wear veils.

Since the days of the ancient Berbers, many other groups have entered and spread out over North Africa. The Greeks, Persians, Romans, and Turks have all invaded Egypt and its neighbors. But no group has had as much impact on North Africa as the Arabs have had. In A.D. 640 a small army of Arab warriors conquered much of the area. Wherever they went, they spread their language and their religion. Soon most of the people in North Africa were speaking Arabic and following the rules of Islam.

One group of people who resisted the Arabs were the Berbers. The Berbers had lived in North Africa for thousands of years before the invasion of the Arabs. Although most Berbers became Muslims, for many years they did not learn to speak Arabic. They continued to use their own language, known as Berber.

GROWING POPULATIONS

Cairo, the capital of Egypt, is an example of the huge, growing cities of North Africa. Its population of about 10 million people is increasing by almost 1,000 people a day. Many people expect Cairo to have more than 12 million people by the year 2000.

Because Cairo is growing so rapidly, it does not have enough running water, sewers, schools, or housing for its people. Al-though Cairo's wealthy citizens live in elegant buildings away from the center of the city, in many poor neighborhoods eight or nine people often share a single room.

Explosive population growth is a major problem throughout North Africa. For example, every ten months Egypt has another 1 million people to feed, house, and educate. Part of the reason for the sharp rise in population is good news. As a result of improved health care, North Africans now live longer than they did.

Schools in North Africa share the same problems with schools in North America or other areas whenever there is a rapid increase in the number of schoolchildren. Many students go to school in shifts. They attend classes for half a day—some from 7:00 to 11:30 in the morning and others from 1:30 to 4:00 in the afternoon. Classes with 45 to 60 students are not unusual.

Housing is also a problem. Tens of thousands of people live in Cairo's cemeteries.

MAP SKILL: All the capital cities of North Africa are port cities. Which capital is on the Atlantic Ocean? Which is on the Nile River?

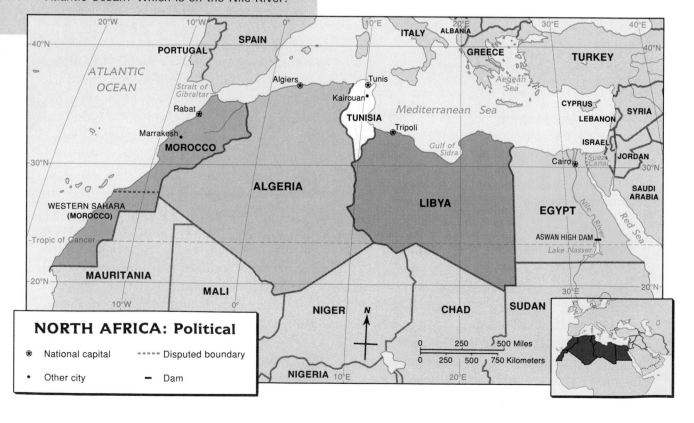

NORTH AFRICA: Political

⊛ National capital

• Other city

----- Disputed boundary

— Dam

They camp in the ancient tombs because they cannot find any better place in which to live. Many people have trouble finding work and getting enough food.

You read in Chapter 17 that North Africa has little arable farmland. Since there are so many people to feed, it is not surprising that food shortages are common. Egypt's president has warned that if the country's population growth does not slow down, "We will have terrible famine, unemployment, and terrorism." Since the 1970s, riots over the high cost of food have shaken cities in Morocco, Algeria, and Tunisia as well as in Egypt.

THE FAMILY

You have read that extended families are common among the Muslims of North Africa. In a typical North African family the bride moves in with her husband's family. Large extended families often share the same household. For example, a Moroccan teenager named Mokhtar lives in a house built hundreds of years ago by his Berber ancestors. His grandfather is the head of the family. An aunt and uncle and their children also live in the house.

High, windowless walls surround most North African houses to give families privacy. Unlike the houses in many suburban neighborhoods of the United States, North African houses have no backyards. Instead homes are built around courtyards.

Although Islamic law allows a man to have four wives if he can support them equally, few Muslim men have more than one wife. Many Muslim nations now make it illegal to have more than one wife. In 1980 Egypt passed a law that allowed a woman to divorce her husband if he took a second wife. Other Muslim countries have similar laws. Many Muslims object. They argue that governments should not interfere with sharia, or the laws of Islam.

High walls surround the homes of many of North Africa's families.

ISLAMIC INFLUENCES

Hajji Ammar Baccar is not a young man. Yet 5 times a day he climbs 101 steps to the top of a minaret, or tower, that rises above the main mosque of the town of Kairouan (kâr wän'), Tunisia. From the top of the minaret, he calls out the Muslim chant "Allah u Akbar!"

Hajji Ammar Baccar is a muezzin, a crier who announces each of the five times of day when Muslims are supposed to

For centuries Muslim **muezzins**, or public criers, have climbed to the tops of minarets to announce the time of prayers.

In 1912 Italy made Libya a colony and ruled it until the end of World War II. Then France and Britain ruled Libya until 1952. As a result, Libya has several different European influences.

All the countries of North Africa are now independent. Yet some of the people in these countries are not happy. They want to cut all ties to their European past and return to a stricter form of Muslim life. For example, in 1985 an Egyptian Muslim leader urged the government to make all Egyptians obey Islamic laws. He said the change was needed to stop "the invasion of Egypt by modern culture."

The question of how much Western culture should be borrowed and retained sparks bitter quarrels in North Africa, as it does in the Middle East. Many of the people in North Africa want to return to stricter Islamic ways.

GROWTH AND CONFLICT

In this lesson you have read that the people of North Africa share several problems caused by a rapidly growing population. Most of the cities in the area are overcrowded, and many countries do not grow enough food to feed their people. You have also read that most of the people in North Africa are Arabs who practice the Islamic religion. In the following lessons you will learn more about these people and how Islam affects North Africa.

stop whatever they are doing and pray. These times are at dawn, at noon, in the afternoon, at sunset, and at night. In cities where the human voice cannot be heard over the roar of traffic, tape-recorded calls to prayer are broadcast over loudspeakers.

Nine out of ten people in North Africa are Muslims. Islam shapes the way they live, work, and play. Islam also has a strong effect on the government, education, and customs of North Africa.

INFLUENCES FROM OTHER LANDS

Between 1830 and 1900 France and Great Britain won control of much of North Africa. In Egypt the British introduced their language, their books, and their ideas of government. In Algeria, Morocco, and Tunisia, which were colonized by France, the French language and customs were introduced. Today English and French are still widely used in North Africa as second languages.

 Check Your Reading

1. Who are the Berbers?
2. Why has North Africa's population been growing so rapidly?
3. How does Islam affect the lives of the people of North Africa?
4. **THINKING SKILL:** Based on your reading of this lesson, what can you conclude about life in North Africa?

390

The Economy

READ TO LEARN

Key Vocabulary

fellahin

Read Aloud

"This is the best place on earth," says Ahmed, an Egyptian farmer in the Nile Delta. The Nile Delta, between Cairo and the Mediterranean Sea in Egypt, is one of the most fertile areas on the earth. "Truly Allah has blessed us," says Ahmed. "Soil, water, sun—we can grow everything!"

As you know, much of North Africa is desert. Little rain falls, and very little of the land is suitable for farming. Therefore, millions of people live crowded together in places like the Nile Delta. Like everyone else in North Africa, they know how important water is to the future of their country.

Read for Purpose

1. **WHAT YOU KNOW:** What major problem faces the people of North Africa today?
2. **WHAT YOU WILL LEARN:** Why are water and oil so important to the economies of the countries of North Africa?

FARMERS AND FOOD SHORTAGES

Although only a tiny part of North Africa can be farmed, most of the people work on the land. More than one third of Egypt's people are **fellahin**, or farmers. Most of them raise crops on small plots, using labor-intensive methods.

Ezzat, an Egyptian boy, lives on his grandfather's farm south of Cairo. When his grandfather dies, the 2.5-acre (1.0-ha) farm will be divided four ways among Ezzat's father and his three uncles. Even now the farm does not produce enough food to feed everyone who lives on it. Although Ezzat's grandfather and one uncle are farmers, his father is a camel driver. Another uncle works in a factory, and the third uncle is looking for a job.

Many North African children never go to high school. Instead they stay home to work on family farms. By the time he was 12 years old, Mokhtar, the Moroccan teenager whom you read about in the last lesson, had to quit school. Like Ezzat he was needed to work on his grandfather's farm. Today Mokhtar's jobs include hauling water from irrigation ditches to the fields and keeping irrigation ditches in good repair. During the walnut harvest he climbs the trees to collect the nuts.

Of the five countries of North Africa, only Morocco once grew enough to feed its people. It even exported nuts, fruits, and vegetables. But a severe drought and a plague of insects hurt Morocco's agriculture in the 1980s. As a result, Morocco had to import food.

The other four North African nations usually have to buy food from different parts of the world. Egypt imports almost half of the food its people eat. The daily bill for food imported into Cairo alone is $10 million. Farms in Algeria can produce only one third of the food that the country needs. The rest must be imported.

Every year the countries of North Africa have to produce more and more food for their growing populations. Yet as the number of people increases, usable farmland is disappearing. Some farmland is being taken over to build new roads and houses. So North Africans have had to find ways of bringing water to remote lands so that they can be farmed. For example, after Egypt's giant Aswan High Dam was built, 30 percent more land could be farmed.

IRRIGATION—NEW AND OLD

For thousands of years, the Nile River regularly overflowed its banks each year in late summer. Egyptian fellahin relied on the flooding river to irrigate their fields. The floodwaters also brought silt, a fine clay that spread over the land and made it much more fertile.

Today the Nile no longer overflows its banks. The Aswan High Dam stops the river's annual floods by storing the water behind huge walls. Then the water is released steadily throughout the year and carried to the fields by canals.

Although the Aswan High Dam provides much-needed water and is also used to create electric power, it has created some problems. The land is now poorer because the rich silt that used to come with the flood waters has stopped. Expensive artificial fertilizers must instead be used. Almost 20 years after the completion of the dam, experts are not certain whether its effects are helpful or harmful.

OIL AND OTHER INDUSTRIES

Unlike Egypt, Libya has no great river. The country is nearly all desert. Yet Libyans are more prosperous than most North Africans. Oil has transformed Libya from a poor desert country into a rich land. Today workers in a Libyan oil field earn more in one month than they earned in a year working as farmers. Oil and a small population keep Libya prosperous.

Libya and Algeria are major oil and natural gas producers. Tunisia, Egypt, and Morocco produce some oil, but they do not have the large reserves of their neighbors.

The Aswan High Dam (*left*) provides a steady supply of water for many Egyptians. Now some farmers can grow as many as three crops a year. Farm animals (*right*) make some farming less labor-intensive.

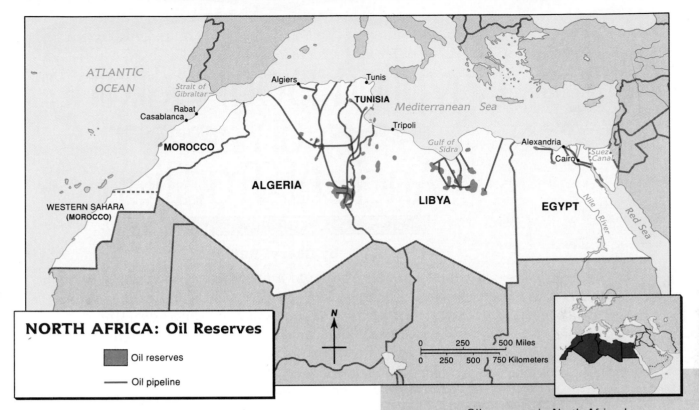

NORTH AFRICA: Oil Reserves

- ▧ Oil reserves
- — Oil pipeline

MAP SKILL: Oil reserves in North Africa have raised the standard of living of its people. Which countries have the most reserves?

Even having small oil reserves, though, can be a great help to a country. For example, Egypt today produces just enough oil so that it does not have to import any from foreign countries. This is an advantage for a country that is trying to develop its industries. Until recently the economy of Egypt was based on the production of just one crop—cotton. Now Egypt is the second-largest industrialized nation in Africa, after South Africa. It has some heavy industries, such as iron and steel manufacturing, and some light industries, such as textile manufacturing.

WATER AND OIL

When the nations of the Middle East and North Africa gained their independence after World War II, they were all poor, undeveloped lands. They have come a long way since that time.

In this lesson you have read how much North Africa depends on two important resources—water and oil. People in North Africa, like people everywhere, need water to live. But to North African countries, having oil is almost as important because it brings in badly-needed money from foreign countries. The economic future of North Africa depends heavily on how the people of this region use their water and oil resources.

 Check Your Reading

1. What are *fellahin*?
2. How has the Aswan High Dam helped Egypt? What problems has it caused?
3. How does the future of North Africa depend on water and oil?
4. **THINKING SKILL:** Do you think that the quotation in the Read Aloud section on page 391 is biased? Why or why not?

Egyptian Boat Building an Ancient Tradition

by Cheryl Haldane

Have you ever tried to build a boat? If you have, you know how difficult it is. The materials you use must be light enough to float, and the bottom of the boat must be watertight. Would it surprise you to learn that thousands of years ago people were already building boats capable of traveling hundreds of miles and carrying thousands of pounds?

As you read in Lesson 2, people have been living along the Nile River, the "superhighway of Egypt," for thousands of years. We will never know when they first tied together bundles of papyrus plant stems to build boats. But we do know that boat building and sailing became important traditions in Egypt. Egyptians today still sail the Nile's waters, and they see some of the same sights their ancestors saw more than 5,000 years ago. As you read this lesson, think about why advances in boat building have played such an important role in human history.

AN AMAZING DISCOVERY

In 1954 a young Egyptian archaeologist was at work beside the huge pyramids just outside of Cairo. His name was Kamal el-Mallakh (kə′ mol el′ mə′ lokh) and he was directing the removal of a pile of sand and rubble next to an ancient wall. El-Mallakh suspected that under the sand and rubble were two pits containing buried boats.

Weeks later, el-Mallakh chiseled a hole in a huge stone his workers had uncovered. After he cut deeper and deeper through the stone, el-Mallakh finally was able to peer into the darkness of one of the pits. At first he could not see a thing, but a sweet smell began to fill his nose. It was the smell of cedar wood. El-Mallakh says that smell made him sure a boat was in the pit. With a little more work, what a boat el-Mallakh discovered.

394

THE KHUFU BOAT

Imagine you are a child in ancient Egypt. You are kneeling to draw water from the Nile in a large pottery jar. When you look up, the beautiful boat you see in the photo at right is gliding past. This boat is towed by another boat, and it is steered by oars held by royal servants of Khufu (kü′ fü), a ruler the ancient Egyptians considered their living god.

Today the boat discovered by Kamal el-Mallakh majestically fills a museum next to the Great Pyramid of Khufu. The boat was built in about 2550 B.C. and is more than 140 feet (43 m) long. That's almost half the length of a football field! Built of cedar wood planks, the Khufu boat makes people catch their breath when they see it. Although at least 4,500 years old, it looks as if it could float on the Nile today.

Khufu's boat is an example of the advanced technology of ancient Egypt. In the diagram on the right you can see how the planks of the hull were sewed together by ropes made from grass. No nails were used. Only the ropes laced back and forth across it and small pieces of wood called tenons kept the hull fastened together.

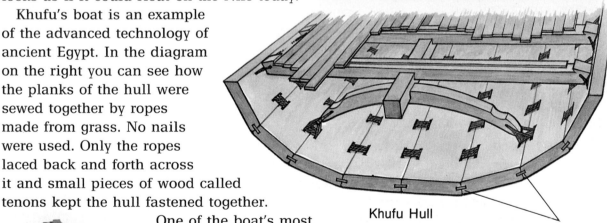

Khufu Hull

tenons

One of the boat's most remarkable features was its "air-conditioned" cabin. Water was poured onto grass mats laid on a frame above the cabin's roof. As the breeze moved air around and under the mats, the water slowly evaporated and cooled the cabin. As you have read, temperatures in North Africa have been recorded as high as 136°F. (58°C). Imagine how nice it must have felt to sit in the air-conditioned cabin on a hot summer day.

395

Building a boat like Khufu's 4,500 years ago was a lot like building a spacecraft today. The best materials and the finest craftworkers were used, and the result was tremendously expensive. The cedar wood came from Lebanon, which was a long journey away by sea. The Egyptians had to trade treasured goods such as gold, perfumes, exotic feathers, and animal skins for the cedar. Then they towed large rafts of cedar logs across the eastern Mediterranean Sea and along the Nile.

THE FIRST SAIL

Early Egyptian advances in boat-building technology influenced the way that boats were built in other parts of the world. It is possible that the sailboat was first developed in Egypt, although we do not know for sure. We do know that the oldest picture of a sailboat comes from the side of an ancient Egyptian vase. The invention of the sail changed the way people traveled. The sail allowed ships to journey farther and faster than they ever had before. The sail may have been one of the inventions the ancient Egyptians passed on to later civilizations around the Mediterranean Sea, such as the ancient Greeks and the Phoenicians.

GREAT VOYAGES

Ancient wall paintings tell us much about how boats were used in ancient Egypt. Some paintings show large ships loaded with cattle and grain, part of expeditions to distant lands such as Punt, which was located in what is now Ethiopia and Somalia. Perhaps the most incredible feat of ancient Egyptian boats was their ability to move gigantic stone monuments from quarries in the south of Egypt to temples farther north. One wall carving, which is drawn below, shows a boat carrying two needle-shaped monuments end to end. The boat would have been built much like the Khufu vessel, with thick planks fastened together with wood and rope. We know that

each of the two monuments was nearly 100 feet (30 m) long, and together they weighed more than 660 tons (598 metric t). This would be the same as a boat carrying a huge airplane loaded with 40 elephants!

LIFE ON THE RIVER TODAY

If you visited Egypt today, you would see some of the same sights a student might have seen in ancient Egypt. Large boats still sail the Nile carrying people, as well as cargoes of bricks, pottery jars, animals, and stone. Of course, today most Egyptians live in modern cities like Cairo, but some families still live on small boats and fish in the Nile. The life-giving river irrigates nearby fields, creating a narrow band of lush green growth in the desert sands.

Picture yourself sailing on the Nile. You are in a small sailboat called a felucca (fə lü′ kə), which is not that different from boats that have sailed the Nile for ages. You smell the earthy scent of the river, and if you only close your eyes, a cool breeze can transport you to another time. The mast creaks as the sail strains against it, and the captain sings softly to himself about the beauty of the river.

Now, like a modern Egyptian, drink your hibiscus tea and eat some honeyed bread. Remember that your river trip is the result of a boat-building tradition that goes back thousands of years.

Why did boat building become an important tradition in ancient Egypt and elsewhere?

The Government

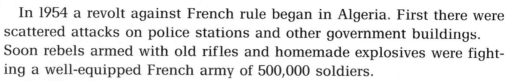

READ TO LEARN

Key Vocabulary   **Key Places**

colonialism   Algeria

Read Aloud

In 1954 a revolt against French rule began in Algeria. First there were scattered attacks on police stations and other government buildings. Soon rebels armed with old rifles and homemade explosives were fighting a well-equipped French army of 500,000 soldiers.

At least one half million Algerians died in the eight-year war that followed. But when the shooting finally stopped, Algeria had won its independence. Although the new nation faced great challenges ahead, its people were proud and hopeful.

Read for Purpose

1. **WHAT YOU KNOW:** What kind of governments are common in the Middle East?
2. **WHAT YOU WILL LEARN:** What problems did many of the countries of North Africa face after gaining their independence?

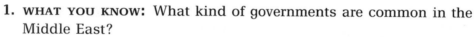

EFFECTS OF FOREIGN RULE

At the beginning of this century, all of North Africa was ruled by European nations. Great Britain controlled Egypt (as you read in Lesson 1). France ruled Tunisia and Algeria, and Italy ruled Libya. Morocco was split into two colonies, one ruled by France and one by Spain.

During more than 130 years of colonial rule in Algeria, the French introduced many improvements, such as modern irrigation systems and good railroads. Yet most Algerians received few of the benefits. Europeans owned the best land and most of the businesses. They also held the highest-paying jobs.

Most Algerians resented colonialism. Colonialism is the control of a country as a colony by another country. Resentment against colonialism led to revolutions like the one described above.

PATTERNS OF GOVERNMENT

No two governments in North Africa are exactly alike, but they all follow similar patterns. Morocco is a kingdom, and the other countries are republics. Yet they all have strong central rule by one leader.

King Hassan II of Morocco has a great deal of political power. He can suspend the legislature and can issue rules and regulations that have the force of law. At the same time King Hassan has worked hard to modernize Morocco. One of his first official acts was to issue a constitution giving equal rights to all citizens.

The president of Egypt is another North African ruler with a great deal of power. Egypt's president can dissolve the legislature of his country. He can also order people to be imprisoned without trial.

In most of the countries of North Africa, single political parties hold great power. For example, in Libya only one political party is permitted. Algeria also had a government that permitted only one political party. But in 1991, Algeria let candidates from other parties run in the national election. More than half the candidates elected wanted a strict Islamic Republic.

Before 1978 Egypt was also a one-party government. Now several small opposition parties hold seats in the Egyptian legislature. However, the Arab Socialist Union, the political party that has governed Egypt for more than 40 years, is still in control.

CONFLICT AND PEACE

North Africa has long been a land of conflict. Egypt, for example, had a long-standing conflict with Israel. Since 1948 Israel has fought four bitter wars against Egypt and other Arab countries.

In 1979 President Anwar Sadat of Egypt broke with his Arab neighbors and made peace with Israel. After 30 years of war he signed a peace treaty that stated that Israel had a right to exist.

Because no other Arab nation would accept the new peace treaty, Sadat's decision isolated Egypt from the Arab world. Even some Egyptians were upset by the treaty. In 1981 a small group of Egyptian terrorists assassinated Sadat. To assassinate is to murder a public figure.

At the time, other Arab nations disagreed with Sadat, but Egypt ended up gaining from the treaty. It regained land that it had lost in the Sinai peninsula, and it gained a certain amount of security from destructive wars.

Anwar Sadat (*left*) of Egypt and Menachem Begin of Israel discuss peace in 1979.

All the governments of North Africa are faced with conflicts. People disagree about how to interpret the laws of Islam. Most of all, they disagree about how governments should deal with rapid population growth and limited resources.

AN UNCERTAIN FUTURE

The countries of North Africa had a troubled past but hope for a better future. You have read that after they won their independence, they all set up new governments. Today the countries' leaders vary from kings to presidents. These leaders have the responsibility of trying to keep their countries at peace in the years ahead.

Check Your Reading

1. Which European nations controlled North Africa during the 1900s?
2. What problems did the newly independent countries of North Africa face?
3. What issue is at the root of the conflict between Israel and the Arab countries?
4. **THINKING SKILL:** Governments change, sometimes very quickly. How could you determine if the information in this lesson is still accurate?

Asking Questions

Imagine that your teacher has divided your class into groups. The teacher tells each group to research and prepare an oral report on one country of North Africa. The reports are due in one week, and each report should last for no longer than ten minutes. Then the teacher asks, "Are there any questions?"

What questions would you ask? How did you know which questions to ask? Questions help you to learn what you want to know. The more skilled you are at asking questions, the easier it will be for you to get the information you need.

Trying the Skill

You have read that nine out of ten people in North Africa are Muslims, and that Islam shapes the way they live, work, and play. Suppose you want to know more about the religion of Islam. List three questions that would help you to get this information.

1. How did you come up with your questions?
2. What information would the answers to your questions provide?

HELPING YOURSELF

The steps on the left will help you to ask questions to learn what you want to know. The example on the right shows one way to use these steps to learn more about the Islamic religion.

One Way to Ask Questions	Example
1. Identify the topic or subject.	The topic is the religion of Islam.
2. Determine what you want to know about the topic.	Do you want to learn facts or to evaluate the accuracy of information?
3. Brainstorm questions that will help you. • To find factual information, ask *who*, *what*, *where*, *when*, and *how*. • To find the meaning or importance of a topic or event, ask *why* or "What conclusions can I draw?" • To evaluate information, ask questions to distinguish fact from opinion, or to identify bias or point of view.	Asking "What are the main beliefs of Islam?" will help you to gather facts. Asking "Why is a pilgrimage to Mecca so important to Muslims?" will help you to understand the importance of this event. Asking "What information is not included?" can help you to determine a writer's bias or point of view.
4. Review your questions to be sure they focus on what you want to know. Cross out those that are not helpful.	A question such as "What is the population of Mecca?" will not help you to learn about Muslim beliefs.
5. Arrange the remaining questions in order, from the easiest to the most difficult.	The easiest questions are usually ones that ask for facts. The facts will help you to answer the more difficult questions.
6. Ask and then answer your questions.	Asking questions will help you to find the information you need.

Applying the Skill

Morocco was once a colony of France. Suppose you wanted to learn about how Morocco became an independent country.

1. Which question would probably be the easiest to answer?
   a. When did Morocco declare its independence from France?
   b. Why did the French want to control Morocco?
   c. How did the events of World War II affect French control of Morocco?
2. For which of the following would you need to ask questions to identify the writer's point of view?
   a. an encyclopedia chart on Morocco
   b. the French governor-general's account of Morocco's struggle for independence
   c. a textbook time line of the history of North Africa
3. What are some questions you would ask to learn how Morocco became an independent country?

Reviewing the Skill

1. Name four steps you can follow to ask good questions.
2. Why is it important for you to ask your own questions?

Arts and Recreation

READ TO LEARN

◼ Key Vocabulary

Ramadan

◼ Read Aloud

Jemaa el Fna—the Assembly of the Dead. What a strange name for a place that is so alive, the noisy, vibrant center of the dusty oasis city of Marrakesh. The broad plaza pulsed day and night, week in and week out, with the beat of drums, the whine and wail of flutes, the twang of three-string instruments—mixed with shouts, singing, and amplified readings from the Koran.

Visitors to Marrakesh, Morocco, have always been fascinated by the bazaar held in the city's big market square. Like so many other things in North Africa, the bazaar in Marrakesh is also influenced by the rules of Islam.

◼ Read for Purpose

1. **WHAT YOU KNOW:** What are some religious holidays that are celebrated in Western Europe?
2. **WHAT YOU WILL LEARN:** How do the arts of North Africa reflect both traditional and modern styles?

TRADITIONS IN ART AND LITERATURE

In a typical North African bazaar, like the one in Marrakesh, you can see metalworkers hammering copper, silver, and other metals just as their ancestors did for hundreds of years. Most of the designs are traditional. North Africans take pride in making things the way their ancestors did.

The arts of North Africa are related to those of the Middle East. For example, Moroccan rugs and Turkish carpets are similar in design.

Egypt has its own artistic traditions. For more than 5,000 years artists in Egypt have created fine wall paintings, elegant jewelry, and other works of art. Many modern Egyptian artists use traditional themes in their work. Like other North Africans they see no reason to believe that "modern" art is better than traditional art.

Let's look at an example. As you know, the Koran commands Muslims to make a *hajj*, or pilgrimage, to the holy city of Mecca at least once in a lifetime. After an Egyptian family makes this important journey, they may paint pictures of the pilgrimage on the outside of their house. On the walls you might see drawings of the airplanes and taxis they took, as well as the places they visited along the way to Mecca.

If you look closely at the pictures, you would notice that people's heads and feet are drawn in profile while their bodies are drawn facing forward. This is the style that ancient Egyptians painted in 4000 years ago.

Islam influences the arts and literature of North Africa, just as it affects many other aspects of life in the area. Egyptian poets, novelists, and playwrights are widely read throughout the Arabic-speaking world. One of their favorite themes is the importance of keeping Islamic traditions alive in a constantly changing world. This idea appears in stories, poems, plays, and many television programs.

Another popular theme with artists is the way modern influences and traditional values challenge one another. Much of the art in North Africa today deals with modern influences on the people of the region. Many artists try to strike a balance between the modern and the traditional.

RELIGIOUS HOLIDAYS

Religious holidays are the most important days of the year for Muslims. Presents are exchanged on Muhammad's birthday, just as they are exchanged by Christians on Christmas.

For those who practice Islam, Ramadan is the most holy month of the year. Like Muslims in other parts of the world, Muslims in North Africa are not supposed to eat, drink, or smoke during the daytime for the entire month of Ramadan. At night they get together for special meals and celebrations. Ramadan is a time of daytime fasting and nighttime feasting. It is also a time of spiritual renewal for Muslims.

As you know, the Koran requires Muslims to pray five times a day. During each of these times, television programming in North Africa is interrupted to allow Muslims time to pray. In countries like Libya, where Islam is followed very strictly, television is regulated by the rules of Islam.

Metalworkers make many fine products that are sold at North African bazaars.

TIES TO THE PAST

As you have read, the arts of North Africans are strongly influenced by Islam. In fact Islamic law plays a large part in nearly every aspect of everyday life. Religious holidays are the most important days of the year for Muslims in North Africa.

Many different kinds of entertainment can be found in the great squares and bazaars of North Africa's cities. As you read at the beginning of this lesson, these "noisy, vibrant" places are filled with the music, arts, and crafts of North Africa.

 Check Your Reading

1. What happens at the bazaar in the city of Marrakesh?
2. What happens during the Muslim month of Ramadan?
3. How do the arts of North Africa reflect both traditional and modern concerns?
4. **THINKING SKILL:** Compare and contrast the role of religion in the lives of the people of North Africa and the people of Western Europe.

NORTH AFRICA: CULTURAL GEOGRAPHY

PEOPLE

- Major ethnic groups: Arabs and Berbers
- Population: rapid growth, overcrowded, often has food shortages and unemployment

- Nine out of every 10 people are Muslims
- Extended families

ECONOMY

- Most North Africans are farmers
- Most North African countries need to import food to feed their people

- Dams are needed for: irrigation, a steady water supply, and electric power
- Libya and Algeria are major producers of oil and natural gas

GOVERNMENT

- North Africa was ruled by European nations for a long time
- Present systems of government: 1 constitutional monarchy, 4 republics
- Most North African countries have one political party that holds great power

- North Africa has long been a land of conflict

ARTS AND RECREATION

- Crafts: metalworking, carpetmaking, and others related to those of the Middle East

- Themes in the arts: Islamic traditions and modern influences
- Religious holidays: Muhammad's birthday, Ramadan

IDEAS TO REMEMBER

- The people of North Africa are mostly Arab and Berber, and most practice the Muslim religion.
- The wise use of water and oil is the key to successful economic development in North Africa.
- Formerly European colonies, the governments of North Africa now include one constitutional monarchy and four republics.
- Many arts and leisure activities in the area are similar to those in the Middle East.

REVIEWING VOCABULARY

Each of the following statements contains an underlined vocabulary word. Number a sheet of paper from 1 to 5. Beside each number write whether the following statements are true or false. If the statement is true, write **T**. If the statement is false, rewrite the sentence using the vocabulary word correctly.

1. A <u>muezzin</u> is a crier in the Islamic world who calls Muslims to prayer.
2. Because it involved only control of the government, <u>colonialism</u> had little effect on the countries of North Africa.
3. During the month of <u>Ramadan</u>, Muslims are not supposed to eat, drink, or smoke during the daytime.
4. The <u>fellahin</u> are a class of merchants and businesspeople who live in North Africa's large urban centers.
5. A <u>muezzin</u> is a pilgrimage to the holy city of Mecca.

REVIEWING FACTS

1. Which group of conquerors has had the most lasting impact on the culture of North Africa?
2. List three effects of the exploding population in the Middle East.
3. What are the two main reasons that most North African countries have difficulty feeding their people?
4. Which countries in North Africa produce the most oil and natural gas?
5. What were some of the effects of French colonialism on Algeria?
6. How does Morocco's constitutional monarchy differ from constitutional monarchies in Europe?
7. Why is Ramadan an important month for Muslims? How do Muslims observe Ramadan?
8. Why did the peace treaty with Israel isolate Egypt from the Arab world?
9. Why did terrorists assassinate Egyptian president Anwar Sadat?
10. Name one example of how religion influences popular art in Egypt.

WRITING ABOUT MAIN IDEAS

1. **Writing a Travel Brochure:** Imagine a journey that begins in Casablanca, Morocco, passes through each country of North Africa, and ends in Mecca, Saudi Arabia. Write a travel brochure for such a trip.
2. **Writing a List:** Write a list of some of the social and political effects of population growth in the countries of North Africa. You may wish to obtain additional information from encyclopedias, newspapers, and magazines.
3. **Writing About Perspectives:** Imagine that you are a Muslim observing Ramadan in North Africa. Write a journal entry describing your day and your feelings about the holiday.

BUILDING SKILLS: ASKING QUESTIONS

1. What does it mean to understand how to ask good questions?
2. What are some steps that could help you to ask good questions?
3. Why is it important to come up with your own questions?
4. Write five questions you might ask to learn more about North Africa.
5. Why is it useful to understand how to ask good questions?

THE MIDDLE EAST AND NORTH AFRICA: PHYSICAL GEOGRAPHY

 LANDFORMS

- Peninsulas: Sinai Peninsula, Arabian Peninsula, Anatolia Peninsula

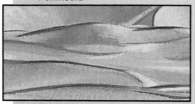

- Deserts: Sahara
- Fertile river valleys: Nile River Valley, Tigris River Valley, Euphrates River Valley

 CLIMATE

- Arid climate: dry

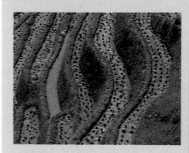

- Temperatures: hot except the Mediterranean coast, Iranian Plateau, and Anatolia, where winters may be long and cold

NATURAL RESOURCES

- Scarce resources: water, arable land
- Fertile land with adequate rainfall is found in Lebanon, the Nile delta, and Yemen
- Forests grow in Atlas Mountains and northern Iran
- Abundant resources: oil and natural gas
- The Middle East produces one third of the world's supply of oil

THE MIDDLE EAST AND NORTH AFRICA: CULTURAL GEOGRAPHY

 PEOPLE

- Most people are Muslim Arabs; Turks, Persians, and Kurds are non-Arab Muslims; non-Muslim groups include Jewish people of Israel and Christians
- Among traditional Muslims women and men lead separate lives
- Major ethnic groups of North Africa: Arabs and Berbers
- Population: rapid growth, has led to overcrowding, often has caused food shortages and unemployment

 ECONOMY

- Oil has brought tremendous wealth to many nations on the Persian Gulf, and to Libya and Algeria
- Farming methods: labor-intensive, modern in Israel and some other regions

- Dams are needed for irrigation, a steady water supply, and electric power

 GOVERNMENT

- Absolute rulers and laws based on Islam are common
- Israel has a parliamentary system
- Some countries are ruled by Islamic law; others combine Islamic law with constitutional law
- Efforts have been made to resolve disputes between some Arab countries and Israel
- North Africa was long ruled by European nations
- Most North African countries have one political party that holds great power

 ARTS AND RECREATION

- Storytellers are highly regarded in the region
- Beautiful calligraphy is used for Arabic and Muslim writings

- Crafts: metalworking, carpetmaking, and others
- Themes in the arts: Islamic traditions and modern influences

REVIEWING VOCABULARY

bazaar	irrigation
colonialism	kibbutz
desert	labor-intensive
fellahin	qanat
Islam	sharia

Number a sheet of paper from 1 to 10. Beside each number write the word or term from the above list that best completes the sentence.

1. The legal systems of most Middle Eastern countries are based on _____.
2. After many years of _____, Algerians revolted against French rule.
3. A _____ is an outdoor marketplace.
4. Farming in most of the Middle East would be impossible without _____.
5. Founded by Muhammad, _____ is the dominant religion of the Middle East and North Africa.
6. Water from a large underground tunnel called a _____ is used to irrigate many farms in Iran.
7. The _____ are a class of Middle Eastern farmers who work small plots of land.
8. Members of an Israeli _____ own and farm the land together.
9. Methods of production that are slower and less efficient than production by machines are called _____.
10. A _____ is a dry, sandy, or rocky region that receives very little rainfall.

WRITING ABOUT THE UNIT

1. **Writing an Essay:** The Middle East is the birthplace of three world religions—Judaism, Christianity, and Islam. It is also the site of nearly constant religious conflict. Write an essay supporting an end to conflict based on the beliefs these three religions hold in common.
2. **Writing About Perspectives:** Imagine that you are the Middle Eastern astronaut who traveled aboard the space shuttle *Discovery* in 1985. You look down on earth and see that the spacecraft is over your country, Saudi Arabia. Describe your feelings in a poem.

ACTIVITIES

1. **Constructing a Bar Graph:** Show the oil production of the world's ten largest oil-producing countries by drawing a bar graph. Use the figures given in the chart on page 374.
2. **Working Together to Make a Scrapbook:** With a group of classmates, gather articles from newspapers and magazines about a current issue in the Middle East or North Africa. Use the articles to make a scrapbook for the rest of the class.

LINKING PAST, PRESENT, AND FUTURE

Do you believe the Islamic world will be able to preserve its culture and modernize at the same time? What adjustments will have to be made? Will those changes be smooth or will they be accompanied by violence and conflict? In what way do you think Islam will have changed by the year 2025?

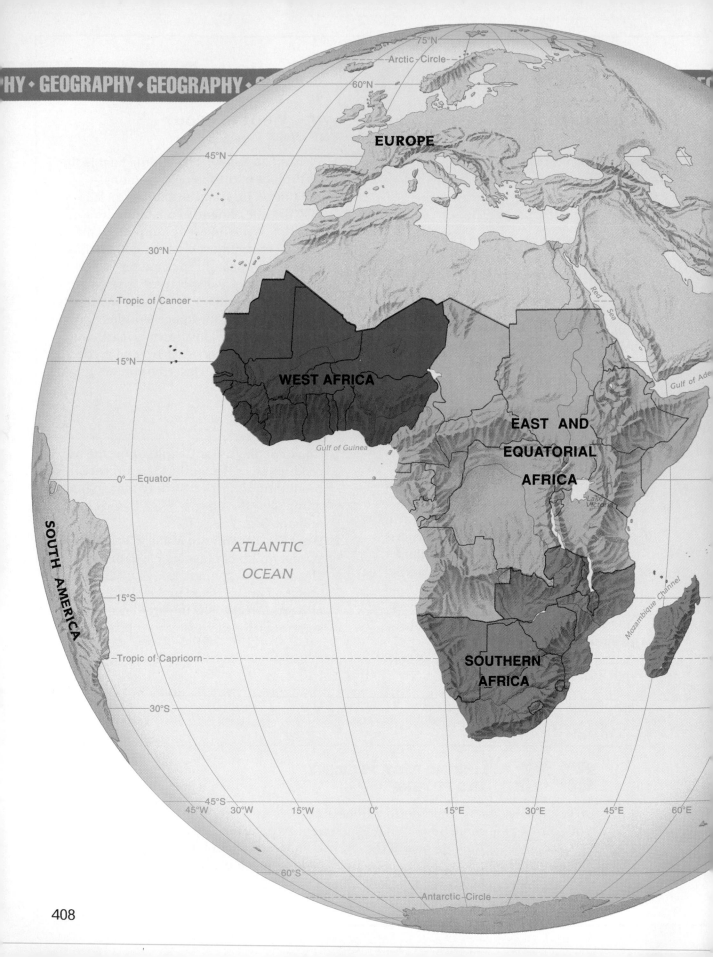

EUROPE

Arctic Circle

75°N

60°N

45°N

30°N

Tropic of Cancer

15°N

Red Sea

Gulf of Ade

WEST AFRICA

EAST AND

EQUATORIAL

AFRICA

Gulf of Guinea

Lake
Victoria

0°   Equator

SOUTH AMERICA

ATLANTIC

OCEAN

Mozambique Channel

15°S

SOUTHERN

Tropic of Capricorn

AFRICA

30°S

45°S

45°W   30°W   15°W   0°   15°E   30°E   45°E   60°E

60°S

Antarctic Circle

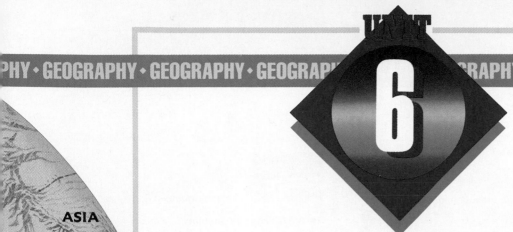

ASIA

INDIAN
OCEAN

90°E

6

SUB-SAHARAN AFRICA

WHERE WE ARE

In the last unit you read about the vast Sahara, the desert that covers much of Northern Africa. Now your journey through the world takes you south of the Sahara to the region with the largest number of countries that have become independent during the past 50 years. This region is known as Sub-Saharan Africa.

Sub-Saharan Africa is divided into three areas: West Africa, East and Equatorial Africa, and Southern Africa. Find these areas on the map. They contain all kinds of land, from harsh deserts to tropical rain forests. As you read about these lands and their peoples, think again about the region in which you live and the others you have studied in this book. How is Sub-Saharan Africa similar to these regions? How is it different?

SUB-SAHARAN AFRICA

ANGOLA
Capital ★
Luanda

Major languages: Portuguese and Ovimbundo
Population: 8.5 million
Area: 481,352 sq mi; 1,246,700 sq km
Leading exports: oil and coffee

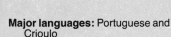

CAPE VERDE
Capital ★
Praia

Major languages: Portuguese and Crioulo
Population: 0.4 million
Area: 1,556 sq mi; 4,030 sq km
Leading exports: fish and bananas

BENIN
Capital ★
Porto-Novo

Major languages: French and Fon
Population: 4.8 million
Area: 43,483 sq mi; 112,620 sq km
Leading exports: fuels and coffee

CENTRAL AFRICAN REPUBLIC
Capital ★ Bangui

Major languages: French and Sango
Population: 3.0 million
Area: 237,362 sq mi; 622,980 sq km
Leading exports: coffee, diamonds, and timber

BOTSWANA
Capital ★
Gaborone

Major languages: English and Setswana
Population: 1.3 million
Area: 231,803 sq mi; 600,370 sq km
Leading exports: diamonds and cattle

CHAD
Capital ★
N'Djamena

Major languages: French and Arabic
Population: 5.1 million
Area: 495,754 sq mi; 1,284,000 sq km
Leading export: cotton

BURKINA FASO
Capital ★
Ouagadougou

Major language: French
Population: 9.4 million
Area: 105,869 sq mi; 274,200 sq km
Leading exports: cotton and manufactured goods

COMOROS
Capital ★
Moroni

Major languages: French, Arabic, and Comoran
Population: 0.5 million
Area: 838 sq mi; 2,170 sq km
Leading export: vanilla

BURUNDI
Capital ★
Bujumbura

Major languages: Kirundi and French
Population: 5.8 million
Area: 10,745 sq mi; 27,830 sq km
Leading export: coffee

CONGO
Capital ★
Brazzaville

Major language: French
Population: 2.3 million
Area: 132,047 sq mi; 342,000 sq km
Leading export: oil

CAMEROON
Capital ★
Yaoundé

Major languages: English and French
Population: 11.4 million
Area: 183,568 sq mi; 475,440 sq km
Leading exports: oil, coffee, and cocoa

CÔTE D'IVOIRE (Ivory Coast)
Capital ★
Yamoussoukro

Major language: French
Population: 12.5 million
Area: 124,502 sq mi; 322,460 sq km
Leading exports: cocoa, coffee, and fuels

DJIBOUTI

Capital ★
Djibouti

Major languages: Arabic and French
Population: 0.4 million
Area: 8,494 sq mi; 22,000 sq km
Leading exports: hides and skins

GHANA

Capital ★
Accra

Major language: English
Population: 15.5 million
Area: 92,101 sq mi; 238,540 sq km
Leading exports: cocoa and gold

EQUATORIAL GUINEA

Capital ★
Malabo

Major language: Spanish
Population: 0.4 million
Area: 10,830 sq mi; 28,050 sq km
Leading exports: cocoa and coffee

GUINEA

Capital ★
Conakry

Major language: French
Population: 7.5 million
Area: 94,927 sq mi; 245,860 sq km
Leading export: bauxite

ERITREA

Capital ★
Asmara

Major languages: Tigrinya and
Arabic
Population: 3.3 million
Area: 36,170 sq mi; 93,679 sq km
Leading exports: salt, leather, and
textiles

GUINEA-BISSAU

Capital ★
Bissau

Major languages: Portuguese and
Crioulo
Population: 1.0 million
Area: 13,946 sq mi; 36,120 sq km
Leading export: peanut products

ETHIOPIA

Capital ★
Addis Ababa

Major language: Amharic
Population: 50.5 million
Area: 435,607 sq mi; 1,128,221 sq km
Leading export: coffee

KENYA

Capital ★
Nairobi

Major languages: English and
Kiswahili
Population: 25.2 million
Area: 224,962 sq mi; 582,650 sq km
Leading exports: coffee and tea

GABON

Capital ★
Libreville

Major languages: French and Fang
Population: 1.2 million
Area: 103,348 sq mi; 267,670 sq km
Leading export: oil

LESOTHO

Capital ★
Maseru

Major languages: Sesotho and
English
Population: 1.8 million
Area: 11,718 sq mi; 30,350 sq km
Leading exports: manufactured goods
and wool

GAMBIA

Capital ★
Banjul

Major languages: English and
Mandinka
Population: 0.9 million
Area: 4,363 sq mi; 11,300 sq km
Leading export: peanut products

LIBERIA

Capital ★
Monrovia

Major language: English
Population: 2.7 million
Area: 43,000 sq mi; 111,370 sq km
Leading exports: iron ore and rubber

MADAGASCAR

Capital ★
Antananarivo

Major languages: French and Malagasy
Population: 12.4 million
Area: 226,656 sq mi; 587,040 sq km
Leading exports: coffee, vanilla, and sugar

NAMIBIA

Capital ★
Windhoek

Major languages: English, Afrikaans, and German
Population: 1.5 million
Area: 318,259 sq mi; 824,290 sq km
Leading exports: diamonds, uranium, and livestock

MALAWI

Capital ★
Lilongwe

Major languages: English and Chichewa
Population: 9.4 million
Area: 45,745 sq mi; 118,480 sq km
Leading exports: tobacco, sugar, and tea

NIGER

Capital ★
Niamey

Major languages: French and Hausa
Population: 8.0 million
Area: 489,190 sq mi; 1,267,000 sq km
Leading export: uranium

MALI

Capital ★
Bamako

Major languages: Bambara and French
Population: 8.3 million
Area: 478,765 sq mi; 1,240,000 sq km
Leading exports: cotton and manufactured goods

NIGERIA

Capital ★
Abuja

Major languages: English, Hausa, Yoruba, and Ibo
Population: 122.5 million
Area: 356,669 sq mi; 923,770 sq km
Leading exports: oil, cocoa, and rubber

MAURITANIA

Capital ★
Nouakchott

Major languages: Arabic and French
Population: 2.1 million
Area: 397,954 sq mi; 1,030,700 sq km
Leading exports: iron ore and fish

RWANDA

Capital ★
Kigali

Major languages: Kinyarwanda and French
Population: 7.5 million
Area: 10,170 sq mi; 26,340 sq km
Leading exports: coffee and tea

MAURITIUS

Capital ★
Port Louis

Major languages: English, Creole, and Hindi
Population: 1.1 million
Area: 718 sq mi; 1,860 sq km
Leading export: sugar

SÃO TOMÉ and PRÍNCIPE

Capital ★
São Tomé

Major language: Portuguese
Population: 0.1 million
Area: 371 sq mi; 960 sq km
Leading export: cocoa

MOZAMBIQUE

Capital ★
Maputo

Major language: Portuguese
Population: 16.1 million
Area: 309,495 sq mi; 801,590 sq km
Leading exports: shrimp, cashew nuts, and sugar

SENEGAL

Capital ★
Dakar

Major languages: French and Wolof
Population: 7.5 million
Area: 75,749 sq mi; 196,190 sq km
Leading exports: fuels, fish, and chemicals

SEYCHELLES

Capital ★
Victoria

Major language: Creole
Population: 0.1 million
Area: 171 sq mi; 443 sq km
Leading exports: fish and cinnamon

TANZANIA

Capital ★
Dar es Salaam

Major languages: Swahili and English
Population: 26.9 million
Area: 364,900 sq mi; 945,090 sq km
Leading exports: coffee and cotton

SIERRA LEONE

Capital ★
Freetown

Major languages: English, Mende, and Temne
Population: 4.3 million
Area: 27,699 sq mi; 71,740 sq km
Leading exports: rutile, diamonds, and bauxite

TOGO

Capital ★
Lomé

Major languages: French, Kabiye, and Ewe
Population: 3.8 million
Area: 21,927 sq mi; 56,790 sq km
Leading export: phosphates

SOMALIA

Capital ★
Mogadishu

Major languages: Somali and Arabic
Population: 7.7 million
Area: 246,201 sq mi; 637,660 sq km
Leading exports: bananas and bauxite

UGANDA

Capital ★
Kampala

Major languages: English and Luganda
Population: 18.7 million
Area: 91,135 sq mi; 236,040 sq km
Leading export: coffee

SOUTH AFRICA

Capitals ★
Pretoria, Cape Town
and Bloemfontein

Major languages: Afrikaans, English, Zulu, Xhosa, and Sesotho
Population: 40.6 million
Area: 471,445 sq mi; 1,221,040 sq km
Leading exports: gold, coal, and minerals

ZAIRE

Capital ★
Kinshasa

Major languages: French, Kiswahili, and Kiluba
Population: 37.8 million
Area: 905,565 sq mi; 2,345,410 sq km
Leading export: copper

SUDAN

Capital ★
Khartoum

Major language: Arabic
Population: 25.9 million
Area: 967,496 sq mi; 2,505,810 sq km
Leading export: cotton

ZAMBIA

Capital ★
Lusaka

Major languages: English, Nyanja, and Bamba
Population: 8.4 million
Area: 290,583 sq ml; 752,610 sq km
Leading export: copper

SWAZILAND

Capital ★
Mbabane

Major languages: siSwati and English
Population: 0.8 million
Area: 6,703 sq ml; 17,360 sq km
Leading exports: food, sugar, and wood products

ZIMBABWE

Capital ★
Harare

Major languages: English, Chishona, and Sindebele
Population: 10.0 million
Area: 150,803 sq mi; 390,580 sq km
Leading exports: tobacco and gold

CHAPTER 20

PHYSICAL GEOGRAPHY OF SUB-SAHARAN AFRICA

FOCUS

For most Africans, land is more than a source of wealth, it is sacred. It gives people life, and so they believe they were entrusted with it and must, in return, treasure it.

This is how one writer described the importance of land to the people of Sub-Saharan Africa. In this chapter you will read about the physical geography of this vast region.

Landforms

READ TO LEARN

Key Vocabulary

basin
rift valley
escarpment
savanna

Key Places

West Africa
East and Equatorial Africa
Southern Africa
Great Rift Valley
Sahel

Read Aloud

According to an ancient African legend, two angry bulls once fought a fierce battle. They pawed and stamped with such rage that they smashed mountains into powdery dirt. Their hoofs churned up giant clouds of red dust that covered the entire land of West Africa.

In this lesson you will read about the red clay landscape of West Africa. You will also read about vast grasslands and thick, green forests in other parts of Sub-Saharan Africa. As you will discover, this is a region of great variety.

Read for Purpose

1. **WHAT YOU KNOW:** How would you describe the physical geography of North Africa?
2. **WHAT YOU WILL LEARN:** What are the major physical features of Sub-Saharan Africa?

SOUTH OF THE SAHARA

Did you know that Africa is the world's second-largest continent? You began to learn about Africa when you read about North Africa in Unit 5. You may recall that the world's largest desert, the Sahara, extends across North Africa from the Atlantic Ocean to the Red Sea. You may also recall that geographers link North Africa together culturally with the area known as the Middle East.

In this unit you will read about Sub-Saharan Africa. This region extends southward from the Sahara and includes most of Africa.

If you look at the map of the region of Sub-Saharan Africa in the Unit Opener on pages 408–409, you can see that this region includes about three fourths of the continent of Africa. Note also that Madagascar, a large island in the Indian Ocean, is included in this region. Within Sub-Saharan Africa there are great extremes of climate, vegetation, and landforms. Although people have created special ways to live in the different environments of this region, some parts of it are so harsh that few people try to live there.

West Africa, East and Equatorial Africa, and Southern Africa are the three areas

415

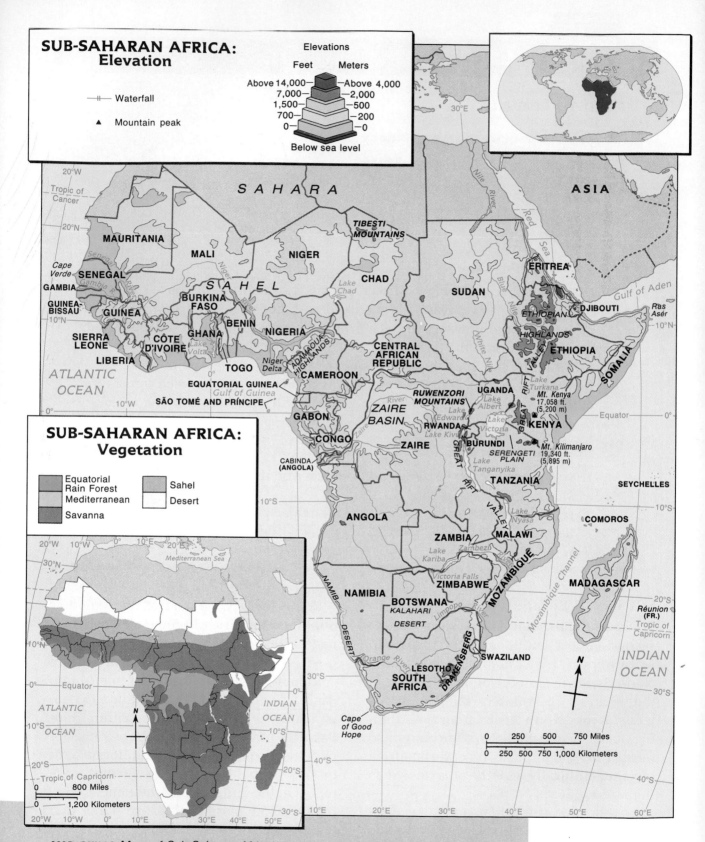

SUB-SAHARAN AFRICA: Elevation

Elevations

Feet	Meters
Above 14,000	Above 4,000
7,000	2,000
1,500	500
700	200
0	0

Below sea level

—⊩— Waterfall

▲ Mountain peak

ASIA

Tropic of Cancer

20°W

20°N

SAHARA

30°E

Nile River

Red Sea

Gulf of Aden

Ras Asér

MAURITANIA

MALI

NIGER

TIBESTI MOUNTAINS

CHAD

SUDAN

ERITREA

DJIBOUTI

Cape Verde

SENEGAL

Senegal River

GAMBIA

Gambia River

GUINEA-BISSAU

GUINEA

SAHEL

BURKINA FASO

Niger River

Lake Chad

ETHIOPIAN

HIGHLANDS

ETHIOPIA

10°N

SIERRA LEONE

GHANA

BENIN

NIGERIA

CÔTE D'IVOIRE

Lake Volta

LIBERIA

TOGO

ADAMAOUA HIGHLANDS

CENTRAL AFRICAN REPUBLIC

SOMALIA

10°N

ATLANTIC OCEAN

10°W

Niger Delta

EQUATORIAL GUINEA

CAMEROON

SÃO TOMÉ AND PRÍNCIPE

Gulf of Guinea

GABON

ZAIRE BASIN

Zaire River

RUWENZORI MOUNTAINS

UGANDA

Lake Albert

White Nile

Blue Nile

Lake Turkana

Mt. Kenya 17,058 ft. (5,200 m)

Equator

0°

CONGO

ZAIRE

RWANDA

Lake Edward

Lake Victoria

KENYA

GREAT RIFT VALLEY

CABINDA (ANGOLA)

Lake Kivu

BURUNDI

SERENGETI PLAIN

Lake Tanganyika

Mt. Kilimanjaro 19,340 ft. (5,895 m)

SUB-SAHARAN AFRICA: Vegetation

▨ Equatorial Rain Forest	▨ Sahel
▨ Mediterranean	☐ Desert
▨ Savanna	

TANZANIA

SEYCHELLES

10°S

ANGOLA

GREAT RIFT VALLEY

Lake Nyasa

ZAMBIA

MALAWI

COMOROS

Zambezi

Lake Kariba

MOZAMBIQUE

MADAGASCAR

20°S

Réunion (FR.)

Tropic of Capricorn

Mediterranean Sea

30°N

20°W 10°W 0° 10°E 20°E

NAMIB DESERT

NAMIBIA

BOTSWANA

KALAHARI DESERT

Victoria Falls

ZIMBABWE

Limpopo River

Mozambique Channel

10°N

0° Equator

ATLANTIC OCEAN

INDIAN OCEAN

INDIAN OCEAN

10°S

20°S

Tropic of Capricorn

0° 800 Miles

0° 1,200 Kilometers

20°W 10°W 0° 10°E 20°E 30°E 40°E 50°E

Orange River

DRAKENSBERG

SWAZILAND

LESOTHO

SOUTH AFRICA

Cape of Good Hope

N

0 250 500 750 Miles

0 250 500 750 1,000 Kilometers

30°S

40°S

10°E 20°E 30°E 40°E 50°E 60°E

MAP SKILL: Most of Sub-Saharan Africa's land is at low elevations. What is the region's largest area of high elevation? What type of vegetation is found in the Zaire Basin?

that make up Sub-Saharan Africa. Find those areas on the Unit Opener map. More than 435 million people live in the more than 45 large and small countries that make up these areas.

A VAST PLATEAU

As the map on page 416 shows, much of Sub-Saharan Africa rises no higher than 7,000 feet (2,000 m) above sea level. There are lowlands along the coasts and rivers, and there is a great plateau that stretches the length of the region. As the map shows, this plateau is broken in East Africa by an area of highlands. The highest mountains of Africa, Mount Kilimanjaro (kil ə mən jär' ō) and Mount Kenya, are found in this region. Both of these towering mountains are volcanoes that are no longer active.

In addition to plateaus, there are huge basins in Sub-Saharan Africa. As you may know, a basin is a large, bowl-shaped dip in the land. Rivers flow into basins from surrounding highlands. The huge Zaire (zä îr') Basin is sometimes called "The Heart of Africa." It is a place of dense rain forests, swamps, and winding rivers. Where is the Zaire Basin on the map?

THE GREAT RIFT VALLEY

The most dramatic landforms in Sub-Saharan Africa are a series of huge north-south cracks in the land called rift valleys. A rift valley is a narrow valley with steep sides that was formed millions of years ago by cracks in the earth's crust. One large area of rift valleys in Sub-Saharan Africa is the Great Rift Valley. This area starts in Mozambique at Lake Nyasa (also called Lake Malawi) and is made up of several systems of rift valleys. North of Lake Nyasa, the western part of the Great Rift Valley bends to the west of Lake Victoria and includes Lake Tanganyika

In Zimbabwe, the Zambezi River plunges over an escarpment to form "The Smoke That Thunders," Victoria Falls.

(tan gən yē' kə), Lake Kivu, Lake Edward, and Lake Albert.

Another system of rift valleys branches to the east of Lake Victoria toward Lake Rudolf, forming the eastern belt of the Great Rift Valley. Still farther north a system of rift valleys cuts through the highlands of Ethiopia and forms the Red Sea.

RIVERS AND ESCARPMENTS

While many people in Sub-Saharan Africa live in the Great Rift Valley, others are clustered along great rivers and their tributaries. Did you know that the Nile River has its source in Sub-Saharan Africa? The Nile, Zaire, and Niger rivers are Africa's longest rivers. They descend from Africa's vast plateau, forming rapids and waterfalls. In fact many African rivers fall over escarpments. An escarpment is a steep cliff at the edge of a plateau.

For example, the Zambezi River plunges 350 feet (100 m) at Victoria Falls in Zimbabwe (zim bäb' wē). People who live near the falls call it "The Smoke That Thunders" because the thundering Zambezi River crashes over an escarpment and constantly sprays water into the air.

417

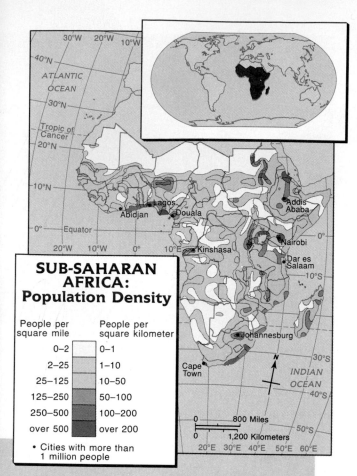

SUB-SAHARAN AFRICA: Population Density

People per square mile	People per square kilometer
0–2	0–1
2–25	1–10
25–125	10–50
125–250	50–100
250–500	100–200
over 500	over 200

• Cities with more than 1 million people

MAP SKILL: Which are the two southernmost cities in Sub-Saharan Africa shown above?

Because they are dramatic and beautiful, waterfalls throughout the world often attract tourists. But waterfalls present a constant challenge to the people who live near them. Huge waterfalls make rivers useless for boat traffic. The great number of escarpments in Sub-Saharan Africa means that there are few navigable rivers.

SAHEL, SAVANNA, AND RAIN FOREST

Just south of the Sahara is a mostly dry area of grasslands known as the **Sahel** (sä' hel). *Sahel* is an Arabic word meaning "border" or "shore." As you might have guessed, this vegetation zone got its name because it borders the Sahara. Parts of the

Sahel are dry and dusty. The dusty red clay of West Africa that you read about in the lesson opener is found in the Sahel.

In addition to the Sahel, Sub-Saharan Africa is famous for two other special zones of vegetation. The largest zone is known as the **savanna**. A savanna is a broad grassland containing scattered trees and shrubs. The savanna covers more than one fourth of the African continent. It is the major farming and livestock-grazing area of Sub-Saharan Africa. Most of the large animals for which Africa is famous—such as lions, elephants, and giraffes—live on the savanna.

The other important vegetation zone in Sub-Saharan Africa is the tropical rain forest. The rain forest forms a curving belt that begins in West Africa and loops south to include all of the Zaire Basin. It rains almost every day in the rain forest, and temperatures are always high.

THE LAND SOUTH OF THE SAHARA

As you have read, Sub-Saharan Africa is a large region, and its people live in a variety of environments. Note from the map on this page that most of the people live near bodies of water. Plateaus, rift valleys, river basins, escarpments, and waterfalls are all found in Sub-Saharan Africa.

Check Your Reading

1. Describe the Great Rift Valley.
2. What is an escarpment?
3. What is the difference between the Sahel and the savanna?
4. **THINKING SKILL:** Classify the terms below into at least two categories. Explain what this information tells about Sub-Saharan Africa.

basin	rain forest	Sahel
escarpment	rift valley	savanna

Reading a Mileage Chart

Key Vocabulary
mileage chart

Suppose you wanted to know how far it is from Lagos, Nigeria, to Nairobi, Kenya. You might refer to a map, using its scale bar to measure the distance between these two cities. But you could use a mileage chart instead. A mileage chart is a table that shows distances between specific places. Some mileage charts show distances by air while others show distances by road, train, or water.

How to Read a Mileage Chart
Look at the mileage chart on this page. First, read the title of the chart. It tells you that the chart shows distances between 5 cities in Sub-Saharan Africa. The title also tells whether the distances are by air or by land. Next, read the labels on the horizontal and vertical axes on the chart. The labels on the horizontal axis list some of the cities in Sub-Saharan Africa in alphabetical order. The labels on the vertical axis list the same 5 cities, also in alphabetical order.

Suppose you want to find the distance between Kampala and Nairobi. Find Kampala on the horizontal axis and place your right index finger on it. Now find Nairobi on the vertical axis, and put your left index finger on it. Move both fingers, one across the chart and one down, until they meet. You have found the distance between the two cities. What is it?

Have you noticed that there is a blank space in each row on the chart? You will

MILEAGE CHART FIVE AFRICAN CITIES

Road Distance in Miles	Jinja	Kampala	Mombasa	Nairobi	Tanga
Jinja		50	668	364	764
Kampala	50		718	414	814
Mombasa	668	718		304	96
Nairobi	364	414	304		401
Tanga	764	814	96	401	

find that the blank space is where each city listed on the vertical axis meets the same city on the horizontal axis. Of course, there is no distance between a city and itself, so this area of the chart is left blank.

Reviewing the Skill
1. What is the purpose of using a mileage chart?
2. How far is it from Mombasa to Nairobi? From Jinja to Mombasa?
3. Which trip would be longer—traveling from Jinja to Nairobi or from Mombasa to Nairobi?
4. If you were to travel from Jinja to Nairobi to Mombasa by car, how many miles would you drive?
5. Why is it useful to understand how to read mileage charts?

Climate and Resources

READ TO LEARN

Key Vocabulary

trade winds   drought
harmattan

Key Places

Kano

Read Aloud

In southwestern Niger there is a type of antelope called an addax that rarely needs to drink water. This is just as well, because most of this region gets only a few inches of rain each year. Some of the scarce water collects in rock pools that attract many kinds of wildlife. Ostriches, baboons, cheetahs, gazelles, and other animals live in this arid climate.

Read for Purpose

1. **WHAT YOU KNOW:** What kind of climate would you expect lands located at the equator to have?
2. **WHAT YOU WILL LEARN:** What are the climates of Sub-Saharan Africa? What are the region's chief natural resources?

THE TROPICS

Africa has more tropical land than any other continent. More than 90 percent of Sub-Saharan Africa lies between the Tropic of Cancer and the Tropic of Capricorn. As you can see from the map on the opposite page, the equator slices through the middle of this region.

Except for its mountainous regions, all of Sub-Saharan Africa is warm or hot all year. There is not much difference between the summer and winter temperatures. However, there is often a great difference between daytime temperatures and nighttime temperatures, especially in the deserts. The variation can be as much as 60°F. (33°C). The highest temperatures in Sub-Saharan Africa occur near the Sahara and in the desert of Somalia, along the Indian Ocean.

Rainfall varies throughout Sub-Saharan Africa. As the map on page 421 shows, rain is scarce in about three fourths of Africa. Many places get enough rain for part of the year. For several months after, they swelter under the tropical sun.

For example, the region around Kano, in northern Nigeria, gets about the same amount of rain every year as does Chicago, Illinois. Yet Chicago is green with trees, grass, and shrubs because moisture is available year-round. Farmers in the areas around Chicago can grow many kinds of crops. In the area around Kano, the rain comes all at once. Then, in the long dry season, plants turn brown. Few crops can grow because of the long dry spell.

WINDS

Sub-Saharan Africa's seasonal patterns of rainy and dry seasons are caused by winds. Sailors called some of these winds trade winds because they determined which way trading ships could sail.

In Sub-Saharan Africa trade winds blow from the Atlantic Ocean, carrying moist ocean air into West Africa. As the winds rise over the escarpments at the edge of the plateau, they drop moisture as heavy rain. This is the reason that rain forests start just inland from the west coast.

A second kind of wind picks up dry, dusty air from the Sahara and carries it to Sub-Saharan Africa. This hot, dry wind, called the **harmattan** (här mə tan′), creates a hot, dry season especially in the north-western part of Sub-Saharan Africa.

Some years the winds shift, resulting in no rainy season in the savannas. Since 1970 the rains have failed several times. **Drought**, or a lack of rain over a long period, has caused plants and crops to die. The results for the people have been disastrous. Millions of people in Ethiopia, Chad, Niger, Mali, Burkina Faso, Somalia, and Senegal have died of hunger-related illnesses after their crops and animals died. More than 240 million Africans live in these areas that have suffered droughts.

INSECTS AND DISEASE

Drought is only one problem that changing trade winds can cause. Another problem is diseases. Mosquitoes and other tropical insects spread malaria, yellow fever, and other illnesses.

One tropical insect, the tsetse (tset′ sē) fly, carries a disease known as sleeping sickness. The tsetse fly also infects cattle, horses, sheep, camels, and other livestock with another disease called nagana. It is usually fatal.

Tsetse flies breed in hot climates that have plenty of rain. They cluster on the banks of streams and rivers. Unfortunately 38 countries in Sub-Saharan Africa have just the right conditions for tsetse flies to thrive. At least 50 million people live in the tsetse-fly area of Sub-Saharan Africa.

MAP SKILL: Hundreds of millions of people in Sub-Saharan Africa have experienced **drought**, or extremely dry conditions. Which parts of the region are always dry?

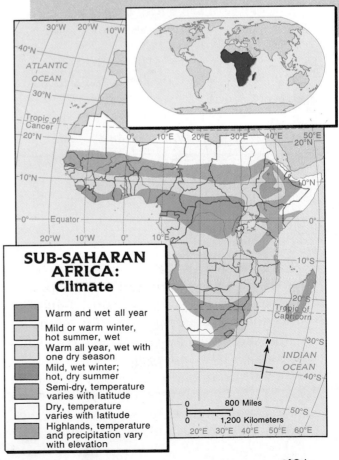

SUB-SAHARAN AFRICA: Climate

- Warm and wet all year
- Mild or warm winter, hot summer, wet
- Warm all year, wet with one dry season
- Mild, wet winter; hot, dry summer
- Semi-dry, temperature varies with latitude
- Dry, temperature varies with latitude
- Highlands, temperature and precipitation vary with elevation

0   800 Miles
0   1,200 Kilometers

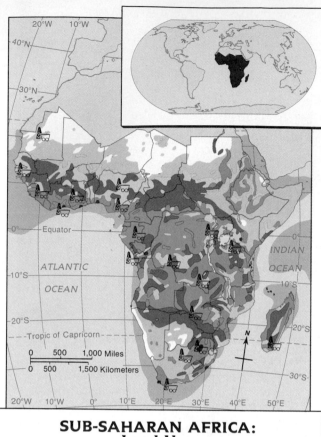

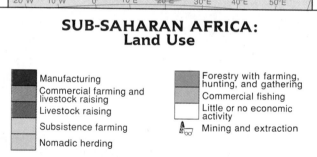

SUB-SAHARAN AFRICA:
Land Use

- Manufacturing
- Commercial farming and livestock raising
- Livestock raising
- Subsistence farming
- Nomadic herding
- Forestry with farming, hunting, and gathering
- Commercial fishing
- Little or no economic activity
- Mining and extraction

MAP SKILL: Much of Sub-Saharan Africa is rich in minerals. In which part of the region does the least amount of mining take place?

mans if tsetse flies did not breed there. Herders like the Masai (mä sī') of East Africa have been very careful to keep their cattle out of the tsetse-fly area. But in recent years, because drought has scorched their traditional lands, some Masai have had to drive their cattle into the danger zone in search of food.

Fortunately some Masai have received help from veterinarians and scientists who are working on the tsetse-fly problem. Governments and health groups are also working hard to find ways to control tropical insects. If killers like tsetse flies can be controlled, Africans can make greater use of the Sub-Saharan region's agricultural resources.

AGRICULTURE

In 1879 a blacksmith named Tete Kwashi (tē tē kwä' shē) returned to his village in Ghana with seeds from a tree he had seen on an island off the west coast of Africa. Tete Kwashi tended the seedlings that sprouted from the reddish-brown seeds. Five years later he harvested his first cacao (kə ka' ō) crop.

Today cacao is the most important crop in both Ghana and in the nearby Côte d'Ivoire. Flavoring for the chocolate ice cream or candy you eat may have come from African trees.

Cacao trees grow only in the tropics. They need at least 50 inches (130 cm) of rain a year and hot weather. The tropical coast of West Africa has just the right conditions for growing cacao.

Cacao is by no means the only successful crop of Sub-Saharan Africa. In addition to cacao, the rain forest provides coffee, rubber, palm oil, and other products. Timber from such trees as mahogany, teak, ebony, cedar, and walnut is also a major resource of the rain forest of Sub-Saharan Africa.

In the tsetse-fly area people cannot keep horses, oxen, camels, or cattle alive. Therefore they have no work animals. Since the people are also usually too poor to buy farm machinery, they must tend their crops by hand.

On the savanna, where herding cattle is a way of life for many people, the tsetse-fly area acts as an invisible wall. Much of the African savanna could support more hu-

422

The savanna is an important grazing area for livestock. In areas that have enough rain, residents can raise grain crops like millet or corn. The migrating wildlife of the savanna is also a resource. Tourists come from all over the world to see a variety of African wildlife in their natural settings.

A WEALTH OF MINERALS

Sub-Saharan Africa is a storehouse of minerals. Copper, iron, gold, uranium, manganese and many other minerals have been found in the region. And many parts of Sub-Saharan Africa have not as yet been fully explored for their minerals.

Look at the map on page 422. You can see that mining takes place all over Sub-Saharan Africa. Zaire is a center of copper mining. South Africa, the richest country in the region, mines gold, diamonds, uranium, and other scarce resources. Nigeria, in West Africa, has valuable petroleum.

WATER RESOURCES

In the last lesson you read that waterfalls can make rivers useless for transportation. But those same waterfalls can be used to create hydroelectric power. Although Africa has many rivers that could be harnessed to make electricity, most of its countries are too poor to spend the large amounts of money needed to build power dams. Only recently have dams been built. For example, a huge dam on the Zaire River provides the power to run Zaire's mines.

Rivers can be used over and over as an energy resource. Unlike oil or coal, this resource is not gone after one use. Africa's rivers, like its mineral treasures, hold great promise for the continent's future.

A CONTINENT OF CONTRASTS

You have read that trade winds help shape the climate patterns and economy of

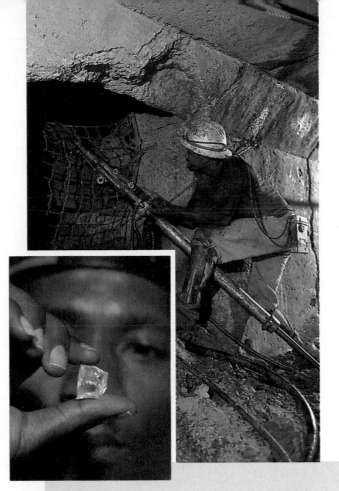

Diamonds (*inset*) are a major mineral resource of South Africa.

Sub-Saharan Africa. You have also read that Sub-Saharan Africa is a region of untapped resources. As agricultural problems are solved and mineral and water resources are developed, the economic growth of the region should increase.

 Check Your Reading

1. What is a drought?
2. How do the trade winds affect Sub-Saharan Africa's climate?
3. What are some of the important agricultural resources of Sub-Saharan Africa?
4. **THINKING SKILL:** Which resources do you think will be developed in Sub-Saharan Africa in the future? Why?

SUB-SAHARAN AFRICA: PHYSICAL GEOGRAPHY

 LANDFORMS

- Highest mountains: Mount Kilimanjaro, Mount Kenya
- Most of Sub-Saharan Africa is a great plateau

- Special features: Zaire Basin, Great Rift Valley, waterfalls
- Rivers: Nile, Zaire, Niger, Zambezi

- Vegetation zones: Sahel, savanna, rain forest

 CLIMATE

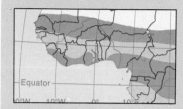

- Mostly tropical, with high temperatures all year
- Rainfall is scarce in about three fourths of the continent

- Trade winds cause rainy and dry seasons
- Tropical diseases include malaria, yellow fever, sleeping sickness

NATURAL RESOURCES

- Tropical crops: cacao, coffee, rubber, palm oil, timber

- Large wildlife preserves attract tourists

- Rich in minerals: copper, iron, gold, uranium, manganese, diamonds
- Many waterfalls that can be harnessed to provide hydroelectric power

IDEAS TO REMEMBER

- The region's plateaus, basins, and rift valleys are covered mainly by savannas and rain forests.
- Most of Sub-Saharan Africa has a tropical climate and its resources include tropical crops, migrating wildlife, and mineral resources.

REVIEWING VOCABULARY

basin   savanna
escarpments   trade winds
rift valleys

Number a sheet of paper from 1 to 5. Beside each number write the word or term from the above list that best matches the definition.

1. A vast region of grasslands in Africa that is similar to prairies in the United States
2. A large bowl-shaped depression named for Zaire in central Africa
3. Low-lying areas bordered by high cliffs that extend through much of the African continent
4. Air currents that strongly influence cycles of rain and drought in Sub-Saharan Africa
5. Steep cliffs that form the boundaries of many of Sub-Saharan Africa's great plateaus

REVIEWING FACTS

1. What is Sub-Saharan Africa? Name its three main regions.
2. What is the Great Rift Valley? Why has this region attracted people throughout history?
3. What is the relationship between escarpments and the lack of navigable rivers in Africa?
4. What is the Sahel? What are two of the main features of this region?
5. Which region of Sub-Saharan Africa is most famous for wildlife?
6. Which vegetation zone is characterized by rain and dense vegetation? In which two African regions is most of this zone located?
7. Name three characteristics of the climate of Sub-Saharan Africa.
8. What effect has drought had on the people of Sub-Saharan Africa?
9. In what way has cacao helped the economies of Ghana and Côte d'Ivoire?
10. What factor has prevented Sub-Saharan nations from developing hydroelectric power?

WRITING ABOUT MAIN IDEAS

1. **Writing a Paragraph:** Write a paragraph describing some of the ways in which the tsetse fly affects the economy of Sub-Saharan Africa.
2. **Writing an Editorial:** Write an editorial about famine in Sub-Saharan Africa.
3. **Writing About Perspectives:** Imagine that you are an African journalist who is traveling from the northern to the southern part of Sub-Saharan Africa. Write a travel article in which you describe the three natural features that you find the most interesting.

BUILDING SKILLS: READING A MILEAGE CHART

1. What is the purpose of using a mileage chart?
2. Look at the mileage chart on page 419. How far is it from Jinja to Kampala?
3. Which trip would be longer—traveling from Tanga to Jinja or from Tanga to Nairobi?
4. Why is it useful to understand how to read mileage charts?

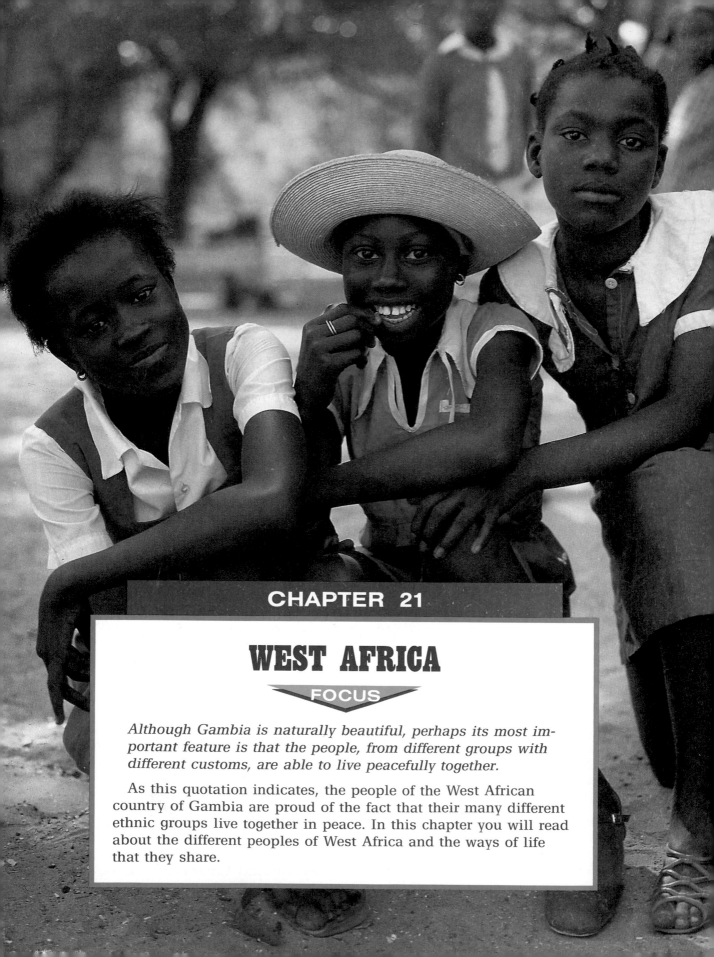

CHAPTER 21

WEST AFRICA

FOCUS

Although Gambia is naturally beautiful, perhaps its most important feature is that the people, from different groups with different customs, are able to live peacefully together.

As this quotation indicates, the people of the West African country of Gambia are proud of the fact that their many different ethnic groups live together in peace. In this chapter you will read about the different peoples of West Africa and the ways of life that they share.

The People

READ TO LEARN

Key Vocabulary

clan

Read Aloud

Once, oh small children round my knee, there were no stories on earth to hear. All the stories belonged to Nyame, the Sky God. He kept them in a golden box next to his royal stool.

That is the way that one West African story about the origin of stories begins. Some West African stories are about forest creatures. Others are about families and their histories. As you will learn in this lesson, family history is very important to the people of West Africa.

Read for Purpose

1. **WHAT YOU KNOW:** What are the three parts of Sub-Saharan Africa?
2. **WHAT YOU WILL LEARN:** What three major influences have helped to shape West African culture?

THE NATIONS OF WEST AFRICA

West Africa has a long history. Hundreds of years ago many powerful black African kingdoms flourished along its rivers. By A.D. 400 the kingdom of Ghana was a rich trading center. Historians believe that great amounts of gold, ivory, and prized woods were bought and sold in the busy marketplaces of ancient Ghana.

Today West Africa is made up of 16 modern nations. They range in size from tiny Gambia to Nigeria, Africa's largest country. Many of these nations are located along the coasts of the Atlantic Ocean and the Gulf of Guinea. West Africa is the most densely populated area of Sub-Saharan Africa.

Did you know that most nations of West Africa have been independent only since the 1960s? Before that time, every country except Liberia was a colony of a European power. However, it is important to realize that even though West Africa is a land of newly independent nations, the cultures of the West African people are very old and rooted in a rich past.

A BLEND OF CULTURES

The cultures of West Africa have had three major influences: first, traditional African practices and beliefs; second, the religion of Islam; and third, European colonialism and Christianity. These influences became uniquely West African.

427

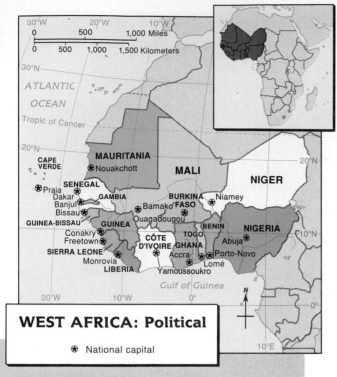

WEST AFRICA: Political

⊛ National capital

MAP SKILL: West Africa is made up of many different countries, large and small. Which large country is located in the northeastern part of the area?

Traditional customs and beliefs are rooted in the rich, ancient past of West Africa. Long ago West Africans developed strict rules for working together so that families in the harsh lands south of the Sahara could survive. Cooperation became more important than success for individuals in the area.

As you may know, the religion of Islam reached West Africa more than a thousand years ago when Arab and Berber traders brought Muslim ideas across the Sahara. As groups of West Africans adopted Islam, they learned Arabic in order to read the Koran, the sacred book of Islam. Islamic scholars taught the children of the rulers of early African kingdoms. Today Islam is the major religion in most of West Africa. Nigeria has about 60 million Muslims, more than any other country in Africa.

The third major influence on the cultures of the people of West Africa was European colonialism and the Christian religion. Europeans reached West Africa in the 1500s. Most West African countries, as you have read, were ruled as colonies for many years by European powers. After the Europeans left about 1960, their languages remained. Today the most frequently spoken European languages are English, French, and Portuguese. Many black West Africans speak one of these languages in addition to the language of their particular ethnic group. In Nigeria, for example, the members of the Hausa, the Ibo, and the Fulani ethnic groups each speak their own language. However, they all use English as a common language. As you can see on the chart on pages 410–413, the official language of many West African nations is English or French.

MANY ETHNIC GROUPS

They are young. When they come back to us, they bring motorcycles, bicycles, and radios. These are things they buy just for themselves. In Dogon culture things are acquired for use by the whole family.

Boua Diabate (bü′ ə dē ə ba′ tē) is a member of the Dogon ethnic group of West Africa. In recent years drought has scorched the Dogon homelands in the Sahel, south of the Sahara. Hundreds of Dogon people have moved to other parts of West Africa in search of food, and so Boua worries about the survival of his culture. Like most West African ethnic groups, family bonds are very strong among the Dogon people.

The Dogon are just one small group in West Africa's patchwork of peoples, cultures, and nations. Hundreds of ethnic groups each have their own customs and special way of life. Family ties are very strong among West Africa's ethnic groups.

The many different ethnic groups of West Africa have developed ways of life to fit the lands they live in. The Fulani and the Tuaregs of the arid savanna herded goats, camels, and cattle. The Ibo and other ethnic groups in the south have had the benefit of richer soil and more rain. They have made their homes in permanent villages as farmers and fishing people. A few groups, like the Yoruba, have traditionally worked as traders and merchants.

MANY LANGUAGES

Because there are so many different ethnic groups in West Africa, there are also many different West African languages. This is typical throughout Africa. Between 800 and 1,000 languages are spoken on the African continent. Varying dialects are spoken in different villages. As you read in Chapter 11, a dialect is a variation of a language spoken by a particular group. In Nigeria alone, more than 250 different dialects are spoken.

Most people in the southern part of West Africa speak a dialect of a group of languages known as the Niger-Congo languages. The majority of these people are black Africans. In the northern part of

There are many different ethnic groups in West Africa. The people in these ethnic groups live in both villages (*bottom*) and large cities such as Lagos, Nigeria (*top*).

West Africa, there are many different mixes of black, Berber, and Arab people. Most of these people speak languages related to Berber or Arabic.

MANY RELIGIONS

The three major influences on West Africa have left a legacy of different religions in the region. Many West Africans practice traditional religions that developed long before the Muslims or Christians arrived. In Burkina Faso, Côte d'Ivoire, Guinea-Bissau, Liberia, and Togo, more than half the people follow various traditional religions.

Many countries today are mainly Muslim. Mauritania, for example, describes itself as an Islamic Republic. Nearly all of its people are Muslim. Gambia, Mali, Niger, and Senegal also have populations that are mostly Muslim.

Only Cape Verde has a population that is mostly Christian. The people of Cape Verde are descended from Portuguese colonists and Africans who were enslaved. The Portuguese colonists brought Roman Catholicism, which remains the chief religion of Cape Verde.

In Nigeria, most members of an ethnic group practice the same religion. The Hausa, Fulani, and Kanuri people, who live mostly in northern Nigeria, are mainly Muslim. Christianity is the major religion of the Ibo and other groups that live mostly in southern Nigeria.

Usually a country's leaders belong to the largest religious group in the nation, but sometimes they do not. In Côte d'Ivoire, for example, about 20 percent of the people are Christian, about 20 percent are Muslim, and the rest practice traditional religions. Yet the Christian leaders of Côte d'Ivoire decided to build a great Roman Catholic cathedral in its capital, Yamoussoukro. It is the largest Roman Catholic cathedral in the world. Côte d'Ivoire's leaders hope that the cathedral will attract many tourists and visitors.

Our Lady of Peace in Côte d'Ivoire is the largest Roman Catholic cathedral in the world.

MIXED LOYALTIES

The newly independent countries of West Africa have found it difficult to encourage people to feel a loyalty to the country. Many Africans have a strong sense of loyalty to their ethnic group. Some have a feeling of loyalty to their religious group. Africans are also loyal to their clan. A clan is a group of families who are descended from one ancestor.

Members of a clan share a common religion and set of values. Being part of a clan gives Africans a sense of belonging.

There is an important reason that many Africans feel stronger loyalties to their ethnic group or to their clan than to their nation. Africans did not create all the borders of their countries. The borders of most African nations were established mainly by the European colonial nations. Often the borders have little to do with where different groups live.

In the years since the countries of West Africa gained independence, some people have begun to develop a new feeling of belonging to a country. Without this feeling, it is hard for a country, especially a new country, to survive.

PEOPLES AND CULTURES

West Africa is a patchwork of peoples and cultures. The region's people are a mixture of black African, Berber, and Arab. They speak many different languages and dialects and belong to hundreds of ethnic groups.

As you have read, three different influences have strongly shaped the West African way of life. The first are customs and traditional beliefs rooted in the rich history of West Africa.

The second influence on West Africa was Islam, which was brought to the area more than a thousand years ago. Today Islam is the major religion in West Africa.

Traditional ways of life are followed in many parts of West Africa. This crowd is attending a Senegalese government rally at which traditional instruments are played.

Finally, the people of West Africa have also been strongly influenced by European colonialism and Christianity. European languages are still spoken in many of the West African countries. Recently some African countries have begun to form feelings of national loyalty.

Check Your Reading

1. Why do many West Africans speak French or English?
2. What three influences have shaped the way of life of the people of the countries of West Africa?
3. What are some groups that claim the loyalties of many people of West Africa?
4. **THINKING SKILL:** List two questions you could ask to learn more about European colonial influences in West Africa. Then provide the answer to one of the questions.

The Economy

READ TO LEARN

◼ Key Vocabulary

desertification
shifting cultivation
slash-and-burn farming

Key Places

Côte d'Ivoire
Senegal
Nigeria

◼ Read Aloud

Louise Able lives in a cacao-growing village in Côte d'Ivoire. As you know, the beans of the cacao plant are used to make chocolate. How, then, can it be possible that Louise has tasted chocolate only twice in her life? The answer is that the cacao beans must be processed before they can be used to make chocolate. Côte d'Ivoire does not have the kind of factories that can turn cacao beans into a chocolate bar. However, as you will read in this lesson, new industrial growth is changing West Africa.

◼ Read for Purpose

1. **WHAT YOU KNOW:** What types of businesses are important to the economy of your community and your state?
2. **WHAT YOU WILL LEARN:** What kinds of economies are found in West Africa?

THE GROWING DESERT

As it is in places all over the world, farming is an important economic activity in West Africa. But in much of this area, farming is becoming more and more difficult because of drought conditions.

As you read in Chapter 20, a dry grassland called the Sahel borders the Sahara to the south. For those nations of West Africa that are located in the Sahel, less rainfall than usual is dangerous. The farming economy of these nations depends on the little rain they already receive. In recent years, however, the rains over the Sahel have failed. As you can imagine, this has created many problems.

The droughts have not just reduced farm production, they have changed the landscape of the Sahel. Desertification, or the expansion of a desert, has crept southward from the Sahara. Desertification is caused by drought coupled with too much grazing by animals and by the cutting down of trees and bushes for firewood. The soil blows away because there is nothing to hold it. If desertification cannot be halted, the Sahel may become part of the Sahara.

SHIFTING CULTIVATION

South of the Sahel lies the savanna. In the savanna parts of West Africa continuing east to Sudan and the Indian Ocean coast, rain provides sufficient moisture for crops and animals. Far more people live in the savanna than in the Sahel.

However, in much of the savanna, the soil is not fertile enough to bear crops every year. People have therefore developed a plan of shifting cultivation. Shifting cultivation allows some fields to rest, lying unplanted, while crops are planted on other fields. While a field is resting, it becomes covered with new grass which helps to restore the soil's precious nutrients. In some areas of the savanna, villagers allow fields to remain unplanted for many years. Other villagers will move their entire village to a place where the fields have not been used for a long time.

Shifting cultivation often depends on slash-and-burn farming. In this type of farming, people first clear a field by cutting down trees and stumps, as you can see in the top drawing. Next they burn the brush. The burning creates ashes that enrich the soil. Finally the people plant crops, such as millet, peanuts, and yams.

Often the farmers use the soil wisely by rotating, or changing, the crops they grow in a field. Each crop uses up different minerals in the soil. If millet is planted in a field one year, peanuts may be planted there the next year. In the third year the field may be planted with a starchy root plant called cassava or manioc. This crop can survive drought, but it uses up minerals in the soil quickly.

The policy of shifting cultivation requires a lot of land. Recently, in order to produce enough food for more people, many villagers have been forced to shorten the rest periods of a large number of their fields. As the fields are replanted again and again, the soil wears out and produces smaller and smaller crops.

CASH CROPS

Most West Africans are subsistence farmers who grow only enough food for their families. Families work together to

SLASH-AND-BURN FARMING

1. Trees and brush are slashed to the ground.

2. The land is burned.

3. Crops are planted.

DIAGRAM SKILL: How is the land prepared in the slash-and-burn farming system?

433

Jobs in West Africa range from traditional farming to modern manufacturing.

grow their food, often sharing fields. Subsistence farmers eat most of what they grow, but some subsistence farmers grow enough produce to sell small amounts in local markets. Women often are in charge of the business of selling farm products in these markets.

However, growing cacao, peanuts, and other cash crops is a very important part of the economies of West Africa's coastal nations. As you may remember, a cash crop is a plant or plant product raised to make money. The prosperous economy of Côte d'Ivoire is based on cash crops such as coffee, cacao, and bananas. The entire economy of Senegal rises or falls with the price that customers pay for peanuts in world markets.

GROWING INDUSTRIES AND CITIES

Most West Africans live in farming communities, and the economies of this region rely heavily on agriculture. However, industries are developing, and cities are growing. West Africa now has 5 cities with more than 1 million people each.

African countries want to sell more than raw materials. Nigeria, Ghana, and Côte d'Ivoire are building mills and factories to process their crops.

Minerals also play an important new role in West Africa. For example, the discovery of oil in Nigeria has provided work in the oil industry for thousands of Nigerians. When people move to take jobs in oil fields or in offices in cities, they leave their old ways of life.

A DEVELOPING AREA

Most West African economies are still in the early stages of development. As you have read, many people are subsistence farmers or use shifting cultivation to produce cash crops. Others find work in the developing industries of West Africa.

Check Your Reading

1. What has caused desertification?
2. How has the drought in the Sahel affected the rest of West Africa?
3. What kinds of economies are found in West Africa?
4. THINKING SKILL: What effect has the growing population of West Africa had on its economy?

The Government

READ TO LEARN

Key Vocabulary
oba

Key Places
Benin
Gambia

Read Aloud

For the Gambia, our homeland,
We strive and work and pray,
That all may live in unity,
Freedom, and peace each day.

These words are taken from the national anthem of Gambia. As you read earlier, Gambia's people are proud of the fact that they "live in unity." This country's small population has six main ethnic groups. Larger West African nations have hundreds of different ethnic groups. In this lesson you will read about how the nations of West Africa strive to unify their people.

Read for Purpose

1. **WHAT YOU KNOW:** For about how long have the nations of West Africa been independent?
2. **WHAT YOU WILL LEARN:** What special problems face the governments of West Africa's nations?

DIFFERENT TRADITIONS

When the English created the colony that is now the nation of Nigeria, they brought together people who governed themselves by very different customs. The Yoruba people were used to obeying kings. The Hausa and Fulani were loyal to Muslim rulers who had great authority over their lives. In sharp contrast, millions of Ibo in the tropical south were used to running their villages democratically.

The Ibo system used a village council of older men to talk over problems and make decisions. These men were called elders. In the council every elder had an equal voice. Other men in the village could also attend the meetings of the council and speak. This tradition of democratic village councils is common in West Africa.

In the past, African women, who have always been important at home and in the marketplace, took little part in government. This tradition is changing slowly. One Muslim woman asked her husband for permission to run for a state council in Nigeria. She won and became the only woman on a council of 350 people.

TRADITIONAL RULERS

West Africa also has a long tradition of rule by kings. In the north these rulers are known as emirs, as they are in some areas

435

Traditional councils are still important in modern Nigeria. They continue to make important decisions for their villages.

of the Middle East and North Africa. In other parts of West Africa, a ruler is known as an **oba**. According to one Egyptian visitor to **Benin**:

It is the oba who is mighty. Though his attendants wear ivory, the oba is decorated in gold.

In the past many emirs and obas were absolute rulers who made decisions for the people in their villages. Today, there are still traditional rulers in West Africa, and many of them are still important. But now most work with the government systems of their nations.

Traditional rulers are most powerful in their own section of a country. An oba may hold a meeting of a council of chiefs in the walled courtyard of his home and discuss present-day concerns. At one such meeting, the council discussed ways to use the country's oil wealth wisely. Local chiefs gave their opinions in turn. One chief summed up what he believed were the most urgent needs: electricity, good drinking water, and medical care for the people of his village.

Traditional rulers are often treated with great respect. Old and new ways blend when the people of the Katsina region of Nigeria gather to honor their emir. Such a gathering is called a *durbar* and includes a horseback ceremony to honor the emir. Wearing flowing robes, riders gallop forward, swords flashing, to within a few feet of the emir. Abruptly, the riders pull up on the reins and the horses stop. The riders raise their right hands in clenched fists, an old salute of loyalty to the emir.

At a modern durbar, an elderly Nigerian man explained that his people have given respect to traditional rulers for many hundreds of years. "You can be a doctor or lawyer in Lagos, but out of respect you come home to ride in the durbar." When the durbar ends, some of the people who attended board jet airplanes to fly home to their regular lives in the city.

THE LEGACY OF COLONIALISM

When West African countries became independent, they found themselves with oddly drawn boundary lines. These borders had been set by the European countries that ruled African colonies. Many modern African countries include ethnic groups that are ancient enemies. Other boundaries have separated people who might have formed one country.

Gambia, for example, might easily join with Senegal, which surrounds it. The two nations remain separate because the former British colony of Gambia is an English-speaking country while the people of Senegal speak French. Senegal was once a French colony.

Newly independent countries have also had to find a way to blend governments influenced by Europe with traditional African systems. Often a national government and traditional rulers have disagreed about how to govern the country.

MODERN NATIONS

After they gained their independence, most West African nations had representative governments, but few of them were truly democratic. Nearly all of them have had either one-party systems or military governments. For a while, only Senegal and Gambia allowed more than one party.

Political parties in West Africa, like those in other regions of Africa often form along ethnic group lines. Some West African leaders argued that because of these ethnic-political ties, many political parties would slow down the task of unifying their country. The leaders claimed that one-party governments were the glue holding together countries with different groups.

The "glue" often came unstuck. Rebellions and overthrown governments have been common. In one nine-year period, the government of Benin was overthrown five

West Africa's rulers have included traditional monarchs (*above*) and modern military leaders, such as Ibrahim Babangida of Nigeria (*below*).

Arts and Recreation

READ TO LEARN

Key Vocabulary

oral tradition   talking drums
griot

Key People

Léopold Senghor
Wole Soyinka

Read Aloud

Mouse may seem small and unimportant, yet she goes all places, and sees all things. Long ago she wove [created] story children from all that she saw. During a quarrel . . . all the story children ran outside. They never returned, and to this day they travel all over the world.

According to this ancient Nigerian legend, Mouse, through the creation of magical beings called "story children," brought stories into the world. As you will read in this lesson, stories and other arts such as music, dance, and sculpture are an important part of daily life in West Africa.

Read for Purpose

1. WHAT YOU KNOW: What are some popular stories and folktales of the United States?
2. WHAT YOU WILL LEARN: In what ways do West Africans make the arts part of their everyday lives?

THE ORAL TRADITION

West African tales are rich with humor, wisdom, and mischief. These tales originated hundreds of years ago when Africa did not have written languages. So the stories were spoken, but not written down. History and literature that is spoken, rather than written, and passed down from person to person is called oral tradition.

Since early African history, stories and poems were not written, storytellers told them aloud to people in the villages. The stories were passed from generation to generation. Much of West Africa's history is preserved in its oral tradition.

The most famous West African storytellers are the griots, who are the "praise singers" and historians of many groups. You will read more about the griot tradition on pages 442–445.

Today there are also many well-known African poets and writers. Léopold Senghor, a poet from Senegal, also served as Senegal's president for many years. Birago Diop, whose poem you can read on page 441, is also from Senegal. In 1986 the Nigerian writer Wole Soyinka (shō ying' ka) became the first African to win a Nobel Prize for literature.

MUSIC AND DANCE

In West Africa skillful dancers and musicians are highly respected. Ceremonial dances mark the main events of human life, such as birth, death, marriage, and even a successful hunt. Dances also mark the seasons of the farming year.

The main musical instrument in West Africa and throughout the African continent is the drum. In some areas there are large orchestras made up only of drums. Talking drums can be made to imitate the sound of human speech. By using these drums, people can send messages over long distances. Some West African languages use different tones to give the words different meanings. A master of the talking drum can produce these tones.

THE MEANING OF MASKS

In many parts of Africa dances and music for important ceremonies are performed by people in masks. These masks are large and elaborately decorated with wood, feathers, leather, and shells.

The masks are much more than decoration. They are believed to have great power. Among traditional West African groups, masks are a way of calling gods and spirits to speak to humans. When a mask is well made, it is believed to take on the spirits of ancestors.

Most West African masks are made mainly of wood, but metal, clay, and ivory are also used. Nigerian artists made bronze masks as early as A.D. 1000.

THE LEGACY OF AFRICAN ART

West Africans make art, music, and dance a part of their daily lives. As you have read, the oral tradition, poetry, music, and dance have helped to preserve the history of West Africa.

Check Your Reading

1. How was history passed down among the early people of West Africa?
2. What is the main musical instrument used in West Africa?

AN AFRICAN POEM

Listen more to things
Than to words that are said.
The water's voice sings
And the flame cries
And the wind that brings
The woods to sighs
Is the breathing of the dead.

Those who are dead have never gone
  away.
They are in the shadows darkening
  around,
They are in the shadows fading
  into day,
The dead are not under the ground.
They are in the trees that quiver,
They are in the woods that weep,
They are in the waters of the rivers,
They are in the waters that sleep.
They are in the crowds, they are in the
  homestead.
The dead are never dead. . . .

Those who are dead have never gone
  away.
They are at the breast of the wife.
They are in the child's cry of dismay
And the firebrand bursting into life.
The dead are not under the ground.
They are in the fire that burns low
They are in the grass with tears to
  shed,
In the rock where whining winds blow
They are in the forest, they are in the
  homestead.
The dead are never dead. —*Birago Diop*

Poems are important in West Africa. This poem expresses the belief that the spirits of the dead are in living things.

3. When are ceremonial dances performed in West Africa?
4. **THINKING SKILL:** Why do you think the instruments and skill for playing the talking drums were developed?

A STORYTELLING TRADITION

by Elza Dinwiddie-Boyd

When you study history in school, you usually read about it in books. Imagine trying to preserve or study history without writing it down. How could it be done? As you read in Lesson 4, in West Africa history was preserved and passed down through time by special storytellers called griots. For hundreds of years the people of West Africa have relied upon griots to keep alive their traditions, beliefs, and history. As you read this lesson think about how the tradition of oral history has helped West Africans to keep records of their past.

AN ORAL HISTORY

As you have read, West Africa includes many countries with people who speak many different languages. All of these people have their own cultures. But one thing they all share is an oral tradition that involves the practice of storytelling. The West African griots are specially trained to remember the history and traditions of their people.

Imagine that you are standing in the main square of a West African town in the 1400s. The square is bustling with activity as people gather to hear the words of a famous storyteller. Suddenly the crowd becomes silent as the griot begins.

I am a griot. It is I, Mamoudou Kouyaté [ma mü' dü kü' yo tā], son of griots, master in the art of [storytelling].

I teach kings the history of their ancestors so that the lives of the ancients might serve them as an example, for the world is old, but the future springs from the past.

My word is pure and free of all untruth; it is the word of my father; it is the word of my father's father. I will give you my father's words just as I received them; royal griots do not know what lying is.

Listen to my word, you who want to know; by my mouth you will learn the history of [our people].

REMEMBERING HISTORY

How does a person become a griot? As you have read, the ideas of clan and family are very important to West Africans. To become a griot a person must be the son or daughter of a griot. Most griots are male, but occasionally a woman can be a griot. Griots begin learning their craft as children. Griot parents teach their children to remember centuries of history. It is not easy. Reciting oral history can take days. Memorizing thousands of stories and historical facts that have added up over many centuries requires fantastic memory skills. It also requires many years of practice.

TALKING BOOKS

In early times griots were cared for generously by the people whose history they preserved. The most experienced griots sat at the courts of kings where they recited the king's family tree as well as important historical events. Although griots can be thought of as talking books, griots also may sing, dance, and play music. They sometimes wear costumes and masks. The words of a griot are supported by the practice known as "call and response." When the griot calls out a well-known verse, the audience sings back a response.

LEARNING HISTORY THROUGH GRIOTS

One twentieth-century writer who paid great attention to the words of griots was Alex Haley. He was an author who traced the history of his family back through time. Haley knew from the storytelling of his grandparents that one of his ancestors, named "Kunta Kinte" (kùn′ tə kin tā′), had been captured in West Africa and brought by ship to North America, where he was enslaved. Haley's search for the story of his ancestors took years of hard work. Along the way, he was able to learn much about his family history. A West African griot helped Haley to locate the village in West Africa where Kunta Kinte was born. After years of research, Haley wrote a book called *Roots*, which is the story of his great-great-great-great-grandfather and of that man's descendants in the United States.

In *Roots*, Haley described the scene in which the West African griot helped him find the village of his ancestors.

> *The old man sat down, facing me, as the people hurriedly gathered behind him. Then he began to recite for me the ancestral history of the Kinte clan, as it had been passed along orally down across centuries from the forefathers' time.*

Haley wrote about the amazement he felt when he heard the name Kunta Kinte spoken from the lips of the griot.

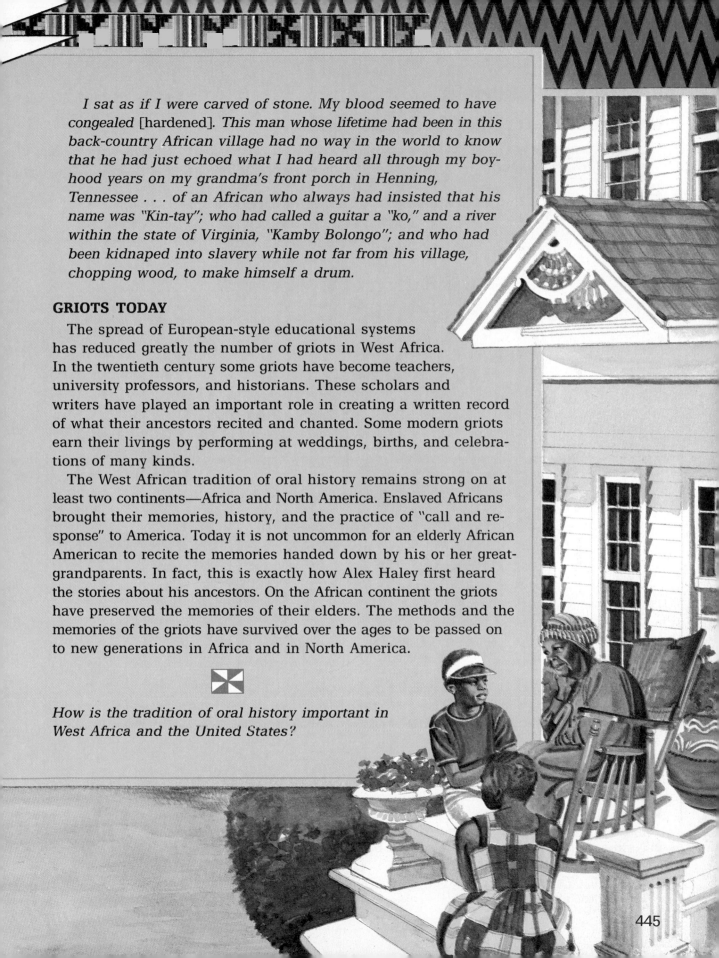

I sat as if I were carved of stone. My blood seemed to have congealed [hardened]. This man whose lifetime had been in this back-country African village had no way in the world to know that he had just echoed what I had heard all through my boyhood years on my grandma's front porch in Henning, Tennessee . . . of an African who always had insisted that his name was "Kin-tay"; who had called a guitar a "ko," and a river within the state of Virginia, "Kamby Bolongo"; and who had been kidnaped into slavery while not far from his village, chopping wood, to make himself a drum.

GRIOTS TODAY

The spread of European-style educational systems has reduced greatly the number of griots in West Africa. In the twentieth century some griots have become teachers, university professors, and historians. These scholars and writers have played an important role in creating a written record of what their ancestors recited and chanted. Some modern griots earn their livings by performing at weddings, births, and celebrations of many kinds.

The West African tradition of oral history remains strong on at least two continents—Africa and North America. Enslaved Africans brought their memories, history, and the practice of "call and response" to America. Today it is not uncommon for an elderly African American to recite the memories handed down by his or her great-grandparents. In fact, this is exactly how Alex Haley first heard the stories about his ancestors. On the African continent the griots have preserved the memories of their elders. The methods and the memories of the griots have survived over the ages to be passed on to new generations in Africa and in North America.

How is the tradition of oral history important in West Africa and the United States?

NATIONS OF WEST AFRICA: CULTURAL GEOGRAPHY

 **PEOPLE**

- Most densely populated part of Sub-Saharan Africa

- Cultural influences: traditional practices and beliefs, Islam, and Christianity

- Many ethnic groups and languages
- Clans provide a deep sense of belonging

ECONOMY

- Expanding desert caused by increasing drought and over-grazing in the Sahel

- Agriculture: both subsistence farming and cash crops

- Cash crops: cacao, peanuts, coffee bananas
- Industrial facilities: mills, food-processing plants, oil wells and refineries in Nigeria

GOVERNMENT

- Nations include several political traditions

- Traditional local governments and fairly new national governments
- National problems include longstanding ethnic enmities and conflicting loyalties
- Some countries are trying to end one-party rule and move toward democracy

ARTS AND RECREATION

- Griots preserve West Africa's rich oral tradition
- Talking drums are means of celebration and of communication
- Decorated masks are used in religious ceremonies to call on gods and spirits
- Present-day writers in many countries are well known throughout the world

IDEAS TO REMEMBER

- The ethnic groups and clans of West Africa have been influenced by traditional African customs, Islam, and European colonialism and Christianity.
- Economies depend mainly on two types of agriculture: subsistence farming and the growing of cash crops.
- National unity has been hard to achieve because of conflicting loyalties and different types of government.
- West Africa's oral tradition, music, dance, and art enrich and preserve community life and history.

REVIEWING VOCABULARY

Each of the following statements contains an underlined vocabulary word or term. Number a sheet of paper from 1 to 5. Beside each number write whether the following statements are true or false. If the statement is true, write true. If it is false, rewrite the sentence using the underlined vocabulary word correctly.

1. An <u>oba</u> is a traditional West African musical instrument that is often used in religious ceremonies.
2. <u>Shifting cultivation</u> is a method of farming in which certain fields are allowed to "rest" between plantings.
3. <u>Griots</u> preserve the stories and history of their people.
4. <u>Desertification</u>, or the expansion of desert, is the result of both natural processes and human activities.
5. <u>Oral tradition</u> involves regular public readings of works of poetry, histories, and other printed materials.

REVIEWING FACTS

1. Why is West Africa called a blend of cultures?
2. Which West African groups are herders? Traders and merchants?
3. What is subsistence farming? Why are cash crops important to the economies of West Africa?
4. How do national boundaries created by colonial powers contribute to conflict and instability in West African countries?
5. In what ways do masks serve religious purposes in West Africa?

◀■▶ WRITING ABOUT MAIN IDEAS

1. **Writing a Paragraph:** You have read that West Africans feel loyal to their families and clans. Write a paragraph describing the importance of clans in West African life.
2. **Writing a Letter:** Imagine you are visiting the savanna in West Africa. Write a letter to a friend describing the farming methods of shifting cultivation and slash-and-burn farming.
3. **Writing an Outline:** Write an outline of the various forms of art, music, and dance that West Africans use to express themselves.
4. **Writing About Perspectives:** Imagine that you are a West African trying to stop the desertification of the Sahel. Write a plan for bringing about change. Discuss at least two changes you would like to make. Why do you think that people might be willing or unwilling to follow your suggestions?

BUILDING SKILLS: DISTINGUISHING FACTS FROM OPINIONS

1. What is a fact? What is an opinion? Write an example of each.
2. What are some steps you could take to identify a fact and an opinion?
3. Why is it important to be able to distinguish between facts and opinions?

CHAPTER 22

EAST AND EQUATORIAL AFRICA

FOCUS

Harambee!

This term, which means "pull together," is the motto of the East African country of Kenya. Since they have dozens of different ethnic groups, the nations of East and Equatorial Africa are always seeking ways to help their peoples live and work together in harmony.

The People

Key Vocabulary

migration
Swahili

Key Places

Zaire

Read Aloud

Less than a hundred years ago, Nairobi, Kenya, was little more than a quiet watering spot for cattle. In fact, in the language of the Masai people who named it, *Nairobi* means "The Place of Cool Waters."

Today "The Place of Cool Waters" is a jam-packed city. On the streets you will still see some Masai people, but you will also find people from many other ethnic groups. Some are African, some are Asian, some are Middle Eastern, and some are European. In this lesson you will read about the many different ethnic groups who have made their home in East and Equatorial Africa.

Read for Purpose

1. **WHAT YOU KNOW:** What causes people to move to new places? What do they hope to find?
2. **WHAT YOU WILL LEARN:** What groups of people settled in East and Equatorial Africa, and how did their languages and cultures develop?

THE NATIONS OF EAST AND EQUATORIAL AFRICA

East and Equatorial Africa is one of the important divisions of Sub-Saharan Africa. In the last chapter you read about West Africa. Now you will learn about the lands near the equator and in the east of Africa.

East and Equatorial Africa is a vast area, larger than the continental United States. It includes ten countries in East Africa: Burundi, Djibouti (ji bü′ tē), Ethiopia, Kenya, Rwanda (rü än′ də), Eritrea, Somalia, Sudan, Tanzania, and Uganda. The region also includes ten countries in Equatorial Africa: Angola, Cameroon, Central African Republic, Chad, Congo, Equatorial Guinea, Gabon, São Tomé and Príncipe (soun tù mä′ and prēn′ si pä), Seychelles (sā shel′), and Zaire.

THE BANTU MIGRATION

Hundreds of ethnic groups share the lands of East and Equatorial Africa. In Sudan alone there are more than 500 groups. Zaire has more than 200 ethnic groups. The ancestors of these people came to East and Equatorial Africa over thousands of years.

About 2,500 years ago a great migration began in and around what is today the country of Cameroon. A migration is a movement of groups of people into new lands. The group of people who migrated

449

EAST AND EQUATORIAL AFRICA: Political

✳ National capital

MAP SKILL: Which important river flows through Sudan?

of East Africa. Among the largest Bantu ethnic groups are the Kikuyu of Kenya and the Baganda of Uganda.

MUSLIM SETTLEMENTS

The Bantu were by no means the only people to migrate into East and Equatorial Africa. Look at the map on this page. Notice how close the country of Djibouti is to the Arabian Peninsula. Also notice that the Nile River runs through the heart of Sudan. It should come as no surprise to learn that the countries of East Africa are strongly influenced by the cultures of the Middle East and North Africa.

In about A.D. 650, Muslim traders began to set up trading posts on the east coast of Africa. Dar es Salaam, now the capital city of Tanzania, was founded by Arabs. Merchants came to this city from as far away as India and Indonesia to buy ivory, gold, and slaves. Some merchants stayed and founded other trade settlements on the coast of Africa.

Muslim traders brought the Arabic language and the religion of Islam to the East African coast. Traders also introduced important food crops, such as yams, coconuts, and bananas. Farmers started planting these crops throughout much of East and Equatorial Africa.

OTHER MIGRATIONS

Many other groups migrated within East and Equatorial Africa. A group known as the Kushites migrated south from Ethiopia into the fertile plateaus of the present-day countries of Uganda, Kenya, and Tanzania. The Kushites were skilled farmers.

Another group of people migrated south from the valley of the Nile River in what is now the country of Sudan. These people knew how to grow grain and keep livestock alive in very dry climates. They were called Nilotes, because they came from

were known as the Bantu. The word *Bantu* means "people." It is used to describe the groups of people that speak the Bantu languages.

The Bantu migration proceeded south and east from Cameroon into Equatorial Africa. In time the Zaire Basin became the center of Bantu kingdoms. Find Zaire on the map on this page. From the Zaire Basin, Bantu people later fanned out into new lands in East and Equatorial Africa.

The Bantu migration was a slow process. In fact, it lasted more than 2,000 years! Over this long period of time the Bantu languages and Bantu customs changed. Today there are about 400 different Bantu languages. Bantu-speaking people form the largest ethnic groups in Equatorial Africa and the southern part

The Kikuyu of Kenya are one of the many Bantu-speaking peoples of East Africa. They are mainly agricultural and have strong ties to their ethnic group and communities.

lands near the Nile River. The Nilotes roamed all over the dry lands of East and Equatorial Africa.

Of course not everyone in East and Equatorial Africa chose to migrate somewhere else. There are people in Ethiopia today who can trace their ancestry back to a thriving civilization of Biblical times. And some Kushite peoples have been in the northern part of Sudan since the days of the Egyptian empire. In the fourth century A.D., Christianity began to spread from Egypt to Ethiopia. By 600 most Ethiopians had become Christians.

In the 1400s and 1500s Europeans came in great numbers to many parts of Africa, including East and Equatorial Africa. Some Europeans came to trade and others came to settle. They brought their languages with them and converted many East and Equatorial Africans outside Ethiopia to Christianity. Eventually European colonies were established in the area and Europeans soon ruled all of East and Equatorial Africa except Ethiopia.

MANY PEOPLE, MANY LANGUAGES

As a result of migrating, trading, and colonialism, ethnic groups tended to blend together. Many present-day East and Equatorial Africans are mixtures of several groups. Their ancestors might be a mix of Bantus, Kushites, and Nilotes. As was true in West Africa, the blend of peoples led to the development of many new languages.

Many people in East and Equatorial Africa are Christians. In Ethiopia, which has some of the oldest churches in the world, people have been practicing Christianity for more than 1,600 years.

One of the most common languages in East and Equatorial Africa is Swahili. It contains Bantu words along with elements of the Arabic and Portuguese languages. Swahili is still changing and acquiring words from other languages. For example, the Swahili word for bicycle, *baisikeli*, comes from English.

Today Swahili is widely spoken in East Africa. In much of the region, English and French are also spoken. Both were introduced during the colonial period.

A BLEND OF ETHNIC GROUPS

In this lesson you have read the story of how East and Equatorial Africa's ethnic groups developed. Many people in this area are descended from Bantus who migrated into the region over the course of more than 2,000 years. Other groups came from the Nile River Valley and the Middle East. Finally Europeans arrived in the 1400s and 1500s, bringing their own languages and customs.

Today East and Equatorial Africa has hundreds of different ethnic groups. They speak many different languages. Swahili is one of the most common, but English and French are also widely used.

 Check Your Reading

1. Who are the Bantu-speaking people?
2. Why were some people in East Africa influenced by the cultures of the Middle East and North Africa?
3. List three groups of people who came to East and Equatorial Africa, and name the routes they took to get there.
4. **THINKING SKILL:** In what ways are the people of East and Equatorial Africa similar to West Africans? In what ways are they different?

452

The Economy

READ TO LEARN

■ Key Vocabulary

famine   barter
malnutrition

■ Read Aloud

Tied to the trunks [of trees] is a scaffolding of poles from which big baskets are hung to catch the fish coming down in the roaring force of water. Wagenya men work like acrobats along the poles. . . .

This is how a visitor described Wagenya fishermen catching fish at a series of waterfalls along the Zaire River. The Wagenya people have been fishing in this way for hundreds of years. To catch fish, they have to cooperate. In East and Equatorial Africa, whether people are subsistence farmers, herders, or fishers, they typically work closely together to get the most out of their land and water.

■ Read for Purpose

1. **WHAT YOU KNOW:** How would you describe the people of East and Equatorial Africa?
2. **WHAT YOU WILL LEARN:** How do the lands in which the East and Equatorial Africans live shape the way they earn their livings?

TRADITIONAL HERDERS

It is hard for non-Africans to understand the importance of cattle to the people of East and Equatorial Africa. Cattle are not just sources of food. They are a status symbol—a sign of a person's wealth and importance. Some of the Luo people, who live along the shores of Lake Victoria, may leave to work in cities—but only long enough to earn money to buy cattle.

Many people in East and Equatorial Africa are nomadic herders of cattle. They move back and forth across the savanna areas of Sudan, Ethiopia, Djibouti, Somalia, and Kenya. When the land becomes too dry in one area, they move across the savanna to another place.

DROUGHT AND FAMINE

Even in the best times the savanna is often harsh and dry. In many parts of the savanna, water and vegetation are scarce. There are many droughts.

Droughts have led to famine and great misery for many people in East and Equatorial Africa. Famine is the widespread and extreme shortage of food. Droughts and famine have caused millions of deaths in Sub-Saharan Africa. Many people here also suffer from malnutrition, a condition that occurs when people have too little food or too little of the right kinds of food. Ethiopia, Somalia, and Sudan have been particularly hard hit by famine and malnutrition in recent times.

The sisal plant is harvested and dried before being twisted into rope or twine.

FARMING PEOPLES

The southern part of East and Equatorial Africa gets more rainfall than the dry savannas to the north. In the southern areas most people work as farmers.

Most people are subsistence farmers, raising only enough to feed themselves. If they do not raise something they need, they **barter**, or swap, for it.

The governments of East and Equatorial Africa have urged people to grow more cash crops, such as coffee, tea, sugarcane, cotton, and sisal. Leaves of the sisal plant are used to make rope and twine.

In many farming villages individuals and families do not own land. In traditional Kikuyu villages of Kenya, for example, village land belongs to the clan. Those yet to be born have the same right to use the land as those presently alive. Therefore, no one may sell a field to an outsider since it belongs to a future Kikuyu.

In many villages farms are owned jointly, either by an extended family or by members of the village. Whole villages may join together to borrow money to buy equipment or seed. Community ownership of land is widespread in East and Equatorial Africa. Families and communities work closely together to get the most out of their land. This is how one Ugandan woman described her life on a farm.

Our old clan forest extends for 28 miles [45 km]. We raise cotton, millet, maize, simsim [a seed for cooking oil], cassava, peanuts, and all our own fruit and garden vegetables. My four sisters and I, my brother, my late mother, my present stepmother, my father, and some of his brothers, all worked in the fields. . . .

INDUSTRIAL DEVELOPMENT

Generally, the countries of East and Equatorial Africa are not industrially well developed. Lack of money to invest in industry and poor transportation are major problems in the area.

There are some exceptions. Lumbering is very important in Congo and in Gabon, which also has very rich iron and manganese deposits. Zaire has developed rich copper mines and is one of the world's largest producers of that metal. On the whole, however, although countries have deposits of valuable resources such as petroleum, gold, diamonds, iron, silver, tin, and aluminum, these resources have yet to be developed.

FACING ECONOMIC PROBLEMS

The standard of living in East and Equatorial Africa tends to be low. The countries of this area have low per capita incomes.

In many parts of East and Equatorial Africa, water for people, animals, and crops is scarce.

The per capita income in Zaire, for example, is about $150 per year. As you have read, per capita income is the average income for each person in a country.

To become more developed economically, the countries of East and Equatorial Africa need to take several costly steps all at once. All the countries need better transportation systems and more dams to produce hydroelectric power. They also need more educated workers. Most people agree on these needs. The problem is finding the money to pay for it all. Most countries of East and Equatorial Africa are deeply in debt.

TRADITION AND DEVELOPMENT

At least three out of four people of East and Equatorial Africa make their living by herding, farming, or fishing. In this lesson you have read about the way of life of some of the people in these traditional kinds of occupations.

You have also read that the economies of the countries of East and Equatorial Africa are still developing. Mineral resources are slowly being tapped. Drought, lack of money for investment, and poor transportation systems have slowed the economic development of this area.

Check Your Reading

1. Where is herding most common in East and Equatorial Africa?
2. What kind of land ownership is common in this area?
3. What are some of the problems slowing the economic development of East and Equatorial Africa?
4. **THINKING SKILL:** What are some alternatives by which East and Equatorial Africans could develop their economies over the next 20 years? Which do you think they will choose? Why?

455

Land Use in East and Equatorial Africa

In the last lesson you read about the importance of farming to the economy of East and Equatorial Africa. In recent years much of the farmland in this area has been destroyed—by drought, overgrazing of cattle, or as a result of the growth of cities. So pressure to open new land for farming and raising cattle is increasing. In their search for land, farmers have established settlements on land reserved for wildlife. In Kenya, where the wildlife is regarded as a unique heritage, the settlers' need for land has created a problem for the government.

The government of Kenya is determined to preserve its wildlife. Huge reserves are set aside for buffalo, lions, jackals, zebras, giraffes, elephants, and other wildlife. The animals, which draw hundreds of thousands of tourists to game parks, are a valuable natural resource for Kenya. With the human population of Kenya expanding rapidly, the situation seems to be getting worse.

POINT

Protect the Wildlife Reserves

Kenya is a widely recognized leader in protecting endangered African wildlife. Since 1977 all big-game hunting has been banned in the country. Kenya's 22,500 square miles of national parks and game preserves are an example to other African countries trying to protect and promote their wildlife.

In 1989 the director of Kenya's Department of Wildlife Conservation and Management, Perez M. Olindo, spoke about the situation in his country. He said that the people of Kenya must be aware that the future of the wildlife in their country depends on cooperating to reduce the threat to animals. He said the government was trying to increase public support for conservation through an educational program. Olindo said:

> The future of wildlife in Kenya is quite bright. The wildlife will be protected in their restricted areas. But the increasing [human] population is definitely a threat. We are trying to give people an economic justification for wildlife occupying up to 15 percent of the country at a time when the [human] population is increasing at about 4 percent [a year] and the land-mass of Kenya is remaining the same.

- What is the Kenyan government's position on protecting wildlife?

COUNTERPOINT

Share the Wildlife Reserves

The competition between people and animals for land is increasing in Kenya. Less than 20 percent of Kenya's land is available for agriculture, complicating the nation's ability to absorb more people. The country's population has one of the highest growth rates in the world.

Some people in Kenya believe that the need for land is more important than the need to save wildlife. Farmers are increasingly moving into areas reserved for animals.

Some members of Kenya's parliament urge the transfer of some of the land from the reserves to farmers and cattle herders. Ncharo Kubo supported the suggestion to provide land in certain game reserves to the farmers.

> Farmers have lived with wild animals and could continue to do so if given land in the parks for farming. In Taita-Taveta wild animals running away from poachers [hunters] were encroaching on the farmers.

Kubo blamed the Kenyan Ministry of Tourism and Wildlife for not extending the benefits of the game parks and reserves to the farmers.

- What reasons are given for opening some game preserves to farmers?

UNDERSTANDING THE POINT/COUNTERPOINT

1. Which side do you think makes the stronger argument? Explain.
2. What opinions might some other groups have about the issue of protecting or opening the wildlife reserves?
3. Can you think of a way in which the two sides could compromise on this issue? Explain.

The Government

READ TO LEARN

Key Vocabulary

civil war

Key People

Jomo Kenyatta

Key Places

Kenya

Read Aloud

In the nineteenth century a Kikuyu medicine man in Kenya had a terrifying vision. He warned his people that pale strangers carrying firesticks would soon come to their land, and that they would be followed by a fire-belching iron snake with as many legs as a centipede.

Not long afterward, white European settlers with guns appeared in Kenya. Later they built a railroad from Mombasa on the Indian Ocean to Lake Victoria. It was the first of many "iron snakes" in Kenya. The "pale strangers" had taken over.

Read for Purpose

1. **WHAT YOU KNOW:** When did most of the countries of West Africa gain their independence from European nations?
2. **WHAT YOU WILL LEARN:** Why have many countries in East and Equatorial Africa had one-party governments?

LESSONS OF COLONIALISM

In 1938 Jomo Kenyatta, a young Kikuyu, told the above story in a book called *Facing Mount Kenya*. When Kenyatta wrote this book, Kenya was a British colony. After Kenya won its independence in 1963, Kenyatta became its first president.

The legacy of European colonialism is strong in East and Equatorial Africa. Every country of Equatorial Africa was once a colony of a European nation. In East Africa only Ethiopia remained an independent nation. Belgium, Germany, Italy, Great Britain, France, and Portugal all held colonies. The chart on page 459 gives the dates that each of these countries gained its independence.

As you read in Lesson 1, the European colonial powers introduced their languages and their customs to East and Equatorial Africa while they governed the area. Europeans also took the best farmlands and mineral resources. For example, the English passed a law that no African could own land in the fertile lands of Kenya and Tanzania known as the White Highlands. Suddenly, only white people could farm what had been the Kikuyus' most fertile fields.

INDEPENDENT NATIONS

Today the countries of East and Equatorial Africa are independent of European rule. Look again at the chart. During what period did the countries of East and Equatorial Africa win their independence?

Leaders like Jomo Kenyatta knew that independence was only the first step in creating stable, lasting governments. The young nations of the region are still trying to pull together and help themselves.

Many of the new countries have been torn apart by civil wars and uprisings. A civil war is a war between people of the same country. Somalia, Ethiopia, Angola, Zaire, Burundi, and Sudan have all had major civil wars and unrest. In 1989 the government of Angola and the rebels agreed to end a 14-year civil war. However, the war started up again in 1993.

ONE-PARTY RULE

After they gained independence, the countries of East and Equatorial Africa faced great challenges. Most needed new schools and transportation systems. Often the economies of the countries could not support these badly needed projects.

Many citizens thought that their new governments could work instant miracles. When miracles did not occur, leaders were forced from office in coups. Coups have been very common in the region.

Most East and Equatorial African leaders believe that stable government is more important than guaranteeing democratic rights to their people. The governments of this area have had one-party systems or dictatorships. In most elections only one candidate's name is listed on the ballot. Power has usually changed only when a leader died or was overthrown in a coup. However changes are coming to this region. In 1990 Zaire ended a 20-year ban on multiple political parties. Other countries in the region are also moving to end one-party rule.

Many people in East and Equatorial Africa believe that things will change only as

INDEPENDENCE IN EAST AND EQUATORIAL AFRICA

Country	Date of Independence
Angola	1975
Burundi	1962
Cameroon	1961
Central African Republic	1960
Chad	1960
Congo	1960
Djibouti	1977
Equatorial Guinea	1968
Eritrea	1993
Ethiopia	Never a colony
Gabon	1960
Kenya	1963
Rwanda	1962
São Tomé and Príncipe	1975
Seychelles	1976
Somalia	1960
Sudan	1956
Tanzania	1961
Uganda	1962
Zaire	1960

CHART SKILL: Jomo Kenyatta (top) was a leader of the independence movement in Kenya. When did Kenya win its independence?

459

Civil wars have been common in East and Equatorial Africa since the independence movements started. These soldiers were training in Angola, where a long-lasting civil war upset much of the country.

young people who are not familiar with colonialism become adults. They think that this new generation of independent citizens will be better able to govern themselves in the future.

UNSTABLE GOVERNMENTS

You have read that all of the countries of East and Equatorial Africa except Ethiopia were once ruled by colonial powers. Without recent traditions and experience of self-rule, many governments of this area have been unstable. Some governments are trying to change one-party systems or dictatorships. But civil wars and coups still take place.

 Check Your Reading

1. Who was Jomo Kenyatta?
2. Why have many governments been overthrown in many of the countries of East and Equatorial Africa?
3. How would you describe a typical government in East and Equatorial Africa today?
4. **THINKING SKILL:** Tell what conclusions you can draw from the following statement: "Many East and Equatorial African leaders believe that stable government is more important than guaranteeing democratic rights to their people."

Arts and Recreation

READ TO LEARN

Key Vocabulary

proverb

Read Aloud

The stars are hearing, the earth is hearing. The people are hearing—all is well, good, sweet. Then laugh, laugh, laugh.

When the Pokot people of East Africa say good-bye, each person repeats this old blessing. Spoken language is one of the most important arts in East and Equatorial Africa.

Read for Purpose

1. WHAT YOU KNOW: What is an example of a saying or proverb that is popular in the United States?
2. WHAT YOU WILL LEARN: How are poems, stories, and other forms of spoken language important in East and Equatorial Africa?

PROVERBS

Most of the groups in East and Equatorial Africa have a rich store of proverbs. A proverb is a short, popular saying that illustrates a truth. The Luyia people, who live by the Great Lakes of East Africa, warn: "Don't laugh at a distant boat being tossed by the waves. Your relative may be in it." This proverb not only warns people against laughing at the misfortune of others, but also shows the strong loyalty to family that the Luyia people feel.

The following are Swahili proverbs from Zanzibar. What do you think is the meaning of each, and what are some of the values expressed?

Ability is wealth.

He who does not listen to an elder's advice comes to grief.

Blood is thicker than water.

A bad brother is far better than no brother.

To stumble is not to fall down but to go forward.

Do not forget what it is to be a sailor because you became a captain.

When elephants fight, the reeds get hurt.

STORYTELLING

Ethnic groups in East and Equatorial Africa did not have systems of writing until outsiders brought them. As you have read, in groups without writing systems, storytellers serve as important teachers, historians, and entertainers.

Storytelling sessions are among the favorite recreational activities of East and Equatorial African people. Stories are often combined with music and dance. Listeners know most of the stories and join in by clapping and singing.

461

Cloth for sale in the East African country of Kenya portrays a gathering of people. Above the cloth are handmade necklaces.

As people gather to hear tales, they gain a strong sense of belonging to a particular group. Stories also help children to understand their place in the world and allow them to feel proud of their past. Through tales and songs, storytellers educate young people in the values and traditions of their ethnic groups.

POETRY

Throughout East and Equatorial Africa, poetry is a major way of expressing feelings, dreams, hopes, and fears. Poetry occupies a special place in everyday life. A Swahili newspaper in Tanzania features a "Poems to the Editor" section next to "Letters to the Editor." The poems are about anything from personal problems to the cost of food.

Among Bantu-speaking people, poets receive a special place of honor. Like the West African griots you read about in Chapter 21, Bantu poets memorize and recite poems that reflect the wisdom of their people. A skilled Bantu poet can talk for several days about ancient Bantu kingdoms. Bantu poets in Rwanda recite epic poems that tell of the great deeds of their ancestors.

TRADITIONAL ARTS

People in East and Equatorial Africa learn the traditions of their ethnic group through proverbs, stories, and poetry. As you have read, young people in traditional villages learn by watching and listening.

 Check Your Reading

1. What is a proverb?
2. About which subjects do Bantu poets often recite poems?
3. What special role do proverbs, stories, and poems play in the lives of the people of East and Equatorial Africa?
4. **THINKING SKILL:** Write three statements of fact from this lesson. What can you conclude about East and Equatorial Africa based on these facts?

462

Making a Graph from a Chart

Key Vocabulary
line graph

In this book information is presented in many different forms. You have already seen that one of these forms is a chart. The chart on this page shows the populations of two cities in East and Equatorial Africa from 1960 to 1990.

Drawing a Line Graph

The same information presented in a chart might also be presented in a different way on a line graph. In this lesson you will read about making a line graph to show the information that appears in the chart on this page.

First, copy a grid like the one below the chart. Next, write a title for the graph. Label the vertical axis "Population (in millions)." Number the vertical axis beginning with 0. Then number each line up to 3 million. Next, label the horizontal axis, "Year." Use each line on the horizontal axis to represent a decade, starting at 1960 and ending at 1990.

To make a population graph of Kinshasa, follow the vertical line labeled 1960 until it reaches halfway between 0 and 1 million. Mark this place with a dot to show that in 1960 the population of Kinshasa was approximately 500,000 (half a million) people. Next, follow the vertical line for 1970 until you reach 1.25 million. Place a dot one quarter of the way between 1 and 2 million. Continue to mark dots at the correct number for all years up to 1990. When you have marked all the dots for Kinshasa, connect the dots with straight lines.

POPULATION PATTERN OF TWO AFRICAN CITIES

	Kinshasa, Zaire	Nairobi, Kenya
1960	500,000	265,000
1970	1,250,000	500,000
1980	2,200,000	800,000
1990	3,000,000	1,700,000

Use a different color to plot the graph for Nairobi. When you have finished plotting the graph for both cities, you will see the direction of population growth at a glance. The line graph also shows the differences in population growth between the two cities.

Reviewing the Skill

1. What does a line graph show?
2. Why must the vertical and horizontal axes of a line graph be labeled?
3. Which city, Kinshasa or Nairobi, had the larger population in 1960?
4. Why is it important to understand how to make a graph from a chart?

EAST AND EQUATORIAL AFRICA: CULTURAL GEOGRAPHY

 **PEOPLE**

- People: hundreds of ethnic groups, many ethnic mixtures
- Bantu–speaking people are the largest ethnic groups

- Swahili—a common language of the area—combines Bantu, Arabic, and Portuguese
- Migrations: Bantu, Muslim traders, Kushites, European settlers

ECONOMY

- Cattle: source of food, a sign of a person's wealth and importance
- Main economic activities: herding, subsistence farming, fishing
- Export products: coffee, tea, sugar, cotton, sisal, copper, lumber, iron, manganese

- Economic needs: better transportation; more hydroelectric power, educated workers, industry

GOVERNMENT

- All except Ethiopia were European colonies until about 30 years ago

- Civil wars and uprisings have been common
- Many are trying to end one-party systems or dictatorships

 **ARTS AND RECREATION**

- Traditional arts include proverbs, storytelling, and poetry
- Literature reflects the wisdom of the people
- Through songs and tales, storytellers teach values and traditions

IDEAS TO REMEMBER

- Several large migrations have caused East and Equatorial Africa to have a variety of peoples, cultures, and languages.
- Herding, farming, and fishing are the major important ways of earning a living.
- Since their independence in the 1960s, most of the area's governments have suffered from civil wars and coups, but many are trying to change.
- Proverbs, stories, and poetry both entertain and teach important values, customs, and history.

REVIEWING VOCABULARY

barter   migration
famine   proverb
malnutrition

Number a sheet of paper from 1 to 5. Beside each number write the word or term from the above list that best completes the sentence.

1. _____ is the movement of large groups of people into new lands.
2. Popular throughout Africa, _____ are short sayings that illustrate important truths.
3. Instead of purchasing something, many Africans _____, or exchange, one good for another.
4. _____ is a condition that occurs when people have too little food or not enough of the right kinds of food.
5. Drought and overgrazing have resulted in _____, or severe food shortages, in large parts of Africa.

REVIEWING FACTS

1. Which ancient African tribe had the greatest impact on the culture of East and Equatorial Africa? How did they achieve this impact?
2. Name three contributions of Muslim traders to East and Equatorial Africa.
3. How does the Swahili language reflect the blend of cultures in East and Equatorial Africa?
4. Why are many herders in the savanna region nomadic?
5. Why do governments in East and Equatorial Africa encourage farmers to raise such crops as cotton and coffee?
6. How does land ownership in East and Equatorial Africa differ from land ownership in the United States?
7. Name four major reasons that explain why most countries in East and Equatorial Africa remain poor despite abundant resources.

8. Name two ways in which European nations affected the countries of East and Equatorial Africa.
9. Why do the governments of most countries in East and Equatorial Africa practice one-party rule?
10. How does the custom of storytelling strengthen the community in East and Equatorial Africa?

◀📝▶ WRITING ABOUT MAIN IDEAS

1. **Writing an Editorial:** Write an editorial titled: "More Democracy, Not Less, Is Needed to Solve the Problems of East and Equatorial Africa."
2. **Writing a Proverb:** The groups in East and Equatorial Africa have a rich store of proverbs. Write your own proverb that illustrates some basic truth about life.
3. **Writing About Perspectives:** Pretend you live in a country in East and Equatorial Africa and want to start a small business. What kind of business could you start that would use both the region's resources and have customers? Write a paragraph explaining your plan.

BUILDING SKILLS: MAKING A GRAPH FROM A CHART

1. How is a graph different from a chart?
2. Look at the chart on page 463. Which city, Kinshasa or Nairobi, had the larger population in 1980?
3. Which labels would you use on a graph showing the same information as the chart on page 463?
4. Why is it helpful to understand how to make a graph from a chart?

465

CHAPTER 23

NATIONS OF SOUTHERN AFRICA

▼ FOCUS

[One must] set goals, to have faith, . . . to be a fighter, to be resilient, to have patience, to have hope. . . .

The South African athlete and writer, Mark Mathabane, tells us what he believes South Africans need to meet their many challenges. As you read, you will discover whether or not you agree with him.

The People

READ TO LEARN

Key Vocabulary
apartheid

Key Places
South Africa   Kalahari Desert

Read Aloud

Yes, this is a good land. Everyone who has come here, from the first blacks to the earliest whites, has found it so. Can we work together to keep it so? That is our test.

These are the words of a store owner in the city of Harare, Zimbabwe. The "test" he speaks of—having whites and blacks live together in peace—is faced by all of the countries of Southern Africa.

Read for Purpose

1. **WHAT YOU KNOW:** Think of some news articles you have read or some television shows you have seen about South Africa. What were these articles or programs about?
2. **WHAT YOU WILL LEARN:** What changes are taking place in the way in which different ethnic groups of Southern Africa live today?

A RICH LAND

Southern Africa is rich in mineral resources, such as gold, copper, diamonds, and coal. The climate of the area is warm and inviting, especially on the southern tip. Much of the region is at high altitudes, so there are few disease-spreading insects. These factors have combined to draw many groups of people to the region.

Blacks greatly outnumber whites in Southern Africa. Yet the country of South Africa, governed by white people, is so rich and powerful that it dominates most of its neighbors. These include Botswana, Lesotho, Madagascar and other islands, Malawi, Mozambique, Namibia, Swaziland, Zimbabwe, and Zambia.

Many ethnic groups have fought for and are still fighting for control of these lands. Let's learn about the major ethnic groups.

BUSHMEN AND BANTUS

A people known as the Bushmen have been living in Southern Africa longer than any other peoples. Hundreds of years ago Bushmen had lived throughout the continent of Africa. Bushmen cave paintings have been found as far north as Ethiopia.

Until recently most Bushmen lived in the Kalahari (kä lə här´ ē) Desert of Botswana and Namibia. Find this area on the map on page 468. Most people would starve to death in this harsh land. Bushmen are skilled at tracking animals and finding food and water. Today many Bushmen live on farms and in towns.

Between 500 and 800 years ago, Bantu peoples migrated to the lands of the Bushmen. This movement was part of the great Bantu migration you read about in Chapter 22. The Bantu drove the Bushmen from

MAP SKILL: There are many Bantu ethnic groups living in Southern Africa. Here, a group of people called the Hereros gathers at a rally in Namibia. They wear traditional clothing. Where is Namibia on the map of Southern Africa below?

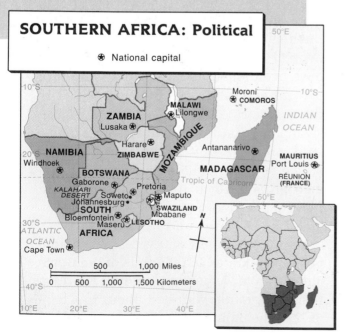

SOUTHERN AFRICA: Political

⊛ National capital

the savanna areas of Southern Africa into the Kalahari Desert.

Today the majority of people in Southern Africa are of Bantu descent. Some of them still live in a traditional way. Extended families are grouped into clans, and these clans live in small villages.

Millions of younger Africans, however, have given up the old ways of living. About one third of Southern Africa's people live in cities. These cities include Johannesburg, Pretoria, and Cape Town in South Africa, and Harare in Zimbabwe. Most of these city dwellers still have parents or grandparents who live in traditional African villages.

EUROPEAN GROUPS

As you have read in this unit, the European influence is strong throughout

468

Sub-Saharan Africa. Southern Africa is no exception.

Dutch settlers arrived on the southern tip of Africa in 1652. They were sent to set up a supply station for European merchant ships traveling between India and Indonesia, and Western Europe. Look at the world map in the Atlas on pages 620-621. Why do you think the southern tip of Africa would be an important location for ships sailing to and from Europe?

The settlers set up a new colony called Cape Colony. More settlers came to the new colony not only from the Netherlands, but from Germany and France as well. As a result of this mixture of groups, a new language was created that contains Dutch, German, and French words. This language is called *Afrikaans*. It also includes many words from Bantu languages.

People of Dutch, German, and French ancestry who speak Afrikaans are called Afrikaners, or Boers. They are the largest group of whites in South Africa.

In 1795 the British took over Cape Colony. Thousands of Boers, not wanting to live under English rule, left the colony. They traveled north over the Drakensberg Mountains and the Orange River and formed two republics, the Transvaal and the Orange Free State. Both are now part of South Africa.

The areas that the Boers claimed for the two republics had large Bantu populations. Years of war between the Bantus and the Boers followed. Later, the Boers fought the British for control of these areas, which were rich in minerals. In more recent times the descendants of these two European groups made up less than 20 percent of South Africa's population, yet they ruled a country that was more than 70 percent black. This situation has caused bitter conflicts.

Black South Africans have had to live in areas with few modern conveniences (*left*). Protests (*right*) eventually led to the end of many apartheid laws.

Blacks and whites live and work together in Harare, Zimbabwe.

RACIAL SEPARATION

From 1948 to 1991, South Africa's laws separated people by race and color. The country recognized four main racial groups: whites, blacks, "coloured," and Asian. People labeled coloured have both black and white, and sometimes Asian, ancestors. Most of them live in Cape Province and speak Afrikaans. Most Asians are descendants of immigrants from India.

The term for South Africa's system of separating racial groups is apartheid (ə pär' tīd), from an Afrikaans word meaning "separateness" or "apartness." Under apartheid laws each of the four racial groups in South Africa had to live in its own area and attend segregated schools.

These rules left most blacks in South Africa poor. Often families were separated for long periods of time while some family members worked in cities. Many black South Africans live without water, electricity, or good housing. Most of them had no hope of improving their lives as long as apartheid rules continued.

In 1991, the South African government announced plans to change some of its apartheid laws. Some schools and other public places became integrated. The total end of apartheid was announced in 1993. That same year a multiethnic council began overseeing the government of South Africa.

Neighboring Zimbabwe also has a majority of blacks and a minority of whites. The black majority has governed Zimbabwe since 1980. Zimbabwe's leaders have worked hard to create a country in which black people and white people can live and work together in peace. As one way to promote understanding among different groups, the Zimbabwe government makes students study other people's languages. Most classes in Zimbabwe's schools are taught in English. However, every student also has to study the languages of the two main Bantu groups of Zimbabwe—Shona and Ndebele.

A MIX OF PEOPLES

In this lesson you have read about some of the different ethnic groups of Southern Africa. A majority of the people of Southern Africa are Bantu-speaking peoples. A small population of Bushmen live in or near the Kalahari Desert. Until recently South Africa was the only country in Sub-Saharan Africa that was ruled by a minority racial group. In the following lessons you will read more about Southern Africa.

Check Your Reading

1. Where do most of the Bushmen live?
2. Who are the Afrikaners?
3. Describe the system of apartheid.
4. **THINKING SKILL:** What effects has apartheid had on black people in South Africa?

The Economy

READ TO LEARN .

Key Vocabulary

township
veld

Key Places

Johannesburg   Zambia
Soweto   Harare

Read Aloud

When Botswana gained its independence in 1966, it was one of the least developed countries on earth. There were few paved roads and not one public high school. Today Botswana is an economic success story. How did it happen? It started with three new diamond mines. To open the mines, Botswana needed help. South African companies gave money to build the mines, in return for part of the profits. South African companies also own part of Botswana's new nickel and copper mines.

All of the economies of the countries of Southern Africa are influenced by South Africa. South Africa has a strong, industrialized economy. Most of the rest of the area, as you will read, is still developing.

Read for Purpose

1. **WHAT YOU KNOW:** What valuable resources are found in Southern Africa?
2. **WHAT YOU WILL LEARN:** How does the economy of South Africa contrast with the economies of most countries of Southern Africa?

SOUTH AFRICA'S DIVERSIFIED ECONOMY

Why is South Africa's economy relatively strong? One reason is that it is diversified. A diversified economy, as you have read, is one that produces a wide range of goods and services. South Africa is a land of farms, mines, and advanced industries.

South Africa has vast mineral resources. It is the world's largest supplier of gold and one of the main sources of diamonds. Look at the maps on page 472. Which other lands have gold and diamonds?

South Africa also has chrome, which is scarce elsewhere. Coal, iron, platinum, and uranium are part of its mineral wealth.

Both blacks and whites work in South Africa's mines, but they are not treated equally. White miners often earn three to five times more than black miners earn.

South Africa also has highly developed industries, particularly in the processing of metals. The Witwatersrand area around Johannesburg is South Africa's industrial center. Less than 100 years old, Johannesburg looks like industrial cities in the United States, such as Cleveland or Pittsburgh. Johannesburg is South Africa's largest city. Soweto has even more residents than Johannesburg, but it is called a township, not a city. In South Africa a township is a racially segregated urban

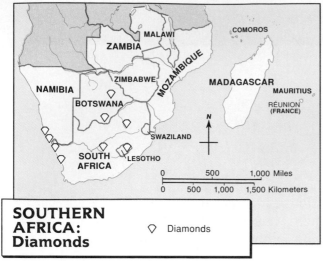

SOUTHERN AFRICA: Diamonds

◇ Diamonds

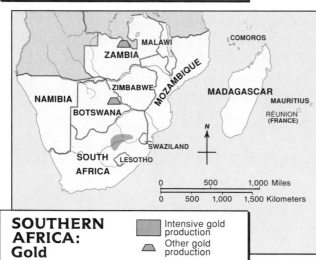

SOUTHERN AFRICA: Gold

▨ Intensive gold production
△ Other gold production

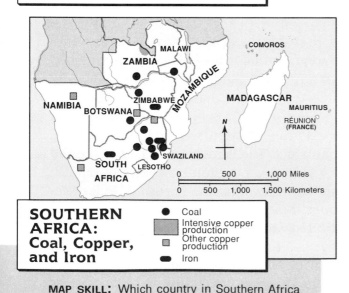

SOUTHERN AFRICA: Coal, Copper, and Iron

● Coal
▨ Intensive copper production
◻ Other copper production
⬤ Iron

MAP SKILL: Which country in Southern Africa has intensive gold production?

area located just outside a city. About 30 percent of South Africa's blacks live in townships. Every day, thousands of blacks from Soweto travel to work in Johannesburg.

South Africa is also an important agricultural nation, even though much of the country's land is not good for growing crops. A vast, dry, treeless plateau called the **veld** covers much of South Africa. Most crops need irrigation in order to grow on the veld.

Despite poor land and lack of water, South African farmers raise a wide variety of products, ranging from sheep for wool to grapes and tea. In fact, South Africa raises enough food to export.

POVERTY

South Africa's economy is developed, but many of its people do not live well. Apartheid separated groups of people, and whites had an unfair advantage. By law, 87 percent of South Africa's land was set aside for white people even though whites made up less than 20 percent of the population. Blacks were allowed to work in cities set aside for whites, but blacks were not permitted to live in them. These land laws were ended in 1990.

Since most jobs in South Africa have been in areas reserved for whites, millions of black people have had to work far from their homes. Others have had to live in temporary quarters and go home only once a week, or even less often.

Now that laws have changed, some blacks are moving into areas that were once reserved for whites. Yet more than three million South Africans continue to live in squatters' towns. A squatter is someone who lives without permission on land he or she does not own. Many squatters' towns in South Africa have no running water, sewers, or electricity.

IN A GIANT'S SHADOW

South Africa is the economic giant of Southern Africa. Most of South Africa's neighbors have concentrated on agriculture or mining and have bought many manufactured goods from South Africa. Selling raw materials and buying more expensive finished goods has left neighboring countries with weak economies.

Zambia has one fourth of the world's copper, and copper and copper products make up nine tenths of Zambia's exports. But copper is less valuable than it once was, and Zambia's reliance on one export product has caused its economy to suffer.

Development of agriculture has been uneven in Zambia. The country has abundant arable farmland, but much of it is still used for subsistence farming. Zambia does not have enough money to develop many goods and services that it needs.

In other parts of Southern Africa, years of war have wrecked normal living and working patterns. In Mozambique, for example, a long war combined with a drought have caused widespread famine, malnutrition, and death.

In Zimbabwe almost 80 percent of the people farm for a living. Zimbabweans raise crops and livestock on farms. Women do most of the farming, partly because many of the men are away working in cities or in mines. Racial segregation has been abolished in Zimbabwe. In its capital, Harare, black and white Zimbabweans live and work together.

As you read on page 471, Botswana's mines are being developed with money from South Africa.

AN ECONOMIC CONTRAST

As you have read, South Africa's economy contrasts with the economies of other countries in Southern Africa. South Africa has a highly developed industrial econ-

These women are among the almost 80 percent of Zimbabweans who farm for a living.

omy in which blacks and whites do not share equally in the wealth. The other countries in the area are still developing economically. With time and effort, South Africa may narrow the huge economic gap between its people. In the other countries of Southern Africa, growth is likely to come as industries expand, farming is modernized, and peace is established.

 Check Your Reading

1. What are some of South Africa's most valuable minerals?
2. How did apartheid affect the economy of South Africa?
3. How quickly has industry developed in different countries of Southern Africa?
4. THINKING SKILL: Compare and contrast the economies of South Africa and Zambia.

The Government

Read Aloud

In the villages and towns of Botswana, citizens have special places called "freedom squares." All over the country, people meet in these squares to debate issues about government. Politicians in the capital city of Gaborone make a point of showing up at the squares to talk and listen. "We haven't learned democracy from America or England," says the country's Vice President, Peter Mmusi. "It is inborn."

Read for Purpose

1. **WHAT YOU KNOW:** What is apartheid?
2. **WHAT YOU WILL LEARN:** What are the major forms of government in Southern Africa?

FORMS OF GOVERNMENT

Many governments in Southern Africa are based on Great Britain's system of government. As you read in Chapter 9, Great Britain has a parliamentary form of government. In a parliamentary system the leader of the political party that wins the most votes in an election becomes prime minister. The prime minister heads the government. Botswana, Mauritius, Namibia, South Africa, Zambia, and Zimbabwe are all republics with parliamentary systems of government.

As in the rest of Sub-Saharan Africa, most of the countries of Southern Africa have won their independence from European control only recently. They are still trying to find systems of government that work well for their people.

Independence did not always mean democracy. Soon after independence, most countries of Southern Africa had one-party systems. Often such parties were headed by a leader whom the people regarded as the "father of the nation," the person who had led the independence movement.

A "SECOND REVOLUTION"

In the early 1990s many countries began a change some people call a "second revolution." This revolution was a move away from one-party government to a multiparty system.

For example, in Zambia, Kenneth Kaunda had led the government since 1964, when the country became independent. In 1991 he was voted out of office when voters were given a choice. As one Zambian woman said, "It's a good idea to have many people, then you let people choose the leader they want."

Many countries in the region are moving toward greater democracy. Botswana, Madagascar, Mauritius, and Namibia have multiparty systems, and Mozambique is moving in this direction.

But some countries have not become more democratic. Lesotho, which began as a constitutional monarchy, has been ruled by military officers since the army seized power there in 1986. Malawi is another exception. Its leader, Kamuzu Banda, has ruled since independence and has declared himself "president for life."

A SOUTHERN AFRICAN KINGDOM

Swaziland is a monarchy ruled by King Mswati (em swä' tē) III, who in 1986 at the age of 18 became the world's youngest monarch. His rule combines traditional customs that Bantu chiefs have followed for centuries with modern government practices.

The king rules with a parliament, and he chooses some of its members. He also settles questions about property ownership and other disputes. These are things that Bantu chiefs have done for centuries.

YEARS OF APARTHEID

You have read that South Africa has several political parties and a parliamentary form of government modeled on Great Britain's system. Yet blacks, who are the majority of South Africans, have not been allowed to vote.

When South Africa became independent from Great Britain in 1961, the country's white minority controlled the government. White people had a privileged position that they did not want to lose. In 1948 they enacted apartheid laws that kept people who were not considered white from voting and from serving in any important government jobs. The apartheid laws also kept blacks, coloureds, and Asians in the poorest jobs, schools, and neighborhoods.

Events in other countries have affected South Africa. Most countries of Sub-Saharan Africa became independent in the 1960s. Black people in the United States began to win a long struggle for equal rights including the right to vote in the parts of the country where voting had been denied them. South Africa's government found it increasingly difficult to find support for the idea that rule by a small minority was acceptable.

Other nations criticized South Africa's policies. So in 1976, the South African government created the first of ten black "homelands" within its borders. Each homeland had its own flag, capital, and official language. But each homeland had very little land and few resources for the needs of the people. The homelands were

South African police sometimes reacted violently to anti-apartheid protests.

said to be independent and ruled by governments made up largely of traditional chiefs.

Most blacks opposed this plan, saying it did not offer true self-rule. They continued to demand full and equal rights in an undivided South Africa. Other nations refused to recognize the homelands as independent countries. Yet South Africa forced more than 3 million people to move into the already crowded homelands.

South Africa's blacks continued to fight for years against apartheid. In response,

Nelson Mandela, a leader of the African National Congress, greets crowds in triumph after his release from imprisonment as a political prisoner.

the South African government declared a state of emergency in 1986. The state of emergency permitted the government to jail more than 20,000 people without any trial. The government also controlled the press.

To protest apartheid many other countries, including the United States, passed sanctions against South Africa. Sanctions are actions taken against a country by other countries to try to bring about change. For example, other countries would not buy or sell goods to South Africa. They would not allow South Africa's athletes to compete in most world sports events because many South African teams were racially segregated.

CHANGE IN SOUTH AFRICA

Sanctions against South Africa did help to change the system of apartheid. Even more important, South Africa's blacks made great efforts to change the system. Their struggle has been supported by many coloureds and Asians as well as a small but significant number of whites.

Desmond Tutu, a black archbishop in South Africa's Anglican Church, has been one of the most important leaders in the fight against apartheid. Tutu urged South Africa's blacks to resist unfair laws without violence. Their methods included boycotts, demonstrations, and hunger strikes. In 1984 Archbishop Tutu won the Nobel Peace Prize for his efforts to end apartheid without violence.

Other groups in South Africa believed that violence was necessary to end apartheid. The African National Congress (ANC), took part in armed conflict. Nelson Mandela, a leader of the ANC, was jailed for 27 years after being convicted of treason for opposing apartheid laws. Another black group, Inkatha, opposed both the white government leaders and the ANC.

Asians and coloureds gained a small voice in the government in 1983, but the 70 percent of the South Africans who were black still had no vote.

By 1990, under the pressure of black resistance and foreign sanctions, South Africa's government began to give in. The state of emergency was declared over, and many apartheid laws were repealed. People no longer had to list their race on government papers. Black people are now allowed to own land in areas that were formerly reserved for whites.

A major change for the future was announced in 1993. Late in that year black and white leaders reached agreement on a new constitution to grant equal rights to blacks. Black citizens finally gained the right to vote for their country's leaders.

CHANGING GOVERNMENTS

You have read that the countries of Southern Africa have different kinds of political systems and that many systems are changing. A "second revolution" is bringing greater democracy to many countries that had one-party governments. The country of South Africa has begun to grant equal rights to the black people who make up 70 percent of its population.

Check Your Reading

1. What was once the most common form of government in Southern Africa?
2. What changes are taking place in the governments of some countries in the region?
3. What has been happening to South Africa's system of apartheid?
4. **THINKING SKILL:** Classify all the countries mentioned in this lesson into three or more groups according to their systems of government. What generalization could you make about the governments of Southern Africa?

FIGHTING FOR RIGHTS

Albertina Sisulu, a black nurse from Soweto, South Africa, protested against the restrictions that were imposed by the white minority government on the black people of South Africa. Albertina was jailed several times for her nonviolent resistance to apartheid.

From 1964 to 1983 Albertina lived under a government ban. A banned person was not allowed to leave the area where he or she lived without police permission. Banned people could not talk to reporters, leave their homes after dark, or attend any gathering of more than two people. For 19 years Albertina could leave her house only to go to work. She raised six children alone because her husband, Walter, was imprisoned for his anti-apartheid activities.

Today the African National Congress is legal, and Albertina Sisulu has been elected one of its leaders. Because of her own experiences, she feels that she can speak for all those people who still suffer from the consequences of apartheid. "It is proper for people to fight for their rights," she says. "I'm doing this for the good of the nation."

Recognizing Bias: Review

Suppose you read a movie review in your school newspaper. The review is so positive that you go to see the movie the following weekend. However, you do not like the film at all. Later you discover that the writer is a fan of the movie's director.

An account that is one-sided often shows bias. It may be exaggerated and filled with emotionally charged words. If you can recognize bias, you will not easily accept a biased account as being true and accurate.

HELPING YOURSELF

One way to recognize bias is to:

1. Recall the definition of *bias*.

2. Recall clues to bias such as exaggerations, emotionally charged words, and a slanted presentation of an issue.

3. Examine the information presented, looking for clues.

4. Ask yourself: Do the clues I have found give a one-sided view for or against something?

5. State the bias, if any.

Applying the Skill

Read the following accounts of a past event in South Africa. Then answer the questions that follow.

A. Police in Cape Town used tear gas to break up a student demonstration near a mainly white university yesterday. More than 2,000 students carrying posters were lined up along a highway to demonstrate their support of a nationwide anti-apartheid campaign.

B. Brutal police action crushed a student anti-apartheid demonstration today. Students who were peacefully parading with posters near the university were attacked without warning. Police savagely fired tear gas and rubber bullets into the crowd of young people. Hundreds of girls and boys ran weeping from the scene.

1. Which account shows bias?
2. What are some clues that alerted you to the bias?
3. Describe the bias in your own words.

Reviewing the Skill

1. What does the word *bias* mean?
2. What are some clues that help you to recognize bias?
3. Why is it important for you to be alert to bias in visual, spoken, or written accounts?

Arts and Recreation

READ TO LEARN

■ Key Vocabulary

mbira

■ Read Aloud

A traditional house of the Ndebele people of South Africa has a thatched roof and walls painted with bright geometric shapes. Bold reds, greens, yellows, and blues seem to burst out of their black outlines.

As in the rest of Sub-Saharan Africa, the arts are woven into everyday life in Southern Africa. In this lesson, you will read about some of these arts and about some of the popular sports of Southern Africa.

■ Read for Purpose

1. **WHAT YOU KNOW:** Have you ever heard music from Africa? How does it compare with other kinds of music you have heard?
2. **WHAT YOU WILL LEARN:** What are some of the popular arts and sports of Southern Africa?

TOWNSHIP MUSIC

Music can be very competitive in South Africa. In black townships, choral groups hold contests with one another. Singers make beautiful melodies and also dance and make people laugh. Groups are judged for their wit as well as for their sound. The song on page 480 is traditional Zulu music.

One of the best known choral groups is Ladysmith Black Mambazo. Through their own recordings and their work with Paul Simon, an American singer and songwriter, they introduced the sounds of South Africa to people in the United States and other parts of the world.

Black South Africans call the kind of songs sung by Ladysmith Black Mambazo "township music." It was born in the all-black townships at the edges of industrial cities. People in these townships created the music by mixing traditional African music with Christian hymns and popular American and British songs they heard on the radio. This combination proved to be very popular not only in Africa, but also in the United States and Great Britain.

TRADITIONAL MUSIC

Some Southern African groups play and sing traditional music. One group, Amampondo, uses only instruments invented in Africa. One of the main instruments used by Amampondo is the mbira (em bîr ə), a finger piano. It is made of metal or bamboo strips tied to a wood bowl. Like some other African instruments, the mbira can "talk," meaning that it can be used to imitate the human voice. Traditionally the mbira is not just for entertainment. The Shona people of Zimbabwe, for example, play mbiras to call the spirits during healing ceremonies.

The Trees Bend

Zulu Folk Song

I - mith' i - go - ba Ka - hle, I - thi, i - thi,
Ee - meet ee - goh - bah, goh - shleh, Ee - thee, ee - thee,

Ku - nya - kaz' a - ma - hla - mvu, Ka - nje, Ka - nje.
Goon - yah - gahz ah - ma - shlam - voo, Gohn - jeh, gohn - jeh.

Zi - phu - mu - la Ka - nja - ni na, I - zi - nyou' e - si -
Zee - pooh - mooh - lah gahn - ja - nee nah, Ee - zeen - yohn eh - seeth -

dle - ke - ni? I mith' i - go - ba Ka - hle, I - thi,
leh - geh - nee?

i - thi, Ku - nya - kaz' a - ma - hla - mvu, Ka - nje, ka - nje.

Translation:
The trees bend nicely; they say,
The leaves are stirring in the breeze. *(Repeat)*

480

South Africa's Ladysmith Black Mombazo has performed with American singer Paul Simon.

SPORTS

Music, of course, is not the only popular recreational activity in Southern Africa. People like to play and watch many different kinds of sports.

Many of the popular sports came from Great Britain. The English brought soccer, rugby (the English form of football), cricket, golf, and tennis to Southern Africa. In just about any country of the area, young people play soccer in empty lots.

Sports are very important to people in South Africa. For many years apartheid laws kept blacks and whites from playing on the same teams in South Africa. To protest this policy, many international sports competitions, such as the Olympics, imposed a sanction against South Africa refusing to let its athletes participate. In 1991, after South Africa promised to end segregation in sports, the International Olympic Committee removed its 21-year ban on letting South Africans compete in the Olympics.

MUSIC AND SPORTS

The popular recreational activities of Southern Africa come from many different sources. As you have read, township music is a combination of African, British, and American forms. Other kinds of popular music are completely African in origin. A traditional African folk song of the Zulu people is found on page 480. Finally, some sports, such as soccer and tennis, come directly from Europe.

Check Your Reading

1. What is township music?
2. How have sanctions helped to change segregation in sports?
3. What are some of the popular arts and sports of Southern Africa?
4. **THINKING SKILL:** Based on this lesson, what conclusions can you draw about music in Southern Africa?

NATIONS OF SOUTHERN AFRICA: CULTURAL GEOGRAPHY

 **PEOPLE**

- South Africa— dominant country of the area

- Bushmen were earliest settlers, followed by Bantus, the largest group

- European settlers are most powerful group and include Afrikaners, or Boers, and British

- Apartheid kept racial groups separate

ECONOMY

- Diversified economy exists in South Africa, which has mineral resources

- White workers earned more than black workers

- Agriculture: irrigated farming in South Africa; subsistence farming; communal farming

- Many workers migrate to South Africa

- Botswana has a rapid growth rate

GOVERNMENT

- Main type: parliamentary

- Monarchy: Swaziland

- Many countries are changing from one-party to multiparty systems

- South Africa has ended its apartheid laws

ARTS AND RECREATION

- Diverse types of music: township music, traditional

- Traditional instruments—such as the mbira—used for entertainment and in religious ceremonies

- Popular sports: soccer, rugby, cricket

- Segregation in team sports has ended in South Africa

IDEAS TO REMEMBER

- Ethnic groups in Southern Africa include Bushmen, Bantu (the largest group), and the powerful white minority.
- South Africa's economy affects the economies of its neighbors.
- Systems of government include many parliamentary governments, democracies, long-time heads of government, and one kingdom. South Africa's government has been forced to move away from the system of apartheid.
- Music and sports include traditional and European influences.

REVIEWING VOCABULARY

apartheid   township
mbira   veld
sanctions

Number a sheet of paper from 1 to 5. Beside each number write the word from the above list that best matches the definition.

1. A dry plateau that covers much of South Africa
2. Afrikaans word that means "separateness" and refers to South Africa's system of racial separation
3. Actions taken to pressure a country to change its policies
4. A musical instrument that can imitate the human voice
5. An area in South Africa in which black people are forced to live

REVIEWING FACTS

1. How did the Bushmen come to live in the Kalahari Desert?
2. How did the Boers respond when the British seized control of Cape Colony in 1795?
3. Into which four racial groups did the South African government classify its people?
4. Name three reasons that explain why South Africa has the most powerful economy in the region.
5. What economic benefits do South African whites gain from the system of apartheid?
6. Name three economic effects that apartheid had on blacks in South Africa.
7. How does Zambia's reliance on one product damage its economy?
8. Which South African country is ruled by a king?
9. Why were the black homelands in South Africa not recognized by the international community?
10. Why is the mbira popular in Southern Africa?

◀◀✏▶ WRITING ABOUT MAIN IDEAS

1. **Writing a List:** Write a list of five or more reasons that explain why living in South Africa is very difficult for black people.
2. **Writing a Letter to the Editor:** Write a letter to the editor explaining your position for or against sanctions against South Africa.
3. **Writing a Journal Entry:** Imagine you are visiting South Africa. Write a journal entry describing the expressions of art and music you observe.
4. **Writing About Perspectives:** Imagine that you live in a country of Southern Africa that has had one ruler since independence. Now for the first time, voters have elected a new ruler. Write an essay telling what you hope will happen and what you worry might happen when the change in government takes place.

BUILDING SKILLS: RECOGNIZING BIAS

1. Define what is meant by *bias*. Give an example.
2. List several steps you might take to recognize bias.
3. Why is it important to recognize bias?

SUB-SAHARAN AFRICA: PHYSICAL GEOGRAPHY

LANDFORMS

- Highest mountains: Mount Kilimanjaro, Mount Kenya
- Most of Sub-Saharan Africa is a great plateau
- Special features: Zaire Basin, Great Rift Valley, waterfalls
- Rivers: Nile, Zaire, Niger, Zambezi are among the most important
- Vegetation zones: Sahel, savanna, rain forest

CLIMATE

- Mostly tropical, with high temperatures all year
- Rainfall is scarce in about three fourths of the continent

- Trade winds cause rainy and dry seasons

NATURAL RESOURCES

- Tropical crops: cacao, coffee, rubber, palm oil, timber
- Wildlife preserves attract tourists
- Rich in minerals: copper, iron, gold, uranium, manganese, diamonds
- Many waterfalls that can be harnessed to provide hydroelectric power

SUB-SAHARAN AFRICA: CULTURAL GEOGRAPHY

PEOPLE

- Three cultural influences: traditional beliefs, Islam, and European colonialism and Christianity
- Hundreds of ethnic groups and many languages: Bantus are one of the largest groups
- South Africa is ending apartheid system that kept racial groups separate

ECONOMY

- Expanding desert caused by drought and overgrazing
- Agriculture: mainly shifting cultivation, slash-and-burn farming
- Economic needs: better transportation; more hydroelectric power, better-educated workers, more industry
- Industrial facilities are still being developed: mills, food-processing plants, oil wells and refineries in Nigeria
- South Africa has a diversified economy

GOVERNMENT

- Many nations have parliamentary systems
- Some nations have one-party rule; others are becoming more democratic
- Almost all countries were European colonies until about 30 years ago
- Under apartheid system, blacks forced to live in Bantu "homelands" lacked rights

ARTS AND RECREATION

- Traditional arts include proverbs, poetry; rich oral tradition
- Music: traditional instruments; modern forms of music like township music are also popular
- Traditional religious ceremonies: decorated masks are used to call on gods

REVIEWING VOCABULARY

apartheid   migration
civil war   oral tradition
desertification rift valleys
drought   sanctions
harmattan   savanna

Number a sheet of paper from 1 to 10. Beside each number write the word or term from the above list that best completes the sentence.

1. In Africa drought and overgrazing have contributed to the expansion of dry land in a process known as _____.
2. _____ explains why Bantu culture spread from Cameroon throughout East and Equatorial Africa.
3. _____ separated the races and kept the white minority in power.
4. A major farming and grazing region, the _____ is a broad grassland covering much of Sub-Saharan Africa.
5. The _____ is a wind that blows from the Sahara over western Africa.
6. Beginning as cracks in the earth, _____ are steep-sided lowlands that extend through much of eastern Africa.
7. Common in Sub-Saharan Africa, _____ is armed conflict between two or more groups within the same country.
8. _____ are actions taken by one country to force change within another country.
9. In West Africa history and literature were preserved through _____ instead of through written language.
10. A _____ is a long period without adequate rain.

WRITING ABOUT THE UNIT

1. **Writing a Paragraph:** Write a paragraph explaining why European languages are often used as the official languages of Sub-Saharan Africa.
2. **Writing Questions for an Interview:** Write a list of questions for an interview with the leader of a country in Sub-Saharan Africa. Focus your questions on political issues and democracy versus one-party rule.
3. **Writing About Perspectives:** You have read how Tanzanians write "poems to the editor" that address issues of concern. Imagine that you live in Sub-Saharan Africa. Write a poem to the editor dealing with an issue that would be important to you.

ACTIVITIES

1. **Working Together to Tell a Story:** Choose a well-known folktale or legend to share with your classmates. Assume the role of a griot and ask other members of the class to be your audience. Tell the story and encourage the rest of the class to respond in the call-and-response technique.
2. **Gathering Information About an Issue in Sub-Saharan Africa:** Choose an important political, economic, or social issue affecting Sub-Saharan Africa. Gather articles about the issue from newspapers and magazines. Then present the information in an oral report to the rest of the class.

LINKING PAST, PRESENT, AND FUTURE

Ancient hatreds, the legacy of colonialism, and decades of misrule have made Sub-Saharan Africa a poor and strife-torn region. What changes would you make to establish political stability and prosperity for Africans?

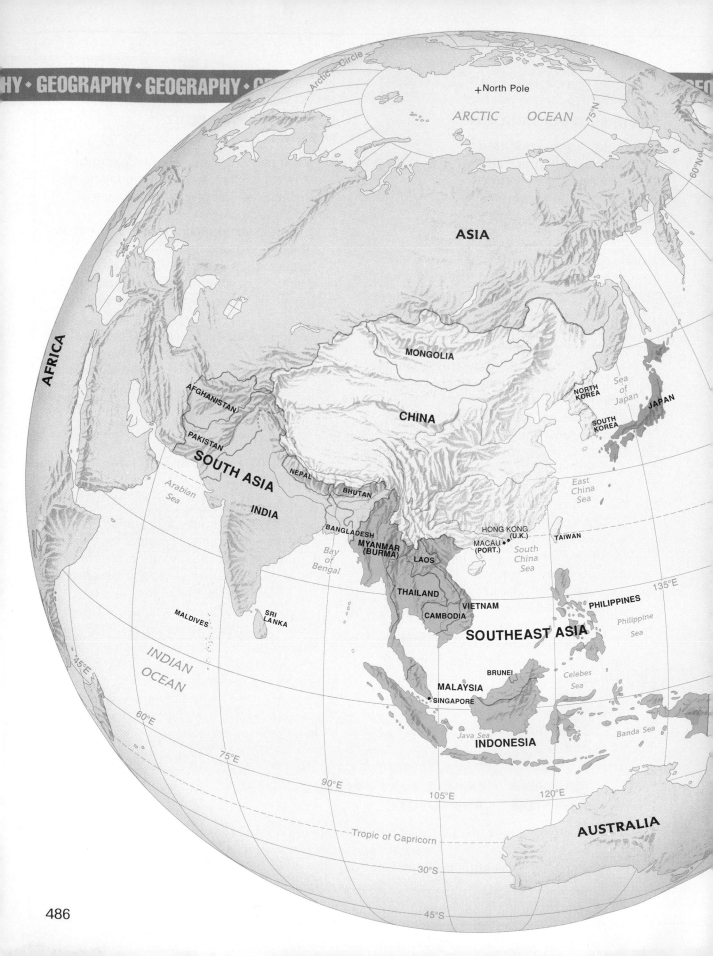

Arctic Circle

+North Pole

ARCTIC   OCEAN

75°N

60°N

ASIA

AFRICA

MONGOLIA

NORTH
KOREA

Sea
of
Japan

JAPAN

AFGHANISTAN

CHINA

SOUTH
KOREA

PAKISTAN

SOUTH ASIA

NEPAL

BHUTAN

East
China
Sea

Arabian
Sea

INDIA

BANGLADESH

HONG KONG
(U.K.)

TAIWAN

MYANMAR
(BURMA)

MACAU
(PORT.)

Bay
of
Bengal

LAOS

South
China
Sea

135°E

THAILAND

MALDIVES

SRI
LANKA

VIETNAM

CAMBODIA

PHILIPPINES

Philippine
Sea

SOUTHEAST ASIA

INDIAN
OCEAN

45°E

BRUNEI

Celebes
Sea

MALAYSIA

SINGAPORE

60°E

Java Sea

Banda Sea

75°E

INDONESIA

90°E

105°E

120°E

AUSTRALIA

Tropic of Capricorn

30°S

45°S

UNIT 7

SOUTHERN AND EASTERN ASIA

WHERE WE ARE

As you have read, the world around us is made up of many different nations, cultures, religions, and ideas. In this unit you will read about Southern and Eastern Asia, a region that is home to more than 3 billion people.

As the map shows, Southern and Eastern Asia stretches from India, Afghanistan, and Pakistan across China to Japan and to North and South Korea. As you read about this region, think about its people and the different economic, political, and social systems they have developed. Then you will understand why Southern and Eastern Asia is one of the most important regions of the world today.

487

SOUTHERN AND EASTERN ASIA

AFGHANISTAN
Capital ★
Kabul

Major languages: Pushtu and Dari Persian
Population: 16.6 million
Area: 251,773 sq mi; 647,500 sq km
Leading exports: natural gas, fruit, and carpets

INDIA
Capital ★
New Delhi

Major languages: Hindi and English
Population: 859.2 million
Area: 1,269,342 sq mi; 3,287,590 sq km
Leading export: machinery

BANGLADESH
Capital ★
Dhaka

Major language: Bengali
Population: 116.6 million
Area: 55,599 sq mi; 144,000 sq km
Leading exports: textiles and jute

INDONESIA
Capital ★
Jakarta

Major languages: Bahasa Indonesia and Javanese
Population: 181.4 million
Area: 741,098 sq mi; 1,919,440 sq km
Leading exports: oil and natural gas

BHUTAN
Capital ★
Thimphu

Major language: Dzonkha
Population: 0.7 million
Area: 18,147 sq mi; 47,000 sq km
Leading export: cement

JAPAN
Capital ★
Tokyo

Major language: Japanese
Population: 123.8 million
Area: 143,749 sq mi; 372,310 sq km
Leading export: machinery

BRUNEI
Capital ★
Bandar Seri Begawan

Major language: Malay
Population: 0.3 million
Area: 2,228 sq mi; 5,770 sq km
Leading export: oil

KOREA, NORTH
Capital ★
P'yongyang

Major language: Korean
Population: 21.8 million
Area: 46,541 sq mi; 120,540 sq km
Leading export: minerals

CAMBODIA
Capital ★
Phnom Penh

Major language: Khmer
Population: 7.1 million
Area: 69,900 sq mi; 181,040 sq km
Leading export: rubber

KOREA, SOUTH
Capital ★
Seoul

Major language: Korean
Population: 43.2 million
Area: 38,023 sq mi; 98,480 sq km
Leading exports: machinery and manufactured goods

CHINA
Capital ★
Beijing (Peking)

Major language: Chinese
Population: 1,151.3 million
Area: 3,705,396 sq mi; 9,596,960 sq km
Leading export: manufactured goods

LAOS
Capital ★
Vientiane

Major languages: Lao and French
Population: 4.1 million
Area: 91,429 sq mi; 236,800 sq km
Leading exports: food and timber

MALAYSIA
Capital ★
Kuala Lumpur

Major languages: Bahasa Malaysia,
  English, and Chinese
Population: 18.3 million
Area: 127,317 sq mi; 329,750 sq km
Leading exports: machinery and
  rubber

MALDIVES
Capital ★
Malé

Major language: Dlvehl
Population: 0.2 million
Area: 116 sq mi; 300 sq km
Leading exports: fish and clothing

MONGOLIA
Capital ★
Ulaanbaatar

Major language: Khalkha Mongolian
Population: 2.2 million
Area: 604,248 sq mi; 1,565,000 sq km
Leading exports: fuels, minerals,
  and machinery

MYANMAR
(Burma)
Capital ★
Yangon
(Rangoon)

Major language: Burmese
Population: 42.1 million
Area: 261,217 sq mi; 676,550 sq km
Leading exports: rice and timber

NEPAL
Capital ★
Kathmandu

Major language: Nepali
Population: 19.6 million
Area: 54,363 sq mi; 140,800 sq km
Leading exports: food products and
  manufactured goods

PAKISTAN
Capital ★
Islamabad

Major languages: Urdu, Punjabi,
  and English
Population: 117.5 million
Area: 310,402 sq mi; 803,940 sq km
Leading exports: cotton products,
  clothing, and rice

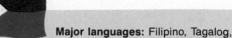

PHILIPPINES
Capital ★
Manila

Major languages: Filipino, Tagalog,
  and English
Population: 62.3 million
Area: 115,830 sq mi; 300,000 sq km
Leading exports: food, copra, and
  minerals

SINGAPORE
Capital ★
Singapore

Major languages: Chinese, English,
  Malay, and Tamil
Population: 2.8 million
Area: 224 sq mi; 580 sq km
Leading exports: machinery and
  petroleum products

SRI LANKA
(Ceylon)
Capital ★
Colombo

Major languages: Sinhala, Tamil,
  and English
Population: 17.4 million
Area: 25,332 sq mi; 65,610 sq km
Leading export: tea

TAIWAN
(Formosa)
Capital ★
Taipei

Major language: Chinese
Population: 20.5 million
Area: 13,892 sq mi; 35,980 sq km
Leading exports: machinery, plastics,
  and textiles

THAILAND
Capital ★
Bangkok

Major language: Thai
Population: 58.8 million
Area: 198,456 sq mi; 514,000 sq km
Leading exports: food and machinery

VIETNAM
Capital ★
Hanoi

Major language: Vietnamese
Population: 67.6 million
Area: 127,243 sq mi; 329,560 sq km
Leading exports: coal and agricultural
  products

489

CHAPTER 24

PHYSICAL GEOGRAPHY OF SOUTHERN AND EASTERN ASIA

FOCUS

I begin to work when the sun rises;
I rest when the sun sets.
I dig a well for my drinking water;
I plow the field to provide my food.

Although it is 3,000 years old, this Chinese folk song describes the lives of many farmers in Southern and Eastern Asia today. As you will read, the region's rivers and fertile river valleys are among its important natural resources.

Landforms

READ TO LEARN

Key Vocabulary

subcontinent
loess
alluvial soil

Key Places

Gobi
Mount Everest
Himalayas
North China Plain
Huang River

Chang River
Mekong River
Ganges River
Indus River
Brahmaputra River

Read Aloud

A hundred mountains
echoed in the jeweled eyes
of a dragonfly. . . .

This poem was written a little over 200 years ago by the famous Japanese poet, Issa. With a few words it describes mountains reflected again and again in the shiny eyes of a dragonfly. In this chapter you will read about the many high mountains of Southern and Eastern Asia, as well as its other landforms.

Read for Purpose

1. **WHAT YOU KNOW:** Which parts of Asia have you already learned about in this book?
2. **WHAT YOU WILL LEARN:** How do the high mountains of Asia affect the rivers and lowlands of South, East, and Southeast Asia?

LAND OF CONTRASTS

The continent of Asia is vast. Larger than North America and South America combined, Asia makes up almost one third of the earth's land. However, in this unit you will read about only part of Asia—the region of Southern and Eastern Asia. About half of Asia's countries are located in this region.

Asia is the only continent that has a subcontinent, a large landmass that is smaller than a continent. Turn to the map on page 492 and look at the southern coast of Asia. You will find a large triangular peninsula there. This peninsula is called the subcontinent of India. The subcontinent includes the countries of India, Pakistan, Bangladesh, Bhutan, and Nepal.

Besides the subcontinent, Southern and Eastern Asia has many distinctive features, several of which contrast greatly with one another. One of the best ways to see these features would be to fly over the land. For example, if you were flying north over India, you would see hundreds of miles of ice-capped mountains at India's northern border. After the mountains end, you would fly over high plateaus and never spot a house or any other sign of human life. The Gobi and Takla Makan deserts, which are located here, are among the driest places on earth. The writer Ross Terrill calls the Gobi, "utterly barren, an unrelieved ginger [colored] waste, baking in the sun."

If you were then to turn and fly east toward the coast, you would see that the land changes greatly. Instead of an empty landscape, you would see densely populated lowland river valleys and thousands of crowded islands. For instance, the island of Taiwan has over 1,500 people per square mile (over 600 per sq km). The view of the islands is very dramatic. You might spot a bright light. This light could mark an active volcano forming a new mountain on an island.

THOUSANDS OF ISLANDS

Many of the islands off Asia's southeastern shore were formed by volcanoes. Some of these islands are very large. If you look at the map below, you can see that several Asian nations are also made up of archipelagoes, or groups of islands. The largest island groups are Indonesia, which has more than 13,500 islands, and the Philippines, which has more than 7,000 islands. Wide seas separate these densely populated archipelagoes.

THE WORLD'S HIGHEST MOUNTAINS

Although Southern and Eastern Asia has many distinctive features, its high mountain ranges are the major physical feature. These huge barriers separate countries and areas within the region.

MAP SKILL: In and near which Asian countries are the Himalayas located?

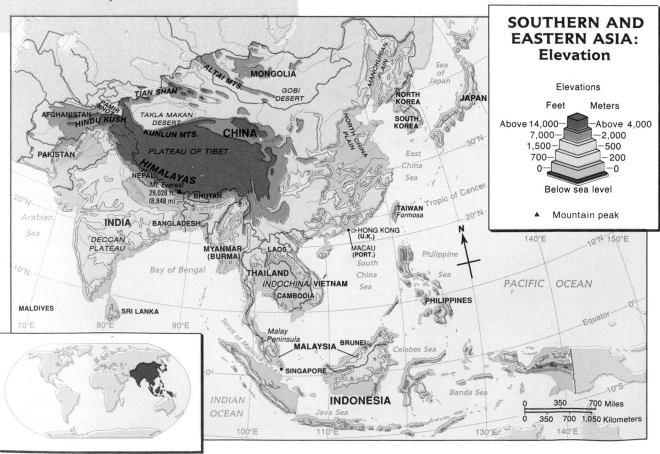

492

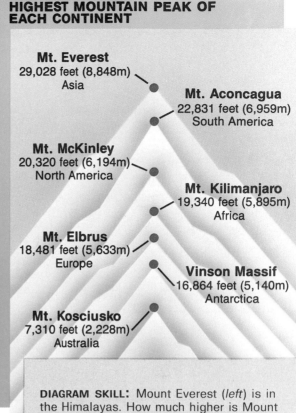

HIGHEST MOUNTAIN PEAK OF EACH CONTINENT

Mt. Everest
29,028 feet (8,848m)
Asia

Mt. Aconcagua
22,831 feet (6,959m)
South America

Mt. McKinley
20,320 feet (6,194m)
North America

Mt. Kilimanjaro
19,340 feet (5,895m)
Africa

Mt. Elbrus
18,481 feet (5,633m)
Europe

Vinson Massif
16,864 feet (5,140m)
Antarctica

Mt. Kosciusko
7,310 feet (2,228m)
Australia

DIAGRAM SKILL: Mount Everest (*left*) is in the Himalayas. How much higher is Mount Everest than South America's highest peak?

These high mountains also affect climate and the fertility of the soil throughout Southern and Eastern Asia.

Nowhere on earth are there higher mountains than those in Asia, as you can see on the diagram on this page. These mountains have long been a challenge to climbers. It was not until 1953 that a New Zealand climber and his Nepalese guide chipped their way up cliffs of ice more than 5 miles (9 km) above sea level in Nepal. Edmund Hillary and Tenzing Norgay were the first to reach the peak of Mount Everest, the world's highest mountain at 29,028 feet (8,848 m). Hillary described the breathtaking view from the top of the mountain.

> [W]herever we looked, icy peaks and somber gorges lay beneath us like a relief map. Perhaps the view was most spectacular to the east, for here the giants Makalu and Kanchenjunga dominated the horizon and gave some idea of the vast scale of the Himalayas. The . . . Himalayas stretched hundreds of miles in a tangled mass of peaks, glaciers, and valleys.

Around Mount Everest are a dozen other peaks in the Himalayas that are almost as high. The Himalayas and nearby ranges form the heart of Asia. Long ago, natural forces deep within the earth thrust this land high above the rest of the continent. People call this high area "The Roof of the World." At the center of the "roof" are the Pamirs (pə mîrz′), a mountain range where several other mountain ranges meet to form a knot called the "Pamir Knot." Now look at the elevation map on page 492. Notice that China, Afghanistan, Pakistan, and Tajikistan meet in this area.

From the Pamirs other mountains reach outward like crooked spokes in a lopsided wheel. For example, the Altai and Tian Shan mountains stretch across northwest China. South of these mountains, the Kunlun Mountains split China into northern and southern China.

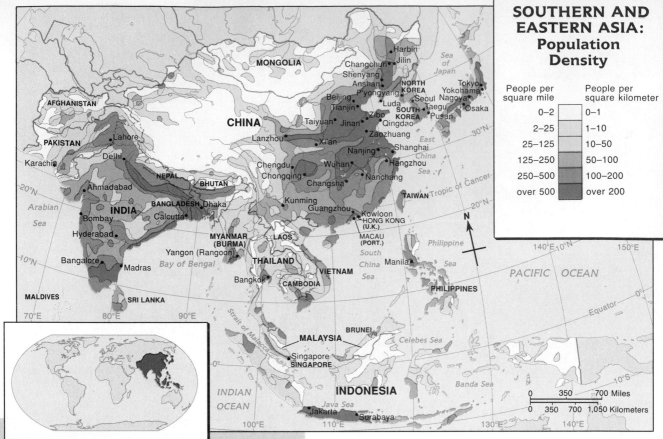

SOUTHERN AND EASTERN ASIA: Population Density

People per square mile	People per square kilometer
0–2	0–1
2–25	1–10
25–125	10–50
125–250	50–100
250–500	100–200
over 500	over 200

MAP SKILL: India has more than 800 million people. Which parts of India have the lowest population densities?

EFFECT OF THE MOUNTAINS

Mountains divide and isolate many parts of Southern and Eastern Asia. Look at the map on page 492 again. How many countries in this part of Asia have mountains on their borders?

Mountains make travel or farming difficult in many countries of the region. Also, where the land is too high, people cannot live in comfort. The climate in these areas is too cold and dry.

Asia's mountains affect the land in one other way. In the high plateaus of Tibet, Mongolia, and western China, dry winds howl across a bleak, arid landscape. As the winds cross Mongolia, they lift bits of dry soil into the air and carry them to the

North China Plain. There the soil drifts to the ground, creating a yellowish topsoil known as **loess** (les). This soil is very fertile and is refertilized each year.

The mountains also block rain-bearing winds blowing from the south. Therefore, north of the mountains and the Plateau of Tibet, Asia has several deserts. The Gobi and the Takla Makan, and other arid areas are located there.

RIVER VALLEYS

As the land slopes away from the highlands at the heart of Asia, it lowers to the sea in hills and plateaus before reaching the plains. Some of these lower areas are among the most fertile and crowded places on earth. They are the valleys of the great rivers that carry soil and water down from "The Roof of the World." Look at the population-density map above. Which areas have the highest population density?

Each spring melting mountain ice renews the major rivers of the region. Two of China's rivers, the Huang River, (or Yellow River) and the Chang River (Yangtze) start in the mountains east of the Plateau of Tibet. As the rivers flow downhill toward the sea, they cut through the plains and often flood them.

Thousands of years ago China's first civilization began along the Huang River in the North China Plain. People learned to farm the rich alluvial (ə lü′ vē əl) soil, or soil deposited by the river as it flows. The Huang River is nicknamed "China's Sorrow" because it has often raged out of control, flooding crops and homes. Today dams along the river help to prevent floods and also provide power.

The Chang is China's longest river and the third longest in the world. The word *chang* means "long" in Chinese.

A third great river of the region also starts in the Plateau of Tibet. This river, the Mekong River, flows south through China into the area called Southeast Asia. You will read more about Southeast Asia in Chapter 28. The river deposits alluvial soil over a large valley, then winds south through tropical rain forests to enter the sea near Ho Chi Minh City, Vietnam.

Other great rivers also flow out of the Plateau of Tibet. Look at the Indian subcontinent on the map on page 492. In the north you will see three long rivers—the Ganges (gan′ jēz) River, Indus River, and Brahmaputra River. They flow across plateaus and plains and through fertile deltas to empty into the sea. These three rivers often flood, leaving behind some of the fertile soil they carry.

THE PATTERN OF THE LAND

As you can see, Southern and Eastern Asia has a pattern of high mountains and great river valleys. This pattern explains

Strangely shaped rocks and lush green fields line the Li River in southern China.

why some parts of the region are crowded and others have few or no people. The mountains also have isolated some of the region's peoples from one another. As a result, their cultures have developed with few outside influences. You will read about some of these cultures in the next few chapters.

 Check Your Reading

1. What is "The Roof of the World"? Which parts of Southern and Eastern Asia does it separate?
2. Why is the Huang River called "China's Sorrow"?
3. Where do many of the region's major rivers originate?
4. **THINKING SKILL:** List two questions you could ask to help you learn more about the major landforms of Asia.

Understanding Great-Circle Routes

Key Vocabulary

great circle
great-circle route

You have read that the equator divides the earth into equal halves, the Northern Hemisphere and the Southern Hemisphere. The equator is also called a great circle. A great circle is any circle that divides the earth into equal halves. Great circles are the largest circles that can be drawn along the earth.

Another great circle is formed by the 0° line of longitude and the 180° line of longitude. It divides the earth into the Eastern Hemisphere and the Western Hemisphere. Every line of longitude and the line of longitude opposite it make up a great circle. The diagram on this page shows how great circles divide the earth in half. Look at the diagram to identify the four hemispheres formed by the two great circles.

Great-Circle Routes

You may recall having read that the easiest way to find true distances is by using a globe. The shortest, most direct route between any two places on the earth lies along a great circle. Such a route is called a great-circle route

Ship and airplane navigators need to know the shortest routes from one place to another. You can understand why navigators of ships and planes use great-circle routes.

A simple exercise will help you to understand great circles and great-circle routes. All you need is a piece of string

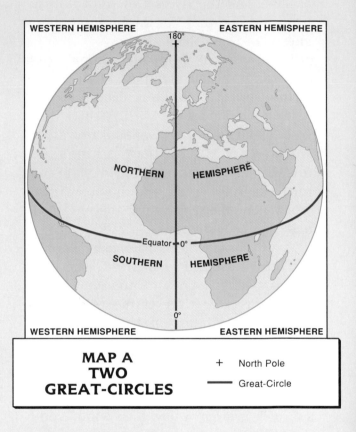

MAP A
TWO
GREAT-CIRCLES

+ North Pole
— Great-Circle

and a globe. Wrap the string tightly around the globe along the equator. Mark the distance on the string with a pen. Now wrap the string tightly around the globe in any other direction. If the distance is the same as that of the equator, you have found another great circle. Any route that is along a great circle is a great-circle route.

Suppose you want to find the great-circle route between Los Angeles and Tokyo. Hold the string against the globe so that is passes through the dots for both cities and pull it tight. The string now shows the great-circle route, or shortest distance, between Los Angeles and Tokyo.

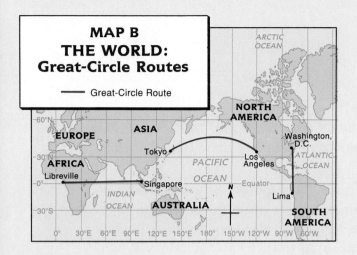

MAP B
THE WORLD:
Great-Circle Routes

—— Great-Circle Route

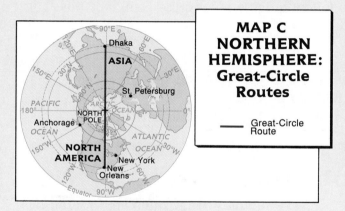

MAP C
NORTHERN
HEMISPHERE:
Great-Circle
Routes

—— Great-Circle
Route

know, every line of longitude is part of a great circle. The equator (0° latitude) is the only line of latitude that is a great circle. On this map, great-circle routes between places on the equator or on the same line of longitude appear as straight lines. Other great-circle routes appear as curved lines. For example, a navigator flying a plane from Lima to Washington, D.C., on the great-circle route would fly directly north throughout the entire trip. On the great-circle flight from Los Angeles to Tokyo, however, a plane would travel northwest at the beginning of the trip, west during the middle of the trip, and southwest at the end of the trip.

Navigators use special maps on which the great-circle routes appear as straight lines. **Map C** is such a special map for great-circle routes passing over the North Pole. To fly the great-circle route from Dhaka to New Orleans, a plane would first travel directly north to the North Pole, then directly south along 90°W to New Orleans.

Using a Great-Circle Route

On maps great-circle routes may appear as either straight lines or curved lines, depending on the map projection. Find the great-circle route between Los Angeles and Tokyo on **Map B**. Is it a straight or curved line?

On the map a straight east-west line appears to be the shortest distance between Los Angeles and Tokyo. The great-circle route appears to be longer. However, the distance along the straight line is nearly 5,800 miles (9,332 km). The real distance along the great-circle route is about 5,430 miles (8,737 km).

On **Map B** all lines of latitude and longitude are shown as straight lines. As you

Reviewing the Skill

1. What is a great circle? What is a great-circle route?
2. Which line of latitude is a great circle? Why is it that no other line of latitude is a great circle?
3. What line of longitude, together with 150°E, makes up a great circle?
4. On **Map B** would the great-circle route between Los Angeles and Washington, D.C., appear as a straight line or as a curved line?
5. In which direction would a plane flying the great-circle route from Singapore to Libreville travel at the beginning of the trip? During the middle of the trip?
6. Why are great-circle routes useful?

497

LESSON 2

Climate and Resources

READ TO LEARN

■ **Key Vocabulary**

monsoons   terraces

■ **Read Aloud**

The clouds advance like . . . elephants, enormous and full of rain. They come forward as kings among tumultuous armies; their flags are lightning, the thunder is their drum. . . .

The Indian poet Kālidāsa (käl′ ē däs′ ə) wrote these words over 1,500 years ago to describe the first dramatic signs of the rainy season in India. People throughout Southern Asia still wait eagerly for the start of the life-giving rains. If the rains fail to appear, so do the crops. When that happens, hunger and famine follow quickly among the people of the crowded lands of this area.

■ **Read for Purpose**

1. **WHAT YOU KNOW:** In what other parts of the world do soaking rains pour down every day for long periods of time?
2. **WHAT YOU WILL LEARN:** Why are land and water precious in Asia?

TROPICAL CLIMATES

The climates of Southern and Eastern Asia are as varied as the landforms of the region. Northern China has long, cold winters and one growing season. The Philippines and Singapore, on the equator, are almost always hot and rainy. The warm temperatures and plentiful rain allow farmers in the tropical part of the region to grow three crops a year.

Not all of tropical Asia has the same climate. Parts of southern Asia, such as India, are hot and dry for much of the year. Other parts may be soaked with cooling rains during some seasons. These areas have three seasons a year. A winter rainy season is followed by a fiercely hot, dry season. Then a summer rainy season usually follows.

MONSOONS

The region's heavy rains are brought by strong seasonal winds called **monsoons** (mon sünz′). In winter, monsoons from the north bring cooler weather. As you can see from the climate map on page 499, summer monsoons blowing from the southwest carry ocean moisture. Summer monsoons dump heavy rains in a wide arc from India on the west to Southeast Asia and southeast China on the east. These rains can fall so steadily that they cause heavy flooding. For example, in Cherrapunji, a city in the northeastern part of India, as much as 41 inches (104 cm) of rain may fall in a single day.

The rains also can come suddenly. One visitor to India recalls a year when the rains were very late.

498

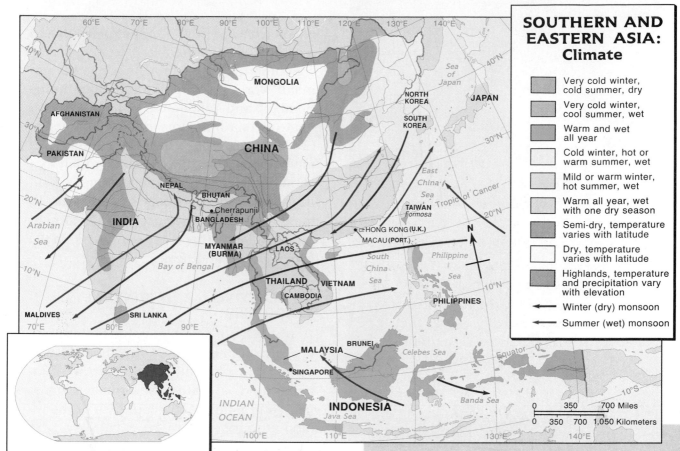

SOUTHERN AND EASTERN ASIA: Climate

- Very cold winter, cold summer, dry
- Very cold winter, cool summer, wet
- Warm and wet all year
- Cold winter, hot or warm summer, wet
- Mild or warm winter, hot summer, wet
- Warm all year, wet with one dry season
- Semi-dry, temperature varies with latitude
- Dry, temperature varies with latitude
- Highlands, temperature and precipitation vary with elevation
- → Winter (dry) monsoon
- ← Summer (wet) monsoon

MAP SKILL: Few countries in Southern and Eastern Asia have areas with dry or semidry climates. Name the countries that do.

I remember on the first of July . . . passing over the causeway that spanned [a dried-up waterway]. How absurdly large [the causeway] looked in that sun-scorched land . . . !

At midday . . . there was a change . . . a damp feeling of softness in the air. . . . A strong wind blew toward us. . . . There was the roar of close thunder, and suddenly the rain came down in bucket-loads. . . . When the fury of the storm had passed away, we went toward the railway station. We only got halfway; the causeway had disappeared under a raging torrent of dark muddy water.

HIGH-ELEVATION AND DESERT CLIMATES

To the north of the tropics, Southern and Eastern Asia has two main types of climate: high elevation and desert. Since much of the central part of Asia is at high elevations, the climate is far colder than

you might expect at such latitudes. The Plateau of Tibet is nearly 2 miles (3.2 km) high and very cold. It also is very dry because the Himalayas and other mountains block most rain from this area. Mongolia, Tibet, and western China have mostly high-elevation climates.

In the steppes and deserts of Mongolia and western China, people once made their livings by moving about to graze their sheep, camels, cattle, or horses. Today one herder says, "We still raise herds of cattle, horses, and sheep, but now we have modern veterinary services. We still live in felt tents, but we have brick houses for the winter." Many people in this area also work in cities and towns in shops, factories, and in service industries.

499

Much of southern China near Vietnam is hilly. Farmers grow rice and other crops in terraces built in the hillsides.

TEMPERATE CLIMATES

Find Japan, North Korea, South Korea, and China on the map on page 499. Most or all of these countries are north of the Tropic of Cancer, which is the southern border of the temperate zone. All four nations have mainly temperate climates. This means that these countries have four seasons similar to those of the eastern United States.

WATER RESOURCES

The region's great rivers are a major resource for its countries. China and India have thousands of miles of navigable rivers and canals. China's longest waterway, the Chang River, allows people to ship

goods from far inland to the great eastern port city of Shanghai.

Southern and Eastern Asia has several major world ports, including Hong Kong, Bombay, and Yokohama. In fact the continent of Asia has more than 80,000 miles (129,000 km) of coastline. It also has many large seas. It is no wonder then that so many people make their living by fishing or working on boats or on docks. In many Asian countries people also farm, or raise fish and other marine animals, in the lakes, rivers, and seas.

AGRICULTURAL AND MINERAL RESOURCES

Arable land, or soil suitable for farming, is scarce in the region. Only about 11 percent of China's land and 15 percent of Japan's land is arable. Nevertheless, most people in many of the countries of the region are farmers.

Farmers have found ways to make the most of their scarce farmland. For centuries, the Chinese and Filipinos have carved big steps, or terraces, into hillsides. Then they plant crops, such as rice, on the flat steps.

Southeast Asia has the richest farmland on the continent. Almost everywhere farmers can be seen working ankle-deep in the waters of flooded rice fields. Rice, Asia's most important crop, thrives in such wet climates.

Crops like wheat grow well in the loess of the North China Plain. There farmers like Ki Quanping (kē' chwän ping') are "in the fields by 5:00 every morning. At midday I shelter from the heat, which gets up to 33°C (92°F.) in the shade, but then I'm back in the fields until dark." Among plentiful products are wheat, millet, maize, sweet potatoes, and cotton.

Despite its size, Southern and Eastern Asia lacks a generous share of the world's

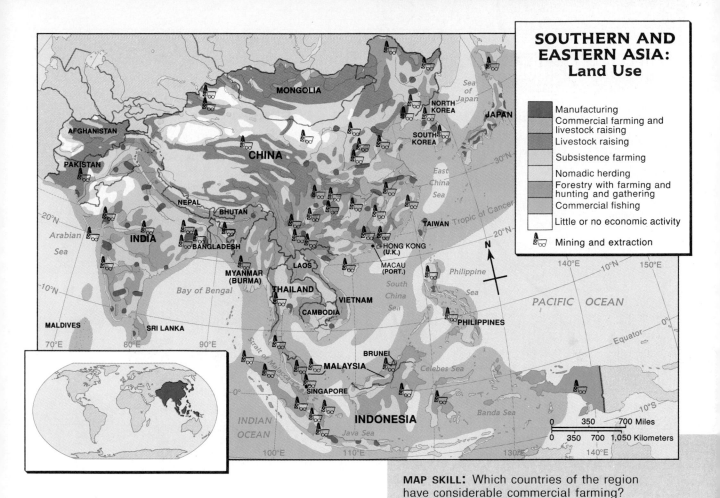

SOUTHERN AND EASTERN ASIA: Land Use

Legend:
- Manufacturing
- Commercial farming and livestock raising
- Livestock raising
- Subsistence farming
- Nomadic herding
- Forestry with farming and hunting and gathering
- Commercial fishing
- Little or no economic activity

 Mining and extraction

MAP SKILL: Which countries of the region have considerable commercial farming?

minerals. Look at the land-use map above. One of the areas with rich natural resources is Southeast Asia, which has large reserves of petroleum. India, China, and several other countries have iron and coal deposits. Which countries have considerable mining?

MANY CLIMATES, LIMITED RESOURCES

Southern and Eastern Asia has a variety of climates. The entire tropical part of the region is affected by monsoons. Since rains carried by the monsoons are blocked by the high mountains between Southern and Eastern Asia, land north of the mountains is dry. Most of the people who live in this area herd animals for a living.

The region has little arable land, yet large numbers of people are farmers. Min-

eral and energy resources are distributed unevenly. Some rivers are used for transportation and some for irrigation. In the next four chapters you will read about how these countries use their resources.

Check Your Reading

1. What are the major climates of Southern and Eastern Asia?
2. How do monsoons help the farmers of Southern and Eastern Asia?
3. Which resources are scarce in Southern and Eastern Asia?
4. **THINKING SKILL:** What effects do the mountains at the heart of Southern and Eastern Asia have on the climate of the region?

501

SOUTHERN AND EASTERN ASIA: PHYSICAL GEOGRAPHY

 LANDFORMS

- Mountains: Himalayas, Pamirs, Altai, Tian Shan, Kunlun

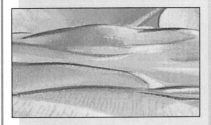

- Deserts: Gobi, Takla Makan, Tarim Basin
- Archipelagoes: Philippines, Indonesia

- Mount Everest is the world's highest mountain
- Major rivers: Huang, Chang, Mekong, Ganges, Indus, Brahmaputra

 CLIMATE

- Temperate climates: northern India, northern and eastern East Asia
- Dry and semidry climates: central China, western South Asia

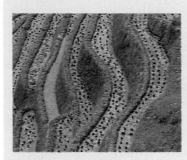

- Highland climates: southwestern China, northern South Asia
- Tropical climates: southern South Asia, Sri Lanka, Maldives, Southeast Asia

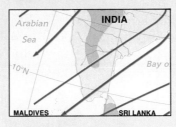

- Monsoons cause both rainy and dry seasons

NATURAL RESOURCES

- Rivers are important for transportation
- Major seaports: Hong Kong, Bombay, Yokohama
- Richest farmland is in Southeast Asia

- Few mineral resources, except in Southeast Asia, which has abundant petroleum

IDEAS TO REMEMBER

- Southern and Eastern Asia has many dramatic landforms, including the world's largest mountains, the driest deserts, and giant archipelagoes.
- The region has a variety of climates, with the most prosperous countries located in the temperate zone, but few areas except for Southeast Asia are rich in natural resources.

REVIEWING VOCABULARY

alluvial soil   subcontinent
loess   terraces
monsoons

Number a sheet of paper from 1 to 5. Beside each number, write the word or term from the above list that best matches the definition.

1. The triangular landmass jutting from southern Asia into the Indian Ocean is the world's only example of this type of landform.
2. Consisting of "steps" carved into the hillside, people in eastern Asia have used this method of increasing scarce farmland for centuries.
3. This term refers to rich soils deposited by rivers.
4. These seasonal winds bring heavy rains in an arc from India and Southeast Asia to Hong Kong and southeast China.
5. This fertile soil in the North China Plain starts out as dust from Mongolia that is carried by winds.

REVIEWING FACTS

1. What is the name of the world's highest mountain? In which mountain range is this mountain found?
2. What is the "Pamir Knot"? Which four countries meet in this region?
3. What explains the presence of deserts in central Asia? What are the names of two of these deserts?
4. Along which river did China's first civilization arise? Name the three great rivers of the Indian subcontinent.
5. How do high elevations affect the climate in Mongolia and western China?
6. How has life changed for people in the steppes and deserts of Mongolia and western China?
7. In which climate zone are Asia's most prosperous countries found?
8. How do farmers in Asia create farms on steep hillsides?
9. Name three major world ports in Asia. In which countries are these ports found?
10. What is Asia's most important crop? In which region are Asia's richest farmlands found?

WRITING ABOUT MAIN IDEAS

1. **Writing a Journal Entry:** Imagine that you are Edmund Hillary. You have just reached the summit of the world's highest mountain. Write a journal entry recording your impressions.
2. **Writing a Travel Narrative:** Write a travel narrative of a journey down the Mekong River, from its source in the mountains of Tibet to its mouth in the South China Sea.
3. **Writing About Perspectives:** Imagine that you live in one of the Asian countries that experience monsoons. Write an eyewitness account describing the arrival of the first of the summer monsoons.

BUILDING SKILLS: UNDERSTANDING GREAT-CIRCLE ROUTES

1. What is a great circle? A great-circle route?
2. Why do ships and planes often follow great-circle routes?
3. Which is the only line of latitude that is a great circle? Explain.
4. What line of longitude, together with 0°, makes up a great circle?

CHAPTER 25

THE NATIONS OF SOUTH ASIA

FOCUS

Because hospitality is an important tradition, . . . Indians are used to being around other people. . . . Life is seldom lonely in India.

In her book about India, Amita Vohtra Sarin describes many Indian traditions. In this chapter you will read about some of these traditions, as well as the beliefs and ways of life shared by many peoples of South Asia.

The People

READ TO LEARN

Key Vocabulary
Hinduism
caste
Brahmans
Sikhism

Key People
Mohandas Gandhi
Benazir Bhutto

Key Places
South Asia
Bangladesh
India
Pakistan
Sri Lanka

Read Aloud

Each time we visited a different part of India it seemed we were visiting a new land. The language, the food, the clothes were all so different.

The speaker, a 17-year-old Indian student named Sanjay Kaul, is describing field trips he had taken in his own country with his school. As you will read, South Asia is an area in which many of its peoples have remained deeply attached to their traditions, especially those of family and religion.

Read for Purpose

1. **WHAT YOU KNOW:** Which regions have you studied that have religious traditions that are over a thousand years old?
2. **WHAT YOU WILL LEARN:** In what ways does religion shape the lives of the people of South Asia?

AN ANCIENT PATCHWORK OF CULTURES

South Asia is formed by the subcontinent of India and its neighbors. The area includes eight countries: Afghanistan, Bangladesh, Bhutan, India, Maldives, Nepal, Pakistan, and Sri Lanka (also known by the island's name of Ceylon).

The subcontinent is the home of some of the world's earliest civilizations. Buried beneath the plains of the Indus River valley are the ruins of cities more than 4,000 years old. The people who formed these civilizations came from many places. Some had developed unique cultures in the area. Others were invaders who struggled into the warm subcontinent through the icy mountain passes on South Asia's northwest border. Each group had its own religious beliefs, customs, and languages. They made South Asia a patchwork of many cultures.

From the 1700s until World War II, the British either ruled or influenced the countries of South Asia. You will read more about the British influence in Lesson 3.

HINDUISM

The Aryans (âr′ ē ənz), one of the first groups to invade the subcontinent, came through the mountain passes about 3,500 years ago. The legends and customs they

505

SOUTH ASIA: Political

⊛ National capital   ┈┈┈ Disputed boundary

• Other city

MAP SKILL: The Ganges River (*above*), which is holy to the Hindus, is India's longest river, at 1,600 miles (2,560 km). Which cities are near the Ganges?

brought later grew into the religion of **Hinduism** (hin′ dü iz əm). Today Hinduism is the major religion of South Asia. The nations of South Asia are shown on the map on this page. In India Hindus make up 80 percent of the population.

Hinduism teaches that there is one great spirit in the universe, but this spirit can appear in the form of different gods. These gods can be worshiped in different ways—in temples, at family shrines at home, or at the Ganges River. The Ganges is holy to all Hindus, and people come from all over South Asia to bathe in its waters.

To Hindus all life is holy and all living things have souls. Hindus have a special respect for cows. No Hindu will eat meat from a cow, and Hindus won't harm cows that wander through streets or villages.

THE CASTE SYSTEM

One important way in which Hinduism affects the lives of South Asians is to divide them into **castes**. Castes are social groups that are ranked from highest to lowest. Hindus believe that a person is born again after death. Depending on the way the person lived, rebirth may return the person into a higher or lower caste or as an animal.

In ancient India people belonged to one of four main castes. These were the Brahmans, or priests; the warriors; the merchants and farmers; and the servants. Over time these castes were divided into more than 3,000 castes.

Below the caste system was a group called the "untouchables." What does the word tell you about the way untouchables were treated? For centuries untouchables were forced to live apart, avoided by other Hindus. They were not even allowed to draw water from a village well. The untouchables did the jobs that no caste members would do, such as cleaning streets and collecting garbage.

Caste affects what people eat and where they live. When caste rules are strictly followed, people marry only someone from the same caste. Rarely do people leave the caste into which they were born.

Some Hindus have tried to change the caste system. Mohandas Gandhi, the leader of India's independence movement, tried to improve the lives of the untouchables. Gandhi called these people *harijans* (här i jänz'), meaning "children of God." Gandhi also appeared in public with *harijans*. Since 1950, Indian law has forbidden citizens from discriminating against *harijans*, but some Hindus find it hard to change.

In large cities, where people of all castes work together, caste has become less important than it was. However, it remains an important part of South Asian life.

OTHER RELIGIOUS GROUPS

Islam came to South Asia many centuries after Hinduism. Today three South Asian nations, Afghanistan, Pakistan, and Bangladesh, have populations that are almost completely Muslim, meaning that the people follow Islam. India also has more than 90 million Muslims. Most of India's Muslim citizens live in the northern part of the country.

Religious differences have caused much conflict in South Asia. In 1947 conflict between Hindus and Muslims in India led to the creation of Pakistan, a separate Muslim country. However, forming the new country did not completely end the tension between the two groups.

Another religion, Sikhism (sēk' iz əm), is a blending of Hinduism and Islam. Founded in the late 1400s, Sikhism is today a separate religion combining some elements of Hinduism and Islam. You will read about the tension between Sikhs and Hindus in Lesson 3.

Mohandas Gandhi was both the political leader and the spiritual leader of India for more than 25 years.

As the graph on this page shows, India has too few Buddhists for Buddhism to be listed as a major religion. You will read about Buddhism in Chapter 26. Although Buddhism began in India, it has not kept as many followers there as it did in East Asia. In South Asia most Buddhists are in Nepal, Bhutan, and other Himalayan areas. Buddhism is also the majority religion in Sri Lanka. Tension between Buddhists and the Hindu minority in Sri Lanka burst into violence in 1988, with some Hindus demanding their own state. Christians are found mainly along India's coasts, where European influence has been strong.

LANGUAGES OF SOUTH ASIA

Even the languages of South Asia have been shaped by religion. The one language spoken by more Indians than any other is Hindi. It evolved from Sanskrit, an ancient language of South Asia still used in Hindu sacred books. Closely related to Hindi is Urdu, the official language of Pakistan and 1 of the 16 official languages of India. Most Sikhs speak Punjabi, the language of the Indian state of Punjab and of Sikh holy writings.

India has hundreds of other languages and dialects. The fact that no one of these languages and dialects is spoken by every Indian helps to explain why today many educated Indians can speak English. In

GRAPH SKILL: One Indian religious group, the Hindus, considers cows sacred and allows them to roam freely (below, right). How many Indians are Hindus? The Ladakh (below) are among the few Buddhist groups in India.

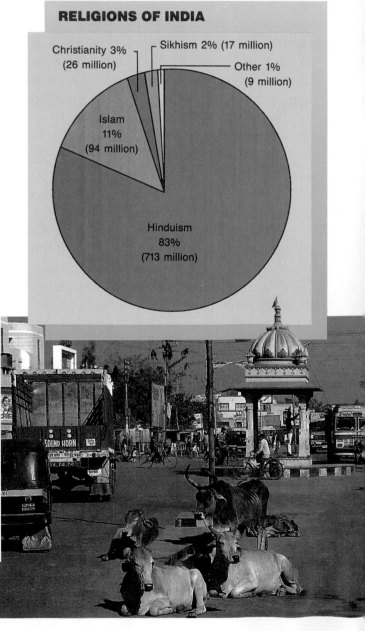

RELIGIONS OF INDIA

Christianity 3% (26 million)

Sikhism 2% (17 million)

Other 1% (9 million)

Islam 11% (94 million)

Hinduism 83% (713 million)

the years Great Britain ruled the area, many Indians and other groups learned English in school. Although the government recently made Hindi the main official language, many Indians still use English.

THE FAMILY

Most South Asians live in villages. A bride often moves in with her husband's extended family. That includes his parents, uncles, brothers, their children, and unmarried sisters. The extended family provides many hands to do the farm work. It also provides aging parents someone to live with and to care for them.

No matter what religious group they belong to, many South Asian families arrange marriages for young people. These families believe that parents know what is best for their children. In the past, newlyweds often met each other for the first time at their wedding. Today, future mates usually meet before the wedding.

In cities young people sometimes arrange their own marriages, often for love. Or they may advertise for a spouse in newspapers. The ads usually mention caste, as well as their education and their occupation.

Women are expected to marry. **Benazir Bhutto** (bü′ tō), the prime minister of Pakistan from 1988 to 1990, married a man chosen by her relatives after she decided to run for office. She first met him five days before they became engaged. "For me, there was no other choice," she said. It was either "no marriage or an arranged marriage."

THE FORCE OF TRADITION

The eight countries of South Asia have many different peoples and customs. Much of this variety stems from one source—a deep attachment to traditional ways of life.

Wearing traditional dress, Benazir Bhutto crossed Pakistan several times in her campaign to become prime minister in 1988.

Hinduism and Islam are among the major religions that influence daily life in South Asia. The clothes people wear, the food they eat—and sometimes even the jobs they have—may be the result of traditions that stretch back for hundreds of years. As you read on, you will learn more about life in South Asia.

Check Your Reading

1. What are the major religions of South Asia?
2. How does religion shape life in India?
3. List some aspects of a Hindu's life that are influenced by the caste system. Explain why this influence may be weaker in cities.
4. **THINKING SKILL:** Classify into two or more groups the ways of life affected by South Asia's religions.

The Economy

READ TO LEARN

Key Vocabulary

Green Revolution
cottage industry

Key Places

Calcutta
Bombay

Read Aloud

That year the rains failed. A week went by, two. We stared at the cruel sky—calm, blue, indifferent to our need. We threw ourselves on the earth and we prayed. . . . But no rain came. . . .

The person who spoke these words, a woman in southern India, lost her land when the monsoon failed to bring rain in the 1950s. She and her husband then moved to a city to find work. In this lesson you will read about the ways in which people earn a living in South Asia.

Read for Purpose

1. **WHAT YOU KNOW:** In what ways might people's lives change when they move from a farm village to a large city?
2. **WHAT YOU WILL LEARN:** In what ways do the land and climate of South Asia shape the ways in which people earn their livings?

FEEDING A LARGE POPULATION

South Asia is rich in natural resources. It has many fertile valleys with plenty of water and a long growing season. There are many mineral deposits. Yet in spite of this abundance, many South Asians are poor. How can this poverty in the midst of abundance be explained?

One explanation is that South Asia has one of the highest population densities on earth. For example, the United States has about 71 people per square mile (about 27 per sq km), and Bangladesh has more than 2,000 people per square mile (more than 800 per sq km).

Bangladesh is one of the most densely populated countries in the world, and it cannot grow enough food to feed all its people. Most people of Bangladesh live under the constant threat of famine and malnutrition. In Chapter 21 you read about the ways in which these problems affect people in Sub-Saharan Africa.

CONTROLLING THE WATER SUPPLY

To end famine and malnutrition, South Asia's farmers have begun programs to produce more food. One such program is aimed at creating a steady supply of water. As you read in Chapter 24, South Asia does not have a regular supply of water. Although most of the subcontinent receives plenty of rain, almost all of it falls during the few months of the summer

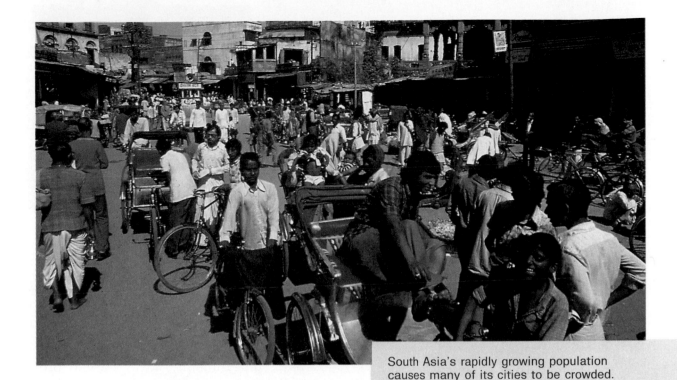

South Asia's rapidly growing population causes many of its cities to be crowded.

monsoon. The rest of the year is almost completely dry. Also, when the rains do come, they are often followed by floods that wash away crops and houses.

No one can tame the wild monsoon, but South Asians are learning to control its effects. Engineers build ditches and high walls to contain floods. They put up dams on the rivers to harness the power of rushing water. Most important, they build reservoirs and irrigation canals to water the fields all year long.

Pakistan needs irrigation for a different reason than India does. Find Pakistan on the Atlas map on page 636. Because the country is located north of the monsoon zone, it receives little rain. Pakistani farmers rely on the Indus River system for water. Each year Pakistan builds more canals and cultivates more areas.

THE GREEN REVOLUTION

In addition to irrigation, some South Asian farmers plant new types of crops and use new farming techniques that re-sult in larger harvests. These changes are known as the Green Revolution because the new techniques produce leafier plants that make the fields look greener.

One of these crops is a new type of rice, South Asia's basic food. Since this new kind of rice grows more quickly than ordinary rice, farmers can now plant more than one crop per year. Some parts of Bangladesh have three rice harvests.

Another new crop is "miracle wheat," grown in areas that are too dry and cool for rice. This new type of wheat is more resistant to many crop diseases than are older types of wheat. Raja Gohar Masud, a farmer in northern Pakistan, says that the land produced very little when he was young. But farmers "have increased production now by using tractors and fertilizers, and also by planting a new [type of] wheat. . . ." Such methods have helped Pakistan to more than double its wheat production since 1967.

Many farmers in South Asia use traditional methods to plant (*above*), harvest, and transport their crops (*right*).

FARM VILLAGES

Many of the new crops and farming techniques are used on bigger farms. However, about 75 percent of South Asians live in small farm villages. Here "women still carry pots of drinking water on their hips. . . ." writes an Indian poet about village life.

Old customs also shape village economies. For example, when an Indian farmer dies, the fields are divided among his sons. In each generation the land is divided again, leaving most farmers with very small plots. The size of the average Indian farm is only about 2 acres (0.8 ha). In the United States the average farm measures about 456 acres (185 ha), although many people have larger or smaller farms.

The farmers working these tiny fields are mostly subsistence farmers, who grow food only for family use. They have little money to spend on modern farm machinery, insecticides, or fertilizers. However, several governments have started programs to help poor farmers to take part in the Green Revolution.

INDUSTRY IN THE HOME

When you think of industry, you are likely to imagine huge factories with hundreds of workers. That type of industry can be found in South Asia, but manufacturing often takes place in people's homes. These small manufacturers, or cottage industries, provide millions of jobs and produce the fine crafted goods for which South Asia has long been known.

The major products from handicrafts include gold and silver jewelry, textiles, and carpets. Have you heard of the luxurious soft wool known as cashmere? It comes originally from the state of Kashmir in northern India.

INDUSTRIAL INDIA

All the countries of South Asia are developing nations, even India, which has many industries. In the hills just outside Calcutta, miners extract coal and iron ore from underground deposits. Nearby factories turn iron into steel, which is then shipped elsewhere to be processed.

Calcutta is also home to the jute industry. The tough fibers of this plant, which is grown mostly in Bangladesh, are used to make rope and burlap bags.

In and around Bombay are numerous textile mills. India also produces automobiles, bicycles, chemicals, computer components, and electronic parts.

ECONOMIC CHALLENGES

India and Pakistan are making major progress in manufacturing. The rest of the area, though, has few factories. Nepal's economy is based on agriculture and tourism. People from all over the world go there to see the majestic Himalayas. Sri Lanka relies heavily on plantations where rubber and tea are grown for export. Afghanistan and Bhutan are isolated mountain lands where herding is the chief occupation.

Every year steady streams of farmers and cottage workers leave the villages of South Asia to seek job opportunities in the large cities. As a result, large cities have grown even larger. Bombay's population, for instance, grew from 1.5 million people in 1941 to over 11 million in 1990.

Unfortunately many villagers do not find the jobs or homes they seek. Many residents of South Asia's cities live on the streets. Despite their growing wealth, most large cities cannot create housing or jobs fast enough for the rapidly increasing numbers of people.

DEVELOPING SOUTH ASIA'S ECONOMIES

South Asia has some of the most densely populated places on earth. As a result, malnutrition and famine remain constant threats although the area has abundant natural resources. New methods

Among India's factories are tractor plants like this one. After they are manufactured, tractors and parts are shipped around the world.

of irrigation and the Green Revolution are producing more food.

India and Pakistan are the most industrialized countries of South Asia, with many large factories as well as cottage industries. Every year thousands of farmers leave their homes to seek better job opportunities in the cities.

Check Your Reading

1. Why is population density a problem in a country like Bangladesh?
2. How have South Asians begun to control their water supplies?
3. If India is becoming more industrially developed, why does it have trouble feeding its people?
4. THINKING SKILL: In what ways might working in a cottage industry be similar to working in a small factory? How might it be different?

513

The Government

Read Aloud

We want freedom for our country, but not at the expense of others.

The great Indian leader Mohandas Gandhi spoke these words before World War II, when South Asia was part of the British Empire. Gandhi hoped to unite all of South Asia into one independent nation. There the many peoples of the area could live together in peace and equality. As you will read, South Asia did gain independence, but not in the way Gandhi had hoped.

Read for Purpose

1. **WHAT YOU KNOW:** Would you find it easy to make your own decisions if someone else had always made decisions for you?
2. **WHAT YOU WILL LEARN:** What types of governments are found in the countries of South Asia?

THE BRITISH LEGACY

The governments of the countries of South Asia vary from democracies to dictatorships. Despite their differences, the countries of South Asia have one thing in common. At one time they were all under the control or influence of Great Britain.

European merchants first entered South Asia in the 1500s. Eventually the British gained control of the local governments. By the middle 1800s the British had made the subcontinent a British colony.

The years of British rule have left their mark on South Asian life. Perhaps the most important British legacy has been the democratic ideal that the people can govern themselves through their elected representatives.

INDEPENDENCE AND PARTITION

Britain contributed to India's independence movement in another way. Starting about 100 years ago, many young Indians went to study in Great Britain. There they learned about democracy and their rights as British citizens. The Indians realized that they did not enjoy equal rights with the British in their home country, India.

One Indian who studied law in London was Mohandas Gandhi. When he returned to India in 1915, Gandhi began a campaign for justice that soon became a fight for independence. Gandhi's fight was unusual because it was fought without violence. He urged peaceful protests against British power. His movement gained the support of much of the world and earned

him the nickname *Mahatma*, which is Hindi for "great soul."

By 1947 the British had agreed to grant India independence, but bitter tensions divided the people. Muslims realized that an independent India would be ruled by a Hindu majority. Many Muslims wanted to live under Islamic law in their own land. Mohammed Ali Jinnah (jin′ ä) led a Muslim group that wanted to establish its own country. At last everyone agreed to a partition, or division, of British India. In 1947 two countries, India and Pakistan, were formed.

After partition many Muslims left India for Pakistan, while Hindus fled Pakistan for India. Violent fights broke out between Hindus and Muslims on the roads and in railroad cars. At least half a million people died. Some Hindus were angry about the partition. One Hindu extremist murdered Gandhi in 1948.

TROUBLED PAKISTAN

Muslim Pakistan was originally two separate sections divided by almost 1,000 miles (1,600 km) of Indian land. Find Pakistan and Bangladesh in the Atlas on page 636. Pakistan was West Pakistan and Bangladesh was East Pakistan.

The people of both Pakistans were mostly Muslim. But they had different languages, economic resources, and ways of life. These differences led to civil war in 1971. With India's help, East Pakistan won its independence and became the nation of Bangladesh.

THE WORLD'S LARGEST DEMOCRACY

India has a huge population—more than 860 million people. Only China has more people, as you will read in Chapter 26. The size of its population causes India sometimes to be called "the world's largest democracy." Most of the electorate goes to the polls to vote. Many go to support local parties and issues.

In 1984 Sikhs demonstrated for rights in New Delhi, the capital (*left*). Unrest spread to Amritsar (*right*), the Sikh headquarters.

India borrowed ideas for government from Britain and the United States. The Indian Parliament meets in New Delhi. The head of the party that wins the most votes becomes the prime minister. India also has a supreme court modeled on that of the United States.

India has 25 states and several territories. Wherever possible, state borders were drawn to include mainly members of one ethnic or religious group. This allows India's peoples to govern themselves at the local level. But it does not prevent conflict from happening.

For example, the northern state of Punjab has more than 10 million Sikhs. Some Sikhs feel that India's central government does not respect their religious and economic rights. They want the Sikhs to form their own country. A number of Sikhs began a terrorist campaign to gain their ends. One attack, in 1984, resulted in the death of India's Prime Minister Indira Gandhi. For the second time in less than 40 years, India had lost a leader to religious violence.

Indira Gandhi was the daughter of Jawaharlal Nehru (jə wä′ hər läl nā′ rü), India's first prime minister and the leader who helped shape modern India. According to Nehru, he "was no believer in kings and princes." Indira Gandhi also believed in democracy. But when India's economic and political problems began to increase in the late 1970s, she took on almost dictatorial powers. After Indira Gandhi's death in 1984, India remained a democracy. Her son, Rajiv Gandhi, was prime minister until 1989. He too was assassinated while campaigning for re-election in 1991.

OTHER GOVERNMENTS

In Bangladesh the government is under the control of army officers. A mili-

516

tary government was also in power in Pakistan until 1988 when free elections were held. Benazir Bhutto, whom you read about in Lesson 1, was the first prime minister chosen under the new laws and the first woman to govern a Muslim country.

Another South Asian country with a democratic system is the island nation of Sri Lanka. There, struggles between the Buddhist Sinhalese, the major group of people on the island, and the Hindu Tamils threaten the nation's stability.

The Himalayan nations of Bhutan and Nepal are among the world's few remaining monarchies. Like Great Britain, these two countries also have representative governments. In each country, a king rules with the help of advisers and an elected assembly. The two nations look to India for economic support, military protection, and guidance in foreign affairs.

In Afghanistan a revolution toppled the king from his throne in 1973. A second revolution in 1978 brought a socialist group to power. When other Afghans rebelled, troops from the Soviet Union crossed the border to keep Afghanistan's socialist government in power. The Soviets took over the capital city of Kabul, but they never were able to control all of Afghanistan. After a long and costly war, Soviet troops began to leave Afghanistan in 1989.

INDEPENDENT SOUTH ASIA

To preserve their independence, the nations of South Asia banded together with other small countries in a worldwide movement of nonaligned nations. These were developing countries that did not want to take sides in the struggles between the United States and its allies and the Soviet Union and its allies. "We in India," said Prime Minister Nehru in 1953, "follow a foreign policy . . . of nonalignment with any power bloc."

King Birendra and Queen Aisswarya of Nepal hold a public audience in the capital.

CHALLENGES OF DEMOCRACY

Until 1947, when India and Pakistan became independent countries, all of South Asia was under either British rule or influence. From the British, South Asians inherited a belief in democracy and independence. However, the new countries often differed on such matters as religion and political systems. Today South Asia's governments include representative democracies, monarchies, and dictatorships.

Check Your Reading

1. Name three nations that were once part of the British colony of India.
2. What kinds of governments are found in the countries of South Asia? Which countries have borrowed British ideas of government?
3. In what ways do you think being nonaligned helped countries preserve their independence?
4. **THINKING SKILL:** Reread the information about Nepal and Bhutan on this page. From this information, what conclusion can you draw about the independence of these two countries?

517

Determining Point of View: Review

Wendy's family recently moved from the city to a house in the country. On the first day in the country Wendy was delighted to see a family of deer on the lawn behind the house. At school Wendy told her classmates about the deer. She was surprised when they said that deer are a nuisance because they eat shrubbery, flowers, and vegetables in the garden.

Point of view is the way a person looks at or feels about something. How a person feels about something can affect the accuracy of what he or she says.

HELPING YOURSELF

The procedure below shows one way to determine point of view.

1. Identify the subject or topic.

2. Identify statements of fact and opinion.

3. Identify information that was left out but could have been included.

4. Identify any biases the writer has.

5. Describe the point of view from which the author writes. Is the writer for or against something?

Applying the Skill

Read the following passage about rail travel in India. Look for clues that will help you to determine the writer's point of view.

The Indian railway system provides service throughout the country. Every visitor to India should take a long train trip. This is the best way to experience the Indian way of life: its beauty, its excitement, and its frustrations. Even though monkeys change the signals, floods wash away the tracks, and cows fall asleep on the tracks, somehow the trains keep running.

1. Which sentences in the above paragraph are statements of fact?
2. Which sentences in the above paragraph are statements of opinion?
3. What biases, if any, does the writer of the paragraph have?
4. What do you think is the writer's point of view?

Reviewing the Skill

1. What is the meaning of the phrase *point of view*?
2. What are some steps you can take to determine a writer or speaker's point of view?
3. Where, outside of school, would it be useful to try to determine the point of view of a writer or a speaker?

Arts and Recreation

READ TO LEARN

Key Vocabulary

Vedas
yoga

Read Aloud

According to the Hindu holy book, the Ramayana, the god Vishnu once came to earth as the prince Rama. Rama was the ideal Hindu. Even while he was in exile, he remained a loyal son, a lover of all living things, and a devoted husband. So greatly was Rama loved that when Rama's wife, Sita, was kidnapped and carried away to an island, the monkeys built a bridge across the ocean to rescue her.

Throughout South Asia stories about Prince Rama are shown frequently on television and in the movies and are told in many forms. Religion plays an important role in the arts and recreation of the area.

Read for Purpose

1. **WHAT YOU KNOW:** What are some movies or television programs that you have seen dealing with religious themes?
2. **WHAT YOU WILL LEARN:** In what ways have both traditional and modern ideas influenced the arts and recreation of South Asia?

A LIVING HINDU TRADITION

The above story of Rama belongs to an epic that is more than 2,000 years old. Even older is the collection of Hindu religious writings known as the Vedas (vā′dəz). The Vedas are a part of the culture found throughout South Asia.

Hindu tales are told through traditional drama, dance, and song. Traveling troupes of actors bring Hindu tales to the villages. "Villagers will watch . . . all night, for as long as 12 hours at a time," wrote one visitor. Audiences know the stories so well that they sometimes yell out an actor's lines before the actor can speak them.

Traditional dances remain popular in both villages and cities. For example, in Nepal's capital city of Kathmandu a dancer paints his face blue because the color identifies the Hindu god Vishnu. People in the audience follow the story because they know the specific meaning of each of the dancer's steps and gestures.

ART AND ARCHITECTURE

South Asians like to create things that are beautiful as well as meaningful and useful in everyday life. For example, Hindus decorate everything, from clothes to statues. Carpenters carve religious designs on roof beams as they build houses. In some villages women paint rice-powder designs on doors to honor Hindu gods.

The Taj Mahal in Agra is one of the most beautiful buildings in the world. Shah Jahan and his wife Mumtaz Mahal are buried there.

Each of South Asia's major religious groups has built magnificent monuments to their gods. Usually every inch of the outside of a Hindu temple is carved and decorated. The carvings illustrate scenes from the Vedas and show many gods.

Buddhist shrines, some of which are more than 1,500 years old, are found in many parts of South Asia. Other Buddhist structures are the sturdy monasteries clinging to the steep Himalayan slopes of Bhutan and Nepal.

MUSLIM INFLUENCE

In Agra, India, Mohammad Husain (hü sän') grinds precious stones into colorful chips. With a hand-turned grinding wheel, he shapes bits of turquoise and other stones into tiny pieces to decorate boxes and tabletops. Husain says his craft has changed little over hundreds of years. His ancestors, he believes, helped decorate the building that has become India's

most famous architectural symbol, the Taj Mahal (täzh' mə häl').

The Taj Mahal was built in the 1600s as the tomb of the wife of the ruler, Shah Jahan. Because he was Muslim, the Taj Mahal is Islamic in design. The tomb is spectacular, with mosaics, domes and slender columns, beautiful gardens, and a large reflecting pool in front. There are no human images because their use in art is discouraged by Islam.

RELIGIOUS HOLIDAYS

South Asia observes many religious holidays. One recent month of March, three American college students were bicycling through Bombay. They noticed that the streets and houses were splashed with purple, red, and pink. As the students rounded a corner, a group of young men threw balloons at them. The balloons burst and the students were drenched with purple dye.

The Americans were "victims" of the prank-filled Hindu festival called *Holi*. It's a day of mischief, when Hindus fling differently colored dyes at everyone and everything in sight.

Holi is only one of many religious celebrations. Each religious community has its own holidays, and cities have their own local celebrations.

CULTURAL EXCHANGE

Many of the area's newer forms of art and recreation have entered South Asia through contact with the British. For example, the English game of cricket has become a favorite sport in India.

Even more popular in India are movies. The film industry is the world's largest, producing hundreds of movies every year. Filmmakers have discovered that movies provide a way for Indians to explore problems of ethnic and religious conflict.

Although India has imported such activities as cricket and filmmaking, it also has given much of its culture to the world. One example is the ancient Hindu practice of **yoga**—a way of training both body and mind through exercise and meditation. Yoga has become popular in the United States and other countries of the world.

The game Indians call *poona* crossed the ocean and was renamed badminton by a British earl. Polo, a sport played on horseback, comes from India. Chess, one of the world's greatest games of skill, originated in India at least 2,500 years ago. One ruler liked the game so much he had huge squares painted on the ground. People stood on the squares of this huge chessboard waiting for him to call out moves.

LIVING WITH PAST AND PRESENT

South Asia combines past traditions with modern ideas. As you have read, ancient tales remain popular and are retold in many forms. Some people have adopted customs from outside the region. Build-

Costumed dancers use special movements to act out Hindu and other religious tales.

ings throughout the area reflect the traditions of Islam, Buddhism, Hinduism, and other religions. Yoga has spread from India to many parts of the world. Arts and crafts, and even sports and festivals, keep alive the traditions of the people of South Asia.

Check Your Reading

1. How do South Asians use both modern and old ways to retell tales?
2. What is the Taj Mahal?
3. Give examples of the cultural exchange between South Asia and Great Britain.
4. **THINKING SKILL:** Based on what you read about Prince Rama on page 519, what can you conclude about the qualities Hindus admire in people?

SOUTH ASIA: CULTURAL GEOGRAPHY

 **PEOPLE**

- Religion is an important part of South Asian culture

Hinduism
83%
(713 million)

- About 80 percent of India's people are Hindus
- Muslims live mainly in Pakistan, Bangladesh, and northern India
- South Asia has many languages and dialects

- Force of tradition remains strong

 **ECONOMY**

- Population grows faster than ability of nations to provide food and jobs
- Green Revolution, with new technology and stronger, more rapidly growing grains, has doubled production of some crops
- Cottage industries produce: jewelry, textiles, carpets

- Other industries: mining, steel, jute, textiles

 **GOVERNMENT**

- All of South Asia was once under the influence of Great Britain

- Religious differences cause conflict
- Religious conflicts led to creation of India and Pakistan

- India is the world's largest democracy
- Other types of government: military dictatorships, constitutional monarchies

 **ARTS AND RECREATION**

- Arts and recreation strongly influenced by religious traditions
- Area has many temples and shrines

- India's Taj Mahal, Muslim in design, is one of the world's most beautiful buildings
- Cricket and other British sports are popular
- Favorite Indian pastimes: yoga, chess, badminton, and polo

IDEAS TO REMEMBER

- Many languages and customs in South Asia reflect religious and cultural traditions.
- Most countries in South Asia are densely populated and have developing economies in which the majority of workers are farmers.
- South Asia today has many types of government—representative democracies, monarchies, and dictatorships.
- South Asian arts and recreation is a mixture of traditional themes and practices with more recent British influences.

REVIEWING VOCABULARY

Each of the following statements contains an underlined vocabulary word or term. Number a sheet of paper from 1 to 10. Beside each number write whether the following statements are true or false. If the statement is true, write true. If it is false, rewrite the sentence using the vocabulary word correctly.

1. Common in South Asia, <u>cottage industry</u> is the small-scale production of goods that takes place inside people's homes.
2. Although they have weakened in recent times, <u>castes</u>, or rigid social classes, are found in parts of South Asia.
3. In ancient India the <u>Brahmans</u> were members of the servant class and belonged to one of the lowest castes.
4. <u>Yoga</u> began in the United States but has become popular in India.
5. <u>Vedas</u> are ancient Hindu religious stories and are still a source of art, entertainment, and worship.
6. The <u>Green Revolution</u> resulted in more production of food crops.
7. <u>Sikhism</u> is a branch of Islam whose beliefs are identical to those of Muslims in other countries.
8. The <u>partition</u>, or division, of British India created the countries of East Pakistan and West Pakistan.
9. <u>Nonaligned nations</u> are developing countries that had close military and economic ties to one of the superpowers.
10. <u>Hinduism</u> teaches that there is only one god and that all people are equal.

REVIEWING FACTS

1. Which eight countries make up the region of South Asia?
2. Why does English continue to be spoken by large numbers of people in India?
3. What is the Green Revolution?
4. What changes have affected the government of Afghanistan since 1973?
5. What is yoga? From which religious tradition does yoga come?

✏ WRITING ABOUT MAIN IDEAS

1. **Writing a Paragraph:** Write a paragraph contrasting the way in which India gained independence with struggles for independence in other countries. Discuss Mohandas Gandhi's role in this struggle.
2. **Writing a Report:** You have read how religious conflict is the source of much unrest in the Middle East. Write a report about religious conflict in South Asia and the impact this unrest has had on South Asian countries.
3. **Writing About Perspectives:** Write an essay giving your opinion of the following statement: "The Green Revolution may fail if the population continues to grow unchecked in South Asia."

BUILDING SKILLS: DETERMINING POINT OF VIEW

1. What does it mean to determine an author's point of view?
2. List at least four steps you could take to recognize a point of view.
3. Why is it important to be able to determine an author's point of view?
4. Locate a statement in the text that expresses a person's point of view. Describe what that point of view is.

CHAPTER 26

CHINA AND ITS NEIGHBORS

FOCUS

With each day the face of China is changing. Hundreds of millions of Chinese are laboring to build the face of the future. The obstacles they face are immense.

China has more than 1 billion people—one fifth of the world's population. As the book *Modern China* tells us, a large population is only one of the challenges facing China. In this chapter you will learn how China and its neighbors are attempting to build their future.

The People

READ TO LEARN

Key Vocabulary

Confucianism
Daoism
Buddhism
pinyin

Key People

Mao Zedong
Confucius
Laozi
Siddhartha Gautama

Key Places

East Asia
Beijing

Read Aloud

Just 80 years ago, any common person who made his way into China's Imperial Palace—the "Forbidden City"—was immediately dragged out again and beheaded. Today 140,000 sightseers a week wander through the palace.

The person describing this change is Sun Jue (sủn′ jü′ ə). He works at the Palace Museum located in Beijing, the capital city of China. The building he mentions used to be the home of China's emperor. Today the palace is the home of art treasures that Mr. Sun calls the "reminders of China's cultural history."

Read for Purpose

1. **WHAT YOU KNOW:** What revolutions have you read about that completely changed a country's way of life?
2. **WHAT YOU WILL LEARN:** What ways of life do the people of East Asia continue to share despite their political differences?

EAST ASIA

Life is changing throughout **East Asia**. East Asia includes China and nearby areas that share many parts of China's culture. As you can see from the map on page 526, these nearby areas are the countries of Mongolia, North Korea, South Korea, Taiwan, and the British colony of Hong Kong. North and South Korea were once one country. Hong Kong is scheduled to become part of China in 1997.

For many centuries China has influenced the ways of life of the peoples in the surrounding areas. Once a great empire, China is today the largest country in East Asia. Its area of 3.8 million square miles (9.8 million sq km) makes China the third-largest country in the world, after Russia and Canada.

CHINA'S BREAK WITH THE PAST

Life changed in almost every way in China after 1949. That was the year the Communist forces under the leadership of **Mao Zedong** (mou′ dze dung′) won control of China in a civil war. At that time, most Chinese people were poor and a few very rich people held most of the country's wealth.

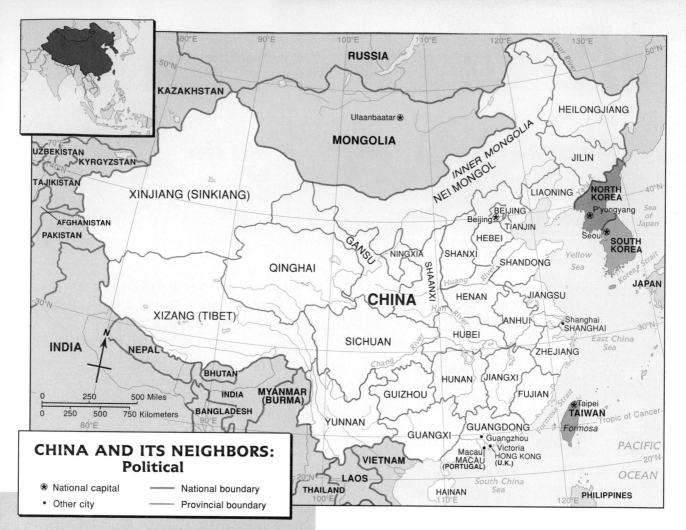

CHINA AND ITS NEIGHBORS: Political

⊛ National capital   —— National boundary

• Other city   —— Provincial boundary

MAP SKILL: China is so large it shares a border with many countries. What country is on China's north-central border?

The new Communist rulers wanted to make all people in China equal. They gave most of the rich people's land to poor farmers. The Communists experimented with new ways of organizing farms and factories and tried to teach everyone to read and write. They wanted to get rid of many ancient traditions and values and to replace them with Communist beliefs.

Have the Communists succeeded in changing China? The answer is yes, in many ways. If you were to visit China you would see fewer poor people and more schools and factories than there were at the end of World War II.

As in the past, the present-day people of China are proud to be Chinese. This sense of pride reflects their long and impressive history. Over the centuries Chinese civilization invented silk, paper, printing, and many other things. China also maintained centuries of peace and prosperity for its people.

EAST ASIA'S TRADITIONAL VALUES

Family loyalty helped to shape the cultures of China and its neighbors. In East Asia the idea of honoring one's parents goes back at least 2,500 years to the time of Kongfuzi, China's great philosopher and teacher. Kongfuzi is known outside Asia as Confucius (kən fū′ shəs).

526

Many East Asian statues and paintings honor Confucius (*right*) and Buddha (*left*).

The teachings of Confucius, known as Confucianism, are a set of rules for behavior. Confucius taught that family members have responsibilities to one another. In the same way, people and their rulers have responsibilities to each other. Confucius also taught respect for learning because he believed that knowledge can bring human beings closer to perfection.

Confucianism remains a strong influence on life in Taiwan, Hong Kong, and South Korea. In those places, family loyalty and respect for elders are important values.

After the Communists took power in China and North Korea, they tried to replace family loyalty with loyalty to the state. But the breaking of family ties went against tradition and met with only limited success. In China today, many staunch Communists still keep the traditions of honoring their parents in many different ways.

FAMILY SIZE

In the past most East Asian families lived close to their relatives. Relatives might live in the same house or near one another in the village.

Large families are traditional, and many East Asian couples would like to have several children. But most of the governments throughout East Asia are trying to slow the rapid growth of their large populations.

In China especially, the size of the population is overwhelming. China's 1 billion people make its population four times as large as that of the United States. The Chinese government has made an effort to slow population growth by passing laws that encourage families to have only one child. These measures have slowed down the increase in population somewhat, but population growth is still a serious problem for China.

DAOISM AND BUDDHISM

In addition to Confucianism, two systems of belief have helped to shape life in East Asia. They are Daoism (dou′ iz əm) and Buddhism (bùd′ iz əm). Daoism teaches that people should accept calmly whatever fate brings. Buddhism teaches that human suffering is caused by selfishness or the desire for things.

Daoism may have been started by a teacher named Laozi (lou′ dzu′), who lived about the same time as Confucius. When things have gone wrong, have you ever heard someone say, "Well, that's the way life is"? That thought is somewhat like that of a Daoist. *Dao* means "the way." Daoists believe that people should leave things alone and not try to change them. Over the centuries Daoism slowly changed into a religion.

Another belief system, Buddhism, was begun by the Indian prince **Siddhartha Gautama** (si där′ tə gô′ tə mə). He believed that the way to overcome suffering is to get rid of selfish desires. Instead of seeking worldly gains, Siddhartha said that people should concentrate on forming good thoughts and good behavior. Siddhartha came to be called the Buddha, which means the "enlightened one."

The Communist governments of East Asia discourage Buddhism and Daoism. The Communist government leaders believe that all religions are old-fashioned and unscientific. Yet Buddhism and Daoism remain important religions in East Asia.

LANGUAGE AND WRITING

Being able to write helped the Chinese to communicate and to unite into an em- pire. The Chinese also introduced their way of writing to their neighbors. The Mongolians and Koreans now have their own systems of writing.

Wherever they live, the people of China can read the same books because written Chinese is the same throughout the country. However, Chinese from different parts of the nation may not be able to understand one another's spoken language. In addition to different languages, China has many dialects. The official dialect is based on that of **Beijing**, the capital.

Chinese writing is not based on an alphabet which represents different sounds, as is English. Chinese writing is based on characters, which represent ideas. The Chinese government recently developed a new system of using our alphabet to write Chinese sounds. This system is called **pinyin**. For example, you may have seen the capital city of China written *Peking*. In pinyin it is now written *Beijing*.

TRADITION, FAMILY, AND LANGUAGE

As you have read, Confucianism, Daoism, and Buddhism have been important belief systems in East Asia. Family loyalty is an important value which has endured in Communist as well as non-Communist countries. The Chinese system of writing has helped to unify their country.

Check Your Reading

1. Why did China's Communist rulers want the Chinese people to break with their past?
2. What is Confucianism?
3. What is Daoism?
4. **THINKING SKILL:** How is the Chinese system of writing different from the alphabet you use?

CHART SKILL: When did pictures of words begin to look like characters?

CHINESE WRITING

Word (in English)	sun	tree	rain
Word (in Pinyin)	ri	mu	yu
Drawing before 1500 B.C.	⊙	米	⑪
Chinese character since 200 B.C.	日	木	雨

LESSON 2

The Economy

READ TO LEARN

Key Vocabulary

aquaculture
iron rice bowl
Pacific Rim

Key People

Deng Xiaoping

Key Places

Hong Kong
Taiwan
South Korea

Read Aloud

I was a farmer like everyone else. Nobody had their own land at that time.

Yin Yengcheng (yung' chung'), who spoke these words, borrowed money to start his own orchard in China in 1978. The Communist government had decided to allow some people to have private plots of land. A few years later Yin's orchard earned a profit, but the village committee would not permit Yin to dig the irrigation pond he needed to increase the size of this orchard. Why? A newspaper article said Yin was the victim of the "red-eyed disease"—jealousy.

In this lesson you will learn why East Asia's economies are changing, some faster than others, and why changes may cause disagreements.

Read for Purpose

1. **WHAT YOU KNOW:** What is the major difference between a communist economic system and capitalism?
2. **WHAT YOU WILL LEARN:** In what ways do most people in East Asia earn their living?

SCARCE LAND

As you read in Lesson 1, in the past many Chinese had been poor, but under the Communists life slowly improved. China's government took over all land and businesses. Like the government of the Soviet Union at that time, China's government made economic decisions for the entire country. The government was also strict about keeping everyone economically equal. It became a serious crime to make a profit or run a private business.

Then in the late 1970s the government discovered that the population was grow-

ing faster than the country's ability to grow food. The government tried to find ways to feed 1 billion people and to slow the growth of the population. That is why it urges families to have only one child, as you read in Lesson 1.

Unfortunately, the country's resources are limited. As you read in Chapter 24, good land is scarce in China. Only about 11 percent of China's land is suitable for farming, and the Chinese are already using every available bit of land. In addition China does not have enough money to buy all the food it needs.

Experts looked for new ways to solve China's food problem. The government started collective farms like those the Soviet Union had. Farmers tried to grow crops on dry land and to raise more cattle in outlying areas. In addition many Chinese dug ponds in order to raise fish. Aquaculture (ak' wə kul chər), or fish farming, is an important source of food throughout East Asia. However, China still needed to have more food.

In the late 1970s China's leader, Deng Xiaoping (dung' shou' ping'), decided to allow a limited amount of private enterprise in China. Some farmers were allowed to work small plots for themselves and to sell their goods at open markets for a profit.

THE SPREAD OF PRIVATE ENTERPRISE

China's new economic program was successful. Villages and towns permitted

This farmer is winnowing rice, or separating the grain from the husks. Rice is a major crop of East Asia.

people to start businesses in their free time. For example, in a small building near the fields, a dozen women might be knitting sweaters for sale or a group might be repairing bicycles and farm machinery for a fee.

Within a few years some Chinese businesses began to take greater risks, often using foreign money and techniques. Many of the private enterprises started in the coastal provinces where people have long been traders. For example, in southern Guangdong Province a small town began its own electric fan company in 1987. Money for the machinery came from a company in Hong Kong. The factory's approximately 2,000 workers produce about 5 million fans a year, which are sold through the company in Hong Kong for a large profit.

In contrast to the fan factory is a giant state-owned computer factory in Hunan Province. Its workers produce only about 5,000 units a year because of frequent shortages of parts and money. The people of Hunan live inland where change is slower. Some Hunanese, who are more traditional in outlook, do not place much value on business as a way to earn a living. Thus they keep prices low and do not compete vigorously for business.

PROBLEMS IN CHANGING THE SYSTEM

Complaints have led the government of China to tighten its control over private enterprises. Some people have much to gain by slowing the program of private enterprise. They include people who gained their jobs as a result of their political beliefs rather than their skills. In these instances factory heads may know little about the type of work that is done in the factory. Also, in the past workers were paid whether or not they worked. This sys-

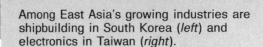
Among East Asia's growing industries are shipbuilding in South Korea (*left*) and electronics in Taiwan (*right*).

tem, called the iron rice bowl because it means a sturdy rice bowl that can be used a long time, gave people lifetime jobs.

Still other Chinese worry about the problems that free enterprise has caused. Some parts of China now have too many goods, while other parts have severe shortages. Many prices have risen steeply. These are only a few of China's problems.

THE PACIFIC RIM

With the exception of Mongolia, China and its East Asian neighbors are among the more than 30 countries of the Pacific Rim. This term refers to all the countries that border the Pacific Ocean. The United States, Canada, and Mexico are Pacific Rim countries. So are Australia, New Zealand, and the countries on the western coasts of Central and South America.

Trade among these countries has grown rapidly. Some of the Pacific Rim countries in Asia have increased their business and trade so much that they are called "economic miracles." Because their workers' wages were low, Hong Kong, Taiwan, and South Korea produced goods more cheaply than other countries. Rising standards of living have increased wages in the "miracle" countries, but this has not diminished their trade.

CONTRASTING ECONOMIES

You have read that in 1949, China's new Communist government started programs to make everyone economically equal. When China's population began to grow faster than the nation's ability to feed its people, its leaders looked for new solutions. One answer was limited private enterprise. Pacific Rim countries Taiwan and South Korea, along with the colony of Hong Kong, have become "economic miracles" by rapidly increasing trade.

Check Your Reading

1. Why did China's government decide to allow limited private enterprise?
2. Give two reasons that the government decided to slow the spread of private enterprise in China.
3. Why do you think Taiwan, Hong Kong, and South Korea are called "economic miracles"?
4. **THINKING SKILL:** List three questions you would ask to find out whether a business in China is privately run.

531

The Government

READ TO LEARN

 Key Vocabulary

autonomous region

 Read Aloud

The glorious history of the People's Republic of China of the past 42 years has proved and will continue to prove that no difficulty can crush or cow the Chinese people. . . . No tempests [disturbances] *will shake their determination to move along the path of building socialism under the leadership of the Communist Party of China.*

These words were spoken by Prime Minister Li Peng in 1991 as he declared that his country would keep a communist government even after the former Soviet Union and the countries of Eastern Europe had ended their commitment to communism.

 Read for Purpose

1. **WHAT YOU KNOW:** What was the role of the Communist party in Eastern Europe and the former Soviet Union?
2. **WHAT YOU WILL LEARN:** What kinds of governments do the countries of East Asia have?

A DIVIDED CHINA

Two internal wars led to the present systems of government in China and Taiwan. The first was a brief revolt that broke out as the emperor's government began to fall apart. The victorious rebels established a republic in 1912.

In the 1920s a civil war began between the Communists and the Nationalists, who had taken control of the government. The Communists won in 1949. Mao Zedong declared that "China has stood up" and was on the road to greatness.

The Nationalists retreated to the island of Taiwan, which had been part of China. Vowing to return to the mainland one day, they formed a non-Communist government-in-exile on Taiwan. They called their government the Republic of China. Until 1971, the United Nations recognized Taiwan's government as the "official China." Taiwan's government is headed by a president and a national assembly. Until 1986, only one political party was allowed.

GOVERNING CHINA

On the mainland the Communists faced a difficult task. In 1949 they had nearly a half billion people to govern, more than any other country at that time. China, renamed the People's Republic of China, was divided into 21 provinces and 5 autonomous regions. The autonomous regions are self-governing areas that are supervised by the central government in Beijing, the capital.

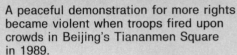
A peaceful demonstration for more rights became violent when troops fired upon crowds in Beijing's Tiananmen Square in 1989.

Most of China's minority groups live in autonomous regions in the sparsely populated north and west. Together, they make up about 5 percent of China's population. One area, Tibet, had been an independent country, but China attacked it and made it an autonomous region in 1950.

The army has remained a powerful force throughout East Asia. In China soldiers have many roles. They may act as police, guides, or even physical laborers. One soldier, Liu Yongshe (lyü' yông' shûr'), says that such "activities not only benefit the people but also remind us that we belong to the people."

The Chinese army played a critical role in 1989. When thousands of students gathered in Beijing to demand more political rights, some of the troops at first refused to break up the crowds because the soldiers considered themselves part of the people. More troops were brought in from other parts of China, and they used force to end the protest. Many students were killed and imprisoned at this time.

ONE-PARTY GOVERNMENT

Officially the head of China's government is the premier. However, the country's real leader is the head of the Communist party. The Chinese Communist party is the only political party allowed in China. Most government officials are members of the Communist party.

China's Communist party and government resemble two pyramids. At the bottom of the party's pyramid are the small Communist cells found in all neighborhoods. At the top of the pyramid is the Central Committee of the Communist Party Congress. The chairman of the Central Committee is the head of the entire party.

In government smaller groups elect people to represent them in larger groups. The largest group is the National People's Congress, the national legislature. It has more than 3,500 members and meets once a year in Beijing. The congress chooses the State Council, which is headed by the premier.

HONG KONG

China claims a number of the areas around it. One of them is Hong Kong. Until 1842 Hong Kong was a relatively unknown island on the southeastern coast of China. In that year the British won from China the right to use Hong Kong as a port. In 1898 the British invaded the mainland and forced the Chinese to cede, or legally give them, all of this area as a British colony for 99 years.

Hong Kong has grown into an important center of world trade and finance. Those who live there have considerable personal freedom. But the governor is appointed by the British government, and there are no elected officials.

Many people have wondered what will happen to Hong Kong when the 99-year lease runs out in 1997. The British have agreed to return the colony to China. Also, the Chinese government has said it would allow Hong Kong to keep its free-market economy. However, some people in Hong Kong cautiously feel that "only the future will tell what will really happen."

MONGOLIA AND KOREA

The homeland of the Mongols was divided into two areas in China: Inner Mongolia and Outer Mongolia. Inner Mongolia remained part of China. But Outer Mongolia gained its independence in 1911. A few years later it became the Mongolian People's Republic with a Communist government and ties to the Soviet Union. When the Soviet Union ended in 1991, Mongolia began to become more democratic.

Like the Chinese on the mainland and Taiwan, the Koreans also have different kinds of government. After World War II Communist troops held the northern part of Korea and formed a Communist system of government. North Korea became the Democratic People's Republic of Korea. South Korea became the Republic of Korea. Most of South Korea's presidents have been military leaders. By 1988 the country, strengthened by economic success, felt less threatened by North Korea, and it held free elections. North and South Korea are members of the United Nations.

CONTRASTING SYSTEMS OF GOVERNMENT

You have read that China and North Korea have governments in which the Communist party makes all important decisions. Taiwan and South Korea have republican forms of government. Democracy has been increasing in Taiwan and South Korea. Hong Kong is a British colony that will be returned to China in 1997.

Skyscrapers line the deep, sheltered harbor of Victoria on Hong Kong Island.

Check Your Reading

1. What role does the army play in China?
2. Explain why Hong Kong is not an independent country.
3. Why did Korea become divided into two countries?
4. **THINKING SKILL:** What caused Taiwan to have a different type of government from that of mainland China?

Reading Political Cartoons

Key Vocabulary
political cartoon
symbol

A cartoon is a drawing that is supposed to make you laugh. Cartoonists draw cartoons to express themselves and amuse others. You can find cartoons in comic books as well as in newspapers and magazines. One kind of cartoon is a **political cartoon**.

A political cartoon is a drawing that focuses attention on important issues and tries to influence public opinion. A cartoon can help you to understand political events. Political cartoonists use visual humor to express their views on an issue. In this lesson you will read about how political cartoonists share their point of view.

Recognizing Symbols

Political cartoonists often use **symbols** as a way to express their ideas. A symbol is a person, an animal, or an object that stands for something beyond itself. For example, a picture of a dove is a symbol of peace. Uncle Sam is a symbol of the United States. Can you think of other symbols for our country? They include the Liberty Bell and the Statue of Liberty.

During the 1800s a cartoonist named Thomas Nast created two symbols that are still used today. He drew an elephant to represent the Republican party and a donkey to stand for the Democratic party. When you look at a political cartoon, look at all the people, animals, and objects in the drawing. To understand a cartoon that

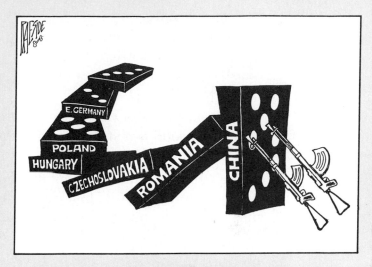

uses symbols, you need to understand what each symbol stands for.

Interpreting a Political Cartoon

Look at the cartoon on this page. A Canadian drew this cartoon about the Chinese government's use of violence to prevent democratic change. The cartoonist has used dominoes to stand for governments of countries. The Eastern European dominoes have fallen over because of democratic change, but the Chinese domino has been propped up with guns. What point do you think the cartoonist is making?

Reviewing the Skill
1. What is a political cartoon?
2. Why do cartoonists use symbols?
3. What symbols can you identify in the cartoon on this page?
4. Do you think the cartoonist approved of what China was doing? Why or why not?
5. Why is it important to be able to understand political cartoons?

Arts and Recreation

READ TO LEARN

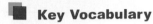

Key Vocabulary

socialist realism
martial arts

Read Aloud

The wise delight in water; the good delight in mountains. The wise move; the good are still. The wise find happiness; the good achieve long life.

The Chinese landscape has inspired the country's poets, painters, and thinkers throughout its history. In the above quote, Confucius explained that mountains and water are not just part of the landscape. They also bring out deep feelings about the proper way to live.

Read to Learn

1. **WHAT YOU KNOW:** Which traditional American sports do you enjoy?
2. **WHAT YOU WILL LEARN:** Which arts and recreation are popular in East Asia today?

BREAKING WITH TRADITION

Before 1949 the arts in China, Korea, and Japan shared some of the same themes and techniques. For example, they shared the same kinds of landscape painting, nature poems, and use of ink and watercolor for painting.

After 1949 China's new leaders said that the arts must "serve the people." In painting, landscapes and other traditional themes had to be replaced by true-to-life views of working people or heroes performing great deeds for the nation. This form of art is called socialist realism. Its purpose is to use the "tremendous energy of the masses" to bring about change. Mongolia and North Korea also make use of socialist realism. Look at the photograph on page 537. It shows a modern Chinese ballet that is performed today.

KEEPING TRADITIONS ALIVE

Western artistic styles and ideas are increasingly popular in Hong Kong, Taiwan, and South Korea. However, traditional arts and crafts continue to thrive. "Window flowers," which are colorful paper cutouts of birds, animals, and flowers, are often hung in windows for good luck. Some people earn their livings at the crafts they learned as children. For example, Kam Wang makes paper dragons in Hong Kong, as his father did in China before 1949.

My father brought our art with him from China. We make lions' heads, dragons, and Chinese lanterns. These objects are used by people to celebrate events in their history or folklore.

Kam's biggest job is making dragon costumes for parades. On holidays, such as the Chinese New Year, many people climb

536

In China, **socialist realism,** has become the main influence in art, dance, and literature.

under the bamboo-and-paper dragon costume and weave and dance through the streets. This holiday falls between January 21 and February 19.

SPORTS AND PHYSICAL FITNESS

Among the sports that are popular in East Asia are swimming, tennis, and table tennis. In China Mao Zedong wanted to end the low value that China's educated classes placed on physical activity. Therefore, he urged people to exercise.

Early in the morning in parks and open spaces, dozens of Chinese move silently in slow, flowing body movements. They are doing taiji quan (tī' jē' chü än'). This form of exercise is sometimes called shadowboxing because people seem to be fighting an unseen enemy.

Martial arts have become very popular. These ancient forms of hand-to-hand combat are methods of self-defense. The best-known martial arts are kung fu of China, karate of Japan, and tae kwan do (tī' kwän' dō') of Korea. These martial arts are practiced to improve physical and mental skills.

ARTS THAT SERVE THE PEOPLE

After the Communists came to power in 1949, Chinese arts were made to "serve the people." The new socialist realist art of China, North Korea, and Mongolia praised workers and heroes of the people. In another break with tradition, China urged its people to exercise and take part in sports. In non-Communist parts of East Asia, both traditional and modern arts continue to flourish.

Check Your Reading

1. Why was the form of art known as socialist realism introduced into China?
2. Name some traditional arts and crafts that are practiced in Hong Kong, Taiwan, and South Korea.
3. List at least three forms of East Asian martial arts.
4. **THINKING SKILL:** What would you do to check the accuracy of what Kam Wang said on page 536?

CHINA AND ITS NEIGHBORS: CULTURAL GEOGRAPHY

 **PEOPLE**

- China's early civilization influenced the cultures of its neighbors

- Major beliefs: Confucianism, Buddhism, and Daoism

- Confucianism taught importance of family loyalty, education, and social harmony

- Communism has changed ways of life in China, Mongolia, and North Korea, but not totally

- Chinese language is written with characters instead of an alphabet

ECONOMY

- Under China's Communist system, the government makes major economic decisions for the whole country

- The capitalist economies of Hong Kong, Taiwan, and South Korea are called "economic miracles"

- China has more than 1 billion people

GOVERNMENT

- Civil war between Communists and Nationalists led to a communist China and a separate government in Taiwan

- China and North Korea: Communist parties are strong

- Taiwan, South Korea: representative democracies under strong leaders

- Hong Kong: rule by British until 1997, when the colony will be returned to China

ARTS AND RECREATION

- Landscape painting and use of ink and watercolor are popular among traditional artists

- Communists replaced much traditional art with socialist realism, art that serves the masses

- Popular East Asian recreations: swimming, table tennis, martial arts

IDEAS TO REMEMBER

- Confucianism, Daoism, and Buddhism remain important beliefs in East Asia, although Communist influence has been strong.
- China has government-run businesses with limited private enterprise, while Hong Kong, Taiwan, and South Korea are newly industrialized.
- China and North Korea are Communist; Taiwan, South Korea, and Mongolia are republics; and Hong Kong will return to China in 1997.
- In the Communist countries of East Asia, many traditional arts have been replaced by socialist realism; elsewhere traditional forms flourish.

REVIEWING VOCABULARY

aquaculture	iron rice bowl
autonomous regions	martial arts
Buddhism	Pacific Rim
Confucianism	pinyin
Daoism	socialist realism

Number a sheet of paper from 1 to 10. Beside each number write the word or term from the above list that best completes the sentence.

1. China's five ____ are self-governing areas that report to Beijing.
2. The ____ are ancient forms of combat used today for self defense.
3. ____ teaches a system of responsibility between family members, government, and people.
4. ____ is a method of raising fish in ponds people have made.
5. All of the East Asian nations except Mongolia are among the more than 30 countries of the ____.
6. ____ is a philosophy that emphasizes accepting the natural flow of life.
7. The ____ system guaranteed lifetime employment to every Chinese person.
8. ____ is a form of art that often portrays people performing heroic deeds on behalf of the "masses."
9. The modern system of writing Chinese words in our alphabet is called ____.
10. ____ teaches that to avoid suffering, one must get rid of one's selfish desires.

REVIEWING FACTS

1. What are the names of the five countries and one British colony of East Asia? Which of these countries is the largest?
2. What are Chinese characters? How has pinyin changed the way Chinese words are written in our alphabet?
3. In which part of China is private enterprise most developed? In which part is it least developed?
4. How is the Chinese Communist party different from political parties in the West?
5. How does socialist realism differ from traditional forms of art in East Asia?

WRITING ABOUT MAIN IDEAS

1. **Writing a Paragraph:** You have read that one of the main goals of the Chinese Communists was "to make all people in China equal." Write a paragraph discussing to what extent that goal has been achieved.
2. **Writing Lists:** In the past, under the iron rice bowl system, all Chinese people were paid whether or not they worked. Write two lists, one of advantages and one of disadvantages of such a system.
3. **Writing About Perspectives:** Many people in the Pacific Rim have experienced great changes in their standard of living. Imagine that you live in one of the Asian Pacific Rim countries. Write about how the changing economy has changed your life in both pleasant and unpleasant ways.

BUILDING SKILLS: READING POLITICAL CARTOONS

1. What is a political cartoon?
2. Why do cartoonists use symbols?
3. Look at the political cartoon on page 535. What do you think the cartoonist is trying to say?
4. Why is it important to be able to understand political cartoons?

CHAPTER 27

JAPAN

FOCUS

Cooperation and harmony help us work together on things we consider most important.

This quote by a Japanese worker expresses an important Japanese attitude. In this chapter you will learn about many of the beliefs and customs that have made the Japanese way of life a unique one.

The People

READ TO LEARN

Key Vocabulary

homogeneous   samurai
Shinto

Key Places

Tokyo

Read Aloud

Use every moment of every day without wasting it.

Tsuneko Tashiro, a Japanese schoolteacher, lives by the saying above. Although it is her own personal saying, it could well be a motto describing the Japanese people. By working very hard for long hours, the Japanese have turned Japan into a bustling, thriving land. In this lesson you will read about the ways of life that made this possible.

Read for Purpose

1. **WHAT YOU KNOW:** What are Confucianism and Buddhism?
2. **WHAT YOU WILL LEARN:** What distinct ways of life have the people of Japan developed?

AN ISLAND NATION

You read in Chapter 24 that Japan is a group of islands off the eastern coast of China. Japan has hundreds of islands, but most people live on four main islands. They are: the largest island Honshu (hon' shü), Shikoku (shi kō' kü), Kyushu (kū' shü), and the least populated one of the four—Hokkaido (ho kī' dō).

Japan's island location kept it safe from invaders. Yet the Japanese were close enough to their Asian neighbors to borrow new ideas and ways of living. During the 600s and 700s the Japanese began to eat with chopsticks and write with Chinese characters. They read about the teachings of Confucius and adopted the Buddhist religion from Korean and Chinese monks.

The Portuguese arrived in Japan in the 1500s. At first the Japanese welcomed these and other Europeans. However, fear-ing that foreign missionaries and traders were gaining too much power in Japan, the country's leaders tried to cut the islands off from the rest of the world. In 1638 the government passed a law forbidding all Japanese citizens from building large ships or going on long voyages. All for-eigners, except the Dutch, were also ex-pelled from the country. This closed-door policy lasted until 1853, when Commo-dore Matthew Perry of the United States Navy sailed into Tokyo Bay and demanded that Japan open its ports to other nations of the world.

Japanese culture continued to develop during this period of isolation. Some ideas from China, Korea, and the West were studied and adopted into the Japanese culture. As you will read, the Japanese bal-anced new and traditional ways of life.

THE PEOPLE AND THEIR BELIEFS

Would you say that most people in your country look and act as you do? Some Japanese would answer yes. The Japanese consider themselves to be a homogeneous group. That is, their appearances and behavior are somewhat similar. Almost all Japanese belong to the same ethnic group. They speak the same language, share the same history, and have similar values.

If you were to ask Japanese people about their religion, many would say that they are not very religious. Then they would probably tell you that they take part in both Shinto (shin' tō) and Buddhist celebrations. Shinto is the oldest of Japan's religions. Shinto followers believe that spirits, or *kami* (kä' mē), dwell in all things in nature, such as mountains, trees, streams, lakes, and rocks.

Most people in Japan are Shinto, Buddhist, and Confucian—all at once. They accept Confucian ideas of an orderly society and duty to family and country. Yet they also like the peaceful beliefs of Buddhism. They combine many beliefs into an outlook on life that is uniquely Japanese.

MEMBERS OF THE GROUP

Some of the values that have developed in Japan are very different from those in Europe or the United States. For example, unlike most Westerners, many Japanese believe that society is more important than any one person. They see themselves as members of a group that makes gains together, rather than as unique individuals striving to get ahead.

At an early age children in Japan are taught loyalty and respect for the common good. They learn that it is important to get along with the group. "A nail that sticks out," goes an old Japanese saying, "must be hammered down."

MANNERS, DUTY, AND LOYALTY

In a land where agreement among people is so important, there is a deep respect for authority and order. Both family members and schoolteachers teach children that everyone has a certain position in society. As a result, some people think the

The *Matsuri* Festival (*right*), celebrating the founding of the city of Kyoto, is a popular Shinto festival. Japanese Children's Day (*left*) is an official holiday.

542

Japanese may be the most polite people in the world. Students bow to teachers, employees bow to their bosses, and friends bow to one another.

Over the centuries the Japanese have worked out a thousand rules of correct behavior. Responsibilities have become very important in this system. People are taught that they have special duties to their families and their leaders.

The idea that every person owes a debt to his or her family is an important part of Japanese culture. To fail to do one's duty causes a person to "lose face." The whole family is shamed and disgraced when one member fails to do his or her duty.

How did such traditions begin? For hundreds of years warriors called samurai (sam′ ů rī) ruled Japan. Samurai were taught to feel a great sense of duty to their families, their rulers, and to their country. Over the years these values have been passed on to other groups.

TOKYO, A CROWDED CITY

Tokyo, the capital of Japan, has one of the largest populations of any city in the world. Together with other nearby cities, Tokyo is part of a megalopolis. You may recall that a megalopolis is an area with so many cities close together that they seem to form one large city.

Most of this megalopolis is densely populated. Often the trains that people ride to work are so crowded that railroad employees have to push people into the cars to make them fit. Because so many other people drive automobiles, traffic jams are a common problem in Tokyo.

A SEPARATE PEOPLE

As the political map on this page shows, Japan stands apart from East Asia. In this lesson you have read how the Japanese developed a distinctive culture. The peo-

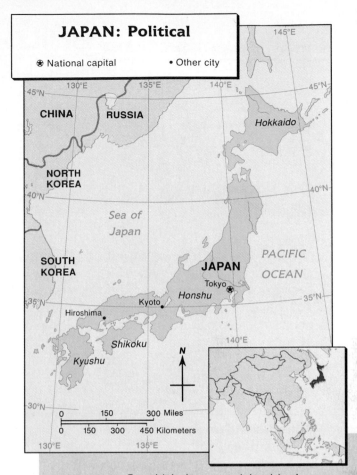

MAP SKILL: On which Japanese island is the city of Kyoto located?

ple of Japan are a mostly homogeneous group whose members share the same basic beliefs, cultural values, and manners. As one Japanese writer explained, "Only when everybody acts the same do individual differences become clear."

Check Your Reading

1. Why did the Japanese develop a culture that was different from those of the rest of Asia?
2. What are some types of belief that many Japanese share?
3. Why is Japan considered to be a nation of "team players"?
4. THINKING SKILL: State one fact and two opinions that you read about in this lesson.

543

Writing a Summary

Key Vocabulary

summary
topic sentence

This book contains information on many subjects. On every page and in every paragraph you have found different facts. You have read about the geography, the economy, the culture, and the government of many different regions in the world. Sometimes it is a challenge to remember all the interesting things that you are reading about.

What Is a Summary?

A good way to help you to remember what you have read is to write a short summary. A summary briefly states the main ideas contained in a piece of writing. Writing a summary helps you to sort out the most important information.

To prepare for writing a summary look for the topic sentences, or the sentences that contain the main ideas. First, read through the entire selection and write down the topic sentences. Often a topic sentence is the first sentence in a paragraph. However, it may also be in the middle or at the end of a paragraph. Notice that the rest of the sentences give supporting details.

When you write a short summary, you will be concerned only with main ideas. In a longer summary, you might want to include some important details.

Summarizing the Lesson

To write a summary of Lesson 1, which is about the Japanese people, first read through the whole lesson. It will help to pay close attention to the bold headings within the lesson. Headings help you to figure out what each section is about. Headings also provide an outline of the main ideas of the lesson.

For example, the second heading in Lesson 1 tells you that one of the main ideas in your summary will have to do with the people and their beliefs. You can find it on page 542. Write down the most important ideas in each section.

As you read each section, ask yourself these questions: "What is the main idea of this paragraph? Which are supporting details?" When you have finished, write a summary using your own words.

Reviewing the Skill

Read the paragraph below. Then write a summary of the article in two or three sentences.

Not long after my arrival [in Japan], I was surprised again by the odd behavior of some Japanese children. They had boxes or jars in one hand, and with the other they were trying to catch some invisible creature. Then I heard the sound of the cicada [an insect] and I realized what they were after. Then, too, I caught my first glimpse of one, held between the thumb and forefinger of a boy. He held it with a mixture of tenderness and unconcern, before putting it in his box with the rest of his crawling collection.

544

The Economy

READ TO LEARN

 **Key People**

Akio Morita

Read Aloud

A Japanese businessman named Akio Morita visited West Germany in the early 1950s. He often stopped to buy ice cream in a small neighborhood shop. One day a waiter told him that the decorative little umbrella stuck in his ice cream came from Japan.

As Morita looked around the ice cream shop, he noticed that the only items with a "Made in Japan" label were the paper umbrellas. He believed that Japan could export better products than the one he saw.

At the time Akio Morita headed a small Japanese company named Sony. Today Sony is a huge electronics company, and Japan is the second-largest industrial power in the world. In this lesson you will read how this dramatic change came about.

Read for Purpose

1. **WHAT YOU KNOW:** Which Japanese goods have you bought most recently?
2. **WHAT YOU WILL LEARN:** What factors helped create Japan's recent economic miracle?

JAPAN'S ECONOMIC MIRACLE

You read in Chapter 11 that many German factories were destroyed at the end of World War II. The same was true in Japan. Most of Japan's cities were shattered by American bombs, including two atomic bombs that were dropped on the cities of Hiroshima and Nagasaki.

Japan built itself into a major industrial power in the years following the war. Today Japanese businesses produce goods and services that make up about 11 percent of the world's economic output. Only the United States produces more. Japanese products now include everything from calculators, computers, videocas-

sette players, and microchips to motorcycles, automobiles, and grand pianos, not just the paper umbrellas you read about at the beginning of this lesson.

The growth of Japan from a ruined land into a modern, prosperous nation has been called a miracle. What makes this development so remarkable is that Japan has very few natural resources. Every year the country must buy most of its oil, iron ore, copper, and lumber from overseas. "We are very different from the rest of the world," explained one Japanese businessperson. "Our only natural resource is the hard work of our people."

QUALITY AND TECHNOLOGY

Many things help to explain the success, shown on the graph on this page. One is the demand for excellence. When asked why Sony can sell so much in the United States, Akio Morita replied that there are many reasons. But the first three reasons are "quality, quality, and quality."

When they do a job, the Japanese try to do it efficiently and artistically. That means not wasting time or effort while making the finest products possible. One Japanese writer explained:

> [W]atching a Japanese assembly line is like watching a ballet performance; every body movement has been worked out to achieve the most efficiency. . . . Everything is calculated to allow the worker to accomplish the most amount of work in one continuous movement.

Another reason for Japan's economic success has been its ability to adapt the technologies of other countries. After World War II hundreds of Japanese businesspeople came to the United States to observe America's best factories. Then they returned home to improve Japan's industries based upon what they had seen.

The Japanese have been careful since then to replace old or out-of-date equipment so that their industries work efficiently.

One kind of technology that the Japanese have used effectively is robots that perform various jobs in factories. Many Japanese factories have installed computer-controlled machines that do some jobs faster and better than a human could. Japan also builds robots to export to other countries.

By 1980 Japan had become the leading producer of automobiles in the world. Japan has also become a world leader in the manufacture of iron, steel, chemicals, and electronic equipment like computers and radios.

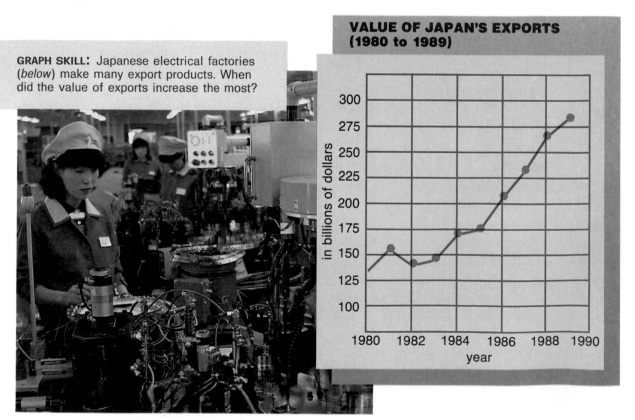

GRAPH SKILL: Japanese electrical factories (*below*) make many export products. When did the value of exports increase the most?

VALUE OF JAPAN'S EXPORTS (1980 to 1989)

in billions of dollars

year

LOYAL, SKILLED WORKERS

An industrial economy needs highly skilled, educated workers. Japan has plenty of them. In Japan all children must go to school for nine years. After junior high school, students take exams that determine which high school they will attend. It is not uncommon for students to spend nearly every waking hour either doing regular homework or studying for the exams. Still, 94 percent of Japan's teenagers enter high school and almost all of them graduate.

Getting into one of the best universities in Japan means passing the most difficult exams of all. Throughout the country, students attend private "cram schools" in addition to regular schools to help them pass these tests with high marks. In some cases students must pass an exam to get into cram school.

If a person goes to work for a large company in Japan, he or she receives extensive training. Many businesses even send employees to foreign universities for additional education.

Large companies find that it pays to spend time and money training workers because few people in these companies change jobs. Once they are hired, workers are part of the company family. Many people expect to work their whole lives for just one company.

In some businesses the workday begins with group exercise and company songs and slogans. Large companies have gyms, swimming pools, and other recreational facilities for their workers. Such training and group activities have made the Japanese work force both highly skilled and loyal. "All of us, every one of us in Japan," one worker said, "believe that the rise or fall of our organization rests on the individual shoulders of each one of us." Each individual is important to the team.

Japanese students study hard to acquire good handwriting. The people in this picture have entered a writing contest.

A STRONG ECONOMY

As you have read, Japan is the second-largest industrial power in the world. After World War II the country turned to technology and quality to modernize its industries. Japan's success also rests with its workers. They are educated, hard working, eager, and reliable.

Check Your Reading

1. Name three factors that contributed to Japan's economic success.
2. What do many Japanese students attend besides regular school?
3. How do Japanese companies maintain worker loyalty?
4. **THINKING SKILL:** From your reading of the lesson, what three factors would you select to explain Japan's economic success? Explain your choice.

Should Japan's Trade Policies Be More Open?

During the last 50 years Japan has demonstrated amazing growth in technological development and manufacturing capacity. All over the world customers buy Japanese cameras, television sets, radios, and other products. In the United States the popularity of Japanese automobiles has increased their sales to about 20 percent of the United States automobile market.

In the 1980s, however, a number of disputes arose between Japan and its trading partners, the United States in particular. The disputes arose because the Japanese maintained a system of quotas and tariffs to limit the amount of goods Japan imports from other countries. Critics say that the Japanese are allowed to sell their goods freely in the United States, but foreign companies wishing to market goods in Japan must fight their way through many difficult barriers.

The Japanese view the issue differently. They say their trade organization, the Ministry of International Trade and Industry (MITI), simply coordinates business activity, protects emerging industries, and studies the U.S. marketplace. Japanese business leaders believe that their success today is a result of their dedication to advanced technology, competitive quality, performance, and design. Which side do you think is right?

POINT ☆

Japan's Trade Policies Are Fair

In an interview, Akio Morita, a leading Japanese industrialist, responded to critics of Japanese policy.

Americans and Europeans do import more Japanese goods than they export to Japan. But that has nothing to do with unfairness; it is simply the result of the free play of the market. To treat us like a closed country is scandalous. Consider the automobile industry: American companies manufactured 250,000 cars in Japan last year, only to sell them to customers in the U.S. They have never really tried to sell us their cars. And the recent agreement to increase Japanese imports of American agricultural goods is not going to bridge the gap. To do that, every Japanese would have to eat several tons of beef and oranges a year.

Japan is the leading country in industrial research and development. . . . Many people think that competitiveness is just a matter of prices, and there they are making a serious mistake. Competitiveness depends on many criteria. Even if it costs a bit more, customers will buy a Japanese brand for its quality, performance, and design.

• What reasons does Akio Morita give to support the idea that Japan's trade policies are fair?

COUNTERPOINT ☆

Japan's Trade Policies Are Unfair

An article in *Fortune* magazine summarizes the point of view held by many American businesspeople.

The U.S. and Japan recently broke off talks aimed at increasing American beef and citrus exports to Japan. . . . American negotiators had demanded an end to all quotas. The Japanese agreed to that, but insisted on the right to impose variable duties. . . . Earlier this year renewal of a pact calling for technological cooperation . . . stalled because the Americans wanted stronger assurances that Japanese technology would be readily available to American scientists.

Robert Strauss, a former trade negotiator with Japan, made these comments.

There [is] no question that Japan must change many of their practices. Japan simply has a terrible "buy Japan" procurement [buying] policy. . . . The Kansai Airport [where Japan has blocked American companies from bidding on an $8 billion project] is a perfect example. The way they have behaved by not buying foreign telecommunications equipment is another example.

• What reasons do some United States leaders give for saying that Japan's trade policies are unfair?

UNDERSTANDING THE POINT/COUNTERPOINT

1. Which side do you think presents the stronger argument? Explain your answer.
2. What are some other groups that might have an opinion on this issue? What opinion might each of them have?
3. Do you think that there is a way for the two sides to reach a compromise? Explain.

The Government

READ TO LEARN

Key Vocabulary

Diet

Key People

Akihito

Read Aloud

On January 1, 1946, Japan's Emperor Hirohito told his people that he did not rule by divine right. His power came from the will of the people, he said, not from God.

Today the Japanese honor their emperor as a symbol of the country. The present emperor, the son of Hirohito, is the one hundred twenty-fifth member of his family to act as emperor of Japan. The family has been serving the country for more than 1,500 years. Think about how long this time is and the great store of tradition it suggests. As you read this lesson, you will see how Japan's government successfully blends a very old monarchy with present-day democracy.

Read for Purpose

1. **WHAT YOU KNOW:** What is a constitutional monarchy?
2. **WHAT YOU WILL LEARN:** How is the Japanese government organized?

ROLE OF THE EMPEROR

For centuries emperors in Japan held no real power. Government leaders and military chiefs ran the nation. The emperor was important to his people mainly as a symbol of the past and of the nation's accomplishments. After World War II, Japan officially became a constitutional monarchy. In 1989, Akihito became emperor after his father, Hirohito, died.

Emperor Akihito remains a symbol of the country today. He presides at ceremonies and greets important visitors. By continuing to live in Tokyo's Imperial Palace, the emperor also serves as a reminder to his people of the strong link between Japan's traditional government and the newer democratic government that was formed after World War II.

THE JAPANESE CONSTITUTION

At the end of World War II, the United States forced Japan to accept a new kind of government. It ordered a group of Americans and Japanese to write a constitution forming a democracy for Japan.

In many ways the Japanese Constitution of 1947 resembles the Constitution of the United States. It guarantees free speech and a free press. Japan is one of the few countries in East Asia that permits its citizens to speak out against the government without fear of punishment.

The Japanese constitution has some unique features. It states that "the Japanese people forever renounce war as a sovereign right of the nation and the threat or use of force as a means of settling international disputes." A sovereign right is a nation's right to act independently. Japan's defense force is not used outside of the country.

THE DIET

Japan's government is also different from that of the United States in other ways. For example, although a democracy, Japan has a parliamentary system of government, much like that of Great Britain. Its legislature, called the Diet, makes all laws for the country. As in Great Britain, the leader of the majority party in the legislature becomes prime minister, or the leader of the government. The prime minister selects a cabinet to give advice.

Until 1989 all Japanese prime ministers and top government officials had been men. In that year two women joined the cabinet. Although their constitution gives women equal rights, the Japanese by custom have not encouraged women to become political leaders.

GOVERNMENT AND BUSINESS

Since the 1950s the government of Japan has actively supported business. The main government agency dealing with foreign trade is the Ministry of International Trade and Industry (MITI). After World War II MITI took the lead in urging Japanese industries to modernize.

MITI doesn't just collect facts and give suggestions. It pushes and prods businesses to follow its advice. In addition MITI helps companies obtain bank loans and contributes money for research. One example of MITI's leadership and support over the last 30 years is the help it has given to make the country's electronics industry a world leader.

A CONSTITUTIONAL MONARCHY

The government of Japan is a mixture of the traditional and modern. In this lesson you have read that the country blends ancient Japanese traditions in a Western-style democracy. At the end of World War II, the government of Japan was completely changed. It adopted a constitution that made the country a parliamentary democracy headed by the emperor. Unlike most of East Asia, Japan has free elections, free speech, and a free press.

Among the important duties of Emperor Akihito and Empress Michiko of Japan is making goodwill visits to other nations.

 Check Your Reading

1. How did the government of Japan change after World War II?
2. Name two unique features of Japan's present constitution.
3. How does the government help business in Japan?
4. **THINKING SKILL:** Classify the provisions of Japan's constitution into two groups. Explain your classification.

Arts and Recreation

READ TO LEARN

Key Vocabulary

sumo wrestling

Read Aloud

Midnight full of stars . . .
dim cherry-petals float on
rice-paddy waters

A famous Japanese poet named Buson wrote these lines over 200 years ago. They are an example of the country's most popular form of poetry, haiku (hī′ kü). Like other types of Japanese art, haiku look simple but are difficult to create. Each short poem reflects a respect for the marvels of nature as well as for traditional forms of art.

Read for Purpose

1. WHAT YOU KNOW: What kind of painting was popular in China?

2. WHAT YOU WILL LEARN: How do the people of Japan combine traditional and new styles in their arts and leisure activities?

ART AS A WAY OF LIFE

In the poem above, Buson sketches a picture of the delicate cherry blossom, a flower admired by the ancient samurai warriors. The cherry blossom not only signals the coming of spring, it also reminds us that nature's beauty is fleeting. To enjoy the flower, a person must stop and look now, before the blossom withers and dies.

The Japanese have long valued "catching the moment." They fill their everyday lives with as much beauty as possible. For example, traditional Japanese food is served in a way that makes it look as good as it tastes, with colors and shapes chosen to balance one another. In school students study both writing and the ancient art of calligraphy, or beautiful writing. Because

the Japanese believe that the way in which a person writes is important, students study calligraphy from third grade through ninth grade.

In their homes the Japanese try to make room for beauty in many detailed ways. Few homes are without a tasteful display of flowers. A Japanese flower arrangement does not use big bunches of many blossoms. Instead it has only a few parts. One might be a twisted branch or a cluster of leaves. The art of flower arranging has been handed down from generation to generation by the Japanese.

The people of Japan also love to be outdoors surrounded by beautiful flowers and trees. In a nation where living space is scarce, small spaces are used for gardens.

552

In some of the most famous Japanese gardens, rocks are an important part of the design. For example, large stones may be surrounded by rounded pebbles that have been raked to resemble waves or other kinds of designs.

TRADITIONAL SPORTS

In sports as in art, the Japanese try to preserve and cherish their past. Yasuhiro Yamashita (yä sü hē′ rō yä mä shē′ tə) is an athlete who practices a traditional sport called judo. Judo and karate are two kinds of martial arts, or methods of unarmed fighting similar to those you read about in China. Judo uses balance and weight to knock over opponents. Karate uses blows struck with the hands and feet. You will read more about the martial arts tradition in the lesson on pages 554–557.

To perform another of Japan's traditional sports, sumo wrestling, a person should weigh about 300 pounds (136 kg). In sumo wrestling two enormously strong players try to force each other to touch the ground with any part of the body other than the feet. However, sumo wrestlers may not pull hair, kick, or punch their opponents during the match.

BASEBALL AND GOLF

While the Japanese love traditional sports, they have also adopted sports from other countries. Among the most popular of these are baseball, golf, and skiing. The Japanese adopted baseball from the United States in 1873.

Golf is a Western sport that has become popular in Japan more recently. But in a country where level land is scarce, it is very costly to play. People in Tokyo have spent up to $900,000 to buy a membership in a golf club. Even as members, they may have to call weeks ahead for a starting time because courses are heavily booked.

Grand champion Wajima stands in a traditional pose of Japan's sumo wrestlers.

TRADITIONAL AND MODERN

Japan's traditional arts are still popular. Haiku poetry is hundreds of years old. As you have read, the Japanese believe that art should be part of everyday life. Thus flower arranging, calligraphy, and gardening are practiced.

Today the Japanese enjoy such traditional sports as karate and sumo wrestling along with baseball, golf, and other Western sports.

 Check Your Reading

1. Name two ways that the Japanese include art in their everyday lives.
2. How might a Japanese person combine a haiku with the art of calligraphy?
3. What is sumo wrestling?
4. **THINKING SKILL:** In what ways might Japanese flower arrangements be different today from those of the past? In what ways might they be the same?

MARTIAL ARTS:
More Than Just Fighting

by Diana Reische

You just read about how the people of Japan have adopted several sports from other countries, such as baseball and golf. You also read about sports that date from earlier periods in Japan's history, such as sumo wrestling and karate. As you read this lesson, think about the tradition of the martial (mär' shəl) arts and their significance to Japanese culture.

LEARNING A MARTIAL ART

Classes are over for the day at your Japanese school, but you do not leave the building. Instead you hurry to the gym, where your after-school club is meeting. You and the other club members are there to practice one of Japan's traditional martial arts. A martial art is a system of fighting and exercise that

stresses self-defense. The goal of such a system is not just winning, but improving yourself through training and self-control.

When your teacher arrives, you bow courteously. So do the other students. Why? Courtesy and discipline are part of learning any martial art. "If you do not master yourself," your teacher always says, "you cannot hope to improve."

A JUDO CLUB

Your club practices judo. This modern sport grew out of an older, rougher

Japanese martial art called jujitsu (jü jit′ sü). Jujitsu is a system of hand-to-hand fighting that includes kicks, throws, and other dangerous moves. How did judo emerge from this rough-and-tumble style?

It was invented by a man named Jigoro Kano (kä′nō) in the late 1800s. As a boy, Kano was sickly, and his parents sent him to study with jujitsu masters to make him stronger. Kano became an expert in this style of fighting. However, as an adult and educator, he wanted to develop a less dangerous sport that could be taught to schoolchildren. Kano called this new martial art *judo*, which means "the gentle or flexible way."

Kano borrowed many moves from jujitsu for his new sport, but he left out the chops and strikes that could seriously harm someone. No hitting, striking, or kicking was allowed. And as its name suggests, judo encouraged a flexible form of fighting. This flexibility has been compared to that of a willow branch heavy with snow. Because the branch bends, it saves itself from breaking under the snow's weight. Yet the branch is not weak. A judo expert learns to use the force of an attacker *against* the attacker: to bend with that force, rather than being broken by it.

Jigoro Kano invented the art of judo.

A WAY TO IMPROVEMENT

The word judo ends in *do*, which means "path" or "way" in Japanese. When you study judo you learn much more than how to defend yourself. You follow a specific training "path" toward improving yourself. Jigoro Kano set down precise moves for every judo fall, throw, lock, or hold.

Yet Japanese martial arts consist of much more than simply learning moves. For inner control, the training draws on a special form of Buddhism, which you read about in Chapter 26. For calming the mind, it draws on yoga, the Hindu method of exercise and meditation that you read about in Chapter 25. And for its code of honor, martial arts training draws on Japan's samurai past.

THE SAMURAI TRADITION

You have already read about the samurai—the great warriors who ruled Japan centuries ago. Their code of honor still influences every Japanese martial art. A samurai was forbidden to win a fight by using dirty tricks or dishonesty. When a modern-day martial arts teacher tells a classroom of students to always perform "with honor and style," the teacher is echoing samurai values.

Women, too, formed part of the samurai tradition. While warriors were away fighting, Japanese women sometimes had to defend themselves from roving bandits. The women trained with weapons that the warriors had left at home because they were too difficult to carry on horseback. One of these was called the *naginata* (nä gē nä′ tä). This weapon consisted of a long wooden shaft with a blade on one end and an iron knob on the other. A woman skilled in using the naginata might fight off a more powerful attacker using a short sword.

Fighting with a naginata remains a popular sport with Japanese women today. In the modern sport, however, the emphasis is on speed and grace, and instead of a blade, the modern weapon contains nothing more dangerous than a curved bamboo tip.

KARATE

While judo, naginata, and many other arts of self-defense emerged from Japan's warrior traditions, one popular martial art came from outside Japan. In the 1600s the Japanese ruled the island of Okinawa (ō kə nä′ wə). Since the Japanese rulers did not allow the Okinawans to carry weapons, the islanders needed to develop a way to protect themselves.

Their solution was to borrow a Chinese fighting style. In China monks often had to defend themselves from bandits. However, they had no wish to carry weapons. For this purpose, a group of monks invented a fighting style called "temple boxing," which involved only the use of bare hands. The Okinawans modified this Chinese style of weaponless fighting into karate, which means "empty hand."

Karate remained an Okinawan art for many years. In the early 1900s, however, a karate expert named Gichin Funakoshi (fü nə kō′ shē) was invited to demonstrate this martial art at the Japanese emperor's palace. The slim, small-boned Funakoshi, who was only 5′1″ (1.52 m), won match after match against much bigger opponents. His fame spread, and when he opened a karate school in Tokyo, students from all over Japan came to attend.

Since then, karate has become popular all over the world. There may be a karate school in your city or town. Many different styles of this sport have developed over the years. Yet Funakoshi's words still sum up the ideals of karate and other Japanese martial arts:

As a mirror's polished surface reflects whatever stands before it and a quiet valley carries even small sounds, so must the student of karate render his mind empty of selfishness and wickedness in an effort to react appropriately toward anything he may encounter.

How do martial arts such as judo, naginata, and karate combine old and new aspects of Japanese culture?

JAPAN: CULTURAL GEOGRAPHY

 PEOPLE

- Japan has a nearly homogeneous population

- Many Japanese believe in Shinto, Confucianism, and Buddhism
- The group is considered to be more important than the individual
- Important values: respect for authority and order, duty to family and rulers

ECONOMY

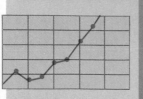

- Japan is the second most productive industrial power in the world
- Few natural resources except for the hard work of its people

- Reasons for economic success: efficiency, quality control, ability to adapt foreign technologies, extensive research to improve products, skilled and loyal workers

GOVERNMENT

- Emperor: an important symbol of the country

- The constitution guarantees the rights of citizens; prohibits the formation of armed forces, except a defensive force
- Parliamentary system includes the Diet (legislature)
- Government supports business

ARTS AND RECREATION

- Popular traditional arts: haiku (poetry), calligraphy, flower arranging

- Art is thought to be an important part of daily life

- Favorite sports: judo, karate, sumo wrestling, baseball, golf

IDEAS TO REMEMBER

- Many of the members of Japan's homogeneous population share common beliefs, values, and customs.
- Japan has become the second-largest industrial nation in the world with the help of its hard-working, well-educated, loyal workers.
- Japan is a constitutional democracy in which the emperor serves as a symbol of the country.
- Traditional arts and sports, such as haiku and sumo wrestling, exist side by side with adopted recreations, such as golf and baseball.

REVIEWING VOCABULARY

Diet

Shinto

homogeneous

sumo wrestling

samurai

Number a sheet of paper from 1 to 5. Beside each number write the word or term from the above list that best matches the definition.

1. A Japanese religious belief that spirits dwell in nature
2. A sport in which participants try to force each other to touch the ground
3. Japanese warriors who were taught to feel a great sense of duty
4. A word that applies to people who share many of the same characteristics
5. The legislative body that makes all national laws in Japan

REVIEWING FACTS

1. Name four things that the Japanese borrowed from their Asian neighbors.
2. How has the samurai tradition influenced Japanese culture?
3. Name two ways in which the Japanese express their sense of loyalty and respect for the common good.
4. What percentage of total world output is contributed by Japan? Which country is ahead of Japan in industrial production?
5. How did Japan's electronic industry become first in the world?
6. Why is education an important part of Japan's economic success?
7. How does the Japanese sense of loyalty help companies in Japan?
8. How was democracy forced on Japan?

9. Why have few Japanese women achieved high positions in government despite the equality given to women in the constitution?
10. How does the Japanese attitude toward art differ from that of Americans and Europeans?

WRITING ABOUT MAIN IDEAS

1. **Writing a Paragraph:** You have read that Japan's homogeneous society is one of the country's key characteristics. Write a paragraph comparing Japanese society with American society.
2. **Writing a Poem:** Haiku is a short, vivid, 3-line poem containing only 17 syllables that often deals with some aspect of nature. Write a haiku that expresses something that is important to you.
3. **Writing About Perspectives:** Imagine that you are away from home, enrolled away in a "cram school." Write a letter to your parents describing your experiences at the school.

BUILDING SKILLS: WRITING A SUMMARY

1. What is a summary?
2. What is a topic sentence?
3. Read Lesson 2 in this chapter. Find 5 topic sentences in the lesson.
4. Use the topic sentences to help you to write a summary of Lesson 2.
5. When might it be helpful to know how to write a summary?

CHAPTER 28

SOUTHEAST ASIA

FOCUS

Wherever you go in Thailand, you are sure to see men in long robes of yellow-orange, ochre, or brown. Their heads and eyebrows are shaven clean, they are barefoot or wearing simple sandals, and often they are carrying small bowls.

Writer Sylvia McNair describes the traditional appearance of Buddhists monks in her book about Thailand. Today many young people continue to study to become monks in Southeast Asia. But life is changing in this part of the world, and countries such as Thailand are learning to balance respect for tradition with the need to change.

The People

READ TO LEARN

Key Places

Southeast Asia   Jakarta

Read Aloud

Tsang Su Yin (dzäng′ sü′ yin′) works for a newspaper in Singapore. Like many of the people who live in this small Southeast Asian country, she was born elsewhere.

"My mother came from the Malay Peninsula," she explains. She also says that during World War II, when the Japanese army invaded the peninsula, her family fled south to India.

"In Bombay, in India," continues Tsang Su Yin, "Mom met and married Dad, who had arrived earlier from Hong Kong. My brother was born in Bombay, and so was I."

Many of the people of Southeast Asia have been forced to relocate at various times. In this lesson you will read about these people, as well as their ways of life.

Read for Purpose

1. **WHAT YOU KNOW:** How did Japan's separation from mainland Asia influence its people and their culture?
2. **WHAT YOU WILL LEARN:** Why has Southeast Asia always been a great crossroads?

CROSSROADS OF SOUTHERN AND EASTERN ASIA

Like the Middle East, Southeast Asia is one of the great crossroads of the world. Southeast Asia separates India and China and stretches about 3,800 miles (6,114 km) from the western border of Myanmar (formerly known as Burma) southeast through Irian Jaya, the western part of the island of New Guinea. It is made up mostly of peninsulas and archipelagoes and includes ten countries: Brunei, Myanmar, Cambodia (formerly known as Kampuchea), Indonesia, Laos, Malaysia, the Philippines, Singapore, Thailand (formerly called Siam), and Vietnam.

THE FIRST SETTLERS IN SOUTHEAST ASIA

Southeast Asia has many different peoples and ways of life. Over thousands of years people and ideas have been introduced there from nearby places.

Given the area's location, it is not surprising that the greatest influences have come from China and India. The first settlers came to Southeast Asia many thousands of years ago during the Ice Age. They were related to the early peoples of Australia and the Pacific.

The next group to arrive were the Malays. They came from Southwest China about 2,500 years ago. These skilled sail-

561

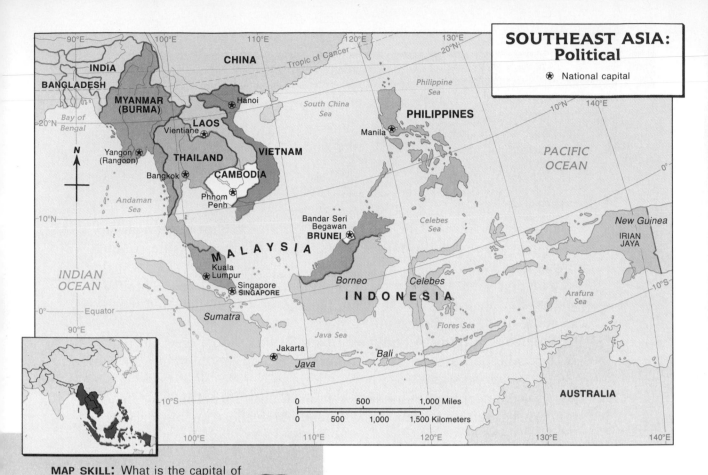

MAP SKILL: What is the capital of Thailand? The children shown here live in the mountains of Vietnam.

ors used the Southeast Asian seas, shown on the map above, as a great sea route.

NEARBY INFLUENCES

The Malays moved farther south when later settlers arrived from China and India. Some people, such as the Vietnamese from southeastern China, brought Chinese ideas and ways of life to Southeast Asia. For example, the Vietnamese wrote with Chinese characters and had adopted the Chinese system of government. The ancestors of the people of Myanmar, Thailand, and Laos, also came from southern China.

During this time merchants from India settled in Burma and the Malay Peninsula. There they introduced soil irrigation and the building of harbors.

Eventually the largest and strongest ethnic groups lived along the river deltas and other lowlands. Small ethnic groups lived in the hills.

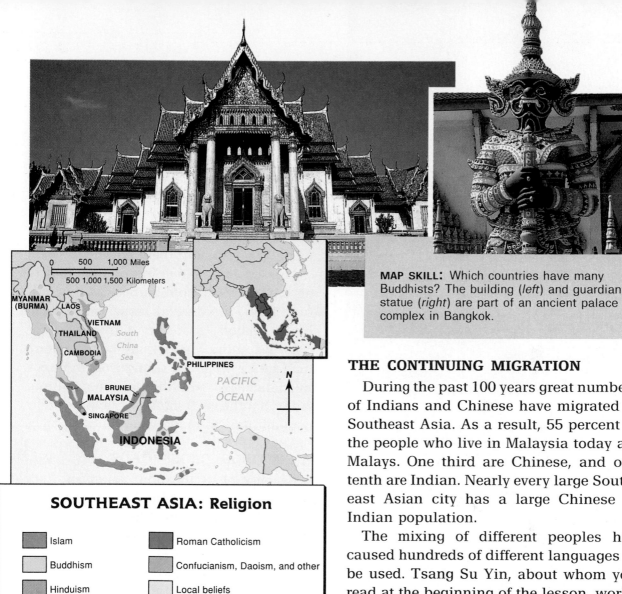

SOUTHEAST ASIA: Religion

- Islam
- Buddhism
- Hinduism
- Roman Catholicism
- Confucianism, Daoism, and other
- Local beliefs

MAP SKILL: Which countries have many Buddhists? The building (*left*) and guardian statue (*right*) are part of an ancient palace complex in Bangkok.

EUROPEAN INFLUENCES

Europeans arrived in the early 1500s. They came in search of spices but stayed to build colonies. In time every country in the area except Thailand was controlled by Europeans—the Portuguese, British, Dutch, Spanish, and French.

Traces of colonialism are still seen in the area. For example, the capital of Indonesia, Jakarta, has canals like those in Amsterdam in the Netherlands. The Spanish introduced Roman Catholicism to the Philippines. Today 85 percent of Filipinos are Roman Catholics.

THE CONTINUING MIGRATION

During the past 100 years great numbers of Indians and Chinese have migrated to Southeast Asia. As a result, 55 percent of the people who live in Malaysia today are Malays. One third are Chinese, and one tenth are Indian. Nearly every large Southeast Asian city has a large Chinese or Indian population.

The mixing of different peoples has caused hundreds of different languages to be used. Tsang Su Yin, about whom you read at the beginning of the lesson, works for an English-language newspaper in Singapore. But English is only one of the four official languages in Singapore. The others are Chinese, Malay, and an Indian language called Tamil. One hundred different languages are used in Myanmar, and Indonesia has as many as 365 languages—one for every day in the year.

RELIGION

It is impossible to travel far in mainland Southeast Asia without seeing Buddhist monks and temples. More than 1,500 years ago, monks and merchants began spreading Buddhism from India to this region. Today Buddhism is the major religion of

563

Like these people of northern Thailand, many rural Southeast Asians live in groups of homes built from wood and bamboo.

Myanmar, Thailand, Cambodia, and Laos.

The region's second major religion, Islam, was brought to the coastal towns of Southeast Asia by Indian and Arab traders in the 1300s. During the next two centuries, Islam spread from the Malay Peninsula to the islands of Southeast Asia. Islam is the official religion of Indonesia and Malaysia.

Many Southeast Asians maintain a variety of traditional beliefs that have evolved over thousands of years. These beliefs include the worshiping of spirits thought to exist in nature—in trees, animals, winds, and rivers. Other Southeast Asians, such as the Vietnamese, have been influenced by Confucianism and Daoism. Many Indonesians on the island of Bali are Hindus.

THE IMPORTANCE OF COOPERATION

Most Southeast Asian families are extended families, and family loyalties are strong. Within the family women hold respected positions. In some places in the area women inherit the property and manage the family income.

No matter which ethnic group they belong to, most Southeast Asians are concerned about the well-being of others. For example, in Indonesia if someone's house washes away in a mud slide, the family doesn't have to ask for aid. They know that neighbors will help them rebuild.

This custom of helping one another is an important part of Southeast Asian culture. Today people work closely together to build schools, roads, and irrigation canals. An entire village may help a young man find a wife or a young woman find a husband. By working in cooperation, many Southeast Asians are helping their communities to modernize.

A CULTURAL CROSSROADS

Because of its location, Southeast Asia has long been a great crossroads. You have read how people, ideas, and ways of life from nearby areas moved to Southeast Asia. The Hindu and Buddhist religions were brought from India. Islam was introduced by Indian and Arab traders. Later, during the colonial period, Southeast Asia came under the influence of different groups of Europeans.

Check Your Reading

1. Why does Southeast Asia have so many different ethnic groups?
2. Which major religions have spread to Southeast Asia?
3. Why did the Europeans come to Southeast Asia?
4. **THINKING SKILL:** From what you read about Southeast Asia, what would most likely happen if villagers decided they needed a community center?

564

The Economy

READ TO LEARN

Key Vocabulary

gross national
   product (GNP)
paddy

Key Places

Singapore
Malaysia
Brunei

Read Aloud

Have you ever heard of the "Four Little Tigers"? The name refers to four Asian places—three countries and one colony—that have strong industrial economies. Three of the "Little Tigers" are located in East Asia. They are Hong Kong, South Korea, and Taiwan. The fourth tiger is located in Southeast Asia. It is the tiny island of Singapore.

In this lesson you will read about the economy of Singapore as well as the economies of other Southeast Asian countries. In the future there may be more "Little Tigers" in the Pacific Rim of Southeast Asia.

Read for Purpose

1. **WHAT YOU KNOW:** Why does Japan have one of the strongest economies today?
2. **WHAT YOU WILL LEARN:** Why are the economies of some Southeast Asian countries booming while others are developing slowly?

BOOMING ECONOMIES

You might wonder how a nation as small as Singapore can have an economy with so much influence. About the size of Chicago in the United States, Singapore is a major financial, industrial, and communications center. It also has the world's second-busiest port, after the city of Rotterdam in the Netherlands.

One reason for Singapore's economic success is its location. You can see from the Atlas map on page 636 that this tiny island is located halfway between India and China. Goods coming from East Asia and other parts of Southeast Asia enter Singapore on their way to Europe, Africa, and the United States.

Located next to Singapore is the area's third-richest country, Malaysia. Malaysia is rich in natural resources. In addition to farm and forest products, it has petroleum and natural gas. Malaysia is also a major exporter of tin.

The sultanate of Brunei is the richest country in Southeast Asia. Its large deposits of oil make Brunei's 220,000 people among the wealthiest in the world. The average yearly income per person is almost $20,000.

Thailand, Indonesia, and the Philippines are not as industrialized as the Four Little Tigers. However, these three countries have natural resources similar to Malaysia's. Their economies are making gains, and foreign companies have increased their trade with these countries.

Singapore, Malaysia, Brunei, Thailand, Indonesia, and the Philippines are working to create a free-trade area to lower tariffs on each other's goods. They plan to invite other Asian nations to join them.

The cartogram on this page shows the gross national products (GNPs) of countries of the region. The GNP is the value of the total goods and services produced by a country during a year. A special kind of map, a cartogram, enables us to compare facts about countries. On the cartogram below, sizes of countries represent their GNPs rather than true area and shape. The cartogram shows the way in which one country's GNP compares with others.

Southeast Asia is rich in resources. It produces more than 80 percent of the world's natural rubber and more than 60 percent of its copper and tin. Money from the sale of these resources and from oil and natural gas is being used to finance industrialization in Southeast Asia.

IMPOVERISHED BY WAR

Unlike the countries you have just read about, Vietnam, Laos, and Cambodia are very poor. Since the end of World War II, they each have been torn apart by a series of terrible wars, which you will read about in Lesson 3. These wars caused hundreds of thousands of educated people to flee to safer countries. The resulting lack of skilled workers has weakened these countries.

Laos and Vietnam have communist economies that were modeled after that of the former Soviet Union. Each government controls its economy and decides what and how much to produce.

Myanmar is also a poor country. However, its economic problems have not been caused by war, but by civil unrest, poor planning, and harmful economic policies.

MAP SKILL: Helping Indonesia's GNP to rise are large factories such as this helicopter factory (right). Does Laos, Singapore, or Indonesia have the highest GNP?

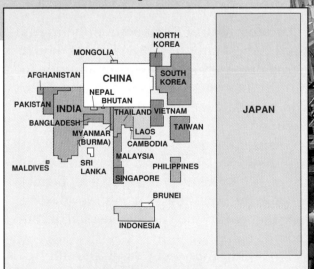

CARTOGRAM:
Gross National Product of
Southern and Eastern Asia

CHANGING WAYS OF LIFE

Some parts of Southeast Asia are changing more slowly. Not so long ago, a visitor described the hill country of Thailand as a place "that has been completely bypassed by time." But now people in even the most remote villages have radios and tape players. Village people now use money instead of relying entirely on barter, and they also pay taxes.

About four out of five people in Southeast Asia live in rural areas. Many of them work small farms. Farming areas are becoming crowded. In the past there was enough land for the children of farmers. Today, however, many of the children of farmers have left the farm areas to move to the cities where they work to earn money, often in the newly established industries. As a result, cities such as Yangon (formerly Rangoon), in Myanmar, Jakarta in Indonesia, and Manila in the Philippines have become very crowded. Even smaller towns and cities are growing rapidly as people who used to live on farms move into them.

PADDY RICE AND PLANTATIONS

Farmers in the lowlands of Southeast Asia plant rice in fields called paddies. First, tiny seedlings are grown in seedbeds and then moved by hand from the seedbeds to the flooded paddy fields. Paddy rice, or wet rice as it is often called, has a higher yield per acre than any other kind of grain.

The lowlands also have large plantations. Most of them are owned by a few families and companies. Although the plantations were started by Europeans, most of them today are controlled by Southeast Asians. Plantation crops are exported. Among the region's major exports are tea, rubber, coffee, bamboo, and sugarcane.

RICH LANDS AND POOR LANDS

The economies of the countries of Southeast Asia are based mainly on farming, mining, and forestry. Singapore has a booming economy, and Brunei and Malaysia are industrializing rapidly. Others, however, have been slower to develop. It will be years before Vietnam, Laos, and Cambodia can fully recover from the devastating effects of the wars in Southeast Asia.

This Indonesian plantation worker is making cuts in rubber trees to get at the latex.

Check Your Reading

1. Why does Singapore have such a strong economy?
2. Why are Vietnam, Laos, and Cambodia economically poor countries?
3. Name three natural resources found in Southeast Asia that are essential to countries all over the world.
4. **THINKING SKILL:** Compare and contrast the countries in this region with booming economies and those with poorer economies.

567

The Government

Key Vocabulary

Vietnam War

Key People

Corazon Aquino

Key Places

Philippines

Read Aloud

I am not embarrased to tell you that I believe in miracles.

In 1986 many people around the world agreed with the speaker, Corazon Aquino. With little political experience, she had just become the president of the Philippines. In this lesson you will discover why this election was so remarkable in the history of Southeast Asia.

Read for Purpose

1. **WHAT YOU KNOW:** What are the two main types of government of the countries in East Asia?
2. **WHAT YOU WILL LEARN:** Why has it been difficult for the nations of Southeast Asia to achieve peace and stability?

DEMOCRACY IN THE PHILIPPINES

The newspaper stories coming from the Philippines in 1986 seemed too amazing to be true. This Southeast Asian country had been ruled by President Ferdinand Marcos, who had been charged with having a corrupt government. In 1986 Corazon Aquino ran against him for the presidency of the Philippines.

During the election the Marcos government had sent troops into most communities to destroy ballot boxes and votes that had been cast for Aquino. The National Assembly of the Philippines then declared Marcos the winner. In response thousands of Filipinos accused the Marcos government of election fraud and formed human chains around the ballot boxes. Soldiers put down their guns and joined the protesters. Faced with such protests, Marcos and his followers were forced to flee the country. Marcos went to Hawaii, where he died in 1989. Meanwhile, Corazon Aquino became the president of the Philippines. Aquino was popular with the people, but there were groups loyal to Marcos that continued to oppose her.

AUTHORITARIAN TRADITIONS

Throughout Southeast Asia the 1986 presidential election in the Philippines offered an example of political hope. Since the end of World War II, most of the countries in Southeast Asia have been run by governments with only one political party. Although these governments vary from communist dictatorships to constitutional monarchies, they have one thing in common: They are run by powerful leaders who make their own rules.

Southeast Asia has a long history of rule by kings or other powerful leaders. People

In 1986 Corazon Aquino (*right, center*) campaigned hard against Ferdinand Marcos (*left*) for the presidency of the Philippines.

made decisions for their villages but had no say in higher levels of government. Moreover, before World War II, nearly all of Southeast Asia had been controlled by Europeans. Only Thailand had avoided European rule and was able to continue governing itself.

For these reasons, most Southeast Asian countries lacked experience in governing themselves when they gained independence after World War II. Where democracy exists, it is fragile. Corazon Aquino almost lost power to military rebels many times before leaving office in 1992.

DIFFERENT GOVERNMENTS

Today the people of the countries of Southeast Asia are trying to work out ways to govern their lands successfully. They hope to preserve traditional ways of life and attitudes while introducing modern ideas. Thailand has a constitutional monarchy, and its government is among the most stable in the area.

Two other Southeast Asian countries have also remained monarchies. Brunei's leader is a sultan, a muslim title for ruler. As an absolute monarch, his word is law in Brunei. Malaysia, however, has an unu-

sual kind of constitutional monarchy. It has a parliamentary system in which the ruler is the country's leading sultan. He is chosen by the nine sultans who head the nine states of Malaysia. The sultan's most important role is as the religious leader of Malaysia's Muslim people.

Indonesia and Myanmar are both republics ruled by military leaders. Singapore has a parliamentary system of government, with a president as head of the country and a prime minister as head of government. Laos and Vietnam have communist governments. Cambodia is a constitutional monarchy.

SOCIAL UNREST

In many places in Southeast Asia, social stability has been rare. One reason has been that old quarrels among the area's ethnic groups have caused much unrest. For example, in Malaysia many of the poorer rural people are Malays, while the wealthier city dwellers and business leaders are Chinese. Recent programs that put government in the hands of the Malays have been criticized by the Chinese as unfair. In Myanmar the Karen ethnic group is fighting bitterly to form their own country.

Over 30 years of war has caused millions of people to become refugees in Southeast Asia.

Communist North Vietnam won the Vietnam War in 1975. It then took control of all of Vietnam. A dictator in Cambodia invaded Vietnam, and Vietnam invaded Cambodia in return. Millions of people were forced to flee from their homes.

In Cambodia, Vietnamese troops occupied most of the country but continued to fight Cambodian refugee fighters. By the late 1980s, though, Vietnam allowed more of the fighting to be done by the forces of the Cambodian government they had placed in power.

It is believed that perhaps as many as 3 million people have died in Cambodia since the 1970s. In neighboring Vietnam there is still great distrust between the people of the north and those of the south. Although the country was united in 1975, it is just beginning to become stable.

MANY KINDS OF GOVERNMENT

The governments of the countries of Southeast Asia range from a republic in the Philippines to an absolute monarchy in Brunei. You have read that most of these governments have one powerful group or leader in control. Most people have few individual rights or freedoms. Social and economic problems make it difficult to set up stable governments. As a result, the future of Southeast Asia remains uncertain.

Unrest is also caused by the great gaps in the standards of living between the rich and the poor in some parts of Southeast Asia. While a few families are very wealthy, most people have little or no land or money. One of the most serious problems faced by Corazon Aquino in the Philippines has been finding a way in which to deal with communist rebels. The rebels have gained support among the nation's many poor plantation workers.

YEARS OF WAR

Much of Southeast Asia is deeply scarred by years of war. The longest and most damaging was the **Vietnam War**, which the United States joined in the early 1960s and withdrew from in 1973. The Vietnam War began as a civil war in South Vietnam between Vietnamese communists and the government troops. After the United States became more deeply involved in the conflict, war also was waged in Laos and Cambodia.

Check Your Reading

1. How does the government of the Philippines differ from most of its neighbors?
2. Why have some countries in Southeast Asia had difficulty in establishing stable governments?
3. Name three problems that many countries of Southeast Asia face today.
4. **THINKING SKILL:** Classify Southeast Asia's governments into two or three groups. Give each group a title.

BUILDING SKILLS

Drawing Conclusions: Review

Suppose you and your family arrive home after spending the weekend away. While you are unpacking your suitcase you notice that the time on your electric alarm clock does not agree with the time on your wristwatch. When you go to the refrigerator for a glass of milk you notice a sour smell coming from the milk carton. Now you draw the conclusion that while you were away the electricity was off in your house.

When you draw a conclusion, you put facts together to arrive at a statement of meaning. A conclusion tells how pieces of information relate, or connect, to one another.

HELPING YOURSELF
Here is one way to draw conclusions.

1. Identify the topic of the information.

2. Examine the information given.

3. Look for ideas or subjects that are common to all the pieces of information.

4. Draw a conclusion stating how the subjects or ideas common to all pieces of information relate, or link, to one another.

Applying the Skill
Read the following pieces of information. Then answer the questions below.

- In 1970 the Kingdom of Cambodia became the Khmer Republic.
- In 1975 the Khmer Republic became Democratic Kampuchea.
- In 1979 Democratic Kampuchea became the People's Republic of Kampuchea.
- In 1989 the People's Republic of Kampuchea became the State of Cambodia.

1. What is the topic of the information given above?
   a. the politics of the People's Republic of Kampuchea
   b. the people of Kampuchea
   c. the history of Cambodia's name
2. What subjects or ideas are common to all the pieces of information?
3. What is one conclusion you can draw from the above information?

Reviewing the Skill
1. What is the meaning of the phrase *draw a conclusion*?
2. Describe four steps that will help you to draw conclusions.
3. In which subjects, other than social studies, do you often find it necessary to draw conclusions? Give an example.

Arts and Recreation

READ TO LEARN

Key Vocabulary

meditate
shadow play
gamelan

Key Places

Indonesia
Java

Read Aloud

On the island of Bali a religious year is 210 days long. Each temple on the island holds a religious festival once a year. Since there are hundreds of temples, there are festivals on Bali on most days. These festivals give the Balinese many opportunities to wear traditional costumes, hear traditional music, and watch traditional plays and dances.

In this lesson you will read about some of the ways in which Southeast Asians enjoy leisure time.

Read for Purpose

1. **WHAT YOU KNOW:** What other areas of the world have numerous religious festivals?
2. **WHAT YOU WILL LEARN:** In what ways has religion influenced the arts and recreational activities of Southeast Asia?

FESTIVALS FOR EVERY SEASON

Many of the oldest festivals in Southeast Asia have to do with farming. Festivals mark the cycle of planting, transplanting, and harvesting rice. In April or May people ask a god or gods to help their newly planted crops. At other festivals people pray or give thanks for rain.

In Thailand Buddhist boys become temporary monks at a rice festival. This festival takes place at the time the seedlings are transplanted from seedbeds to the flooded paddy fields. After the festival the boys go to monasteries to live, pray, and work together for a few months. The boys also spend a period of time meditating, or thinking deeply, while they are at the Buddhist monastaries.

SHADOW PLAYS AND MUSIC

When a child in Indonesia spends the evening watching a shadow play, he or she isn't just being entertained. Puppets are used to act out well-known stories by casting shadows. The leather puppets in the plays are called *wayang* (wä' äng), which means "shadow." The puppets are held up behind a cloth screen that is stretched between two bamboo poles. A light behind the screen casts the shadows.

These puppet dramas are part of the education of most Indonesian children. Shadow plays are used to teach moral and religious values. Most tell the stories of ancient Hindu rulers, gods, and heroes.

An important part of every shadow play is the music, which is performed by a

In Indonesian **shadow plays**, light shining on a puppet (*left*) casts a shadow such as the one shown on the right.

gamelan (gam′ ə lan). A gamelan is an orchestra of drums, gongs, bells, chimes, cymbals, and xylophones made of bamboo and metal. A gamelan orchestra has no conductor. The drums set the pace, and the other players join in. Traditionally music was not written down, but taught by a master musician to a student.

In recent years the government of Indonesia has been trying to get people to move from **Java**, a large island that is extremely crowded, to islands that have fewer people. As soon as a new village is built, the people start saving money to support a village gamelan. The Indonesians believe that a village without a gamelan can't have a proper festival.

SPORTS AND RECREATION

Among the favorite sports in Southeast Asia are badminton and basketball. As in Japan, many traditional sports are also very popular. One is Thai boxing. Boxing in Thailand is a different sport from boxing that is practiced in the United States. Thai boxers wear gloves and trade punches, but they also use their elbows and knees and make lightning-fast kicks.

The waters off Southeast Asia's islands and peninsulas have some of the world's best underwater viewing. In addition to this activity, snorkeling, scuba diving, and water sports of all kinds are popular with tourists from around the world.

LOCAL TRADITIONS

Religion plays an important part in the arts and recreation of Southeast Asia. As you have read, festivals are held throughout the year in the area. Traditional art forms, such as shadow plays and gamelans, are still favorite forms of entertainment. Performed at festivals, they help to keep alive local traditions. Both traditional and modern sports are popular.

 Check Your Reading

1. Give two examples of the ways in which religion has influenced the arts in Southeast Asia.
2. What is a shadow play? What does it teach the children of Indonesia?
3. Why do you think gamelans are popular throughout Southeast Asia?
4. **THINKING SKILL:** Based on this lesson, what conclusions can you make about the recreation of the people of Southeast Asia?

573

SOUTHEAST ASIA: CULTURAL GEOGRAPHY

PEOPLE

- The cultures of Southeast Asia were influenced by those of China, India, and Europe
- Southeast Asia has hundreds of languages
- Major religions: Buddhism, Islam

- Values: family loyalty, cooperation, concern for well-being of others

ECONOMY

CHINA
NEPAL
BHUTAN
SOUTH KOREA
THAILAND VIETNAM
ANMAR (BURMA) LAOS TAIWAN
CAMBODIA
MALAYSIA
SRI LANKA PHILIPPINES

- Booming economies: Singapore (trade), Brunei (oil)
- Major resources: rubber, copper, tin, oil, natural gas
- Years of war and civil unrest have caused poverty in: Cambodia, Laos, Vietnam, Myanmar

- Agriculture: small farms, paddies, and plantations (in lowlands)

GOVERNMENT

- Tradition of authoritarian rule
- Only Thailand was never a European colony
- Monarchies: Thailand, Brunei, Malaysia, Cambodia

- Republics: Philippines, Indonesia, Myanmar; parliamentary system: Singapore; Communist: Laos, Vietnam

- The area has many refugees

ARTS AND RECREATION

- Arts are used to teach important religious values in Southeast Asia

- Religious festivals and shadow plays are popular traditional practices
- Gamelan: traditional orchestra in Indonesia
- Popular sports: badminton, basketball, Thai boxing

IDEAS TO REMEMBER

- Southeast Asia is a cultural crossroads, combining ideas and ways of life from southern China, India, the Middle East, and Europe.
- Some countries in Southeast Asia are rapidly developing, while others suffer the effects of years of war.
- Most Southeast Asian countries are ruled by one powerful group or leader and have found it difficult to form stable governments.
- Religious traditions influence the art and recreation of Southeast Asia.

REVIEWING VOCABULARY

gamelan	meditate
gross national	paddy
product	shadow play

Number a sheet of paper from 1 to 5. Beside each number write the word or term that best matches the definition.

1. A field where rice is grown
2. The total amount of goods and services produced in a country during a year
3. To think deeply about important matters
4. Puppet drama that is part of the education of Indonesian children
5. An Indonesian orchestra that plays music

REVIEWING FACTS

1. Which two Eastern civilizations have had the greatest impact on Southeast Asia?
2. In which Southeast Asian countries is Buddhism the dominant religion?
3. Which five European countries established colonies in Southeast Asia?
4. What are the names of the three wealthiest countries in Southeast Asia? The three poorest?
5. What effect has population growth had on the rural economy of Southeast Asia?
6. Name four exports from plantations in Southeast Asia.
7. Who became president of the Philippines in 1986?
8. Which country in Southeast Asia avoided European rule?
9. How has the gap between the rich and the poor strengthened communist rebel movements in the Philippines?
10. How does a gamelan orchestra differ from an orchestra in the United States?

WRITING ABOUT MAIN IDEAS

1. **Writing an Essay:** Using Singapore as an example, write an essay with the title: "A Country Doesn't Have to Be Big to Be Prosperous."
2. **Writing a Narrative:** Write a narrative of the events leading up to the overthrow of Ferdinand Marcos in the Philippines and the coming to power of Corazon Aquino.
3. **Writing a List:** You have read that Southeast Asia has many natural resources. Yet it also contains some of the world's poorest countries. Write a list of reasons explaining this paradox.
4. **Writing About Perspectives:** What would it be like to have to flee from your country and start a new life where the language and customs are different? Imagine that you had to leave your country in Southeast Asia. Write a paragraph describing some of the ways in which you would have to change your life.

BUILDING SKILLS: DRAWING CONCLUSIONS

1. What does it mean to "draw a conclusion"?
2. Explain the process involved in drawing a conclusion.
3. Why is the ability to draw conclusions important?

SOUTHERN AND EASTERN ASIA: PHYSICAL GEOGRAPHY

 LANDFORMS

- Mount Everest is the world's highest mountain
- Deserts: Gobi, Takla Makan, Tarim Basin
- Archipelagoes: Phillippines, Indonesia
- Major rivers: Huang, Chang, Mekong, Ganges, Indus, Brahmaputra

 CLIMATE

- Temperate climates: northern India, northern and eastern East Asia
- Dry and semi-dry climates: central China, western South Asia
- Highland climates: southwestern China, northern South Asia
- Tropical climates: southern South Asia, Sri Lanka, Maldives, Southeast Asia
- Monsoons cause both rainy and dry seasons

NATURAL RESOURCES

- Rivers are important for transportation
- Major seaports: Hong Kong, Bombay, Yokohama
- Richest farmland is in Southeast Asia
- Few mineral resources, except in Southeast Asia, which has abundant petroleum

SOUTHERN AND EASTERN ASIA: CULTURAL GEOGRAPHY

 PEOPLE

- Religions: Hinduism, Buddhism, Islam, Confucianism, Daoism, Shinto
- Communism has changed ways of life in China, Mongolia, North Korea, Vietnam, Cambodia, and Laos
- Japanese values: respect for authority and order, duty to family and rulers

 ECONOMY

- Population often grows faster than ability of nations to provide for people
- Under China's Communist system, the government owns most of the land
- The capitalist economies of Hong Kong, Taiwan and South Korea are called "economic miracles"
- Japan is the second most productive industrial power in world
- Years of war have caused poverty in Cambodia, Laos, Vietnam, Myanmar

 GOVERNMENT

- Many different kinds of government in the region, from India (world's largest democracy) to China (huge independent communist power)
- Other types of governments: military dictatorships, monarchies
- Japan: parliamentary system includes the Diet (legislature)
- Tradition of authoritarian rule in Southeast Asia

 **ARTS AND RECREATION**

- Arts and recreation strongly influenced by religious traditions; India's Taj Mahal is one of the world's most beautiful buildings
- Popular traditional arts: painting, poetry, flower arranging
- Popular East Asian recreations: chess, swimming, tennis, martial arts, baseball, golf

REVIEWING VOCABULARY

Buddhism	monsoons
castes	nonaligned nations
Confucianism	samurai
cottage industry	Shinto
Diet	socialist realism

Number a sheet of paper from 1 to 10. Beside each number write the word or term from the above list that best completes the sentence.

1. _____, a major religion of Asia, teaches that one must give up selfish desires in order to overcome suffering.
2. _____ is a form of art that often shows people at work on farms or in factories.
3. _____ are rigid social classes that define a way of life for people in India.
4. _____ are seasonal winds that have a great influence on the climate of Southern and Eastern Asia.
5. The _____ is Japan's national legislature.
6. Japanese _____ were taught to feel a great sense of duty to their country.
7. _____ emphasizes respect for others and the performance of one's duty.
8. By not joining a particular power bloc, _____ tried to avoid being drawn into great power rivalries.
9. _____ is a type of small-scale production that makes up a large percentage of India's total output.
10. _____ is the oldest of Japan's religions.

WRITING ABOUT THE UNIT

1. **Writing an Essay:** Write an essay contrasting the methods that Mao Zedong and Mohandas Gandhi used to achieve sweeping changes in their countries.
2. **Writing a Scenario:** A scenario is a brief description, similar to a news story, of an event or condition. The story is often a projection based on current trends. Write a scenario for an Asian country or region for the year 2010.
3. **Writing About Perspectives:** If you were living in a poor country in Asia, what would you do to try to improve the economy? In writing your answer to this question, tell how your solution would affect different groups of people in the country.

ACTIVITIES

1. **Constructing a Collage:** Locate pictures and photographs of Asia in magazines and travel brochures. Construct a collage to show how the modern and the traditional mix in this continent.
2. **Working Together to Create a Dialogue Between Members of Different Religions:** Work together to role-play a dialogue between a member of an Eastern religion, such as Buddhism, and a member of a Western religion, such as Christianity. In your dialogue highlight similarities and differences between the religions.

LINKING PAST, PRESENT, AND FUTURE

Many people believe that countries in Asia, such as Taiwan, South Korea, and Japan are becoming more powerful economically. Do you think this area will surpass the West as the world's foremost economic power?

ASIA

PACIFIC   OCEAN

45°N

MICRONESIA

PAPUA
NEW
GUINEA

MELANESIA

Arafura Sea

Timor Sea

Coral
Sea

INDIAN
OCEAN

AUSTRALIA

Tasman
Sea

NEW
ZEALAND

International Date Line

150°E

135°E

120°E

165°E

105°E

180°

90°E

165°W

75°E

60°E

60°S

Antarctic Circle

75°S

ANTARCTICA

South
Pole +

UNIT
8

THE PACIFIC

WHERE WE ARE

In your journey through the world around us, you have seen almost all of the world's continents, from North and South America to Europe, Asia, and Africa. But there are two continents that you have not yet studied. Can you guess which ones they are?

If you guessed Australia and Antarctica, you're right. These two continents make up much of the region known as the Pacific. As you can see from the map, this is a vast region, made up not only of these two continents, but also of thousands of small islands. What makes this region different from all the others you have studied? In the following chapters you will find out.

THE PACIFIC

KIRIBATI

Capital ★ Tarawa

Major languages: Gilbertese and English
Population: 71,000
Area: 277 sq mi; 717 sq km
Leading export: fish

AUSTRALIA

Capital ★ Canberra

Major language: English
Population: 17.5 million
Area: 2,967,900 sq mi; 7,686,850 sq km
Leading export: wheat

MARSHALL ISLANDS

Capital ★ Jamuro

Major language: English
Population: 50,004
Area: 70 sq mi; 181.3 sq km
Leading exports: agricultural products and handicrafts

FIJI

Capital ★ Suva

Major language: English
Population: 0.7 million
Area: 7,054 sq mi; 18,270 sq km
Leading export: sugar

MICRONESIA
FEDERATED STATES OF

Capital ★ Kolonia

Major languages: English, Trukese, Yapese, and Kosrean
Population: 107,662
Area: 270 sq mi; 700 sq km
Leading export: copra

NAURU

Capital ★ Yaren

Major language: Nauruan
Population: 8,100
Area: 8 sq mi; 20 sq km
Leading export: phosphates

TONGA

Capital ★ Nuku'alofa

Major languages: Tongan and English
Population: 0.1 million
Area: 270 sq mi; 700 sq km
Leading exports: copra and bananas

NEW ZEALAND

Capital ★ Wellington

Major languages: English and Maori
Population: 3.5 million
Area: 103,738 sq mi; 268,680 sq km
Leading exports: lamb and wool

TUVALU

Capital ★ Funafuti Atoll

Major languages: Tuvaluan and English
Population: 9,000
Area: 10 sq mi; 26 sq km
Leading export: copra

PAPUA NEW GUINEA

Capital ★ Port Moresby

Major languages:
English, Pidgin English, and Hiri Motu
Population: 3.9 million
Area: 178,259 sq mi; 461,690 sq km
Leading exports: gold, copper, and silver

VANUATU

Capital ★ Port-Vila

Major languages: Bislama, English, and French
Population: 0.2 million
Area: 5,699 sq mi; 14,760 sq km
Leading export: copra

SOLOMON ISLANDS

Capital ★ Honiara

Major language: English
Population: 0.3 million
Area: 10,985 sq mi; 28,450 sq km
Leading exports: copra and copper

WESTERN SAMOA

Capital ★ Apia

Major languages: Samoan and English
Population: 0.2 million
Area: 1,104 sq mi; 2,860 sq km
Leading exports: copra, cocoa, and bananas

CHAPTER 29

PHYSICAL GEOGRAPHY OF THE PACIFIC

FOCUS

They call her a young country, but they lie,
She is the last of lands, the emptiest. . . .

This is the way that the Australian poet A. D. Hope wrote
about his country. Rudyard Kipling used very similar words to
describe New Zealand: "last loneliest, loveliest . . . apart. . . . "
These writers called Australia and New Zealand the last places
on earth because they are so far from other lands. In this chapter
you will read about Australia, New Zealand, and the thousands of
small islands of the Pacific region.

LESSON 1

Landforms

READ TO LEARN

■ **Key Vocabulary**

outback
atoll
iceberg

Key Places

Australia
Oceania
Great Barrier Reef

Polynesia
Micronesia
Melanesia

■ **Read Aloud**

The lands of the Pacific region vary greatly, but they have one important feature in common. Wide expanses of ocean surround them all. Thousands of years ago, the first explorers of the Pacific must have had enormous confidence. They sailed into the empty spaces of the Pacific with no guarantee of finding anything. In the end, after sailing huge distances in small, open boats, they found islands that no human had ever seen before.

■ **Read for Purpose**

1. WHAT YOU KNOW: If you could live in any area, which geographic features would you choose to live near? Mountains? The seashore? Rivers? Why would you choose these features?
2. WHAT YOU WILL LEARN: In what ways does the geography of Australia differ from that of the rest of the Pacific region?

AN ISOLATED REGION

Australia is the world's smallest continent. It is about the same size as the United States, not including Alaska. The small continent of Australia is like an enormous island, with 23,000 miles (37,000 km) of coastline.

The rest of the Pacific region is made up of islands. There are large islands, such as New Zealand, but there are also thousands of small islands that dot the Pacific Ocean. All of the islands of the Pacific are known collectively as Oceania.

The Pacific region is made up mostly of water, with very little land. It includes only 3.3 million square miles (8.5 million sq km) of land—less than 6 percent of the earth's land surface. This land is scattered over a vast ocean. On a map most of the islands may appear to be close together, but in fact they are very far apart. Australia and New Zealand are more than 1,000 miles (1,609 km) apart. Because of such vast distances, various ways of life have developed in distinct ways in the Pacific.

AUSTRALIA

Winds and rain have scraped, sanded, and washed the surface of Australia for millions of years. They have worn the land down to make it the flattest, lowest continent on earth. There are no volcanoes or rugged new mountains on the continent. Australia is not only the smallest, but also the oldest continent.

Most Australians live on the coastal rim

583

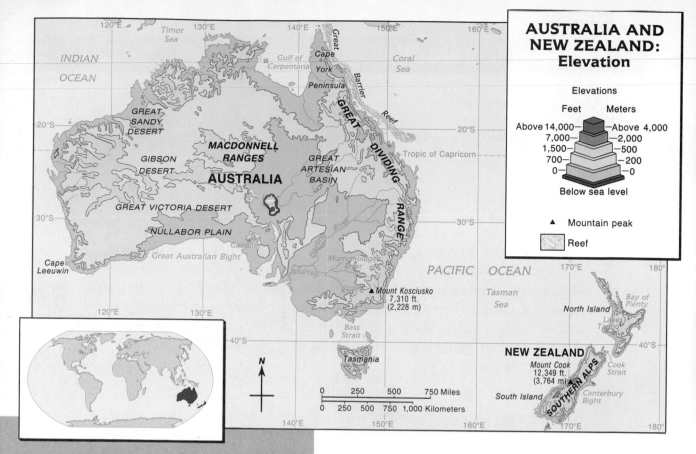

**AUSTRALIA AND
NEW ZEALAND:
Elevation**

Elevations

Feet   Meters

Above 14,000 —   — Above 4,000
7,000 —   — 2,000
1,500 —   — 500
700 —   — 200
0 —   — 0

Below sea level

▲ Mountain peak

    Reef

MAP SKILL: What area of high elevation lies along Australia's east coast? Name a mountain peak in this area.

of their land. Inland there are three main regions: the huge Western Plateau, the Central Plains (or Central Eastern Lowlands), and the Eastern Highlands.

All the large cities of Australia, except Perth, are on the east coast. It is like the east coast of the United States, a narrow, fertile strip with an ocean on one side and low mountains to the west.

Not far inland a system of low mountains, hills, and highlands parallels the east coast. This area is the Great Dividing Range. Part of it looks blue when viewed from a distance. The color comes from the eucalyptus (ū kə lip′ təs), or gum trees, that cover the Blue Mountains. Sunlight glints off the oily leaves of the trees, making a blue haze.

As the map above shows, most of Australia's major rivers begin in the Great Dividing Range in the northeast. The Murray River and its branches, especially the Darling River, form the continent's major river system. Find the Murray River on the map above. Australia has few other rivers.

THE OUTBACK

You have read that Perth is the only large city in Australia that is not on the east coast. Separating Perth from other cities is the huge, arid area Australians call the outback. There wasn't even a paved road between Perth and Adelaide until 1976. An Australian writer has said of the outback:

It is a hard land, even today. Times change, but the Australian heartland never does. . . . Most of it lies as it has for countless millennia [thousands of years], sunk in a coma of ancient waterlessness.

584

In some parts of the outback huge outcroppings of red rock rise out of the flat land. They are old rocks that were too strong to erode. One of them, Ayers Rock, is 1.5 miles (2.4 km) long.

In the outback, where there are few roads or gas stations, Australians use airplanes for everyday transportation. They run errands and visit friends by plane. Even their ambulances are airplanes.

THE GREAT BARRIER REEF

Australia contains not only a famous dry area, but also an underwater wonderland. Just off the northeast coast of Australia lies the Great Barrier Reef. A reef is a ridge of rocks near the surface of a sea.

The Great Barrier Reef is as large as the British Isles, yet it is comprised of tiny sea creatures called polyps. These little creatures live in huge colonies in the sea, and when they die, coral reefs are built up from their skeletons. The reefs keep growing as living polyps attach themselves to the coral skeletons.

The water temperature of the Great Barrier Reef never falls below 68°F. (18°C), and the water has very little dirt in it. The conditions of the Great Barrier Reef resemble a gigantic outdoor aquarium. Some 1,500 kinds of fish live amid its coral.

PACIFIC ISLANDS

Like the Great Barrier Reef, many of the islands of Oceania are made of coral. Some of them are called atolls. Atolls are doughnut-shaped coral reefs looped around an area of still, warm water. Most atolls are formed by coral buildup on the rims of sunken volcano craters.

Low coral islands lack fertile soil. Only a few plants can grow on such islands, so they cannot support many people. The people of Oceania bring soil from other islands to grow plants on some atolls.

Red-orange Ayers Rock rises out of the flat Australian outback. Ayers Rock is one of the most popular attractions among tourists visiting Australia.

Other Pacific islands are actually the tops of mountains that start below the sea. These mountains are part of the great mountain chains that circle the world. They just happen to be located mostly underwater.

Some of the islands that are part of these mountain chains rise far above sea level. They have varied landscapes of mountains, rivers, and valleys. Many of them are also volcanic. The lava that comes from the volcanoes forms fertile soil, so volcanic islands have many kinds of vegetation. They can support more people than can atolls.

POLYNESIA, MICRONESIA, AND MELANESIA

The islands of Oceania can be sorted into three main groups. The name of each group tells something about its islands. Polynesia means "many islands," but the name makes most people think of a warm, sunny climate, palm trees, and sandy beaches. Polynesia includes Tahiti, American Samoa, and, far to the east, Easter Island. Hawaii, the westernmost state of the United States, is located within the area of Polynesia. The map on pages 620–621 of the Atlas shows the location of many Pacific islands.

Polynesia is spread over a huge stretch of ocean, which covers 15 million square miles (39 million sq km). The isolation of all the islands in this area, as well as their small size, has limited their economic development.

Can you guess the size of the islands of Micronesia from the name? *Micronesia* means "tiny islands." Micronesia contains more than 2,000 islands. Most of these islands are atolls.

Melanesia means "black islands," a name given to the islands possibly because of the dark vegetation of their hillsides. Melanesia lies south of the equator, west of Polynesia, and northeast of Australia. Fiji and the Solomon Islands are part of Melanesia.

Papua New Guinea, the eastern half of the island of New Guinea, is the largest country in Melanesia. It has a rugged, mountainous terrain. Heavy rainfall in the mountains collects in streams that cross swamps and forests.

NEW ZEALAND

There is one large Pacific island country that you have not yet read about—New Zealand. New Zealand has everything from mountains and waterfalls to seashores and hot springs. In this land, which is about the size of Colorado, peo-

MAP SKILL: How would you describe the population density of Australia and New Zealand compared to other regions?

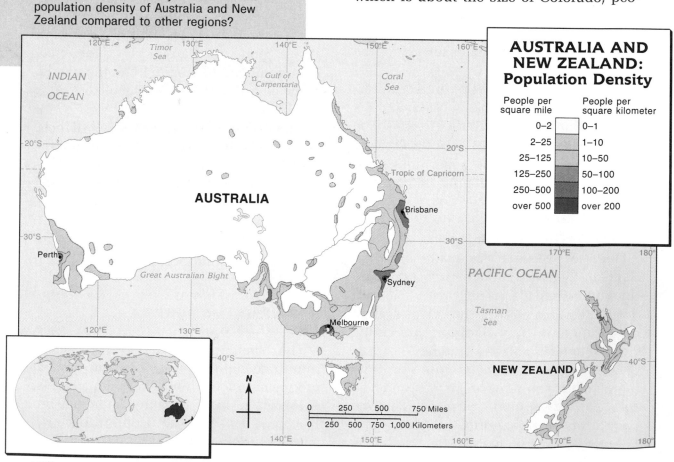

AUSTRALIA AND NEW ZEALAND: Population Density

People per square mile	People per square kilometer
0–2	0–1
2–25	1–10
25–125	10–50
125–250	50–100
250–500	100–200
over 500	over 200

ple are never more than 80 miles (129 km) from the coast. As the map on page 586 shows, much of New Zealand's population is along its coastlines.

The coastlines have one magnificent area of scenery after another. Mountainsides plunge straight down to the sea. Glaciers have scraped out mountain lakes, coastal fjords, and deep harbors. The city of Auckland, located at the base of a long peninsula, has not one, but two very fine harbors.

New Zealand has two main islands, North Island and South Island. South Island is larger than North Island and has a major mountain range, the Southern Alps. Mount Cook, New Zealand's highest peak, offers a very rare sight—snow in the Pacific region.

THE SOUTHERNMOST CONTINENT

Before leaving the Pacific region, we need to take a look at a continent that you have not yet read about in this book—Antarctica. This continent at the South Pole is in total contrast to the tropical and subtropical islands of the Pacific. All but 2 percent of its land is covered permanently with a thick cap of ice that spreads beyond the land. Ice shelves extend far into the surrounding ocean.

In 1987 part of one ice shelf in Antarctica broke off to become an iceberg that is larger than the state of Delaware. Icebergs are large bodies of ice that have broken away from glaciers. A scientist said of this iceberg:

> If you could somehow transport it to California and melt it, it would supply all the water needs of Los Angeles for the next 675 years.

If all the ice in Antarctica were to melt, the world's oceans would rise at least 160 feet (50 m). In some places, the ice pack is 2 miles (3.2 km) thick.

Explorers have visited many parts of the frozen continent of Antarctica.

CONTINENTS AND ISLANDS

In this lesson you have read that the land area of the Pacific region consists of two continents, Australia and Antarctica, and many large and small islands. These islands are divided into three groups: Polynesia, Micronesia, and Melanesia. In the next lesson you will read about the region's climate and resources.

Check Your Reading

1. Of the seven continents, which is the smallest?
2. What are Polynesia, Micronesia, and Melanesia?
3. Describe the physical geography of Antarctica.
4. **THINKING SKILL:** Compare and contrast Australia's physical geography with that of other parts of the Pacific region.

Reading Maps of the Ocean Floor

Earth is sometimes called the water planet. The reason that this name is used for the earth is that much of it—about 71 percent of the planet's surface—is covered by water!

The ocean is a major factor in the geography of the Pacific. As you have read, this region includes a lot of water. To understand more about its geography, then, it is helpful to be able to read the special photographs and maps showing details of the ocean floor. The ocean floor is the part of the earth's crust that lies below sea level. Have you ever wondered what the ocean floors look like? You may

be surprised to learn that the ocean floor has many different features.

Maps of the earth's land areas are the most common kinds of maps. Less common are maps of the ocean floor. Until about 60 years ago, it was thought that the ocean floor was a nearly flat plain. Scientists have discovered, however, that the different parts of the ocean's floor are extremely varied.

Ocean Floor Features

The surface of the ocean floor is just as varied as the surface of the earth above sea level. Mountain ranges, basins, plains, ridges, canyons, and valleys are all found there. You can see such features in the special photograph below. Called a Seasat photograph, it shows the roughness of the ocean floor.

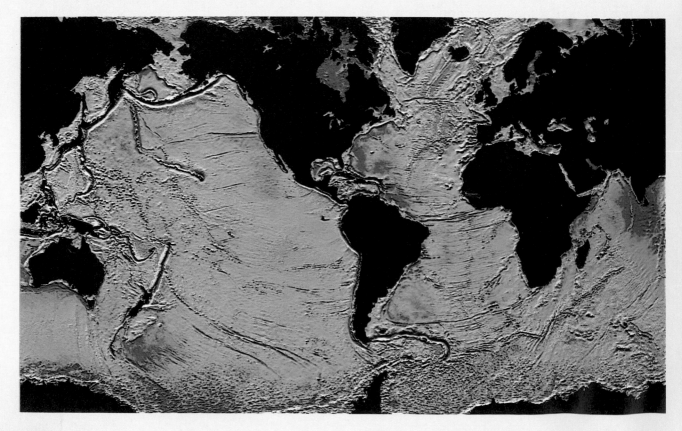

Using Seasat photographs, such as the one on page 588, scientists have been able to make more accurate maps of the ocean floor. The photograph was taken by a satellite in space. If you look closely you can see the deep trenches, or valleys, of the ocean floor. Trenches are the deepest parts of the ocean floor. Look at the photograph and find the trenches that run in the Pacific Ocean near Asia and Australia. You can also see the many ranges of hills that lie across the ocean floor in the Pacific region and other parts of the world.

Contour Maps

Elevation and features of the ocean floor are shown by contour maps. As you read in Chapter 17, contour maps outline landforms with lines or different colors showing different elevations. You may recall that these lines are called contour lines. A contour line on a map connects areas of the same elevation.

As you may recall, contour lines that are drawn close together mean that the land is very steep. Contour lines show height both above sea level and below sea level on land maps. On sea maps contour lines show height only below sea level. As shown on **Diagram A** on this page, the measurement of the depth below sea level in feet is preceded by a minus sign ($-$).

Map A and **Map B** also show Fin Island. Note that both maps are contour maps. What is the difference between **Map A** and **Map B**? As you can see, the contour lines shown on **Map A** show land above sea level. The contour lines shown on **Map B** show land below sea level. What is the contour interval on these maps? You may recall that contour intervals are the differences in elevation between the contour lines. As shown on both of the maps, the contour interval is 20 feet.

FIN ISLAND: Contour Lines

Fin Island
60'
40'
20'
0' (Sea Level)
20
40
60
80
DIAGRAM A

MAP A
Fin Island
X 60'
40
20
0' (Sea Level)

MAP B
.Y
Fin Island
0' (Sea Level)
20
40
60
80

Reviewing the Skill

1. What is one difference between a physical map and a contour map?
2. Compare a contour line and a contour interval.
3. Look at the Seasat photograph and name the deepest parts of the Pacific.
4. If you wished to have a picnic and to take a swim, and then an easy climb to the highest point on Fin Island, which map would you use to choose the best site? Explain the reason for your choice.
5. On maps **A** and **B**, what is the difference in elevation between points **X** and **Y**?
6. How do maps of the ocean floor help you to better understand the earth's surface?

589

Climate and Resources

READ TO LEARN

Key Vocabulary
typhoon
copra

Key Places
Queensland
Papua New Guinea
Samoa

Read Aloud

Like much of the rest of Australia, the place suffers from earth-cracking droughts, blistering heat, surging brown floods and explosive brushfires. Such land forms its people—and draws them together.

This is the way that one writer described part of Queensland, Australia. Most places in the Pacific region have a wet climate, but Australia often bakes under cloudless skies. For instance, the city of Sydney has about 340 days of sunshine a year. By contrast rain falls year-round on the green islands of the rest of Oceania.

Read for Purpose

1. **WHAT YOU KNOW:** Why can a good climate be considered a resource?
2. **WHAT YOU WILL LEARN:** How do the climate and natural resources of the Pacific affect the way of life of the people of the region?

CLIMATE "DOWN UNDER"

If you were lucky enough to vacation in New Zealand or Australia, you'd find that the seasons are the reverse of what you are used to. In the lands of the Southern Hemisphere, "down under" the equator, winter starts in June. Summer runs from December to February.

Climates within Australia also are different from what you might expect. Queensland, a state on the northeast coast, is hotter and drier than places on the south coast. This is because Queensland is located nearer the equator.

CLIMATE IN OCEANIA

In Chapter 8 you read that lands near large bodies of water often have milder climates than do lands far from water. Oceans affect the climate. In lands near large bodies of water, temperatures don't rise or fall as much because water absorbs and holds both heat and cold. Oceans make winters warmer and summers cooler.

The climate of New Zealand and the other islands of Oceania is greatly affected by both the Pacific Ocean and by wind currents. For example, Samoa is in the tropics, yet it is much cooler than land at the same latitude in Africa. Moist ocean breezes cool the Pacific islands.

Usually islanders welcome the ocean breezes. Yet some ocean winds are dangerous. Powerful windstorms called typhoons strike this region two or three times a year. Typhoons are whirling tropical hurricanes. In a typhoon very high winds churn around a center of low air pressure.

THE "LUCKY COUNTRY"

Australia has been called the "Lucky Country." It is an uncrowded land with abundant natural resources.

As you have read, the outback is one of the least settled areas of Australia. Ranchers in the outback graze livestock on vast landholdings. They need about 40 acres (16 ha) of land to graze one head of sheep because the land is so dry that little vegetation grows. Peter Cannon says that the 600,000-acre (243,000-ha) ranch he manages in the outback is not large—the one "next door" is nearly 2 million acres (800,000 ha)! It's no wonder some Australian ranches, which are called stations, make Texas ranches seem small.

Land for ranching is by no means Australia's only natural resource. Look at the land use map on page 592. It shows that mining is a major industry in Australia. People who want to earn money in mining must leave the coastal areas and head inland. Drilling for oil and mining Australia's bauxite, diamonds, iron, copper, lead, silver, and zinc are all done on the country's inland deserts.

In addition to these minerals, Australia has many other natural resources. Although there are few rivers that can be used to create electric power, Australia has many other energy sources. There is abundant coal, oil, and natural gas. Australia also has large amounts of uranium, which is used in creating nuclear power.

GREEN AND BOUNTIFUL NEW ZEALAND

Water is a major resource for New Zealand. The country gets plenty of rain, and there is abundant water for electric power. The high rainfall in New Zealand also en-

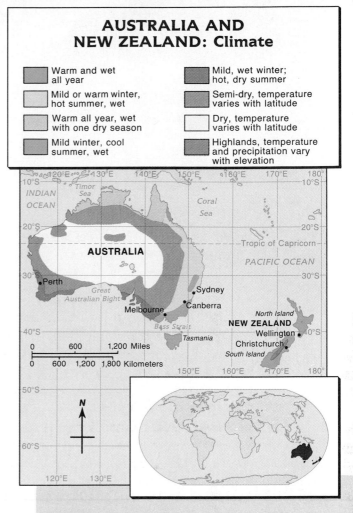

AUSTRALIA AND NEW ZEALAND: Climate

- Warm and wet all year
- Mild or warm winter, hot summer, wet
- Warm all year, wet with one dry season
- Mild winter, cool summer, wet
- Mild, wet winter; hot, dry summer
- Semi-dry, temperature varies with latitude
- Dry, temperature varies with latitude
- Highlands, temperature and precipitation vary with elevation

MAP SKILL: How does the climate on the eastern coast of Australia differ from the climate in the interior of the country?

courages the growth of forests. About one fourth of the country is covered with large forests.

New Zealand has both good soil and a variety of climates. Farmers can grow fruits that need cooler climates, like apples. They can also raise fruits that need subtropical warmth. The cool highlands of New Zealand that you see on the map above are perfect for sheep raising.

THE TROPICAL ISLANDS

In the islands of Oceania near the equator, it would not be possible to raise sheep.

591

MAP SKILL: Sheep are raised in many parts of Australia and New Zealand. According to the map, what is the most common economic activity in these two countries?

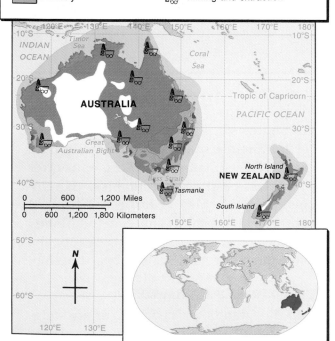

AUSTRALIA AND NEW ZEALAND: Land Use

- Manufacturing
- Commercial farming and livestock raising
- Livestock raising
- Forestry
- Commercial fishing
- Hunting and gathering
- Little or no economic activity
- Mining and extraction

Sheep could not survive the hot monsoon climate of places like Papua New Guinea.

There are thousands of islands in Oceania, and no two are exactly alike. Some have few natural resources. Other larger island countries, like Papua New Guinea, have some mineral resources. Yet the beauty of the islands is itself a resource, for it draws many tourists. Many years ago one visitor to the island of Samoa wrote home:

> There's only one thing on earth as beautiful, and that's Samoa by moonlight. . . . You lie on a mat in a cool Samoan hut, and look on the white sand under the high palms and a gentle sea, and the black line of the reef a mile out, and the moonlight over everything, floods and floods of it. . . .

OTHER ISLAND RESOURCES

As you have read, volcanoes are active on some of the Pacific islands. Though volcanoes are dangerous when they erupt, they yield a valuable resource. Volcanic ash and lava wear down into rich soil. The volcanic islands are the most fertile of Oceania. Many of them are covered with dense rain forests.

Island countries such as Papua New Guinea also have many more mineral resources than the smaller coral islands. Papua New Guinea has the most varied resources of any of the Pacific islands. It has deposits of copper, gold, and silver, as well as good farmland. Yet the land is so rugged that most resources have not yet been developed.

THE TREE OF LIFE

You have read that the sandy coral soil of many of the Pacific Islands is not good for farming. But one plant that will grow in this soil is the coconut palm tree. People in the island countries of the Pacific call it the "Tree of Life."

Islanders use the "meat" inside the coconut to flavor fish and to make cakes and puddings. People who live on tiny coral islands that do not have rivers often drink the milk inside the coconut instead of water.

The hardwood trunks of the coconut palms are used for the beams of houses and the masts of boats. The fronds, or leaves, of the palm trees are used to thatch roofs. They are also woven into mats, baskets, and hats.

Today an important coconut product for export is copra, the dried meat of a coconut. Crushed copra yields an oil used in the making of margarine, soap, shampoo, cosmetics, and other products.

PACIFIC CLIMATES AND RESOURCES

You have read that since the Pacific region is in the Southern Hemisphere, the seasons are reversed from the way they are in our part of the world. Most of the region is tropical or semitropical, with plenty of rain year-round. Australia, however, is mostly dry, except on its coastal rim.

Natural resources are unevenly spread in the region. Australia has abundant minerals, including major energy sources. New Zealand has excellent agricultural resources, as well as a variety of climates. Most islands of Oceania have limited natural resources.

Check Your Reading

1. How does the Pacific Ocean affect the climate of Oceania?
2. What are the important mineral resources of Australia?
3. How do the region's climate and natural resources affect how people live?
4. THINKING SKILL: What conclusion can you draw from the quote on page 592?

★ PEOPLE WHO MAKE A DIFFERENCE ★

Conserving the Rain Forests

In 1979 John Seed was living on a farm in New South Wales, Australia, when he learned that the nearby rain forest was going to be cut down by loggers. At one time forests had nearly covered the Australian continent. Now only a small percentage of the forested acres remained.

John decided to do something about the planned logging. First he met with state and national politicians. Then he organized people in his community by writing petitions and demonstrating at the logging sites. The protest grew in size and strength until finally the state government stopped the logging.

Since then John has taken his campaign to the national level. Because of his efforts, preservation of the rain forests in Tasmania and Queensland were important issues in the national elections of 1983 and 1987. The people of Australia voted into office a prime minister who supported conservation of the rain forests. In 1987 the federal government announced that more than 2 million acres (809,400 ha) of rain forest would be permanently protected.

Today John travels all over the world, helping people to understand the role of the rain forests in maintaining the future of our planet.

THE PACIFIC: PHYSICAL GEOGRAPHY

 LANDFORMS

- Continents: Australia (world's smallest) and Antarctica
- Islands of Oceania: New Zealand; thousands of small islands
- Australia has three main areas: Western Plateau, Central Plains (or Central Eastern Lowlands); Eastern Highlands

- Island groups of Oceania: Polynesia, Micronesia, Melanesia
- Antarctica: huge frozen continent

 CLIMATE

- Australia mostly dry; others get plenty of rain
- Ocean moderates climates

- Typhoons: tropical hurricanes that strike 2-3 times a year

NATURAL RESOURCES

- Australia: abundant land for ranching; minerals such as bauxite, iron, silver, coal, oil, natural gas, uranium
- New Zealand: water, forests, good soil

- Tropical islands: natural beauty
- Coconut: the "Tree of Life" for island countries

IDEAS TO REMEMBER

- The Pacific region is made up of numerous islands and two continents—Australia and Antarctica.
- Most of the islands of the Pacific have tropical climates and limited resources; Australia and New Zealand are exceptions.

REVIEWING VOCABULARY

atoll   outback
copra   typhoon
iceberg

Number a sheet of paper from 1 to 5. Beside each number write the word or term from the above list that best matches the definition.

1. Whirling tropical storms that strike the region of Oceania several times each year
2. The vast, dry interior region of Australia in which few people live
3. Coral islands that encircle a small, warm body of water
4. Dried meat of the coconut used for export
5. Floating "islands of ice" that often form when ice packs break up

REVIEWING FACTS

1. What is the general name for the islands of the Pacific Ocean? What are the names of the two largest landmasses in this region?
2. What are the names of Australia's three main regions? Where are most of Australia's large cities located?
3. What is the Great Barrier Reef? How did the reef form?
4. What are the two main types of islands in Oceania? Which of these has the most fertile soil?
5. Which American state is part of Polynesia?
6. What are the names of the two main islands of New Zealand? What is the name of the mountain range on the southern island?
7. Why is the northern coast of Australia hotter and drier than the southern coast?
8. What are the two most important industries of the Australian outback?
9. Name the economic benefits that New Zealand enjoys because of its abundant water resources and cool climate.
10. Why is the coconut palm tree called the "tree of life" in Oceania?

WRITING ABOUT MAIN IDEAS

1. **Writing a Travel Brochure:** Write a travel brochure describing places to visit in Australia's outback, such as the great stations or the red rock outcroppings.
2. **Writing a Survival Manual:** Write a survival manual for people who are shipwrecked on a small, deserted island in the Pacific.
3. **Writing About Perspectives:** Imagine that you have just completed a long stay in New Zealand and have visited many towns and scenic places. Write a paragraph of your observations describing New Zealand's land and people.

BUILDING SKILLS: READING MAPS OF THE OCEAN FLOOR

1. Compare the surface of the ocean floor with the surface of the earth above sea level.
2. Name one kind of map used to show the surface of the ocean floor.
3. How do contour maps of the ocean floor differ from contour maps of land above sea level?
4. Who might find maps of the ocean floor useful?

CHAPTER 30

NATIONS OF THE PACIFIC

FOCUS

Most people [in our part of the world] are outgoing, friendly, and fond of the "great outdoors." They also like to treat everyone as equals.

Special environments and events draw people to work hard together and to treat others as friends. In this chapter, you will read about the peoples and different ways of life that make the nations of the Pacific region distinctive.

LESSON 1

The People

READ TO LEARN

■ **Key Places**

Tahiti

■ **Read Aloud**

I felt as though I had been transported to the Garden of Eden. Everywhere we found hospitality, peace . . . and every appearance of happiness. What a country! What a people!

The French navigator Louis-Antoine de Bougainville wrote this glowing description after seeing the island of Tahiti for the first time. Yet his words could have been written about any of the Pacific islands. In this lesson you will read about the groups of people who live in this "Garden of Eden."

■ **Read for Purpose**

1. **WHAT YOU KNOW:** What is the name for the thousands of islands that dot the Pacific Ocean?
2. **WHAT YOU WILL LEARN:** Who were the first groups of people to live in the lands of the Pacific?

AUSTRALIA'S ABORIGINES

The first settlers of the Pacific region came in several groups over a long period of time.

Historians believe that the earliest known Australians came from Asia more than 50,000 years ago. English explorers called these people *Aborigines* (ab ə rij' ə nēz), which means "the first people to live in a place." The Aborigines call themselves the *Koori* (kü' rē). This name comes from one of their words for human.

For thousands of years the Aborigines survived by hunting, fishing, and gathering wild seeds, nuts, and fruits. They made tools of stone, wood, or shell.

When the first Europeans settled in Australia in 1788, there were about 300,000 Aborigines living there. Many were attacked and killed by the European explorers. Others died from diseases that came to the continent with the newcomers.

In spite of the hardships, however, the Aborigine culture survived. Today some Aborigines live in Australia's busy cities. Others choose to live in the outback, trying to continue the ways of their ancestors.

MELANESIANS AND MICRONESIANS

After the Aborigines, another wave of settlers sailed across the Pacific and landed on the islands of Melanesia. You can see from the map on page 598 that Melanesia is located north and east of Australia. The rugged land in most of this area separated groups of Melanesians

The Economy

Key Vocabulary

station

Key Places

Melbourne
New Zealand

Read Aloud

Once a week the "Tea and Sugar" train stops in Rawlinna, a place that appears to be a speck on the map of the Nullarbor Plain, a bleak, unpopulated plateau that cuts Western Australia off from the east. The "Tea and Sugar" links tiny communities made up mostly of railroad workers to the outside world. It is one way that Australians have overcome the problems of distance and isolation in building their economy. As you will read, other countries of the Pacific face similar challenges.

Read for Purpose

1. **WHAT YOU KNOW:** When did Europeans first explore the Pacific?
2. **WHAT YOU WILL LEARN:** What economic challenges do the people of the Pacific face today?

THE AUSTRALIAN ECONOMY

Like the United States, Australia has a developed economy that includes a mixture of farming, mining, manufacturing, and service industries. Today over 85 percent of the country's people live in urban areas. In the many skyscrapers of big cities like Sydney and Melbourne, people earn their living in such areas as banking, insurance, law, and medicine.

Only 6 percent of Australians work on farms or stations, which are huge cattle or sheep ranches. Yet farm exports like wool help to keep the country's standard of living high. Every year millions of sheep are loaded onto ships that haul them to markets around the world. Australian sheep supply the world with more than one third of the wool used for clothing.

You read in Chapter 29 that Australia is a land of abundant minerals. Australia leads the world in the production of iron ore. It also ranks among the top producers of copper, nickel, and aluminum.

A LAND OF FARMS

New Zealand is neither as prosperous nor as industrialized as Australia. Farming and ranching is still the most important part of the country's economy. For every person living in New Zealand, there are at least 20 sheep.

New Zealand is the world's largest exporter of wool. You may own a sweater or jacket made with wool from sheep on a New Zealand sheep station. New Zealand also exports lamb, beef, and such dairy products as butter and cheese.

Because of its variety of climates, New Zealand has almost every kind of farm. In

600

Sydney, Australia, is a modern, industrialized city. The famous Sydney Opera House (*right*) is a center for many of the arts.

addition to cattle and sheep stations and dairy farms, there are large orchards in which apples, pears, and nectarines are grown. Some farmers also raise flowers to sell overseas. On the Canterbury Plains, one of the few flat areas in New Zealand, farmers grow wheat and other grains.

ISLAND ECONOMIES

On many of the Pacific islands, tourism is the main source of income. In the days before jet planes, the South Pacific seemed liked an exotic, faraway land. Today, however, people can travel by plane and within hours be on a tropical beach.

Despite money from tourism, however, the economies of most of the Pacific islands are still developing. In Papua New Guinea, for example, farming, fishing, and forestry are the main sources of income.

The island of Tonga also has a developing economy. It exports mostly bananas and copra, the dried meat of coconuts. Yet Tonga's imports greatly outnumber its exports. The government of Tonga hopes that money brought in by tourism will help make up the difference.

THE PACIFIC ISLANDS AT WORK

As you have read, the Pacific region has a variety of economic systems. Australia has a developed economy based on farming, mining, manufacturing, and service industries. New Zealand's economy, based on farming and ranching, is less developed. The remaining Pacific islands have traditional economies.

Check Your Reading

1. Why does Australia have a high standard of living?
2. What products does New Zealand sell to countries around the world?
3. Describe the economy of a typical Pacific island country.
4. THINKING SKILL: List some of the goods produced in Australia and in the other nations of the Pacific. Now group the goods. What do your groups tell you about the economies of this region?

Decision Making: Review

Each day you make many decisions. Some decisions are small, such as which clothes you are going to wear. Other decisions are more important, such as whether or not to join a particular team at school.

When you make a decision, you select from among a number of alternatives, or options, one that will help you to achieve a goal or goals. If you are clear about your goal and carefully evaluate all possible alternatives, you will be more likely to make good decisions.

HELPING YOURSELF
One way to make a decision is to:

1. Identify and clearly define the goal(s) you wish to achieve.

2. Identify all possible options by which you can achieve your goal(s).

3. Predict the likely consequences, both immediate and long range, of each option.

4. Evaluate each consequence by determining whether it will benefit or harm you or others.

5. Choose the best option.

Applying the Skill
Read the example below. Then answer the questions that follow.

Imagine that your teacher has assigned a research project on which students can work together in pairs or in small groups. This project is a good opportunity for you to improve your social studies grade. Your two best friends ask you to work with them. A classmate who has just moved into your neighborhood also asks you to work with her. This new classmate is one of the smartest and most creative students in your school. You must decide with whom you want to work. Your teacher will ask about your plans soon, so you must make your decision.

1. What is your goal?
2. What are your options?
3. What might the consequences be of each option?
4. Which option would you choose? Why?

Reviewing the Skill
1. List some steps you can follow to make a good decision.
2. When you make a decision, why should you have a clear understanding of your goal(s)?
3. Why should you think of as many options as possible before making a decision?

The Government

READ TO LEARN

Key Vocabulary

trust territory

Key Places

Canberra
Northern Territory

Guam

Read Aloud

When the Queen of England visits Australia, she is not an outsider because she is also the head of state of the land "down under." Although it is an independent nation, Australia is also part of the British Commonwealth of Nations and, like Canada, recognizes the British monarch as its leader. The same is true of New Zealand, Papua New Guinea, and Fiji. These countries were once English colonies. When they gained their independence, they kept some of their ties to Great Britain.

In recent years many other nations of the Pacific have gained their independence. As you will read, the governments that these nations have established combine traditional island values with Western principles of democracy and justice.

Read for Purpose

1. WHAT YOU KNOW: What do many of the governments of Southeast Asia have in common?
2. WHAT YOU WILL LEARN: On what principles are the governments of the nations of the Pacific based?

GOVERNING AUSTRALIA

Australia's government was shaped by hundreds of years of British rule of the country. Like the British government, the Australian government values the rights and liberties of its people. Like the people of the United States, Australians saw the advantages of a federal system of government for their country.

The government of Australia is a democratic monarchy. Australia's legislature is a parliament, like Great Britain's. The government is headed by a prime minister, who is the leader of the political party with the most seats in the parliament.

Australia has six large states: New South Wales, Victoria, Queensland, South Australia, Western Australia, and Tasmania. There are also two territories that are run by the federal government. They are Canberra, which is the nation's capital, and the Northern Territory. Recently much of the Northern Territory was set aside for Aborigines.

Australians have long been strong believers in democracy and equality. Australia was the first nation to allow every adult male to vote, and one of the first to allow women to vote. Australia also introduced the use of secret ballots in elections.

Today all major democracies use secret ballots so that people cannot be frightened into voting a particular way. Australians believe that voting is so important that anyone who does not vote must pay a fine.

NEW ZEALAND AND THE PACIFIC ISLANDS

New Zealand also has a parliamentary system of government, with elected representatives in its legislature and a prime minister. Like Australia, New Zealand is a member of the British Commonwealth of Nations.

Until recently many Pacific island countries were controlled by European powers. Since most island nations had very few people, they were easily taken over by more powerful countries. For example, Palau, in Micronesia, was ruled first by Spain, followed by Germany, then Japan, and finally New Zealand.

After World War II the United Nations decided to make Palau a trust territory. A trust territory does not belong to any outside power. Rather, its government is controlled by another country until that country decides the trust territory is ready to govern itself.

Some Pacific islands, such as Guam (gwäm), are still trust territories of the United States. The United States has naval bases on some of these islands.

ISLAND TRADITIONS OF GOVERNMENT

The governments of most Pacific island nations are a mixture of ancient customs and Western principles of democracy. For thousands of years most islanders lived in villages that were headed by several chiefs. The chiefs ran not only the village government, but the economy as well.

Many island nations include chiefs in their present systems of government. For example, Vanuatu has an elected legislature and a council of chiefs. The council advises the government on how to save many of their traditional ways. Similarly, Tonga is a kingdom ruled by a monarch and a council. Half of the council are nobles, while the other half are elected by the people of Tonga.

The United States has large navy bases on the islands of Midway (*left*) and Guam.

Polynesians traditionally lived in large family clans known as *aigas*. An *aiga* might have several chiefs and hundreds of members. From the chiefs the *aiga* chose one person as *matai*, or high chief.

This system of government is still used in Samoa. The *matai* is in charge of the *aiga's* communal land and sits on the village council. In Western Samoa only *matai* have the right to vote for government officials to represent them.

GOVERNMENT IN THE PACIFIC

There are many forms of government in the Pacific region. But, as you have read, most of these nations have representative assemblies. Australia, New Zealand, Papua New Guinea, and Fiji are part of the British Commonwealth of Nations. Although the British monarch is the head of state, each country elects its own prime minister and parliament.

In many of the island nations of the rest of the Pacific, most governments are a mixture of old and new. Together, traditional island chiefs and government officials try to solve each country's problems.

 Check Your Reading

1. What system of government is used in Australia today?
2. Name two democratic practices that are followed in Australia.
3. How does Western Samoa combine the new and the old in its government?
4. **THINKING SKILL:** How are the governments of Great Britain and Australia similar? How are they different?

Arts and Recreation

TRADITIONAL ARTS

In the days before European explorers arrived in the Pacific region, warriors in opposing clans danced and chanted before they went into battle. You can imagine how they sounded by watching a Samoan canoe race today. Two dozen young men in a single canoe yell fierce chants to the beat of drums as they bend over their oars. The boats seem to fly over the water.

Some chants tell the history of families. Wi Huata (wē hü ä' tä) is an Episcopal priest in New Zealand. He is also a Maori who can tell the history of 50 generations of his family in a chant. To help recall the chant, he moves his fingers across a spear carved with his family's history.

Keeping their cultural identity alive is very important to the Maori and other Pacific peoples. The Aborigines of Australia have an ancient art tradition that you can read about on pages 608–611. Traditional art connects Pacific peoples to the past.

ENJOYING THE MODERN ARTS

At the center of the spectacular harbor in Sydney is a building like no other in the world. It looks like a flock of great white birds with their wings extended, ready to soar over the water. This building is the Sydney Opera House. It was planned to be an eye-catching building. Australians hoped to show outsiders that they not only appreciate the fine arts, but that they can also create beautiful architecture.

Several Australians have become world-famous opera stars, like Joan Sutherland. The country has also produced many other world-famous entertainers. From movie stars such as Paul Hogan and Mel Gibson, to singers such as Olivia Newton John, Australian entertainers are recognized all over the world today.

SPORTS

In the warm climate of the Pacific region, outdoor sports are available year-

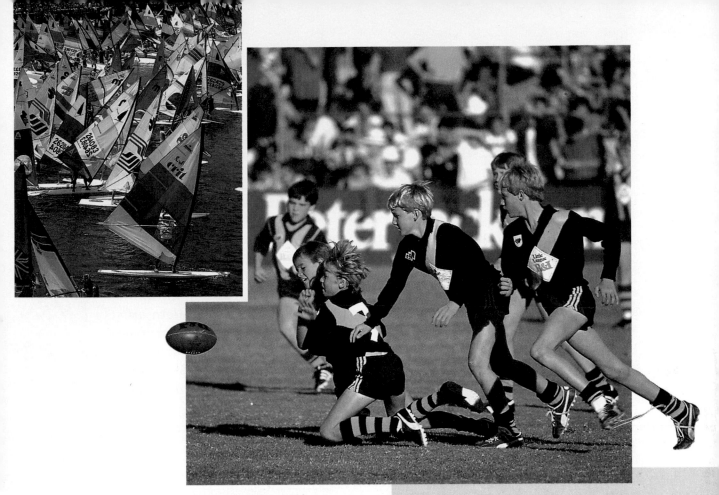

Australian children play a game of football, a game that is similar to rugby. Wind surfing is also a popular sport in the Pacific.

round. In Australia, for example, it seems as if everyone hikes, swims, surfs, or plays tennis or golf. Australians like to watch sports, but they will almost always say, "I'd rather give it a go myself."

There's no question about the most popular sport in New Zealand. "Kiwis," as New Zealanders are sometimes called, love to play rugby. As you have read, the game of rugby is much like American football. In addition to rugby players, New Zealand has also produced world-class distance runners and mountain climbers.

PACIFIC ARTS AND SPORTS

The arts and leisure of the Pacific region are a mixture of ancient and modern. On the same island you can enjoy a new movie or hear a family's history through a traditional chant.

As you have read, sports are enormously popular in this region of sunny days and warm temperatures. From sailing and swimming to golfing and hiking, the people of the Pacific love to be outdoors.

 Check Your Reading

1. How do some New Zealanders try to preserve their past?
2. How is the Sydney Opera House unique?
3. What are some popular outdoor activities in the Pacific region?
4. **THINKING SKILL:** What effect do you think the climate of the Pacific has had on the development of the popular sports of the region?

ABORIGINE PAINTING

by Carrie Evento

As you read in Chapter 29, the first people to live in Australia were the Aborigines. The Aborigine way of life has changed greatly. Despite change, Aborigines are holding on to many of their traditions. Some Aborigine artists continue to paint in the traditional ways of their ancestors. Many of these modern artists paint on the bark of trees and on rock walls just as Aborigines who lived long before them did. With their paintings, Aborigine artists keep an important part of their culture alive. As you read, think about why traditional ways of painting are so important to Aborigine artists.

AN ABORIGINE ARTIST AT WORK

Bluey Ilkirr, an Aborigine artist, props a long forked branch against the tall trunk of a stringybark tree. With an ax in one hand, he climbs up the branch until he is next to the tree trunk, about 20 feet (6 m) above the ground. Ilkirr reaches up and wedges the blade of the ax under the bark. Pulling down, he removes a large strip of bark in one piece from the tree.

Ilkirr spends weeks preparing the strip of bark for painting. He weighs it down with stones to make it flat and scrapes it clean.

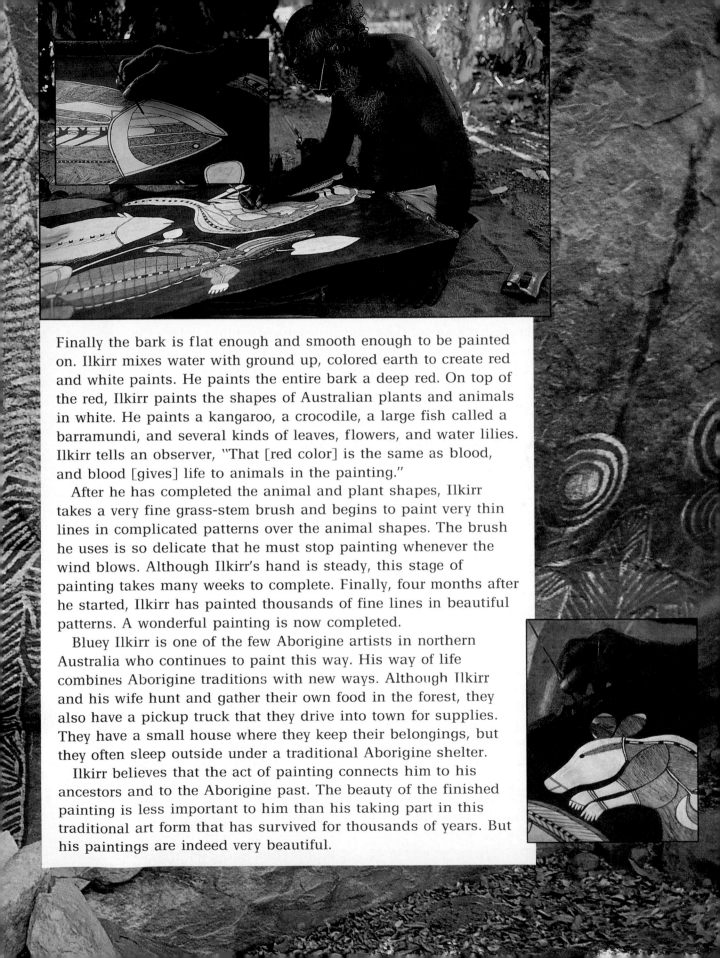

Finally the bark is flat enough and smooth enough to be painted on. Ilkirr mixes water with ground up, colored earth to create red and white paints. He paints the entire bark a deep red. On top of the red, Ilkirr paints the shapes of Australian plants and animals in white. He paints a kangaroo, a crocodile, a large fish called a barramundi, and several kinds of leaves, flowers, and water lilies. Ilkirr tells an observer, "That [red color] is the same as blood, and blood [gives] life to animals in the painting."

After he has completed the animal and plant shapes, Ilkirr takes a very fine grass-stem brush and begins to paint very thin lines in complicated patterns over the animal shapes. The brush he uses is so delicate that he must stop painting whenever the wind blows. Although Ilkirr's hand is steady, this stage of painting takes many weeks to complete. Finally, four months after he started, Ilkirr has painted thousands of fine lines in beautiful patterns. A wonderful painting is now completed.

Bluey Ilkirr is one of the few Aborigine artists in northern Australia who continues to paint this way. His way of life combines Aborigine traditions with new ways. Although Ilkirr and his wife hunt and gather their own food in the forest, they also have a pickup truck that they drive into town for supplies. They have a small house where they keep their belongings, but they often sleep outside under a traditional Aborigine shelter.

Ilkirr believes that the act of painting connects him to his ancestors and to the Aborigine past. The beauty of the finished painting is less important to him than his taking part in this traditional art form that has survived for thousands of years. But his paintings are indeed very beautiful.

THE DREAMTIME

Many of the subjects painted by Bluey Ilkirr and other Aborigine artists come from a period in the past that the Aborigines call the Dreamtime. According to Aborigine belief, the Dreamtime was the period during which everything in nature was created. This includes people, landforms, plants, and animals.

The Gagudju, an Aborigine group from northern Australia, believe that at the beginning of the Dreamtime a spirit named Warramurrungundji came out of the sea. She created the people and gave them their language. Other spirits followed her in the forms of animals. Marrawuti, a giant eagle, carried water lilies and planted them in the water. Ginga, a crocodile, made some of the rocky areas near where the Gagudju live.

Aborigines believe that when these spirits were finished creating, they made themselves part of the land. Ginga, the crocodile, became a rock shaped like the back of a crocodile. Warramurrungundji became a large white rock. For thousands of years Aborigine artists have been making rock paintings at many of the places where they believe that the creator spirits placed themselves in the land. These rock paintings show the creator spirits of the Dreamtime as well as many animals still found in Australia.

At a place called Kakadu in northern Australia, there is a rock face more than 200 feet (61 m) long that is covered with Aborigine paintings. The photo of a fish at the top of this page, and the background photo are paintings from Kakadu. Scientists believe that some of the paintings are more than 20,000 years old. The Gagudju believe that the earliest paintings at Kakadu were made by the creator spirits. One Gagudju says, "The [spirits] showed Aborigine people how to hunt kangaroos, how to paint, and many other things."

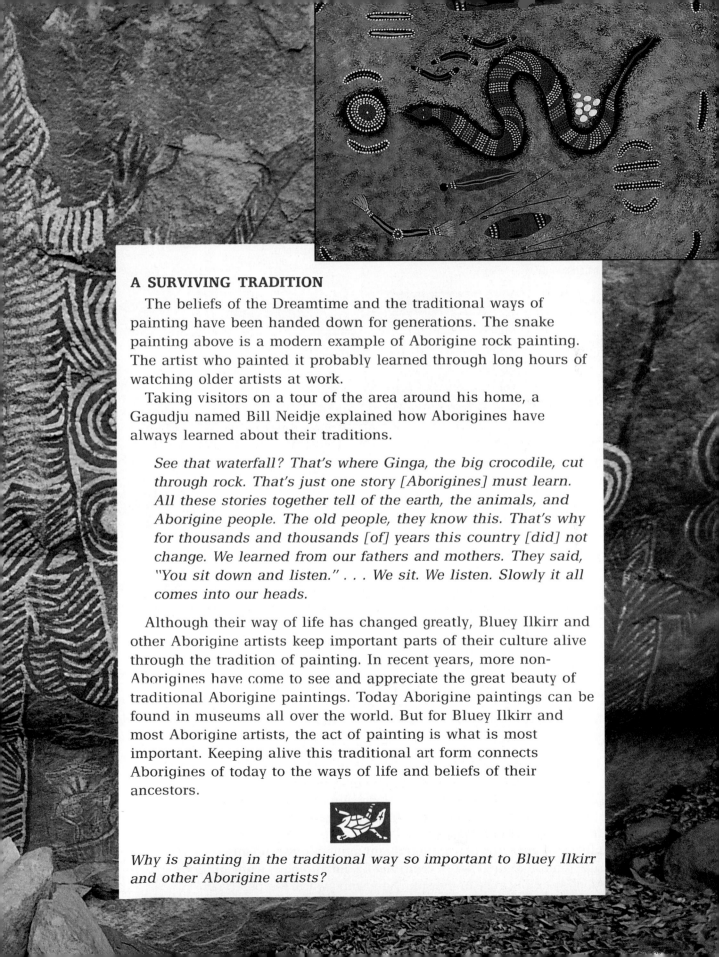

A SURVIVING TRADITION

The beliefs of the Dreamtime and the traditional ways of painting have been handed down for generations. The snake painting above is a modern example of Aborigine rock painting. The artist who painted it probably learned through long hours of watching older artists at work.

Taking visitors on a tour of the area around his home, a Gagudju named Bill Neidje explained how Aborigines have always learned about their traditions.

> See that waterfall? That's where Ginga, the big crocodile, cut through rock. That's just one story [Aborigines] must learn. All these stories together tell of the earth, the animals, and Aborigine people. The old people, they know this. That's why for thousands and thousands [of] years this country [did] not change. We learned from our fathers and mothers. They said, "You sit down and listen." . . . We sit. We listen. Slowly it all comes into our heads.

Although their way of life has changed greatly, Bluey Ilkirr and other Aborigine artists keep important parts of their culture alive through the tradition of painting. In recent years, more non-Aborigines have come to see and appreciate the great beauty of traditional Aborigine paintings. Today Aborigine paintings can be found in museums all over the world. But for Bluey Ilkirr and most Aborigine artists, the act of painting is what is most important. Keeping alive this traditional art form connects Aborigines of today to the ways of life and beliefs of their ancestors.

Why is painting in the traditional way so important to Bluey Ilkirr and other Aborigine artists?

NATIONS OF THE PACIFIC: CULTURAL GEOGRAPHY

PEOPLE

- Australian Aborigines: original inhabitants; some live traditional life today
- Micronesians and Melanesians: farmers; extended family groups or clans

- Polynesians: expert sailors and shipbuilders; settled Tahiti, Samoa, Hawaii, New Zealand
- Europeans: first arrived in 1500s; first settled in Australia in 1788; introduced English language and customs

ECONOMY

- Australia: developed economy; urban, with large cities like Sydney and Melbourne

- Australian sheep ranching provides one third of world's wool; mining is also a major industry
- New Zealand: farming and ranching; world's largest wool exporter
- Islands: tourism key source of income; developing economies; subsistence farming

GOVERNMENT

- British Commonwealth countries: Australia, New Zealand, Papua New Guinea, Fiji

- Australia: democratic monarchy; parliamentary system; country made up of six states and two territories
- Trust territories: temporarily controlled by outside country; for example, Palau, Guam
- Many islands have traditional governments with village chiefs

ARTS AND RECREATION

- Traditional culture: chants retell histories of clans

- Australia has produced world-famous entertainers in opera, movies, popular music

- Outdoor sports are popular

IDEAS TO REMEMBER

- People who settled in Australia and the Pacific islands developed distinct cultures because of their isolation from the outside world.
- Australia and New Zealand have the most developed economies in the region; in the Pacific island countries tourism is important.
- Among the forms of government in the Pacific are parliamentary systems, monarchies, and mixtures of traditional and modern governments.
- Arts and recreation in the Pacific combine the old and new, while outdoor sports are popular because of the sunny days and warm temperatures.

REVIEWING VOCABULARY

Each of the following statements contains an underlined vocabulary word or term. Number a sheet of paper from 1 to 5. Beside each number write whether the following statements are true or false. If the statement is true, write "true." If it is false, rewrite the sentence using the vocabulary word correctly.

1. Stations are huge cattle or sheep ranches in New Zealand and Australia.
2. Although a trust territory does not belong to an outside power, its government is controlled by a foreign country.
3. Only 6 percent of Australians work on farms or stations.
4. Several Pacific islands, such as Guam, are trust territories of the United States.
5. Trust territories are controlled by another country until the trust territory decides to govern itself.

REVIEWING FACTS

1. Describe two effects that European settlement had on Australia's aborigines.
2. What effect did Melanesia's rugged landscape have on the region's culture?
3. Describe two features of traditional culture that are still maintained in rural Melanesia.
4. Why have the ancient Polynesians often been compared to the Vikings?
5. Who were the first British settlers in Australia? When did these settlers arrive?
6. Why is Australia's economy called a developed economy?
7. Name two things that are similar about the governments of Australia and the United States.
8. How are the governments of New Zealand and Australia similar?
9. What are *aigas*? What are *matais*? On which Polynesian island are these institutions still found?
10. What does a Samoan canoe race have in common with traditional warfare in the Pacific islands?

WRITING ABOUT MAIN IDEAS

1. **Writing a Legend:** You read about a Polynesian legend describing the "paradise" of Tahiti. Write a legend describing the arrival of Europeans in Australia from the standpoint of the aborigines.
2. **Writing a Proposal:** A proposal is a document that makes recommendations to create, improve, or change something. Write a proposal entitled "A Plan for Developing the Economies of the Pacific Islands."
3. **Writing a Report:** Write a report about the status of both the aborigines in Australia and the Maoris in New Zealand. You may wish to use encyclopedias, magazines, and newspapers to supplement the information presented in the text.
4. **Writing About Perspectives:** Imagine a conversation between two New Zealanders: one of Maori ancestry, the other of European ancestry. Write something each might tell the other about the important traditions of his or her people.

BUILDING SKILLS: DECISION MAKING

1. Use your own words to define *decision making*.
2. List the steps you might follow in making a sound decision.
3. Why is it important to know how to make decisions?

THE PACIFIC: PHYSICAL GEOGRAPHY

 LANDFORMS

- Two large continents (Australia and Antarctica), thousands of islands (Oceania)
- Antarctica: huge frozen continent

 CLIMATE

- Australia mostly dry; others get plenty of rain
- Ocean moderates climates

- Typhoons: tropical hurricanes that strike 2-3 times a year

NATURAL RESOURCES

- Australia: abundant land for ranching; minerals such as bauxite, iron, silver, coal, oil, natural gas, uranium
- New Zealand: water, forests, good soil
- Tropical islands: natural beauty
- Coconut: the "Tree of Life" for island countries

THE PACIFIC: CULTURAL GEOGRAPHY

PEOPLE

- Original inhabitants and early settlers: Australian Aborigines, Melanesians, Micronesians, Polynesians
- Europeans: first arrived in 1500s; first settled in Australia in 1788; introduced English language and customs

ECONOMY

- Australia: developed economy; urban, with large cities like Sydney and Melbourne

- Sheep ranching: major industry in Australia and New Zealand
- Islands: tourism key source of income; developing economies; subsistence farming

GOVERNMENT

- British Commonwealth countries: Australia, New Zealand, Papua New Guinea, Fiji
- Trust territories: temporarily controlled by outside country; for example, Palau, Guam
- Many islands have traditional governments with village chiefs

ARTS AND RECREATION

- Traditional culture: chants retell histories of clans
- Australia has produced world-famous entertainers in opera, movies, popular music

- Outdoor sports are popular

REVIEWING VOCABULARY

atoll trust territory
copra typhoon
outback

Number a sheet of paper from 1 to 5. Beside each number write the word or term from the above list that best completes the sentence.

1. Consisting of the dried meat of the coconut, _____ is a major export product for many Pacific islands.
2. The government of a _____ is controlled by another country until that country feels the land is ready for self-government.
3. A whirling tropical hurricane, or _____, strikes Oceania several times a year.
4. A doughnut-shaped coral reef, or _____, may have formed on the rim of a submerged volcano in Oceania.
5. The _____ is an arid, desolate region in the interior of Australia where few people live.

WRITING ABOUT THE UNIT

1. **Writing a Paragraph:** You read that Australia is the oldest continent. Write a paragraph that describes the evidence for this idea.

2. **Writing a Letter:** Imagine that you are a scientist stationed in Antarctica. In a letter to a friend, write your observations about the frozen continent.
3. **Writing About Perspectives:** Imagine that you are the leader of the first group of Polynesians to land on the island of Tahiti. Write a diary entry describing your new island home.

ACTIVITIES

1. **Working Together to Construct a Regional Data Chart:** Work together to construct a chart showing data for Australia, New Zealand, and the United States. The three countries should be listed at the left of the chart. At the top of the chart, from left to right, the following categories should appear: area (in square miles and kilometers); population; population density (number of persons per square mile/square kilometer); GNP (gross national product); and per capita income (expressed in dollars). Use almanacs to obtain this information.
2. **Presenting an Oral Report:** Use juvenile nonfiction books and encyclopedias to research coral reef formation. Present your findings in an oral report to the rest of the class.

LINKING PAST, PRESENT, AND FUTURE

Some of the things that have attracted countless newcomers to Oceania, from ancient Polynesian seafarers to modern tourists, are the mild climate, abundant food, and natural beauty of the islands. Many of these islands are now struggling to develop their resources to meet the needs of growing populations. Do you think that Oceania will be able to remain a "paradise" in the face of such change? What will islands like Samoa and Tahiti be like in the twenty-first century?

Conclusion

In this book you have studied the planet earth, from the farthest northern reaches of Canada to the outback of Australia. You have seen how people interact in the world's eight regions: the United States and Canada, Latin America, Western Europe, Eastern Europe and Northern Asia, the Middle East and North Africa, Sub-Saharan Africa, Southern and Eastern Asia, and the Pacific. What have you learned about our world?

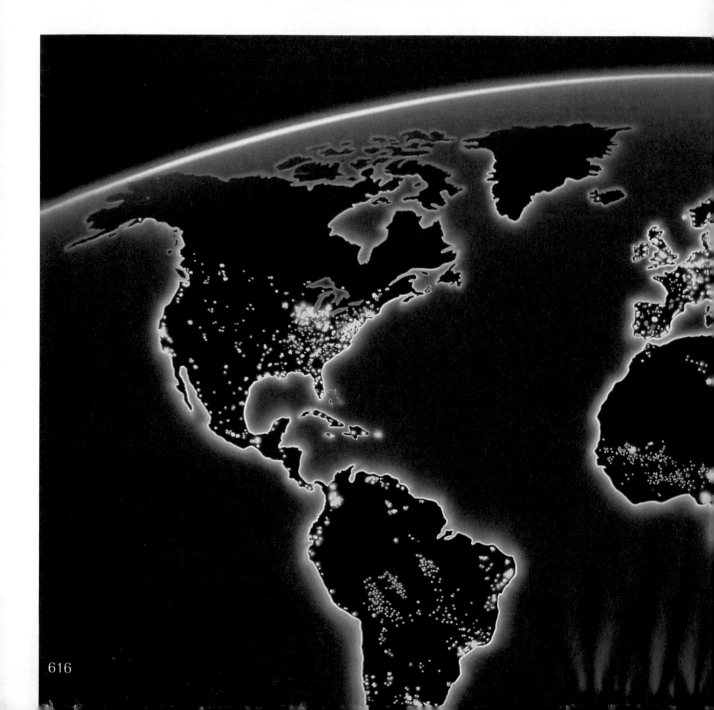

THE EARTH AT NIGHT

Look at the map on this page. It shows what the earth looks like at night, based on satellite photographs. The bright yellow spots on the map are sources of light. Most are from urban areas but some come from other sources, such as fires used in slash-and-burn farming. The bright lights around Japan are from huge floodlights used by fishing fleets to attract squid.

As you look at the map, think about what you have read in this book. Can you see how some of the important concepts you have learned are shown on the map?

Look at the eastern United States and Western Europe. Their dense population is shown by the tight grouping of bright lights. Similarly, you can see by the lights that most of Canada's people live along its southern border with the United States.

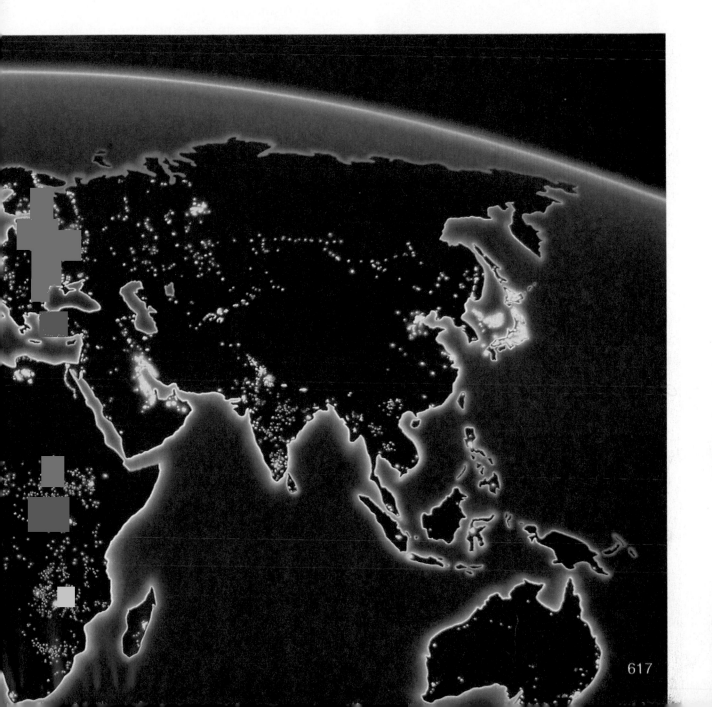

617

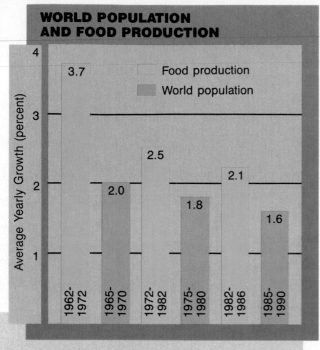

WORLD POPULATION AND FOOD PRODUCTION

Average Yearly Growth (percent)

- Food production
- World population

3.7 — 1962-1972
2.0 — 1965-1970
2.5 — 1972-1982
1.8 — 1975-1980
2.1 — 1982-1986
1.6 — 1985-1990

GRAPH SKILL: By what percentage did annual food production increase from 1982 to 1986?

Can you find the Nile River Valley? As you may remember, it is in the northeastern part of Africa, near the Arabian Peninsula. You can follow the outline of the river on the map by the lights from the many towns along its banks. In contrast, look at the vast dark expanses of the Sahara, home to so few people.

In Unit 4 you read about how the Trans-Siberian Railroad links the remote parts of Russia. Can you find the railroad on this map? It is indicated by the lights of the cities and villages along its route.

In Unit 2 you read about the pros and cons of the effort to develop Brazil's rain forest. Many of the lights shown in South America are from forest fires that have been set to clear the rain forest.

These are just some of the things this map shows about life on our planet. As you study the map further, think about other ways in which it reflects what you have learned about the world.

WORKING TOGETHER

As we move toward the twenty-first century we on planet earth face many great challenges. You have read about some of them, such as the acid rain that threatens to kill forests in the United States, Canada, and Western Europe. At times it may seem that these problems are too big to be solved. Is there a future for our planet? Yes, if the people of the earth work together to guarantee it.

We are already meeting some of the challenges. Look at the graph on this page. It shows that although the world's population is growing quickly, food production is growing even faster. If we can keep producing food at this pace, we will be able to feed a world population of more than 10 billion people 100 years from now!

THE FUTURE

Right now people from all over the world are working together in ways that you probably cannot even imagine. American, Canadian, Russian, Italian, Norwegian, and Chinese scientists are exploring Antarctica and measuring the far-reaching effects of air pollution. UNICEF—the United Nations Children's Fund—is working to house, feed, and clothe nearly 1 billion children in more than 100 countries. And in cities and towns all over our country, people are organizing efforts to recycle important natural resources such as aluminum. Recycling programs enable us to use natural resources over and over again.

In the future it will be your responsibility to make sure that these efforts continue. As one scientist has noted:

Our ability to look back on ourselves from outer space symbolizes the unique perspective we have on our environment. . . . With this knowledge comes a responsibility . . . to manage the human use of planet earth.

REFERENCE SECTION

THE WORLD
Political

NORTH
AMERICA

CANADA

UNITED STATES

GREENLAND
(DENMARK)

ALASKA
(U.S.)

Arctic Circle

ARCTIC OCEAN

80°N

60°N

40°N

PACIFIC
OCEAN

MIDWAY ISLANDS
(U.S.)

Tropic of Cancer

HAWAII (U.S.)

20°N

MEXICO

BERMUDA
(U.K.)

ATLANTIC
OCEAN

AZORES
(PORT.)

See inset below

Caribbean Sea

CAPE
VERDE

KIRIBATI

0°   Equator

GALAPAGOS
ISLANDS
(ECUADOR)

ECUADOR

VENEZUELA

GUYANA
SURINAME
FRENCH GUIANA (FR.)

COLOMBIA

SOUTH
AMERICA

WESTERN
SAMOA

AMERICAN
SAMOA
(U.S.)

PERU

BRAZIL

TONGA

FRENCH

BOLIVIA

20°S

POLYNESIA
(FR.)

Tropic of Capricorn

EASTER ISLAND
(CHILE)

PARAGUAY

CHILE

URUGUAY

40°S

ARGENTINA

PACIFIC
OCEAN

FALKLAND ISLANDS
(U.K.)

60°S

Antarctic Circle

180°   160°W   140°W   120°W   100°W   80°W   60°W   40°

80°S

ANTARCTICA

180°   160°W   140°W   120°W   100°W   80°W   60°W   40°

Central America
and West Indies

90°W

80°W

FLORIDA
(U.S.)

Gulf of Mexico

BAHAMAS

70°W

Tropic of Cancer

Tropic of Cancer

60°W

20°N

CUBA

TURKS AND CAICOS ISLANDS (U.K.)

ATLANTIC
OCEAN

20°N

MEXICO

BELIZE

CAYMAN
ISLANDS
(U.K.)

JAMAICA

HAITI

DOMINICAN
REPUBLIC

PUERTO RICO (U.S.)

VIRGIN ISLANDS (U.K.)
ST. KITTS AND NEVIS
ANTIGUA AND BARBUDA

GUADELOUPE (FR.)

GUATEMALA

HONDURAS

VIRGIN
ISLANDS
(U.S.)

DOMINICA

MARTINIQUE (FR.)

EL SALVADOR

N

Caribbean   Sea

SAINT LUCIA

BARBADOS

PACIFIC
OCEAN

NICARAGUA

ARUBA
(NETH.)

NETHERLANDS
ANTILLES
(NETH.)

SAINT VINCENT AND
THE GRENADINES

GRENADA

BONAIRE

CURAÇAO

TRINIDAD
AND TOBAGO

10°N

10°N

COSTA
RICA

0   250   500 Miles

0   250   500   750 Kilometers

PANAMA

COLOMBIA

SOUTH AMERICA

VENEZUELA

GUYANA

SURINAME

80°W

70°W

60°W

620

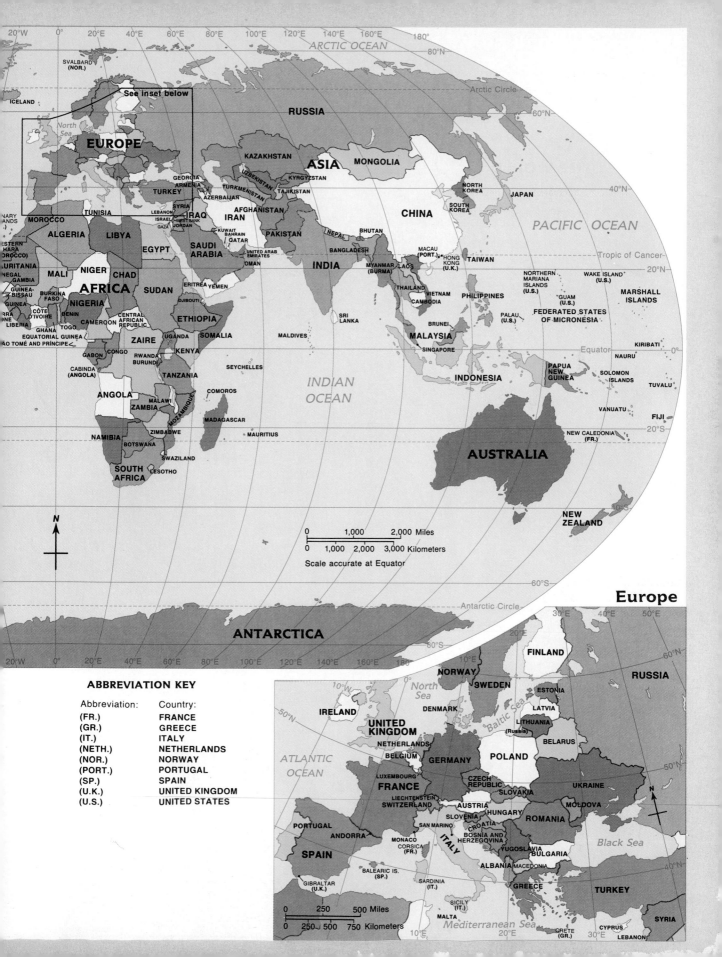

ARCTIC OCEAN

SVALBARD
(NOR.)

ICELAND

See inset below

North
Sea

EUROPE

RUSSIA

Arctic Circle

80°N

60°N

ASIA

MONGOLIA

KAZAKHSTAN

40°N

UZBEKISTAN
KYRGYZSTAN

NORTH
KOREA

GEORGIA
ARMENIA
TURKEY

TURKMENISTAN
TAJIKISTAN

AZERBAIJAN

JAPAN

SOUTH
KOREA

CHINA

PACIFIC OCEAN

TUNISIA

MOROCCO

LEBANON
SYRIA
IRAQ
ISRAEL WEST BANK
JORDAN
GAZA

AFGHANISTAN

IRAN

ALGERIA

LIBYA

EGYPT

KUWAIT
BAHRAIN
QATAR

SAUDI
ARABIA

UNITED ARAB
EMIRATES
OMAN

PAKISTAN

NEPAL

BHUTAN

BANGLADESH

MACAU
(PORT.)

HONG
KONG
(U.K.)

TAIWAN

Tropic of Cancer

20°N

WAKE ISLAND
(U.S.)

CANARY
ISLANDS
(SP.)

WESTERN
SAHARA
(MOROCCO)

MAURITANIA

SENEGAL
GAMBIA

MALI

NIGER

CHAD

AFRICA

SUDAN

INDIA

ERITREA

YEMEN

MYANMAR
(BURMA)

LAOS

THAILAND

VIETNAM

CAMBODIA

NORTHERN
MARIANA
ISLANDS
(U.S.)

GUAM
(U.S.)

PHILIPPINES

MARSHALL
ISLANDS

GUINEA-
BISSAU

GUINEA

SIERRA
LEONE

LIBERIA

BURKINA
FASO

NIGERIA

CÔTE
D'IVOIRE

GHANA

TOGO
BENIN

CAMEROON

CENTRAL
AFRICAN
REPUBLIC

ETHIOPIA

DJIBOUTI

SRI
LANKA

MALDIVES

BRUNEI

MALAYSIA

SINGAPORE

PALAU
(U.S.)

FEDERATED STATES
OF MICRONESIA

EQUATORIAL GUINEA

SÃO TOMÉ AND PRÍNCIPE

GABON

CONGO

ZAIRE

UGANDA

RWANDA
BURUNDI

KENYA

SEYCHELLES

INDIAN
OCEAN

KIRIBATI

NAURU

Equator

0°

CABINDA
(ANGOLA)

TANZANIA

COMOROS

SOLOMON
ISLANDS

TUVALU

ANGOLA

ZAMBIA

MALAWI

MOZAMBIQUE

MADAGASCAR

PAPUA
NEW
GUINEA

INDONESIA

VANUATU

FIJI

NAMIBIA

ZIMBABWE

BOTSWANA

MAURITIUS

NEW CALEDONIA
(FR.)

20°S

SWAZILAND

SOUTH
AFRICA

LESOTHO

AUSTRALIA

N

NEW
ZEALAND

| 0 | 1,000 | 2,000 Miles |
| 0 | 1,000 | 2,000 | 3,000 Kilometers |

Scale accurate at Equator

60°S

Antarctic Circle

ANTARCTICA

80°S

Europe

ABBREVIATION KEY

Abbreviation:	Country:
(FR.)	FRANCE
(GR.)	GREECE
(IT.)	ITALY
(NETH.)	NETHERLANDS
(NOR.)	NORWAY
(PORT.)	PORTUGAL
(SP.)	SPAIN
(U.K.)	UNITED KINGDOM
(U.S.)	UNITED STATES

FINLAND

NORWAY

SWEDEN

RUSSIA

North
Sea

ESTONIA

IRELAND

DENMARK

LATVIA

Baltic Sea

LITHUANIA
(Russia)

UNITED
KINGDOM

BELARUS

NETHERLANDS

GERMANY

POLAND

ATLANTIC
OCEAN

BELGIUM

LUXEMBOURG

FRANCE

CZECH
REPUBLIC

UKRAINE

LIECHTENSTEIN

SLOVAKIA

SWITZERLAND

AUSTRIA

HUNGARY

MOLDOVA

SLOVENIA

ROMANIA

PORTUGAL

SAN MARINO

CROATIA

ANDORRA

MONACO

ITALY

CORSICA
(FR.)

BOSNIA AND
HERZEGOVINA

YUGOSLAVIA

BULGARIA

Black Sea

SPAIN

ALBANIA

MACEDONIA

TURKEY

GIBRALTAR
(U.K.)

BALEARIC IS.
(SP.)

SARDINIA
(IT.)

GREECE

SYRIA

SICILY
(IT.)

| 0 | 250 | 500 Miles |
| 0 | 250 | 500 | 750 Kilometers |

MALTA

Mediterranean Sea

CRETE
(GR.)

CYPRUS

LEBANON

N

THE WORLD
Physical

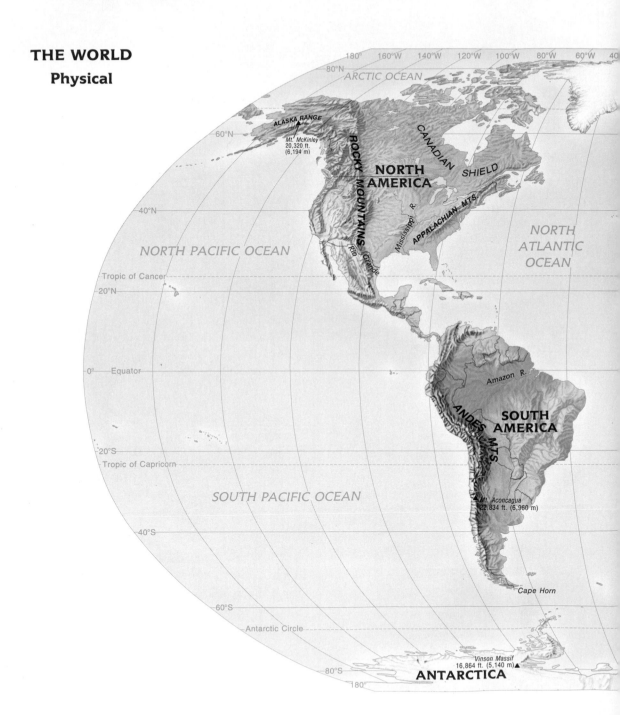

ARCTIC OCEAN

180° 160°W 140°W 120°W 100°W 80°W 60°W 40

80°N

60°N

ALASKA RANGE
Mt. McKinley
20,320 ft.
(6,194 m)

CANADIAN SHIELD

ROCKY MOUNTAINS

NORTH
AMERICA

40°N

Mississippi R.

APPALACHIAN MTS.

NORTH
ATLANTIC
OCEAN

NORTH PACIFIC OCEAN

Rio Grande

Tropic of Cancer

20°N

0° Equator

Amazon R.

SOUTH
AMERICA

ANDES MTS.

20°S

Tropic of Capricorn

SOUTH PACIFIC OCEAN

Mt. Aconcagua
22,834 ft. (6,960 m)

40°S

Cape Horn

60°S

Antarctic Circle

Vinson Massif
16,864 ft. (5,140 m)

80°S

180°

ANTARCTICA

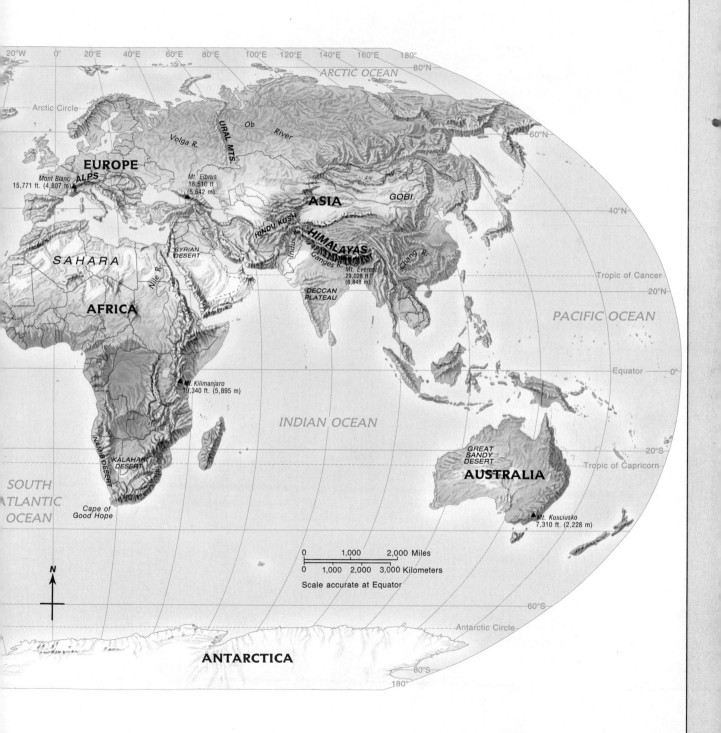

20°W | 0° | 20°E | 40°E | 60°E | 80°E | 100°E | 120°E | 140°E | 160°E | 180°

ARCTIC OCEAN

80°N

Arctic Circle

60°N

Volga R.
URAL MTS.
Ob River

EUROPE

ALPS
Mont Blanc
15,771 ft. (4,807 m)

Mt. Elbrus
18,510 ft.
(5,642 m)

ASIA

GOBI

40°N

HINDU KUSH
HIMALAYAS
SYRIAN DESERT

SAHARA

Indus R.
Ganges R.
Mt. Everest
29,028 ft.
(8,848 m)

Chang R.

Tropic of Cancer

20°N

Nile R.

DECCAN
PLATEAU

AFRICA

PACIFIC OCEAN

Mt. Kilimanjaro
19,340 ft. (5,895 m)

Equator
0°

INDIAN OCEAN

NAMIB DESERT

KALAHARI
DESERT

GREAT
SANDY
DESERT

20°S

SOUTH
ATLANTIC
OCEAN

AUSTRALIA

Tropic of Capricorn

Cape of
Good Hope

Mt. Kosciusko
7,310 ft. (2,228 m)

N

0   1,000   2,000 Miles
0   1,000   2,000   3,000 Kilometers
Scale accurate at Equator

60°S

Antarctic Circle

ANTARCTICA

80°S

180°

623

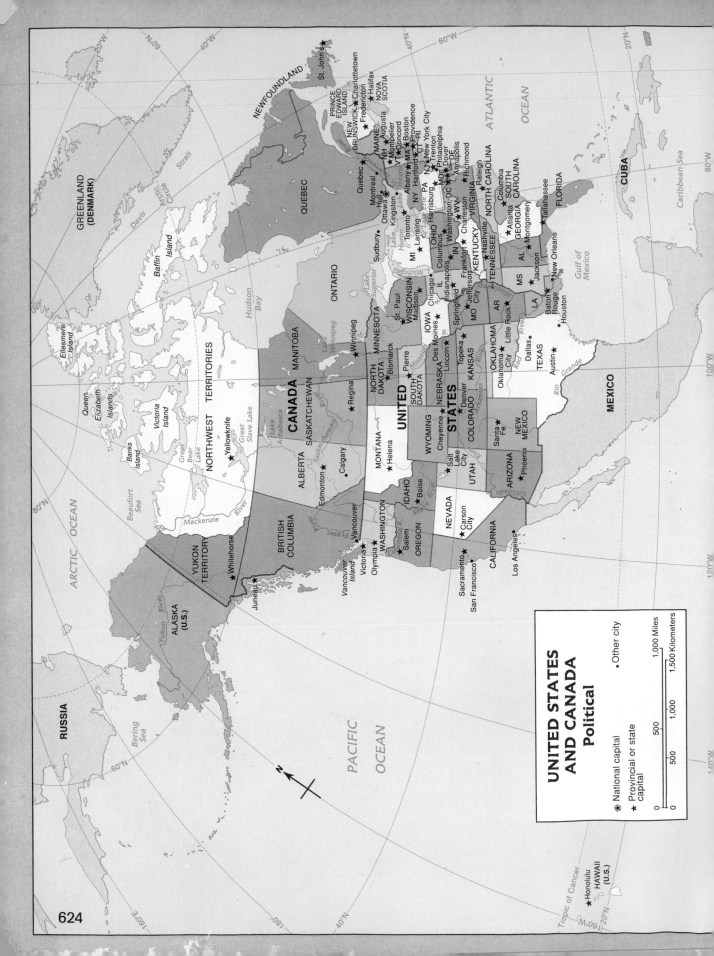

UNITED STATES AND CANADA
Political

⊛ National capital
★ Provincial or state capital
• Other city

		500		1,000 Miles
0	500	1,000		1,500 Kilometers

GREENLAND (DENMARK)

ARCTIC OCEAN

RUSSIA

Bering Sea

PACIFIC OCEAN

Beaufort Sea

ALASKA (U.S.)

Yukon River

Juneau ★

Whitehorse ★

YUKON TERRITORY

NORTHWEST TERRITORIES

Yellowknife ★

Great Bear Lake

Great Slave Lake

Banks Island

Victoria Island

Queen Elizabeth Islands

Ellesmere Island

Baffin Island

Davis Strait

Hudson Bay

Mackenzie River

Lake Athabasca

BRITISH COLUMBIA

Vancouver Island

Victoria ★

Vancouver

Fraser River

ALBERTA

Edmonton ★

Calgary •

SASKATCHEWAN

Regina ★

Saskatchewan River

MANITOBA

Winnipeg ★

Lake Winnipeg

ONTARIO

Sudbury •

QUEBEC

NEWFOUNDLAND

St. John's ★

PRINCE EDWARD ISLAND
Charlottetown ★

NEW BRUNSWICK
Fredericton ★

NOVA SCOTIA
Halifax ★

Quebec ★

Montreal

Hull
Ottawa ⊛

Kingston

Toronto ★

Lake Ontario

Lake Erie

Lake Huron

Lake Superior

Lake Michigan

CANADA

UNITED STATES

WASHINGTON
Olympia ★
Columbia R.

OREGON
Salem ★

Columbia River
Snake River

IDAHO
Boise ★

MONTANA
Helena ★

NORTH DAKOTA
Bismarck ★

SOUTH DAKOTA
Pierre ★

Missouri River

MINNESOTA
St. Paul ★

WISCONSIN
Madison ★

MI
Lansing ★

NEVADA
Carson City ★

CALIFORNIA
Sacramento ★
San Francisco •
Los Angeles •

UTAH
Salt Lake City ★

WYOMING
Cheyenne ★

COLORADO
Denver ★

NEBRASKA
Lincoln ★

IOWA
Des Moines ★

KANSAS
Topeka ★

ARIZONA
Phoenix ★

NEW MEXICO
Santa Fe ★

OKLAHOMA
Oklahoma City ★

TEXAS
Austin ★
Dallas •
Houston •

Rio Grande

Red River

Arkansas River

Colorado River

MISSOURI
Jefferson City ★

ARKANSAS
Little Rock ★

LA
Baton Rouge ★
New Orleans •

MS
Jackson ★

AL
Montgomery ★

Mississippi River

ILLINOIS
Springfield ★
Chicago •

IN
Indianapolis ★

OHIO
Columbus ★

KENTUCKY
Frankfort ★

TENNESSEE
Nashville ★

GEORGIA
Atlanta ★

FLORIDA
Tallahassee ★

SOUTH CAROLINA
Columbia ★

NORTH CAROLINA
Raleigh ★

VIRGINIA
Richmond ★

WV
Charleston ★

Washington, D.C. ⊛

MD
Annapolis ★
DE
Dover ★

PA
Harrisburg ★
Philadelphia •

NJ
Trenton ★

NEW YORK
Albany ★
New York City •

CT
Hartford ★
RI
Providence ★

MA
Boston ★

VT
Montpelier ★
NH
Concord ★

MAINE
Augusta ★

ATLANTIC OCEAN

MEXICO

Gulf of Mexico

CUBA

Caribbean Sea

HAWAII (U.S.)
Honolulu ★

Tropic of Cancer

N

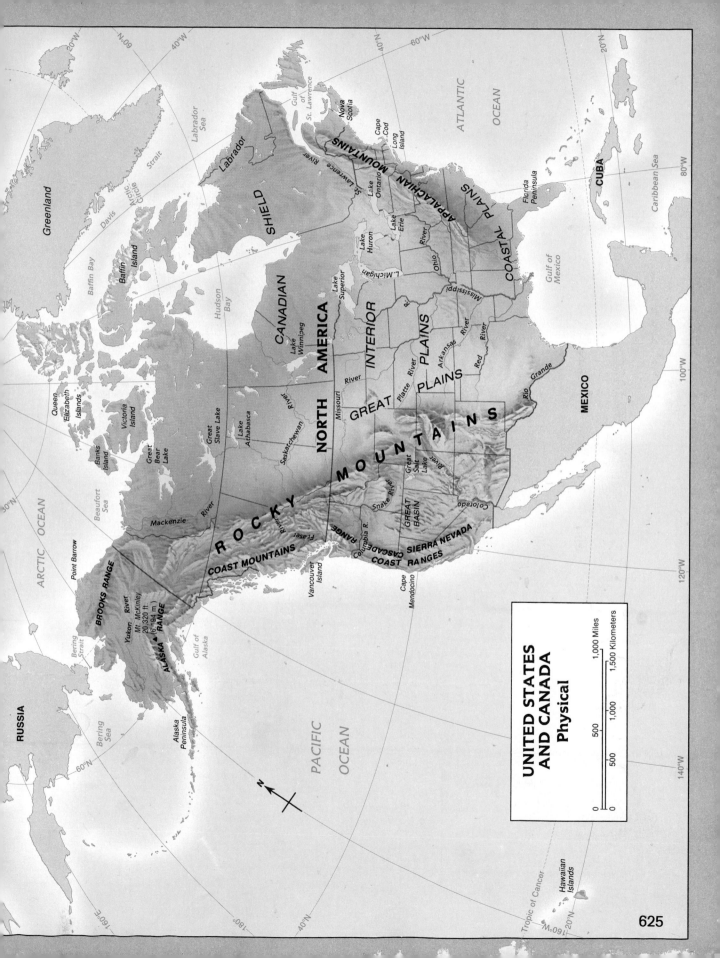

UNITED STATES AND CANADA Physical

RUSSIA

Bering Strait

ARCTIC OCEAN

Point Barrow

Beaufort Sea

Banks Island

Victoria Island

Queen Elizabeth Islands

Greenland

Baffin Bay

Davis Strait

Baffin Island

Labrador Sea

Arctic Circle

CANADIAN SHIELD

Labrador

Gulf of St. Lawrence

Nova Scotia

Cape Cod

Long Island

APPALACHIAN MOUNTAINS

ATLANTIC OCEAN

CUBA

Caribbean Sea

Florida Peninsula

Gulf of Mexico

COASTAL PLAINS

St. Lawrence River

Lake Ontario

Lake Erie

Lake Huron

L. Michigan

Lake Superior

Ohio River

Mississippi

INTERIOR PLAINS

GREAT PLAINS

NORTH AMERICA

Lake Winnipeg

Saskatchewan River

Lake Athabasca

Great Slave Lake

Great Bear Lake

Mackenzie River

Missouri River

Platte River

Arkansas River

Red River

Rio Grande

Colorado

MEXICO

ROCKY MOUNTAINS

Great Salt Lake

River

GREAT BASIN

Snake River

Columbia R.

CASCADE RANGE

SIERRA NEVADA

COAST RANGES

Cape Mendocino

Fraser River

COAST MOUNTAINS

Vancouver Island

Hudson Bay

BROOKS RANGE

Yukon River

Mt. McKinley 20,320 ft (6,194 m)

ALASKA RANGE

Gulf of Alaska

Bering Sea

Alaska Peninsula

PACIFIC OCEAN

Tropic of Cancer

Hawaiian Islands

N

Scale

1,000 Miles

500

0

1,500 Kilometers

1,000

500

0

625

LATIN AMERICA
Political

★ National capital   • Other city

| 0 | 400 | 800 Miles |

| 0 | 400 | 800 | 1,200 Kilometers |

626

NORTH
AMERICA

Baja
California

Gulf of California

SIERRA MADRE OCCIDENTAL

SIERRA MADRE ORIENTAL

Gulf of Mexico

30°N

Tropic of Cancer

Cuba

Greater Antilles

Hispaniola

Yucatán Peninsula

15°N

Caribbean Sea

Lesser Antilles

CENTRAL

Lake Nicaragua

AMERICA Isthmus of Panama

Guajira Peninsula

Gulf of Panama

Lake Maracaibo

Orinoco R.

GUIANA HIGHLANDS

LLANOS

Magdalena River

Cauca River

Galapagos Islands

Equator

0°

Rio Negro

AMAZON

Amazon River

Marajó Island

Cape São Roque

Japurá

River

Gulf of Guayaquil

Marañón R.

BASIN

Amazon River

Aguja Point

PACIFIC

Ucayali

Purus

River

Madeira R.

Tapajós R.

Xingu River

Tocantins River

Araguaia River

Parnaíba River

São Francisco River

SOUTH

MATO GROSSO PLATEAU

OCEAN

River

AMERICA

Lake Titicaca

BRAZILIAN

15°S

Lake Poopó

HIGHLANDS

ANDES MOUNTAINS

Pilcomayo R.

Paraguay R.

GRAN CHACO

River

ATACAMA DESERT

Salado River

Paraná River

Tropic of Capricorn

ANDES MOUNTAINS

Mt. Aconcagua
22,834 ft.
(6,960 m)

Uruguay River

Paraná River

30°S

ATLANTIC

PAMPAS

Rio de la Plata

Blanca Bay

OCEAN

San Matías Gulf

Chiloé Island

PATAGONIA

Gulf of San Jorge

45°S

N

Strait of Magellan

Falkland Islands

Tierra del Fuego

Cape Horn

South Georgia

LATIN AMERICA
Physical

0   400   800 Miles
0   400   800   1,200 Kilometers

627

WESTERN EUROPE
Political

⊛ National capital   • Other city

| 0 | | 150 | | 300 Miles |
0 | 150 | 300 | 450 Kilometers |

ICELAND
⊛ Reykjavík

ARCTIC OCEAN

FAEROE
ISLANDS
(DEN.)

SHETLAND
ISLANDS
(U.K.)

ATLANTIC
OCEAN

FINLAND

⊛ Helsinki

NORWAY
• Bergen
Oslo ⊛

SWEDEN
⊛ Stockholm

• Göteborg

North
Sea

Baltic
Sea

Glasgow • • Edinburgh
UNITED
• Belfast
KINGDOM
• Dublin ⊛
IRELAND   • Liverpool

DENMARK
Copenhagen ⊛

• Hamburg

NETHERLANDS
Amsterdam •
• London   • Hannover   • Berlin ⊛

GERMANY

Antwerp •
Brussels •   • Essen
BELGIUM   • Cologne
LUXEMBOURG   • Bonn   • Leipzig
Le Havre •   • Dresden
⊛ Luxembourg
Paris •

• Nantes   • Munich
                          LIECHTENSTEIN   ⊛ Vienna
FRANCE   Zürich •   • Vaduz   AUSTRIA
           Bern •
• Bordeaux Lyon •   SWITZERLAND
                     • Milan
Bilbao •   • Venice
Bay of
Biscay   MONACO •   SAN MARINO
• Porto   Marseille • Monaco-   • San Marino
PORTUGAL Andorra • Ville
          la Vella ANDORRA
SPAIN
• Madrid   ITALY
          • Barcelona
⊛ Lisbon   CORSICA
                    (FR.)
          • Valencia   ⊛ Rome
                    SARDINIA
• Cordoba   (IT.)   • Naples
• Seville
          • Cartagena
GIBRALTAR   BALEARIC
(U.K.)   ISLANDS
                    (SP.)   GREECE
                                  • Thessaloniki
                    SICILY
                    (IT.)   ⊛ Athens

MALTA • Valletta

Mediterranean
Sea   CRETE
                   (GR.)

AFRICA

628

WESTERN EUROPE
Physical

0   150   300 Miles
0   150   300   450 Kilometers

ARCTIC OCEAN

Iceland

Arctic Circle

Lofoten
Islands

LAPLAND

Norwegian
Sea

Scandinavian Peninsula

Gulf of
Bothnia

Faeroe
Islands

Shetland
Islands

N

Gulf of Finland

ATLANTIC

OCEAN

North
Sea

Baltic
Sea

British
Isles

Jutland
Peninsula

Elbe

English Channel

NORTH EUROPEAN PLAIN

River

Rhine

Seine

River

Loire

River

River

Danube

River

Bodensee

Jura
Mts.

Lake
Geneva

Bay of
Biscay

Garonne River

Mt. Blanc
15,771 ft.
(4,807 m)

A L P S

Po

River

APENNINES

PYRENEES

Ebro

River

Corsica

Adriatic
Sea

Balkan
Peninsula

Tagus

River

Iberian

Rhône River

Italian Peninsula

Sardinia

Tyrrhenian
Sea

Peninsula

Balearic
Islands

Aegean
Sea

Strait of Gibraltar

Ionian
Sea

Rhodes

Sicily

Mediterranean

AFRICA

Sea

Crete

629

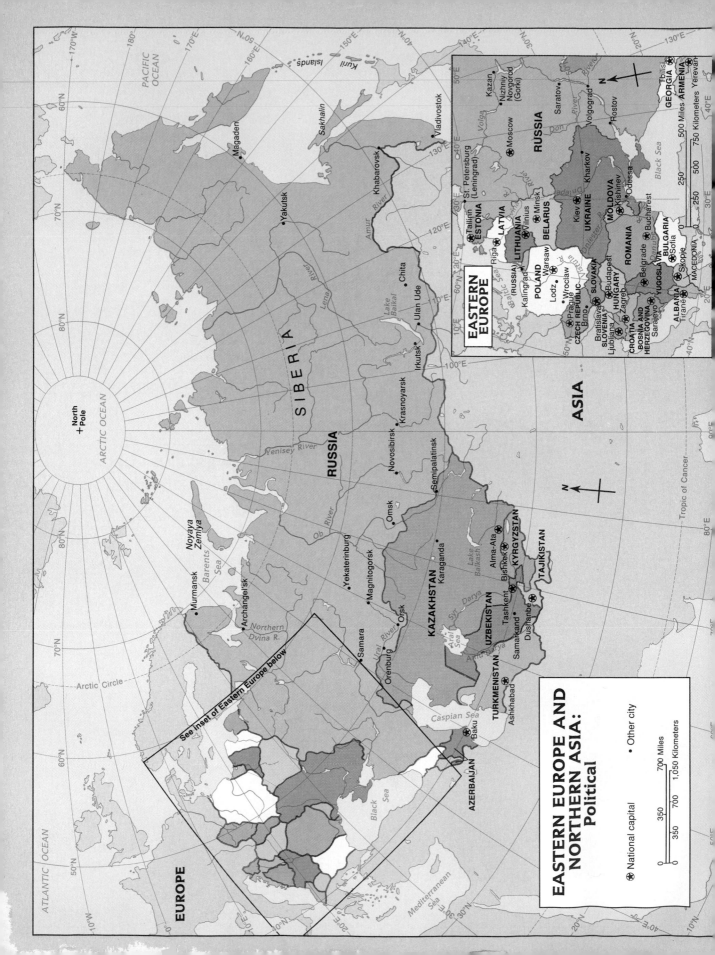

EASTERN EUROPE AND NORTHERN ASIA: Political

⊛ National capital   • Other city

0   350   700 Miles
0   350   700   1,050 Kilometers

EASTERN EUROPE

N

0   250   500   750 Miles
0   250   500 Kilometers

RUSSIA

Moscow

Kazan
Nizhniy Novgorod (Gorki)
Saratov
Volgograd
Rostov

St. Petersburg (Leningrad)
Tallinn
ESTONIA
LATVIA
Riga
LITHUANIA
Vilnius
Minsk
BELARUS
Kiev
UKRAINE
Kharkov
Odessa
Kishinev
MOLDOVA
Bucharest
ROMANIA
BULGARIA
Sofia
Skopje
MACEDONIA
ALBANIA
Tiranë
YUGOSLAVIA
Belgrade
Sarajevo
BOSNIA AND HERZEGOVINA
CROATIA
Zagreb
SLOVENIA
Ljubljana
HUNGARY
Budapest
SLOVAKIA
Bratislava
Brno
CZECH REPUBLIC
Prague
Wroclaw
Lodz
Warsaw
POLAND
Kaliningrad (RUSSIA)

Volga River
Don River
Dnieper River
Dniester
Vistula
Drava
Danube
Dvina

GEORGIA
Tbilisi
ARMENIA
Yerevan

Black Sea
Baltic Sea

Eastern Europe and Northern Asia (main map)

ARCTIC OCEAN
North Pole
PACIFIC OCEAN
ATLANTIC OCEAN
Mediterranean Sea
Black Sea
Caspian Sea
Barents Sea
Aral Sea
Lake Baikal
Lake Balkhash

Kuril Islands
Sakhalin
Novaya Zemlya

EUROPE
ASIA
SIBERIA
RUSSIA

Arctic Circle
Tropic of Cancer
North Pole

Magadan
Vladivostok
Khabarovsk
Yakutsk
Chita
Ulan Ude
Irkutsk
Krasnoyarsk
Novosibirsk
Omsk
Semipalatinsk
Yekaterinburg
Magnitogorsk
Orsk
Samara
Orenburg
Murmansk
Archangel'sk

Amur River
Lena River
Yenisey River
Ob River
Ural River
Syr Darya
Amu Darya
Northern Dvina R.

KAZAKHSTAN
Karaganda
Alma-Ata
KYRGYZSTAN
Bishkek
TAJIKISTAN
Dushanbe
UZBEKISTAN
Tashkent
Samarkand
TURKMENISTAN
Ashkhabad
AZERBAIJAN
Baku

See inset of Eastern Europe below

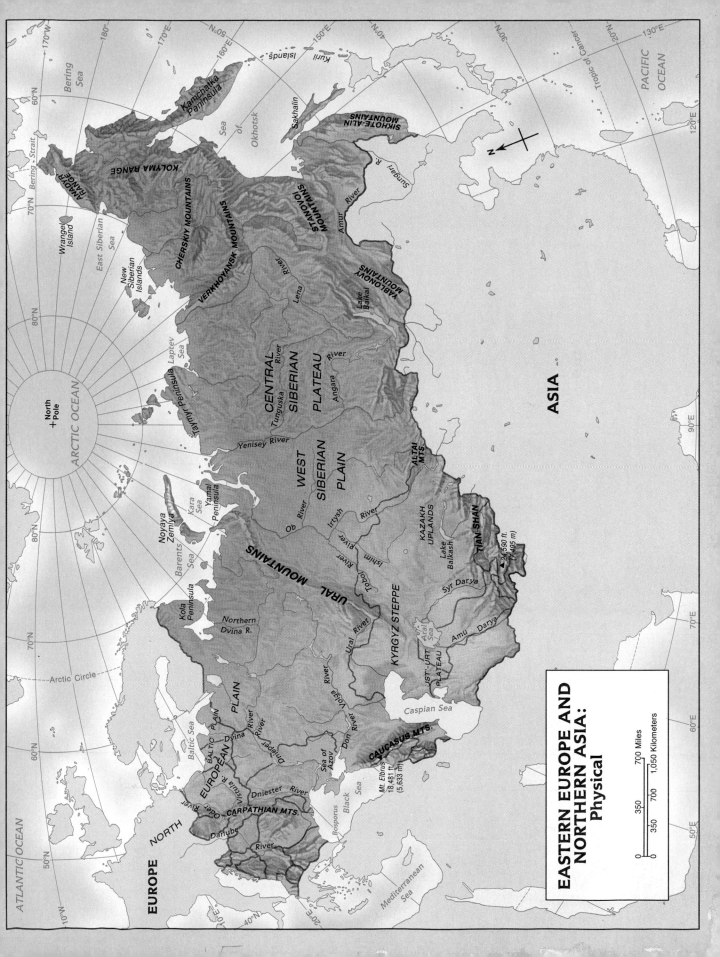

EUROPE

ASIA

ATLANTIC OCEAN

ARCTIC OCEAN

North Pole

PACIFIC OCEAN

Bering Sea

Bering Strait

Wrangel Island

East Siberian Sea

New Siberian Islands

Kamchatka Peninsula

Sea of Okhotsk

Kuril Islands

Sakhalin

ANADYR RANGE

KOLYMA RANGE

CHERSKY MOUNTAINS

VERKHOYANSK MOUNTAINS

STANOVOY MOUNTAINS

SIKHOTE-ALIN MOUNTAINS

YABLONOVY MOUNTAINS

Amur River

Sungari River

Lena River

River

Lake Baikal

Laptev Sea

Taymyr Peninsula

CENTRAL SIBERIAN PLATEAU

Tunguska River

Angara River

Yenisey River

WEST SIBERIAN PLAIN

Novaya Zemlya

Kara Sea

Yamal Peninsula

Ob River

Irtysh River

Tobol River

Ishim River

ALTAI MTS.

KAZAKH UPLANDS

Lake Balkhash

TIAN SHAN

24,590 ft. (7,495 m)

Barents Sea

Kola Peninsula

Northern Dvina R.

URAL MOUNTAINS

Ural River

KYRGYZ STEPPE

Syr Darya

Amu Darya

Aral Sea

UST-URT PLATEAU

Arctic Circle

Baltic Sea

NORTH EUROPEAN PLAIN

BALTIC PLAIN

Dvina River

River

Dnieper

Volga River

Don River

Caspian Sea

Sea of Azov

CAUCASUS MTS.

Mt. Elbrus 18,481 ft. (5,633 m)

Oder River

Vistula R.

Dniester River

CARPATHIAN MTS.

Danube River

Bosporus

Black Sea

Mediterranean Sea

N

EASTERN EUROPE AND NORTHERN ASIA:
Physical

0   350   700 Miles
0   350   700   1,050 Kilometers

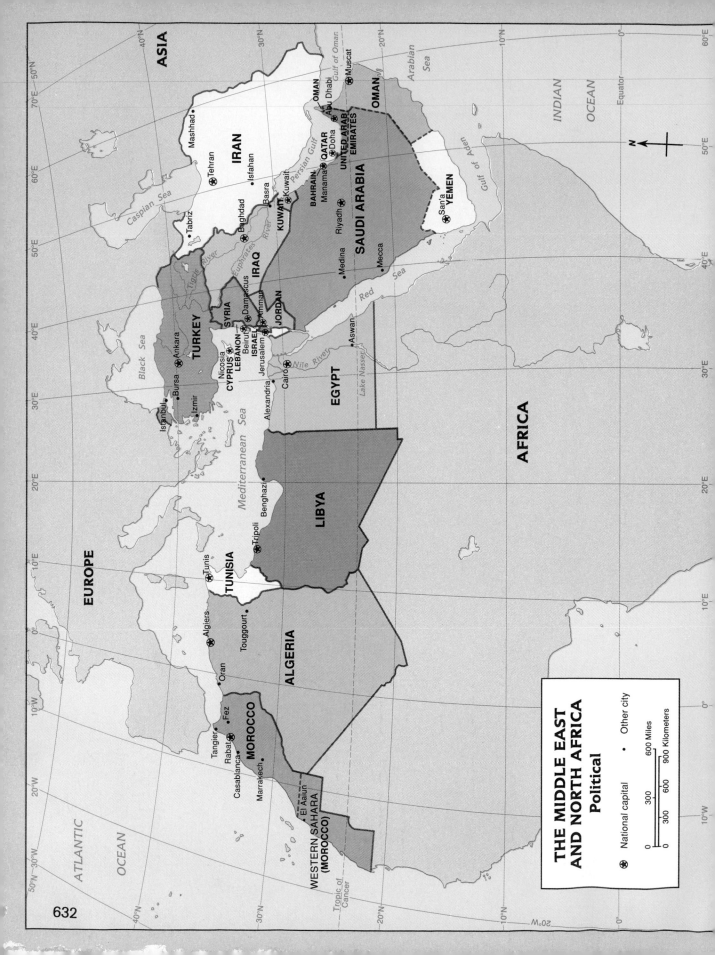

THE MIDDLE EAST
AND NORTH AFRICA
Political

⊛ National capital   • Other city

0   300   600 Miles
0   300   600   900 Kilometers

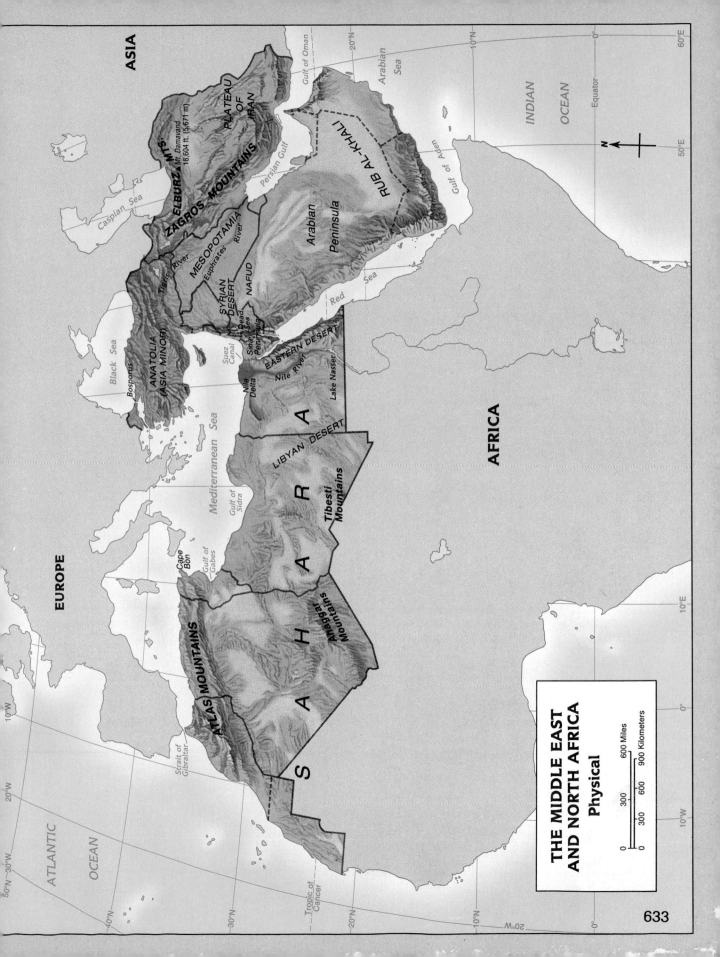

ASIA

PLATEAU
OF
IRAN

ELBURZ MTS.
Mt. Damavand
18,604 ft. (5,671 m)

ZAGROS MOUNTAINS

RUB AL-KHALI

Gulf of Oman

Arabian
Sea

INDIAN

OCEAN

Equator

Caspian Sea

Tigris River

MESOPOTAMIA

Euphrates River

SYRIAN
DESERT

NAFUD

Persian Gulf

Arabian
Peninsula

Gulf of Aden

Dead Sea

Sinai
Peninsula

Black Sea

Bosporus

ANATOLIA
(ASIA MINOR)

Suez
Canal

EASTERN DESERT

Nile River

Red Sea

Nile
Delta

Lake Nasser

AFRICA

Mediterranean Sea

Gulf of
Sidra

LIBYAN DESERT

S A H A R A

Tibesti
Mountains

EUROPE

Cape
Bon

Gulf of
Gabes

ATLAS MOUNTAINS

Ahaggar
Mountains

Strait of
Gibraltar

ATLANTIC

OCEAN

50°N
40°N
30°N
20°N
10°N
0°

30°W
20°W
10°W

0°
10°E

60°E
50°E
40°E
30°E
20°E
10°E

20°N
10°N

Tropic of
Cancer

20°W

THE MIDDLE EAST
AND NORTH AFRICA
Physical

600 Miles
300
0

900 Kilometers
600
300
0

633

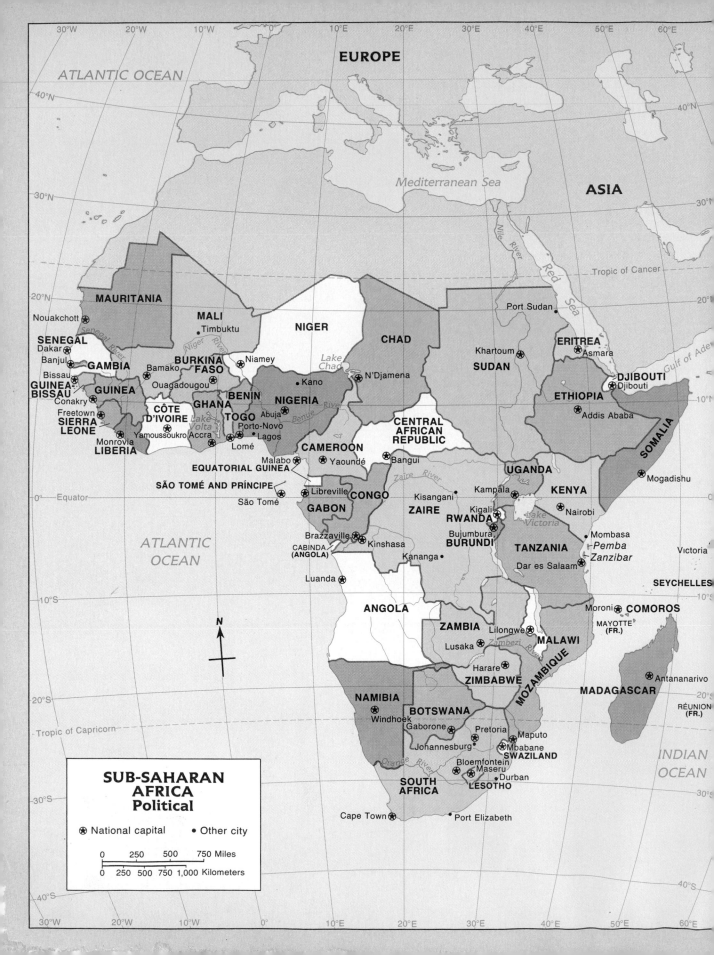

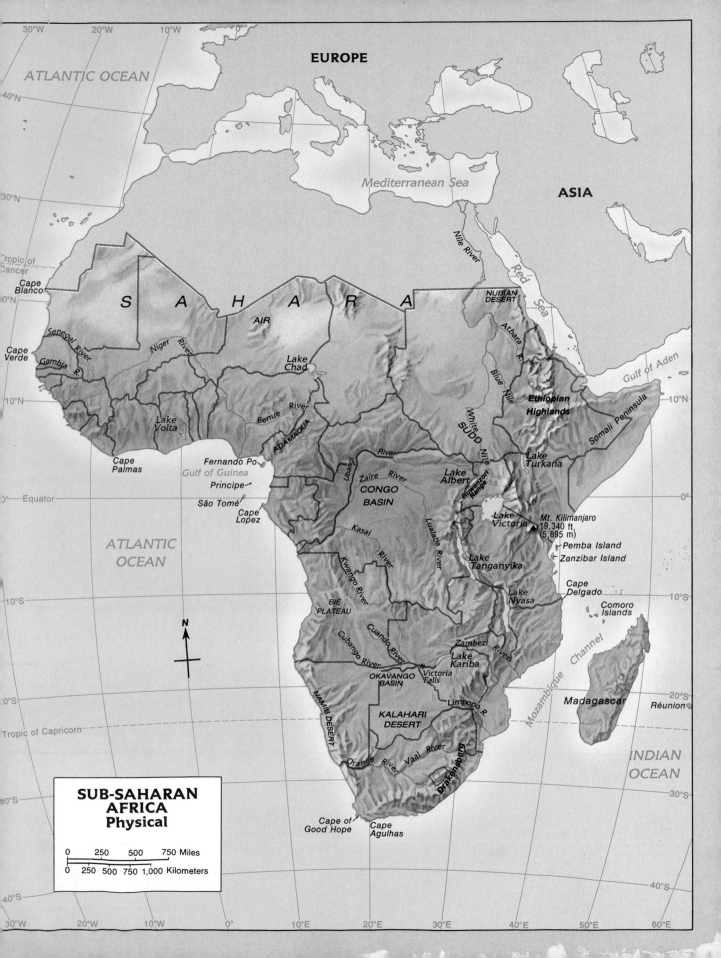

ATLANTIC OCEAN

EUROPE

Mediterranean Sea

ASIA

30°N

Tropic of Cancer

Cape Blanco

S A H A R A

AIR

NUBIAN DESERT

Nile River

Red Sea

Gulf of Aden

Cape Verde

Senegal River

Niger River

Gambia R.

Lake Chad

Athara R.

Blue Nile

Ethiopian Highlands

10°N

Lake Volta

Benue River

ADAMAOUA

White Nile

SUDD

Somali Peninsula

Lake Turkana

Cape Palmas

Fernando Po

Gulf of Guinea

Principe

São Tomé

Cape Lopez

Ubangi

River

Zaïre River

CONGO BASIN

Kasai

Lualaba River

River

Lake Albert

Ruwenzori Range

Lake Victoria

Mt. Kilimanjaro 19,340 ft. (5,895 m)

Pemba Island

Zanzibar Island

Equator

ATLANTIC OCEAN

Kwango River

Lake Tanganyika

Cape Delgado

BIÉ PLATEAU

Lake Nyasa

Comoro Islands

Cubango River

Cuando River

Zambezi River

Lake Kariba

OKAVANGO BASIN

Victoria Falls

Mozambique Channel

Madagascar

Réunion

NAMIB DESERT

KALAHARI DESERT

Limpopo R.

Orange River

Vaal River

Drakensberg

INDIAN OCEAN

Cape of Good Hope

Cape Agulhas

SUB-SAHARAN AFRICA
Physical

0   250   500   750 Miles

0 250 500 750 1,000 Kilometers

N

30°W 20°W 10°W 0° 10°E 20°E 30°E 40°E 50°E 60°E

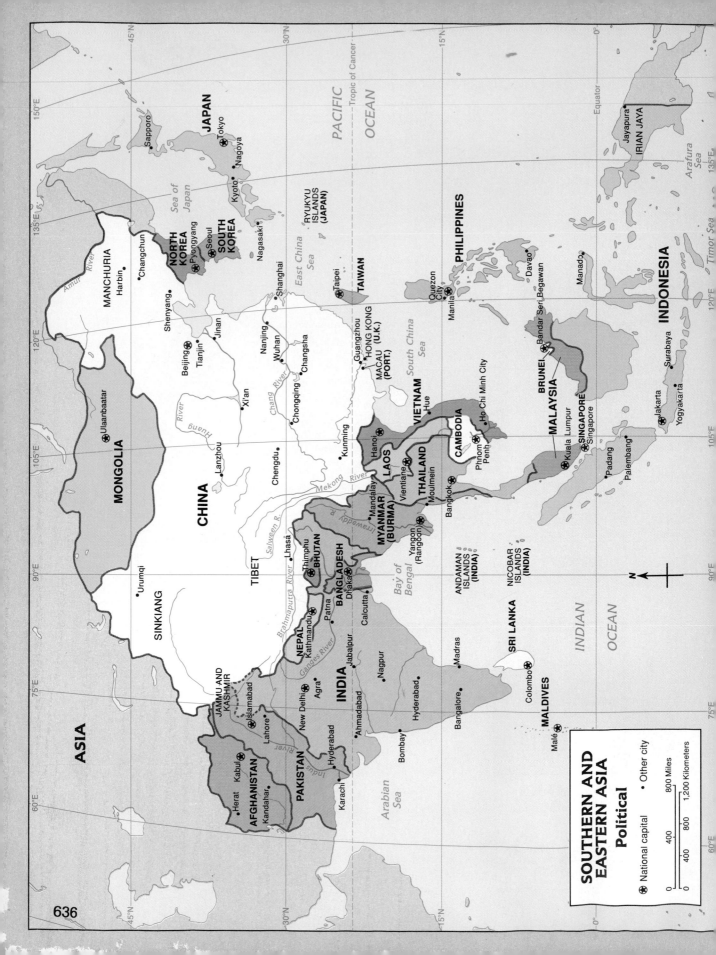

SOUTHERN AND
EASTERN ASIA

Political

⊛ National capital   • Other city

	400		800 Miles
0	400	800	1,200 Kilometers

636

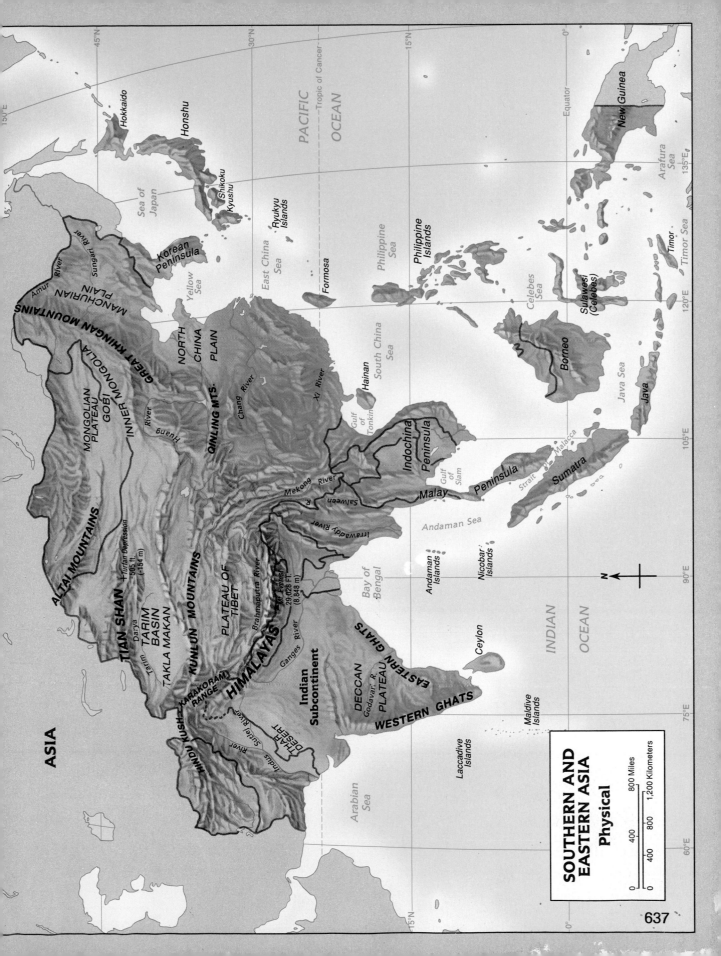

ASIA

PACIFIC

OCEAN

Tropic of Cancer

New Guinea

Hokkaido

Honshu

Sea of
Japan

Shikoku
Kyushu

Ryukyu
Islands

Arafura
Sea

Korean
Peninsula

MANCHURIAN
PLAIN

Sungari River

Amur River

East China
Sea

Philippine
Sea

Philippine
Islands

Timor

Timor Sea

GREAT KHINGAN MOUNTAINS

INNER MONGOLIA

NORTH
CHINA
PLAIN

Yellow
Sea

Formosa

Celebes
Sea

Sulawesi
(Celebes)

MONGOLIAN
PLATEAU

GOBI

QINLING MTS.

Chang River

Huang River

Xi River

Hainan

South China
Sea

Gulf
of
Tonkin

Borneo

Java Sea

Java

ALTAI MOUNTAINS

TIAN SHAN

Turfan Depression
-505 ft.
(-154 m)

TARIM BASIN

TAKLA MAKAN

Tarim
Dar-ya

KUNLUN MOUNTAINS

PLATEAU
OF
TIBET

Mt. Everest
29,028 FT.
(8,848 m)

Brahmaputra River

Mekong River

Salween R.

Indochina
Peninsula

Gulf
of
Siam

Malay Peninsula

Strait of Malacca

Sumatra

HIMALAYAS

HINDU KUSH

KARAKORAM
RANGE

Ganges River

Irrawaddy River

Andaman Sea

Andaman
Islands

Nicobar
Islands

N

Indus River

Sutlej River

THAR
DESERT

Indian
Subcontinent

Bay of
Bengal

Ceylon

INDIAN

OCEAN

DECCAN
PLATEAU

Godavari R.

EASTERN GHATS

WESTERN GHATS

Maldive
Islands

Arabian
Sea

Laccadive
Islands

Equator

135°E

120°E

105°E

90°E

75°E

60°E

45°N

30°N

15°N

0°

15°S

15°E

SOUTHERN AND
EASTERN ASIA
Physical

800 Miles

1,200 Kilometers

400

800

0

400

0

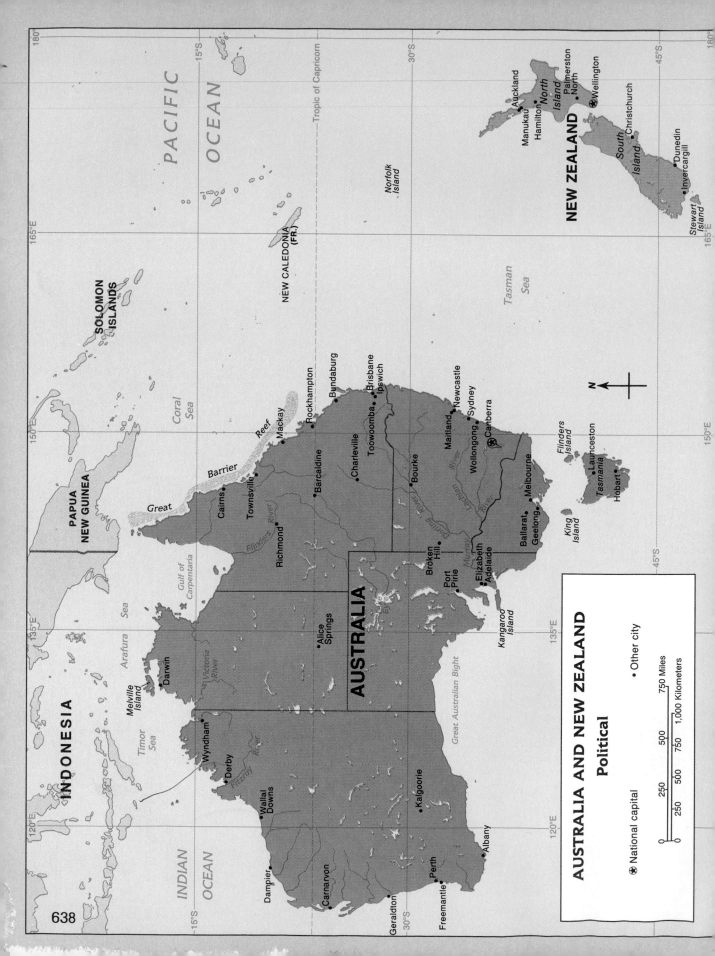

PACIFIC OCEAN

PAPUA NEW GUINEA

INDONESIA

SOLOMON ISLANDS

NEW CALEDONIA (FR.)

Coral Sea

Arafura Sea

Timor Sea

Gulf of Carpentaria

Reef

Barrier

Great

Darwin

Melville Island

Wyndham

Derby

Wallal Downs

Fitzroy River

Victoria River

Dampier

Carnarvon

Geraldton

Perth

Freemantle

Albany

Kalgoorie

Alice Springs

Richmond

Flinders River

Cairns

Townsville

Mackay

Rockhampton

Bundaburg

Brisbane

Ipswich

Toowoomba

Charleville

Barcaldine

Bourke

AUSTRALIA

Darling River

Murray River

Murray River

Broken Hill

Port Pirie

Elizabeth

Adelaide

Kangaroo Island

Great Australian Bight

Newcastle

Sydney

Canberra

Maitland

Wollongong

Melbourne

Ballarat

Geelong

King Island

Flinders Island

Launceston

Tasmania

Hobart

Tasman Sea

Norfolk Island

NEW ZEALAND

Auckland

Manukau

Hamilton

North Island

Palmerston North

Wellington

Christchurch

South Island

Dunedin

Invercargill

Stewart Island

INDIAN OCEAN

Tropic of Capricorn

N

AUSTRALIA AND NEW ZEALAND
Political

⊛ National capital   • Other city

0   250   500   750 Miles

0   250   500   750   1,000 Kilometers

120°E   135°E   150°E   165°E   180°

15°S   30°S   45°S

PACIFIC OCEAN

INDONESIA

PAPUA NEW GUINEA

SOLOMON ISLANDS

Coral Sea

Arafura Sea

Timor Sea

NEW CALEDONIA (FR.)

Norfolk Island

Tasman Sea

NEW ZEALAND

North Cape

Bay of Plenty

North Island

Lake Taupo

Cook Strait

Cape Farewell

Mt. Cook 12,350 ft. (3,742m)

South Island

Canterbury Bight

SOUTHERN ALPS

Stewart Island

Foveaux Strait

GREAT DIVIDING RANGE

Great Barrier Reef

Cape York

Torres Strait

YORK PENINSULA

CAPE

Mitchell River

Flinders River

Gulf of Carpentaria

Groote Eylandt

BARKLY TABLELAND

GREAT ARTESIAN BASIN

Warburton River

Cooper Creek

Lake Eyre

Lake Torrens

Lake Gairdner

EYRE PENINSULA

Spencer Gulf

Kangaroo Island

Great Australian Bight

AUSTRALIA

MACDONNELL RANGES

SIMPSON DESERT

Lake Amadeus

Lake Hopkins

Lake Mackay

Lake Disappointment

GIBSON DESERT

GREAT SANDY DESERT

KIMBERLY PLATEAU

KING LEOPOLD RANGES

Fitzroy River

Ord River

Daly River

Victoria River

Cape Londonderry

Joseph Bonaparte Gulf

Melville Island

GREAT VICTORIAN DESERT

NULLABOR PLAIN

Lake Cowan

Lake Barlee

Lake Carnegie

Gascoyne River

Murchison River

Ashburton River

Northwest Cape

Cape Leeuwin

INDIAN OCEAN

Darling River

Murrumbidgee River

Lachlan River

Murray River

Mt. Kosciusko 7,330 ft. (2,228m)

Cape Howe

Flinders Island

Bass Strait

King Island

Tasmania

Southwest Cape

Tropic of Capricorn

N

AUSTRALIA AND NEW ZEALAND
Physical

250   500   750 Miles

250 500 750 1,000 Kilometers

DICTIONARY OF
GEOGRAPHIC TERMS

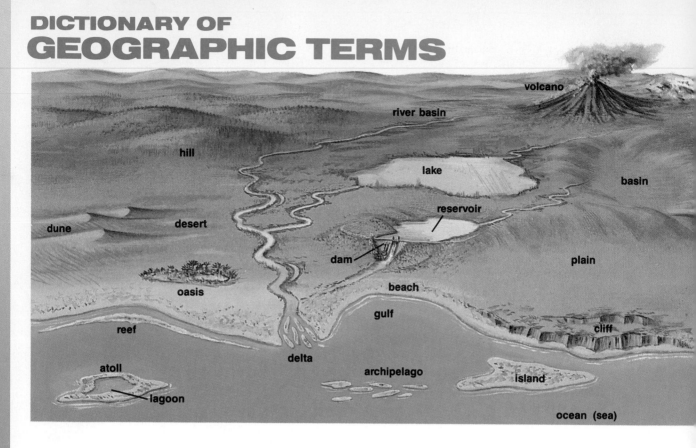

archipelago (ar kə pel i gō) A large group or chain of islands.

atoll (at′ ôl) A ring-shaped coral island or string of islands, surrounding a lagoon.

basin (bā′ sin) An area of low-lying land surrounded by higher land. *See also* **river basin**.

bay (bā) Part of an ocean, sea, or lake, that extends into the land. A bay is usually smaller than a gulf.

beach (bēch) The gently sloping shore of an ocean or other body of water, especially that part covered by sand or pebbles.

butte (būt) A small, flat-topped hill. A butte is smaller than a plateau or a mesa.

canal (kə nal′) A waterway built to carry water for navigation or irrigation. Navigation canals usually connect two other bodies of water.

canyon (kan′ yən) A deep, narrow valley with steep sides.

cape (kāp) A projecting part of a coastline that extends into an ocean, sea, gulf, bay, or lake.

cliff (klif) A high, steep face of rock or earth.

coast (kōst) Land along an ocean or sea.

dam (dam) A wall built across a river to hold back the flowing water.

delta (del′ tə) Land formed at the mouth of a river by deposits of silt, sand, and pebbles.

desert (dez′ ərt) A very dry area where few plants grow.

dune (dün) A mound, hill, or ridge of sand that is heaped up by the wind.

fjord (fyôrd) A deep, narrow inlet of the sea between high, steep cliffs.

foothills (fut′ hilz) A hilly area at the base of a mountain range.

glacier (glā′ shər) A large sheet of ice that moves slowly over some land surface or down a valley.

gulf (gulf) Part of an ocean or sea that extends into the land. A gulf is usually larger than a bay.

harbor (här′ bər) A protected place along a shore where ships can safely anchor.

hill (hil) A rounded, raised landform, not as high as a mountain.

island (ī′ lənd) A body of land completely surrounded by water.

isthmus (is′ məs) A narrow strip of land bordered by water, that connects two larger bodies of land.

lagoon (lə gün′) A shallow body of water partly or completely enclosed within an atoll; a shallow body of sea water partly cut off from the sea by a narrow strip of land.

lake (lāk) A body of water completely surrounded by land.

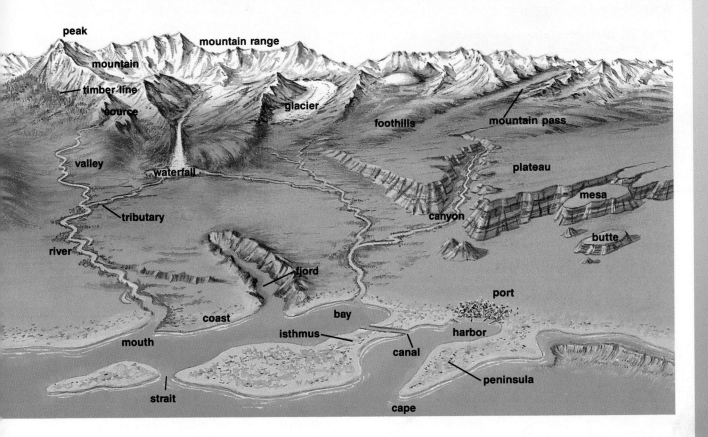

In the illustration, the following labels appear:

peak, mountain range, mountain, timber line, glacier, source, foothills, mountain pass, valley, waterfall, plateau, mesa, tributary, canyon, butte, river, fjord, port, coast, bay, isthmus, harbor, mouth, canal, peninsula, strait, cape

mesa (mā′ sə) A high, flat landform rising steeply above the surrounding land. A mesa is smaller than a plateau and larger than a butte.

mountain (mount′ ən) A high, rounded or pointed landform with steep sides, higher than a hill.

mountain pass (mount′ ən pas) An opening or gap through a mountain range.

mountain range (mount′ ən rānj) A row or chain of mountains.

mouth (mouth) The place where a river empties into another body of water.

oasis (ō ā′ sis) A place in the desert made fertile by a steady supply of water.

ocean (ō′ shən) One of the earth's four largest bodies of water. The four oceans are really a single connected body of salt water that covers about three fourths of the earth's surface.

peak (pēk) The pointed top of a mountain or hill.

peninsula (pə nin′ sə lə) A body of land nearly surrounded by water.

plain (plān) A large area of flat or nearly flat land.

plateau (pla tō′) A high, flat landform that rises steeply above the surrounding land. A plateau is larger than a mesa and a butte.

port (pôrt) A place where ships load and unload goods.

reef (rēf) A ridge of sand, rock, or coral that lies at or near the surface of a sea.

reservoir (rez′ ər vwär) A natural or artificial lake used to store water.

river (riv′ ər) A large stream of water that flows across the land and usually empties into a lake, ocean, or other river.

river basin (riv′ ər bā′ sin) All the land drained by a river and its tributaries.

sea (sē) A large body of water partly or entirely surrounded by land; another word for *ocean*.

source (sôrs) The place where a river or stream begins.

strait (strāt) A narrow waterway or channel connecting two larger bodies of water.

timber line (tim′ bər līn) An imaginary line on mountains, above which trees do not grow.

tributary (trib′ yə ter ē) A river or stream that flows into a larger river or stream.

valley (val′ ē) An area of low land between hills or mountains.

volcano (vol kā′ nō) An opening in the earth through which lava, rock, gases, and ash are forced out.

waterfall (wô′ tər fôl) A flow of water falling from a high place to a lower place.

GEOGRAPHIC TERMS

641

GAZETTEER

This Gazetteer is a geographical dictionary that will help you to pronounce and locate the places discussed in this book. Latitude and longitude are given for cities and some other places. The page number tells you where each place appears on a map.

PRONUNCIATION KEY

a	cap	êr	clear	oi	coin	ü	moon
ā	cake	hw	where	ôr	fork	ū	cute
ä	father	i	bib	ou	cow	ûr	term
är	car	ī	kite	sh	show	ə	about, taken,
âr	dare	ng	song	th	thin		pencil, apron,
ch	chain	o	top	th	those		helpful
e	hen	ō	rope	u	sun	ər	letter, dollar,
ē	me	ô	saw	ù	book		doctor

A

Abuja (ä bü′ zhä) The capital of Nigeria since 1991; 8°N, 7°E. (p. 428)

Afghanistan (af gan′ ə stan) A country in South Asia. (p. 486)

Africa (af′ ri kə) The world's second-largest continent. It lies south of Europe between the Atlantic and Indian oceans. (p. 5)

Albania (al bā′ nē ə) A country in southeastern Europe on the Adriatic Sea. (p. 294)

Algeria (al jêr′ ē ə) A country in western North Africa. (p. 356)

Alps (alps) A major European mountain system, extending in an arc from the Mediterranean coast east to the Balkan Peninsula. (p. 184)

Altai (al′ tī) A mountain range of Asia, extending from the south-central part of Russia east into western Mongolia. (p. 492)

Amazon River (am′ ə zon riv′ ər) The longest river in South America and the second-longest river in the world. It flows from the Andes across Brazil into the Atlantic Ocean. (p. 108)

Amsterdam (am′ stər dam) The capital and largest city of the Netherlands, in the west-central part of the country; 52°N, 4°E. (p. 222)

Anatolia (an ə tō′ lē ə) A peninsula in western Asia, bordered by the Black and Mediterranean seas. It is also known as Asia Minor. (p. 356)

Andes Mountains (an′ dēz moun′ tənz) A major mountain system stretching along the west coast of South America. They form the longest mountain chain in the world. (p. 108)

Antarctica (ant ärk′ ti kə) The fifth-largest continent. Ice-covered, it surrounds the South Pole and lies mainly within the Antarctic Circle. (p. 5)

Appalachian Highlands (ap ə lā′ chē ən hī′ ləndz) The hills and low mountains that stretch along much of the east coast of North America. (p. 40)

Arabian Peninsula (ə rā′ bē ən pə nin′ sə lə) A large peninsula in southwestern Asia. (p. 356)

Arctic Islands (ärk′ tik ī′ ləndz) Islands lying in the Arctic Ocean north of North America. (p. 40)

Arctic Ocean (ärk′ tik ō′ shən) The world's smallest ocean. It surrounds the North Pole and lies north of the Arctic Circle. (p. 5)

Argentina (är jən tē′ nə) A country in southern South America. (p. 108)

Armenia (är mē′ nē ə) A country in Eastern Europe. Armenia was a republic of the Soviet Union from 1936 until 1991, when it became independent. (p. 306)

Asia (ā′ zhə) The largest continent, bounded on the west by Europe, on the east by the Pacific Ocean, and on the south by the Indian Ocean. (p. 5)

Asia Minor (ā′ zhə mī′ nər) A peninsula in western Asia, bordered by the Mediterranean and Black seas. It is also known as Anatolia. (p. 356)

Atacama Desert (ä tə kä′ mə dez′ ərt) A cold desert that extends along the Pacific Coast of South America from southern Peru to central Chile. (p. 108)

Athens (ath′ ənz) The capital and largest city of Greece. It was once the most important and powerful city of ancient Greece; 38°N, 24°E. (p. 186)

Atlantic Coastal Plain (at lan′ tik kōs təl plān) The low land plain extending along the east coast of the United States. (p. 40)

Atlantic Ocean (at lan′ tik ō′ shən) The second-largest ocean. It separates North America and South America from Europe and Africa. (p. 5)

Atlas Mountains (at′ ləs moun′ tənz) A mountain range extending along the northwestern coast of Africa. (p. 356)

Australia (ôs trāl′ yə) The world's smallest continent, bounded by the Indian and Pacific oceans. (p. 5)

Austria (ôs′ trē ə) A country lying mainly in the Alps of Central Europe. (p. 184)

Azerbaijan (ä zər bī jän′) A country in the Caucasus Mountain region of Eastern Europe. Azerbaijan was a republic of the Soviet Union from 1939 until 1991, when it became independent. (p. 306)

B

Bahrain (bä rān′) An island country off the Arabian Peninsula in the Persian Gulf; a world center for oil and banking. (p. 356)

Balkan Peninsula (bôl′ kən pə nin′ sə lə) A large peninsula in southern Europe bounded by the Black, Aegean, and Adriatic seas. (p. 184)

Baltic Sea (bôl′ tik sē) An inland sea in northern Europe. (p. 178)

Bangladesh (bang glə desh′) A country in eastern South Asia, on the Bay of Bengal. (p. 486)

Barbados (bär bā′ dōs) An island country, part of the Lesser Antilles group in the Caribbean Islands. (p. 142)

Basel (bä′ zəl) An important commercial city on the Rhine River in northwestern Switzerland; 48°N, 8°E. (p. 234)

Beijing (bā jing′) The capital of the People's Republic of China in the northeastern part of the country. It was formerly called Peking; 40°N, 116°E. (p. 494)

Belarus (be lä rüs′) A country in Eastern Europe. Belarus was a republic of the Soviet Union from 1922 until 1991, when it became independent. (p. 306)

Belgium (bel′ jəm) A country in the Low Countries of Western Europe, on the North Sea. (p. 184)

Belize (be lēz′) A country on the northeastern coast of Central America, on the Caribbean Sea. (p. 142)

Benin (be nēn′) A country on the Gulf of Guinea in West Africa. (p. 416)

Berlin (bər lin′) The capital of Germany, located in the northeastern part of the country; 52°N, 13°E. (p. 186)

Bhutan (bü tän′) A country in eastern South Asia, on the border between India and China. (p. 486)

Black Sea (blak sē) An inland sea between Europe and Asia. (p. 178)

Bohemia (bō hē′ mē ə) A historic region and ancient kingdom in western Czech Republic (p. 343)

Bombay (bom bā′) The largest city and chief port of India, on the west coast; 19°N, 73°E. (p. 494)

Bonn (bon) The capital city of the former West German state; 50°N, 7°E. (p. 234)

Bosnia and Herzegovina (boz′ nē ə and hûrt sə gō vē′ nə) A republic in the central part of Yugoslavia that became independent in 1991. (p. 332)

Brahmaputra River (brä mə pü′ trə riv′ ər) A major river of southern Asia, flowing south from Tibet into the Bay of Bengal. (p. 492)

Brasília (brə zēl′ yə) The capital of Brazil in the east-central part of the country; 16°S, 48°W. (p. 110)

British Isles (brit′ ish īlz) A group of islands off the western coast of Europe, made up of Great Britain, Ireland, and some small islands. (p. 178)

Brittany (brit′ ə nē) A historic region in northwestern France, between the English Channel and the Bay of Biscay. (p. 218)

Brunei (brü nī′) A country on the northern coast of the island of Borneo in Southeast Asia. (p. 486)

Bucharest (bü kə rest) The capital and largest city of Romania, in the south-central part of the country; 44°N, 26°E. (p. 296)

Bulgaria (bul gâr′ ē ə) A country in Eastern Europe, on the Black Sea coast of the Balkan Peninsula. (p. 294)

C

Cairo (kī′ rō) The capital and largest city of Egypt, in the northeastern part of the country on the Nile River; 30°N, 31°E. (p. 358)

Calcutta (kal kut′ ə) A port city in northeastern India, on the Bay of Bengal; 23°N, 88°E. (p. 494)

Canadian Shield (kə nā′ dē ən shēld) The plains and hills that surround Hudson Bay and cover about half of Canada. (p. 40)

Canberra (kan ber′ ə) The capital of Australia in the southeastern part of the country; 35°S, 149°E. (p. 591)

Cape Town (kāp toun) A port city on the southwestern coast of South Africa; 34°S, 18°E. (p. 468)

Caribbean Islands (kar ə bē′ ən ī′ ləndz) Islands of the Caribbean Sea, also known as the West Indies. They are made up of the Greater Antilles, the Lesser Antilles, and the Bahamas. (p. 100)

Caspian Sea (kas′ pē ən sē) The largest inland body of water in the world, located in south-central Asia. (p. 294)

Catalonia (kat ə lō nē ə) A historic region and former principality in northeastern Spain, bordered by France to the north and the Mediterranean Sea to the east. (p. 259)

Caucasus Mountains (kô′ kə səs moun′ tənz) A mountain range that forms part of the southern boundary between Europe and Asia. (p. 294)

Central America (sen′ trəl ə mer′ i kə) The part of North America lying south of Mexico and north of South America. (p. 142)

Central Asia (sen′ trəl ā′ zhə) A large, dry area in the central parts of Asia including the countries of Kazakhstan, Kyrgyzstan, Tajikistan, Turkmenistan, Uzbekistan, China, and Mongolia. (p. 294)

Central Europe (sen′ trəl yür′ əp) Part of Western Europe including West Germany, Switzerland, and Austria. (p. 178)

Central Plateau (sen′ trəl pla tō′) A large plateau in central Mexico. (p. 108)

Chaco (chä′ kō) A dry, lowland area of South America covering much of Paraguay, eastern Bolivia, and northern Argentina. (p. 108)

Chang River (chäng riv′ ər) The longest river in China, flowing from Tibet east into the East China Sea. It is also known as the Chang Jiang and the Yangtze River. (p. 492)

China (chī′ nə) A country in East Asia. (p. 486)

Coastal Plains (kōs′ təl plānz) The lowland plains of the United States lying along the Atlantic Coast (Atlantic Coastal Plain) and the Gulf of Mexico coast (Gulf Coastal Plain). (p. 40)

Continental Divide (kon tə nən′ təl di vīd′) An imaginary line formed by the peaks of the Rocky Mountains in North America. It separates the rivers flowing eastward across the land from those flowing westward across it. (p. 40)

Copenhagen (kō′ pən hā gən) The capital and largest city of Denmark, located on a small island off the southwestern coast of Sweden; 56°N, 12°E. (p. 188)

Corsica (kôr′ si kə) A French Island in the Mediterranean Sea, south of France. (p. 184)

Costa Rica (kos′ tə rē′ kə) A country in Central America where the population is mainly of Spanish descent. (p. 108)

Côte d'Ivoire (kōt dē vwär′) A country in West Africa, on the Gulf of Guinea. (p. 416)

Croatia (krō ā′ shə) A country in Eastern Europe. It was a republic in northern Yugoslavia until it became independent in 1991. (p. 332).

Cuba (kū′ bə) An island country, part of the Greater Antilles group in the Caribbean Islands. (p. 108)

Czechoslovakia (Chek ə slə vä′ kē ə) A country in Eastern Europe that split into two countries, the Czech Republic and Slovakia, in 1993. (p. 294)

D

Danube River (dan′ ūb riv′ ər) The second-longest river of Europe. It flows from southern Germany east into the Black Sea. (p. 184)

Denmark (den′ märk) A country in Scandinavia, in Western Europe, with coasts on the North Sea and the Baltic Sea. (p. 184)

Dnieper River (nē′ pər riv′ ər) River flowing through Eastern Europe into the Black Sea. (p. 294)

Dominican Republic (də min′ i kən rə pub′ lik) A country in the Caribbean Sea, on the eastern part of the island of Hispaniola in the Greater Antilles. (p. 108)

Drakensberg Mountains (drä′ kənz bûrg moun′ tənz) Mountain range in southeastern Africa. (p. 417)

E

East Africa (ēst af′ ri kə) An area in Africa stretching along the east coast from Egypt south to Mozambique. (p. 408)

East and Equatorial Africa (ēst and ē kwə tôr′ ē əl af′ ri kə) Part of Sub-Saharan Africa stretching from the Sahara Desert south to Mozambique, Zimbabwe, and Namibia. (p 408)

East Asia (ēst ā′ zhə) The part of Asia that includes China, Japan, Mongolia, North Korea, South Korea, Taiwan, and Hong Kong. (p. 486)

Eastern Europe (ēs′ tərn yür′ əp) The part of Europe that lies between Western Europe and Northern Asia. (pp. 288–289)

Eastern Hemisphere (ēs′ tərn hem′ i sfêr) The half of the world that lies east of 0° longitude and includes Europe, Asia, Africa, and Australia. (p. 6)

Edmonton (ed′ mən tən) The capital and largest city of Alberta, Canada; 54°N, 114°W. (p. 82)

Elbe River (el′ bə riv′ ər) A river flowing from Central Europe into the North Sea. (p. 184)

England (ing′ glənd) The largest political division of the United Kingdom. England is located in the southern part of the island of Great Britain. (p. 202)

English Channel (ing′ glish chan′ əl) A narrow body of water between the island of Great Britain and northwestern Europe. (p. 194)

Equatorial Africa (ē kwə tôr′ ē əl af′ ri kə) The part of Sub-Saharan Africa that lies along the equator in the central part of the continent. (p. 408)

Eritrea (êr ə trē′ ə) A country of East Africa that was part of Ethiopia from 1952 to 1993. (p. 416)

Estonia (es tō′ nē ə) A country on the Baltic Sea in northern Europe. It was a republic of the Soviet Union from 1940 until its independence in 1991. (p. 306)

Euphrates River (ū frā′ tēz riv′ ər) A river in the Middle East flowing from Turkey to Iraq, where it joins the Tigris River to empty into the Persian Gulf. (p. 356)

Eurasia (yü rā′ zhə) The large landmass on which Europe and Asia are located. (p. 5)

Europe (yür′ əp) The sixth-largest continent. It lies between the Atlantic Ocean and Asia, from which it is separated by the Ural and Caucasus mountains. (p. 5)

F

Faeroe Islands (fâr′ ō ī′ ləndz) A group of Danish islands in the North Atlantic Ocean, lying between Iceland and the Shetland Islands. (p. 184)

Fátima (fat′ ə mə) A village and pilgrimage center in central Portugal; 40°N, 10°E. (p. 250)

Fertile Crescent (fûr′ təl kres′ ənt) A fertile, crescent-shaped area of the Middle East. It was the site of several early civilizations. (p. 359)

GAZETTEER

644

Finland (fin′ lənd) A country in Scandinavia, in Western Europe, between the Scandinavian Peninsula and Russia. (p. 184)

Flanders (flan′ dərz) A historic region in west-central Western Europe, comprising parts of present-day Belgium, France, and the Netherlands. (p. 228)

Florence (flôr′ əns) A city in central Italy that became a great center of art and ideas during the Renaissance; 44°N, 11°E. (p. 250)

Formosa (fôr mō′ sə) The former name for Taiwan, an island off the southeast coast of China. (p. 486)

French Guiana (french gē an′ ə) An overseas department of France, on the northeastern coast of South America. (p. 108)

G

Gambia (gam′ bē ə) An English-speaking country on the Atlantic coast of West Africa, totally surrounded by French-speaking Senegal. (p. 416)

Ganges River (gan′ jēz riv′ ər) A river in northern India and Bangladesh, flowing from the Himalayas into the Bay of Bengal. (p. 492)

Geneva (jə nē′ və) A city in southwestern Switzerland; 46°N, 6°E. (p. 234)

Georgia (jôr′ jə) A country in the Caucasus Mountain region of Eastern Europe. Georgia was a republic of the Soviet Union from 1936 until 1991, when it became independent. (p. 306)

Germany (jûr′ mə nē) A country in Central Europe with coasts on the North Sea and the Baltic Sea. From the end of World War II until 1990, Germany was split into East Germany and West Germany. (p. 184)

Gibraltar (ji brôl′ tər) A British crown colony near the southern tip of Spain; 36°N, 5°W. (p. 250)

Gobi (gō′ bē) A large desert in Central Asia. (p. 492)

Grand Canyon (grand kan′ yən) A wide, deep canyon on the Colorado River in the western part of the United States; 36°N, 112°W. (p. 40)

Great Barrier Reef (grāt bar′ ē ər rēf) The largest barrier reef in the world, lying off the northeastern coast of Australia. (p. 584)

Great Dividing Range (grāt di vīd′ ing rānj) Highlands extending along the eastern coast of Australia. (p. 584)

Great Britain (grāt brit′ ən) One of the British Isles, in Western Europe. Great Britain is part of the United Kingdom, and contains the provinces of England, Scotland, and Wales. (p. 202)

Great Lakes (grāt lāks) Five large freshwater lakes lying along the border between Canada and the United States. They are Lake Superior, Lake Huron, Lake Michigan, Lake Erie, and Lake Ontario. (p. 40)

Great Plains (grāt plānz) The western, nearly treeless part of the Interior Plains of North America. (p. 40)

Great Rift Valley (grāt rift val′ ē) A series of valleys in eastern Africa extending from the Red Sea south to Mozambique. (p. 416)

Greater Antilles (grā′ tər an til′ ēz) The islands, excluding the Bahamas, making up the western part of the West Indies, or Caribbean Islands. (p. 108)

Greece (grēs) A country in the eastern part of Southern Europe. (p. 184)

Greenland (grēn′ lənd) The largest island in the world, located off the northeast coast of North America. It is part of Denmark. (p. 188)

Guam (gwäm) An island in the western part of the Pacific Ocean. Guam is a trust territory of the United States. (p. 621)

Guatemala (gwä tə mä′ lə) A country in Central America. (p. 108)

Gulf Coastal Plain (gulf kōs′ təl plān) The low-lying plain that borders the Gulf of Mexico. (p. 40)

Gulf of Guinea (gulf əv gin′ ē) A large arm of the Atlantic Ocean on the coast of west-central Africa. (p. 416)

Gulf of Mexico (gulf əv mek′ si kō) An arm of the Atlantic Ocean lying between the United States and Mexico. (p. 40)

Gulf Stream (gulf strēm) A special "river" that flows in the Atlantic Ocean. It brings warm water from the Gulf of Mexico to the Atlantic coast of Europe. (p. 193)

H

Haiti (hā′ tē) A country in the Caribbean Islands, on the western part of the island of Hispaniola in the Greater Antilles. (p. 108)

Harare (hə rär′ ā) The capital and largest city of Zimbabwe; 18°S, 31°E. (p. 468)

Helsinki (hel′ sing kē) The capital and largest city of Finland, located in the southern part of the country; 60°N, 24°E. (p. 272)

Himalayas (him ə lā′ əz) The world's highest mountain system, forming part of the northern boundary of the Indian subcontinent. (p. 492)

Hiroshima (hêr ə shē′ mə) A port city in southwestern Japan on the island of Honshu. In 1945 it was the first city to be devastated by an atomic bomb; 34°N, 132°E. (p. 543)

Hokkaido (ho kī′ dō) The northernmost and second-largest island of Japan. (p. 543)

a cap; ā cake; ä father; är car; âr dare; ch chain; e hen; ē me; êr clear; hw where; i bib; ī kite; ng song; o top; ō rope; ô saw; oi coin; ôr fork; ou cow; sh show; th thin; th those; u sun; u̇ book; ü moon; ū cute; ûr term; ə about, taken, pencil, apron, helpful; ər letter, dollar, doctor

Hong Kong (hong′ kong′) A British crown colony off the southeastern coast of China. It will return to Chinese control after 1997; 22°N, 115°E. (p. 486)

Honshu (hon′ shü) The largest island of Japan. (p. 543)

Huang He (hwäng′ hù) A large river that flows across north China. It is also known as the Huang River and the Yellow River. (p. 492)

Hungary (hung′ gə rē) A country in Eastern Europe. (p. 294)

I

Iberian Peninsula (ī bêr′ ē ən pə nin′ sə lə) A large peninsula of southwestern Europe that includes Spain and Portugal. (p. 184)

Iceland (īs′ lənd) An island country in the northern Atlantic Ocean. (p. 184)

India (in′ dē ə) A country in South Asia. (p. 486)

Indian Ocean (in′ dē ən ō shən) The third-largest ocean. It lies south of Asia between Australia and Africa. (p. 5)

Indonesia (in də nē′ zhə) A country in Southeast Asia, located in the Malay Archipelago. (p. 486)

Indus River (in′ dəs riv′ ər) A river in South Asia, flowing from Tibet into the Arabian Sea. (p. 492)

Interior Plains (in têr′ ē ər plānz) Plains covering much of the central part of North America. (p. 40)

International Date Line (in tər nash′ ən əl dāt līn) An imaginary line running approximately along the line of longitude at 180°, in the middle of the Pacific Ocean, marking the time boundary between one day and the next. (p. 204)

Ireland (īr′ lənd) One of the British Isles, in Western Europe. Ireland contains the Republic of Ireland and the province of Northern Ireland, which is part of the United Kingdom. (p. 184)

Israel (iz′ rā əl) A country in the Middle East, lying between the Mediterranean Sea and the Jordan River, founded in 1948 as a Jewish homeland. (p. 356)

Italian Peninsula (i tal′ yən pə nin′ sə lə) A long peninsula in Southern Europe on which Italy is located. (p. 184)

Italy (it′ ə lē) A country in Southern Europe. Italy includes the Italian Peninsula and the islands of Sardinia and Sicily. (p. 184)

J

Jakarta (jə kär′ tə) The capital and largest city of Indonesia. It is a major seaport on the island of Java; 6°S, 107°E. (p. 494)

Java (jä′ və) A large island of Indonesia, in the Malay Archipelago. (p. 562)

Jerusalem (jə rü′ sə ləm) The capital of Israel and a holy city for Jews, Christians, and Muslims; 31°N, 31°E. (p. 370)

Johannesburg (jō han′ əs bûrg) An important industrial city in northeastern South Africa; 26°S, 29°E. (p. 418)

Jordan River (jôr′ dən riv′ ər) A river in the Middle East, flowing between Jordan and the West Bank into the Dead Sea. (p. 378)

Jutland Peninsula (jut′ lənd pə nin′ sə lə) A peninsula in the northern part of Western Europe that is located between the North and Baltic seas. (p. 184)

K

Kalahari Desert (käl ə här′ ē dez′ ərt) A large desert in southern Africa. (p. 416)

Kano (kä′ nō) A city in north-central Nigeria; 12°N, 9°E. (p. 634)

Kazakhstan (kä zäk stän′) A country in Central Asia. Kazakhstan was a republic of the Soviet Union from 1936 until 1991, when it became independent. (p. 306)

Kenya (ken′ yə) A country in East Africa. (p. 416)

Kiev (kē′ ev) The capital and largest city of Ukraine; 50°N, 30°E. (p. 296)

Kremlin (krem′ lin) The buildings that are the seat of government for Russia and were the seat of government for the Soviet Union. (p. 322)

Kunlun Mountains (kùn′ lùn′ moun′ tənz) A mountain chain in western China. (p. 492)

Kyrgyzstan (kêr′ giz stän) A country in Central Asia. Kyrgyzstan was a republic of the Soviet Union from 1936 until 1991, when it became independent. (p. 306)

Kyushu (kū′ shü) The third-largest island of Japan, the southernmost of the four largest islands. (p. 513)

L

Lake Lugano (lāk lü gä′ nō) A lake on the border between Switzerland and Italy; 46°N, 9°E. (p. 234)

Lake Titicaca (lāk tit i kä′ kə) The largest lake in South America and the highest navigable lake in the world. It is located in the Andes on the border of Peru and Bolivia; 16°S, 71°W. (p. 108)

Lake Victoria (lāk vik tôr′ ē ə) The largest lake in Africa, located in the east-central part of the continent. (p. 408)

Lapland (lap′ land) A region in northern Europe that includes northern Norway, Sweden, and Finland, and northwestern Russia. (p. 272)

Latin America (lat′ in ə mer′ i kə) The parts of the Western Hemisphere where Spanish and Portuguese are widely spoken. The region includes Mexico and Central America, South America, and the Caribbean Islands. (p. 31)

Latvia (lat′ vē ə) A country on the Baltic Sea in northern Europe. Latvia was a republic of the Soviet Union from 1940 until 1991, when it became independent. (p. 306)

Lesser Antilles (les′ ər an til′ ēz) The islands, excluding the Bahamas, making up the eastern part of the West Indies, or Caribbean Islands. (p. 108)

Lithuania (lith ü ā′ nē ə) A country on the Baltic Sea in northern Europe. Lithuania was a republic of the Soviet Union from 1940 until 1991, when it became independent. (p. 306)

Lofoten Islands (lō′ fōt ən ī′ ləndz) Island group of Norway, off the northwestern coast of Norway. (p. 272)

London (lun′ dən) The capital of the United Kingdom. London is located in southeastern England on the Thames River; 52°N, 0°longitude. (p. 12)

Low Countries (lō kun′ trēz) An area in the west-central part of Western Europe that is made up of the Netherlands, Belgium, and Luxembourg. (p. 218)

Luxembourg (luk′ səm bûrg) One of the Low Countries in Western Europe. (p. 184)

M

Macedonia (mas ə do′ nyə) A country in Eastern Europe. It was a republic in the southern part of Yugoslavia until it became independent in 1991. (p. 332)

Madrid (mə drid′) The capital and largest city of Spain, located in the central part of the country; 40°N, 4°W. (p. 186)

Malay Peninsula (mā′ lā pə nin′ sə lə) A long, narrow peninsula extending from Southeast Asia into the Indian Ocean. (p. 492)

Malaysia (mə lā′ zhə) A country in Southeast Asia, located partly on the Malay Peninsula and partly on the island of Borneo. (p. 486)

Marbella (mär bā′ yä) A popular vacation town in southern Spain; 37°N, 5°W. (p. 250)

Marrakesh (mar ə kesh′) A city in the central part of Morocco; 32°N, 8°W. (p. 388)

Mecca (mek′ ə) A city in western Saudi Arabia. Mecca was the birthplace of Muhammad and is the holiest city of Islam; 21°N, 40°E. (p. 370)

Mediterranean Sea (med i tə rā′ nē ən sē) A large, nearly landlocked arm of the Atlantic Ocean lying between Europe, Asia, and Africa. (p. 178)

Mekong River (mā′ kong riv′ ər) A river in Southeast Asia, flowing from western China southeast into the South China Sea. (p. 492)

Melanesia (mel′ ə nē′ zhə) One of three main divisions of the Pacific islands. Melanesia lies south of Micronesia and west of Polynesia. (p. 578)

Melbourne (mel′ bərn) A port city in southeastern Australia; 38°S, 145°E. (p. 586)

Mexico (mek′ si kō) A Latin American country in North America. (p. 122)

Mexico City (mek′ si kō sit′ ē) The capital and largest city of Mexico; 19°N, 99°W. (p. 110)

Micronesia (mī krə nē′ zhə) One of three main divisions of the Pacific islands. Micronesia is located north of Melanesia and west of Polynesia. (p. 578)

Middle East (mid′ əl ēst) The southwestern part of Asia that stretches from Turkey to Iran. (p. 350)

Minsk (minsk) The capital city of Belarus. Minsk is also the headquarters of the Commonwealth of Independent States; 53°N, 27°E. (p. 296)

Mississippi River (mis ə sip′ ē riv′ ər) The longest river in North America and the fourth longest river in the world. It flows south across the interior United States into the Gulf of Mexico. (p.40)

Moldova (mol dō′ və) A country in Eastern Europe. Moldova was a republic of the Soviet Union from 1940 until 1991, when it became independent. (p. 306)

Mongolia (mong gō′ lē ə) A vast area in east-central Asia, extending from northern China to Siberia and including Inner Mongolia and the country of Mongolia. (p. 492)

Montenegro (mon tə neg′ rō) A republic in the southern part of Yugoslavia. (p.332)

Moscow (mos′ kou) The capital and largest city of Russia. 56°N, 38°E. (p. 296)

Mount Aconcagua (mount ak ən kä′ gwə) The highest mountain in South America, located in the Andes Mountains between Argentina and Chile at 22,834 feet (6,960 m); 33°S, 70°W. (p. 108)

Mount Athos (mount ath′ os) A small peninsula in northeastern Greece on which several monasteries are located. (p. 250)

Mount Cook (mount kůk) The highest mountain in New Zealand, in the central part of the Southern Alps on South Island. Its elevation is 12,349 feet. (3,764 m); 44°S, 170°E. (p. 584)

Mount Everest (mount ev′ ər əst) The highest mountain in the world. It is located in the Himalayas on the border between Nepal and Tibet at 29,028 feet (8,848 m); 33°N, 87°E. (p. 492)

Mount Kilimanjaro (mount kil ə mən jär′ ō)) The highest mountain in Africa, located in northern Tanzania at 19,340 feet (5,895 m); 3°S, 37°F. (p. 416)

Mount McKinley (mount mə kin′ lē) The highest mountain in North America, located in south-central Alaska at 20,320 feet (6,194 m); 63°N, 151°W. (p. 40)

Munich (mū′ nik) A city in southern Germany; 48°N, 11°E. (p. 234)

a cap; ā cake; ä father; är car; âr dare; ch chain; e hen; ē me; êr clear; hw where; i bib; ī kite; ng song; o top; ō rope; ô saw; oi coin; ôr fork; ou cow; sh show; th thin; <u>th</u> those; u sun; ů book; ü moon; ū cute; ûr term; ə about, taken, pencil, apron, helpful; ər letter, dollar, doctor

GAZETTEER

N

Nepal (nə pôl′) A country in South Asia, located on the southern slopes of the Himalayas. (p. 486)

Netherlands, the (ne<u>th</u>′ ər ləndz) One of the Low Countries in Western Europe, on the North Sea. (p. 184)

Netherlands Antilles (ne<u>th</u>′ ər ləndz an til′ ēz) Dutch islands lying off the coast of Venezuela that are part of the Lesser Antilles of the Caribbean Islands. (p. 108)

New Brunswick (nü brunz′ wik) A province in eastern Canada. (p. 82)

New Zealand (nü zē′ lənd) An island country in the southern Pacific. (p. 578)

Niger River (nī′ jər riv′ ər) A river in West Africa, flowing from the Sierra Leone-Guinea border into the Gulf of Guinea. (p. 416)

Nigeria (nī jêr′ ē ə) A country on the Gulf of Guinea in West Africa. (p. 416)

Nile River (nīl riv′ ər) The world's longest river, flowing from east-central Africa north into the Mediterranean Sea. (p. 356)

Normandy (nôr′ mən dē) A historic region in northwest France, bordering the English Channel. (p. 218)

North Africa (nôrth af′ rik ə) Region consisting of the Muslim countries of Africa lying along the Mediterranean coast. (p. 350)

North America (nôrth ə mer′ ik ə) The world's third-largest continent, lying between the Pacific and Atlantic oceans. (p. 5)

North China Plain (nôrth chī′ nə plān) A large fertile plain lying north of the Qin Ling Mountains in eastern China. (p. 492)

North Island (nôrth ī′ lənd) The smaller and more northerly of the two main islands of New Zealand. (p. 584)

North Pole (nôrth pōl) The northernmost point on the earth; the northern end of the earth's axis, at 90°N. (p. 6)

North Sea (nôrth sē) A large arm of the Atlantic Ocean, between Great Britain and mainland Europe. (p. 184)

Northern Asia (nôr′ <u>th</u>ərn ā′ zhə) The part of Asia east of the Ural Mountains and the Caspian Sea. (p. 294)

Northern Ireland (nôr′ <u>th</u>ərn īr′ lənd) A province of the United Kingdom located in the northeastern part of Ireland. (p. 202)

Norway (nôr′ wā) A country in Western Europe, located in the western part of the Scandinavian Peninsula. (p. 184)

O

Oceania (ō shē an′ ē ə) Islands of the Pacific Ocean including Polynesia, Melanesia, Micronesia, and many other islands. Australia and New Zealand are sometimes considered part of Oceania. (p. 598)

Oinoussai (ē nü′ sā) A small Greek island in the Aegean Sea, lying near the Turkish coast; 39°N, 26°E. (p. 250)

Orinoco River (ôr ə nō′ kō riv′ ər) A large river of northwestern South America that flows into the Atlantic Ocean. (p. 108)

Ottawa (ot′ ə wə) Canada's capital, located in the province of Ontario in the southeastern part of the country. (p. 82)

P

Pacific Mountains (pə sif′ ik moun′ tənz) A mountain system in the United States and Canada that lies between the Pacific Ocean and the Rocky Mountains. (p. 40)

Pacific Ocean (pə sif′ ik ō′ shən) The world's largest body of water, lying between Asia and Australia on the west and North America and South America on the east. (p. 5)

Pakistan (pak′ ə stan) A country in South Asia, on the Arabian Sea. (p. 486)

Palestine (pal′ ə stīn) A historical area in the Middle East, lying between the Mediterranean Sea and the Jordan River. It was the homeland of the Jews in biblical times and a British protectorate that became the nations of Israel and Jordan. (p. 372)

Pamirs (pä mêrz′) A mountain region of Asia bordering Afghanistan, Tajikistan, Pakistan, and China. Several mountain ranges meet here to form the "Pamir Knot." (p.492)

Pampas (päm′ pəz) Grass-covered plains of South America that cover much of central Argentina and parts of Uruguay. (p. 108)

Panama (pa′ nə mä) A country of Central America, between the Atlantic and Pacific Oceans. (p. 108)

Panama Canal (pan′ ə mä kə nal′) A ship canal across the Isthmus of Panama connecting the Atlantic and Pacific oceans. (p. 151)

Panama Canal Zone (pan′ ə mä kə nal′ zōn) A strip of land on both sides of the Panama Canal that, from 1903 to 1978, was a United States territory. Panama controls most of the Canal Zone and will gain complete control of it in the year 2000. (p. 151)

Papua New Guinea (pap′ ù ə nü gin′ ē) A country in the Pacific, located on the eastern part of the island of New Guinea and several nearby islands. (p. 578)

Paris (par′ is) The capital city of France and one of Western Europe's great cultural centers; 49°N, 2°E. (p. 186)

Patagonia (pat′ ə gō′ nē ə) The southern part of Argentina. (p. 108)

Persian Gulf (pûr′ zhən gulf) A body of water located between the Arabian Peninsula and Iran. (p. 356)

Philippines (fil′ ə pēnz) A country located on an archipelago in Southeast Asia, separated from the mainland by the South China Sea. (p. 486)

Plateau of Iran (pla tō′ əv i ran′) A plateau located in the northeastern part of Iran, in the Middle East. (p. 30?)

Plateau of Tibet (pla tō′ əv ti bet′) A high, dry plateau in southwestern China, north of the Himalayas. (p. 492)

Poland (pō lənd) A country in Eastern Europe, on the Baltic Sea. (p. 332)

Polynesia (pol ə nē′ zhə) One of the three main island groups of Oceania in the Pacific Ocean. (p. 579)

Popocatépetl (pō pō kä tā′ pə təl) A volcano in southern Mexico, near Mexico City; 19°N, 99°W. (p. 108)

Portugal (pôr′ chə gəl) A country in Southern Europe, in the western part of the Iberian Peninsula. (p. 184)

Puerto Rico (pwer′ tō rē′ kō) An island in the Greater Antilles of the West Indies. It is a commonwealth of the United States. (p. 108)

Pyrenees (pir ə nēz) A mountain range in the southwestern part of Western Europe, extending from the Bay of Biscay to the Mediterranean Sea. (p. 184)

Q

Quebec (kwi bek′) The capital city of the province of Quebec in eastern Canada; 46°N, 71°W. (p. 82)

Queensland (kwēnz′ lənd) A state of Australia, in the northeastern part of the country. (p. 590)

R

Red Sea (red sē) A narrow sea located between the Arabian Peninsula and northeastern Africa. (p. 350)

Rhine River (rīn riv′ ər) A river in Western Europe that flows from eastern Switzerland into the North Sea. (p. 184)

Rio de Janeiro (rē′ ō dā zhə nâr′ ō) A large port city in southeastern Brazil; 23°S, 43°W. (p. 110)

Río de la Plata (rē′ ō dā lä plä′ tə) A river system in east-central South America. It is actually the mouth of the Paraná and Uruguay rivers and their main tributaries and empties into the Atlantic Ocean. (p. 108)

Riviera (riv ē âr ə) A narrow strip of land along the Mediterranean coasts of France, Monaco, and Italy, famous as a vacation spot. (p. 220)

Riyadh (rē yäd′) The capital and largest city of Saudi Arabia, located in the central part of the country; 25°N, 47°E. (p. 358)

Rocky Mountains (rok′ ē moun′ tənz) A long, rugged mountains that stretch along the western part of North America from Alaska to Mexico. (p. 40)

Romania (rō mā′ nē ə) A country in Eastern Europe, on the Black Sea coast of the Balkan Peninsula. (p. 294)

Rome (rōm) The capital and largest city of Italy, located on the Tiber River in the central part of the country; 42°N, 13°E. (p. 186)

Rotterdam (rot′ ər dam) A city in the southwestern Netherlands and the busiest port in the world; 51°N, 4°E. (p. 186)

Ruhr Valley (rür val′ ē) The valley of the Ruhr River, a major tributary of the Rhine River in northwestern Germany. (p. 238)

Russia (rush′ ə) A country in Eastern Europe and Northern Asia. Russia was a republic of the Soviet Union from 1922 until 1991, when it became independent. (p. 306)

S

Sahara (sə har′ ə) The largest desert in the world, covering much of northern Africa. (p. 623)

Sahel (sä′ hel) A dry grassland that stretches across Africa just south of the Sahara Desert. (p. 416)

Samoa (sə mō′ ə) An archipelago in Polynesia, about halfway between New Zealand and Hawaii. (p. 598)

San Francisco (san frən sis′ kō) A port city in west-central California, on the Pacific Ocean; 38°N, 122°W. (p. 43)

San Pedro de Macorís (san pā′ drō dā mä kô rēs′) A city in the southeastern Dominican Republic; 19°S, 69°W. (p. 142)

Santiago de Compostela (sän tē ä′ gō də kom ... Spain; 43°N, 9°W. (p. 250) A pilgrimage center in northwestern ...

Sardinia (sär din′ ē ə) An Italian island in the Mediterranean Sea, southwest of the Italian Peninsula. (p. 184)

Scandinavia (skan də nā′ vē ə) A large peninsula in Western Europe, including the countries of Norway and Sweden. Denmark, Iceland, and Finland are also considered part of Scandinavia. (p. 178)

Senegal (sen i gôl′) A country on the western part of Africa. It is the westernmost part of Africa. (p. 416)

Serbia ... A republic in the Atlantic coast of ... Yugoslavia. (p. 332)

Shikoku (shi kō′ kü) The smallest of the four main islands of Japan. (p. 543)

a hat; ā age; ä far; e let; ē equal; ėr term; i it; ī ice; o hot; ō open; ô order; oi oil; ou out; u cup; ů put; ü rule; ch child; ng long; sh she; th thin; ŦH then; zh measure; ə represents a in about, e in taken, i in pencil, o in lemon, u in circus

between the Ural Mountains and the Pacific Ocean. It includes the Asian part of Russia. (p. 294)

Sicily (sis' ə lē) An Italian island in the Mediterranean Sea off the southwestern tip of Italy. (p. 184)

Siena (sē en' ə) A city in central Italy; 43°N, 11°E. (p. 264)

Sinai Peninsula (sī' nī pə nin' sə lə) A small peninsula in northeastern Egypt, bordered by the Mediterranean Sea on the north and the Red Sea on the south. It is a bridge between Asia and Africa. (p. 356)

Singapore (sing' ə pōr) An island country in Southeast Aisa off the southern tip of the Malay Peninsula. (p. 486)

Slovenia (slō vēn' ē ə) A country in Eastern Europe. It was a republic in northwestern Yugoslavia until it became independent in 1991. (p. 332)

South Africa (south af' ri kə) A country in Southern Africa. (p. 416)

South America (south ə mer' i kə) The world's fourth largest continent. It lies between the Pacific and Atlantic oceans. (p. 160)

South Asia (south ā' zhə) The part of Asia made up of the Indian subcontinent and nearby lands. (p. 486)

South Korea (south kə rē' ə) A country in eastern Asia, occupying the southern half of the Korean Peninsula. (p. 486)

Southeast Asia (south ēst' ā' zhə) The part of Asia lying between South Asia and East Asia. (p. 486)

Southern Africa (suth' ərn af' ri kə) The part of Sub-Saharan Africa that is south of East and Equatorial Africa. It is the southernmost part of the continent. (p. 408)

Southern Europe

Stockholm (stok' hōm) The capital and largest city of Sweden, located on the eastern coast; 59°N, 18°E. (p. 272)

Sub-Saharan Africa (sub' sə har' ən af' ri kə) The part of Africa lying south of the Sahara. (p. 31)

Sweden (swē' dən) A country in Western Europe, located in the eastern part of the Scandinavian Peninsula. (p. 184)

Switzerland (switz' ər lənd) A country in Central Europe. (p. 184)

Sydney (sid' nē) The largest city and chief port of Australia, on the eastern coast of the country; 34°S, 151°E. (p. 586)

T

Tahiti (tə hē' tē) The largest of the Society Islands, located in French Polynesia, midway between Australia and South America; 18°S, 150°W. (p. 598)

Taiwan (tī wän') An island off the southeastern coast of China, between the Formosa Strait and the Philippine Sea. It is also known as Formosa. (p. 486)

Tajikistan (tä jik' i stän) A country in Central Asia. Tajikistan was a republic of the Soviet Union from 1929 until 1991, when it became independent. (p. 300)

Takla Makan (täk' lə mə kän') A large desert in northwestern China. (p. 492)

Tarim Basin (dä rem' bä' sin) A dry region in northwestern China, lying between the Tian Shan and the Kunlun Mountains. (p. 367)

Tenochtitlán (tā nōch tē tlän') Capital of the Aztecs. It was situated where Mexico City stands today. (p. 120)

Thingvellir (thing' vel ər) A small settlement and plain in southwestern Iceland, about 25 miles (40 km) east of Reykjavik; 64°N, 21°W. (p. 272)

Tian Shan (tē än' shän') A mountain system of central Asia, extending from western China. (p. 492)

Tibet (ti bet') An autonomous region of China, north of the Himalayas. (p. 492)

Tigris River (tī' gris riv' ər) A river in southwest Asia, flowing from eastern Turkey to southern Iraq, where it joins the Euphrates River and flows into the Persian Gulf. (p. 356)

Tokyo (tō' kē ō) The capital and largest city of Japan.

South Island (south ī' lənd) The more southerly of the two main islands of New Zealand. (p. 584)

South Pole (south pōl) The southernmost point on earth; the southern end of the earth's axis. (p. 6)

Soviet Union (sō' vē et ūn' yən) A former country in Eastern Europe and Northern Asia. The Soviet Union existed from 1922 until 1991, when it was replaced by 15 independent countries. (p. 258–284)

Plateau of Iran (plə tō′ əv i ran′) A plateau located in the northeastern part of Iran, in the Middle East. (p. 356)

Plateau of Tibet (plə tō′ əv ti bet′) A high, dry plateau in southwestern China, north of the Himalayas. (p. 492)

Poland (pō lənd) A country in Eastern Europe, on the Baltic Sea. (p. 332)

Polynesia (pol ə nē′ zhə) One of the three main island groups of Oceania in the Pacific Ocean. (p. 579)

Popocatépetl (pō pō kä tā′ pə təl) A volcano in southern Mexico, near Mexico City; 19°N, 99°W. (p. 108)

Portugal (pôr′ chə gəl) A country in Southern Europe, in the western part of the Iberian Peninsula. (p. 184)

Puerto Rico (pwer′ tō rē′ kō) An island in the Greater Antilles of the West Indies. It is a commonwealth of the United States. (p. 108)

Pyrenees (pir′ ə nēz) A mountain range in the southwestern part of Western Europe, extending from the Bay of Biscay to the Mediterranean Sea. (p. 184)

Q

Quebec (kwi bek′) The capital city of the province of Quebec in eastern Canada; 46°N, 71°W. (p. 82)

Queensland (kwēnz′ lənd) A state of Australia, in the northeastern part of the country. (p. 590)

R

Red Sea (red sē) A narrow sea located between the Arabian Peninsula and northeastern Africa. (p. 350)

Rhine River (rīn riv′ ər) A river in Western Europe that flows from eastern Switzerland into the North Sea. (p. 184)

Rio de Janeiro (rē′ ō dā zhə nâr′ ō) A large port city in southeastern Brazil; 23°S, 43°W. (p. 110)

Río de la Plata (rē′ ō dā lä plä′ tə) A river system in east-central South America. It is actually the mouth of the Paraná and Uruguay rivers and their main tributaries and empties into the Atlantic Ocean. (p. 108)

Riviera (riv ē âr ə) A narrow strip of land along the Mediterranean coasts of France, Monaco, and Italy, famous as a vacation spot. (p. 222)

Riyadh (rē yäd′) The capital and largest city of Saudi Arabia, located in the central part of the country; 25°N, 47°E. (p. 358)

Rocky Mountains (rok′ ē moun′ tənz) The high, rugged mountains that stretch along the western part of North America from Alaska south to New Mexico. (p. 40)

Romania (rō mā′ nē ə) A country in Eastern Europe, on the Black Sea coast of the Balkan Peninsula. (p. 294)

Rome (rōm) The capital and largest city of Italy, located on the Tiber River in the central part of the country; 42°N, 13°E. (p. 186)

Rotterdam (rot′ ər dam) A city in the southwestern Netherlands and the busiest port in the world; 51°N, 4°E. (p. 186)

Ruhr Valley (rūr val′ ē) The valley of the Ruhr River, a major tributary of the Rhine River in northwestern Germany. (p. 238)

Russia (rush′ ə) A country in Eastern Europe and Northern Asia. Russia was a republic of the Soviet Union from 1922 until 1991, when it became independent. (p. 306)

S

Sahara (sə har′ ə) The largest desert in the world, covering much of northern Africa. (p. 623)

Sahel (sä′ hel) A dry grassland that stretches across Africa just south of the Sahara Desert. (p. 416)

Samoa (sə mō′ ə) An archipelago in Polynesia, about halfway between New Zealand and Hawaii. (p. 598)

San Francisco (san frən sis′ kō) A port city in west-central California, on the Pacific Ocean; 38°N, 122°W. (p. 43)

San Pedro de Macorís (san pā′ drō dā mä kō rēs′) A city in the southeastern Dominican Republic; 19°S, 69°W. (p. 142)

Santiago de Compostela (sän′ tē ä′ gō də kom pō stel ä) A pilgrimage center in northwestern Spain; 43°N, 9°W. (p. 50)

Sardinia (sär din′ ē ə) An Italian island in the Mediterranean Sea, west of the Italian Peninsula. (p. 184)

Scandinavia (skan də nā′ vē ə) Area in northwestern Europe including the countries of Norway, Sweden, Denmark, and their dependents. Iceland and Finland are also considered part of Scandinavia. (p. 178)

Scandinavian Peninsula (skan də nā′ vē an pə nin′ sə lə) A large peninsula in the northern part of Western Europe. (p. 184)

Senegal (sen i gôl′) A country on the Atlantic coast of West Africa. (p. 416)

Serbia (sûr′ bē ə) A republic in the western part of Yugoslavia. (p. 332)

Shikoku (shi kō′ kü) The smallest of the four main islands of Japan. (p. 543)

a cap; ā cake; ä father; är car; âr dare; ch chain; e hen; ē me; êr clear; hw where; i bib; ī kite; ng song; o top; ō rope; ô saw; oi coin; ôr fork; ou cow; sh show; th thin; th those; u sun; u book; ü moon; ū cute; ûr term; ə about, taken, pencil, apron, helpful; ər letter, dollar, doctor

Siberia (sī bêr′ ē ə) A vast region in Russia lying between the Ural Mountains and the Pacific Ocean. It includes the Asian part of Russia. (p. 294)

Sicily (sis′ ə lē) An Italian island in the Mediterranean Sea off the southwestern tip of Italy. (p. 184)

Siena (sē en′ ə) A city in central Italy; 43°N, 11°E. (p. 264)

Sinai Peninsula (sī′ nī pə nin′ sə lə) A small peninsula in northeastern Egypt, bordered by the Mediterranean Sea on the north and the Red Sea on the south. It is a bridge between Asia and Africa. (p. 356)

Singapore (sing′ ə pôr) An island country in Southeast Aisa off the southern tip of the Malay Peninsula. (p. 486)

Slovenia (slō vēn′ ē ə) A country in Eastern Europe. It was a republic in northwestern Yugoslavia until it became independent in 1991. (p. 332)

South Africa (south af′ ri kə) A country in Southern Africa. (p. 416)

South America (south ə mer′ i kə) The world's fourth-largest continent. It lies between the Pacific and Atlantic oceans. (p. 160)

South Asia (south ā′ zhə) The part of Asia made up of the Indian subcontinent and nearby lands. (p. 486)

South Korea (south kə rē′ ə) A country in Eastern Asia, occupying the southern part of the Korean Peninsula. (p. 486)

Southeast Asia (south ēst′ ā′ zhə) The part of Asia lying between South Asia and East Asia. (p. 486)

Southern Africa (suth′ ərn af′ ri kə) The part of Sub-Saharan Africa that is south of East and Equatorial Africa. It is the southernmost part of the continent. (p. 408)

Southern Europe (suth′ ərn yür′ əp) The countries of the southern part of Western Europe. (p. 350)

South Island (south ī′ lənd) The larger and more southerly of the two main islands of New Zealand. (p. 584)

South Pole (south pōl) The southernmost point of the earth; the southern end of the earth's axis; at 90°S. (p. 6)

Soviet Union (sō′ vē et ūn′ yən) A former country of Eastern Europe and Northern Asia. The Soviet Union existed from 1922 until 1991, when it was replaced by 15 independent countries. (pp. 288–289)

Soweto (sə wā′ tō) A black township in South Africa, near Johannesburg; 26°S, 27°E. (p. 471)

Spain (spān) A country in Southern Europe, on the Iberian Peninsula. (p. 184)

Sri Lanka (srē läng′ kə) An island country in South Asia, off the southern tip of India. (p. 486)

St. Lawrence Seaway (sānt lôr′ əns sē′ wā) The St. Lawrence River and its system of dams, locks, and canals that connect the Great Lakes with the Gulf of St. Lawrence. This waterway allows large ships to travel between interior North America and the Atlantic Ocean. (p. 49)

Stockholm (stok′ hōm) The capital and largest city of Sweden, located on the eastern coast; 59°N, 18°E. (p. 272)

Sub-Saharan Africa (sub′ sə har′ ən af′ ri kə) The part of Africa lying south of the Sahara. (p. 31)

Sweden (swē′ dən) A country in Western Europe, located in the eastern part of the Scandinavian Peninsula. (p. 184)

Switzerland (switz′ ər lənd) A country in Central Europe. (p. 184)

Sydney (sid′ nē) The largest city and chief port of Australia, on the eastern coast of the country; 34°S, 151°E. (p. 586)

T

Tahiti (tə hē′ tē) The largest of the Society Islands, located in French Polynesia, midway between Australia and South America; 18°S, 150°W. (p. 598)

Taiwan (tī wän′) An island off the southeastern coast of China, between the Formosa Strait and the Philippine Sea. It is also known as Formosa. (p. 486)

Tajikistan (tä jik′ i stän) A country in Central Asia. Tajikistan was a republic of the Soviet Union from 1929 until 1991, when it became independent. (p. 306)

Takla Makan (täk′ lə mə kän′) A large desert in northwestern China. (p. 492)

Tarim Basin (dä′ rem′ bä′ sin) A dry region in northwestern China, lying between the Tian Shan and the Kunlun Mountains. (p. 637)

Tenochtitlán (te nôch tē tlän′) Capital of the Aztecs. It was located where Mexico City stands today. (p. 120)

Thingvellir (theng′ vet lêr) A small settlement and plain in southwestern Iceland, about 25 miles (40 km) east of Reykjavik; 64°N, 21°W. (p. 272)

Tian Shan (tē än′ shän′) A mountain system of central Asia, extending from Kyrgyzstan into western China. (p. 492)

Tibet (ti bet′) An autonomous region in southwestern China, north of the Himalayas. (p. 526)

Tigris River (tī′ gris riv′ ər) A river in southwestern Asia, flowing from eastern Turkey to southeastern Iraq, where it joins the Euphrates River to empty into the Persian Gulf. (p. 356)

Tokyo (tō′ kyō) The capital and largest city of Japan, in the east-central part of the island of Honshu; 36°N, 140°E. (p. 494)

Tropic of Cancer (trop′ ik əv kan′ sər) An imaginary line around the earth at latitude 23° 27′N. (p. 25)

Tropic of Capricorn (trop′ ik əv kap′ ri kôrn) An imaginary line around the earth that is at latitude 23° 27′S. (p. 25)

Turin (tùr′in) A city in northwestern Italy, an important automobile-manufacturing center; 45°N, 8°E. (p. 186)

Turkmenistan (tûrk men′ i stän) A country in Central Asia. Turkmenistan was a republic of the Soviet Union from 1929 until 1991, when it became independent. (p. 306)

U

Ukraine (ū krān′) A country in Eastern Europe. Ukraine was a republic of the Soviet Union from 1922 until 1991, when it became independent. (p. 306)

Ural Mountains (yür′ əl moun′ tənz) A mountain system traditionally forming part of the boundary between Europe and Asia. (p. 294)

Uruguay (yür′ ə gwā) A country on the southeastern coast of South America. (p. 108)

Uzbekistan (ùz bck′ i stan) A country in Central Asia. Ukraine was a republic of the Soviet Union from 1924 until 1991, when it became independent. (p. 306)

V

Vatican City (vat′ i kən sit′ ē) An independent state within the city of Rome. It is the world headquarters of the Roman Catholic Church; 42°N, 12°E. (p. 250)

Venezuela (ven ə zwā′ lə) A country in the northern part of South America, on the Caribbean Sea. (p. 108)

Victoria Falls (vik′ tôr ē ə fôlz) A spectacular waterfall in Southern Africa, on the Zambezi River between Zimbabwe and Zambia; 18°S, 26°E. (p. 416)

Vienna (vē en′ ə) The capital and largest city of Austria, on the Danube River in the northeastern part of the country; 48°N, 16°E. (p. 186)

Virgin Islands (vûr′ jin ī′ ləndz) A group of islands in the West Indies, divided politically between the United States and Great Britain; 18°N, 64°W. (p. 142)

Volga River (vôl′ gə riv′ ər) The longest river in Europe, located in Russia. It flows from the Ural Mountains into the Caspian Sea. (p. 294)

W

West Africa (west af′ ri kə) The part of Sub-Saharan Africa that makes up the southern part of the continent's northwestern "bulge." (p. 408)

West Bank (west bangk) An area in the Middle East, west of the Jordan River. It has been occupied by Israel since 1967. (p. 378)

Western Europe (wes′ tərn yür′ əp) The countries that make up the western part of Europe. (p. 31)

Western Hemisphere (wes′ tərn hem′ i sfêr) The half of the world that lies west of the prime meridian and includes North America and South America. (p. 6)

West Indies (west in′ dēz) Islands in and around the Caribbean Sea, also known as the Caribbean Islands. They are made up of the Greater Antilles, the Lesser Antilles, and the Bahamas. (p. 142)

West Siberian Plain (west si bêr′ ē ən plān) A vast plain, one of the largest flat areas in the world, located in Siberia. (p. 294)

Witwatersrand (wit wôt′ ərz rand) An area in South Africa noted for its rich deposits of gold and other minerals. Several industrial cities, including Johannesburg, are located there. (p. 471)

Y

Yucatán Peninsula (ū kə tän′ pə nin′ sə lə) A peninsula in southeastern Mexico and northeastern Central America that juts between the Gulf of Mexico and the Caribbean Sea. (p. 108)

Yugoslavia (ū gō slä′ vē ə) A country in Eastern Europe, on the eastern shore of the Adriatic. (p. 294)

Z

Zagros Mountains (zag′ rəs moun′ tənz) A mountain range in western Iran. (p. 356)

Zaire (zä êr′) A country in Equatorial Africa. (p. 416)

Zambia (zam′ bē ə) A country in Southern Africa. (p. 416)

Zanzibar (zan′ zə bär) An island in the Indian Ocean, off the coast of Africa, that is part of Tanzania; 6°S, 40°E. (p. 635)

a cap; ā cake; ä father; är car; âr dare; ch chain; e hen; ē me; êr clear; hw where; i bib; ī kite; ng song; o top; ō rope; ô saw; oi coin; ôr fork; ou cow; sh show; th thin; th those; u sun; ù book; ü moon; ū cute; ûr term; ə about, taken, pencil, apron, helpful; ər letter, dollar, doctor

GAZETTEER

GLOSSARY

This Glossary will help you to pronounce and understand the meanings of the Key Vocabulary in this book. The page number at the end of the definition tells where the word first appears.

PRONUNCIATION KEY

a	cap	êr	clear	oi	coin	ü	moon
ā	cake	hw	where	ôr	fork	ū	cute
ä	father	i	bib	ou	cow	ûr	term
är	car	ī	kite	sh	show	ə	about, taken,
âr	dare	ng	song	th	thin		pencil, apron,
ch	chain	o	top	th	those		helpful
e	hen	ō	rope	u	sun	ər	letter, dollar,
ē	me	ô	saw	ù	book		doctor

A

absolute ruler (ab' sə lüt rü' lər) A ruler with complete power whose authority cannot be questioned. (p. 377)

acid rain (as' id rān') Rain mixed with chemicals from the burning of coal and other fuels. Acid rain pollutes waterways and kills wildlife and trees. (p. 88)

alluvial soil (ə lü' vē əl soil) Soil deposited by a river as it flows. (p. 495)

almanac (ôl' mə nak) A reference book that contains up-to-date facts on many subjects. (p. 89)

altiplano (äl ti plän' ō) A high, cold, flat area between two mountain ranges in Bolivia and Peru. (p. 109)

apartheid (ə pär' tīd) A system used in South Africa to separate people of different races by law. (p. 470)

aquaculture (ak' wə kul chər) Fish farming. (p. 530)

aquifer (ak' wə fər) An underground layer of rock, sand, or gravel that holds water or carries it to springs or wells. (p. 363)

arable (ar' ə bəl) Good for farming. (p. 47)

archipelago (är kə pel' i gō) An island group, such as the West Indies. (p. 109)

arid (ar' id) Dry. (p. 362)

atlas (at' ləs) A reference book that contains a variety of maps and information about places in the world. (p. 89)

atoll (at' ôl) A doughnut-shaped coral reef looped around an area of still, warm water. (p. 585)

autonomous region (ô ton' ə məs rē' jən) An area within a country, such as China, that is self-governing but supervised by the central government. (p. 532)

autonomy (ô ton' ə mē) The right to self-government. (p. 259)

B

barter (bär' tər) To swap. (p. 454)

basin (bā' sin) A large, bowl-shaped dip in the land. (p. 417)

bazaar (bə zär') An outdoor market. (p. 375)

bias (bī' əs) A tendency to favor one point of view over another. (p. 242)

Brahmans (brä' mənz) The priestly caste in the Hindu caste system. (p. 507)

Buddhism (bùd' iz əm) A system of belief in Asia that teaches that suffering is caused by selfishness. (p. 527)

buffer zone (buf' ər zōn) A region between two hostile powers. (p. 340)

C

cabinet (kab' ə nit) Members of a government, either a parliament or an executive branch, who help run the government by giving advice and helping to carry out the laws. (p. 91)

call and response (kôl and ri spons') A traditional African way of telling a story in which the storyteller calls out part of a well-known story and the listeners call out or sing out a response. (p. 443)

calligraphy (kə lig' rə fē) A beautiful form of writing that features graceful, flowing lines. (p. 382)

calypso (kə lip' sō) A style of music developed in the Caribbean by enslaved Africans who sang while they worked. (p. 154)

campesino (kam pə sē' nō) Village farmer in Mexico. (p. 124)

canal (kə nal') A waterway that is dug to provide a water route for travel or irrigation. (p. 222)

canton (kan′ tən) A small political unit in Switzerland, similar to a state or province. (p. 241)

capital goods (kap′ i təl güdz) Products that are used by industries to make other goods. (p. 315)

capitalism (kap′ i tə liz əm) An economic system in which businesses are owned by individuals rather than by the government. (p. 62)

cardinal directions (kär′ də nəl di rek′ shənz) The four primary directions: north, south, east, and west. (p. 7)

caste (kast) A social group among the Hindus that identifies a person according to the occupation of his or her ancestors. (p. 506)

caudillo (kou dē′ yō) In South America, a local military leader who gained power in his local area after the country gained its independence. (p. 170)

censor (sen′ sər) To examine something to decide if it may be made public. (p. 327)

chancellor (chan′ sə lər) Title of the prime minister in Germany. (p. 240)

chart (chärt) An organized way of presenting information in rows and columns. (p. 253)

checks and balances (cheks and bal′ əns əz) The system by which each branch of government limits the power of the others. (p. 67)

civil war (siv′ əl wôr) A war between people of the same country. (p. 459)

civilization (siv ə lə zā′ shən) A culture in which learning and government reach high levels. (p. 119)

clan (klan) A group of families who are descended from the same ancestor. (p. 431)

climate (klī′ mit) The kind of weather a place has over a long period of time. (p. 23)

climograph (klī′ mə graf) A graph that shows information about the temperature and precipitation in a particular location over a period of time. (p. 301)

coalition (kō ə lish′ ən) A temporary union between different political parties that agree to work together for a common purpose. (p. 258)

colonialism (kə lō′ nē ə liz əm) The control of a country as a colony by another country. (p. 398)

command economy (kə mand′ i kon′ ə mē) An economic system in which the government makes and organizes most economic decisions. (p. 315)

commercial farming (kə mûr′ shəl fär′ ming) A type of farming where crops are grown for sale. (p. 124)

commonwealth (kom′ ən welth) A self-governing territory, such as Puerto Rico. (p. 150)

Commonwealth of Independent States (kom′ ən welth əv in di pen′ dənt stāts) An organization formed in 1991 by some of the countries that had been members of the Soviet Union to foster cooperation in economic and governmental concerns. (p. 317)

Commonwealth of Nations (kom′ ən welth əv nā′ shənz) A group of independent nations once ruled by Great Britain; they consider the British monarch to be the head of their governments. (p. 92)

communism (kom′ yə niz əm) The system developed by Karl Marx in the 1800s in which all property is owned in common. (p. 147)

Confucianism (kən fū′ shə niz əm) The teachings of Confucius, including the importance of honoring one's parents, of being honest, respecting others, working hard, and acquiring learning. (p. 527)

constitutional monarchy (kon sti tü′ shən əl mon′ ər kē) A government headed by a king or queen, in which the monarch's powers are limited by a constitution that guarantees the people's rights. (p. 209)

consumer goods (kən sü′ mər güdz) Products bought by individuals for personal use. (p. 315)

continent (kon′ tə nənt) A large body of land, separated or nearly separated from another by water. (p. 5)

Continental Divide (kon tə nen′ təl di vīd′) An imaginary line in the Rocky Mountains that separates rivers flowing east from those flowing west. (p. 42)

contour interval (kon′ tür in′ tər vəl) The difference in elevation between two contour lines on a contour map. (p. 361)

contour line (kon′ tür līn) A line on a contour map that connects areas of the same elevation. (p. 360)

contour map (kon′ tür map) A map that shows the elevation and landforms of a place. (p. 360)

cooperative (kō op′ ər ə tiv) A business organization owned by its members. (p. 275)

copra (kō′ prə) The dried meat of a coconut. (p. 593)

cottage industry (kot′ ij in′ də strē) Manufacturing on a small scale that takes place in people's homes. (p. 512)

coup (kü) A sudden seizing or overthrowing of a government. (p. 171)

culture (kul′ chər) The way of life of a group of people, including their beliefs, customs, rules, and ways of relating to each other. (p. 28)

cultural geography (kul′ chər əl jē og′ rə fē) The study of people and their ways of life. (p. 18)

custom (kus′ təm) A practice from the past that people continue to observe. (p. 29)

cylindrical projection (sə lin′ dri kəl prə jek′ shən) A type of map projection in which distances measured along the equator are correct, but become more distorted as they near the poles. (p. 188)

Cyrillic (sə ril′ ik) Relating to the alphabet used for the languages of Russian, Ukrainian, Bulgarian, and certain other mostly Slavic languages. (p. 333)

D

Daoism (dou′ iz əm) A system of belief, formulated in Asia, that teaches that people should accept their fate calmly. (p. 527)

dateline (dāt′ līn) The words at the beginning of a news article that tell when and where the story was written. (p. 345)

GLOSSARY

democracy (di mok' rə sē) A government in which decisions are made by the citizens. (p. 66)

desert (dez' ərt) A dry, sandy region with very little plant or animal life. (p. 356)

desertification (di zûrt' i fi kā' shən) The expansion of a desert. (p. 432)

developed economy (di vel' əpt i kon' ə mē) An economy that has many different economic activities. (p. 64)

developing economy (di vel' ə ping i kon' ə mē) An economy that is only partly industrialized. (p. 124)

dialect (dī' ə lekt) A local variation of a language. (p. 235)

dictator (dik' tā tər) A ruler who has total control over a country and usually rules by force. (p. 147)

dictionary (dik' shə ner ē) A reference book that gives meanings of words and tells how to pronounce them. (p. 89)

Diet (dī' it) The national legislature in Japan. (p. 551)

dike (dīk) A huge wall used to keep back the sea. (p. 222)

discrimination (di skrim ə nā' shən) The unfair treatment of a person or a group of people by another person or group. (p. 58)

distortion (di stôr' shən) The shrinking, stretching, and changes in shape of places that results when a globe is represented on the flat surface of a map. (p. 188)

distribution map (dis' trə bū shən map) A map that shows how such things as population, rainfall, language, and religion are distributed in parts of the world. (p. 13)

diversified economy (di vûr' sə fīd i kon' ə mē) An economy in which a wide range of goods are produced. (p. 275)

drought (drout) A lack of rain over a long period of time. (p. 421)

E

Edda (ed' ə) A long Viking poem about the early Scandinavian gods. (p. 282)

editor (ed' i tər) One of the people who runs a newspaper. (p. 345)

editorial (ed i tôr' ē əl) An article in which the people who run a newspaper give their opinion on an important issue. (p. 345)

elevation (el ə vā' shən) Height above sea level. (p. 25)

encyclopedia (en sī klə pē' dē ə) A reference book that contains information about many subjects written in the form of articles. (p. 89)

environment (en vī' rən mənt) All the surroundings of a place, including the land and water, weather patterns, and plants and animals that live there. (p. 22)

equal-area projection (ē' kwəl âr' ē ə prə jek' shən) A type of map projection good for comparing different places on the earth because sizes and shapes are shown fairly accurately and distances are nearly correct. (p. 189)

equator (i kwā tər) The imaginary line that divides the earth halfway between the North Pole and the South Pole. (p. 6)

erosion (i rō' zhən) The gradual wearing down of the earth's surface by water or wind. (p. 41)

escarpment (e skärp' mənt) A steep cliff at the edge of a plateau. (p. 417)

ethnic group (eth' nik grüp) A group of people who share a language, history, or place of origin. (p. 29)

European Community (yùr ə pē' ən kə mū' ni tē) An organization of western European nations formed after World War II to promote free trade and to link transportation routes among themselves; also known as the Common Market. (p. 223)

executive branch (eg zek' yə tiv branch) The branch of the government that carries out the laws. (p. 68)

export (eks' pôrt) Any item sold to another nation. (p. 64)

extended family (ek stend' əd fam' ə lē) A family that contains, in addition to parents and their children, other relatives, such as cousins, aunts, uncles, and grandparents. (p. 122)

F

famine (fam' in) A widespread and severe shortage of food. (p. 453)

feature article (fē' chər är' ti kəl) In a newspaper, a detailed report on a person, an issue, or an event. (p. 345)

federal system (fed' ər əl sis' təm) The division of power between the national and local governments. (p. 67)

fellahin (fel ə hēn') Farmers in Arab countries. (p. 391)

fjord (fyôrd) A deep narrow inlet of the sea between high cliffs. (p. 186)

fossil fuel (fos' əl fū' əl) Fuel that is made from the remains of plants and animals that died thousands of years ago and is found underground. Examples are coal, petroleum, and natural gas. (p. 27)

free enterprise (frē en' tər prīz) In a capitalist economy, the freedom to own property and run a business largely free of government control. (p. 62)

freedom of expression (fre' dəm əv ek spresh' ən) The freedom to express all aspects of an individual's life. (p. 70)

G

gamelan (gam' ə lan) An Indonesian orchestra of drums, gongs, bells, chimes, cymbals, and xylophones, in which there is no conductor. (p. 573)

gaucho (gou' chō) A cowhand in South America who herds cattle on the Pampas. (p. 161)

geography (jē og' rə fē) The study of the earth's landforms, its plants and animals, its climates, and the relationship of people to their natural environment. (p. 15)

glasnost (glas' nōst) A policy of "openness" in the former Soviet Union. (p. 327)

global grid (glō bəl grid) The lines of latitude and longitude on a map or globe. (p. 51)

graph (graf) A type of diagram that shows numbers in picture form, such as a bar graph. (p. 253)

great circle (grāt sûr′ kəl) Any circle that divides the earth into equal halves. (p. 496)

great-circle route (grāt sûr kəl rïit) A route between two places that falls along a great circle. (p. 496)

Green Revolution (grēn rev ə lü′ shən) New farming techniques used in South Asia and elsewhere that produce larger harvests. (p. 511)

grid map (grid map) A map that is divided into squares identified by letter and number to help people locate places or points of interest. (p. 13)

griot (grē′ ō) A traditional storyteller or "praise singer" in West Africa. (p. 440)

gross national product (grōs nash′ ən əl prod′ əkt) The total value of all goods and services that a nation produces each year. (p. 566)

guest worker (gest wûr kər) A person who moves to another country to find work and who is usually not permitted to become a citizen of the other country. (p. 218)

Gulf Stream (gulf strēm) A special "river" that flows in the Atlantic Ocean, bringing warm water from the Gulf of Mexico to the Atlantic coast of Europe. (p. 192)

H

hajj (häj) The pilgrimage that every Muslim is supposed to make at least once to Mecca, the birthplace of Muhammad. (p. 370)

harmattan (här mə tan′) A seasonal wind that carries dry, dusty air from the Sahara to Sub-Saharan Africa. (p. 421)

headline (hed′ līn) Words printed in large type across the top of a newspaper article to catch the reader's attention. (p. 345)

hemisphere (hem′ i sfêr) Half of the earth. The Northern and Southern hemispheres are divided by the equator, and the Eastern and Western hemispheres by the prime meridian. (p. 5)

high latitudes (hī lat′ i tüdz) The lands around the North and South poles, with the earth's coldest temperatures. (p. 115)

Hinduism (hin′ dü iz əm) The oldest and widest-spread religion in South Asia. (p. 506)

Holocaust (hol′ ə kôst) The killing of more than 6 million Jewish people by German and its allies during World War II (1939–1945). (p.235)

homogeneous (hō mə jē′ nē əs) Similar; of the same kind. (p. 542)

hydroelectric power (hī drō i lek′ trik pou′ ər) Electricity that is produced by the force of rapidly moving water, as at a waterfall or dam. (p. 49)

I

iceberg (īs′ bûrg) A large body of ice that has broken away from a glacier. (p. 587)

icon (ī′ kon) A painting of a saint or a religious leader. (p. 311)

immigrant (im′ i grənt) A person who moves to a country other than the one where he or she was born. (p. 56)

import (im′ pôrt) An item brought in from another country. (p. 64)

Impressionism (im presh′ ə niz əm) A style of painting started in France in the late 1800s, in which artists tried to capture the feeling of a place during one moment in time. (p. 228)

Industrial Revolution (in dus′ trē əl rev ə lü′ shən) In Western Europe, the gradual changeover from home-made goods to the production of goods by machine in factories. The changeover was so sweeping that it is considered a revolution. (p. 206)

intermediate directions (in tər mē′ dē it di rek′ shənz) The directions halfway between the cardinal directions: northeast, northwest, southeast, and southwest. (p. 7)

International Date Line (in tər nash′ ə nəl dāt līn) An imaginary line located halfway around the world from the prime meridian. It marks the end of one day and the beginning of the next. (p. 205)

iron rice bowl (ī′ ərn rīs bōl) A system of employment in China under which people expect to be guaranteed jobs for life. (p. 531)

irrigation (ir i gā′ shən) The watering of dry land with the use of streams, canals, or pipes. (p. 358)

Islam (is′ lam) One of the world's great religions, founded by Muhammad. (p. 369)

Islamic republic (is lam′ ik ri pub′ lik) A nation that is governed by the religious laws of Islam. (p. 378)

J

judicial branch (jü dish′ əl branch) The branch of the government that interprets the laws. (p. 68)

junta (hùn′ tə) A group of army officers who rule a country after the army takes control. (p. 170)

---

a cap; ā cake; ä father; är car; âr dare; ch chain; e hen; ē me; êr clear; hw where; i bib; ī kite; ng song; o top; ō rope; ô saw; oi coin; ôr fork; ou cow; sh show; th thin; th those; u sun; ù book; ü moon; ū cute; ûr term; ə about, taken, pencil, apron, helpful; ər letter, dollar, doctor

GLOSSARY

K

kibbutz (ki buts') A collective farm in Israel, where the members own and work the land together. (p. 376)

L

labor-intensive (lā' bər in ten' siv) A term that describes a situation in which people, rather than machines, do the work. (p. 375)

landform (land' fôrm) A physical feature of a place. (p. 23)

landform map (land' fôrm map) A physical map that shows how the earth's surface varies from place to place. (p. 11)

landlocked (land' lokt') Entirely surrounded by land. (p. 195)

large-scale map (lärj skāl map) A map that shows detailed information about a place because the map includes only a small area. (p. 225)

latitude (lat' i tüd) Line on a map or globe that extends east and west and shows distance from the equator. (p. 50)

legislative branch (lej' is lā tiv branch) The branch of the government that makes the laws and decides how much money the government can spend. (p. 68)

line graph (līn graf) A type of graph that uses a line to show changes in the amount of something over time. (p. 463)

loess (les) A yellowish soil that is very fertile. (p. 494)

longitude (lon' ji tüd) A measure of the distance east or west from the prime meridian. (p. 50)

low latitudes (lō lat' i tüdz) Areas located near the equator that have generally hot temperatures. (p. 115)

M

Magna Carta (mag' nə kär' tə) A document signed by King John of Great Britain in 1215 that limited the powers of the monarch. (p. 209)

malnutrition (mal nü trish' ən) A condition caused by a lack of food or of the right kinds of food. (p. 453)

map key (map kē) The guide that appears on a map to explain what its symbols stand for. (p. 9)

martial arts (mär' shəl ärts) Forms of self defense and exercise, such as karate and kung fu, that are based on ancient Asian methods of hand-to-hand combat. (p. 537)

Maroon (mə rün') In Jamaica, a descendant of slaves who escaped from the Spanish to set up an independent community. (p. 143)

mbira (em bêr' ə) A South African finger piano. (p. 479)

meditate (med' i tāt) To think deeply. (p. 572)

megalopolis (meg ə lop' ə lis) A region that is so crowded with cities and suburbs that it appears to be one large city. (p. 59)

meridian (mə rid' ē ən) A line of longitude. (p. 50)

mestizo (mes tē' zō) A person of mixed Indian and Spanish ancestry. (p. 120)

metropolitan area (met rə pol' i tən âr' ē ə) A large city and its surrounding suburbs and towns. (p. 123)

middle latitudes (mid' əl lat' i tüdz) Areas farther from the equator than those in the low latitudes, with generally cooler temperatures and changing seasons. (p. 115)

migration (mī grā' shən) A movement of a group of people into new lands. (p. 449)

mileage chart (mī' lij chärt) A table that shows distances between specific places. (p. 419)

mixed economy (mikst i kon' ə mē) An economy that has both private enterprises and government-run businesses. (p. 207)

monarchy (mon' ər kē) Any government headed by a hereditary ruler, such as a king or queen. (p. 92)

monsoons (mon sünz') Seasonal winds that bring heavy rainstorms or hot, dry weather. (p. 498)

mosaic (mō zā' ik) A pattern or picture made up of many small pieces of stone or glass. (p. 81)

moshav (mō shäv') A cooperative farm in Israel, in which each farmer owns his or her own land but sells produce through the cooperative. (p. 376)

muezzin (mü ez' in) The crier who calls Muslims to prayer five times each day. (p. 389)

mural (myùr' əl) A work of art on the wall of a building. (p. 131)

N

nationalism (nash' ə nə liz əm) A strong love for and pride in one's country or ethnic group. (p. 332)

nationalize (nash' ə nə līz) To place an industry under the control or ownership of the government. (p. 206)

natural resources (nach' ər əl rē' sôrs əz) Materials found in nature that people can use, such as water or soil. (p. 25)

neutral (nü' trəl) Refusing to take sides in a war or dispute. (p. 241)

news article (nüz är' ti kəl) In a newspaper, a story about an event that has just taken place. (p. 345)

nonaligned nations (non ə līnd' nā' shənz) Developing countries that do not take sides in the struggles between the world's superpowers. (p. 517)

O

oasis (ō ā' sis) A green, fertile, well-watered spot in a desert. (p. 358)

oba (ō' bə) A traditional ruler in some West African areas. (p. 436)

ombudsman (om' bədz mən) A government official in Sweden, whose job is to hear people's complaints about a government service or action, to inform government representatives of the complaints, and to push for action. (p. 278)

one-crop economy (wun' krop' i kon' ə mē) An economy that depends on a single crop for income. (p. 145)

GLOSSARY

oral tradition (ôr′ əl trə dish′ ən) History and literature that is spoken and passed down from person to person. (p. 440)

outback (out′ bak) A huge, arid area in central Australia where few people live. (p. 584)

P

Pacific Rim (pə sif′ ik rim) All the countries that border on the Pacific Ocean, including many countries of Asia, North America, and South America, as well as Australia and New Zealand. (p. 531)

paddy (pad′ ē) A type of field in which wet rice is grown. (p. 567)

parallel (par′ ə lel) A line of latitude on a map or globe. (p. 50)

parliamentary democracy (pär lə men′ tə rē di mok′ rə sē) A country with a representative national legislature called a parliament. (p. 91)

partition (pär tish′ ən) A division, as in the division of British India into India and Pakistan. (p. 515)

per capita income (pər kap′ i tə in′ kum) The amount of income each person would have if the country's total income were divided equally among all its people. (p. 166)

perestroika (pâr əs trô i kə) In the former Soviet Union and Eastern Europe, a plan for economic restructuring, including reducing the amount of government control over businesses. (p. 315)

permafrost (pûr′ mə frôst) In Arctic lands, a layer of soil that is permanently frozen, found below a thin layer of topsoil. (p. 44)

petrochemical (pet rō kem′ i kəl) A chemical, such as ammonia or benzene, that is made from petroleum. (p. 124)

petroleum (pə trō′ lē əm) Oil. (p. 364)

physical geography (fiz′ i kəl jē og′ rə fē) The study of the earth's surface, the climate, plant and animal life, and other factors that affect the earth. (p. 18)

physical map (fiz′ i kəl map) A map that shows the earth's natural features, such as continents, oceans, mountains, and deserts. (p. 10)

pilgrimage (pil′ grə mij) Journey to a sacred place. (p. 263)

pinyin (pin′ yin′) Presently, the official method of writing Chinese words in English. (p. 528)

plantation (plan tā′ shən) A large farm that grows crops for sale. (p. 145)

point of view (point əv vū) The way a person looks at or feels about something. (p. 280)

polar climate (pō′ lər klī′ mit) A type of climate found in the areas around the North and South poles, where the weather is generally cold. (p. 25)

polder (pōl′ dər) A lowland area reclaimed from the sea in the Netherlands. (p. 222)

political cartoon (pə lit′ i kəl kär tün′) A drawing that focuses attention on an important issue and tries to influence public opinion. (p. 535)

political map (pə lit′ i kəl map) A map that shows political divisions such as countries and states as well as cities. (p. 10)

pollution (pə lü′ shən) Dirty and unpure elements in the environment. (p. 239)

population density (pop yə lā′ shən den′ si tē) The number of people per square mile or square kilometer in a given land area. (p. 43)

prejudice (prej′ ə dis) An unfavorable opinion that is formed unfairly about a group of people without knowing all the facts. (p. 58)

premier (pri mêr′) The title given to the prime minister in France and some other countries. (p. 226)

prime meridian (prīm mə rid′ ē ən) The starting line for measuring longitude. (p. 6, 50)

prime minister (prīm min′ ə stər) The leader of the political party that has the majority of members in a parliament. (p. 91)

projection (prə jek′ shən) A way of showing locations on the earth on a flat map. (p. 188)

proverb (prov′ ərb) A short, popular saying that illustrates a truth. (p. 461)

province (prov′ ins) A self-governing area within a nation, similar to a state in the United States. (p. 82)

Q

qanat (kä′ nât) In Iran, underground tunnels for carrying water from the mountains to irrigate land. (p. 363)

quota (kwō′ tə) A fixed amount as for buying or producing goods. (p. 335)

R

rain forest (rān′ fôr′ ist) A dense tropical forest in a region with high annual rainfall. (p. 113)

Ramadan (ram ə dän′) The ninth month of the Muslim year, a month in which Muslims fast from sunrise to sunset. (p. 403)

reasoned opinion (rē′ zənd ə pin′ yən) A type of opinion based on evidence or reasons. (p. 162)

GLOSSARY

a cap; ā cake; ä father; är car; âr dare; ch chain; e hen; ē me; êr clear; hw where; i bib; ī kite; ng song; o top; ō rope; ô saw; oi coin; ôr fork; ou cow; sh show; th thin; <u>th</u> those; u sun; ů book; ü moon; ū cute; ûr term; ə about, taken, pencil, apron, helpful; ər letter, dollar, doctor

reference (ref′ ər əns) Having to do with information to be referred to, as in a reference book; reference books include dictionaries and almanacs. (p. 89)

reform (ri fôrm′) To make a change for the better. (p. 315)

reggae (reg′ ā) A style of music that began in Jamaica and combines elements of rock 'n' roll, blues, and calypso. (p. 154)

region (rē′ jən) A large area with common features that set it apart from other areas. (p. 20)

relief (ri lēf′) A variation in elevation. (p. 361)

Renaissance (ren ə säns′) A period of rebirth in Europe during the 1300s and 1400s that included great activity in the arts. (p. 261)

republic (ri pub′ lik) A government in which voters elect officials to represent them. (p. 66)

reunification (rē ū nə fi kā′ shən) The act of uniting again or the results of that act. (p. 234)

rift valley (rift val′ ē) A narrow valley with steep sides formed millions of years ago by cracks in the earth's crust. (p. 417)

river system (riv′ ər sis′ təm) The land drained by a river and its tributaries; also known as a river basin. (p. 109)

Roman Catholicism (rō′ mən kə thol′ ə siz əm) The branch of the Christian religion that is under the authority of the pope in Rome. (p. 83)

S

saga (sä′ gə) A long story first told by people in Iceland about their early kings and heroes. (p. 282)

samizdat (säm′ ēz dät) A system of publishing and distributing censored or unapproved literature secretly in the former Soviet Union. (p. 310)

samurai (sam′ ù rī) A member of a class of warriors who once ruled Japan. (p. 543)

sanctions (sangk′ shənz) Actions taken against a country by other countries to try to get that country to change. (p. 475)

satellite (sat′ ə līt) One of several countries in Eastern Europe that were closely tied to the former Soviet Union. (p. 331)

savanna (sə van′ ə) A broad grassland containing scattered trees and shrubs. (p. 418)

scale (skāl) The measurement used to indicate the proportion that distances on a map have to the real distances they represent. (p. 7)

sect (sekt) A religious group that is outside the mainstream of large, organized religions. (p. 144)

separatism (sep′ ər ə tiz əm) A movement to break away from a nation or province. (p. 83)

shadow play (shad′ ō plā) A type of entertainment in Indonesia in which puppets are used to act out well-known stories and to teach moral and religious values. (p. 572)

sharia (shə rē′ ə) Islamic law, based on the Koran as interpreted by Muslim scholars. (p. 378)

shifting cultivation (shift′ ing kul tə vā′ shən) A method used in farming in which a field periodically is not planted so new grasses can grow and replace nutrients in the soil. (p. 433)

Shinto (shin′ tō) Japanese religion which teaches that spirits dwell in all things in nature. (p. 542)

siesta (sē es′ tə) A long afternoon nap, commonly taken by people in Southern European lands. (p. 251)

Sikhism (sēk′ iz əm) A religion blending Hinduism and Islam, founded in the 1400s. (p. 507)

slash-and-burn farming (slash and bûrn fär′ ming) A type of farming where a field is cleared of its trees and stumps and then the brush is burned, creating ash which enriches the soil. (p. 433)

small-scale map (smôl skāl map) A map that shows a large area in a small space. (p. 224)

socialist realism (sō′ shə list rē′ ə liz əm) A form of art practiced in communist countries which shows true-to-life scenes and heroes of the country performing great deeds. (p. 536)

Soviet (sō′ vē et) Referring to people, customs, the government, or the country of the former Soviet Union. (p. 305)

standard of living (stan′ dərd əv liv′ ing) A measure of the amount of goods and services available to the people in a country. (p. 238)

station (stā′ shən) A ranch for raising sheep or cattle in Australia or New Zealand. (p. 600)

steppes (steps) Dry, grassy plains, found south of the taiga in Russia, Ukraine, and parts of Eastern Europe. (p. 299)

subcontinent (sub kon′ tə nənt) A large landmass that is smaller than a continent. (p. 491)

subsistence farming (sub sis′ təns fär′ ming) A type of farming in which the farmer raises only enough food to feed his or her own family. (p. 124)

summary (sum′ ə rē) A brief statement that tells the main ideas contained in a piece of writing. (p. 544)

sumo wrestling (sü′ mō res′ ling) Traditional Japanese sport in which two large, very strong men try to force each other to touch the ground with any part of their body except their feet. (p. 553)

Swahili (swä hē′ lē) A common language in East and Equatorial Africa, containing Bantu words and elements of Portuguese and Arabic. (p. 452)

symbol (sim′ bəl) A person, an animal, or an object that stands for something beyond itself. Symbols are often used in political cartoons. (p. 9, 535)

T

taiga (tī′ gə) In Russia, a vast region of evergreen trees, south of the tundra. (p. 299)

talking drums (tô′ king drumz) Traditional African drums that can be made to imitate the sound of human speech. (p. 441)

tariff (tar′ if) A tax on imports. (p. 88)

GLOSSARY

technology (tek nol′ ə jē) The methods, tools, and machinery that are used to meet human needs. (p. 64)

temperate climate (tem′ pər it klī′ mit) A type of climate found in the areas that are farther from the equator than the tropics, where there are changing seasons and mild weather that is neither too hot nor too cold. (pp. 25, 45)

terraces (ter′ is əz) Large steps carved into hillsides to allow planting. (p. 500)

terrorism (ter′ ə riz əm) The use of violence and the threat of violence, usually to gain political ends. (p. 260)

timberline (tim′ bər līn) The elevation above which trees cannot grow because of the cold climate. (p. 47)

time zone (tīm zōn) One of the 24 areas into which the earth is divided to compensate for the earth's rotation of 15° per hour. (p. 204)

topic sentence (top′ ik sen′ təns) One of the sentences that contains the main ideas in a piece of writing. (p. 544)

Tour de France (tür′ də frans′) A 2,500-mile (4,023-km) bicycle race that winds around the perimeter of France. (p. 229)

township (toun′ ship) In South Africa, a segregated area in which blacks live and, despite its size, is not officially considered a city. (p. 471)

trade winds (trād windz) Winds that cause seasonal patterns of rainy and dry seasons. (p. 420)

tropical climate (trop′ i kəl klī′ mit) A type of climate found in the areas just north and south of the equator, where the weather is usually hot. (p. 25)

trust territory (trust ter′ i tôr ē) An area that an outside country controls until it decides the trust territory is ready to govern itself. (p. 604)

typhoon (tī fün′) A whirling tropical hurricane. (p. 590)

V

value judgment (val′ ū juj′ mənt) A type of opinion based on a person's judgment about the worth or value of something. (p. 162)

Vedas (vā′ dəz) A collection of Hindu religious writings. (p. 519)

vegetation (vej i tā′ shən) Plant life. (p. 26)

veld (velt) A vast, dry, treeless plateau that covers much of South Africa. (p. 472)

Vietnam War (vē et näm′ wôr) A war that began as a civil war in Vietnam in the 1950s and that eventually spread into Laos and Cambodia. (p. 570)

vineyard (vin′ yərd) An area used for growing grapes. (p. 221)

W

Warsaw Pact (wôr′ sô pakt) A military alliance that bound the nations of Eastern Europe to the Soviet Union until 1991. (p. 340)

welfare state (wel′ fâr stāt) A country in which the government takes responsibility for the well-being of all its citizens. (p. 211)

Y

yoga (yō′ gə) A Hindu way of training both body and mind through exercise and meditation. (p. 521)

a cap; ā cake; ä father; är car; âr dare; ch chain; e hen; ē me; êr clear; hw where; i bib; ī kite; ng song; o top; ō rope; ô saw; oi coin; ôr fork; ou cow; sh show; th thin; <u>th</u> those; u sun; ủ book; ü moon; ū cute; ûr term; ə about, taken, pencil, apron, helpful; ər letter, dollar, doctor

INDEX

Page references in italic type that follow an *m* indicate maps. Those following a *p* indicate photographs, artwork, or charts.

INDEX

INDEX

CREDITS

COVER: Barnett–Brandt Design
Photography: Front, **John Riley/Folio Inc.**
Back, © **Tony Stone Worldwide**

MAPS: R.R. Donnelley and Sons Company Cartographic Services

CHARTS AND GRAPHS: Tom Cardamone Associates, Inc.

ILLUSTRATION CREDITS: **Alex Bloch** pp. 34, 554–557; **Allan Eitzen** pp. 60, 126, 162, 242; **Howard S. Friedman** pp. 16–17, 113, 116 (center, top), 357, 640–641; **Ignacio Gomez** p. 89; **Gershom Griffith** pp. 400, 433, 480; **Joe LeMonnier** pp. 74–77; **Maria Pia Marrella** pp. 264–267; **Leonard Morris** p. 140; **Ann Neumann** pp. 52, 96, 98, 116, 138, 156, 174, 176, 198, 214, 230, 246, 268, 284, 286, 302, 328, 346, 348, 366, 384, 404, 406, 424, 446, 464, 482, 484, 502, 538, 558, 576, 594, 614; **Hima Pamoedjo** pp. 42, 71, 120, 279, 345, 441, 544; **Rodica Prato** p. 262; **Larry Raymond** pp. 442–445; **Blanche Sims** pp. 280, 324; **Joel Snyder** pp. 394–397.

PHOTOGRAPHY CREDITS All photographs are by Macmillan/ McGraw-Hill School Division (MMSD) except as noted below.

i: John Riley/Folio, Inc. **Table of Contents:** iii: t. Hans Wendler/The Image Bank; m. Miami Herald Cross/Black Star; b. Dilip Mehtal/ Contact Press Images/Woodfin Camp & Associates. iv: t. Robert Frerck/Odyssey Productions m. Luis Villota/The Stock Market; b.m. Leonar Morris; b. Robert Frerck/Woodfin Camp & Associates. v: t. Tibor Bognar/The Stock Market; t.m. R. Steedman/The Stock Market; m.m. Sepp Seitz/Woodfin Camp & Associates; b.m. Bob Krist/Black Star; b. Viesti Associates. vi: t. Marcello Bertinetti/Photo Researchers, Inc.; t.m. Paolo Koch/Photo Researchers, Inc.; b.m. Sovfoto/Tass; b. John Eastcott/Yva Momatiuk/Woodfin Camp & Associates. vii: t. Thomas Hopker/The Image Bank; t.m. R. & S. Michaud/Woodfin Camp & Associates; m.m. Geoff Juckes/The Stock Market; b.m. James Sugar/Black Star; b. Pedrocoll/The Stock Market. viii: t. Bertrand/Explorer Photo Researchers, Inc.; t.m. Robert Frerck/ Odyssey Productions; m. Fong Siu Nang/The Image Bank; b.m. Tardos Camesi/The Stock Exchange; b. Wolfgang Kaehler. ix: t. Harvey Lloyd/The Stock Market; t.m. Wolfgang Kaehler; b.m. Lindsay Hebberd/Woodfin Camp & Associates; b. Robert Frerck/Odyssey Productions. **Chapter 1:** 4: Nancy Sheehan. 14: NASA. 18: l. Ken Sakamoto/Black Star; r. Roger Miller/The Image Bank. 20: Eddie Hironaka/The Image Bank. 21: t.l. Mike Yamashita/Woodfin Camp & Associates; b.l. Kate Bader; m. Wolfgang Kaehler; l. Alberto Rossi/ The Image Bank; b.r. Terry Madison/The Image Bank. 25: Rick Ridgeway/Adventure Photo. 27: t.l. Breck Kent; m. Breck Kent; t.r. Brian Peterson/The Stock Market; b.r. Breck Kent; b.l. Breck Kent. 29: Robert Frerck/Odyssey Productions. 32: t.l. NASA; b.l. Eddie Hironaka/The Image Bank; m. Rick Ridgeway/Adventure Photo; t.r. Robert Frerck/Odyssey Productions. 36: t.r. Pete Saloutos/The Stock Market; b.l. Karl Hentz/The Image Bank; m. Bob Thomason/Tony Stone Worldwide; b.r. Steve Elmore/The Stock Market; t.l. Charles Krebs/The Stock Market. 37: b.l. Grant Faint/The Image Bank; b.r. Nick Nicholson/The Image Bank; t.r. Stuart Dee/The Image Bank; t.l. Michelle Burgess/The Stock Market; m. Susan McCartney/Photo Researchers, Inc. 38: Hans Wendler/The Image Bank. 41: t. Dan Routh/The Stock Market; b. David Muench Photography. 42: Annie Griffiths/ Woodfin Camp & Associates. 44: l. John Eastcott, Yva Momatiuk/Woodfin Camp & Associates; r. John Eastcott, Yva Momatiuk/Woodfin Camp & Associates. 47: l. Bill Ross/Westlight/ Woodfin Camp & Associates; r. Chris Sorenson/The Stock Market. 52: t.l. Annie Griffiths/Woodfin Associates; b.r. Chris Sorenson/The Stock Market. **Chapter 2:** 54: Miami Herald Cross/Black Star. 56: t. Viesti Associates; b. Jeff Dunn/The Picture Cube; c. Bob Daemmrich/ Stock Boston. 57: David Barnes/The Stock Market; Steve Proehl/The Image Bank. 63: l. Courtesy: Junior Achievement/Tom Hollyman; m. Leif Skoogfors/Woodfin Camp & Associates; r. Michael A. Keller/The Stock Market. 64: Al Satterwhite/The Image Bank. 67: Linda Schaefer/ Black Star. 69: Courtesy of Matthew Rothman. 72: l. Adam J. Stoltman/Duomo; m. Steven E. Sutton/Duomo; r. Adam J. Stoltman/ Duomo. 73: l. Steve Satushek/The Image Bank; r. Jonathon Blair/ Woodfin Camp & Associates. 74: Steve McCutcheon. 76: Jeff Schultz/ Alaska Stock Images; b. Jeff Schultz/Alaska Stock Images. 77: t. Jeff Schultz/Alaska Stock Images. 78: t.l. Miami Herald Cross/Black Star; b.l. Bob Daemmrich/Stock Boston; b.m.l. Al Satterwhite/The Image

Bank; t.r. Adam J. Stoltman/Duomo; b.r. Steve Satushek/The Image Bank. **Chapter 3:** 80: Dilip Mehta/Contact Press Image/Woodfin Camp & Associates. 83: Robert Frerck/Odyssey Productions. 84: l. Doug Wilson/Black Star; m. J.P. Laffont/SYGMA; t.r. Ken Ross/Viesti Associates; b.r. Timothy Eagan/Woodfin Camp & Associates. 87: (both) Cominco, Ltd. 91: l. Bob Anderson/Masterfile; r. Robert Frerck/ Woodfin Camp & Associates; l. Tim Graham/SYGMA. 94: l. Focus on Sports; t.r. D.S. Henderson/The Image Bank; b. Porterfield Chickering/Photo Researchers, Inc. 95: DC Productions/The Image Bank. 96: t.l. Stuart Dee/The Image Bank; m.l. Doug Wilson/Black Star; b.l. Ken Ross/Viesti Associates; m.m.l. Cominco, Ltd; m.m.r. Robert Frerck/Woodfin Camp & Associates; t.r. Susan McCartney/ Photo Researchers, Inc.; b.r. Focus on Sports. 98: Steve Satushek/ The Image Bank. **Chapter 4:** 106: Robert Frerck/Odyssey Productions. 109: Kal Muller/Woodfin Camp & Associates. 110: Claus C. Meyer/Black Star. 112: Loren McIntyre. 114: t.l. Claus C. Meyer/ Black Star; b.l. Kal Muller/Woodfin Camp & Associates; m. Claus C. Meyer/Black Star; r. Randy Taylor/SYGMA. **Chapter 5:** 118: Luis Villota/The Stock Market. 120: t.l. Steven D. Elmore/The Stock Market; b.l. Robert Frerck/Odyssey Productions; t.r. Robert Frerck/ Odyssey Productions. 121: t. Nik Wheeler/Black Star; b. Robert Frerck/Odyssey Productions. 124: Robert Frerck/Odyssey Productions. 125: t. Robert Frerck/Odyssey Productions; b. Randy Taylor/SYGMA. 129: t. Keith Dannemiller/Black Star; m. S. Dorantes/ SYGMA; b. Cindy Karp/Black Star. 130: t. & b. OAS (Organization of American States). 132: t. Robert Frerck/Odyssey Productions; b. Robert Frerck/Odyssey Productions. 133: Courtesy of Maria Teresa Pomar. 134–135: t. The Detroit Institute of Arts. 135: b. Nathanial Tarn/Photo Researchers, Inc. 136: Cameramann, Int'l. 137: t. James Hackett/Leo deWys; (inset) Dirk Bakker, Chief Photographer/The Detroit Institute of Arts. 138: t.l. Robert Frerck/Odyssey Productions; b.l. Nik Wheeler/Black Star; l.m.t. Robert Frerck/Odyssey Productions; r.m.t. S. Dorantes/SYGMA; b.m.t. Keith Dannemiller/Black Star; t.r. Robert Frerck/Odyssey Productions; b.r. Robert Frerck/Odyssey Productions. **Chapter 6:** 143: Robert Frerck/Odyssey Productions. 144: t. Andrew Holbrooke/Black Star; b. Dan Miller/Woodfin Camp & Associates. 147: Tibor Bognar/The Stock Market. 150: t. UPI/Bettman Newsphotos; b. K. Dannemiller/Black Star. 151: Harvey Lloyd/The Stock Market. 152: top (inset) David Hamilton/The Image Bank; b. (inset) D.C. Promotions/The Image Bank; Robert Frerck/Woodfin Camp & Associates. 153: t. Eric Neurath/Stock Boston; b. David Madison/Duomo. 155: t.l. Dale Ware, Ph.D./D.D.B. Stock Photo; t.r. Judy Leeta/Shooting Star; b. David Madison/Duomo. 156: t.l. Dan Miller/Woodfin Camp & Associates; b.l. Andrew Holbrooke/Black Star; b.l.m. Tibor Bognar/The Stock Market; t.r.c. K. Dannemiller/Black Star; t.r. Eric Neurath/Black Star; b.r. David Madison/Duomo. **Chapter 7:** 158: Robert Frerck/Woodfin Camp & Associates. 161: l. Robert Frerck/Woodfin Camp & Associates; r. Alan Reininger/Woodfin Camp & Associates. 165: t.l. Claus C. Meyer/Black Star; t.r. Luis Padilla/The Image Bank; b. Arturo A. Wesley/Black Star. 167: t.r. Robert Frerck/ Odyssey Productions; l. Wolfgang Kaehler; b.r. Robert Frerck/ Odyssey Productions. 168: l. Claus Meyer/Black Star; r. Loren McIntyre. 171: UPI/Bettmann Newsphotos. 173: l. Dan Helms/Duomo; r. Claus Meyer/Black Star. 174: t.l. Robert Frerck/Odyssey Productions; b.l. Arturo A. Wesley/Black Star; c.l. Robert Frerck/ Odyssey Productions; m. UPI/Bettmann Newsphotos; b.r. Dan Helms/ Duomo; t.r. Claus C. Meyer/Black Star. 176: Kal Muller/Woodfin Camp & Associates. **Chapter 8:** 182: Tibor Bognar/The Stock Market. 185: Chuck O'Rear/Westlight/Woodfin Camp & Associates. 187: Ira Block/The Image Bank. 190: M. Philippot/SYGMA. 193: O. Brown, R. Evans & M. Carle/University of Miami Rosensteil School of Marine & Atmospheric Sound. 195: Farrell Grehan/Photo Researchers, Inc. 197: l. Gary Cralle/The Image Bank; r. Michael Pasdzior/The Image Bank. 198: l. Chuck O'Rear/Westlight/Woodfin Camp & Associates; m.t. O. Brown, R. Evans & M. Carle/University of Miami Rosensteil School of Marine & Atmospheric Sound; t.r. Michael Pasdzior/The Image Bank; b. Farrell Grehan/Photo Researchers, Inc. **Chapter 9:** 200: R. Steedman/The Stock Market. 203: Madere/The Image Bank. 207: t. Stuart Franklin/SYGMA. b. Stuart Franklin/SYGMA. 208: top Tom Bean/DRK Photo Photo; b. (inset) D'Lynn Waldron/The Image Bank. 210: l. Her Majesty Queen Elizabeth; m. Universal Pictorial Press, London/Photoreporters; r. David Jones/Press Association LTD. 211: Peter Turnley/Black Star. 213: l. Martha Swope/Assoc.; r. The Folger Shakespeare Library/Washington, D.C. 214: t.l. R. Steedman/The Stock Market; m.l.t. Stuart Franklin/SYGMA; m.l.b. D'Lynn Waldron/The Image Bank; m.r.t. Universal Pictorial Press Photo, London/Photoreporters; r.b. The Folger Shakespeare Library, Washington, D.C. **Chapter 10:** 216: Sepp Seitz/Woodfin Camp & Associates. 219: l. Thomas Craig/Black Star; r. J. Messerschmidt/The Stock Market. 220: l. Bob Krist/Black Star: r.

Laffont/SYGMA; r. Steve Dunwell/The Image Bank. 551: NOVA/SYGMA. 553: John Launois/Black Star. 554: SALMOIRAGHI/The Stock Market. 555: Courtesy: Martial Arts Supply Co. 556: t. Orion Press; b. Kyoto News Service. 557: David Madison. 558: b.l. Ken Straiton/The Stock Market; t.l. Sekai Bunka Photo; l.m. Claude Charlier/Black Star; r.m. NOVA/SYGMA; r. John Launois/Black Star. **Chapter 28:** 560: Wolfgang Kaehler. 562: Lindsay Hebbard/Woodfin Camp & Associates. 563: l. Wolfgang Kaehler; r. Wolfgang Kaehler. 564: Lindsay Hebbard/Woodfin Camp & Associates. 566: Chuck O'Rear/Woodfin Camp & Associates. 567: r. (inset) Wolfgang Kaehler; l. Wolfgang Kaehler. 569: (inset) Ken Sakamoto/Black Star; r. Christopher Morris/Black Star. 570: Chauvel/SYGMA. 573: l. Mike Yamashita/Woodfin Camp & Associates; r. (inset) Hans Hoffer/APA Woodfin Camp & Associates. 574: t.l. Wolfgang Kaehler; b.l. Lindsay Hebberd/Woodfin Camp & Associates; b.m.l. Wolfgang Kaehler; t.m.r. Christopher Morris/Black Star; b.m.r. Cauvel/SYGMA; r. Hans Hoffer/APA/Woodfin Camp & Associates. 576: t. Robert Frerck/Odyssey Productions; b. George Holton/Photo Researchers. **Chapter 29:** 582: Lindsay Hebberd/Woodfin Camp & Associates. 585: Peter Vorlicek/

The Stock Market. 587: l. Lynn Johnson/Black Star; r. (inset) Lynn Johnson/Black Star. 592: Eastcott/Momatiuk/Woodfin Camp & Associates. 593: David J. Cross. 594: l. Lindsay Hebberd/Woodfin Camp & Associates; t.m. Peter Vorlicek/The Stock Market. **Chapter 30:** 596: George Holton/Photo Researchers, Inc.; Robert Frerck/Odyssey Productions. 599: Joe Viesti. 601: Harvey Lloyd/The Stock Market. 604: U.S. Navy. 605: l. Morton Beebe/The Image Bank; r. (inset) AP/Wide World. 607: l. (inset) David Moore/Black Star; r. P. Robert Gravey/Black Star. 608: t.l. George Holton/Photo Researchers, Inc.; t.r. Claudia Parks/The Stock Market; b. Belinda Wright. 608–609: David Hancock. 609: Belinda Wright; 610: Belinda Wright. 609–610: David Hancock. 611: t. Ken Ross/Viesti Associates. 612: l. Joe Viesti; l.m. Eastcott/Momatiuk/Woodfin Camp & Associates; t.r. Harvey Lloyd/The Stock Market; b.r. P. Robert Gravey/Black Star. 614: t.l. Lindsay Hebberd/Woodfin Camp & Associates; b.l. Joe Viesti; b.m.l. Eastcott/Momatiuk/Woodfin Camp & Associates; b.r. Robert Gravey/Black Star. 616–617: From: "Managing Planet Earth" © 1989 by Scientific American, Inc. George V. Kelvin, all rights reserved.

ACKNOWLEDGMENTS, continued from page ii

The New York Times, May 8, 1989. Copyright © 1989 by the New York Times Company. Reprinted by permission. Excerpt from "In Kenya, Man and Beast Compete for Free Land" by Sheila Rule from *The New York Times,* August 2, 1987. Copyright © 1987 by The New York Times Company. Reprinted by permission. Excerpt from "Alumnus Football" from THE FINAL ANSWER AND OTHER POEMS BY GRANTLAND RICE, selected by John Kieren. Excerpt from "Byebye" from THE MAGIC ORANGE TREE AND OTHER HAITIAN FOLKTALES by Diane Wolkstein. Copyright © 1978. Reprinted by permission of Alfred A. Knopf, Inc. "A hundred mountains . . ." from MORE CRICKET SONGS, Japanese Haiku, translated by Harry Behn. Copyright © 1971 by Harry Behn. All Rights Reserved. Reprinted by permission of Marian Reiner. "This Land Is Your Land," words and music by Woody Guthrie. TRO- © Copyright 1956 (renewed), 1958 (renewed), and 1970 Ludlow Music, Inc., New York, NY. Used by permission. Excerpt from an article from *L'Express,* Paris. Published in *World Press Review,* 200 Madison Ave., New York, NY 10016. Used by permission. Excerpts reproduced from WE LIVE IN MEXICO by Carlos Somonte with the kind permission of Wayland (Publishers) Limited, 61 Western Road, Hove, East Sussex BN3 1JD, England. Excerpts reproduced from WE LIVE IN CANADA by Jack Brickenden with the kind permission of Wayland (Publishers) Limited, 61 Western Road, Hove, East Sussex BN3 1JD, England. Time-Life

Books for excerpt from WILD ALASKA by Dale Brown. Copyright © 1972, 1973 Time-Life Books. Reprinted with permission. Excerpt from MARTIAL ARTS: A COMPLETE ILLUSTRATED HISTORY by Michael Finn. Copyright © 1988 by The Overlook Press. Reprinted with permission. Excerpt from "The First Australians" by Stanley Breeder, from *National Geographic,* February 1988. Copyright 1988 by The National Geographic Society. Reprinted with permission. "Oh Caterina!" Translation and versification by M. R. de Saettone and Augustus D. Zanzig. From SONGS TO KEEP. Used by permission of World Around Songs. "The Trees Bend" from AFRICAN SONGS, published by World Around Songs. "My Country" by Mikhail Lermontov from TWO CENTURIES OF RUSSIAN VERSE, edited by Avrahm Yarmolinsky. Used by permission of the Estate of Avrahm Yarmolinsky. "An African Poem" by Birago Diop was first published as "Souffles" in LEURRES ET LUEURS (Presence Africaine, Paris, 1960) and also appears as "Breath" in A BOOK OF AFRICAN VERSE edited by Reed and Wake (London: Heinemann Educational Books Ltd., 1964). Reprinted by permission. Excerpt from "Politics After the Coup" interview with Roy Medvedev in NEW LEFT REVIEW, Sept./Oct. 1991. Reprinted with permission. Random House, Inc. for excerpt from WINDOW OF OPPORTUNITY by Graham Allison and Grigory Yavlinsky. Copyright © 1991. Reprinted by permission of the publisher.